Organization Theory

Robert C. Ford   *University of Alabama—Birmingham*

Barry R. Armandi   *State University of New York—Old Westbury*

Cherrill P. Heaton   *University of North Florida*

Organization Theory

AN INTEGRATIVE

APPROACH

HARPER & ROW, PUBLISHERS, New York
Cambridge, Philadelphia, San Francisco, Washington,
London, Mexico City, São Paulo, Singapore, Sydney

Sponsoring Editor: Jayne L. Maerker
Project Editor: Ellen Meek Tweedy
Text Design Adaptation: Maria Carella
Cover Design: Joan Greenfield
Cover Photo: Courtesy, TRANSAMERICA
Text Art: Fine Line Illustrations, Inc.
Production Manager: Jeanie Berke
Production Assistant: Paula Roppolo
Compositor: ComCom Division of Haddon Craftsmen, Inc.
Printer and Binder: R. R. Donnelley & Sons Co.
Cover Printer: Phoenix Color Corp.

Organization Theory: An Integrative Approach
Copyright © 1988 by Harper & Row, Publishers, Inc.

Library of Congress Cataloging-in-Publication Data

Ford, Robert Clayton, 1945–
   Organization theory.

   Includes bibliographies and index.
   1. Organization. 2. Management. I. Armandi,
Barry R. II. Heaton, Cherrill P. III. Title.
HD31.F5726   1988   302.3′5   87–23796
ISBN 0–06–042124–X

87 88 89 90 9 8 7 6 5 4 3 2 1

To the students

This book's for you—with thanks and high hopes that you'll enjoy learning about this fascinating field.

Contents

Preface

This book is designed for organization theory and management courses. To use it successfully, the reader does not need any special background. Outside the academic setting, the book should be helpful in management training courses offered to industry personnel, government agencies, health care organizations, and other groups.

Organization Theory: An Integrative Approach is organized around a coherent model of organization theory (often called OT). This model enables us to present the field of organization theory in a sensible, orderly fashion. The book is divided into four parts. Part 1 describes and defines the field of organization theory, offers some historical background, and explains the importance of goals to organizational success. Part 2 devotes separate chapters to the five strategies by which organizations differentiate their work: specialization of labor, departmentalization, the line-staff distinction, delegation, and decentralization. These five strategies are each analyzed from three perspectives: classical, human relations, and modern.

Part 3 employs those same three perspectives to analyze the five strategies by which organizations coordinate their differentiated efforts: the hierarchy of authority and leadership, formalization, committees, span of control, and communication. The chapters in Part 4 cover four major determinants of organizational design: the organization's size, technology, environment, and life-cycle stage.

Discussion questions, case materials, and suggested additional readings appear at the end of each chapter.

We think this book has two primary advantages. First, our organization theory model gives it a focus that most organization theory books do not have. Second, as suggested in the dedication, *Organization Theory: An Integrative Approach* is *student oriented.* We have tried to make the book readable, relevant, and interesting to present and future managers. Our hope is that students will *understand* the material, *enjoy* it, and *apply* it—take it to work with them. Let us know whether we have succeeded.

We appreciate the comments and suggestions of the organization theory students who critiqued preliminary drafts. For their insightful and detailed review of the entire manuscript, we thank V. V. Baba, Concordia University, Montreal; Janice Beyer, New York University; J. Bruce Prince, Concordia University, Montreal; Charles B. Shrader, Iowa State University; Linda L. Neider, University of Miami, Coral Gables; David M. Flynn, SUNY at Albany; James E. Estes, University of South Carolina; Charna Blumberg, University of Texas at Arlington.

And finally, we thank our wives: Barbara Ford, Barbara Armandi, and Marieta Heaton; they keep us organized.

Robert C. Ford
Barry R. Armandi
Cherrill P. Heaton

Organization Theory

An Introduction

to Organization

Theory

Organization Theory: An Integrative Approach deals with the structural factors of organizations (Parts 2 and 3) and the major influences on those factors (Part 4). Part 1 provides the background necessary to understand these later sections.

Part 1 consists of three chapters. Chapter 1 introduces and defines the field of organization theory. It describes the three major schools of organizational thought—classical, human relations, and modern—and presents an organization theory model that serves as a basis for dividing the book's material into chapters.

Chapter 2 offers a chronological view of how organizations—particularly American organizations—have developed. That development has not been random; it reflects a series of necessary, logical, rational responses to problems that organizations have faced and solved. Those solutions have become a part of the body of knowledge known as organization theory.

We need to know where organizations and organization theory come from. We also need to know why organizations exist at all. Chapter 3 shows that organizations exist in order to achieve goals.

Organization Theory: Some Background

This chapter introduces the field of organization theory and explains some of the difficulties involved in conclusively defining just what organization theory is. Every organization must *differentiate* its work into separate parts or tasks and then *integrate* the work by bringing the separate parts back together again. The classical, human relations, and modern schools or perspectives represent three different approaches to differentiation and integration. In this chapter, we tie these various concepts together in an integrative model that will serve as the organizational pattern for the book.

THE FIELD OF ORGANIZATION THEORY

Organization Theory: So What?

Organizations and You   From the time you got out of bed this morning until you go to sleep tonight, you will be encountering organizations and their members. Some organizations may make you angry: The bus company didn't keep to its schedule, so you missed your ride; the school registrar told you that an obscure organizational policy requires you to take the one course you detest and prohibits you from taking your favorite. Other organizations may make you happy: The placement service calls to say that Xerox wants to interview you; the campus Honor Society sends a note saying that you have qualified for membership.

Many other organizations have affected you today, but you may not have noticed them or may have taken them for granted because they were uneventfully doing just what they were supposed to do: You used the telephone company to make a call without difficulty; you ate your breakfast this morning without thinking about the chain of organizations that got your favorite cereal to you—a farm produced the grain, a market got the grain to the manufacturer, then a distributor used a trucker to send the product over roads (built and maintained by other organizations) to the supermarket.

As these simple examples suggest, vast numbers of organizations affect our lives and aid us in overcoming the very real human limitations we all share. Indeed, the purpose of organizations is to allow individual persons to overcome their limitations and accomplish goals that they would not even attempt alone.

Primitive People: Guarding and Growing   Primitive people learned very early on that individual self-sufficiency was nearly impossible; that there were many advantages to banding together, dividing up tasks and responsibilities, and coordinating these diverse efforts. How successfully the primitive group divided and coordinated its tasks often determined whether the group survived.

As an example, consider guarding the group and growing the group's food. If everyone guards and no one grows, the group may be safe while it starves. If everyone grows and no one guards, the group may be annihilated by another group while it plants or harvests its crop. If all group members make individual decisions about whether to guard or grow, a random pattern of guarding and growing might result. The group might or might not be safely guarded; it might or might not grow enough food. The members of such an uncoordinated, unstructured group would probably resemble the characters in a Three Stooges movie—constantly bumping into each other and getting in each other's way.

If such a situation continued to exist, the group would risk extinction. To survive, a primitive group would have to master the basics of organizational design very quickly.

What Is Organization Theory?

Organization theory is simply defined as the study of how people organize. But what is an *organization?* According to Daniel Katz and Robert Kahn, "an organization is a social device for efficiently accomplishing through group means some stated purpose."[1] Howard E. Aldrich defines an organization as a "goal-directed, boundary-maintaining activity system."[2] Robert H. Miles sees an organization as "a coalition of interest groups, sharing a common resource base, paying homage to a common mission, and depending upon a larger context for its legitimacy and development."[3] Chris Argyris says that an organization is a group of people, divided up into parts, that engages in "three kinds of activities: (1) achieving objectives, (2) maintaining the internal systems, and (3) adapting to the external environment."[4]

These different definitions have a common element: they all see an organization as *a group of people who join together to work toward achievement of a specific purpose or goal.*

Peter M. Blau and W. Richard Scott distinguish between social organizations in general and the more formal organizations that we shall be studying. Social organizations emerge wherever people group together. Some social organizations "are deliberately established for a certain purpose. . . . Since the distinctive characteristic of these organizations is that they have been formally established for the explicit purpose of achieving certain goals, the term 'formal organizations' is used to designate them."[5]

A *theory* is a general set of statements whose accuracy or truthfulness can be tested through research. Therefore, more explicitly defined, organization theory is a general set of testable statements concerning goal-directed groups of people. This text on organization theory presents the findings of researchers who have, over the years, expressed and then tested statements concerning organizations. It will also include some untested (and occasionally untestable) material: the common sense, opinions, experience, beliefs, and ideas of the people who study, own, manage, and work in organizations. In brief, we hope to present the best that is known and thought about designing and structuring organizations.

Organization theorists use information and methods from a variety of other fields: sociology, psychology, economics, anthropology, political science, and such business areas as finance, accounting, and marketing. Sociology helps in understanding the structure of organizations, the relationships between organizations, and the relationships of organizations to society. Within the domain of psychology lie the behavior and motivation of groups. Economics aids in understanding organizational resources and their allocation. Political science has contributed to our understanding of bureaucracies and organizational politics. Anthropology shows the importance of culture, values, and norms in organizations. The business areas demonstrate how one type of organization—profit oriented—operates within society, particularly capitalistic society.

Some Complications

An understanding of the preceding definitions and descriptions does not completely equip us to explore the world of organizations since they still leave much to be explained. For example, is General Motors best described, studied, and discussed as a single monolithic organization or as the sum of its individual suborganizations, including such diverse groups as a small team of design engineers who spend their time exploring options on a computerized design board, the gigantic Lordstown Assembly Plant, the corporate headquarters, and the local Pontiac dealer? Which GM units are we talking about when we describe an organization as "a group of people who join together to work toward achievement of a specific purpose or goal"?

Further, what is the "specific purpose or goal" toward which these groups are working? Is it the stated corporate purpose of GM, or is each group pursuing its own goal independently (for instance, "to design the most highly automated production facility ever seen, regardless of its profitability," or "to break all previous records for car production, regardless of quality")?

Levels of Analysis   These questions all arise out of the two basic organization theory questions: First, in order to develop a theory of organizations, what is the most appropriate unit to analyze? Figure 1.1 gives a picture of some possibilities. As the figure reflects, an organizational worker is usually a part of a work unit. That unit is usually a part of a department or shop which in turn is a part of a plant or division. All of these groups are "organizations," but they may not contain all of the components that organization theorists have found worth studying in order to determine how people can best join together to achieve a common purpose. The foregoing groups are all encompassed by the "organization" circle.

Other names for the middle three levels are micro, meso, and macro. The *micro* (or "small," as in microscope) level in organization theory is the *formal work group*—either the department/shop or the work units within it—and the relationship of individuals to those groups. In studies at this level, part of the field called *organizational behavior,* the design of the entire organization is frequently ignored.

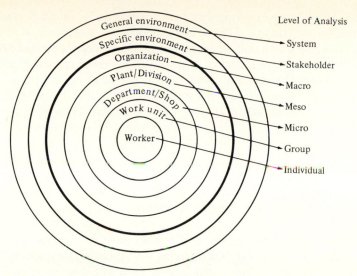

Figure 1.1   Choosing the level of analysis.

The *macro* level studies the organization as a whole. Of course, the organization is itself a group, but it is also a collection of other groups. At the macro level of focus, this collection acting as a whole is examined. Also considered part of the macro level are the organization's interactions with other organizations and with society. Some theorists refer to a *meso* level between the micro and macro levels. The meso level includes such relatively self-sufficient organizational units as divisions. However, micro and macro serve the purposes of most writers.

Whether a given subject of study is micro or macro depends upon one's perspective. The individual is micro and the universe is macro, but distinctions in between are not always so clear-cut. For example, in organization theory, studies of the overall organization are considered macro. In economics, studies of the organization are considered micro, and studies of a nation's economy are macro.[6]

Just beyond the macro or organizational level are those external persons and groups that are not, strictly speaking, a part of the organization as it goes about its daily activities but that do have a stake in the organization's success or failure; stockholders, suppliers of raw materials, and distributors of finished products would be some examples. Finally, at the systems level, the organization and its stakeholders (persons and groups with a stake in the organization's activities) are segments of society as a whole, and they interact constantly with other social elements.

Usefulness of Levels   The levels of analysis make an important contribution to organization theory when the results of different studies are compared. A meaningful comparison is possible only if the compared organizations are on roughly the same level. Otherwise, we are comparing apples and oranges. For example, consider three studies on "centralization of decision-making authority." If one researcher studies a group of General Motors accountants, another studies the GM Chevrolet division, and yet another looks at the huge multinational GM corporation itself, three different levels are evident. Comparisons of "centralization" in these different groups might not be very meaningful. Therefore, by making sure that organizations compared are at the same level of analysis, we hope to avoid drawing improper conclusions.

Once we know which unit we are talking about, we ask the second basic organization theory question: What universal organizational characteristics (if any) will allow us to build a theory that not only *de*scribes the nature of organizations but, perhaps more importantly, *pre*scribes what organizations *should* ideally look like if they wish to accomplish their goals and purposes as effectively and efficiently as possible?

Organizing the Study of Organizations

Clearly, we need some way to organize the study of organizations. But because this field of inquiry is relatively new, the definitions and classifications needed to bring order to our study are still very much a matter of debate.

Size or Technology?   Some theorists recommend classifying organizations by size, the belief being that big (or small) organizations have more in common with each other than they do with small (or big) organizations. Critics of this approach find it lacking because organizations of similar size do not always share similarities in structure and design. Others have proposed that organizations be classified according to similarities in technology or clientele. As the text will later show, the validity of these classification criteria is also debatable. For instance, one might expect that hospitals—with roughly similar technology and clientele—would resemble each other in organizational design and structure. However, a sample gathered from the real world of hospitals will quickly refute that expectation; designs and structures are highly varied. A rural general-care hospital may look very different from an urban university teaching hospital.

Goals?   Perhaps we could classify organizations according to their goals. Even better, and continuing to use hospitals as an example, perhaps we could (1) classify according to goals, (2) distinguish successful from unsuccessful hospitals by determining which hospitals have achieved their common goal and which have not, and (3) look to see whether the organizational structures of the successful hospitals are different from those of the unsuccessful hospitals. Then we would really be getting somewhere.

But now comes the hard part. Just what is the goal or purpose of a hospital? Most answers to this question would be something like "To provide excellent health care." This answer, however, leads to further questions. What is *excellent* health care, and how can we know it when we see it? If Mercy Hospital has more doctors, nurses, and beds, and spends more money per patient on drugs than University Hospital does, is Mercy Hospital offering better health care—or is it simply poorly managed and inefficient?

The goal of most organizations is to do whatever they do in an excellent fashion. In the runaway best-seller *In Search of Excellence: Lessons from America's Best-Run Companies* (1982), by Thomas J. Peters and Robert H. Waterman, Jr., companies of acknowledged excellence were examined in order to determine how they got that way. These firms also became fair game for follow-up reports in later years. Unfortunately, several fell on bad times and were unable to sustain their excellence.[7]

So, defining organizational excellence or effectiveness is difficult in itself. Since *change* is the one inevitability in the world of organizations—effective and ineffective alike—those structures that lead to excellence or effectiveness today may lead to failure tomorrow, and the reasons may not be at all clear.

Theory into Practice   Organization theorists try to stay in touch with reality by leaving the ivory tower frequently to examine the real world of organizations. Practicing organizational realists—owners and managers—are not always so ready to accept theories conceived and constructed in academic offices, even though they may be based on real-world observations and findings.

Some years ago, a noted organization theorist had a rare opportunity to study the founding and design of an organization that would progress from being a plan on paper to 14,000 employees in 10 short years. This would be organizational design in action—a chance to see how the following questions were answered: How are design issues considered and resolved? What is the logic underlying the structural decisions that have to be made? What are the steps in the rational structuring of a large organization in a technologically complex industry? In exchange for the opportunity to observe, the theorist offered to make the major literature, key findings, and cumulative expertise of the organization theory field available to the president who had been hired to put together the new organization.

The president made the structural decisions as follows: He viewed the new situation as similar to, but larger than, the organization he had just left. Therefore, he took the familiar structure of his former employer and adapted it to the needs of his new employer. When pressed for the rationale behind certain structural decisions that flew in the face of standard organizational principles, he would only reply that he thought his way might work better, given the personalities of the organizational members involved.

This example illustrates another difficulty in the search for the universal truths of organizational design. Organizers Smith, Jones, and Brown may structure their similar organizations quite differently and with equally successful results. When researchers go in to study their three organizations, they will find varying solutions to similar organizational dilemmas. Until someone (perhaps one of this book's readers) is able to develop a comprehensive, defensible way to classify effective designs and differentiate them from ineffective designs, we can offer *guidance* but no final answers.

The preceding paragraphs reflect some confusion and frustration. However, their purpose is not to confuse and frustrate the reader, but rather to spark an interest in the exciting and challenging field of organization theory. We are surrounded by organizations. They affect nearly everything we do. Yet our understanding of organizations is far from complete. We know much about what works and what doesn't work, but many aspects of organization still beg for explanation. So as we journey through the waters of organization theory, though our route is only partly charted, we invite the reader to join us and to enjoy the trip.

The Historical Basis

The logic of this text is based in history. From the earliest times, a major motive driving each organization's creator has been to achieve certain goals—goals that could only be attained by finding and using methods for accomplishing more than the organization's creator could accomplish personally.

Dividing the Work   The first structural devices of early, small organizations—families and tribes—provided a way of *dividing up the work* to be done. The organization's creator personally oversaw the operations performed by organization members, and so needed no other structural devices. The organizational head could observe and either correct faulty performance or dismiss those members performing unsatisfactorily.

Sharing Authority   As time went on and organizations became larger, organizational leaders needed to share some of their own duties and responsibilities, to find people who could take their places and act in their interests. Since organizers realized the dangers of simply trusting others to act as the organizers would have them act, the need arose to design a method for sharing authority and power. And so there came into existence, out of necessity, such concepts as delegation, decentralization, and line-and-staff relationships.

Coordination   Organizations continued to grow even larger, beyond the creator's ability to see all, know all, and be in all places at all times. The organizer's need to check on and keep track of numerous activities and people became progressively more important and, at the same time, more difficult. Quite naturally, coordinating devices—such as hierarchical reporting relationships, rules and regulations, committees, spans of control, and, especially, communications—became topics of increasing interest and concern.

This text progresses along a similar path. We describe the methods by which organizational creators (1) divide up organizational tasks and the powers necessary to execute them, and then (2) tie them all back together again in order to reach the organizational goal as established by its creator. These twin areas of concern, to be discussed in Parts 2 and 3, are usually called *differentiating* (dividing up the organizational tasks and power) and *integrating* (putting all the divided pieces back together into a unified whole again).

Tangible and Intangible Issues   Some of the issues involved in studying organizations are concrete and tangible: We can go into an organization and look at an organizational chart, a committee member, or a piece of computer output. Other parts of these twin areas, differentiation and integration, are abstract and intangible: They are processes, flows, or concepts, such as the knowledge that information provides, and the managerial philosophy upon which highly specialized tasks are founded. However, most organizational parts—whether related to differentiation or integration—are a mixture of the concrete and abstract, the tangible and intangible.[8]

THREE SCHOOLS OF THOUGHT

The early writers on organizations confronted the question of why some organizations seemed to be more effective than others. In those quieter times, answers were perhaps a bit easier to find than they are in the dynamic present. Nevertheless, their concerns are essentially the same ones facing theorists and managers today and are an appropriate focus of study for the student preparing to go out and join an organization that must interact successfully with other organizations. How to run a committee effectively, how to share power and authority intelligently, how to ensure effective communications—these concerns are just as real today as they were in the early 1900s.

The Classical School

A group of writers—Frederick W. Taylor, Henri Fayol, Harrington Emerson, James D. Mooney, Alan C. Reiley, Luther Gulick, and Lyndall Urwick among them—that has come to be called the *classical school* developed the basic principles of organization theory during the early decades of this century.

Underlying Assumptions   The classical writers sought to discover a set of universal principles that could lead to organizational effectiveness. Their approach was to observe organizations, and deduce the guidelines or principles that distinguished successful from unsuccessful organizations. Here are some assumptions underlying their efforts.

1. The effectiveness of a principle or procedure is to be measured solely in terms of *productivity*.
2. Most workers do not like to work. Work is contrary to human nature. Most workers lack intelligence, judgment, and motivation. Therefore, they need close, detailed supervision and firm direction that will encourage them to perform work activities contrary to their nature. Otherwise, they will not work at maximum effectiveness, and production will suffer.
3. Workers must understand the limits of their jobs and must be forced to remain within those limits.
4. If they must work, humans prefer to be assigned a definite task, and they prefer to be told just how to do it—rather than use any of their own discretion.
5. Worker tasks should be made as simple as possible. Such tasks are easier to master and lead to greater productivity.
6. Workers should be viewed objectively and impersonally, without regard to personal characteristics or problems.
7. Workers work for money. Their incentives to work harder and better should be monetary.

Classical principles of organization take these assumptions into account. In the view of the classicists, the assumptions embody universal human characteristics, and therefore the principles can be universally applied. Lyndall Urwick summed up some of these ideas in 1937:

There are principles which can be arrived at inductively from the study of human experience of organization, which should govern arrangements for human association of any kind. These principles can be studied as a technical question, irrespective of the purpose of the enterprise, the personnel composing it, or any constitutional, political or social theory underlying its creation. They are concerned with the method of subdividing and allocating to individuals all the various activities, duties and responsibilities essential to the purpose contemplated, the correlation of these activities, and the continuous control of the work or individuals so as to secure the most economical and the most effective realization of purpose.[9]

We shall now explain two other schools of thought regarding the structure and maintenance of organizations. Both find fault with the classical school—one because the classicists *ignore the individuality and needs of the people,* the other because they *ignore the characteristics and requirements of specific situations.*

The Human Relations School

From 1924 through 1932, a group of Harvard investigators studied employees of the Western Electric Company's Hawthorne Works. Their intention was to examine the effects of different physical conditions (such as lighting levels) on employee production. Their findings, published in F.J. Roethlisberger and W.J. Dickson's *Management and the Worker* (1939), led to a separate school of thought—the human relations or human behavior school—regarding how organizations and their managers should operate.

Roethlisberger and Dickson were surprised to find that the introduction of more difficult physical conditions into the workplace *increased* production, rather than decreased it as they had expected. Further experiments and interviews revealed that *social and emotional factors*—not changes in the physical conditions—caused the variations in output.

The Hawthorne Effect   The Hawthorne experimenters were informative, courteous, considerate, friendly, and personally interested in the workers. During their industrial experience, the workers had never known such treatment. They were therefore willing to cooperate and eager to produce *in spite of* more difficult conditions. The positive response of experimental subjects to a new and interesting situation in which they know that they are the focus of attention has come to be called, appropriately, the Hawthorne effect.

Conclusions   In *Management and the Worker,* Roethlisberger and Dickson drew these conclusions about the way people work:

1. Work is a *social* activity as well as a physical activity. People in business and industrial organizations tend to develop informal social organizations.
2. The informal social organization within the work environment:
   a. creates and enforces its own norms and codes of behavior,
   b. helps define the status of its members and determine their behavior,
   c. helps fulfill the needs of members for recognition, a sense of belonging, and security. These needs are *more important* in determining worker morale and productivity than the physical conditions in the job environment.[10]

These conclusions are in dramatic contrast to the assumptions of the classical school, that virtually ignored the worker as a person and the organization as a social system. Stimulated by the Hawthorne studies, managers began to see problems they didn't know existed—problems based on human feelings and interactions, problems that the human relations school sought to address and solve.

Humanizing the Classical Principles   Although critics of the Hawthorne research advanced several reasons for the production increases other than the Hawthorne effect and the social aspects of the situation, the research is still important because it emphasized the significance of the human elements in the workplace.

In the years since the Hawthorne studies were reported, a major contribution of the human relations or behavioral school has been to humanize the principles of the classical school. Although the behavioral movement is more concerned with personal and interpersonal reactions and interactions than it is with how organizations should be structured, the human relations point of view has had an ongoing influence on the structural concerns of organization theory. The classical principles of organization, formulated during the early decades of this century, continue to influence all organizations, particularly large ones. Since the publication of the Hawthorne results in 1939, and the formation of the Committee on Human Relations in Industry in 1943, human relations principles have kept managers aware that workers are people, not machines.

The Modern Perspective

The newest school of thought influencing organization theory is a mixture of *systems theory* and *contingency theory.* In fact, the modern school is often called the systems/contingency school. Impressed by the explanatory power of systems in the physical sciences during the 1960s, social scientists have sought to apply this idea to organizational social systems.

Systems theorists do not break organizations or work down into small elements; instead they tend to generalize, to look at the "big picture." The classical school seemed to examine individual workers and other organizational components in isolation. The systems school feels that in order to understand an organization, you should view it as a *system* and should observe its components *interacting* with one another.

Closed and Open Systems   A system is a set of interacting objects. If the objects never change and if they do not interact with the environment outside the system, then the system is said to be *closed.* Other than our universe, there are no known perfectly closed systems in nature. The standard example of a nearly closed system is the heating system of a house, composed of a thermostat, furnace, and radiators. An organization is not a closed system, since its parts and people may often change and since the organization is always interacting with other groups, such as the government, unions, customers, suppliers, and so on.

An *open* system *does* interact with its environment. Corporations, hospitals, colleges, and families are all open systems. Although all systems with which we come into contact during our lives are open, some are more nearly closed than others. A prison, cruise ship, or space shuttle is more nearly closed than a department store or national park. Open-system thinking has made an important contribution to organizational theory because it stresses the considerable effects of environmental influences on organizations.

Interrelationships   The systems approach suggests that *all systems are interrelated.* Therefore, investigating anything in isolation from its larger context is improper. Individuals do not exist in isolation. They are influenced by all objects and people with whom they interact. The behavior of the individual worker must therefore be considered within the context of the worker's organization. Likewise, the organization can be most effectively structured with reference to its social system, governmental pressures, market forces, historical trends, and employee expectations.

Systems theorists have shown persuasively that every organization is a *social system* whose parts are interrelated and interdependent. A change in any part of the organization can affect the organization as a whole. The environment within which the organization operates can also affect the organization's performance.

Contingency Theory   Contingency theory also recognizes that organizations are systems of interrelated parts. Since no two organizations are ever identical, the appropriate organizational design—in terms of differentiating and integrating principles, methods, and techniques—can be determined only by looking at *the unique environment* in which *the unique organization* finds itself. According to contingency theory, universally accurate answers to the classical organization questions *do not exist.*

Systems theory and contingency theory relate to each other this way: Systems thinking tells us that everything has some relationship to everything else. That concept is interesting but, as it stands, not especially useful to organizational designers. Contingency thinking makes the concept useful by seeking to identify *which* factors, among the infinite factors related to the organization in some way, are most relevant and *how* they operate in making their relevance felt. On which factors is the success of organizational design most contingent? Four important contingency factors discussed later in the book are size, technology, environment, and life-cycle stage.

Organization Theory and Organizational Behavior

Actual and Perceived Structure   One dilemma of organizational theorists we do not address is the difference between *actual* and *perceived* structure. For various reasons, organizational members may perceive the same structural component differently. A person who wants to work independently may perceive a 1-to-20 ratio of supervisors to subordinates as too tight. Such a person may consider *any* supervisory oversight to be more than necessary. A highly dependent, unsure subordinate requiring constant attention may view a 1-to-5 ratio as too loose.[11]

Although the impact of perceived structure is becoming increasingly important in the organization theory literature, full treatment of the issue should probably fall in the domain of organizational behavior.

The OT/OB Distinction   This distinction between individual perception and organizational reality is neither easily dismissed nor unimportant. Indeed, it raises the entire issue of where to draw the line between organization theory (OT) and organizational behavior (OB).

In many respects, OB textbooks describe organizational members and groups *without* considering the structural dimensions that shape these groups or place these individuals in particular organizational jobs. On the other hand, organization theory tends to describe and analyze organizational structures without much concern for the individuals who inhabit them. The net result is the creation of a rather artificial boundary between these two subfields of the management discipline. The confused student may wonder why the artificial boundary was ever drawn.

Levels and Distinctions   Figure 1.1 showed several possible levels of organizational analysis. Most textbook authors choose to write at either the macro (OT) level or at the micro (OB) level. Our book seeks to encompass both the macro and micro approaches somewhat by moving—within each differentiating and integrating chapter—from the early or classical writers, to the human relations writers, to the modern writers.

The classical writers tended to ignore individual differences and group influences on organizational structures. Then the pendulum swung in the other direction, as the human relations writers tended to focus on individuals without worrying much about the organization itself. The modern writers recognize the limitations that the human differences within the organization place on structural rationality and, additionally, they go *beyond* the human factors to consider the influences of technology, size, and external environment on structure. By including all three perspectives, we can (to an extent) integrate the micro and macro approaches.

The early writers sought universal truths, applicable to all organizations. They believed that certain universal principles governed the organizational structure of such diverse institutions as large urban hospitals and small rural furniture factories. Modern organizational scholars seek to identify categories, orders, and classes of organizations and hope to find, if not "truths," at least relatively stable organizational principles within those classes. The modern scholar believes that the large hospital's organizational structure is no more likely to resemble the furniture factory's than the horse's structure is likely to resemble the butterfly's. Just as the biologist believes it unreasonable to expect all living things to be similar, so the modern organization theorist believes it unreasonable to expect all organizations to be similar. The butterfly and the horse are different *classes* of living things; the factory and the hospital are different *classes* of organizations.

Contingency Classifications   But *why* are the hospital and the factory placed in different classes? Upon what bases or criteria can or should organizations be classified? Modern contingency writers focus much of their attention on the latter question.

Contingency refers to "contingent," meaning "subject to," or "dependent upon." The modern school applies a general systems logic to organizations: all things are related, all aspects affect each other. The modernists seek to identify which design issues, which structural concerns (for example, degree of decentralization, span of control, and degree of job specialization) are subject to/dependent upon/contingent upon what factors or influences (for example, organizational size, technology, human differences, environment, and stage in the organizational life cycle).

Although so-called contingency factors have been used as the basis for organizational classification schemes, little agreement exists as to which factors provide the most helpful, most explanatory basis of classification. Contingency theorists in the OT field are still working toward more reliable statements of how the contingency factors are related to the designing of organizations.[12]

Each chapter in Part 2, Differentiation, and Part 3, Integration, will include contingency notions as they apply to the specific design feature that is the chapter's subject. Part 4 will cover these postulated contingency factors in greater detail.

PLAN OF THE BOOK

This chapter has provided an overview of the organization theory field. Chapter 2 will give a brief historical account of how organizations have resolved certain problems related to their design. We shall see that as markets grew and technology became more complex, so did organizations. Organization theory evolved in a trial-and-error, survival-of-the-fittest fashion.

The biggest step forward seems to have occurred when nineteenth-century organizations and their owners accepted the concept of professional management. That concept—developed in the bureaucracies of government and church, and later in the railroads—permitted small organizations to grow large.

In the twentieth century, the most significant contributions to organization theory have been made by the classical school, the human relations school, and the modern school. Each chapter in Parts 2 and 3 will deal with a differentiation or integration strategy. That strategy will be discussed in light of contributions made by the three schools.

The OT-Model

The Organization Theory (OT) Model in Figure 1.2 (and on the inside covers) embodies this book's pattern and approach. As can be seen in the center of the figure, organizations exist in order to achieve goals and objectives. Related to goal achievement are organizational effectiveness and efficiency. *Effectiveness* means the degree to which an organization achieves its goals. *Efficiency* means the degree to which the organization makes economical use of its resources. Effectiveness answers this question: *"To what extent* is the organization achieving its goals?" Efficiency answers such questions as, *"How economically* is the organization using its resources? *How economically* are organizational inputs being converted into outputs?" Efficiency and effectiveness do not necessarily go together. An inefficient organization may achieve its goals, and an efficient organization may fail to meet its goals.

To be effective and efficient, organizations must accomplish two ends simultaneously: (1) divide up the organization's functions among its members (differentiation), and (2) keep all the divided functions focused on the organization's goals (integration). The model includes five differentiating strategies and five integrating strategies. This text devotes a chapter to each strategy.

No Pure Strategies   Despite that twofold division, the truth is that no pure differentiating device or pure integrating device exists, because each device or strategy contains elements of both differentiation and integration. To the extent that this is so, our OT-Model is an oversimplification (as is any model).

The model's logic rests on a need to organize the literature and the material of organization theory and structure. In a very real sense, *all* structural devices are premised on the idea that the organizational leadership can't do everything and be everywhere at once; yet the leadership is responsible for "everything," for all activities, for seeing to it that the organizational membership is united in its pursuit of organizational goals.

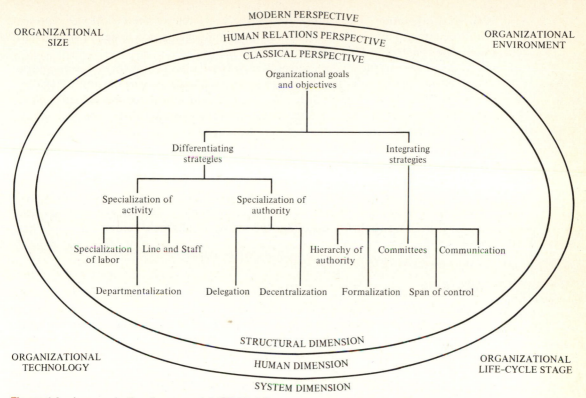

Figure 1.2   An organization theory model (OT-Model).

For these reasons, dividing up the organization's tasks always implies a need to oversee and control their execution. Consequently, for every differentiating device, the organization needs a corresponding integrating device to ensure that what is divided up is also brought back together again. For example, tasks are specialized, but the specialized efforts must be coordinated by a leader through some such leader-initiated strategy as direct oversight, a machine-speed setting, a rule, a performance standard, or a measure of output.

The Three Perspectives

The OT-Model also indicates the three perspectives from which the differentiation and integration strategies will be viewed. Each strategy will be examined as it was put forth by the classical school (with its emphasis on the organization's *structural* dimension), as it has been modified by the human relations school (with its emphasis on the *human* dimension), and as it has been further modified and affected by the modern school (with its emphasis on the *systemwide* dimension).

The modern perspective takes into account the structural concerns of the classical school, the human factors, and in addition such factors as the organization's size, technology, environment, and life-cycle stage. In determining effective organizational design, the modern organization theorist understands that the best design for a hospital may not be the best design for a pizza parlor, a prison, a day-care center or the General

Motors Corporation. The factors outside the last circle of the OT-Model represent those determined by research to be of significant influence on the design of an organization. The chapters in Part 4 deal with these factors.

As we present the modern perspective, we shall discuss how these factors contribute to answering two questions commonly addressed by the systems/contingency theorists: (1) What factors significantly influence optimum organizational design? and (2) How do those factors affect the structural dimension (located within the inner circle) and the human dimension (located within the next circle)? The modern theorist considers the structural and human issues but seeks to go beyond them in discovering how structural, human, and environmental factors all interact in such a way that optimum organizational performance will be the result.

For some differentiating and integrating strategies, a unified and consistent modern perspective has not yet evolved. Organization theory is still a relatively new field; in many areas we shall be suggesting the paths to solutions, rather than presenting solutions themselves.

DISCUSSION QUESTIONS

1. What is an organization? What is organization theory?
2. Did you and your friends ever start up an organization—a secret club, a lemonade stand, a sports team? If so, how did you structure your organization?
3. Distinguish between micro and macro analysis. Does the distinction seem important to you?
4. Why do theorists *classify* organizations? Discuss the complications involved in classifying organizations.
5. What are some underlying assumptions of the classical writers? Offer a critique of these assumptions.
6. Why did the human relations school develop? What were its major differences from the classical school? Which school do you prefer?
7. What is the systems/contingency approach? What has it added to our knowledge of how organizations function?
8. Distinguish between organization theory and organizational behavior. How definite is the dividing line between them?
9. In terms of Figure 1.1, discuss several modern organizations with which you are familiar.
10. Distinguish between organizational effectiveness and organizational efficiency. Why might an efficient organization fail? How might an inefficient organization succeed?

■ *JOHNSON MANUFACTURING COMPANY*

Basically, things were satisfactory at Johnson Manufacturing Company. The production workers seemed satisfied, their output was acceptable if not exceptional, and company profits were rising steadily.

But President Polly Johnson expected more from the company and its workers. She had only recently taken over the top job and wanted exceptional output and outstanding profits. After spending considerable time observing the production line from her office window, she concluded that the production workers were doing too much talking, laughing, and socializing on the job. She estimated that output would increase by 10 to 20 percent if the employees stuck strictly to business.

She called in her three vice presidents, explained the situation, and asked for advice. Vice President Taylor tended to take what he called the "classical" approach to organizational problems. Vice President Hawthorne thought of her general orientation as "human-relations centered." Vice President Boulding, fresh out of a prestigious graduate business program, had a "modern perspective" on organizations.

What advice would these three vice presidents give to President Johnson? What advice would you give?

■   ### LET'S GET ORGANIZED

Henry and Elizabeth Keller enjoyed a good discussion of current events and frequently invited other couples to their home for lively talk about the issues of the day. After several months and numerous discussions, they decided that they benefited most from the intelligence and insight of the Lewallens, Shaffers, Wileys, and Christophers. These ten people met once a week for about six months, at a different couple's home each week. They soon realized that one topic was more important to them than any other: drug abuse. Each couple had one or more children who had experienced a drug problem.

Eventually the Kellers concluded that if the five couples could expand the group, they might actually *do* something about drug abuse, rather than simply having stimulating talk. The next time the couples met, Elizabeth Keller voiced the suggestion: "Let's get organized. Let's start Parents Against Abusing Drugs."

All of the others agreed except the Wileys. They objected strongly. "You can organize if you want to," said Marge Wiley, "but if you do, it'll be without Steve and me."

The Kellers went ahead with the plan anyway. They sent notices to the other four couples, giving the date and time of an "organization meeting" of "Parents Against Abusing Drugs (PAAD)." The notice went on to say that officers would be elected, bylaws proposed, and membership criteria determined.

Were the ten people an organization even before they held an "organization meeting"? What will be the probable advantages and disadvantages of the new setup? Why do you think the Wileys might have opposed "organizing" so strongly?

NOTES

1. Daniel Katz and Robert Kahn, *The Social Psychology of Organizations* (New York: Wiley, 1966), p. 16.
2. Howard E. Aldrich, *Organizations and Environments* (Englewood Cliffs, NJ: Prentice-Hall, 1979), p. 4.
3. Robert H. Miles, *Macro Organizational Behavior* (Santa Monica, CA: Goodyear Publishing, 1980), p. 5.
4. Chris Argyris, *Integrating the Individual and the Organization* (New York: Wiley, 1969), p. 120.
5. Peter M. Blau and W. Richard Scott, *Formal Organizations: A Comparative Approach* (San Francisco: Chandler Publishing Company, 1962), p. 5.
6. As an example of how these different levels can provide a basis for analysis and discussion, see Gregory Moorhead, "Organizational Analysis: An Integration of the Macro and Micro Approaches," *Journal of Management Studies* 18 (April 1981): 191–218.
7. For examples of such follow-ups, see "Who's Excellent Now?" *Business Week,* 5 November

1984; and Kenneth E. Aupperle, William Acar, and David E. Booth, "An Empirical Critique of *In Search of Excellence:* How Excellent are the Excellent Companies?" *Journal of Management* 12 (Winter 1986): 499–512.

8. For several other approaches to the dividing up of organizational aspects, see Henry Mintzberg, *The Structuring of Organizations: A Synthesis of Research* (Englewood Cliffs, NJ: Prentice-Hall, 1979); Moshe Telem, "The Process Organizational Structure," *Journal of Management Studies* 22 (January 1985): 38–52; and Dan R. Dalton et al., "Organization Structure and Performance: A Critical Review," *Academy of Management Review* 5 (January 1980): 49–64.

9. Lyndall Urwick, "Organization As a Technical Problem," in *Papers on the Science of Administration*, ed. Luther Gulick and Lyndall Urwick (1937; reprint ed., Clifton, NJ: Augustus M. Kelly, 1973), p. 49.

10. F.J. Roethlisberger and W.J. Dickson, *Management and the Worker* (Cambridge, MA: Harvard University Press, 1939), Part V.

11. For examples of research that examines the differences between perceived and actual structure, see Richard Blackburn and Larry L. Cummings, "Cognitions of Work Unit Structure," *Academy of Management Journal* 25 (December 1982): 836–854; and Stewart Ranson, Bob Hinings, and Royston Greenwood, "The Structuring of Organizational Structures," *Administrative Science Quarterly* 25 (March 1980): 1–17.

12. For examples of some contemporary classification schemes, see William B. Carper and William E. Snizek, "The Nature and Types of Organizational Taxonomies: An Overview," *Academy of Management Review* 5 (January 1980): 65–75; W. Alan Randolph and Gregory G. Dess, "The Congruence Perspective of Organization Design: A Conceptual Model and Multivariate Research Approach," *Academy of Management Review* 9 (January 1984): 114–127; Richard S. Blackburn, "Dimensions of Structure: A Review and Reappraisal," *Academy of Management Review* 7 (January 1982): 59–66; and Danny Miller, *Organizations: A Quantum View* (Englewood Cliffs, NJ: Prentice-Hall, 1984).

ADDITIONAL READINGS

Bagozzi, Richard P., and Lynn W. Phillips. "Representing and Testing Organizational Theories: A Holistic Construal." *Administrative Science Quarterly* 27 (September 1982): 459–489.

Child, John. "Predicting and Understanding Organization Structure." *Administrative Science Quarterly* 21 (December 1976): 661–674.

Cullen, John B., Kenneth S. Anderson, and Douglas D. Baker. "Blau's Theory of Structural Differentiation Revisited: A Theory of Structural Change or Scale?" *Academy of Management Journal* 29 (June 1986): 203–229.

Hage, Jerald. "An Axiomatic Theory of Organizations." *Administrative Science Quarterly* 10 (December 1965): 289–320.

Lincoln, Yvonna S., ed. *Organizational Theory and Inquiry: The Paradigm Revolution.* Beverly Hills: Sage Publications, 1985.

Miner, John B. "The Validity and Usefulness of Theories in an Emerging Organizational Science." *Academy of Management Review* 9 (April 1984): 296–306.

Price, James L., and Charles W. Mueller. *Handbook of Organizational Measurement.* Boston: Pitman, 1985.

Wholey, Douglas R., and Jack W. Brittain. "Organizational Ecology: Findings and Implications." *Academy of Management Review* 11 (July 1986): 513–533.

The History of Organization Theory

We begin this chapter with a discussion of how the early religious and military groups were organized. Next, the evolution of early American organizations is covered, paying particular attention to the development of the railroads in the nineteenth century. The beginnings of bureaucracy, in both public and industrial organizations, are then outlined, and the major contributors to the classical school of organization theory are identified. Finally, we present the reasons for the emergence of the modern corporation, using the du Pont and General Motors organizations as illustrations.

BIBLICAL AND EARLY MILITARY ORGANIZATIONS

An organization is a group of people joined together to achieve a specific purpose. According to this definition, the first prehistoric family of cave dwellers and General Motors both qualify as organizations. What we now know about organizations represents the wisdom derived from many centuries of thought and trials and errors in the organizing of people, tasks, and resources.

Moses Organizes the Tribes

In biblical times, the basic ideas of organization had already been developed. In Chapter 18 of Exodus, the *Bible* tells of how Moses organized the tribes and delegated authority. Jethro, the father-in-law of Moses, noticed that Moses spent all day, every day, making decisions and judgments for his people. Realizing that the job was too big for one man, Jethro gave this advice:

> Thou shalt provide out of all the people able men, such as fear God, men of truth, hating covetousness; and place such over them, to be rulers of thousands, and rulers of hundreds, rulers of fifties, and rulers of tens. And let them judge the people at all seasons: and it shall be that every great matter they shall bring unto thee, but every

Organizing in Ancient Times

Part of mankind's tremendous development over the centuries has been brought about by the ability to organize. The following examples, displaying our ancestors' organizing capabilities, show that the accomplishments of ancient times were not accidental.

1. In 3100 B.C., to build his capital of Memphis, King Menes of Egypt carried out a vast engineering scheme that actually diverted the course of the Nile River.
2. Excavations at Mohenjo Daro, Harappa, and Kalibanga in Pakistan and India have disclosed that systems of town planning were in operation 4500 years ago. The streets of these ancient cities were straight and the blocks rectangular. They also had superior water supply and drainage systems.
3. The Suez Canal's construction was begun in Pharaoh Necho's reign (608–593 B.C.) and completed by the Persian conqueror Darius.
4. The ancient Romans would change some streets to one-way traffic during peak hours. The city of Pompeii used an arm-waving traffic policeman to cope with congestion. Street signs were used in Babylon more than 2500 years ago. At Nineveh, the capital of Assyria, "no parking" signs were displayed.
5. The library at Alexandria, destroyed during the Egyptian campaign of Julius Caesar, was also a university and research institute. The university had faculties of medicine, mathematics, astronomy, literature, and other subjects. A chemical laboratory, an astronomical observatory, an anatomical theatre for operations and dissections, and botanical and zoological gardens were some of the facilities of this educational institution, where 14,000 pupils studied.
6. The early Egyptians displayed incredible construction skills in their building of the pyramids. For example, the Great Pyramid of Cheops covers 13 acres and contains 2,300,000 stone blocks weighing an average of 2.5 tons apiece. Over 100,000 men worked for 20 years to build the pyramid. Such a project required sophisticated organizational concepts. Great quantities of stone had to be quarried, shaped, moved, and placed properly. Managers had to plan, organize work teams, coordinate the men and the material, provision and support this vast work force, and keep everyone working towards the common goal. How many modern-day construction firms would have enough confidence in their organizational expertise to bid on such a project?

In all deliberate undertakings, even those occurring before the time of recorded history, some form of organization had to be employed to reach the desired goals efficiently.

Based on Andrew Tomas, *We Are Not the First* (New York: Bantam, 1971), pp. 8–19.

small matter they shall judge: so shall it be easier for thyself, and they shall bear the burden with thee.

So Moses chose able men out of all Israel, and made them heads over the people, rulers of thousands, rulers of hundreds, rulers of fifties, and rulers of tens. And they judged the people at all seasons: the hard causes they brought unto Moses, but every small matter they judged themselves.

Moses did as any good modern organization manager does. He delegated authority for handling smaller matters so he could have time to deal with larger concerns.

Early Military Organizations

As organizations grow, they develop new needs. These needs often lead to improvements in organizational design. The armies of Philip of Macedon (382–336 B.C.) and of his son Alexander the Great (356–323 B.C.) illustrate how better organizational design can arise out of the necessities of a situation—that is, if someone is on hand who can cope successfully with the situation.

Philip of Macedon   Until Philip of Macedon's time, armies had little need for detailed organizational structure. Long-range military strategy and tactics had not been developed. Most fighting took place as one group raided another group. A self-contained military force would head out with a month's supply of food, engage the enemy, and either beat them or get beaten. The military objective was limited and the time horizon was short, so armies felt no need for elaborate support units.

Philip built an army organization with a general staff, an engineering corps, and a baggage train. In addition, he established early versions of the three arms branches: infantry, cavalry, and artillery.

Alexander the Great   Upon Philip's death, Alexander took over this structured force and made it into an all-terrain, flexible, mobile fighting organization without equal. He added propaganda and intelligence functions to his father's core staff.

In an army so specialized that some men become highly trained cavalry officers, other men must be assigned more ordinary duties and must also be supervised. Therefore, Alexander had to develop appropriate concepts of organizational design in order to maintain his army's combat-effectiveness.

Alexander's army is a typical example of how organizational concepts develop. Alexander had several problems: He had to assert his control over his father's empire, he had to carry on numerous wide-ranging compaigns, and he wanted to let his fighting prowess be widely known. Therefore, he created new types of fighting units, improved his support services, devised a more appropriate and more complex organizational structure, and added a public relations/propaganda staff unit to advertise his might and to convince opponents that fighting him would be useless.

The Arsenal of Venice

The modern assembly-line, mass-production technique commonly credited to Henry Ford's process for building the Model T can be seen as far back as the mid-1400s. The city-state of Venice developed a shipbuilding facility covering 60 acres and employing between 1000 and 2000 workers. Although the ships were rather small by present-day warship standards—approximately 100 feet long—they were the standard fighting ships of the day.

These vessels were produced in an assembly-line fashion. An unfinished and unprovisioned vessel was towed past a series of warehouses stocked with the equipment necessary to complete and outfit a battle-ready vessel. As the ship passed by the long warehouse area, the arms and equipment were placed on board in the proper outfitting sequence. At one point, the Arsenal prepared 100 ships for battle in about 75 days. In a demonstration for Henry III of France in 1574, the Arsenal assembled, launched, and completely armed a warship in one hour.

To produce at such incredible levels, the Arsenal needed superb organizational skills to match its assembly-line techniques. Inventory procedures kept the necessary numbers and kinds of ship parts on hand. Personnel practices were used to hire, train, supervise, evaluate, and pay all levels of personnel. Standardization of parts allowed the assembly-line procedures to flow smoothly, without the delays of hand-fitting parts to a particular ship. Finally, cost-accounting techniques kept control over the thousands of parts and people required to build the ships. The Arsenal reflected amazing organizational skills in a time without courses or textbooks on the subject.

THE EVOLUTION OF AMERICAN ORGANIZATIONS

The development of nineteenth-century American industry, with its increasingly large and complex organizations, provides a familiar example of organizational growth and evolution in response to changing needs. The experience was not unique to America. The process of industrialization from simple crafts to highly specialized industries developed in a similar fashion within other cultural settings.[1]

Organizational Design and Market Growth

The Crafts   At the time of the American Revolution, many organizational structures were very simple—often one-man operations. A craftsman, such as a silversmith or a blacksmith, would first acquire enough money to buy his tools and learn his trade. He would then serve a small population center.

The craftsman's ability to make a lot of money was limited for several reasons. He could not go very far from his shop because transportation systems were slow, and any time spent in selling would be time taken away from producing. In addition, the craftsman's product was worth no more (except to the very rich) than it would cost customers to make it for themselves. Finally, he might make a reasonable profit, but he could not charge too much for fear of attracting competition.

The Westward Movement   Figure 2.1 shows how the speed of travel westward increased during the 1800–1857 period. Consider New York to Illinois as an example. The trip took six weeks in 1800 and three weeks in 1830. Thanks to the development of the railroads, the trip took only two days in 1857. Many eastern craftsmen took advantage of improved transportation to enter untapped markets.

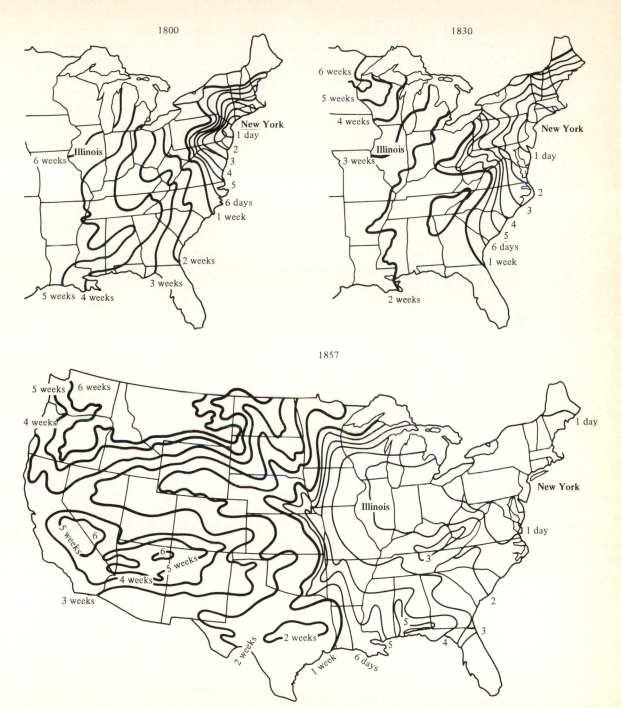

Figure 2.1 Rates of travel from New York: 1800, 1830, and 1857. (*Source:* Adapted from Charles O. Paullin, *Atlas of the Historical Geography of the United States* [Washington, DC: Carnegie Institute and American Geographical Society, 1932], plate 138A, B, C. Used by permission.)

Expansion by Specialization   Another way to do more business was to expand by specializing the operation into production and sales. The craftsman would continue to produce, but he would hire someone to sell his output. As population centers grew, so did many craft-type organizations. These organizations increased production by hiring apprentices and journeymen. They distributed the greater number of products by making some organizational members responsible strictly for sales. Many nineteenth-century organizations met the needs of their growing markets by expanding in this manner.

Limits on Growth   If a mid-nineteenth-century eastern firm made a quality product, sold it at a fair price, and could ship it cheaply and quickly, that firm could sell to the population moving westward. Some firms grew through the use of "Yankee Peddlers," who brought a miscellaneous selection of otherwise unobtainable merchandise to the developing nation's outlying areas.

Some organizations found it difficult to sell products beyond their immediate areas. For example, Ohio River valley residents would not pay the freight on furniture made in Boston. Rather than pay the price for the product plus the cost of shipping, they could make their own furniture or could hire a local craftsman to make it. So, some expanding firms in growing eastern areas began to need an understanding of organizational design. Many craftsmen moving west did not yet need that understanding.

Importance of Market Size   To sum up, whether or not a firm needed to understand the principles of organizational design and structure depended largely on *the size of its market*. Some firms grew to considerable size in the East. Others profitably went west with the population. Still others catered to small, select eastern markets or to markets in smaller western population centers.

Early Organizational Techniques

The Crafts   The early craftsmen gathered raw materials, crafted them, and marketed their products. As markets grew, craftsmen had to get help—from family members or from apprentices. The supervision technique these craftsmen used to coordinate their helpers was simply "eyeball contact." The motivational technique was an appeal to kinship, personal loyalty, or the laws and customs of apprenticeship.

The craftsman or master merchant divided up the tasks and oversaw the operation to keep it heading toward his personal goals. He did not need to define the organization's goals because its goals and his goals were usually identical. Occasionally the different personalities and needs of group members might require a slight difference in the goals of the organization and the goals of the craftsman/owner/entrepreneur. However, the usual pattern of personal or family ties between the owner and his workers meant that everyone was probably working toward the same goal.

Providers of Capital   Many products could be created and sold by individuals or small groups having relatively little capital. However, certain nineteenth-century enterprises—such as the railroad and textile industries—required many people working together and more capital than any one person could provide. The money needed in these so-called "capital intensive" industries was supplied by a new type of craftsman—one who specialized in the "crafting" of money.

Rather than working with raw wood or silver, these craftsmen took money and put it to efficient, skillful use. Their finished products were capital growth and profitability, rather than handsome furniture and beautiful bowls. An early example of what the money craftsmen could produce was the Lowell, Massachusetts textile industry, financed by the money of Boston merchant traders. By pooling their money resources, these specialists in capital investment enabled the textile industry to buy expensive machinery that could use the waters of New England rivers as a power source.

ORGANIZING THE RAILROADS

Best exemplifying the early craft of capital management were the railroads. Early in their development, they required large sums of capital, many employees, and more refined techniques of management and organization than craft-type trades needed. The first railroads were a simple extension of horse-drawn rail traffic. Then the railroad boom of the 1840s and 1850s drastically changed the extent and nature of the industry.[2]

Railroad, Telegraph, and Telephone

The first American railroads were built in the 1830s and 1840s. These roads were rarely more than 50 miles long, so operating them presented few complex organizational problems.

Once railroad technology improved, the railroads rapidly displaced canal boats as carriers of passengers and freight. Nine thousand miles of track had been built by 1850; 30,000 miles by 1860; 70,000 by 1870; and 200,000 by 1900.

The 1840–1900 period also saw the development and expansion of telegraph and telephone services. By 1860, 50,000 miles of telegraph wire were in operation; in 1880, the total was 291,000 miles. The growth of the nation's telephone network in 1880–1900 was similarly explosive. From the outset, telegraph service was dominated by Western Union and telephone service by American Telephone & Telegraph (the Bell system).

New Organizational Forms

Technological developments made swift expansion of the railroad, telegraph, and telephone industries possible. This rapid expansion, in turn, demanded new organizational forms and methods. Railroads had to coordinate unprecedented numbers of employees and passengers, pieces of equipment, and amounts of freight. By 1855 the Erie Railroad had 4,000 employees; by 1890 the Pennsylvania Railroad had 50,000 employees. When a railroad employed only 50 or 100 people, one owner/entrepreneur could run it. Once the railroads experienced geographical dispersion—vastly expanding their miles of track and numbers of employees—one-person management was no longer feasible.

As discussed above, the telephone and telegraph systems had to handle huge numbers of messages moving throughout the country. In order to survive, these new industries had to create management structures, administrative procedures, financial accounts, and internal communication methods. *Size* alone had created a need for new ways of organizing people and tasks.

Coordinating Difficulties

Elements other than increasing size were also having an impact on the early railroads. The need for large amounts of capital and the increased specialization of labor and equipment also made coordination more difficult. Earlier industries, with their simple technology, requiring moderate amounts of capital, and located at one site, had considerable flexibility in training and scheduling people and in using equipment. For example, if a textile worker called in sick, other workers could be reallocated with little or no time lost in training and reassignment. In addition, supervisors could conveniently oversee their workers and make on-the-spot decisions to reallocate workers from one task to another, in the event of a production breakdown or bottleneck.

Because of their physical dispersion and many specialized tasks, large railroads did not have that decision-making flexibility. Some spur-of-the-moment reactions to new situations were possible, but in most instances, the railroads needed predetermined plans to coordinate the activities and efforts of many people in many places. Railroad managers had to be sure that the crossing guard would show up in some remote hamlet when he was supposed to, that the engineer got Old 97 out of Old 98's way at exactly the right time, and so forth.

To sum up, managers in one-site, single-process industries could often make impromptu decisions to solve problems. The far-ranging nature of the railroads required precise coordination to avoid disasters, and a new emphasis on forethought, planning, and control.

Dealing with Uncertainty

We have been discussing how different industries deal with the *uncertainty* caused by large size and geographical dispersion. Organizations try to stabilize themselves by reducing or eliminating the impact of uncertainty on their internal operations. In the case of the railroads in the nineteenth century, wider geographical spread and numerous specialized activities acted to increase the uncertainty surrounding their organizational effort. This increased uncertainty, in turn, made greater attention to coordinating or integrating the different organizational components essential. When uncertainty is minimal, managers can focus on the specialized activities into which the organizational effort is divided. After all, if the owner/entrepreneur knows what the organization's goals are and properly divides up and assigns the tasks necessary to achieve those goals, coordinating the tasks should not be overly difficult.

Let's consider the textile industry in greater detail. Technological breakthroughs in power sources and in spinning and weaving equipment made possible simple textile factories. Textile technology continued to develop rather slowly, and few changes in organizational structure were necessary. In these simple textile mills, workers were regimented and easily supervised, uncertainty was minimal, and coordination was routine. Nor did the marketplace for textiles create much uncertainty. After an initial surge, growth of demand for textiles was continuous, but gradual. A company would build its mills and would then grow steadily and methodically.

The situation was different for the railroads. Because of their explosive growth, wide geographical spread, large number of employees, specialized technology and people, and the *high cost of making mistakes,* railroads were forced to develop innovative organizational structures and methods.

THE DEVELOPMENT OF BUREAUCRACY

The story of how significant American organizations grew and developed is not confined to the railroad, telegraph, and telephone industries. After the Civil War, many other business organizations were evolving as small-scale firms (like Carnegie Steel and Singer Sewing Machines) grew larger, and larger-scale businesses in certain industries (like Standard Oil of Ohio and U.S. Rubber) formed combinations and trusts.

Nineteenth-century American government was also experiencing growth pains, as the old-fashioned politics of patronage and loosely knit government structures gave way to liberal pressure for reform. Although the two movements (in business and government) achieved parallel accomplishments in organizational design, structure, principles, and concepts, their biographers were different. The writers on developments in business evolved into what is known as the *classical school* of management thought. Early writers on developments in government, coming from such fields as sociology and political economy, evolved into the *bureaucratic school* of management thought.

Although we now tend to consider the classical school and the bureaucratic school as distinct fields of study, researchers and writers in the two areas do overlap. Throughout our history, scholars and practitioners in business have been actively involved in government affairs. Worthwhile administrative concepts developed in either business or government soon cross from one area to the other. So it was that many bureaucratic concepts were used by the classical writers, and many classical concepts found their way into the bureaucracy.

Administration Through Bureaus

Bureaucracy is a method for administering a government or business through departments (bureaus) and their subdivisions. The activities of these departments are carried out by means of fairly fixed routines.

Rome   The history of bureaucracy extends back to the military divisions of ancient Rome and to the early Roman Catholic Church. Both the Church and the military achieved consistent administrative policy and practice.

Government Bureaucracy   Modern government bureaucracy (and its accompanying notion of "civil service") can be traced back to the Prussia of Frederick William I (king from 1713–1740) and to the East India Tea Company. Both Frederick and the management of the Tea Company needed methods for achieving consistent, rational administration of large government groups.

In order to maintain his army of mercenaries, Frederick established several new taxes—on manufacturers, members of the landed aristocracy, products at their points of sale, and any persons entering certain towns. To collect these varied taxes, he needed a trained, steadily expanding middle-class bureaucracy. These bureaucrats eventually shared power with the aristocrats they taxed.

Directors of the East India Tea Company discovered that too many Britons transplanted to India tended toward graft, corruption, and brutalization of the natives. The British government named a Control Board, which established a well-paid civil service system to eliminate the bribes and other scandalous aspects of the East India operation. By the early 1800s, the administrative concepts that this elite civil service group developed for selecting and compensating personnel were brought back to England.

U.S. Government   By 1840 or so, the United States government had also come to grips with the problem of how to run an increasingly large government efficiently. Up until that time, the government largely operated under a patronage system—elected officials brought their cronies in to help them run the government. Since these administrative personnel owed their jobs to the officials who appointed them, they did what those officials told them to, whether or not it was in the best interests of the nation.

This system of administration did not cause serious difficulties when our government was relatively small. But as government grew in size and complexity, the patronage system became less satisfactory. Whether the organization is a railroad or a government, the methods that work with 50 or 500 employees may not work with 50,000.

Max Weber   The characteristics of the large-scale bureaucracies that developed during the late nineteenth and early twentieth centuries, as described by social scientist Max Weber (1864–1920), frequently called the "father of modern bureaucracy," follow:

1. *Rational job structure.* Jobs are structured and labor is divided on rational principles.
2. *Hierarchy.* Personnel and bureaus are organized on a hierarchical basis.

Thomas Jenckes and the Bureaucracy

James K. Polk took office as president in 1845. He immediately replaced 13,500 of the country's 16,000 postmasters. Not surprisingly, this huge personnel turnover led to poor postal service.

After several pieces of Thomas Jenckes's mail were either lost or stolen, he began to try to reform the postal system. He then moved on to attack the patronage system in general throughout the federal government. The English civil service system greatly influenced Jenckes, and he urged the adoption in this country of a similar system—a professional administrative organization, based on competition rather than patronage.

Throughout the mid-nineteenth century, many people became increasingly dissatisfied with governmental corruption, disorganization, and mismanagement. In response, Congress passed the Pendleton Act in 1883, which established the Civil Service Commission, the foundation of modern American governmental bureaucracy.

3. *Written formalization.* The rules, decisions, and actions of the bureaucracy are formalized in writing.
4. *Competence.* Organizational managers and workers are selected on the basis of their competence, rather than family, wealth, or some other characteristic.
5. *Owners and managers separated.* In private bureaucracies, owners hire managers to run the organization. In public bureaucracies, the people elect representatives who hire managers to run the government.
6. *Rules.* The office is managed by following general rules. These rules are impersonal, uniformly applied, and can be learned.[3]

Bureaucracy to Reduce Uncertainty

Organizations want to minimize uncertainty. The owners and operators of the early railroads used trial and error to derive methods that would reduce uncertainty. Early bureaucrats were able to minimize uncertainty by superimposing regularity and predictability on human variability. As Warren Bennis stated, in his now-classic attack on bureaucracy:

> Bureaucracy thrives in a highly competitive, undifferentiated, and stable environment, such as the climate of its youth, the Industrial Revolution. A pyramidal structure of authority, with power concentrated in the hands of few with the knowledge and resources to control an entire enterprise was, and is, an eminently suitable social arrangement for routinized tasks.[4]

Reasons for Uncertainty   Nineteenth-century organizational uncertainty had three interrelated causes. First was the increase in organizational *size.* More organizational members meant greater organizational coordination problems. Second was the *geographical dispersion* of organizational members and the people with whom they had to interact. Third, some organizations also had to deal with the complexity of *evolving technology.*

Contrast the uncertainties facing the manager of a short, single-track railroad using horse-drawn carriages and the manager of an intracontinental railroad with 50,000 employees performing countless specialized, complex tasks. Or contrast the uncertainties facing the mayor of a small town in upstate Maine with those facing the mayor of New York City. In the private and public sectors, uncertainty increases as the three factors mentioned above increase. As industrialism spread throughout America in the nineteenth century, specialized technology and a concentrated population of workers were required, which caused coordination problems within industrial organizations and within the urban environments of which these organizations were a part.

Bureaucracy in Industry

After a period of trial and error, the early railroads resolved their problems of growth and its accompanying uncertainty quite well. The rest of the industrial sector had a more difficult time. For the first half-century of their development, the railroads attracted most of the money craftsmen. Consequently, the growth of most other nine-

teenth-century industrial organizations was limited by the ability of individual entrepreneurs to manage their operations, either directly or through family ties.

Direct Supervision by Owner/Entrepreneurs   The organization and management of
nineteenth-century businesses (other than the railroads) were based on a fairly simple
principle: Only the owner/entrepreneur and his blood relations could be trusted to
carry out the management and coordination tasks required by the organization. This
principle reflected the classical economic idea that only the man with something to
lose—his invested capital—could properly make business decisions. Anyone other
than the owner and his family was merely a hired hand—unable to understand organizational objectives and unmotivated to pursue them. Why should the hired hand
care? He had no money or reputation at stake. He could always go to work for
someone else.

The railroads solved this problem by separating management from ownership/
control. Most other early industrial organizations did not have such a separation. Like
Josiah Wedgwood's pottery-making organization, they typically grew out of one person's craft or skills, so their memberships were limited to the number of workers and
their supervisors that one owner/entrepreneur and his family could directly manage.
As his organization grew and prospered, the craftsman/owner/manager had to decide
whether to stop crafting and start managing. The choice between being a craftsman and
being a manager was not an easy one for a nineteenth-century owner to make. Many
craftsmen, in industries not affected by major technological developments, chose to
remain small to avoid these problems.

Effects of Improved Technology   By the late 1800s, the major expansion phase of the
railroads was over. Railroad expansion led to large-scale production of commonly used
items (foodstuffs, structural steel, agricultural equipment), as manufacturers were able
to use the railroads to transport their products inexpensively.

A nineteenth-century company could expand its market in two ways: (1) it could
reduce its shipping costs, so that its products could be competitively priced even though
they were sold far away from the manufacturing site, or (2) it could reduce its production costs and increase its efficiency by specializing its production methods. By the late
1800s, the benefits of cheaper transportation and reduced shipping costs had largely
been realized. The money merchants then turned their attention to specializing their
production methods.

THE CLASSICAL SCHOOL: MAJOR CONTRIBUTORS

During the early decades of the twentieth century, the classical principles of organization theory were developed, as theorists observed managers meeting and solving their
specific challenges and problems. Ernest Dale refers to the successful early twentieth-
century industrial leaders as "the great organizers." They set objectives, then divided
up and accomplished the work according to the practical requirements of their unique
situations, not according to any universal truths about organizing. According to Dale:

> The great organizers devised some "principles," or rather guiding criteria, of their
> own. . . . conceived and applied mostly "without benefit of clergy," that is, without

reference to a great book on organization and without the influence of a "guru," or crusading missionary. . . . These criteria were developed through the challenge of specific problems and possibly are not applicable beyond them.[5]

The academic theorists, however, tried to go beyond noting what worked for a single firm, to derive organizational principles that might have broader applicability.

Frederick W. Taylor

Frederick Winslow Taylor (1856–1915), often called the "father of scientific management," argued forcefully for using scientific procedures to solve the management and organizational problems of evolving mass production industries. By 1911 Taylor had formalized his principles into four categories:

1. Study each job scientifically, to find the best way of doing it.
2. Find the best man for the job, then use the best methods to train him.
3. Cooperate and interact with the workers, to be sure that they stick to the "best way" of doing the work. Give them financial incentives to follow the prescribed methods.
4. Workers should work, and managers should manage. Find and train the best workers and managers; such a division of labor should benefit both groups.[6]

Henri Fayol

The Frenchman Henri Fayol (1841–1925) wrote his classic work, *General and Industrial Management,* in 1916, but it was not widely known in the United States until a translation appeared in 1949.

Frederick W. Taylor's scientific management stressed the immediate gains in productivity resulting from scientifically investigating and prescribing the *worker's* task. Fayol's broader, long-term approach focused on the *manager's* task. As general manager of a large mining corporation, Fayol observed and analyzed those factors that seemed most to influence his organization's effectiveness. He then derived a five-component process involving 14 universal principles.[7] These are Fayol's five managerial functions:

1. *Planning* the organization's tasks.
2. *Organizing* the people, money, and material necessary to perform these tasks.
3. *Commanding* the people assigned to the tasks.
4. *Coordinating* their activities to ensure proper direction.
5. *Controlling* the processes, procedures, and people involved.

Based on his extensive observation of people and organizations, Fayol derived 14 universal management principles which provided the basis for organizing management knowledge. (See the accompanying box.) Fayol provided the first important theory of organizations. He offered a logical, comprehensive method for dividing up and then reintegrating the organization's work.

Henri Fayol's Principles of Administration

1. *Division of work.* Adam Smith saw specialization as appropriate and necessary for pin-making. Fayol saw that specialization could improve managerial efficiency as well.
2. *Authority and responsibility.* The manager has the power of authority. He has the equal responsibility for the use he makes of that power.
3. *Discipline.* Effective managers produce or induce good discipline. They encourage obedience and diligence, and they punish insubordination.
4. *Unity of command.* Each person has only one boss and reports only to that boss.
5. *Unity of direction.* A group of activities having the same objective must have only one boss and only one plan for achieving that objective. Plans must be coordinated, rather than overlapping.
6. *Subordination of individual interest to the general interest.* Managers must promote this principle by example and by counteracting violations.
7. *Remuneration.* Fair and reasonable payment plans are necessary (but they are not a substitute for good management).
8. *Centralization.* Centralization refers to the organization's tendency to keep decision-making authority near the top. Under decentralization, the organization delegates decision-making authority down through the organization. The manager must determine how much centralization or decentralization the organization needs.
9. *Scalar chain.* All employees should be aware of the organizational hierarchy, the different levels in the chain of command. Communications should generally flow through the formal chain of command. Persons on the same level may communicate directly across the chain, to avoid the necessity of sending a message up through the chain of one person's superiors and then down through the chain of the other's superiors.
10. *Order.* All people and things have their place and should be in that place.
11. *Equity.* The manager must be fair and firm, but friendly.
12. *Stability of personnel.* For best results, organizations should encourage the long-term stability of both managers and workers. Rapid turnover is destructive of organizational goals.
13. *Initiative.* Managers must be able to originate projects and complete them.
14. *Spirit.* Managers must work together harmoniously and must encourage harmony and unity within their people.

Henri Fayol, *General and Industrial Management,* trans. Constance Storrs (London: Pitman, 1949), pp. 19–42.

Harrington Emerson

Another early contributor to organization theory was Harrington Emerson, whose books on efficiency—*The Twelve Principles of Efficiency* (1912) and *Efficiency As a Basis for Operation and Wages* (1919)—influenced early twentieth-century railroads and manufacturing firms. Particularly significant were his observations, derived from his study of the German army's general staff, about the importance of staff assistance to line managers and operators.

Emerson stressed the importance of assigning special staff to advise high-ranking organizational officials about their assigned lines of duty. But because these special staffs were too often far removed from the people actually doing the work, Emerson recommended that a general staff be available to advise *all* organizational members, from the president to the line workers. This early champion of staff assistance maintained that firms willing to spend money on staff personnel could actually save money over the long run.[8]

Mooney and Reiley

In 1931 two GM executives, James D. Mooney and Alan C. Reiley, published *Onward Industry: The Principles of Organization and Their Significance to Modern Industry* (republished in 1939 as *The Principles of Organization*). Using their study of governments, the Roman Catholic Church, industry, and the military as a basis, they formulated four principles of organization.

1. *Coordination.* Achieve the coordination necessary to meet organizational goals by using sound management/organizational principles and by maintaining morale.
2. *Scalar chain.* Define the chain of authority, and assign specific duties to the organization's subdivisions.
3. *Specialization.* Group duties by function.
4. *Line/staff.* Recognize that line executives need advice and ideas from staff experts.

These principles, derived from the workings of actual organizations, added support to Fayol's concepts.

Gulick and Urwick

Luther Gulick and Lyndall Urwick published *Papers on the Science of Administration* in 1937. Gulick explains the importance of organizational structure:

> I hope I have convinced you that organizing is part of the mechanics of management, that we should *begin* by making a technically correct structure without reference to individuals as such. My conviction that this is so is not due to an indifference to people as people or to any doubt as to the overwhelming importance of the individual in our society, but to the belief that it is just by dealing with organization in this way that we can deal with human beings most justly and kindly.
>
> You have also probably noted that there is nothing novel in principle in dealing with organization in this way. To take organizing problems in this order, carefully segregating the mechanics from the dynamics, is just a special application of one of F.W. Taylor's fundamental principles of management—the separation of planning from performance.[9]

The early organizers had to adapt their structures to the environments within which they operated and accommodate the managerial personalities with whom they dealt. The classical theorists believed that, ideally, the right structure should first be established, and then filled with the right people.

Practitioners and Theorists

The great classical organizers were pragmatic problem solvers. They often took over and expanded organizations that were just emerging from the control of founder/ entrepreneurs. They created their organizational structures in response to specific challenges. The great classical organization theorists took the broader perspective, trying to find those organizational principles and practices that might have general applicability. The organizers and the theorists of the classical era both made essential contributions to the evolving field of organization theory.

THE EMERGENCE OF THE MODERN CORPORATION

Two examples will serve to show how circumstances forced one-person or one-family organizations in the early twentieth century to change with the changing times.

Consolidation at du Pont

Control by Cooperative Action   At the turn of the century, one of the most powerful groups of cooperating businesses was the Gunpowder Trade Association, dominated by E.I. du Pont de Nemours & Co.[10] Because it held stock in its major competitors, du Pont was able to establish prices and production schedules for explosives. In 1902 all of the E. I. du Pont partners and most of the supervisory force were du Ponts.

Since du Pont controlled prices and production schedules within the industry, the company felt no compelling need to improve manufacturing processes or purchasing and marketing techniques. Therefore, the efforts of the several companies controlled by du Pont were not properly coordinated. Henry du Pont, president of the company from 1850 to 1889, handled the administration of the company and of the Gunpowder Trade Association by himself, writing nearly all business correspondence in longhand.

Reorganization   Following the death of President Eugene du Pont in 1902, the company was reorganized by Alfred, Coleman, and Pierre du Pont. The du Ponts began a program of consolidation and centralization. They bought and traded for the stock of many small explosives firms and formed the E.I. du Pont de Nemours Powder Co. to take over the combined properties.

Once the acquisitions were complete, the du Ponts needed an administrative structure to coordinate the buying, manufacturing, shipping, and selling of explosives. They consolidated production in a few large plants. They established a nationwide marketing organization as well as administrative departments for each major product: black powder, smokeless powder, and dynamite. They added a research department. And they constructed a large office building in Wilmington, Delaware out of which the new departments operated.

Professional Managers   The six major executives of the new company were Coleman du Pont (president), Alfred du Pont (general manager), Pierre du Pont (treasurer), J. Amory Haskell (sales), Hamilton M. Barksdale (manufacture of high explosives), and Arthur J. Moxham (research and development). These men turned a family-run, feudal type of industrial monopoly into a modern, professionally run organization.[11]

The backgrounds of these executives are important for us to consider. Coleman du Pont, Pierre du Pont, and Arthur Moxham had formerly built street railway systems with the Lorain Steel Company. J. Amory Haskell had worked for the Baltimore and Ohio Railroad. These men were able to transfer the organizational experience of the railroads to a different industry. When the du Pont organization grew so large that the family could no longer handle it, professional management specialists and a more efficient administrative structure became necessary.

Growth at General Motors

Thanks to an exploding demand for automobiles and the engineering genius of William C. Durant, General Motors rapidly became an industrial giant in the early twentieth century. In 1918 the du Ponts invested $50 million in General Motors. When GM had financial trouble during the economic recession of 1920, they turned to du Pont for help. Here again, the experience gained in one industry was transferred to another.

Decentralized Control   Henry Ford increased his production capacity by expanding his existing facilities. In contrast, GM founder William C. Durant expanded his production capacity by acquiring many scattered facilities for automobile manufacture. Durant's acquisitions operated more or less independently because he saw no need for centralized control. By 1920 Durant had assembly plants, parts companies, and equipment companies in many areas of the country, but he still showed little concern about the company's overall operating structure. Financial reverses forced Durant to resign in late 1920, and Pierre du Pont became GM's president.

Autonomous Divisions   Alfred P. Sloan, Jr., president of a GM subsidiary, submitted a new organizational plan to Pierre du Pont, calling for autonomous operating divisions—such as Chevrolet, Cadillac, Frigidaire, and GM Trucks—and a central office made up of general executives and staff specialists. His plan was accepted, and its main features characterized GM's organizational structure for several decades.

Organizations in Transition   Du Pont and General Motors are illustrations of two companies that, with some variations, made a successful transition from being organizations dominated by one family or one man to being the large, major corporations we know today. The change from family management to professional management was accompanied by a heightened emphasis on two elements that have been important to organizations since primitive times: specialization and coordination.

Increased Specialization

In *The Wealth of Nations* (1776), Adam Smith used pin making to illustrate the benefits of specialization as a means of *differentiating* or dividing up the organization's tasks. By 1900, specialization was not only economically sensible but economically necessary, to make use of the increasingly sophisticated production processes required to manufacture increasingly complex products.

Consider an organization producing a large volume of electric motors. The organization could laboriously teach each member of its largely uneducated work force to make a motor single-handedly. Or it could quickly specialize tasks into simple repetitive operations. The market demand for electric motors required the latter approach. The greater the demand, the greater the specialization that was possible. Once the demand for automobiles had sufficiently intensified, Henry Ford was able to establish a large-scale assembly-line operation—consisting of many specialized tasks—to meet it.

Improved Coordination: Professional Managers

Increased specialization required improved coordination. Whenever a task becomes specialized, some mechanism—either a master craftsman's knowledge or an organizational design—must *integrate* the separate parts and bring them together. Modern organizations achieve this coordination by allocating responsibility and authority among a professional group of managers. The change from craft organizations to modern industrial organizations came about as owners, entrepreneurs, money merchants, and employees began to accept the concept of a *professional management staff, loyal to the organization.*

As discussed earlier, the idea that only the persons who risked their own capital could properly make decisions was predominant in the eighteenth and nineteenth centuries. The realization that a hired hand without capital at risk could also work loyally and make decisions in the organization's best interests was an important, major transition that allowed previously family-dominated organizations to grow. With their expansion of the railroads, the craftsmen of capital proved that this new idea could work. Today, this concept is generally accepted by all types of organizations, large and small.

SUMMARY

From biblical times through the beginnings of organizational structuring in the military, history reflects the increasing specialization of organizational components in response to changing needs.

As many American crafts eventually gave way to mass production in the nineteenth century, organizations became larger and more complex. Technological developments made rapid expansion possible in the telephone, telegraph, and railroad industries. The railroads in particular developed organizational strategies for dealing with the uncertainties resulting from increasing size and geographical dispersion.

The growth of bureaucracy, particularly in the U.S. government, mirrored the organizational changes in industry. These new concepts were developed and discussed by the following major contributors to the classical school of organizational thought: Frederick W. Taylor, Henri Fayol, Harrington Emerson, James D. Mooney, Alan C. Reiley, Luther Gulick, and Lyndall Urwick.

In the early twentieth century, many organizations experienced the transition from domination by a single owner/entrepreneur or family to professional management. The du Pont and General Motors corporations are examples of firms that successfully made that transition through the use of professional managers, increased specialization of tasks, and improved coordination of efforts.

DISCUSSION QUESTIONS

1. What lessons about organization can be learned from (a) Philip of Macedon, (b) the Arsenal of Venice, (c) Moses?
2. Many nineteenth-century American crafts became twentieth-century mass-production industries. Discuss the importance to that trend of (a) increasing specialization, (b) the Westward movement, and (c) the "money craftsmen."
3. Discuss the place of the railroads in the development of American organizations.
4. Outline the history of bureaucracy. How is its development similar or dissimilar to the development of classical organization theory?
5. What are the components of bureaucracy, as laid out by Max Weber? Are they the components of the modern bureaucracies with which you are familiar?
6. Who were the major contributors to the classical school of organizational thought, and what were their major contributions?
7. Which of Fayol's 14 principles of administration still seem useful?
8. What important point about organizations is illustrated by the major managerial and organizational changes at the du Pont corporation in the early twentieth century? Why are du Pont's accomplishments important to the development of large-scale modern organizations?
9. What was the major contribution of Alfred P. Sloan, Jr. to the structuring of large organizations? Do organizations still use his approach?

■   ### CLUETT MOWING MACHINES

Bob Cluett's mowing machine manufacturing company had grown so fast that he hadn't really taken time to be sure that his production-line workers were doing their jobs as efficiently as possible. When Mike Thaler of Efficiency Unlimited proposed a time-and-motion study as a means of achieving greater efficiency, Cluett enthusiastically gave his approval. The day before the time-and-motion experts were due to begin their work, Bob Cluett explained to his production employees just what was going to be done and why: "We want to help you to do a better job, a more efficient job. Efficiency Unlimited isn't here to spy on you; they'll watch you, make suggestions, and then we'll see where to go from there." The production employees didn't seem happy about the idea, and Cluett didn't understand why.

At closing time, a group of senior employees led by Charlotte Hunt went to Cluett's office. "Mr. Cluett," Hunt began, "we don't like the idea of being watched and timed. We do our best, and no efficiency hotshot ought to be able to tell us what to do. Some of the folks think this is just a way to eliminate some jobs and get more work out of us for the same money. You always treated us like human beings before this. Now you seem to want to treat us like machines, and we don't like it."

Why do you think the workers are so resistant to the idea of "improving their efficiency"? Do you think their fears may be justified? If you were Bob Cluett, would you go ahead with the study tomorrow? Postpone it? Cancel it entirely?

■   ### BAN THE BUREAUCRATS

The police guarding the front of the White House had a problem. They knew Jeffrey Snowdon well. He had been carrying protest signs on the sidewalk for many months. Usually

Snowdon behaved himself, but over the past couple of weeks he had begun accosting any pedestrian wearing a grey-flannel suit, striking official limousines with his protest signs, and generally intensifying his nuisance level.

Patrolman James Smith finally got fed up. "Jeffrey, what are you so hot about? What's the trouble? What's the problem?"

"The problem, Officer Smith, is obvious: *too many bureaucrats.* We have no rugged individualists left, no self-made men or women, no do-it-yourselfers. The bureaucracies are sapping our individuality, forcing us to conform, and turning us into carbon copies of each other. Would John Wayne join a bureaucracy? Would Ernest Hemingway? Amelia Earhart? I say down with bureaucracies! Get rid of 'em all!"

If you were Patrolman Smith, what arguments would you use to persuade Jeffrey Snowdon that bureaucracies play an important role in society and should not be banned?

NOTES

1. For an account of how the industrial revolution affected the British pottery industry, see "The Ecological Theory of Bureaucracy: The Case of Josiah Wedgwood and the British Pottery Industry," *Administrative Science Quarterly* 29 (September 1984): especially pp. 340–341.
2. The following section is indebted to Alfred D. Chandler, Jr., *The Railroads* (New York: Harcourt, Brace & World, 1965), pp. 82–97.
3. Max Weber, "Bureaucracy," in *Max Weber: Essays in Sociology,* ed. and trans. H.H. Gerth and C. Wright Mills (New York: Oxford University Press, 1946), pp. 196–244.
4. Warren Bennis, *Beyond Bureaucracy* (New York: McGraw-Hill, 1966), p. 9.
5. Ernest Dale, *The Great Organizers* (New York: McGraw-Hill, 1960), p. 27.
6. Frederick W. Taylor, *Principles of Scientific Management* (New York: Harper & Brothers, 1911), pp. 36–37.
7. Henri Fayol, *General and Industrial Management,* trans. Constance Storrs (London: Pitman, 1949), Part II.
8. For additional information about Harrington Emerson, see Dale, *The Great Organizers,* pp. 20–22, to which the foregoing account is indebted.
9. Luther Gulick, "Notes on the Theory of Organization," in *Papers on the Science of Administration,* ed. Luther Gulick and Lyndall Urwick (1937; reprint ed., Clifton, NJ: Augustus M. Kelly, 1973), p. 15. For an expansion of Gulick's ideas about organization, see L. Urwick, *The Elements of Administration* (New York: Harper & Row, 1944).
10. The following account is indebted to Alfred D. Chandler, Jr., *Strategy and Structure: Chapters in the History of the American Industrial Enterprise* (Cambridge, MA.: The M.I.T. Press, 1962), Chapter 2.
11. For further information on the advent of professional management at du Pont, see Ernest Dale and Charles Meloy, "Hamilton MacFarland Barksdale and the du Pont Contributions to Systematic Management," *Business History Review* 36 (Summer 1962): 129–152.

ADDITIONAL READINGS

Crozier, Michel. *The Bureaucratic Phenomenon.* Chicago: University of Chicago Press, 1964.
Gent, Michael J. "Theory X in Antiquity, or the Bureaucratization of the Roman Army." *Business Horizons* 27 (January/February 1984): 52–56.

George, Claude S., Jr. *The History of Management Thought.* 2d ed. Englewood Cliffs, NJ: Prentice-Hall, 1972.

Hine, Charles De Lano. *Modern Organization: An Exposition of the Unit System.* New York: The Engineering Magazine Co., 1912.

Lawrence, Barbara S. "Historical Perspective: Using the Past to Study the Present." *Academy of Management Review* 9 (April 1984): 307–312.

Merrill, Harwood F., ed. *Classics in Management.* New York: American Management Association, 1960.

Merton, Robert K. et al., eds. *Reader in Bureaucracy.* New York: Free Press, 1952.

Metcalf, Henry C., and Lyndall Urwick, eds. *Dynamic Administration: The Collected Papers of Mary Parker Follett.* New York: Harper & Row, 1942.

Parker, L.D. "Control in Organizational Life: The Contribution of Mary Parker Follett." *Academy of Management Review* 9 (October 1984): 736–745.

Pusateri, C. Joseph. *A History of American Business.* Arlington Heights, IL: Harlan Davidson, 1984.

Selznick, Philip. "An Approach to a Theory of Bureaucracy." *American Sociological Review* 19 (February 1943): 47–54.

———. "Foundations of the Theory of Organization." *American Sociological Review* 13 (February 1948): 25–28.

Stinchcombe, Arthur L. "Bureaucratic and Craft Administration of Production: A Comparative Study." *Administrative Science Quarterly* 4 (September 1959): 168–187.

Urwick, Lyndall F. *The Pattern of Management.* Minneapolis: University of Minnesota Press, 1956.

———. "Organization and Theories about the Nature of Man." *Academy of Management Journal* 10 (March 1967): 9–15.

Weber, Max. *The Theory of Social and Economic Organization.* Edited by Talcott Parsons. Translated by A.M. Henderson and Talcott Parsons. New York: Oxford University Press, 1947.

Wren, Daniel A. *The Evolution of Management Thought.* 3d ed. New York: Wiley, 1987.

Organizational Goals

An organization is a group of people who come together in order to accomplish a common purpose. Using this description, the importance of common purposes—or goals—to the theory of organizations becomes apparent.

This chapter begins by asking questions about the three elements in our definition of an organization: Who are the people? How and why did they come together? What is their common purpose? It shows how organizational goals evolve, and several traditional goal definitions are explored. Then, organizational goals are explained in terms of official versus operative goals, and nonoperational versus operational goals. Official goals are what the organization *says* it is trying to do; operative goals are what the organization *is* trying to do. Nonoperational goals are nonmeasurable and general; operational goals are measurable and specific. Most organizations have official, operative, nonoperational, and operational goals. Since all organizations (and all levels within organizations) have more than one goal, the problems that can result from multiple goals are then discussed.

Finally, goals are considered in terms of inducements (offered by organizations) and contributions (supplied by members). Organizations must translate their general goals into specific tasks. The successful organization considers the personal goals of members, then offers them the combination of inducements that will encourage them to contribute their best efforts to completing tasks necessary to organizational goal achievement.

PEOPLE AND PURPOSES

We have defined an organization as a group of people who come together to accomplish a common purpose. To understand how organizations can best be designed, we need to examine the three parts of that definition more closely: (1) Who are the people? (2) How and why did they come together? and (3) What is their common purpose?

Who Are the People?

The Boundary   The first question is related to the organizational boundary, drawn between the people inside the organization and the people outside it. The location of the organizational boundary affects and is affected by the answers to the remaining two questions as well. For example, assume that we define the organization's people, its members, as those *physically* within a certain boundary. Determining how and why they came together and identifying their common purpose become organization-specific (or, at worst, geographic-specific) issues. If the organizational membership consists of all the people employed by Harry's Pizza or all the students in the Central High School marching band, then the common purpose of the membership can probably be determined without much difficulty. But if the organization consists of all those people *interested in* or *affected by* or having some *stake in* the pizza parlor or the band, then finding their common purpose is more complicated.

The Stakeholders   These organizational *stakeholders* are much more a part of the organization proper than are the people randomly chosen from the population in general. But their inclusion does muddy up the task of defining the organization's purpose or goal.[1] As will soon become evident, limiting organizational membership to the *employees* of Harry's Pizza or the *students enrolled for credit* in the marching band does not automatically enable us to determine their common purpose despite what we may initially assume.

Establishing the Boundary   Where to establish the boundary between those inside and those outside the organization is not a minor issue. If we define the organization narrowly, we are likely to hear one set of goals specified. If we broaden the definition, extending the boundary, we may observe other goals, similar to but not exactly the same as our first set of goals. The seniors on the football team may have as their common purpose "To win the conference championship this year." Other groups—the non-seniors on the team, coaches, student body, alumni, local gamblers—may also want the team to win the championship. But they may have other goals that are not congruent with, or that may even conflict with, the common purpose of the team's seniors. The coaches may want to build character and sportsmanship; the students may want to watch exciting, wide open games; the alumni may want to crush traditional rivals; and local gamblers may want to beat each week's point spread.

Previously, corporations could often consider their boundaries to be the corporate walls and their organizational members to be only those persons on the payroll. Now, however, corporations are expected to be socially responsible, to consider the interests of external people and groups affected by corporate activities, so the location of the corporate boundary and the common purposes of the people within it are harder to establish.[2]

The Effects of Environment   The issue of social responsibility is just one part of the whole question of the organization's relationship to its environment. Do organizational managers determine organizational goals (as they like to think)? Or do they merely react to environmental pressures, like the pressure to be socially responsible? Does the organization have *any* real control over its circumstances, or is it merely driven by the environmental forces to which it reacts?

The environment—individuals, groups, and institutions beyond the organization's strict boundaries—is always an influence to some extent on organizational goal setting and achievement. No organization—no matter how well organized and no matter how smooth-talking and dynamic its CEO—will survive for long if the common purpose of its members is, for example, "To market surplus army tanks as commuter vehicles in the USA." Our government will simply not permit public purchase of armed tanks for use on the public roads by anyone who happens to have the purchase price of a tank. An organization's goals must be congruent with society's goals. If the general public or powerful social institutions—such as the government, organized religion, or educational institutions—disagree with an organization's goals, they will apply pressure to change those goals. The organization can then either comply or resist. If the external group exerting the pressure is powerful enough, the organization must comply or collapse.

To sum up:

1. The organization's goals will be seen differently, depending on where the boundary is drawn between the people considered inside and those considered outside the organization.
2. Even though the people inside the organization may be the major forces in determining organizational goals, the people in the environment outside the organization will also exert an influence. No matter what the people inside want to do, their goal statements—their common purposes—will to some extent be a compromise with the people outside the organizational boundary.

How and Why Did the People Come Together?

Rational Choice   The second question arising from our definition of organization is: How and why did the people come together? The employees of Harry's Pizza and the members of the Central High School marching band probably decided to join those organizations on a rational, logical basis. They weighed the advantages of organizational membership against the disadvantages of not joining or the comparative advantages of spending their time with another organization or perhaps just staying home and watching TV. Mary can't work evenings at both Harry's Pizza and Ralph's Burgers. Bob can't play in the band and also play on the football team. Choosing to join and stay with one organization rather than another is usually a rational, logical act.

Of course, people are not always rational and logical. Perhaps Mary works at Harry's Pizza because she simply does not know that she could do similar work at Ralph's Burgers for more money. Perhaps Bob's parents take the rational decision away from him because they won't let him play football.

Whose Rationality?   Furthermore, judgments about the rationality of a decision may depend on who is doing the judging. Steve's salary is cut, he is demoted, he must now work the graveyard shift, and he is told that he will never rise from his new position.

From the rational point of view, Steve should probably leave this organization and join another one. Yet, Steve stays on and the rational observer doesn't understand why. However, perhaps Steve doesn't think any other jobs are available so no matter how bad his situation has become, it is better than being unemployed. Perhaps Steve knows of a better job several hundred miles away, but he stays in this one because his son likes the high school, his wife likes their community, and they have a 6 percent 30-year home mortgage that Steve hates to give up.

The literature of organization theory generally assumes that organizational members act rationally, as the theorist conceives of rationality. Yet, people are unique, and one person's rational behavior may be another person's quirky, eccentric, or demented behavior. In a large organization with many members, defining "rational behavior" for the entire organizational membership may be nearly impossible.

Rationality and Goal Setting   So, the rationality or irrationality of individual organizational members varies, depending on one's viewpoint. This variability further compounds the difficulty of setting goals "rationally" at the organizational level. The rational or irrational behavior of the organization's members, and particularly its leaders, will presumably define how rationally or irrationally the organization itself acts. Organization member Johnson may stay with the organization because he is unable or unwilling to consider other choices. Similarly, the organization itself may establish and pursue certain goals and strategies because it is unwilling or unable to see the need for shifting goals or strategies. In brief, organizations and their members may act irrationally when compared to the standards of rationality that an intelligent, aware, objective observer might establish.

Hambrick-Mason Model   The model developed by Donald C. Hambrick and Phyllis A. Mason depicts how individual differences and limitations affect the rationality of the organization as a whole, as it sets goals and performance standards, then tries to achieve them. The model (see Figure 3.1) demonstrates how a manager chooses from the available strategies. It is to be read from left to right. At the far left is the general situation, including the elements (stimuli) that could conceivably affect the manager. But the manager cannot possibly perceive and comprehend *all* of these stimuli. The manager may well omit consideration of *relevant* stimuli simply by virtue of this inability to perceive everything.

Between the situation and the eventual decision or strategic choice arising out of it are several filters that affect the final choice. Two are the manager's cognitive base (facts and information that the manager already knows) and the manager's values. Both serve to filter out most of the stimuli in the situation. Of those that do pass through, some are filtered out by the manager's limited field of vision; the manager cannot attend to all stimuli coming through the cognitive-base and values filters. Since perception is a selective process, only a few perceptions are actively subjected to the manager's interpretations. These perceptual interpretations, in conjunction with the values that bear on the situation, determine the manager's eventual strategic choice. Being human, managers are not all-knowing. Their human limitations keep their decisions from being totally rational. And the same holds true for the organization's other members.

This lengthy discussion of rationality started with the question of how and why

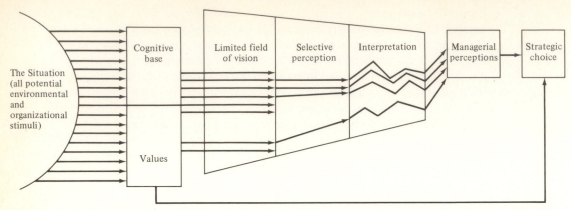

Figure 3.1   Limitations on the "rationality" of strategic choices. (*Source:* From Donald C. Hambrick and Phyllis A. Mason, "Upper Echelons: The Organization as a Reflection of Its Top Managers," *Academy of Management Review* 9 [April 1984], p. 195. Used by permission.)

organizational members come together, because answering that question can best help us to determine and understand their common purpose. Although their motives for coming together are "rational," that rationality—as Figure 3.1 shows—is not limitless. The natural limits that our humanness places on our rational decision-making ability should constantly be kept in mind by students and other organization theorists.

Involuntary Members   Some members become a part of organizations for reasons over which they do not have complete control. Hospital patients, prison inmates, and students in a required course do not join their organizations because they want to, but because they have to. Most members do join organizations by using a weighing process similar to that used by our examples of Harry's Pizza employees and Central High School marching band members. But we should not lose sight of the exceptions.

What Is the Common Purpose of the Organization's Members?

Determining Goals   This last question is the one to which this chapter is primarily devoted. Organizations are goal-seeking devices. How do we determine what a given organization's goals are? Even though an organization is, in reality, an entity made up of people, many discussions seem to imply that it can have a purpose of its own—apart from the purposes of the people within it. Reading the grand and global statements of purposes, missions, and goals in the annual reports of many large organizations reinforces this illusion. A hospital talks of "providing outstanding health care to the citizens of the county"; a charity talks of "ending birth defects"; a school aims to "provide quality education for our children"; and a corporation says "We intend to maximize our profits."

These goals are greater than any single generation of organizational members can fulfill, so, in a sense, the organization *can* have purposes of its own, larger and longer lasting than the purposes and careers of the present organizational membership. Such goals will continue to stimulate successive generations of organizational employees. They can provide an overriding purpose that draws people who "believe in what this organization stands for" to join, stay, serve, cooperate, and contribute.

Accomplishing Goals   Grand and global purpose statements may be somewhat useful in informing people inside and outside the organization of what the organization's primary goal, purpose, or mission is. Unfortunately, they are so general as to be of little use if we try to answer the question: Did you *accomplish* your goal? Goal attainment means effectiveness. Effective organizations reach their goals (or at least make significant progress towards them), and ineffective organizations do not.

Presumably, people join an organization in order to *achieve* a common purpose, to *attain* a common goal. But which purpose? Whose goal? And since goal statements are often quite vague, what is the criterion by which we may know that a goal has or has not been reached?

"To Learn the Material"   This issue is not easy to resolve. For example, assume that several students in an organization theory class join together to form a study group. Their common purpose is to learn the course material. We have said that effective organizations are those that reach their goals. Although "to learn the course material" sounds clear enough, is it a sufficiently specific goal that we will know when it has been achieved?

In order to know whether they have even come close to achieving their common purpose, the students will have to wait until the course is over, the study group is disbanded, and the grades are posted. Similarly, the profit-making corporation with "profit maximization" as its goal must often wait for weeks or months to see whether its "profit-maximizing" actions have in fact led to "maximum" profits. The corporation, however, can examine one period's results and make whatever changes seem necessary to improve the profit picture; the study group, with only one shot at performance—the final exam—does not have the luxury of modifying its learning activities and procedures in subsequent periods.

In our example of the study group trying to "learn the material," a myriad of problems arise as we try to determine the specifics of whether the *group* has met the *group's* goal. Does "learning the material" mean that all group members must get a grade of A? Or that everyone must achieve at least a C? Does the common purpose imply that all members should participate and exert effort equally? Or can some do most of the giving, and others most of the taking?

The Outside Observer   Simple and clear goal statements are usually more complicated than they appear, especially when organizational members try to determine whether they have achieved their goal. When a researcher-observer-theorist who is not a real organizational member seeks to measure whether or not the organization has reached its goal, the problem becomes even more difficult. The outside observer might watch the study group through a one-way mirror or from a corner of the group's meeting room. Such observations will certainly allow the observer to draw some conclusions about how the group operates. A subsequent tallying of the grades will provide a certain measure of whether the group was able to achieve its goal, as the observer defined it. But the external observer cannot really measure, understand, or even perceive the goals of the individual members, or know whether the group viewed the final grades as an acceptable goal achievement.

In a similar sense, the observer studying organizations as they try to achieve their goals is looking at the tip of the iceberg. What the observer is actually observing and measuring are typically the *public statements* of organizational goals, rather than the many unspoken goals that the members are trying to satisfy by coming together to engage in organizational activity.

Goals and Structures   To sum up the importance of goals and purposes: The goals of any organized group influence the decisions that the group makes about how to reach those goals. Until we know what the goal is, how can we put together an organization that will have the best chance of reaching that goal? How can we decide what types of people ought to be doing which things, how to structure or design the relationships of these people to each other, if we don't know the organizational goal?

Even if we do know the group's general goal, we need more specific information to structure the group properly. Consider the guarding-and-growing example in Chapter 1. Part of the group cultivates the land, while other members stand guard. The group's common desire to *survive* brought them together; yet, simply having this common desire does not automatically lead to a well-designed societal structure in which the various guarding-and-growing jobs are created and filled. The general goal—group survival—must be interpreted and translated into specific tasks if the group is to structure itself rationally and effectively.

Trial and Error   One view of organizational formation is that organizations specify their goals, then rationally establish the structures that will best enable achievement of those goals. Other writers argue that a trial-and-error process is more apt to occur in real life. According to this view, those organizations fortunate enough to mesh with their environmental circumstances will survive and perpetuate their organizational schemes; those unlucky enough to be at odds with their environments will—regardless of their goals and structures—die out, from organizational starvation or being overrun by stronger groups.[3] In brief, a natural selection process permits the survival of those groups and organizations which happen to fit best with the environment; the unfit organizations are eliminated. The dominance of this process makes it futile to spend much effort on precise definition of organizational goals or on many of the other issues raised in this text.

Rational Design   While the foregoing argument has interesting aspects, we choose the rational approach. We believe that organizations can and should be designed rationally; that some organizations should be designed one way and some another; that organizational goals can and should be stipulated; and that those goals should serve as the driving force for organizational design.[4] True, the environmental reality within which the organization operates is largely beyond its control. But effective organizational leadership can perceive that environmental reality and operate successfully within it, to compete for the societal resources needed to survive and grow.

Real, True, Operational Goals   Another question relevant to this chapter is: What are the organization's *real* goals, regardless of what the annual report *says* the goals are? Which goal statements actually determine what the organization does, how its members spend their time? Goal statements like "have a good time," "pass the course," "provide high-quality health care," or "maximize profits" all fail to answer such questions as: Should we take action A or action B? Should we meet to study on Thursday night or

Monday night? Should we put 12 ounces or 14 ounces of cheese in our pizza? The problem of specifying which goals the organization actually pursues—regardless of its goal statements—falls to those organizational decision makers who decide just what the organization will and won't do.

For instance, the organization's global statement in a glossy publication sent to stockholders may be: We are committed to making a high-quality product for a profit. Those organizational members responsible for the production process translate this goal into meaningful terms for the production workers by *rewarding or failing to reward* high production levels regardless of quality, high quality levels regardless of production, or something in between. If high production is the "real" goal, then those organizational members believing in high production regardless of quality stay on and are rewarded; those believing in high quality either leave or change their beliefs; and those who don't really care, so long as they can figure out the system well enough to enjoy its rewards, behave as the decision makers seem to want them to.[5]

THE EVOLUTION OF ORGANIZATIONAL GOALS

The academic debate about organizational goals and purposes has become quite complex.[6] For our purposes, however, we shall assume that the typical organization seeks, through its leadership, to accomplish three primary goals: profit, growth, and survival. To survive, an organization must maintain its legitimacy by convincing affected groups and persons that its continued existence is necessary and desirable. It can therefore be argued that the overriding goal of all organizations is survival, with profit and growth merely being vehicles by which survival is assured. Nevertheless, we include survival as one of the three factors—rather than as the overriding one—because, while the desire to survive is always a background goal of the other two, it is frequently in the *distant* background.

Consider a location at which ten retail stores in a row have failed. Susan Roebuck, a young and excited entrepreneur, sets up an eleventh retail store at that location. She would probably not claim that the driving force behind her entrepreneurial act was survival. On the other hand, if Bob Bureaucrat heads a federal agency under threat of congressional extinction, then survival is going to be prominent in that organization's goal structure. Seymour M. Hersh's *The Price of Power: Kissinger in the Nixon White House* (1983) offers numerous illustrations of agency heads who simply wanted their agencies to survive, as Kissinger accumulated more and more decision-making power.

To sum up: We postulate that organizations seek to achieve three primary goals—profit, growth, and survival—with the emphasis among the three depending upon the organization's stage of development in its life cycle and upon the leadership's interpretation of what activities will best lead to achieving the overall purpose that brought the group together in the first place.

Profit, Growth, and Survival

Profit   One way to understand goals is to reflect back on the historical evolution of organizations that was presented in the previous chapter. The early entrepreneur/owner/sole employee/top manager had no difficulty in defining and communicating the goal of his silversmith or blacksmith shop: to make a profit. His desire for profit caused him to risk his capital and to exert his efforts.

"Profit" is traditionally considered only in terms of its accounting definition: Revenues minus Costs equals Profit. However, in governments, churches, charities, and volunteer groups, this definition will not work. In such organizations, economic profit is not typically part of the goal structure, nor the reason for the organization's creation. The same is true even of many "for-profit" entrepreneurial organizations. Many entrepreneurs set up a business not only to make money but also to be their own boss, to engage in meaningful work, or for many other reasons of which money is only a part.

The following general definition might be more appropriate to such organizations: Personal Rewards minus Efforts equals Profit. This more subjective and generalized sense of profit better describes the organizational goal of, let us say, Daniel C. Beard, the founder of the Boy Scouts of America, during that organization's early years.

A familiar goal statement based on the profit motive is *profit maximization*. Under this definition, the firm aims all its efforts toward making as much profit as possible. However, this definition is not as clear-cut as it seems. For example, profit-maximizing behavior this year may hurt long-run profits if the firm maximizes profits by emphasizing quantity at the expense of quality. In short, even if management establishes profit maximization as a goal, determining what decision or combination of decisions will lead to that goal is quite difficult. In a single-product situation, profit maximization assumes that managers can identify the point in the production run where the marginal cost of producing equals the marginal revenue gained from production. Envision (if you can) a Chrysler plant manager pointing at a car and saying, "That's the unit where marginal cost equals marginal revenue. Stop the line." When a firm is turning out many products, the problem is even more complicated.

Since profit maximization as a goal has practical difficulties, top management often establishes its target in the form of profit levels that seem desirable and achievable (rather than maximal).

Growth   Once the business was earning a reasonable profit, the small-scale entrepreneur often wanted to become a larger-scale entrepreneur—in other words, to grow. Within the eighteenth-century social system, "growth" quickly became associated with "success" and "progress" as a good and desirable quality. Without getting into a philosophical discussion of whether society should value growth, the fact remains that society does value it. "Think big" and "Bigger is better" are two popular American slogans. Growth is important to most organizational goal structures. Small entrepreneurs—successful in the competitive marketplace and rewarded for their efforts by profits—think in terms of expansion almost as a reflex action. The university adds new curricula and degree programs, the small church adds a new sanctuary, the small hospital adds more beds. Market success leads to profits and other resources, which serve jointly as an inducement to grow and as a means of financing growth.

Profit and growth are not always compatible goals. In order to grow tomorrow, the entrepreneur might have to resist taking today's profit out of the business.

Survival   Of course, the entrepreneur can enjoy neither profit nor growth if he does not survive. The entrepreneur has perhaps gone through a long apprenticeship period.

He realizes the difficulty involved in acquiring the skills and tools of a new craft. Therefore, he might want his firm just to survive even if both profit and growth are small.

The entrepreneur's dual desires to survive and to make a profit might at times conflict. For example, consider a downtown business district struck by a sudden rainstorm. A store owner thinking only of immediate or short-run profit might get away with selling umbrellas at outrageously high prices. However, once the sun comes out, people are going to realize that they have been taken in and will do as little business with that store as possible. The store owner will find that profit-maximizing behavior in the short run (during the rainstorm) can lead to bankruptcy in the long run (when people have other options). In short, even the entrepreneur motivated primarily by profit must realize that a "get it while you can" pricing policy may not lead to long-run survival.

The organization's drive to survive is also explainable in systems terms. Organizations are founded in order to achieve goals. However, according to the natural system model (briefly discussed in Chapter 1), the organization soon takes on the characteristics of an organism, with needs and goals of its own. And like any other organism, the business or government organization has self-preservation—survival—as a primary goal.[7]

The Organizational Life Cycle

The related goals of profit, growth, and survival seem to embrace the overall goal structures of most organizations. However, the emphasis which a firm places on the three goals will shift over time. A general, descriptive model showing this shifting emphasis through a typical organization's full life cycle appears in Figure 3.2. Not all organizations pass through all stages. Indeed, only about one-half of all new business organizations survive longer than one and a half years, and only one-quarter see a sixth birthday. Relatively few for-profit or not-for-profit organizations survive long enough to travel the full life-cycle path.[8]

Profit to Growth   Figure 3.2 shows that management emphasizes different goals during different phases of the firm's life cycle. In the early years of a firm's history, the owner/entrepreneur is oriented mainly toward profits and less toward growth and survival. Once profits are assured, the firm can shift its emphasis to growth. This critical shift from a profit orientation to a focus on growth is usually accompanied by an organizational shift from management by the founder/owner/entrepreneur and his family to management by a professional administrative group.

This was illustrated by Robert C. Hazard, Jr., who moved from Best Western hotels to Quality Inns in 1980. A risk taker and innovator, Hazard expanded the Best Western chain from 800 hotels to 2597. He wanted to continue the company's rapid expansion, but the elected board of hotel owners wanted to slow down and solidify their gains. Then, the Quality Inns chain, financially stable after several years of losses, and still in the early stages of its life cycle, hired Hazard—with his entrepreneurial attitude and tactics—away from Best Western. The new Best Western president emphasized cost cutting, tight budgets, and controlled expansion rather than go-go growth. On the

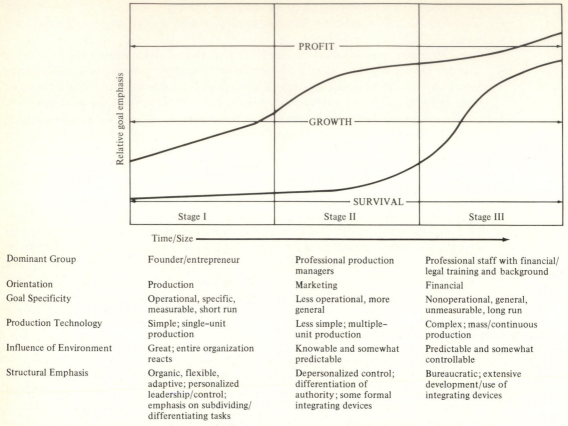

	Stage I	Stage II	Stage III
Dominant Group	Founder/entrepreneur	Professional production managers	Professional staff with financial/legal training and background
Orientation	Production	Marketing	Financial
Goal Specificity	Operational, specific, measurable, short run	Less operational, more general	Nonoperational, general, unmeasurable, long run
Production Technology	Simple; single–unit production	Less simple; multiple–unit production	Complex; mass/continuous production
Influence of Environment	Great; entire organization reacts	Knowable and somewhat predictable	Predictable and somewhat controllable
Structural Emphasis	Organic, flexible, adaptive; personalized leadership/control; emphasis on subdividing/differentiating tasks	Depersonalized control; differentiation of authority; some formal integrating devices	Bureaucratic; extensive development/use of integrating devices

Figure 3.2   Relative emphasis on three different goals during the organizational life cycle.

other hand, within two months of taking over, Hazard was planning to more than double the number of Quality Inns franchises from 345 to nearly 750.

The reason for such shifts in organizational management is simple and logical. By definition, an entrepreneur is a person who takes the risk of starting and managing a business in hopes of making a profit. At some point, age forces the entrepreneur to step aside. Perhaps the founder's descendants will carry on for a while, but eventually they too will give way to managers who run the business for them. While owner/entrepreneurs may be willing to sacrifice growth for profit, professional managers want a wide range of rewards that only growth can supply. Growth justifies salary increases, executive perquisites, and Lear jets.

Growth leads to increased status; if you manage a large company, you must be smart (even if your company's return on investment is low). Most managers would rather run a bankrupt intercontinental railroad than a flourishing corner candy store. Finally, only through growth can the power associated with size be obtained. The president of the bankrupt railroad may well be granted an appointment to see the President of the United States. The candy store owner will probably get a polite refusal.

Once the owner/entrepreneur is no longer the firm's sole leader, the desire for growth to achieve size often becomes the organization's dominant goal. This pattern emerges in nonprofit organizations as well as profit-making organizations. The founders of such groups as the Boy Scouts, the Red Cross, and religious organizations set high-minded humanitarian and spiritual goals ahead of profit or growth. As the founders are replaced by professional managers, the original goals remain important, but growth often slowly emerges as an equally important goal. This new goal makes sense, from the managerial point of view. Growth confirms the wisdom of managerial decisions, as more followers are attracted, joining in the achievement of the organizational purpose. If the organization keeps growing, the management group must be a winner and their cause must be right and true.[9]

Survival   In the latter stages of an organization's existence, a desire to survive dominates the desire to profit and to grow.[10] Consider the marketing life cycle of a single product. Most products eventually reach a market saturation and maturation stage, characterized by fierce competition and price cutting. Consumers may even begin to view the product as a general commodity rather than as a specific name-brand item, which has, for instance, happened to Coca-Cola. During this stage, the company tries to help its products survive by intensifying its marketing efforts. For example, Coca-Cola strives to protect the name "Coke" and to distinguish their beverage from other colas. To survive, the company must prevent "Coke" from becoming a generic term used to describe all cola drinks.

    The organization's life cycle does not necessarily have to coincide perfectly with the life cycles of its products. True, the state of the market for the products or services may influence the organization's culture, internal structure, and strategy. Nevertheless, a very dynamic Stage I (profit-dominated) organization could be contending with a mature product market; for example, MCI is a newcomer to the mature long-distance phone call market. Conversely, a declining Stage III firm could be benefiting from an evolving, expanding market, as is American Telephone & Telegraph in telecommunications.

    The important relationship between product, environment and organizational goals and structure will be discussed at length later. For the moment, we simply want to point out that any organization's focus on its goals is a changing, evolutionary process.

Goals and Other Organizational Characteristics

Stage I and Stage III   Certain characteristics of organizations tend to vary directly with changes in goal focus. For example, Figure 3.2 shows some characteristics that the Stage I, profit-oriented organization tends to have:

1. It is entrepreneurial, dominated by the founder.
2. It is product oriented.
3. It has specific, measurable goals.
4. Its production technology is simple, geared to produce single units.
5. It is greatly affected by environmental forces and changes.
6. Its structure is flexible and organic. Leadership and control are personalized. Differentiation of tasks is stressed.

The Stage III, survival-oriented organization tends to have different characteristics, many of them opposite to those of the Stage I organization:

1. It is managed by professionals, typically staff-trained people from the financial and legal departments.
2. It is finance oriented.
3. It has general, nonoperational goals.
4. Its technology is complex, geared toward mass production or continuous production.
5. Although affected by the environment, it can soften the effects by predicting and controlling the environment to an extent.
6. Its structure is bureaucratic. It emphasizes integrating the efforts of organizational members.

These differences can be better perceived by imagining a spectrum, with Paul Revere making silver bowls at one end and the International Silver Corporation at the other. Paul has designed the organization to reach his personal goals; he supervises his employees by one-on-one contact; and he feels quite helpless to do anything but respond to the environmental forces and conditions that affect his small organization. However, the goals are *his,* and he directs the organization's members to accomplish them. Those who choose to accept Paul's goals and methods, stay; those who do not, leave. The organization's small size and the nature of silver bowl technology force certain structural devices and design strategies upon Paul Revere, but most of the devices and strategies arise out of his personal preferences.[11]

International Silver, a large conglomerate, must deal with the increased technological complexity resulting from highly specialized and sophisticated equipment and processes. It must integrate its many parts efficiently. It must be aware that its size and actions are going to cause some public scrutiny. It will tend to be more bureaucratic, more set in its ways and procedures. It will tend to be managed by highly trained specialists, such as financial analysts and lawyers.

An interesting example of how an entire growth industry achieved influence within its political environment is provided by the semiconductor industry. In its early days of explosive growth and political innocence, the industry did not seem to be aware that it should or could try to affect its political environment. According to *Business Week:*

> The American Electronics Assn. didn't even have a Washington office until 1980. And it took the semiconductor industry nearly two decades to figure out that it needed to make things work on the Hill. For the first 15 years of its life, the industry was totally ignorant of the world outside its little silicon kingdom.
>
> "Intel, National Semiconductor, AMD were around 10 to 12 years old in 1978," says a source who was closely associated with them at the time. "They were incredible. They didn't know anything—on international matters or Washington politics."
>
> The Semiconductor Industry Assn. was first set up in 1977 and cut its political teeth on a 1979 investigation by the International Trade Commission into the pricing and volume of Japanese imports. The semiconductor group went on to press for a reduction in Japanese duties on U.S. semiconductor imports and for a 25%

R&D tax credit in the Reagan Administration's first tax package in 1981. And it got both.[12]

Renewing the Life Cycle   Many organizations are born, move through the three stages, and then die—but not all organizations. An organization can be "reborn" in several ways. One organization may take over another one. Or the directors of a mature organization may replace its top management, to inject a new and youthful spirit. A well-known illustration is Lee Iacocca's rejuvenation of Chrysler Corporation. Decentralization of a centralized structure may regenerate the organization. Operating managers have known for years that small, self-contained, return-on-investment centers can to some extent recreate the excitement and energy of the Stage I owner/entrepreneur firm. In other cases, a change from decentralization to centralization may also have an energizing effect.

Further Influences on Goals

Any organization's goals are dynamic rather than static. They reflect the changing values, needs, and training of the dominant group or coalition (top management, in business and industrial organizations).[13] Although the organization's goals can, to a certain extent, be whatever the dominant group decides, that group is not completely free to choose any goals it wishes. Compromises must often be made in light of several influences: the social system, competition, other organizational members (in particular the owners), the organization's physical environment, and technological limitations.

The Social System   The organization must consider society's expectations and requirements. For example, unless the organization is a street gang, it will try not to break any laws. Automobile manufacturers will not enclose instructions in the owner's manual on how to remove pollution control devices no matter how much consumers want that information. More generally, organizations are finding that an increasingly greater sense of "social responsibility" is expected of them. Therefore, firms make contributions to education and the arts, hire and train minorities, try to protect the environment, respond to consumer complaints, and so on. Of course, society's expectations, laws, and norms of behavior change over time. The levels of socially responsible behavior expected of today's business firm or government official are vastly different from what they were only a few years ago.

Competition   Economic necessity (or economic reality) also affects the dominant group's ability to superimpose its goals on the rest of the organization. Organizations compete for economic resources as well as for the good will of society. If an organization's leadership makes bad economic decisions, competitors will take quick advantage of its mistakes. The organization must use its resources efficiently to achieve an acceptable level of economic performance. A business organization that does not meet minimal return-on-investment or profitability criteria cannot continue to exist. Nor can a charity that uses all of its funds to pay executive salaries. The organization must remain constantly aware that other groups and organizations are competing for the same resources—whether they be funds, materials, customers, employees, reputation, or societal approval. These resources are not limitless, and many different organizations continuously bid for them.

Other Organizational Members   The goals of other organizational members are often the most significant constraint on the dominant group's ability to achieve its own goals. When one person is the sole owner/worker, then individual and organizational goals do not conflict. When the organization expands to more than one person, the original member will have to give up something in order to induce the new members to join. The original member may offer shared ownership, a straight salary, decision-making power, an opportunity to perform noble deeds, or some other of the many tangible and intangible rewards that encourage people to join organizations. Organizational founders and the dominant managerial groups who follow them must sacrifice some degree of their own goal attainment in order to give the additional members some kind of payment for their services. Whatever inducements must be offered inhibit the ability of the organization's dominant group to do as they desire.[14] We will expand upon the inducements/contributions idea later in this chapter.

If the organization's owners are different from its managers, then the owners' desires may affect which goals management tries to achieve. The president of a state-owned university must answer to state officials much as the president of a profit-oriented public corporation must answer to stockholders. Up to a point, the corporation's dominant group may be able to trade profits for growth or for executive perquisites, but unless profits are forthcoming, the stockholders will eventually exert their influence on management.

Environment and Technology   The organization's achievable goals may be restricted by its physical environment and technology. No organization can build a stable structure on a live volcano or a nuclear reactor on the San Andreas fault. Because of technological limitations, certain goals simply cannot be achieved, no matter how badly the dominant group wants to achieve them. Although technological constraints are gradually losing significance in an era in which hearts can be manufactured and people can travel to the moon, some feats remain technologically impossible.

Constraints on the Dominant Group   The constraints on the dominant group's ability to choose freely which goals it wants to achieve are pictured in Figure 3.3. Inside the box, the dominant group has considerable latitude to choose what it wishes to do. But the group eventually encounters limits on this freedom of choice in all directions. If the dominant group does not equitably share the rewards of organizational effort, the employees may strike. If the organization uses its resources inefficiently, society may withdraw its support. And so on, for each limiting factor. The point is that the dominant group has flexibility to establish its own goals, to work toward achieving them, and to reward itself for that achievement. But that flexibility is not unbounded.[15]

MAKING GOALS USEFUL

Most goal statements and most discussions of goals (including ours, so far) are quite general. For an organization to use its goal statements to guide its design or structure

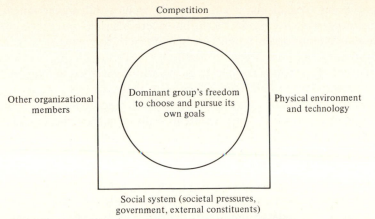

Figure 3.3   Constraints on dominant group's goal selection.

and the actions of its members, the organization must translate its general goal statements into specifics. As sociologist Charles Perrow notes below, in his distinction between official and operative goals, this translation helps the organization to see where it should go and how to get there.

Official and Operative Goals

According to Charles Perrow, *official* goals are "the general purposes of the organization as put forth in the charter, annual reports, public statements by key executives, and other authoritative pronouncements."[16] In contrast, *operative* goals "designate the ends sought through the actual operating policies of the organization; they tell us what the organization actually is trying to do, regardless of what the official goals say are the aims."[17]

Official goals are what the organization formally *says* it wants to achieve while operative goals are what the organization is actually *trying* to achieve. In some organizations, there is a great disparity between the two. For example, the official goal of a city government might be to provide for the health and welfare of all its citizens (a goal whose achievement might cost millions of dollars). The city's operative goal might be to stay within a limited budget. Although city administrators make the official goal well known, they are actually trying to achieve the operative goal.

Goal Displacement   This distinction between official and operative goals can lead to goal displacement. When the official and operative goals are not the same, we say that the operative goals have *displaced* the official goals. Displaced goals are usually unintended by management. Indeed, they may not even know that new goals have displaced the official ones.

Goal displacement can occur in any organization whose leaders put their personal goals ahead of organizational goals. For example, managers can insist to company directors that they are trying to maximize stockholder dividends, when they may in fact be trying primarily to establish their own power, gratify their own egos, and fatten their own paychecks. Goal displacement can easily occur within a government bureaucracy. Bureaucrats tend to live rigidly by the bureaucracy's rules and procedures. Over time, they lose sight of the organization's goals, and strictly following the organization's rules and procedures becomes a goal in itself.

This displacement is familiar to people who have stood in long lines at the motor vehicle bureau only to find, after a long wait, that they have the wrong form, or are at the wrong window, or that the office has just closed down for the lunch hour. The motor vehicle bureaucrats have unintentionally displaced the organization's official goal of serving the public efficiently with a new one: following the rules and procedures handed down by other bureaucrats.

Positive Goal Displacement   Goal displacement need not always have negative results. Organizational members occasionally feel stifled creatively and, on their own, initiate different goals. The goal of the March of Dimes for instance, is to eliminate all birth defects. The organization's resources should presumably be used to attain this admirable goal. But suppose a young medical researcher feels that, since everyone else is trying to achieve this goal, she should branch off and try to find a cure for cancer. She begins using the resources at her disposal to attain her goal and, after intensive research and experimentation, does so. In this case, goal displacement has had a positive result.

Organizational Effectiveness   The distinction between official and operative goals further leads us to the concept of organizational effectiveness—*the degree to which the organization achieves its stated, official goals.* In effective organizations, the operative goals are the same as the official goals. In an ineffective organization, the official and operative goals are not the same. If this difference leads to waste and improperly used resources—that is, to inefficiency—the organization should try to make member goals congruent with organizational goals. On the other hand, if the difference leads to positive organizational achievements (such as in the March of Dimes example), then eventually the organization's management may reexamine the official goals and perhaps incorporate these operative goals into them.

In either event, official and operative goals should be as identical as possible. To be effective, an organization should *actually* be trying to do what it *says* it is trying to do. If it is not, then managers should either change the direction of organizational effort or change the organization's goals.

Organizational Efficiency   Effectiveness refers to the degree of goal attainment. Efficiency refers to how economically the organization converts its inputs into the desired outputs. Efficiency is most often measured in such financial terms as revenues and costs. However, for some organizations, costs and benefits cannot be measured in dollar terms. For example, a hospital might consider "patients treated" or "patients cured" as its output.

Efficiency is a goal of all organizations. But an efficient organization may not necessarily be effective. To understand this principle, consider again the motor vehicle agency where you may stand in a line for hours. The method for processing papers may be efficient, but customer satisfaction—presumably an organizational goal—is not being effectively achieved. Similarly, an organization may view the attainment of certain goals, no matter how long it takes, as more important than efficiency. A social worker who spends two hours with an irate client has perhaps not made the most efficient use of his time (in terms of processing cases), but he may have achieved a more important goal: customer satisfaction.

Nonoperational Goals

The distinction between nonoperational and operational goals is even more useful in making design and structural decisions. A nonoperational goal is one whose degree of achievement cannot be objectively measured. An example would be a New Year's resolution to "be a better student." By definition, every person but one can be a better student than someone else, and even this year's worst student can satisfy the goal by becoming a better student next year.

In the business world, many well-intentioned goal statements are nonoperational. For example, the following statements, coming from actual corporate annual reports, embody official goals:

1. To expand opportunities in natural resources and industrial markets.
2. To manage the company's assets productively.
3. To provide fair and consistent returns to stockholders on their investment.
4. To produce quality goods and services that are in the best interests of the global economy.
5. To offer the customer the best possible products and services.
6. To operate in a manner that contributes to the improvement of society and is sensitive to the natural and human environment.

These official goal statements are impressive and worthy. Yet they are nonoperational. No method exists for measuring the extent to which they have been achieved.

Operational Goals

Achievement of operational goals *can* be measured fairly objectively. The goal itself may or may not be appropriate or worthwhile, official or operative, but at least the organization and all its members know whether the goal has been reached. Organizations need to break down such nonoperational goals as profit, growth, and survival into operational goals. The organization can then recognize whether it is accomplishing these operational goals—whether it is an "effective" organization.

For instance, du Pont has translated the traditional—but nonoperational—goal of profit maximization directly into a specific measure of return on investment (ROI) for every product (for example, 20 percent before taxes). If a product cannot achieve the targeted ROI, as happened to Rayon and Corfam, it is dropped. Although the required ROI may be somewhat arbitrary, it is at least a measurable, commonly understood standard that permits quick determination of whether goals have been attained.

Size and Goals   Organizational size frequently affects goal setting. Large organizations with many members, processes, and products often have to express official goals in general terms that can serve as common themes that appeal to and unite diverse organizational interests. Such organizations must then translate these general nonoperational goals into specific operational goals so that all members can understand how their roles fit into the total organizational pattern. One way to do this is to set ROI criteria for each unit as specific expressions of the general corporate goal. Government bureaucracies might use budget methods to accomplish the same purpose. Another method is through means-end chains.

Means-End Chains   Managers can and should play an important role in converting nonoperational company goals into more specific, understandable goals for their subordinates. One way to envision how specific job activities relate to general, nonoperational goals is in terms of means-end chains.

General goals are transmitted down from the top throughout the organization. As managers on each level are given goals, they translate them into more specific terms for their subordinates. As lower-level goals are met, they become the means for meeting succeedingly higher-level goals. The worker becomes the means whereby the supervisor achieves his ends; the supervisor becomes the means whereby the manager achieves his ends. And so the means-end chains move back up through the organization to the board of directors, which established the organization's goals in the first place.

Figure 3.4 depicts a typical means-end chain. Examining the chain from bottom to top, we see that each unit's accomplishment of its ends becomes the means whereby the next higher level accomplishes its ends.

Some real-life problems may occur in this ideal state. The means-end chain has many links and as we will discuss in Chapter 13, Communications, each link represents a potential misunderstanding. Therefore, people at the bottom of the chain may or may not be engaging in activities that will enable the top levels to achieve organizational goals. Another problem is the inevitable time lag. By the time all of the links in the chain have adjusted to a shift in goals and objectives at the top, opportunities may have been missed.

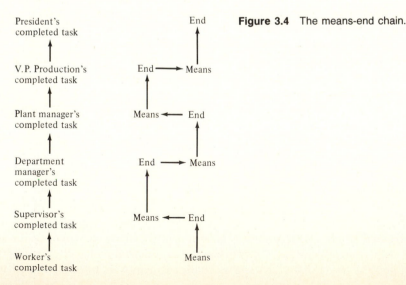

Figure 3.4 The means-end chain.

MULTIPLE GOALS

Multiple Operational Goals

Even if goals can be made operational, the multiplicity of goals in the modern business organization adds complications. Organizations often cannot exert maximum effort in favor of all goals at the same time. Which ones should receive priority?

Consider a personnel department that is told to design programs to reduce product defects by 15 percent and to reduce industrial accidents by 10 percent. In complying, there may well be a "cycle of emphasis" problem. In April the department publicizes a quality-control program. The desired quality level is achieved, but the accident rate rises. In May the department focuses successfully on safety, but quality slips. Failure to achieve one of the operational goals causes it to become the focus of the month, limited personnel prevents adequate attention to *any* goal, and so the cycle continues.

This example points up some of the difficulties managers may face when trying to rank multiple operational goals. Managers are held accountable for reaching several goals. Which is most important? On which should emphasis be placed? Managers may make their decisions not on the basis of what is best for the company, but in light of their own personal goals and their perceptions of what their own managers want or expect. The organizational reward system is also a big factor in successful achievement of operational goals. Managers will usually concentrate their energies where the payoffs are largest. If the bonus plan is based on quantity produced, for instance, then managers may try to achieve their quotas *without* proper regard for product quality or employee safety.

Departmental versus Overall Goals

Another problem with multiple operational goals is that as organizational units focus on their own goals, they may lose sight of overall goals. For example, in many organizations the sales personnel and the credit department maintain a running argument. The sales force argue that they could perform much better if credit restrictions were not so "unrealistically tight." The credit personnel argue that sales wants to endanger the firm's assets by extending credit "to every warm body."

In trying to meet or exceed its own goals, each department may be undercutting the firm's total effectiveness. The general principle to keep in mind is: The more departmental goals an organization establishes, the more its managers will be tempted to maximize those goals *at the expense of* overall organizational goals. The operational goals of departments are in a sense ends in themselves; but, more importantly, they should serve as a means of achieving the goals of the organization as a whole.

Multiple Nonoperational Goals

Over a period of time, managers may use simple trial and error to resolve this balancing problem for multiple operational goals. The balancing problem for multiple *nonoperational* goals is much more difficult. For instance, all companies must translate the multiple nonoperational goals of profit, growth, and survival into more meaningful, operational terms. These general goals must be made specific, to direct effort and to facilitate performance evaluation within such important organizational areas as market share, employee development, new product research, social responsibility, and the like.

Defining operational goals within such areas is not easy. Establishing specific goals that are consistent with all three general goals—profit, growth, and survival—is even more difficult. Let us use social responsibility as an example of a major area within which nonoperational goals must be made operational.

Social Responsibility Just what responsibility does a business organization have to society? Consider Corporation XYZ's goal of operating "in a manner which contributes to the improvement of society." Does this goal translate into political gifts for favored candidates, closing down plants rather than pollute the air, and donating money to colleges? Or is simply providing people with jobs enough? Furthermore, can the answers to these questions be made consistent with profit, growth, *and* survival? What action will society take against firms not meeting an acceptable level of social responsibility? Are any effectiveness measures available to organizational decision makers wanting to know when the costs of social responsibility are in some sense balanced by the benefits?

Difficult as these questions are, they must be answered if a company is to know what it is doing in the area of social responsibility, and why.

BALANCING INDUCEMENTS AND CONTRIBUTIONS

To encourage and maintain continuing involvement in organizational activities, the dominant coalition offers members *inducements*. In exchange, members are expected to make *contributions* to organizational goals.[18] Just as primitive man expected only a share of the slain animal, modern man expects only a share of the automobile factory's returns. The member and the organization have expectations about what constitutes "a fair day's contributions for a fair day's inducements." When these expectations fail to match up, adjustments will be made. In the most extreme case, a dissatisfied member will leave the organization. In a less extreme case, the member may reconsider and accept the inducements presently offered, request additional or different inducements, reduce his contributions, offer to increase contributions if inducements are also increased, and so on.

Every organizational member experiences this very personal and dynamic process of balancing inducements with contributions. The inducements that members demand depend on their own estimates of what their contributions are worth to the accomplishment of the organization's goals. The inducements that organizations offer to members are similarly determined. If the member and the organization agree on the worth of the member's contribution, the best interests of both are easily met.

In addition, the values that members place on inducements depend upon how well those inducements enable them to fulfill their personal goals. If they are fulfilled, the quality and quantity of contributions will be enhanced.

A balancing of inducements with contributions occurs at all levels of all organizations. If managers believe that the only thing workers want from the job is a paycheck, they are likely to become confused when workers ask for more job variety, responsibility, or participation in decision making. Autocratic business managers who become chairpersons of voluntary organizations experience the same confusion. They cannot understand why volunteers don't always do exactly as they are told to do. The successful volunteer chairperson will find out what inducements volunteers consider to be a worthwhile trade for their contributions.

The Changing Values of Inducements

By offering inducements, organizations elicit contributions that help to accomplish group goals. The values and expectations attached to both inducements and contributions are constantly changing. For instance, as a reasonable contribution in exchange for the inducement "opportunity for advancement," many organizations used to demand that new junior executives move from one plant or office location to another every few months. Such training programs often created emotional turmoil for potential executives and their families. Organizations now find that "opportunity for advancement" is often not a sufficient inducement to encourage this particular contribution. Therefore, more and more organizations are offering training programs in one location, appealing to potential managers who consider rapidly rotating assignments too disrupting to other important aspects of their lives.

As the beliefs, values, and customs of organization members change, so will their attitudes toward inducements and contributions. The ability of organizational leaders to recognize and respond to these changes will have considerable impact on the organization's performance.

The Organization's Responsibility: Providing the Link

Goal statements of most large organizations are very broad, reflecting the great diversity of their members' beliefs, values, needs, and goals. The organization's dominant group or coalition provides the link between the organization's general goals and the specific goals of organization members. The coalition does this by knowing the inducements that the organization can offer, learning the personal goals of group members, and then offering those inducements that will encourage members to make their most worthwhile contributions. Individual and organizational goals rarely mesh perfectly. However, if supervisors are trained to recognize the needs and aspirations of group members, and if they have some latitude in combining and offering specific types of inducements that different members prefer, then members should be willing to make the contributions necessary to accomplish organizational goals.

Inducements and Contributions Affect Goal Definition   In the process of making organizational goals operational, managers actually help to shape and define those goals. Like other employees, managers have their own reasons for joining organizations, staying with them, and exerting effort on the organization's behalf. These reasons affect and become part of goals as managers define them for subordinates.

The president of AT&T and the president of Pat's Pizza Palace both put their personal stamp on the goals of the organizations they lead. As goals are passed down through the organizations in the means-end process, succeeding members redefine these goals in terms of their own goals, inducements, and contributions. Each person's own definition of the appropriate balance of inducements-contributions influences the way in which that person makes (or does not make) organizational goals operational. Whether the official goal *as stated* becomes the operative goal *in fact* depends on how well it corresponds to the employees' definition of the inducements-contributions balance.

SUMMARY

Three questions arise out of our definition of "organization": Who are the people in the organization? How and why did they come together? And what is their common purpose? Organizational goals evolve through a profit-growth-survival cycle. There are a number of influences on goals, including society, competition, organizational members other than the dominant group, the physical environment, and technology. Organizations usually have official, operative, operational, and nonoperational goals. Official goals are what the organization says it is trying to do. Operative goals are what the organization is actually trying to do. Operative goals often displace official goals in organizations. Operational goals are specific and measurable. Nonoperational goals are general and nonmeasurable. We explored some advantages (and some difficulties) of making nonoperational goals operational. Specific job activities can be related to general goals by using means-end chains. The achievement by each organizational level of its goals (ends) becomes the means whereby the next higher level achieves its goals.

Multiple goals, whether operational or nonoperational, can create multiple problems for organizations. The social responsibility of organizations is a typical area within which nonoperational goals must be made operational. A balance of the organization's inducements with the member's contributions is necessary to achieve organizational goals.

DISCUSSION QUESTIONS

1. What is the organizational boundary? How is it related to organizational goals?
2. Discuss some of the problems involved in trying to determine the goals of a given organization.
3. Identify and briefly discuss the three major goals of most organizations.
4. How can a "nonprofit" organization show a profit?
5. Why does growth eventually become more important than profit to the typical organization?
6. In Figure 3.2, the growth stage is projected as bulging out rather dramatically. According to the argument in the text, why does this bulge occur? Do you agree or disagree with this explanation? Cite some examples from the current business literature to support your point.
7. What are the important changes as the organization moves from one life-cycle stage to another?
8. "Organizational goals are dynamic, not static." Explain this statement.
9. Other than the organization's stage in the life cycle, what are the major influences on organizational goals? Which is most important, and why?
10. How free is a typical organization's dominant group to set that organization's goals?
11. Distinguish between official and operative organizational goals.
12. What is goal displacement, and why is it important? Discuss its negative and positive aspects.
13. What does "organizational effectiveness" really mean? Can an organization be effective without also being efficient? Why or why not?

14. Distinguish between operational and nonoperational goals. Why is this distinction important?

15. What is the means-end chain? How does it tie the organization together?

16. What is the inducements-contributions concept? What does it tell us about organizational goals?

17. What kinds of inducements can the organization's dominant group offer in order to persuade organizational members to support and work toward achievement of the dominant group's goals?

18. Who or what is the dominant group or coalition? Why do we use these terms instead of "chief executive" or "boss"?

19. How may the goals of the dominant group differ from those of other groups important to the organization (e.g., stockholders, lower-level managers)? In reviewing current business news, can you find illustrations of these differences?

20. Consider any organization of which you have been a member. Pick several major concepts in this chapter and show how they are related to the organization and your relationship to it.

■   *PROFIT? GROWTH? SURVIVAL?*

Four business administration students were having a discussion at the Student Center about the primary goal of business firms.

Jim said emphatically, "Corporations are in business to make as much money as they can. Profit maximization is the primary goal, and everything else is secondary."

Will agreed, up to a point: "For a public corporation, profits are a *necessity,* but the primary *goal* of any business is to *grow*. No business wants to stay small and unimportant. Company officials and stockholders want growth, for the feeling of progress and accomplishment it brings and for the profits that will eventually accompany growth."

Jane said, "There's something to what you both say. Any company needs profits, and any company would like to grow. But *survival* is the primary goal, because without it you can't have profit *or* growth."

Betty said, "No matter what you learned in class, you are all kidding yourselves. 'Primary goals' are just for looks anyway. No matter how specific an organization's goals, no matter how carefully it plans, no matter how hard it works to meet those goals, the environment within which the organization markets its product or service will determine the organization's destiny. Organizations react to environmental forces, regardless of goals. To succeed, a business organization doesn't need to establish goals; it needs to be lucky enough to be in the right place at the right time and take advantage of the opportunities presented to it."

With whose position would the company's stockholders most likely agree? The CEO? The employees? Where do you stand on the issue?

■   *FACULTY ACTIVITIES AT NORMAL STATE UNIVERSITY*

The state evaluation team had exhaustively studied the operation of the English Department at Normal State University. They presented a report to Dean Edward Healy that was highly favorable except for one area. According to the state consultants:

"Your English faculty are conscientious and hard working, but they don't seem to have any objectives at the beginning of a semester other than to 'do the best job I can at my instruction, research/scholarship, and service functions.' We suggest that you and the faculty think more specifically about both what they intend to accomplish and are required to accomplish. Here are our recommendations.

"First, all of you should acquire a better understanding of Normal State University's goals. What is Normal State trying to accomplish? Then, before each semester starts, try to tie faculty activities into those university goals. Come to an agreement with all faculty members about the specific activities they are to engage in and what they are expected to accomplish in their three important areas of responsibility. Agree on what percentage of time will be devoted to each area. At the end of the semester, check back to see how well actual accomplishments match intended accomplishments and evaluate individual faculty members on that basis. Only in these ways can you (1) link individual faculty objectives and activities with institutional goals and (2) base faculty evaluations on meaningful criteria."

Is such a plan feasible? If you were Dean Edward Healy, would you accept, modify, or reject the plan? How do you think faculty members will react to it? What might some of the university's goals be? What faculty objectives and activities might lead to the accomplishment of those goals?

HARTSELL MANUFACTURING COMPANY

While he was still in college, Bill Hartsell decided that printed circuit board modules with integrated-circuit chips could be used in many devices, ranging from computers to washing machines. When he graduated, he borrowed some money, rented an old garage, bought surplus equipment from the government, and started Hartsell Manufacturing Company. The garage was cold in the winter and hot in the summer, but Bill was highly motivated and worked 12 to 16 hours a day, 6 or 7 days a week.

The hard work paid off. Bill added an assembly line to install components on the circuit boards and increased his staff from 3 to 20. He made a determined effort to hire young people, old people, women, minorities, and the handicapped, and he paid them as well as he could. Bill felt a genuine sense of responsibility to his employees and to the community. After five years, Bill had 300 employees working two shifts.

Bill hired three recent MBA graduates, intending to move them into responsible management positions after a training period. At his first meeting with them, Bill made his position plain: "No one at Hartsell Manufacturing works harder than I do. I'm the first to arrive and the last to leave. I work most weekends. I'm paying you well. I'm offering you a chance for rapid advancement. But don't think in terms of a 40-hour work week. I want you to work as hard as I do and act as if this business were your own. Is that clear?"

In unison the three responded, "Yes, sir, Mr. Hartsell." Three months later they had all left and taken jobs with General Motors, U.S. Steel, and General Electric.

What, if anything, was wrong with Mr. Hartsell's approach? Were his expectations for his new employees unrealistic? If so, why? What inconsistencies, if any, do you see between the goals of the three new employees and Mr. Hartsell's goals? Could those inconsistencies have been resolved? How?

STATE MENTAL HEALTH AGENCY

Sally Johnson is a supervisor in a state agency offering mental health services. Once a year, she must evaluate each of her 12 case workers. After a recent evaluation session with Judy Adams, Johnson realized that the agency had a problem.

Judy Adams has been with the agency for two years. She is bright and dedicated, always willing to help co-workers when they get behind. She has mastered her job and performs it with confidence. In the evaluation conference, supervisor Johnson told Adams that her work was outstanding, her attitude excellent, and her leadership skills widely recognized. Johnson said that she was giving Adams the highest appraisal rating in the department.

Then Adams asked her supervisor two tough questions: "What rewards do I get for doing a good job? And where do I go from here?" Adams mentioned the unfairness of the state compensation system and said that the distinctions between state salaries were too small to reward outstanding performance. While she had not been pushed to the desperation point, she was very troubled by the state's unwillingness to recognize economic realities.

She went on to say that, although she really liked her work and received much personal satisfaction from it, she thought she might be ready for something different—possibly a supervisor's job. Because of her desire for fair pay and more responsibility, she said frankly that she was about to investigate other job opportunities.

After the interview, supervisor Johnson thought about what she might do. What inducements could she offer that would keep Adams with the agency?

NOTES

1. For a full discussion of the stakeholder concept, see Ian I. Mitroff, *Stakeholders of the Organizational Mind* (San Francisco: Jossey-Bass, 1983).

2. For a comprehensive discussion of the social responsibility issue, see Keith Davis and William C. Frederick, *Business and Society: Management, Public Policy, Ethics* (New York: McGraw-Hill, 1984).

3. For a review and comparison of several perspectives on organization, see David Ulrich and Jay B. Barney, "Perspectives in Organizations: Resource Dependence, Efficiency, and Population," *Academy of Management Review* 9 (July 1984): 471–481.

4. For a further discussion of the "rational" approach to organization theory, see Alan Bryman, "Organizational Studies and the Concept of Rationality," *Journal of Management Studies* 21 (October 1984): 391–408.

5. For a discussion of production versus quality in American and Japanese firms, see David A. Garvin, "Quality Problems, Policies, and Attitudes in the United States and Japan: An Exploratory Study," *Academy of Management Journal* 29 (December 1986): 653–673.

6. For a thorough review of the issues, see W. Graham Astley and Andrew H. Van de Ven, "Central Perspectives and Debates in Organization Theory," *Administrative Science Quarterly* 28 (June 1983): 245–273.

7. For further information on the organization as a natural system, see Alvin W. Gouldner, "Organizational Analysis," in *Sociology Today,* ed. Robert K. Merton, Leonard Broom, and Leonard S. Cottrell (New York: Basic Books, 1959), pp. 400–428; and Stephen Strasser et al., "Conceptualizing the Goal and System Models of Organizational Effectiveness: Implications for Comparative Evaluation Research," *Journal of Management Studies* 18 (July 1981): 321–340.

8. For a full discussion of organizational life cycles, see John R. Kimberly et al., *The Organizational Life Cycle: Issues in the Creation, Transformation, and Decline of Organizations* (San Francisco: Jossey-Bass, 1980).

9. In his study of one innovative organization's birth and early development, John R. Kimberly

concluded that innovative features leading to short-run organizational success were incompatible with longer-run survival requirements. See Kimberly, "Issues in the Creation of Organizations: Initiation, Innovation, and Institutionalization," *Academy of Management Journal* 22 (September 1979): 437–457.

10. For a discussion of the latter stages of organizational life, see David A. Whetten, "Organizational Decline: A Neglected Topic in Organizational Science," *Academy of Management Review* 5 (October 1980): 577–588.

11. Guy Geeraerts points up the different attitudes toward organizational structure commonly held by owners and managers. See Geeraerts, "The Effect of Ownership on the Organization Structure in Small Firms," *Administrative Science Quarterly* 29 (June 1984): 232–237.

12. *Business Week,* 21 January 1985, p. 75.

13. For a discussion of the idea that "coalitions" form in organizations, see William B. Stevenson et al., "The Concept of 'Coalition' in Organization Theory and Research," *Academy of Management Review* 10 (April 1985): 256–268. These authors point out both the relative recency and the ambiguity of the coalition concept in the organizational literature. For numerous examples of how some organizational leaders have handled the compromises of the goal-setting process, see Ernest Dale, *The Great Organizers* (New York: McGraw-Hill, 1960).

14. For a discussion of some implications of the fact that different organizational members and groups have different goals, see Michael Keeley, "Impartiality and Participant-Interest Theories of Organizational Effectiveness," *Administrative Science Quarterly* 29 (March 1984): 2–3. For additional discussion of how multiple constituencies affect organizational goal setting and effectiveness, see Raymond F. Zammuto, "A Comparison of Multiple-Constituency Models of Organizational Effectiveness," *Academy of Management Review* 9 (October 1984): 606–615; and Gerald R. Salancik, "A Single Value Function for Evaluating Organizations with Multiple Constituencies," *Academy of Management Review* 9 (October 1984): 617–625.

15. For further discussion of the dominant group's interactions with other organizational constituencies, see the sources cited in the previous footnote as well as Terry Connolly, Edward J. Conlon, and Stuart Jay Deutsch, "Organizational Effectiveness: A Multiple-Constituency Approach," *Academy of Management Review* 5 (April 1980): 211–217.

16. Charles Perrow, "The Analysis of Goals in Complex Organizations," *American Sociological Review* 26 (December 1961): 855.

17. Ibid.

18. For further information on inducements-contributions theory, see Petro Georgiou, "The Goal Paradigm and Notes Toward a Counter Paradigm," *Administrative Science Quarterly* 18 (September 1973): 291–310.

ADDITIONAL READINGS

Berenbeim, Ronald. *From Owner to Professional Management: Problems in Transition.* New York: The Conference Board, 1984.

Burgelman, Robert A. "Designs for Corporate Entrepreneurship in Established Firms." *California Management Review* 26 (Spring 1984): 154–166.

Cameron, Kim S. "Effectiveness as Paradox: Consensus and Conflict in Conceptions of Organizational Effectiveness." *Management Science* 32 (May 1986): 539–553.

Cameron, Kim S., and David A. Whetten, eds. *Organizational Effectiveness.* New York: Academic Press, 1983.

Cyert, Richard M., and James G. March. *A Behavioral Theory of the Firm.* Englewood Cliffs, NJ: Prentice-Hall, 1963.

Delacroix, Jacques, and Glenn R. Carroll. "Organizational Foundings: An Ecological Study of the Newspaper Industries of Argentina and Ireland." *Administrative Science Quarterly* 28 (June 1983): 274–291.

Goodman, Paul S., and Johannes M. Pennings, eds. *New Perspectives on Organizational Effectiveness.* San Francisco: Jossey-Bass, 1977.

Hall, Richard H. "Professionalization and Bureaucratization." *American Sociological Review* 33 (February 1968): 92–104.

Hambrick, Donald C., and Phyllis A. Mason. "Upper Echelons: The Organization as a Reflection of Its Top Managers." *Academy of Management Review* 9 (April 1984): 193–206.

Harrigan, K.R., and M.E. Porter. "End-Game Strategies for Declining Industries." *Harvard Business Review* 61 (July/August 1983): 111–120.

Lewin, Arie Y., and John W. Minton. "Determining Organizational Effectiveness: Another Look, and an Agenda for Research." *Management Science* 32 (May 1986): 514–538.

Littler, D.A., and R.C. Sweeting. "Developing a New Business: Its Organisation, Planning and Control." *Journal of General Management* 10 (Autumn 1984): 4–23.

Mintzberg, Henry. "Who Should Control the Corporation?" *California Management Review* 27 (Fall 1984): 90–115.

Price, James L. *Organizational Effectiveness: An Inventory of Propositions.* Homewood, IL: Richard D. Irwin, 1968.

Schein, Edgar H. "The Role of the Founder in Creating Organizational Culture." *Organizational Dynamics* 12 (Summer 1983): 13–28.

Stevenson, H.H., and D.E. Gumpert. "The Heart of Entrepreneurship." *Harvard Business Review* 63 (March/April 1985): 85–94.

Stevenson, H.H., D.E. Gumpert, and Jose Carlos Jarrillo-Mossi. "Preserving Entrepreneurship as Companies Grow." *Journal of Business Strategy* 7 (Summer 1986): 10–23.

Thompson, James D. *Organizations in Action: Social Science Bases of Administrative Theory.* New York: McGraw-Hill, 1967.

Want, Jerome H. "Corporate Mission." *Management Review* 75 (August 1986): 46–50.

CENTRAL PROGRAM SERVICE CENTER

The Central Program Service Center (CPSC) is one of six regional social security administration centers responsible for processing a wide variety of social security claims. CPSC receives claims based on social security number sequence, which in turn is determined by the claimant's state of residence when the number was issued. The claims are most often received from social security district offices of the 11 Central states which issue the social security numbers over which CPSC has jurisdiction. But because there is usually such a long time lag between the issuance of a number and the actual filing of a claim (about 45 years, on average), and because the U.S. population is so mobile, CPSC receives a significant amount of casework from outside the 11 Central states.

Social security claimants file claims through the vast network of social security administration district and branch offices. The main functions of the CPSC are (1) to process claims that cannot be fully processed by the district offices, and (2) to process cyclical claims adjustments which can be more efficiently processed through larger-scale specialized operations. The basic goal of CPSC is to provide fast, high-quality service to the public and to other SSA components and government agencies in a manner consistent with social security law and policies.

As is typical of most federal agencies, CPSC's basic structure is hierarchical, almost military. It is headed by a GS-16 Program Center Director, assisted by a GS-15 Director of Operations and a GS-15 Director of Management, each with specific responsibilities to the Director as regards their operating components. These components consist of two branches, each headed by a GS-14 Branch Manager. Each branch consists of three operating sections, each headed by a GS-13 Section Manager who has responsibility for six operating modules. The operating module is the basic claims processing component. Each module is headed by a GS-12 Module Manager who has two GS-11 Assistant Managers. These relationships are shown in Figure C1.1.

The modular concept is a relatively recent innovation among the SSA program service centers. Before 1974, casework responsibilities were divided between the GS-10 Claims Authorizers and the GS-8 Benefit Authorizers. The higher-grade Claims Authorizers had primary responsibility for adjudicating initial claims and had more decision-making responsibility than the Benefit Authorizers, even though the two functions overlapped.

Because of that overlap and because of the great case flow traffic between the two positions, top management decided to break up the old authorizer sections and place both Claims and Benefit Authorizers, along with support personnel, into 36 mini-program service centers called *operating modules.* The idea was to make case processing more efficient by allowing closer communication between the two authorizer positions. Module Managers could now control a case from its beginning to completion, within a module. The modules proved to be effective; they increased productivity and cut processing time.

Within the modules, *clusters* of two to four desks are arranged so the Authorizers face each other for easy communication. Benefit Authorizers outnumber Claims

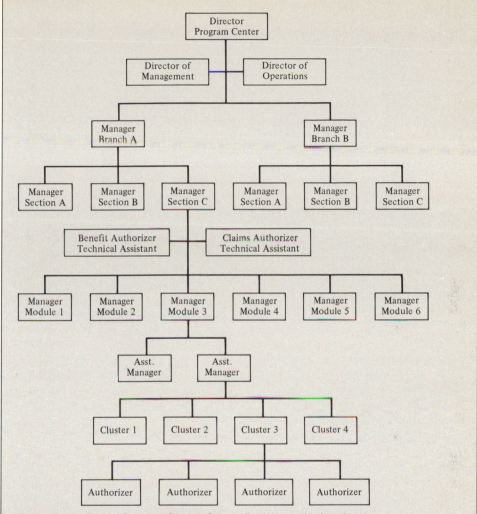

Figure C1.1   Central Program Service Center: Partial organization chart.

Authorizers by 3 to 1. Ideally, each cluster contains a Claims Authorizer, but often the decision as to who sits in which cluster is influenced by such factors as personalities, smoking/nonsmoking, and so forth. Consultation with someone in another cluster is always available.

　　A high priority of the social security administration is the ready access of information on any given claim at any given time. Therefore, a claim is tracked from the minute an application is filed at a district or branch office, through its arrival and processing at a program service center, and even to its storage and eventual destruction at a federal record center site. Admittedly, SSA has lagged behind the private

(continued)

sector and other government agencies in converting to an efficient on-line data system. Therefore, the SSA usually deals with pieces of paper, rather than computerized data. SSA is gradually replacing this antiquated system with the claims modernization process, designed to reduce the amount of paper and to put as much information as possible on-line.

This change will have significant impact on program service centers and how the Authorizers perform their jobs. Paper and loosely bound manuals will be replaced where possible by computer terminals. Unfortunately, the administration's budgetary constraints will not allow each Authorizer to have a terminal; several people will have to share. This development will require cluster members to work even more closely together. Thus, the claims modernization process will impose certain constraints upon Authorizers at the same time as it makes information more accessible.

The Module Manager and the two Assistants are responsible for controlling the flow of casework through a module and for ensuring that work flow goals are met. Because the jobs of the Authorizers are highly technical, the module management staff is not required or expected to maintain technical expertise, even though that staff rates the Authorizers on their performance. To help assess the performance of the Authorizers, each module is assigned a GS-11 Claims Authorizer Technical Assistant and a GS-9 Benefit Authorizer Technical Assistant. These Technical Assistants (TAs) are rotated throughout the modules in a process section every three to six months.

Both the quality and the quantity of each Authorizer's work are assessed. An Authorizer's completed casework is tallied daily and accumulated into monthly totals. The average number of cases worked per *day* in the preceding month then determines the number of cases pulled for quality assessment in the following *month*. For example, if an Authorizer has an average daily production *quantity* of 20 cases in April, then 20 cases will be pulled for *quality* review in May. The daily average for May will determine the cases pulled for quality review in June, and so on.

The present assessment system at CPSC has evolved over a period of years. Up through the late 1960s, technical workers had to maintain a daily quota of cases at an acceptable accuracy rate. This method was discredited as nonproductive and unpopular and was eventually abandoned. Throughout the early and mid-1970s, a period of high agency growth, assessments of technical work were based essentially on subjective managerial observations, an unsatisfactory system because managers who were not expected to be technically proficient were expected to evaluate technical work.

In the late 1970s, a new system was phased in. Once a month, a single day's work was assessed for quantity and another day's work was assessed for quality. This system was replaced in 1984 by one in which 100 percent of an Authorizer's cases are counted for quantity, and the numerical daily average of cases from the previous month is assessed for quality. These quality cases are pulled in small numbers from several days within the month. Management is pleased with this assessment system, and statistics indicate an increase of about 20 percent in Authorizer productivity under the system.

Here are the details of the assessment system. All completed cases are collected from the Authorizers three times a day: at 7 A.M., 10 A.M., and 2 P.M. The clerk picking up the cases counts them and lets the Authorizer know the figure tallied. The clerk takes the cases to a central area where they are sorted in order to be read into the next process or file location. At this point, the Assistant Manager has the option of pulling cases from an Authorizer's stack and sending them to a Technical Assistant for quality assessment. The selection is randomized, and the Authorizer does not know when or how many cases are being reviewed.

The TA receives the case along with an assessment sheet prepared by the Assistant Manager. The TA then reviews the case, annotating on the assessment sheet how difficult the case is and whether the case was done correctly or incorrectly. Correct cases are released to the next area. Incorrect cases are judged upon degree of error—how serious the error is, and whether the error would affect the payment of benefits. The TA writes a brief analysis of the error, describing the incorrect action taken, the correct action that should be taken, and citing references upon which the error determination was based. The Assistant Manager then reviews the incorrect cases, makes comments upon the assessment sheet, and returns the cases and the assessment sheet to the Authorizer to make necessary corrections. The Authorizer signs the assessment sheet, acknowledging its receipt, and returns it to the Assistant Manager; the sheet becomes part of the Assistant Manager's file. An Authorizer can appeal to the Technical Assistant, who has the authority to change an error determination. If the TA refuses, the Authorizer may appeal to the Assistant Manager, the Manager, the Section Manager and, theoretically, on up to the Director of the social security administration.

The assessment system is important in the CPSC workplace, because it is the basic element in determining an Authorizer's performance rating. The assessment system determines two of the three critical elements upon which performance appraisals are based: quantity and quality of casework. The third major element, job knowledge, is indirectly derived from the assessments of the other two elements.

The assessment system allows the establishment of performance levels based upon statistical models. For instance, quantity performance is evaluated in terms of how many cases an Authorizer produces per day. An outstanding Authorizer will produce 24 or more cases a day, an above-average Authorizer 20 to 23, an average Authorizer 14 to 19, and a below-average Authorizer 13 or lower. Quality performance is based upon degree of accuracy: 95 percent or better accuracy is outstanding, 91 to 94 percent is above average, 85 to 90 percent is average, and lower than 85 percent is below average.

The system gives managers quantitative measurements upon which to base performance appraisals. An Authorizer's performance appraisal is the single most important factor in determining promotions, performance awards, and step increases. Thus, an Authorizer's career is highly dependent upon these statistics.

Relate this personnel assessment system to organizational goal achievement in the Central Program Service Center. Can you suggest improvements in the system?

HIGGINS ENGINEERING, INCORPORATED

Higgins Engineering, Incorporated (HEI), a small firm located in Orlando, Florida, provides engineering design services and manufactures prototype hardware for Or-

(continued)

lando's high-tech industry. The firm is owned and operated by Richard Higgins, who has a Ph.D. in engineering. After eight years with Boeing and seven years with NASA, Higgins opened HEI. He wanted to be his own boss. He felt he needed more freedom as an engineer.

In the beginning, HEI had only three employees: Richard Higgins, owner and company president; Jo Ann Higgins, Richard's wife and the firm's accountant; and Ed Eaton, a model maker and machinist. The operation began in a small two-room, rented office with two machines and an engineer's drawing board. HEI continued that way for about a year and a half, until Higgins decided to expand and hire additional shop personnel. The firm continued to grow, employing more people and adding new machinery. After the fourth year of operation, HEI employed 20 people and had 10 production machines.

As the firm grew, Richard had to turn over some of the managerial and office functions to another person. Shop foreman Harry Gibson began bidding jobs; ordering, receiving, and controlling materials; controlling production schedules; and inspecting and shipping parts. When the firm was relatively small and Harry was able to perform all of these functions, control was quite easy. Harry knew what was going on throughout the firm at all times, and Richard Higgins had only to ask Harry in order to get an instant update.

However, HEI continued to grow, and additional personnel were hired to handle the office functions. Carol Jones was placed in charge of buying and production control. Joe Milligan was then hired to do the actual buying, with Carol monitoring production and deciding what to order. Alice Christopher was hired as shipping and receiving clerk. Lars Larson was placed in charge of job-book administration and time-card approval. Then, in order to fulfill a requirement in certain Army contracts, Harry Gibson was removed as shop foreman and replaced by Martha Jarvis.

The increase in personnel, coupled with Gibson's removal, created control problems for Richard Higgins. In the past, he could get an update about anything by asking one person one question. Now he might have to ask five people five questions, and the answer might be rather long in coming. This situation worried Richard, because he wanted to know what was going on *right now.*

To compound the difficulties brought about in the office by growth, Richard had a very negative attitude about the office staff's productivity and importance. He felt that the machinists in the machine shop made all of the money for him and that the activities of the office staff were of secondary importance. Therefore, Richard told the office staff to do whatever it took to keep the machinists working. This requirement created many problems for the office staff. They frequently had to stop their regular work to solve minor emergencies brought to them by the machinists. Never knowing when they might have to drop everything kept the office staff from planning or organizing effectively.

In an attempt to combat this problem, Carol Jones developed a detailed procedure manual to be followed by the office staff. After management approval, the manual was distributed to the staff. The job duties of each office staff member were outlined, as were the office staff procedures necessary to go from bidding a job to shipping the completed parts. The procedures in the manual were followed for about two weeks, but then the office staff—under pressure from Richard Higgins to keep the machinists working and happy—reverted to the old ways.

Richard Higgins continued to be frustrated that he could no longer get instantaneous updates. Sometimes he would want information so badly that he would interject himself into the office system and put an office staff member to work to get the information for him as quickly as possible. Higgins usually got the information, but the office system was so disrupted as a result that it often took days to straighten it out. During that time, Higgins might want additional quick information, and the system would be disrupted even more.

The replacement of Harry Gibson with Martha Jarvis as shop foreman caused additional problems for HEI. Harry had about 18 years' experience as a machinist but only 3 years' experience as a foreman when he was replaced. He had been hired by HEI to supervise the other machinists, quote jobs, and do some machine work. Shortly after Harry's hiring, HEI procured some Army contracts. They required a shop foreman with at least five years of supervisory experience. Harry didn't have it, so Richard Higgins demoted him.

The Army contracts were time-and-materials contracts under which HEI was reimbursed according to the number of hours utilized or the amount of material purchased. Companies bid on a contract by writing a proposal specifying the number of hours and amount of material required to complete the contract. A company's proposal also had to contain a description of how the company would fulfill the contract, including the company's expertise and delivery ability. HEI was usually not the low bidder, but it won contracts because of its engineering expertise and prompt delivery.

The hourly rate covered the direct wages, the overhead, and a profit margin. Under these Army contracts, the contractor had to utilize all hours or the contractor did not get the money. This provision encouraged HEI to use all contract hours whether or not they were needed to complete an Army contract. Because the typical contract contained more than enough hours, and because HEI's hourly rate was higher than most, HEI profited greatly from these contracts.

The Army contracts did much to support HEI. But for some reason, Richard Higgins did not seem to realize their importance. Don Jones, vice president responsible for controlling the Army contracts, tried to convince Richard that these contracts were crucial to HEI's success. Richard and Don had many disagreements over the handling of the contracts. Richard would often want to put aside various tasks needed to complete the Army contracts in order to complete small contracts in which he had a personal interest. Don pushed very hard to get the Army contracts completed on time, since timely delivery was a major reason for HEI's having gotten the contracts.

Although this case reflects several difficulties at HEI, discuss the situation in terms of organizational goals: planning to meet them and communicating them to employees.

Differentiating

Strategies

PART
2

Part 2 examines the differentiating strategies that organizations use to break down their work. Three strategies shown in the OT-Model (specialization of labor, departmentalization, and the line-staff distinction) represent a *horizontal* differentiation of the organization's *activities.* The other two strategies (delegation and decentralization) represent a *vertical* differentiation of the organization's *authority.*

Specialization of labor refers to *the number of different specialties or occupations* within the organization. Walk into an organization's personnel department and count the number of *different* job descriptions; you will then know how specialized that organization's work force is. IBM has thousands of job descriptions. Phil Gold's candy store may have only one, if Phil is the sole owner/employee.

Specialization of labor involves horizontal differentiation at the individual level. *Departmentalization* refers to horizontal differentiation at the level of the larger organizational group in which the individual worker is placed according to some logic. The degree of horizontal differentiation into departments at any given organizational level is reflected in the organization chart.

The *line-staff* distinction is the third horizontal differentiation strategy. *Line* positions are concerned with the organization's main operations. They contribute *directly* to achieving the organization's primary goals. *Staff* positions offer advice and service to the line. For instance, if the president of a large corporation is responsible for more functions than she can fulfill directly, she may divide or differentiate her duties by forming a staff of three, headed by an "executive assistant to the president."

The line-staff distinction is primarily a specialization of *function:* The line makes the product or provides the service, and the staff advises and supports the line. However, the distinction may also involve a specialization of *authority.* As the line-staff discussion in Chapter 6 will show, line authority and staff authority are different. Nevertheless, the primary distinction is between the functions of the line and the functions of the staff, so we shall discuss this distinction as a type of functional specialization, rather than authority specialization.

Vertical differentiation occurs within the organization's up-and-down dimension and refers primarily to the number of managerial levels and the authority that accompanies them. This series of levels is commonly referred to as the "hierarchy of authority" or simply "the hierarchy." As an example, a typical small manufacturing firm may have three managerial levels: the president, the division heads, and the department heads. As the organization grows and prospers, it may add managers by dividing current managerial levels into more managers (further horizontal differentiation at the managerial level) or by introducing a new layer of management (further vertical differentiation).

Because these managers use their authority to blend together the separate efforts of the organization's workers and work units, the hierarchy of authority will be discussed in Part 3 as an *integrating* strategy. *Within* the hierarchy, however, two techniques are used to *differentiate* the organizational authority vertically as it runs down through the organization: delegation and decentralization.

Delegation is the vertical differentiation of authority on a one-to-one basis. For example, if President Mary Baron gives some of her *work duties* to her four vice presidents, she is increasing the specialization of labor at the presidential level and is practicing job enlargement at the vice-presidential level. If she gives some of her *authority* to each vice president, then she has practiced delegation.

If delegation is practiced not just one-to-one but as an organizational philosophy, that orientation is called *decentralization* of authority. The idea of decentralization is to push decision-making power *down* through the organization.

To summarize: Specialization of labor, departmentalization, and the line-staff distinction (Chapters 4, 5, and 6) are methods of specializing organizational *functions.* Delegation and decentralization are methods of specializing organizational *authority* within the authority hierarchy. Chapter 7 covers delegation, and Chapter 8 covers decentralization.

Specialization of Labor

This chapter begins with the contributions of two early writers, Adam Smith and Emile Durkheim, on the most basic of the differentiating strategies: specialization of labor (or division of labor, as it is also called). Specialization of labor is a cornerstone of classical organization theory. The classical section of the chapter describes the many advantages of specialization to organizations that make and sell products. From the human relations perspective, carrying specialization too far becomes harmful to the worker as a human being. Several methods and proposals for overcoming the dehumanizing effects which often accompany specialization are then discussed.

The modern school has not yet put forth a systematic view that avoids the dehumanization of specialization while preserving its economic advantages. Most of the recent efforts seek to build on the successes that the Japanese participative management style seems to have achieved.

EARLY CONTRIBUTORS

The organization must differentiate its tasks. Of the five differentiating strategies covered in Part 2, the specialization of labor has been the most significant. Older than recorded history itself, specialization of labor can be seen in prehistoric relics discovered by archaeologists.[1] Objects of flint and bone fashioned by early man indicate different aptitudes and degrees of skill among those making them. Remains of villages built during Neolithic times for specialized flint miners have been discovered in Belgium. Pottery, statuettes, and other objects made by the artisans of Egypt and other ancient empires further illustrate a developing specialization of labor. The remnants left behind by all former civilizations offer evidence of a specialization of functions.

The ancient writer Xenophon describes specialization in Ancient Persia:

For in small towns the same workman makes chairs and doors and plows and tables. . . . And it is, of course, impossible for a man of many trades to be proficient in all of them. In large cities . . . one trade alone, and very often even less than a whole trade, is enough to support a man: one man, for instance, made shoes for men, and another for women; and there are places even where one man earns a living by only stitching shoes, another by cutting them out. . . . He who devotes himself to a very highly specialized line of work is bound to do it in the best possible manner.[2]

Adam Smith and Emile Durkheim were two early writers on specialization, Smith discussing specialization's benefits to production organizations and Durkheim discussing its benefits to society.

Adam Smith

The first chapter of Adam Smith's *The Wealth of Nations* (1776) was entitled "Of the Division of Labor." Specialization had long been recognized as a useful concept, but never before had it been written about so forcefully. Here is Smith's famous pin-making illustration:

> To take an example, therefore, from a very trifling manufacture; but one in which the division of labor has been very often taken notice of, the trade of the pin-maker; a workman not educated to this business (which the division of labor has rendered a distinct trade), nor acquainted with the use of the machinery employed in it (to the invention of which the same division of labor has probably given occasion), could scarce, perhaps, with his utmost industry, make one pin in a day, and certainly could not make twenty. But in the way in which this business is now carried on, not only the whole work is a peculiar trade, but it is divided into a number of branches, of which the greater part are likewise peculiar trades. One man draws out the wire, another straights it, a third cuts it, a fourth points it, a fifth grinds it at the top for receiving the head; to make the head requires two or three distinct operations; to put it on is a peculiar business, to whiten the pins is another; it is even a trade by itself to put them into the paper; and the important business of making a pin is, in this manner, divided into about eighteen distinct operations, which, in some manufactories, are all performed by distinct hands, though in others the same man will sometimes perform two or three of them. I have seen a small manufactory of this kind where ten men only were employed, and where some of them consequently performed two or three distinct operations. But though they were very poor, and therefore but indifferently accommodated with the necessary machinery, they could, when they exerted themselves, make among them about twelve pounds of pins in a day. There are in a pound upwards of four thousand pins of a middling size. Those ten persons, therefore, could make among them upwards of forty-eight thousand pins in a day. Each person, therefore, making a tenth part of forty-eight thousand pins, might be considered as making four thousand eight hundred pins in a day. But if they had all wrought separately and independently, and without any of them having been educated to this peculiar business, they certainly could not each of them have made twenty, perhaps not one pin in a day; that is, certainly, not the two hundred and fortieth, perhaps not the four thousand eight hundredth part, of what they are at present capable of performing in consequence of a proper division and combination of their different operations.[3]

Division of labor, illustrated so convincingly in this example by Adam Smith, was to become not only the foundation on which classical economic theory was built but also a cornerstone for builders of organizations.

Emile Durkheim

Adam Smith had stressed the *economic* benefits of specialization. Emile Durkheim, in *The Division of Labor in Society* (1893), examined its social implications.

Social Solidarity   Durkheim proposed that division of labor is a sign of an advanced society. Of course, specialization separates people by assigning them different jobs. But Durkheim maintained that specialization also promotes the solidarity of society. He wrote:

> The division of labor unites at the same time that it opposes; it makes the activities it differentiates converge; it brings together those it separates. . . . The individuals among whom the struggle is waged must already be solidary and feel so. That is to say, they must belong to the same society.[4]

What Durkheim says of societies is also true of the organizations within social systems. Members can perform different specialized tasks while still comprising a single, unified, "solid" organization. A corporation assigns many different tasks—such as producing, selling, maintenance, and accounting—yet all the tasks and the people who do them reside within that one corporation.

Differentiation versus Division of Labor   Durkheim draws a helpful distinction between pure differentiation of effort and specialization of labor. A criminal is a specialist, but his activities are pure differentiation (that is, they are simply *different*) because they do not contribute to societal solidarity.

Similarly, an organization can use differentiation which may or may not be an effective division of labor, as Durkheim uses that term. If the organization simply divides up work for the sake of dividing it up, the results will not be particularly effective. In the early 1980s, the Polish Workers Union achieved an effective, highly unified organization based on a meaningful division of labor. In fact, their name was "Solidarity." In contrast, we can find many organizations where jobs have multiplied and tasks have become increasingly specialized *without* regard for their contribution to organizational effectiveness. Such pointless multiplicity and make-work projects are types of differentiation that do *not* contribute to organizational solidarity. The effective organization has high solidarity, a meaningful division of labor, and close correspondence between official and operative goals. The ineffective organization has low solidarity, less meaningful differentiation of effort, and a wide disparity between official and operative goals.

Now that we have an overview of what specialization is, we can turn to the classical perspective on the subject.

THE CLASSICAL PERSPECTIVE

Frederick W. Taylor, Lyndall Urwick, Henri Fayol, and most of the other so-called "classical" writers on organization theory were practicing managers. As such, they sought to make wide-ranging generalizations about management, based on their observations of what *worked*. Many of their conclusions are related to organization theory as well as to management. After examining their early contributions to the idea of specialization in business, we shall add Max Weber's ideas about specialization of labor in bureaucracies, as observed in government settings.

Frederick W. Taylor

An early classical writer on management, mentioned briefly in Chapter 1, Frederick W. Taylor (1856–1915) is frequently called the "father of scientific management." The scientific school believed that scientific procedures could solve the management and organizational problems of the mass production industries evolving in the nineteenth and early twentieth centuries.

In their review of classical organization theory, James G. March and Herbert A. Simon point out why Frederick W. Taylor's scientific management also led to the design of simple, routine, repetitive tasks. They maintain that Taylor "set himself substantially the general task of organization theory: to analyze the interaction between the characteristics of humans and the social and task environments created by organizations."[5] Although that was Taylor's self-appointed task, circumstances forced a much narrower focus upon him. According to March and Simon, "Because of the historical accidents of their positions and training, and the specific problems they faced in industry, Taylor and his associates studied primarily the use of men as adjuncts to machines in the performance of routine productive tasks."[6]

Planning and Doing   Two of Taylor's scientific management principles involved specialization. First, he recommended dividing the labor of industrial organizations between those who *plan* the work (management) and those who *do* the work (labor). Let planners plan, managers manage, and workers work. Such a division of labor should result in more efficient operations, to the greater good of all.

Functional Foremanship   Second, the work of management should be divided up according to *functions* (or subjects, or particular kinds of work), with different managers responsible for personnel matters, raw materials, transportation, and so forth. This idea was known as *functional foremanship*. Each foreman had as few functions as possible to perform and to supervise.

How would this system work in practice? Consider a worker whose workday consisted of performing four operations in one task, over and over. These operations would be designed by four different experts in the planning department. The worker performing them would be supervised by the four shop foremen who specialized in those operations.

Henri Fayol

One of Henri Fayol's (1841–1925) 14 principles of management was the division of labor. Like Taylor, Fayol believed a worker should ideally be assigned one task and then should perform only that task. Workers would then become expert at particular jobs, and organizational efficiency, productivity, and profitability would result.

Lyndall Urwick

Papers on the Science of Administration (1937), edited and contributed to by Luther Gulick and Lyndall Urwick, laid the foundation for the classical school of organization theory. In his later work *Notes on the Theory of Organization* (1952), Urwick confirmed the early classical belief that the organization's members should specialize. Urwick said, "The activities of every member of every organized group should be confined, as far as possible, to the performance of a single function."[7] Like Taylor, Urwick felt that specialization was natural and beneficial to the individual, the organization, and society.

As a manager himself, Urwick did see practical limitations on the extent to which labor could be divided. First, the organization's tasks should not be so narrowly divided up that the work force sits around half the time with nothing to do—because they have finished their specialized tasks. Second, a very narrow division of a task may be impossible because of union constraints or because a trained labor pool might not exist. Third, further division of labor, though theoretically beneficial, may have physical limitations. One person should type an entire memo, rather than 26 people who each specialize in a different letter of the alphabet. Finally, specialization should not be carried so far that something vital is destroyed or lost. For example, milking the back half of the cow in the barn while the front half grazes in the meadow might be preferable, from an efficiency standpoint. But such a division would not be very effective because it would kill the cow. As Urwick maintains, if the work divided bleeds, then specialization has gone too far.

Dangers of Managerial Specialization

Urwick and Fayol believed that all organization members—workers and managers alike—should have as few functions to perform as possible, *but not so few as to interfere with the overriding need for integration and coordination of the total organizational effort.* Managers could not achieve that integration and coordination if they were differentiated into narrow specialties; they needed a broader view.

Taylor's "functional foremanship" embodied a degree of specialization that violated the hierarchy of authority, under which each employee receives instructions from only one boss. Fayol had favored the hierarchy as early as 1916. In his *Notes on the Theory of Organization,* Urwick asserted that the most important organizational consideration is a need for "a clear-cut chain of command from the top to the bottom of the undertaking."[8] These writer/managers were not willing to give up the coordinating advantages of the hierarchy to achieve the advantages of greater managerial specialization.

Max Weber and Bureaucracy

Bureaucracy as the Ideal Type   Sociologist Max Weber (1864–1920), a contemporary of Taylor and Fayol, also tried to answer managerial questions by carefully observing what worked and what did not. Weber felt that the ideal organizational type is the bureaucracy: the organization that handles its tasks and achieves its goals by subdividing into a hierarchy of bureaus or departments. He examined the characteristics of typical bureaucracies and used them as standards against which he compared other organizations. He wrote:

> The fully developed bureaucratic mechanism compares with other organizations exactly as does the machine with the non-mechanical modes of production. Precision, speed, unambiguity, knowledge of the files, continuity, discretion, unity, strict subordination, reduction of friction and of material and personal costs—these are raised to the optimum point in the strictly bureaucratic administration.[9]

Bureaucracy and Specialization   One characteristic of Weber's ideal bureaucracy has direct relevance to specialization. Each organization, he said, should have a specific sphere of competence, involving "(a) a sphere of obligations to perform functions which have been marked off as part of a systematic division of labor; and (b) the provision of the incumbents with the necessary authority to carry out these functions."[10] Organization members must be experts in their jobs and must know the limits of their duties, rights, and power.

Advantages of Specialization: The Classical View

Many advantages of specialization are implied in the writings of the classical school. The following are some specific advantages which arise from specialization and simplification of work:

Time required to learn the task is reduced. The more specialized a job is, the simpler it generally becomes, and consequently, the faster it can be learned. Many workers could never learn how to build an engine or a transmission, much less an entire car. Almost any worker can rapidly learn a highly specialized task such as tightening a nut on the fourth bolt of each automobile coming down the assembly line. Not much time will be required to learn the three steps in the operation: locating the bolt, locating the nut, and turning the wrench.

Waste created by learning the task is reduced. The easier the job is to learn, the fewer mistakes will be made, and consequently, the fewer production defects will occur. This principle applies not only to the quantity of defects but also to their cost. If Bob Workman is trying to learn how to rebuild a car engine, he may destroy many intricate, costly engines while he learns (if he ever learns). If he is trying to learn the simpler operation of carburetor rebuilding, his learning will produce fewer, less costly defects.

Skill is gained by repeating a task. In general, the more times we do something, the better we become at it. This skill improvement can be represented by a learning curve. Psychologists developed these curves to show the relationship between number of attempts and level of skill achieved. A typical learning curve appears in Figure 4.1. The fact that employees repeating a task get better at it is not surprising. What is significant is that improvement in performance often follows such a regular pattern that it can be predicted. These predictions are very helpful in pricing and production planning because they can be used to estimate how long a new project will take and how much it will cost.

During the aerospace boom of the 1960s, companies bidding on large government

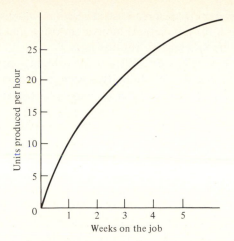

Figure 4.1 A learning curve.

contracts used learning curves to decide how much to bid. Any company wanting to build a bomber or missile would have to start at the least productive point on the curve. Yet a bid based on the cost of producing the first unit would be unrealistic and noncompetitive, because production costs would eventually drop as workers learned their tasks. Therefore, standard learning curves were used to calculate the average time and costs of the work force as they learned by producing 100 planes, 1000 missiles, or whatever.

Time lost in changing from one task to another is reduced. No matter how simple a task is, it requires a certain amount of concentration. Whenever workers move from one task to another, they must shift their mental gears. Even if the tasks are similar, the mind requires adjustment time. As an example, consider a student taking notes on one professor's lecture and then moving along to take notes on another professor's lecture. The tasks are similar, but the mind adjusted to the style, gestures, tone, humor, volume, and subject matter of the first lecturer must readjust for the second lecturer. Time is lost whenever anyone assigned two tasks must drop one set of procedures and skills and then adopt another set.

Time lost in changing tools is reduced. The more specialized the task, the less likely the need to change tools. For instance, during a surgical operation, in which every second may be critical, different members of the surgical team are responsible for using different instruments, instead of the chief surgeon using all of them.

The likelihood of specialized tools and methods being developed is increased. The more specialized the task, the easier it is to focus on it and to think about just what is being done. True, many people doing highly specialized jobs (such as assembly-line work) know their jobs well enough to do them while daydreaming. However, many workers do think about their jobs, especially about how to make them easier.

Workers often like to "tinker" with their jobs, to outdo the "experts" who designed them. Workers may consider the perfectly engineered job with its ideal tools as a challenge to their ingenuity. They make modifications or invent their own gadgets that speed up the operation and increase efficiency far beyond the engineered standard. Most of these unauthorized but effective tools and tricks are securely hidden when the plant efficiency expert walks by. Nevertheless, if they really are an improvement, they eventually find their way into common, widespread use. These innovations are a direct outgrowth of greater intimacy with the job, natural human curiosity, and the thinking time available when doing a highly specialized, routine task.

Individual skills are used more efficiently. When work is highly specialized, the employer need hire only the amount of skill or ability that each job requires. This idea is attributed to scientific management pioneer Charles Babbage, who said over 150 years ago:

> The master manufacturer, by dividing the work to be executed into different processes, each requiring different degrees of skill or force, can purchase exactly that precise quantity of both which is necessary for each process; whereas, if the whole work were executed by one workman, that person must possess sufficient skill to perform the most difficult and sufficient strength to execute the most laborious of the operations.[11]

Consider the word-processing center in the modern office, for example. Under the old arrangement, five managers might have five personal secretaries, each one performing all secretarial functions. A word-processing center is essentially a centralized secretarial operation. Under this setup, the five secretaries are arranged in a pool, each specializing in a particular function. One answers the phone, one types, one transcribes, one takes dictation, and one files. Each secretary becomes more skilled at one function and, more importantly, the cost of the overall secretarial operation decreases because the costs of hiring vary from secretarial function to function. A personal secretary must be skilled in typing, taking dictation, and filing. The cost of the most expensive necessary skill (perhaps typing, for instance) determines the secretary's hourly wage for each hour on the job, whether or not the expensive skill is being used. In a word-processing center, the exact amount of each skill can be purchased so the cost of overall secretarial support can be reduced.

Specialization permits more convenient supervision of work. Whether the task is producing a product or performing a service, specialized workers perform one or a few tasks repeatedly. Thus, a supervisor can quickly become aware of both the end product and the work behavior and readily pick up any deviations. For example, old-time telephone switchboards had long banks of operators doing the same task. The supervisor could easily see what all the operators were doing and could look for exceptions from the norm.

Specialization reduces the need for supervisor expertise. The more specialized the worker's task, the easier it is for the supervisor to understand and manage the work efficiently. Just as specialization reduces the learning time and cost for workers to master a task, so too does it enable supervisors to gain enough expertise about the specialized tasks to supervise effectively the workers doing them. For instance, in order to oversee and coordinate the work of nuclear engineers, the supervisor must be an expert in nuclear engineering (and must be paid accordingly). But if building a nuclear reactor were broken down into a specialized assembly-line operation, supervisors would not need to know as much about nuclear engineering as a whole.

Specialization helps to pinpoint responsibility. When one person specializes in one or a few tasks, then assigning praise or blame for good or poor work becomes easier.[12] Making specialized workers more accountable for their performance is a simpler process. If a car comes off the assembly line without headlights, the persons at fault can be identified quickly. Conversely, in organizations with nonspecialized managers and workers, the blame for errors such as missed deadlines is often difficult to place.

The foregoing advantages of specialization have been overwhelmingly important in increasing the productivity of organizations, industries, and societies. These efficiencies are primarily responsible for the vast rise in the standard of living experienced by industrial countries in the first half of the twentieth century. From automobile assembly-line workers like those in Figure 4.2 to heart specialists, from Midas Muffler to Burger King, the advantages of specialization seem clear.

THE HUMAN RELATIONS PERSPECTIVE

Emile Durkheim was well aware of the criticisms concerning specialization of labor. He wrote:

> It has been accused of degrading the individual by making him a machine. . . . Every day he repeats the same movements with monotonous regularity, but without being interested in them, and without understanding them. He is no longer anything but an inert piece of machinery, only an external force set going which always moves in the same direction and in the same way. . . . One cannot remain indifferent to such a debasement of human nature.[13]

Durkheim denied the charges, saying that the debasing effects resulted not from specialization itself but from "exceptional and abnormal circumstances":

> The division of labor presumes that the worker, far from being hemmed in by his task, does not lose sight of his collaborators, that he acts upon them, and reacts to them. He is, then, not a machine who repeats his movements without knowing their meaning. . . . He feels that he is serving something.[14]

To the later classical writers, organization owners, and managers (from about 1910–1940), specialization of labor sounded great. Like Durkheim, they all tended to minimize the human-related costs associated with routine, repetitive, highly specialized jobs: dissatisfaction, boredom, absenteeism and high turnover, increased supervision, product defects, equipment damage, and even vandalism and sabotage. The loss of human dignity also added to organizational costs and eventually adversely affected growth.[15]

A contemporary dimension of this issue is the large number of white-collar workers, middle managers, and professionals today in highly specialized, routine, monotonous jobs. The high turnover rate and the emergence of stress-related problems among these groups indicate that specialization may have costs across all organizational levels.

The Hawthorne Studies

Workers Are People, Not Machines   The human relations school's concern with the impact of highly specialized jobs on the worker emanated from the famous studies at

Figure 4.2   A traditional automobile assembly line. (Courtesy of the Motor Vehicle Manufacturers Association of the United States, Inc. Used by permission.)

Western Electric's Hawthorne plant near Chicago.[16] The Hawthorne studies led to the remarkable conclusion that the physical conditions of the work environment were less important in obtaining high productivity than were the *humanistic* aspects of the job.

The classical writers assumed that focusing on task design and increasing the degree of job specialization would invariably lead to higher productivity. If the one best

Specialization and Worker Dissatisfaction

Here is Donald F. Roy's description of what he experienced as he used a punching or "clicking" machine to punch shapes out of plastic.

It was evident to me, before my first workday drew to a weary close, that my clicking career was going to be a grim process of fighting the clock, the particular timepiece in this situation being an old-fashioned alarm clock which ticked away on a shelf near George's machine. I had struggled through many dreary rounds with the minutes and hours during the various phases of my industrial experience, but never had I been confronted with such a dismal combination of working conditions as the extra-long workday, the infinitesimal cerebral excitation, and the extreme limitation of physical movement. The contrast with a recent stint in the California oil fields was striking. This was no eight-hour day of racing hither and yon over desert and foothills with a rollicking crew of "roustabouts" on a variety of repair missions at oil wells, pipe lines, and storage tanks. Here there were no afternoon dallyings to search the sands for horned toads, tarantulas, and rattlesnakes, or to climb old wooden derricks for raven's nests, with an eye out, of course, for the tell-tale streak of dust in the distance which gave ample warning of the approach of the boss. This was standing all day in one spot beside three old codgers in a dingy room looking out through barred windows at the bare walls of a brick warehouse, leg movements largely restricted to the shifting of body weight from one foot to the other, hand and arm movements confined, for the most part, to a simple repetitive sequence of place the die . . . punch the clicker . . . place the die . . . punch the clicker, and intellectual activity reduced to computing the hours to quitting time. It is true that from time to time a fresh stack of sheets would have to be substituted for the clicked-out old one; but the stack would have been prepared by someone else, and the exchange would be only a minute or two in the making. Now and then a box of finished work would have to be moved back out of the way, and an empty box brought up; but the moving back and the bringing up involved only a step or two. And there was the half hour for lunch, and occasional trips to the lavatory or the drinking fountain to break up the day into digestible parts. But after each momentary respite, hammer and die were moving again; click . . . move die . . . click . . . move die.

Before the end of the first day, Monotony was joined by his twin brother, Fatigue. I got tired. My legs ached, and my feet hurt. Early in the afternoon I discovered a tall stool and moved it up to my machine to "take the load off my feet." But the superintendent dropped in to see how I was "doing" and promptly informed me that "we don't sit down on this job." My reverie toyed with the idea of quitting the job and looking for other work.

The next day was the same: the monotony of the work, the tired legs and sore feet and thoughts of quitting.

Donald F. Roy, "Banana Time: Job Satisfaction and Informal Interaction," in *Management Readings Toward a General Theory,* ed. William B. Wolf (Belmont, CA: Wadsworth Publishing Co., 1964), p. 128.

way to do a task could be discovered and the workers trained to do the task that way, then obviously they *would* do it exactly that way. The Hawthorne experimenters showed that the focus should be not so much on the task as on the person doing it.

Group Aspects of Work   The Hawthorne studies also made clear that workers act not only as individuals nor as organization-directed employees, but also as members of the *informal organization*—the group. Within Western Electric's work units, the *group* set the quota and penalized group members who produced much above or below that quota. In short, management can use time-and-motion studies and other tools of scientific management to specialize the job ideally, but group influences can readily outweigh the planning department's ideal. In fact Elton Mayo, a major contributor to the Hawthorne experiments, maintained that because corporate leaders ignored the importance of social relationships, factory social systems broke down, resulting in the economic disaster known as the Great Depression.

The Assembly Line   Following publication of the Hawthorne results in 1939, the human relations movement advanced in several directions—all spurred on by tales of intense boredom on assembly lines and all designed to *humanize the workplace. The Man on the Assembly Line* (1952) by Charles R. Walker and Robert H. Guest is a classic presentation of the assembly line's human disadvantages.[17] In addition to the assembly line's physical drudgery and limited opportunities for individual and group interaction, they found that many workers resented being forced to specialize. As one worker put it, "I'd like to be able to do a whole fender myself from the raw material to the finished job. It would be more interesting."[18] Some of Walker and Guest's recommendations—job enlargement and job rotation—will be discussed shortly.

Job Satisfaction

Although this book discusses the impact of the human relations school on the five differentiating and five integrating factors of most importance to organizations, that school's primary target for attack has been specialization of labor. Chris Argyris's book *Integrating the Individual and the Organization* (1964), Rensis Likert's *The Human Organization: Its Management and Value* (1967), and Douglas McGregor's *The Human Side of Enterprise* (1960) are solid appeals for the humanization of work. These authors attempt to show how to humanize the organization for people in specialized jobs, who are uninvolved in decision making and have little control over their work. Human relations theorists were also concerned with the meaning and nature of job satisfaction.

Inducements and Contributions   Here is the human relations argument, phrased somewhat differently. Any organization exists only because its members decide, for their own reasons, to participate in its affairs. Therefore, an issue of major interest becomes: What can be done to induce members to make their maximum contribution toward achieving the organization's goals?[19] This question, which echoes the major concern of the previous chapter on organizational goals, is important because it reverses the premise of the classical position that *the organization* determines the terms and conditions to which members must conform if they want to continue their affiliation.

The position of the humanists is the opposite: the organization's *members* determine the terms and conditions under which they are willing to work toward achieving the organization's goals.

Humanizing the Workplace   This change in emphasis leads to a different perspective on job specialization. The classical school wondered how to make the job *efficient.* The humanists wondered how to make the job *satisfying to the person doing it,* as well. Ideally, the worker will achieve job satisfaction *and* the organization will achieve its goals. Satisfied workers are useless if the organization fails. Conversely (at least in the present social setting), firms that fail to offer their workers some reasonable level of job satisfaction cannot expect to succeed. The human relations movement spurred considerable research and effort into discovering what aspects of the workplace satisfied or dissatisfied workers, so that improvements could be made.

Overcoming Worker Dissatisfaction

The many approaches to alleviating or eliminating the dehumanizing aspects of labor specialization can be loosely grouped under four headings which are chronological in their development: *job rotation, job enlargement, job enrichment,* and, most recently, *quality of work life.*

Job Rotation   This approach is premised on the idea that job variety can reduce the boredom and dehumanizing influences of jobs. Workers can be switched from one specialized job to another, allowing them to learn and use a variety of skills rather than concentrating on only one.

Job Enlargement   Too much specialization can be reversed by "unspecializing," that is by adding more tasks to the worker's job. For example, instead of having one worker put on the wheel and another tighten the bolts, have each worker do both.

Shortcomings   Job rotation and job enlargement may be carried so far that they eliminate the economic benefits of specialization. In addition, merely adding more tasks or rotating jobs can often lead to as much monotony and boredom as were present in the original job. The changes may be interesting at first, but routine jobs remain boring even if the worker does several of them instead of just one. Furthermore, employees accustomed to daydreaming on the job may resent having to *think* as they do more tasks or change routines. They may also view job enlargement as a job "speed-up," a management attempt to get more work out of each worker without paying more.

Job Enrichment   One of the later techniques proposed by human relations theorists for overcoming worker dissatisfaction with specialization was job enrichment—the use of techniques, approaches, and devices that enable employees to feel a personal pride and a sense of craftsmanship in whatever they produce, rather than feeling anonymous, as producers of mass-produced items. As one small example, look at the bottom of a grocery bag, and you may see the name of the worker who produced it.

A classic illustration of job enrichment has been occurring in Sweden at the Volvo plant in Kalmar. Some years ago, the traditional assembly line was broken down into work centers, with employee teams deciding on production rates, individual tasks, team membership, break times, and so on. From both the morale and economic standpoints, results have generally been positive.

The efforts to introduce job-enrichment strategies have had mixed results. Predictably, some workers want their jobs enriched, and some do not. Even when employees are not suspicious of management's motives, reactions to job enrichment programs vary. An additional barrier to job enrichment is managerial resistance to sharing decision-making power with workers with its subsequent loss of status (or so some managers feel). For example, when General Foods let workers at a pet-food plant perform certain managerial functions—making job assignments, scheduling coffee breaks, interviewing prospective employees, and even deciding pay raises—the managers' reactions ranged from indifference to hostility. Said a former manager, "The system went to hell. . . . It was too threatening to too many people."[20]

Although efforts to decrease monotony and job boredom through job enrichment are not always successful, they are still worth trying—from the human relations point of view.

Quality of Work Life

Some recent ideas for overcoming the specialization problem are grouped under the general heading, *quality of work life* (QWL). Although QWL programs include a wide variety of methods for increasing the employee's interest in the job, most QWL efforts emphasize *worker participation,* particularly *group participation,* as the means of improving overall work-life quality. This idea has gained considerable acceptance on the basis of its association with the Japanese economic success story. Over the past 20 years, American and other Western industrial organizations have looked with envy on the Japanese economy's growth and the productivity of its manufacturing sector. According to Theodore H. White,

> Today not a single consumer radio is made in America, although Americans invented the modern radio; not a single black-and-white television set is made here, although America invented television. . . . Almost all our video-cassette recorders are made in Japan; so are most hand-held calculators, watches, a huge share of our office machinery, and most high-fidelity equipment.[21]

In 1986 our trade deficit with Japan was $58.6 billion. For the year ending March 31, 1987, the Japanese trade surplus was over $100 billion.

The economic success of the Japanese has generated a tremendous interest in the Japanese system of managing their organization members. Their jobs are apparently as specialized in their work design as are our jobs; why are the Japanese workers so much more productive than ours? One answer to that question seems to be the opportunities for participation which improve the quality of the Japanese work life.

American companies have come to realize that managers and employees must work together if American productivity and product quality are going to match foreign competition. As a result, employee participation has become central to many organizational philosophies.

Including Workers in Planning   Job rotation, job enlargement, and job enrichment are done *to* the workers by management. QWL programs are supposed to be set up in cooperation *with* the workers. These programs counteract one aspect of job specialization that appears to create worker unhappiness: lack of worker involvement in job planning.

One classical principle was separating the *planning* of work from the *doing* of work. A by-product of this separation was that workers could not identify with their work. Rather than using their own mental abilities, workers were treated like machines, to be programmed by more knowledgeable managers who would prescribe the best work methods.

QWL programs seek to develop worker interest and tap worker knowledge by *including the worker in planning.* Frederick W. Taylor specialized the work by separating the planning from the doing; the QWL programs reunite the two activities.

The Quality Circle   One QWL program is the quality circle (QC). Originally designed for quality control by the American statistician Arthur Demming, the QC was further developed and its uses broadened by the Japanese. It is now widely used in the United States. The basic idea is to group production employees into circles or teams, to plan the job and discuss job-related problems. The hope is that the group will develop enthusiasm for the work as well as a sense of mutual responsibility for product quality. The QC attempts to achieve greater productivity and worker satisfaction by (1) having employees participate in decision making, (2) treating them as adults by asking them to solve problems directly related to what they do all day, and (3) encouraging them to form close-knit, familylike, supportive groups—both on and off the job.

Jerome M. Rosow sums up the progress American organizations have made in recent years towards encouraging employee participation:

> Today, the validity of employee participation is no longer in question, and the various forms of consultative and decision-making groups introduced into American enterprises during the last decade—quality circles, employee involvement teams, labor-management committees, semiautonomous work teams—have become commonplace.[22]

Theory Z   In his book *Theory Z: How American Business Can Meet the Japanese Challenge,* one of the more popular efforts to uncover the secrets of Japanese managerial success, William G. Ouchi suggests ways in which American corporations can profitably adapt the management and organizational styles of Japanese corporations.[23] Theory Z is offered as an extension of Douglas McGregor's Theory X-Y.[24] The Theory X manager sees people as lazy, irresponsible, constantly needing prodding, and motivated by fear. The Theory Y manager assumes that people are hard-working, conscientious, responsible, and motivated by various rewards. Theory Z carries Theory Y to the participative level, in assuming that workers and managers should *share responsibility for the job.*

As an illustration, *all* employees of Hitachi Ltd. must work in a factory for two years. Part of the time they work on the assembly line, learning what the blue-collar life is like. They also work in the accounting, computer-design, and engineering departments, to learn how products are made and how planning decisions affect the factory.

Such efforts narrow the gap between managers and workers and give all employees more knowledge to help share job responsibility.[25]

Here is how Ouchi sums up the major difference between the Japanese and American organizations:

> In the United States we conduct our careers between organizations but within a single specialty. In Japan people conduct careers between specialties but within a single organization. This is a fundamental difference in the way that our two nations have dealt with the problem of industrialization. In the United States companies specialize their jobs and individuals specialize their careers. As a result a semiconductor specialist, a portfolio manager, or a personnel manager can be moved from company A to company B and within five days all can be working effectively. Full productivity takes longer but contributions begin right away. In Japan it is difficult to take a worker from one company, move that person to another company, and expect him ever to be fully productive. Japanese do not specialize only in a technical field; they also specialize in an organization, in learning how to make a specific, unique business operate as well as it possibly can.[26]

J. Bernard Keys and Thomas R. Miller maintain that three fundamental factors underlie the Japanese management practices: a long-run planning horizon, a commitment to lifetime employment, and collective responsibility.[27] The specific practices and their underlying factors are presented in Figure 4.3.

The New Assembly Line The Japanese success in using a participative system to overcome the monotony of the standard assembly-line organizational method has encouraged American organizations to try different approaches also. The automotive assembly line, once the classic illustration of boring, repetitive, routine jobs, is now becoming a proving ground for the new strategies.

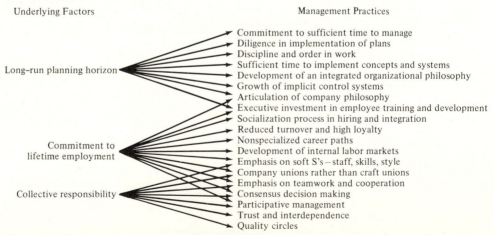

Figure 4.3 Fundamental factors underlying Japanese management practices. (*Source:* From J. Bernard Keys and Thomas R. Miller, "The Japanese Management Theory Jungle," *Academy of Management Review* 9 [July 1984], p. 349. Used by permission.)

Within its $5 billion Saturn Corporation subsidiary, General Motors is using Japanese strategies to compete with the Japanese automakers. According to *Business Week,* "Saturn may become the boldest experiment ever in self-management and consensus decision making—going far beyond anything in Japanese or European factories."[28] At Saturn, scheduled to start producing small cars in 1989, union workers and management will be full partners, participating jointly on all planning and operating committees. The basic work units, teams of 6 to 15 United Auto Workers members, will operate without foremen. These units will decide who does what job, maintain equipment, order supplies, set relief and vacation schedules, control their variable costs, and perform their own quality inspections. Fully 80 percent of the Saturn workers will have jobs for life, if they want them. The entire Saturn complex will be run not by a plant manager but by a committee consisting of UAW and company officials.

The Saturn experiment seems to foreshadow where "specialization" is actually heading. We now examine specialization from the perspective of the modern organization theorist.

THE MODERN PERSPECTIVE

Chapter 1 gave a brief explanation of systems theory. In systems terms, according to Paul R. Lawrence and Jay W. Lorsch, an organization is:

> A system of interrelated behaviors of people who are performing a task that has been differentiated into several distinct subsystems, each subsystem performing a portion of the task, and the efforts of each being integrated to achieve effective performance of the system.[29]

This definition speaks of both differentiation and integration. Differentiation is the division of the organization/system into subsystems that specialize according to the environment's requirements. Integration is the process of unifying the subsystems to achieve the system/organization's goals.

The classical approach to specialization ignored the human element, specializing as much as possible to achieve productivity gains. The human relations approach showed conclusively that, after a point, the cost of specialization in human terms is so great as to outweigh the economic gains of specialized labor. The attitude of modern scholars is essentially that of the human relations school. The following three criticisms of specialization, offered in 1977 by John Child, are based on the human relations position:[30]

1. Highly specialized jobs do not satisfy today's workers. In modern industrial societies, most workers fulfill their basic material needs adequately. They now require greater on-the-job satisfaction through personal involvement in the work and in decision making.
2. Workers in modern industrial nations are more educated—have more abilities and training—than ever before. Specialized tasks usually require low-level abilities. When well-educated, well-trained workers—especially young ones—cannot work up to their abilities, they become frustrated.

3. When workers become frustrated, they suffer from stress and other debilitating mental-health problems. The result is absenteeism, high turnover, strikes and sabotage—particularly on assembly lines. One automobile plant achieved temporary efficiency by paring the average task down to *36 seconds*. After continuous and boring repetition of the same functions, the workers retaliated through strikes, slowdowns, and sabotage. Although well paid, they couldn't stand the monotony.

Defining Specialization

The modern approach is to clarify the definition of specialization, then determine how much specialization is appropriate to each specific work situation. The organization identifies and rationally considers the key factors in each work situation, determines how these factors can best be accommodated within the organizational structure, and then establishes the appropriate degree of specialization. An early effort in this direction was the work of the Aston School.

The Aston School   Working in Aston, England during the 1960s, D.S. Pugh and his associates listed 16 specialized activities, exclusive of normal production activities, that are carried out within *all* production organizations.[31] The Aston list can be used to determine how specialized the nonproduction activities in a given production organization are. In a simple organization, a few people might handle all 16 tasks. A complex organization might have one or more separate departments for each of the 16 specialties. The Aston list appears in Table 4.1.

Two Dimensions of Specialization

In an effort to clarify the modern viewpoint on specialization, Henry Mintzberg has distinguished two dimensions: horizontal and vertical.[32] Horizontal specialization refers to how "broad" a worker's job is and corresponds to the more usual meaning of specialization. When Donald F. Roy punched shapes out of plastic, he was specializing very narrowly—doing one repetitive task all day long without thinking much about it. The other extreme might be a "utility" worker in an automobile plant who gets to do a different (though fairly routine) job each day.

   Mintzberg's second dimension, vertical specialization, refers to the "depth" of the job. A job has "depth" of specialization if the worker has control over the work and has to *think* about the work as it is being done. The jobs of a plastic puncher or Adam Smith's pin-maker have little depth; the work of a brain surgeon has much depth. Figure 4.4 illustrates the two dimensions.

How Much Specialization?

Most modern scholars *believe* in the validity of the human relations approach but can offer little statistical, experimental data to *prove* it. The problem is that what satisfies one worker or group of workers may not satisfy another worker or group of workers. Each organization is a unique combination of elements, a unique system—as is each organizational member. What works in Japan may not work in America. In fact,

Table 4.1 ASTON SCHOOL SPECIALIZATION TYPES, EXCLUSIVE OF
PRODUCTION-FLOW FUNCTIONS.

No.	Example of title	Activities
1	Public relations and advertising	Develop, legitimize, and symbolize the organization's charter
2	Sales and service	Dispose of, distribute, and service the organization's outputs
3	Transport	Carry outputs and resources from place to place
4	Employment	Acquire and allocate human resources
5	Training	Develop and transform human resources
6	Welfare and security	Maintain human resources and promote their identification with the organization
7	Purchasing	Obtain and control materials and equipment
8	Maintenance	Maintain and erect buildings and equipment
9	Accounts	Record and control financial resources
10	Production control	Control the quantity of work flow and see that quotas are met
11	Inspection	Control quality of materials, equipment, and outputs
12	Methods	Assess and devise better ways of producing outputs
13	Research and development	Devise new outputs, equipment, and processes
14	Organization	Develop and carry out administrative procedures
15	Legal/Insurance	Deal with legal and insurance requirements
16	Market research	Acquire information on field in which organization operates

Source: Reprinted from "Dimensions of Organization Structure," by D.S. Pugh, D.J. Hickson, C.R. Hinings, and C. Turner, published in *Administrative Science Quarterly* 13 (June 1968) by permission of *Administrative Science Quarterly.* Copyright © 1981 Cornell University. All rights reserved.

the high *variability* in the reactions of organizational members to specialization is probably the biggest stumbling block in determining the optimal degree of specialization.

The human relations school believes that all workers want to be "fulfilled" in their work. Mitchell Fein makes a contingency-type objection to such a blanket belief. He says that the human relations principles regarding job fulfillment are valid "only for those workers who *choose* to find fulfillment through their work. In my opinion, this includes about 15–20 percent of the blue-collar work force."[33] The remaining 80–85 percent seek fulfillment outside their jobs. For them, Fein says, the techniques proposed by the human relations school to humanize the workplace have little relevance. Indeed, if Fein's percentages are correct, the human relations writers may be practicing the very

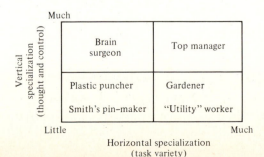

Figure 4.4 Mintzberg's two dimensions of specialization. (*Source:* After Henry Mintzberg, *The Structuring of Organizations: A Synthesis of Research,* © 1979, pp. 80, 443. Adapted by permission of Prentice-Hall, Inc., Englewood Cliffs, NJ)

opposite of their stated beliefs by urging the introduction of such techniques for *all* workers, whether they want them or not.

Human Costs versus Production Costs   Progressing towards a contingency solution to specialization problems requires establishing specialization's actual costs and benefits—to both the organization and its members. Figure 4.5 portrays what the analysis would theoretically look like. As an organization specializes, efficiencies will evolve and production cost per unit will drop. But the human cost per unit will rise, because of monotony, absenteeism, high turnover, sabotage, wasted materials, and other costs associated with workers getting bored, mad, or otherwise disenchanted with the assembly line or other highly specialized task. In short, too little specialization results in higher production costs; too much specialization causes higher human costs. The organization should therefore try to reach the optimum point, at which human costs and production costs are both as low as possible. Implementing the model in Figure 4.5 is, of course, easier said than done, but organizations must make the attempt.

Job Requirement Categories   Louis E. Davis suggests three job-related characteristics that can often lead to worker satisfaction and keep down the negative human costs of specialization.[34]

1. *Autonomy:* Design jobs so that workers can regulate and control their own environment. Let them organize and monitor their own work, rather than having supervisors do it. Evaluate them on *results,* rather than on how well they stick to the rules.
2. *Growth:* Organizations grow because their people develop. Jobs should enable workers to learn, develop, and grow. If they don't, then worker boredom and dissatisfaction will result.
3. *Variety:* If jobs have variety, then workers stay alert and responsive. If jobs are boring and repetitious, workers become mentally fatigued, make mistakes, and lose efficiency.

From the worker's point of view, these three job characteristics are usually desirable. But from the organization's point of view, offering autonomy, growth, and

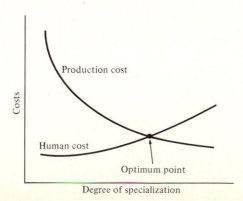

Figure 4.5 Human costs of specialization vs. production costs.

variety may not be consistent with specialization of labor and its economic advantages. A contingency approach would somehow find a balance, where both the worker and the organization are reasonably satisfied.

Organizational Size and Specialization

According to Peter M. Blau, increasing an organization's size by hiring more employees affects its task differentiation in various ways.[35] Here are some effects of increasing organizational size.

1. Specialization of labor also increases, but *at a decelerating rate.* Consider Organization A with one employee who does ten tasks. If the organization adds another employee, it may divide the original employee's job exactly in half, so the organization has doubled both its number of employees and its number of different jobs—that is, its degree of job specialization. However, a successful organization will eventually start hiring more people to do exactly *the same* job. At that point, the number of employees starts to increase at a faster rate than specialization of labor does.

2. With increasing size, the administrative component increases. Organization A added an employee without increasing the organization's administrative component. If Organization A continues to add workers, it must soon hire someone to coordinate their work. As size and division of labor continue to increase, Organization A will be hiring a host of new managers to control the new people and run the new departments or branch offices.

As organizations add employees, they increase their division of labor (at a decreasing rate), which increases the need for supervisors and managers. Taking all of these factors into account, the organization must decide just what size will best enable it to reach its goals. This subject will be discussed fully in Chapter 14, Size.

Hard empirical data showing a relationship between specialization and performance are scarce.[36] Nevertheless, the search for a connection goes on.

SUMMARY

Two early contributors to the literature of specialized labor were Adam Smith and Emile Durkheim. Smith summed up specialization's advantages by using pin making as an illustration. Durkheim believed that true division of labor (rather than simple differentiation of tasks) is found only in advanced societies and that society's members are *unified* by temporarily dividing their work efforts.

Representing the classical viewpoint were Frederick W. Taylor, Henri Fayol, and Lyndall Urwick. All agreed that labor of the *workers* should be narrowly divided. Taylor differed from the others in believing that the work of managers should also be specialized insofar as possible, even though that might result in each worker reporting to several bosses who were each expert in one of the worker's tasks. Max Weber's belief in specialization's advantages for bureaucracies was presented, as well as ten specific advantages of specialization.

The human relations school offers various methods of overcoming specialization's disadvantages by humanizing the workplace: job rotation, job enlargement, job enrichment, quality of work life programs, the quality circle, and Theory Z. The Japanese organizational successes, and corresponding productivity gains, have caused American organizations to study the Japanese business practices intensely. In many instances, the Japanese have employed human relations principles first proposed in this country; today, American organizations are repatriating those principles.

The modern or systems/contingency approach to specialization has not progressed very far. Today's employee wants opportunities for autonomy, growth, and variety. But the modern corporation is a system which, in addition to workers and managers, has a board of directors who are often more interested in decreasing costs and increasing profits than they are in enriching the lives of their workers. Modern organizations must try to find the optimum point at which both production costs and human costs are as low as possible.

DISCUSSION QUESTIONS

1. Why do you think Adam Smith's "famous pin-making illustration" has become so famous as an example of the division of labor's benefits?
2. What did Emile Durkheim contribute to our understanding of the division of labor and specialization?
3. What was Frederick W. Taylor's concept of functional foremanship? How did it work? Was it a good idea?
4. What were the limitations of division of labor as perceived by Lyndall Urwick?
5. In the classical view, what are specialization's advantages?
6. How does specialization within an organization reduce the need for supervisory skills?
7. What did the Hawthorne studies tell us about specialization?
8. The human relations writers perceived difficulties in the classical division of labor. What solutions did they offer? What further problems did these solutions present?
9. What is "quality of work life"? Have you worked for any organization that was interested in it? Describe any successful QWL examples you can find in the current business literature.
10. How do you account for the success of Japanese industrial organizations in recent years?
11. What is the modern attitude toward specialization of labor?
12. Which criticisms of specialization seem valid to you?
13. Distinguish between horizontal and vertical specialization.
14. What are specialization's costs and benefits? Can you suggest any ways to measure them?
15. How does specialization influence organizational design?
16. If you ran an organization, how would you try to implement the ideas portrayed in Figure 4.5?
17. How is organizational size related to specialization?

■ *FIDELITY INSURERS*

Fidelity Insurers is one of the largest insurance companies in the world. Sybil Rose, underwriting manager of the southern regional office, has a problem. The executives and the sales force want the applications for new insurance to be processed by the underwriting department much more quickly. Rose finally concludes that the typing section is a bottleneck in the process.

The section has 11 typists. Most of them are recent high school graduates with no prior work experience and only minimal typing skills. The company starts them at a level 1 salary of $160 a week. One senior typist receives a level 2 salary of $200 a week.

The section has an average daily backlog of about 600 cases, and most cases sit in the area for from three to eight days before being typed. An experienced typist can handle 70 or 80 cases a day, but because of the inexperienced staff, output in the typing section averages 50 cases a day. The typists work mandatory overtime two nights a week and every other Saturday.

Not only is inadequate output a problem. Quality is also below Sybil Rose's standards. Many cases must be retyped, and much correspondence goes out untidy or even unintelligible.

The typists know that their performance is not good, and their morale is very low. Their supervisor argues that the root of the problem is inexperience and says that everything will improve "in time."

Sybil Rose has tried various solutions designed to increase the volume handled, without success:

1. Overtime has not improved matters. In fact, Rose realizes that mandatory overtime has decreased morale and increased turnover.
2. Temporary help from other departments has not helped. Temporary people are not sufficiently familiar with forms, procedures, and terminology.

Rose recently interviewed a group of typists and gathered these comments:

1. We are ranked at level 1, the lowest in the company. Since we have a marketable skill, we feel that we should make more than unskilled employees (mail openers and messengers) make. Yet they are also at level 1.
2. Although we type the work of the underwriters, we are physically and psychologically isolated from them. Our only contact with them is negative—when they point out our errors. They do not know us individually and have no sympathy with our problems.
3. We do not get enough instruction and training. We have no idea how our work relates to the work of other sections. We are part of the underwriting division, but we do not even know what "underwriting" is.
4. Our work is monotonous. Most of what we do is to fill in blanks and type names and addresses on preprinted forms.
5. We have little opportunity for advancement. All we can hope for is advancement to level 2.
6. We are constantly pressured and criticized. We are told that because of the high work volume, nobody has time to train us. Because we do not have enough training, we make errors and are criticized. We are always rushed, so we make more errors. If we slow down to improve quality, the work piles up and we are criticized for that.

What might Sybil Rose do to straighten out the situation in the typing section?

AJAX NUCLEAR POWER PLANT

Ajax Nuclear Power Plant supplies power to an extended geographical area. Its employees are highly trained and well paid. They have to *know* a lot about nuclear power to qualify for their jobs, but they don't have to *do* very much in their highly automated power plant.

Mary Avila is a plant safety officer. She has a degree in engineering with additional training in nuclear power plant safety. She knows just what to do if monitoring devices indicate an irregularity in the system.

While sitting in a control booth one day, Mary Avila came to a conclusion: "I am highly trained and well paid simply to sit here. I am a dial watcher, and my dial always reads 70 kilo-ergs. There's got to be more to work life than this."

How can the Ajax Nuclear Power Plant management make Avila's job more interesting for her? If they don't, what might some consequences be?

GENERAL MANUFACTURING AND PROCESSING COMPANY

In the mid-1980s, General Manufacturing and Processing Company was having problems with workers' negative attitudes and low productivity at its Hartwell, Alabama plant. In order to turn things around, GMP decided to change the operation of the Hartwell plant completely. The plant would be run with a minimum of supervision. The workers themselves would take over such traditional management prerogatives as making job assignments, scheduling coffee breaks, interviewing prospective employees, and even deciding on pay raises.

The new system eliminated several layers of management and supervisory personnel and assigned three areas of responsibility—processing, packaging/shipping, and office duties—to self-managing teams of 7 to 14 workers per shift. The workers rotated between the dull and the interesting jobs. The teams made all necessary management decisions.

The new system was a success in many ways. Unit costs of 10 percent less than under the old system translated into a savings of $2 million per year. Turnover was only 5 percent, and the plant went two years, eight months before its first lost-time accident. From the humanistic standpoint, quality of work life and economic results were good.

Notwithstanding the plan's success, by 1989 the plant began the transition back to a traditional factory system. GMP introduced more specialized job classifications and more supervisors, and reduced opportunities for employee participation. The company added seven management positions to the plant, including controller, plant engineering manager, and manufacturing services manager. Management took back the right to make decisions about pay raises.

Professor Andrew Stubbs analyzed what had happened at Hartwell for his organization theory class: "The basic problem was that in this functional organization, many managers became nervous about what functions they would keep if the workers themselves assumed so many responsibilities. In addition, they resented being left out; upper-level management's enthusiasm for enriching the jobs of the workers didn't take into account the feelings of the middle managers. Where was their enrichment?"

Do you agree with the professor's assessment of what went wrong? What does the General Manufacturing and Processing Company's experience tell you about applying QWL and QC principles in real life?

NOTES

1. The following examples are supplied by Georges Friedmann, *The Anatomy of Work* (New York: The Free Press, 1961).
2. Ibid., p. 2.

3. Adam Smith, *The Wealth of Nations*, Book I (Chicago: Henry Regnery Company, 1953), pp. 8–9.

4. Emile Durkheim, *The Division of Labor in Society*, trans. George Simpson (New York: The Free Press, 1964), p. 276.

5. James G. March and Herbert A. Simon, *Organizations* (New York: Wiley, 1958), p. 12.

6. Ibid., p. 13.

7. Lyndall Urwick, *Notes on the Theory of Organization* (New York: American Management Association, 1952), p. 20.

8. Ibid., p. 66.

9. Max Weber, "Bureaucracy," in *Max Weber: Essays in Sociology*, ed. and trans. H.H. Gerth and C. Wright Mills (New York: Oxford University Press, 1946), p. 214.

10. Max Weber, *The Theory of Social and Economic Organization*, ed. Talcott Parsons, trans. A.M. Henderson and Talcott Parsons (New York: Oxford University Press, 1947), p. 329.

11. Charles Babbage, *On the Economy of Machinery and Manufactures* (London: Charles Knight, 1832), p. 176.

12. For further discussion of this point, see Gareth R. Jones, "Task Visibility, Free Riding, and Shirking: Explaining the Effect of Structure and Technology on Employee Behavior," *Academy of Management Review* 9 (October 1984): 684–695.

13. Durkheim, *The Division of Labor in Society*, p. 371.

14. Ibid., p. 372.

15. See Jon L. Pierce, Randall B. Dunham, and Richard S. Blackburn, "Social Systems Structure, Job Design, and Growth Need Strength: A Test of a Congruency Model," *Academy of Management Journal* 22 (June 1979): 223–240. See also W. Philip Kraft and Kathleen L. Williams, "Job Redesign Improves Productivity," *Personnel Journal* 54 (July 1975): 393–397.

16. F.J. Roethlisberger and W.J. Dickson, *Management and the Worker* (Cambridge, MA: Harvard University Press, 1939), Part V.

17. Charles R. Walker and Robert H. Guest, *The Man on the Assembly Line* (Cambridge, MA: Harvard University Press, 1952).

18. Ibid., p. 154.

19. For further discussion of this point, see Chester I. Barnard, *The Functions of the Executive* (Cambridge, MA: Harvard University Press, 1938).

20. *Business Week*, 28 March 1977, p. 78.

21. Theodore H. White, "The Danger from Japan," *The New York Times Magazine*, 28 July 1985, p. 40.

22. Jerome M. Rosow, "Employee Participation Grows Up," *Enterprise*, June 1985, p. 14.

23. William G. Ouchi, *Theory Z: How American Business Can Meet the Japanese Challenge* (Reading, MA: Addison-Wesley, 1981), p. 58.

24. See Douglas McGregor, *The Human Side of Enterprise* (New York: McGraw-Hill, 1960).

25. For additional information, see Susan Chira, "Business Schools, Japanese Style," *The New York Times*, 4 August 1985, p. 34.

26. Ouchi, *Theory Z*, p. 33.

27. J. Bernard Keys and Thomas R. Miller, "The Japanese Management Theory Jungle," *Academy of Management Review* 9 (July 1984): 342–353.

28. "How Power Will Be Balanced on Saturn's Shop Floor," *Business Week*, 5 August 1985, p. 65.

29. Paul R. Lawrence and Jay W. Lorsch, "Differentiation and Integration in Complex Organizations," *Administrative Science Quarterly* 12 (June 1967): 3.

30. John Child, *Organization: A Guide to Problems and Practice* (London: Harper & Row, 1977), pp. 32–33.

31. D.S. Pugh, D.J. Hickson, C.R. Hinings, and C. Turner, "Dimensions of Organization Structure," *Administrative Science Quarterly* 13 (June 1968): 65–106.

32. Henry Mintzberg, *The Structuring of Organizations: A Synthesis of Research* (Englewood Cliffs, NJ: Prentice-Hall, 1979), Chapter 4.

33. Mitchell Fein, *Approaches to Motivation* (Hillside, NJ: American Institute of Industrial Engineering, 1970), p. 37.

34. Louis E. Davis, "Readying the Unready: Postindustrial Jobs," in *A Contingency Approach to Management: Readings,* John W. Newstrom, William E. Reif, and Robert M. Monczka, (New York: McGraw-Hill, 1975), pp. 133–134.

35. Peter M. Blau, "A Formal Theory of Differentiation in Organizations," *American Sociological Review* 35 (April 1970): 201–218.

36. For a summary of findings on this point, see Dan R. Dalton et al., "Organization Structure and Performance: A Critical Review, *Academy of Management Review* 5 (January 1980): 57–58.

ADDITIONAL READINGS

Crocker, Olga, Cyril Charney, and Johnny Sik Leung Chir. *Quality Circles: A Guide to Participation and Productivity.* New York: Facts on File Publications, 1984.

Glisson, Charles A. "Dependence of Technological Routinization on Structural Variables in Human Service Organizations." *Administrative Science Quarterly* 23 (September 1978): 383–395.

Hackman, J. Richard, and Greg R. Oldham. *Work Redesign.* Reading, MA: Addison-Wesley, 1980.

Hage, Jerald, and Michael Aiken. "Routine Technology, Social Structure and Organization Goals." *Administrative Science Quarterly* 14 (September 1969): 366–376.

Klein, Janice A. "Why Supervisors Resist Employee Involvement." *Harvard Business Review* 62 (September/October 1984): 87–95.

Lawler, E.E., III, and S.A. Mohrman. "Quality Circles after the Fad." *Harvard Business Review* 63 (January/February 1985): 64–71.

Schlesinger, Leonard A., and Barry Oshry. "Quality of Work Life and the Manager: Muddle in the Middle." *Organizational Dynamics* 13 (Summer 1984): 4–19.

Sethi, S. Prakash. *The False Promise of the Japanese Miracle: Illusions and Realities of the Japanese Management System.* Boston: Pitman Publishing Inc., 1984.

Sethi, S. Prakash, Nobuaki Namiki, and Carl L. Swanson. "The Decline of the Japanese System of Management." *California Management Review* 27 (Summer 1984): 35–45.

Wood, Robert, Frank Hull, and Koya Azumi. "Evaluating Quality Circles: The American Application." *California Management Review* 26 (Fall 1983): 37–53.

Departmentalization

The previous chapter was concerned with the first, most basic classical differentiating strategy: specialization of labor. This chapter explains the nature and logic of a second way in which organizational activities can be specialized: departmentalization, or the grouping of specialized tasks.

Small organizations pay little conscious attention to formal departmentalization. Indeed, the natural human tendency for people interested in and competent in the same activities to cluster together usually creates a departmentalized organization even without any formal definition of job duties and reporting structures. As small organizations grow larger, there is seldom a clear-cut signal indicating that *now* is the moment for formal departmentalization. But the time inevitably comes when the growing organization must group together employees who are performing similar tasks.

Departmentalization, one type of horizontal differentiation, contributes to the complexity of an organization's structure. Departmentalization is also labeled functional complexity, functional differentiation, and divisionalization. The concept of departmentalization from the perspectives of the classical, human relations, and modern schools will be discussed in this chapter.

THE NATURE OF DEPARTMENTALIZATION

Departmentalization is the process of splitting the organization into subdivisions. It is the organization-wide division of labor, the strategy for clustering specialized tasks into defined units. Employees are placed into logical groupings that management determines can most efficiently achieve the organization's goals. Figure 5.1 displays the departmental structure of a typical manufacturing organization. In this illustration, the grouping is by function; activities and resources are clustered on the basis of similar expertise.

If the organization's primary groupings are not further divided, they will probably be called departments. If they are subdivided, the primary groups may be called divisions and their subdivisions may be called departments. For example, the marketing

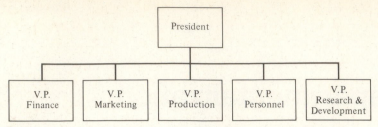

Figure 5.1 Departmentalization of a typical manufacturing organization.

division may have departments of sales, merchandising, distribution, and advertising. The personnel division may have departments of training and development, employment, equal employment opportunity, benefits, compensation, and labor relations. If the organization is quite large, further departmentalization may occur within these subdivisions. Very large organizations, or those with many different products or markets, may also use a special clustering strategy called strategic business units (SBU) or profit centers. Chapter 8, Decentralization, will discuss this clustering strategy as it applies to the overall organization. The present discussion stresses strategies for handling unit-level problems.

Historical Overview

Departmentalizing is an important task for designers of organizations. The logical grouping of jobs requires an in-depth understanding of the reasons for putting tasks together in certain ways and not putting them together in other ways.

Owner/Entrepreneurs   Early organizations managed by owner/entrepreneurs had few departmentalization problems because only a very few people did all jobs necessary for attaining organizational goals and they were under the close supervision of the owner/chief craftsman. The entrepreneur easily divided up the work, grouped the workers, and made any necessary adjustments.

The Need for Formal Grouping   In a larger organization, the grouping and supervision cannot be so casual. For example, as a combat group becomes larger, it must be organized into companies, battalions, and squads. Increased technological complexity can also make more formal grouping necessary, as in the case of musket production.

An Example: Musket Making   When muskets were handmade by skilled craftsmen, an organization's total musket manufacturing capacity depended on how many craftsmen it had. If a few more muskets per month were needed, the organization hired a few more craftsmen.

   As the population (and the demand for muskets) began to increase more rapidly, musket-making firms had to develop a system capable of producing many more muskets—without waiting the several years required for new apprentices to become qualified musket makers. The Springfield Arsenal in Massachusetts solved this problem by (1) dividing musket making into simple, quickly learned, specialized tasks, and (2) departmentalizing those tasks into the specific functional groupings necessary for producing a musket: stock makers, barrel borers, etc. Nowadays, we are accustomed to seeing the employees of mass-producing organizations grouped by type of task. However, the method developed by the Springfield Arsenal was a significant innovation.

One result of departmentalization was the need for standard musket parts. All parts produced by one department had to fit into all assemblies of the next department. This requirement demanded the introduction into the work situation of people to inspect for quality. Furthermore, since the departments worked on partially finished muskets shipped to them by other departments, someone had to be sure that a smooth flow of work was maintained; otherwise a departmental group might be sitting around with nothing to do. Such supervision problems were a long way from those that a craftsman like Paul Revere faced in his silversmith shop. Problems such as these, arising as the nation's small craft industries developed into large mass-production industries, caused the classical school's interest in the formal aspects of departmentalization.

THE CLASSICAL PERSPECTIVE

Once the organization had achieved specialization of labor, the focus became how to develop clustering strategies to group these specialized tasks efficiently. That focus was the classical school's next logical concern.

Lyndall Urwick stressed the importance of clear demarcation lines between the organization's different tasks, positions, and groups of activities:

> If we accept the danger of overlapping functions and the importance of definition, it is clear that one of the first tasks in organizing any complex of activities is to decide how we shall determine the limits of different groups of activities, different positions. Indeed it would not be a bad short definition of organizing to describe it as "fixing the limits of positions."[1]

Three Departmentalization Methods

Urwick advanced three broad methods for "fixing the limits of positions": unitary, serial, and functional. A departmentalization scheme is *unitary* if it depends on a single, common, mutually exclusive way of putting tasks into departments or units. A task is either in the unit or it is not, without any possible debate. Examples are departmentalization by customer (men, women, children) and by region (eastern division, western division). A customer cannot be both a man and a woman; a branch plant cannot be in both the East and the West.

The second departmentalization method is *serial.* If a product is made in a series of steps, the organization might decide to assign a different employee group to each step, as is done on an assembly line. Serial departmentalization is not a unitary method because decisions about where tasks should be grouped are sometimes arbitrary. A hubcap manufacturing unit, for instance, might reasonably be assigned either to the wheel production department or to the automotive trim department.

The *functional* method is really a special case of the unitary method, because employees are grouped in such a way that their tasks contribute to only one of the organization's functions. For example, three functions are common to many organizations: production, distribution, and finance. Therefore, all tasks in such organizations fall under one of those primary divisions.

Now let us look at these three general departmentalization methods more closely.

Unitary Departmentalization

The six unitary methods of departmentalizing are by person, product, area, customer, date or time, and number. Each method provides a clear, unambiguous, mutually exclusive basis for dividing up organizational activities so that each unit can be supervised and held accountable.

Person   Departmentalizing by person simply means taking all of the organization's personnel and splitting them into groups and subgroups. For instance, a fixed number of soldiers comprises an army platoon. The platoon sergeant is responsible for all the men on his roster, and only for those men.

Product   A second unitary departmentalization method, often favored in manufacturing organizations, is by product. A plant producing stringed instruments may be broken down into departments making guitars, banjos, mandolins, ukuleles, and so on. Similarly, companies like General Motors and Procter & Gamble can divide up their activities by product, with each division being responsible for a different brand. Product departmentalization and functional departmentalization are the two most widely used methods for establishing the primary divisions in large organizations.

Area   Groupings can be determined by geographical area. A national corporation might decide, for example, to group its efforts into four geographical regions. This arrangement could resemble a division by numbers (if each region contains roughly the same number of square miles) or a division by product (if a different product is produced or grown in each region). The four NCAA basketball regional semifinal tournaments or the branch offices of a state bank are examples of area departmentalization.

Customer   Departments can be set up according to the types of customers they serve. In many sales-oriented organizations, each customer group has unique characteristics. For example, customers for small and large data processing systems have more differences than mere size of machine capacity. Applications, sophistication, familiarity with computers, and technical competence also differ greatly. The two customer types require entirely different sales approaches and organizational structures.

Date or Time   Children are assigned to schools on the basis of their birth dates. Workers in some organizations are assigned to different time-of-day shifts. A hospital might develop three separate, parallel organizational units to handle the first, second, and third shifts.

Number   The last unitary departmentalization scheme is by number. Organizations handling voter registration, insurance claims, and social security payments might allocate work simply by using numbers.

Each of these six departmentalization methods permits the establishment of mutually exclusive units. A small customer is not a large customer; a 4-year-old is not a 5-year-old; social security number 148-22-6571 is not number 266-72-0634.

Advantages   Creating unitary forms of departments has certain advantages and disadvantages:

ADVANTAGES	DISADVANTAGES
Member perception of unit's purpose	Excessive competition
Cross-functional training	Duplication of work
Cross-unit competition	Uneven workload spread

One advantage is that unitary departmentalization helps department members to see the unit's overall purpose. Chevrolet marketing people (in a unit organized by product, Chevrolets) can perceive and identify with the unit's goals more easily than they could if they were functionally organized as a marketing department for all General Motors products and reported to a marketing vice president on the GM corporate staff. Similarly, the french-fry maker in a small-town McDonald's (a unit determined by geographical area) can identify with the unit's purpose more readily by reporting to the local manager than to a french-fry production vice president at corporate headquarters.

A second advantage is the potential for maximizing cross-functional training within the unit. By its very nature, the unit cluster encourages unit members to know what other members are doing. The interdependent, interpersonal relationships in the unit facilitate cross-training, allowing people to learn a variety of functional skills.

A third advantage of unitary departmentalization is that it creates the opportunity for cross-unit competition: stores can compete for highest profits, platoons for best rifle scores, and geographic divisions for making sales quotas. The unitary form builds motivation through competition and facilitates objective performance comparisons.

Disadvantages   On the other hand, competition among units may pass the healthy point and become fierce and unproductive. For example, if a sales territory is divided up along customer lines, some aggressive salespeople may fudge the customer definitions enough to be competing with their fellow salespeople. An organization whose personnel fight among themselves leaves a negative impression on customers.

Another disadvantage is that placing certain functions in all units, rather than centralizing those functions, may lead to duplication of work. Each unit in a restaurant chain, United Fund agency, or government subdivision might have its own purchasing department or agent, even though centralized purchasing might be more efficient. A staff person purchasing for the entire organization could acquire specialized knowledge about important purchasing areas and, by buying in volume, get better prices than the individual units.

A final disadvantage is that the workload for some functions may be less evenly spread under the unitary method. In the national office, a claims specialist may handle a constant flow of insurance claims. Asking the different regional units to handle their own claims may create periods of inactivity, followed by periods of excessive activity. The migration of people every winter from North to South creates an annual problem for Florida insurance claim handlers. A national claims-handling department, however, would not be affected by that population shift.

Serial Departmentalization

In many organizations, some input must go through a series of stages in order to be transformed into some output. These stages can be the basis for departmentalization. The serial method breaks down into two types: process and machine.

Process   When departmentalizing by process, the organization subdivides its work into stages and then groups the knowledge, skills, and tools needed for completing each stage. The classic illustrations come from the mass-production industries. For example, plants that produce large steel objects are usually organized serially: foundry, forge, machine shop, finishing shop, subassembly, main assembly, and paint shop.

Machine   Groups can also be organized according to the machinery or equipment used at a certain production stage. In a weaving operation, all the dyeing machines, carding machines, and looms are grouped together in their own departments.

Functional Departmentalization

The third method for departmentalizing activities is by function. As organizations have evolved, many of them have seen the three-way grouping of activities into the production, distribution, and finance functions as a rational way of organizing basic activities. Functional departmentalization was the favorite form of the classical school, and it continues to be widely used.

Advantages   A major advantage of clustering by function is ease and effectiveness of supervision. A functional career path often gives supervisors experience in doing many of the jobs they supervise. A personnel manager typically supervises people involved with wage and salary administration, affirmative action programs, training, and performance review—all parts of the traditional educational background and career experience of a personnel manager. In contrast, a supervisor under the unitary form of departmentalization is more likely to supervise diverse job functions.

A second advantage is also related to career development. A fairly clear career track can be defined within most organizational functions. For example, an Engineer I or Bookkeeper I can see the advancement paths for engineers and accountants on the organization chart. Functional personnel can perceive the training, background, and experience that they will need in order to move up the ladder. Although employees working under the unitary departmentalization form can foresee their career paths to an extent, their opportunities for cross-training make the paths less certain. Unitary departmentalization under the Japanese model is an exception, in that career and development opportunities are limited. The Japanese worker knows at the outset what the highest attainable position is and that the path to it is deliberately slow and predetermined. Many American companies seeking to reduce the number of middle-management layers are considering the use of this model.

A third advantage of the functional form is that it permits intense specialization where needed. People working in distinct functional areas can concentrate on learning, using, and improving their functional skills. An accountant who is also required to spend half of her time typing address labels is going to be a less efficient accountant than one who does accounts receivable all day long.

Many professional associations are structured along functional lines. These associations encourage advancement and specialized development through educational programs, seminars, technical publications, and accreditation standards. Each employee is encouraged to become increasingly expert in a small part of the organization's activities.

Disadvantages   Functional clustering has disadvantages as well. An obvious disadvantage is functional myopia. People can get so wrapped up in their functional specialties that they lose sight of how those functions fit into the overall organizational purpose. The organization's goals sometimes get lost in the effort to achieve what is good for sales, or production, or the budget, or any other function. In *On a Clear Day You Can See General Motors,* John De Lorean argued that the decline of General Motors was directly related to the rise within GM of the financial experts who could see the world only through financial eyes.

A second disadvantage is a career block that sometimes develops for functionally trained people. If the traditional career path becomes blocked because someone ahead doesn't move up or out, then the lower-level employee gets locked into position. Consider junior underwriter Tom Smith, hoping to be promoted eventually to underwriting superintendent. If the two people standing between Smith and that job are clearly not promotable, then Smith had better get used to his junior position because that's where he's going to stay—unless, of course, he quits.

Similarly, many top-level functional experts find themselves locked out of the organization's senior management jobs that require production, marketing, or other expertise not available in highly specialized career paths. The personnel director of a nuclear engineering firm or a university may be ineligible for promotion to the CEO position because the personnel director's specialty skills are not sufficiently related to the organization's overall goals.

A final problem is the authority conflict that the functional form sometimes creates. Personnel manager Joan Brown at ABC's Seattle plant takes orders from the plant manager. What is the authority relationship between Joan Brown and the corporate vice president for personnel in Detroit? Brown reports to the plant manager, yet she realizes that her career in personnel is tied directly to the vice president's opinion of her work. If a conflict develops between the plant manager and the corporate vice president, Brown could be caught in the middle. Should she carry out corporate personnel policies to the letter, no matter what the plant manager says? Or should she be loyal to the plant manager even when the manager's directives are contrary to corporate policy? The fuzzy line of authority in such situations need not cause problems; the reporting relationships can be made clear enough to avoid them.

Even with the functional method's disadvantages, many organizations still favor functional departmentalization to make primary organizational divisions.

Varying Strategies   Organizations with multiple structural levels often use a variety of departmentalization strategies. The first major division is usually made on either a functional or a product basis. Subsequent divisions will be made to suit the organization's goal-seeking needs.

Figure 5.2 is a partial organization chart of Tipple Wine Company. The four primary divisions are functional. Below these divisions, the company employs numerous other strategies for clustering its activities and resources.

THE HUMAN RELATIONS PERSPECTIVE

Classical-Human Relations Differences

As reflected in the OT-Model on the inside covers, the classical perspective on departmentalization considered the structural dimension. The preceding discussion of that perspective makes no mention of *the people* involved. The human relations school criticized the classical school for ignoring the individual when the classicists specialized labor. Similarly, the human relations school felt that the classical school ignored

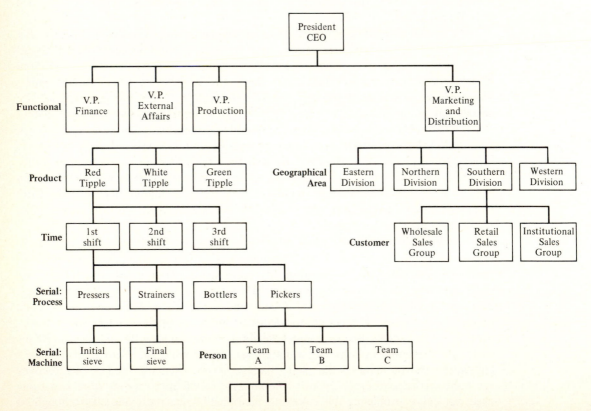

Figure 5.2 Tipple Wine Company: Partial organization chart with departmentalization strategies indicated.

individual variations, interpersonal relationships, and the informal group when they grouped organizational activities.

Real-World Coordination Needs   Real-life departmentalization offers countless coordination problems that the classicists did not acknowledge. In their review of classical principles, James G. March and Herbert A. Simon commented:

> One peculiar characteristic . . . of all the formalizations of the departmentalization problem in classical organization theory is that, if taken literally, problems of coordination are eliminated. Since the whole set of activities to be performed is specified in advance, once these are allocated to organization units and individuals the organization problem posed by these formal theories is solved.[2]

In brief, if persons and tasks are clustered properly, *there should be no coordination problems.* March and Simon pointed out that many real-world activities, rather than lending themselves to prior specification and prediction, are instead interdependent—in terms of when and how they may be done—with other activities. Consequently, human intervention is required to coordinate these interdependent events. Since the humans doing and coordinating the work are not robots and have varying degrees of communication skill, any theory of departmentalization not allowing for human variations is defective.

Who versus What   A second factor not considered by the classical school is that both the people being departmentalized and those running the departments have varying skills, interests, and degrees of influence. An organization will occasionally departmentalize not according to management's ideas about organizational structure but on the basis of a particular executive's interest, influence, training, or capability. For instance, instead of sending all trainees to a training department, an organization may send some of them to departmental managers whose interests and talents seem most apt to result in the achievement of training objectives. The army sometimes assigns soldiers to receive advanced combat training from the officers who will lead them in battle.

This strategy has obvious disadvantages. If managers control certain activities and people because of their personal characteristics and interests, the organization may be at a disadvantage when these managers leave the organization or move on to other assignments. Then the subordinates assigned to these managers may become orphans, and the activities in which the departed managers took an interest may be abandoned.

The Formal and Informal Organizations   A third important distinction emerged in the dispute between the classical and human relations schools: the difference between the formal organization and the informal organization. As described and discussed by the classicists, the formal organization is the organizational design established by management. This official organizational structure is represented in a variety of organizational publications—manuals, policies, procedures, job descriptions, and so forth. The formal design is often depicted in a formal organization chart, like the one for Tipple Wine Company in Figure 5.2, which showed the lines of authority and communication.

The human relations school acknowledged the existence and significance of the formal organization. But they also stressed the importance of the informal organization—the *unofficial* system of relationships resulting from the social and other interpersonal interactions and work patterns of members. For example, people working in the same department usually socialize with one another. The special relationships that subsequently develop may hurt or help the organization. The informal group may devise a better way to do the job. Or, for its own reasons, it may also keep the job from being done. William F. Whyte's classic study, "The Social Structure of the Restaurant," shows how the restaurant's official department structure overlays and is affected by interpersonal relationships and status concerns of restaurant employees.[3]

The informal organization is socially important for most workers. As industrialization and mobility increased, families often became dispersed. For many workers, the extended family was replaced by organizational social groups—both formal (company towns, picnics, softball teams) and informal (weekend gatherings, card parties, dinners). As traditional social groups became more difficult to form, the informal organization took on greater importance for workers.

Of the informal organization at the Hawthorne plant (described in *Management and the Worker* by F.J. Roethlisberger and W.J. Dickson), Philip Selznick made these comments:

> The informal structure of the worker group grew up out of the day-to-day practices of the men as they groped for ways of taking care of their own felt needs. There was no series of conscious acts by which these procedures were instituted, but they were no less binding on that account. These needs largely arose from the way in which the men defined their situation within the organization. The informal organization served a triple function: (a) it served to control the behavior of the members of the worker group; (b) within the context of the larger organization (the plant), it was an attempt on the part of the particular group to control the conditions of its existence; (c) it acted as a mechanism for the expression of personal relationships for which the formal organization did not provide. Thus the informal structure provided those avenues of aggression, solidarity, and prestige-construction required by individual members.[4]

Chester I. Barnard saw informal structures within formal organizations as serving three functions: (1) providing a means of communication and establishing norms of conduct between superiors and subordinates, (2) maintaining cohesiveness through regulating the willingness to serve and the stability of objective authority, and (3) maintaining the feeling of personal integrity, self-respect, and independent choice. While giving each member the feeling of independence, the informal group is in fact subtly controlling the behavior of its members.[5]

The formal organization chart in Figure 5.2 (p. 110) can be contrasted with the presentation in Figure 5.3: the social interaction of a picking team within the formal Tipple organization. The evolution of social patterns within the informal organization does not necessarily have any relationship to positions on the formal chart.

Types of Groups

For the human relations theorists, the significance of the formal organization was not that it clustered people into departments but that it brought them together into *groups*.

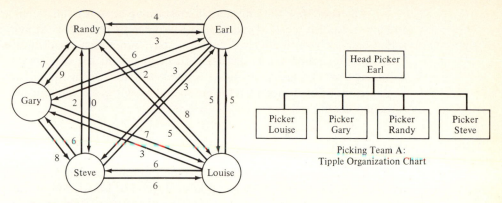

Picking Team A: Observed social interaction
frequencies among pickers in a day (arrows
indicate who initiated contact)

Figure 5.3 Tipple Wine Company, Picking Team A: Social-interaction frequencies and formal chart relationships.

The group is central to the human relations perspective. After all, a division or a department is in a sense nothing more than a group of people, and an organization is a group of groups. Therefore, the human relations school proposed to study organizational groups, rather than those formal groupings called "departments" by the classicists.

The true study of groups falls within the disciplines of psychology, sociology, and—more recently—organizational behavior. Let us examine some characteristics of groups as determined by scholars in these fields.[6]

Three types of groups exist within organizations: functional groups, task groups, and interest groups.

Functional Groups   The organization brings functional groups together, more or less permanently, to achieve certain organizational objectives. Functional groups are officially sanctioned and normally receive a continuous stream of resources. Whether they are called departments, divisions, sections, or areas, they are the formal groupings into which the organization's people and tasks are differentiated. Examples would be the nation's Department of Defense, a company's purchasing department, and a college's sociology department.

Task Groups   The organization brings task groups together *temporarily* to complete specific projects. The members then return to their functional groups. A company committee to examine equal employment opportunity problems, a bipartisan task force to study crime in America, and a project team assigned to recommend quality control improvements are examples.

Interest Groups   Both the functional group and the task group are part of the formal organization. Interest groups are formed by the workers themselves. The common factor may be age or gender, or it may be an interest in cards, opera, baseball, or ceramics. The life span of interest groups varies. If group members are transferred or get tired of the group, it will be short-lived. But it may last indefinitely.

At a major New York firm, an interest group became a functional group. Female employees banded together and formed a Women's Committee. At first, they concentrated on their own job-related concerns: pay, promotion opportunities, and so on. Then they branched out to discuss with management the concerns of *all* workers. Realizing that the group provided a good way to keep in touch with employees, management officially accepted the group and used it as a communications vehicle and sounding board.

THE MODERN PERSPECTIVE

The modern perspective seeks to determine those factors which combine to result in the most effective departmentalization strategy. The foundation of this perspective is *knowing and specifying the organization's goals.* Activities can be effectively arranged into departments only in light of organizational purposes.

Need for a Contingency Viewpoint

An Unstable World   The human relations school had serious reservations about the classical perspective on departmentalization. Classical attempts to define all activities precisely and group them appropriately sometimes seemed to assume a static, stable, predictable world that didn't exist in reality. The assumption of such a stable organizational environment might at one time have been reasonable; by the 1950s, when the human relations movement began to have great impact, that stability had vanished.

The classicists did not always consider the *evolution* of organizations fully. Their prescriptions were often static rather than dynamic, incapable of adjusting to the complexity and turbulence of the times. Many classical prescriptions were a good basis for organizational departmentalization but, in and of themselves, could not cope with a complex, ever-changing world.

Crossing Departmental Boundaries   Today's organizational groupings must interrelate across formal departmental boundaries. As a simple example, consider unitary departmentalization by product in a musical instrument factory. The guitar and mandolin departments may require the same raw materials, share the same tools and machinery, and depend on the same service department to clear out the finished instruments. An automobile manufacturer may use the same engine in models produced by different automotive divisions. While all of Urwick's departmentalization schemes are still found today, their purity rarely exists.

Mixed Departmental Strategies   A point deserving emphasis is that different departmentalization strategies can be *mixed* throughout the organization's various levels, as they were in Tipple Wine Company (Figure 5.2). An organization can be functional at the vice-presidential level, unitary at the branch plant level, and serial at the production level. The organization must focus on the goals of specific areas and levels, then departmentalize accordingly.

Even at the same organizational level, departmentalization schemes are frequently mixed. A company making four major products might departmentalize by product at the vice-presidential level, with each product vice president reporting directly to the chief executive officer (CEO). But Bill Terry, the vice president for finance (a functional, rather than a product, department), will probably also report directly to the CEO. Since Terry makes recommendations concerning the allocation of capital to all product divisions, he cannot very well report to the vice president of any one product division. If he did, he might show an understandable bias toward the vice president who is filling out his performance appraisals and signing his payroll checks.

Relative Importance and Organization Chart Position   Bill Terry's location on the chart illustrates an important point about how the various groups, units, and departments are arranged on the organization chart itself. By looking at their chart positions, we ought to be able to determine the relative importance of each group to the achievement of organizational goals. Almost always, regardless of other grouping strategies used, the finance function will report directly to the chief executive officer. The management of financial resources has become critically important for most organizations. Therefore, CEOs want whoever is performing the finance function to report directly to the top, without any other groups intervening.

Because they are vital to a given organization's success, other functions may similarly report directly to the CEO: quality control in a pharmaceutical firm, safety at NASA or a nuclear plant, and public relations at a university.

The Benefits of Grouping   Henry Mintzberg offers four benefits of grouping into departments or other units:

1. Grouping establishes a system of supervision. Each group has a supervisor, and these supervisors make up the system of formal authority by which the efforts of groups are directed and coordinated.
2. Groups share common resources, facilities, and equipment rather than requiring each position or subunit to have its own resources.
3. Grouping facilitates performance measurement. If group members share resources, then the costs of group production can be measured. If group members contribute to produce the same products or services, their outputs can be jointly measured. Measurement of the group's joint performance encourages group coordination of activities, so that the group will do well on the performance measure.
4. Grouping encourages "mutual adjustment." Sharing resources leads to working closely together, communicating informally, and coordinating by mutual adjustment.

The negative side of these benefits is that close coordination and cooperation *within* the group may create coordination problems *between* groups.[7]

No One System Is Best   Modern organization theorists realize that no one departmentalization system is best. They share that realization with classicist Lyndall Urwick, who argued for a contingency approach to departmentalization years ago. Urwick said that the first or primary division—the main principle of departmentalizing at the highest levels—is of great significance. Yet, he said, "There is apparently no one most effective system of departmentalization." The best system will depend "upon the results which are desired at a given time and place. . . . An organization is a living and dynamic entity. . . . A principle of organization appropriate at one stage may not be appropriate at all during a succeeding stage. . . . Time is an essential element in the formula."[8]

Product versus Function   The following example supports the assertion that no single departmentalization structure is best, even in very similar operations. Arthur H. Walker and Jay W. Lorsch studied two plants that were nearly alike except that one was structured by product and the other by function.[9] Table 5.1 presents some differences between Plant F (functional basis) and Plant P (product basis).

In most respects, the product form seems to have the edge. Even so, the functional plant had a higher production rate. However, over the three-year study period, the product plant *increased* its productivity by 23 percent, while productivity at the functional plant increased by only 3 percent. Walker and Lorsch make this important point about functional versus product departmentalization:

> The functional organization seems to lead to better results in a situation where stable performance of a routine task is desired, while the product organization leads to better results in situations where the task is less predictable and requires innovative problem solving.[10]

Table 5.1   CONTRASTING CHARACTERISTICS: PLANT F AND PLANT P

Characteristic	Plant F: functional	Plant P: product
Goal orientation	Specialists interested in specialties.	Specialists interested in plant product goals.
Time orientation	Short-term issues, daily problems.	Longer-term issues, greater variety of time orientation.
Organizational formality	More formal, jobs more defined, rules and procedures relied on.	Less formal, job definitions more vague, low reliance on rules and procedures.
Integration	Often a problem.	Sometimes a problem.
Communication	Less frequent, more formal, use memos and phone calls.	Frequent, less formal, face to face, open, spontaneous.
Conflict resolution	Some confrontation of conflict, but also smooth it over, avoid it, or kick it upstairs.	Much confrontation of conflict, managers resolve conflict themselves.
Performance	Higher production, greater efficiency, lower cost, but low increase in production, less improvement of plant capabilities.	Lower production, less efficiency, higher cost, but high increase in production and improved plant capabilities.
Managerial attitudes	Managers less involved in their work, feel less stress, more satisfaction.	Managers more involved in their work, feel more stress, less satisfaction.

Source: Reprinted by permission of the *Harvard Business Review.* Exhibit from "Organizational Choice: Product vs. Function" by Arthur H. Walker and Jay W. Lorsch (November/December 1968). Copyright © 1968 by the President and Fellows of Harvard College; all rights reserved.

Duncan Summary   Robert Duncan has summarized the strengths and weaknesses of the product and functional forms. That summary appears in Table 5.2. Although the relationship is not one to one, the advantages of one form seem to be the disadvantages of the other, which accounts for the difficulty that some firms have in making a choice.

James D. Thompson confirms the "no-best-way" idea by pointing out that in complex organizations, their departmental components

> serve different purposes for the larger organization, they employ several processes, they frequently serve more than one clientele, and for the most part they are geographically extended. The question is not which criterion to use for grouping, but rather in which *priority* are the several criteria to be exercised.[11]

Departmentalization Determinants

If no one system is best, what are the determinants that point toward the best systems in given situations? We shall describe a few.

Inseparable Activities   Some activities are so tightly linked that they must be in the same department. A conveyor belt that feeds into an integrated assembly operation should probably be grouped with the assembly operation, even if arguments for assigning it elsewhere can be made.

The fact that a flow of related activities must somehow be differentiated into departments sometimes leads to interesting debates about how the differentiations should be made. For example, organizing a social services delivery function can lead to considerable discussion about how the different provider groupings should be departmentalized.

Table 5.2   FUNCTION VERSUS PRODUCT: STRENGTHS AND WEAKNESSES

Characteristic	Functional structure	Product structure
Environment	Best in stable environment. Slow response time to change.	Best in fast-changing, unstable environment. Responds well to change.
Economies of scale	Achieves economies of scale within functions: same location, same facilities.	Lower economies of scale within functions.
Skill development	In-depth skill development and specialization for employees.	Less opportunity for in-depth skill development and specialization.
Size	Does best in small to medium-size organization.	Does best in large organization.
Number of products	Does best with one or few products.	Does best with several products.
Coordination	Less effective coordination among units and functions.	Highly effective coordination among units and functions.
Innovation	Less innovation.	More innovation.
Goals	Restricted view of organizational goals, good accomplishment of functional goals.	Broader view of organizational goals.
Hierarchy	Hierarchy may become overloaded with decisions to make.	Hierarchy less important in decision making.

Source: Adapted by permission of the publisher from "What Is the Right Organization Structure? Decision Tree Analysis Provides the Answer," by Robert Duncan, *Organizational Dynamics* 7 (Winter 1979): 64, 66, © 1979 American Management Association, New York. All rights reserved.

Achieving Control   Some activities must be separated from others over which they serve as controls. Organizations need to separate electronic data processing from payroll, credit checking from retail sales, and quality control from production. In each case, failure to separate the activities could permit a subunit to put its own goals ahead of the organization's. Checks will be processed faster if the data processing people not only print them but sign them; sales will always be higher if every customer qualifies for credit; and production will always run faster if product quality goes unchallenged. But in all of these situations, keeping responsibilities separated is so important to organizational goal achievement that any other benefit is overshadowed.

Conversely, some activities *must* be grouped together so that one department or manager can control them. As we have pointed out, organizations commonly require the finance, accounting, and internal audit operations to report directly to the chief executive officer—regardless of what strategy is used for departmentalizing the rest of the organization.

Degree of Uncertainty   The degree of uncertainty about future conditions that the organization may face can lead to different types of departmentalization. Paul R. Lawrence and Jay W. Lorsch examined three industries: plastics (much uncertainty), foods (some uncertainty), and containers (not much uncertainty). They found that the higher the uncertainty level, the greater the number of departments.[12]

Importance of Goals and Priorities

According to the systems/contingency school, an organization should be departmentalized in light of its unique situation and the factors affecting it. Yet, one primary criterion does exist: the owner/entrepreneur or chief executive officer must choose the departmentalization strategy *that will best enable the organization to meet its goals as that person understands them.* For example, the CEO who places high priority on differentiating the organization's expertise into distinct categories will set up *functional* departments. The CEO who wants to combine the organization's talents into groups that can best serve the needs of specific customer types may reject functional departmentalization and use *unitary* departmentalization, by customer type, if that design can be made to fit the firm's overall strategy.

As organizations make their departmentalization decisions, taking organizational goals and other factors into account, they will constantly find themselves involved in trade-offs—a balancing of advantages and disadvantages—similar to those reflected in Tables 5.1 and 5.2 for product departmentalization and functional departmentalization. In Chapter 8, a detailed review of decentralization as an organization-wide departmentalization strategy, other trade-offs will be covered. However, one additional trade-off bears mention here: coordination versus cost, as reflected in James D. Thompson's categorization of technological processes.

Coordination versus Cost   The work of many organizational departments is interdependent—the departments depend on each other to carry out their daily work. Which types of interdependence have the lowest and highest coordination costs? James D. Thompson has discussed the coordination costs associated with three types of interdependence: reciprocal, sequential, and pooled.[13] The pattern of *reciprocal* inde-pendence is circular: one department's output becomes the next department's input, which is then sent back as input to the originating department. The designing and engineering of cars follows this pattern. One department designs the car, another builds a prototype, and a third tests it. Based on the test results, the design is modified and another prototype is built, then tested, and so on. A similar process takes place as bills pass back and forth between the Senate and House of Representatives.

In *sequential* interdependence, work flows from one position to the next in some sequence; the output of one department becomes the input of another, whose output becomes the next department's input. An automobile assembly line illustrates sequen-tial interdependence, as the unfinished product moves from station to station.

Pooled interdependence occurs when all of the same jobs are grouped together. The most common example is the typing pool. The three types of interdependence are shown in Figure 5.4.

The coordination costs of the different interdependence types are: pooled, lowest; sequential, medium; reciprocal, highest. According to Thompson, organizations in the early stages of their development structure their departments along reciprocal lines. This departmentalization method has the highest coordination costs because of com-munications problems, reliance on the other departments, and lost time due to unneces-sary duplication. As the organization's work flow grows larger, it often moves to sequential interdependence. Finally, to economize, the organization turns to the pool concept. Pooled interdependence minimizes coordination and other costs since the jobs are in one area and are standardized. Furthermore, absence of any one worker will not halt the work flow.

The Impact of Technology   As technology becomes increasingly sophisticated, organi-zations must develop elaborate departmentalization schemes. More departments are required to house the increasing, improving technology. Then even more departments are required to coordinate the blossoming of technological activities. When Avis began using a computer system to handle its car rental reservations, it developed a small

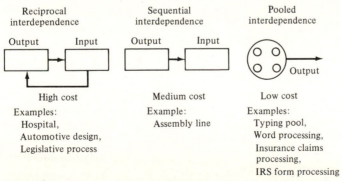

Figure 5.4 Thompson's types of interdependence and their costs. (*Source:* Based on James D. Thompson, *Organizations in Action: Social Science Bases of Administrative Theory* [New York: McGraw-Hill Book Co., 1967].)

"information services department." In the 1960s and early 1970s, as demand for car rentals skyrocketed, Avis had to continue increasing its computer facilities. Eventually the small department that served the company became a huge division which may now be *driving* the company. The impact of technology on organizational structure is the subject of Chapter 15.

Project and Matrix Management

Complex modern technology has caused organizations to try new grouping methods. Project management—and its variant, matrix management—is designed to cope with the modern need for an organization that can conceptualize and complete a large-scale, technologically complex project like a nuclear submarine, a supersonic bomber, or a sophisticated weapons system. The form can also be ideal for organizations such as engineering design firms and hospital specialty teams that want to remain fluid and adaptable as they confront rapidly changing markets for their products and services.

Pradip N. Khandwalla offers the following comment concerning the matrix/project form:

> The more customized and varied the products or services provided to the organization's clientele; the faster the rate of innovation or introduction of new products, projects, or services by the organization; the tighter the operating schedule; and the more sophisticated the technology of operations, the more the organization will tend to develop a matrix, project structure.[14]

Project Management

Project management has become an important organizational strategy for managing undertakings that are (1) definable, in terms of a specific goal, product, or accomplishment; (2) unique, or unfamiliar to the parent organization; (3) large or complex; and (4) quite important. If the undertaking does not have these characteristics, the organization's regular structure should be able to take care of it.

A project team is formed by borrowing employees from their regular work units and assigning them temporarily to the project manager's authority. Unlike many organizational activities, a project is not an ongoing effort; it has a definite beginning and end. The project manager must use the borrowed employees to complete the project on schedule and within cost and performance standards. The life-cycle stages of a typical project are presented in Figure 5.5.

The project team usually varies in size and composition during the course of the project. As expertise is required, specialists from the organization's functional areas work with the project on temporary assignment. When the team member's duties on the project are completed, the member returns to the home department.

Although frequently classified as a "modern" departmentalization strategy, the project form was used by large construction firms as early as 1910. A construction company will often sign a contract to complete a complex piece of work by a strict deadline. The company must meet the deadline or pay severe penalties. According to Russell Robb,

The organization for such an undertaking will not be the same as for deliberate construction systematized in all details for the lowest total construction-cost. It may be necessary to cut "red tape" that would be desirable in other situations, it may pay to take the chances of less thorough deliberation of plans, the lines of authority even may be changed—all because the relative importance of factors is changed. The harmony of the organization is upset, and modifications must be made to suit the new conditions.[15]

Jetcraft Company   As is true of many modern organizational concepts, project management was a logical solution to a problem faced in the aerospace industry. To illustrate, consider an imaginary manufacturer of long-range passenger jet planes: Jetcraft Company. Jetcraft's present structure, straightforward and functional, is shown in Figure 5.6.

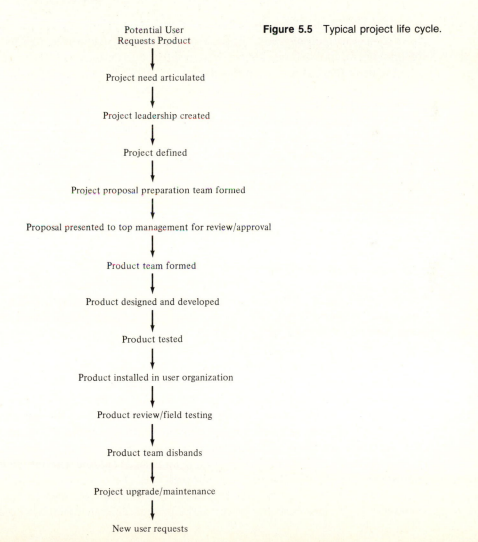

Figure 5.5   Typical project life cycle.

Potential User
Requests Product

↓

Project need articulated

↓

Project leadership created

↓

Project defined

↓

Project proposal preparation team formed

↓

Proposal presented to top management for review/approval

↓

Product team formed

↓

Product designed and developed

↓

Product tested

↓

Product installed in user organization

↓

Product review/field testing

↓

Product team disbands

↓

Project upgrade/maintenance

↓

New user requests

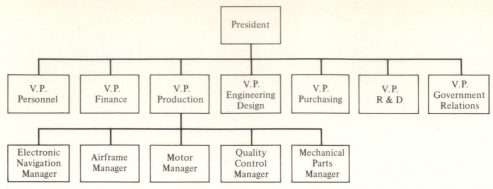

Figure 5.6   Jetcraft Company organization chart.

Creating a temporary organization   Companies producing salt and snuff do not have to deal with obsolescence. In the aerospace industry, however, rapidly advancing technology inevitably forces almost every product into obsolescence. Jetcraft's management realizes that the firm's continued existence depends on its ability to keep securing contracts for new products to replace expiring contracts for obsolete products. To get a contract, Jetcraft must submit the low bid.

Let us suppose that Florida Airways wants a new and different passenger plane. Rather than form a new division to produce an aircraft that may not yet be more than a drawing on a piece of paper, and for which a competitor may win the bid anyway, Jetcraft creates a temporary organization. People are borrowed from the company's functional areas long enough to prepare a bid.

The project manager   The project manager asks for the necessary people: (1) a personnel specialist, to estimate whether the current work force has the necessary skills, what it would cost to train new people, and so forth; (2) a research and development specialist, to estimate the time, money, and people required to develop the project; (3) an engineer, to match equipment with expected needs and to estimate the costs of R&D designs; (4) a finance specialist, to determine the project's expected costs and benefits; and so on. In short, the project manager assembles a miniature organization—perhaps even a duplicate in structure of Jetcraft itself.

Submitting the bid   The specialists put their talents together, and a bid is determined and submitted. The project organization disbands, and people go back to their regular jobs. If Jetcraft does not win the bid, the company has made a large investment of money for nothing. However, human costs and disruption to the organization have been minimal. No large division is standing by, waiting to spring into action if the bid is successful, or waiting to be laid off if the bid is unsuccessful. Project management is the only way for Jetcraft to get involved in large-scale bidding without relying entirely on outside expertise or temporary employees.

If Jetcraft wins the bid, the organization will follow through on the project in whatever way seems best. For a very large project, Jetcraft might set up a separate, basically self-contained division to handle it. If the project is small, another project team might be assembled. Project size, then, largely determines how the group working on the project should be structured.

Centralized Project Management: BellSouth   Turning a project over to a team is usually viewed as a decentralizing strategy. However, in some instances a centralized approach to managing large projects has proven effective.

BellSouth is one of the seven regional holding companies created by the 1984 divestiture of AT&T. BellSouth owns two operating companies: South Central Bell and Southern Bell. The continuing demands of these companies for new and updated computerized information systems led to the creation of Information System Services (ISS), a centralized project management unit that coordinates the development and installation of these systems.

Coordination by ISS   Under ISS coordination, projects are undertaken and performed by interdepartmental teams that specialize in planning, design, implementation, and operation. Each team is headed by a professional project manager from the ISS staff. Figure 5.7 shows how the teams are involved over the life cycle of ISS information-system projects. Each project management team specializes in a particular life-cycle stage. The planning team develops the proposal. Once that task is performed, the planning team dissolves and its ISS project manager moves on to plan another project. Then the design team develops detailed systems configurations, determines systems components, develops interfaces among systems, and creates design specifications. The implementation team then obtains hardware and software, implements work flows, and converts data bases. Finally, the operation team performs maintenance or enhancements, and identifies and corrects deficiencies.

In Figure 5.7 the arrows on the right side indicate that any team may refer the project back to the previous team for needed alterations. This recycling feature is designed to prevent problems from becoming a permanent part of the system.

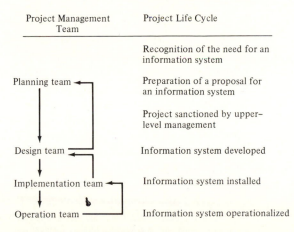

Figure 5.7   ISS information systems project: Team responsibilities during project life cycle.

Advantages   Centralized project management at BellSouth is said to have five advantages:

1. Including a project management function in the organizational structure creates a career path for persons specializing in the management of projects. Such an arrangement creates a pool of experienced project managers capable of managing projects of various types.
2. The availability of well-trained, experienced project managers avoids the delays that frequently result because project managers selected from different departments may not possess necessary management and coordination skills.
3. Following installation of a system or creation of a product, centralized support continues to be available. If modification becomes necessary, the user can request it from the project management organization.
4. Centralized project management ensures the broad view and efficiently establishes priorities, integrates systems, and avoids overlaps and duplication.
5. Centralized project managers do not experience split loyalty between the project and their home units. Under decentralized project management, project managers return to their home units when the project ends. Therefore they may, while working on the project, keep the interests of their functional units in mind, rather than overall organizational needs.[16]

Comparisons, Advantages, and Disadvantages   Table 5.3 compares the functional and project viewpoints. Examining a proposed undertaking in light of these viewpoints should help to determine whether or not it is adaptable to the project management form.

Matrix Management

Project management was developed to allow organizations to cope with large-scale but finite situations without a permanent reorganization. Matrix structures are more difficult to institute but allow even more flexibility.

Matrix organization forms are used for organizational projects and activities requiring specialists to report to more than one supervisor. For example, an engineer might be working on three different projects under three different project directors, as well as reporting to the head of the engineering department. This situation violates the unity-of-command principle and, consequently, is upsetting to classical theorists who cannot imagine keeping four bosses happy.

Matrix management gets its name from its chart, which looks like a grid or matrix. Figure 5.8 shows a typical arrangement. The design, electrical, chemical, and civil engineers working on projects A, B, and C all report to their respective project directors, as well as to their chief engineers.

Matrix management can work only if the authority and responsibility of all managers are clearly defined. Consider ABC Company's Project X. Project manager Brown, chief design engineer Jones, and design engineer Smith must work together and must agree on their authority relationships. Manager Brown has authority for the overall design and execution of the project. If the project is being undertaken for a customer, manager Brown deals with the customer. Manager Brown also handles the

Table 5.3 A COMPARISON OF THE PROJECT AND FUNCTIONAL VIEWPOINTS

Organizational characteristic	Project viewpoint	Functional viewpoint
Line-staff organization	Line functions become support positions. A web, rather than a chain, of authority-responsibility relationships exists.	Line functions are directly responsible for accomplishing objectives. The line commands, the staff advises and supports.
Scalar principle	Some vertical authority relationships, but emphasis is on a horizontal and diagonal work flow.	Chain of authority runs through organization from superior to subordinate. All important business is conducted up and down the chain.
Superior-subordinate relationship	Superior-subordinate relationship not so important. Relationships are peer to peer, associate to associate, manager to technical expert.	Superior-subordinate relationship is most important. All important business is conducted through the superior-subordinate pyramid.
Organizational objectives	Multilateral objectives. Project is joint venture of many relatively independent groups.	Unilateral objectives. Parent unit defines objectives, uses subunits to achieve them.
Unity of direction	Project manager manages across functional and organizational lines to accomplish interorganizational objectives.	General manager manages "downward," heads up a group of activities that are part of the organization's plan.
Equality of responsibility and authority	Project manager's responsibility may exceed authority. Functional manager, not project manager, may have authority over pay, promotion, etc., of project members.	Attempt is made to equalize functional manager's responsibility and authority.
Time duration	Limited.	Unlimited.

Source: Adapted from David I. Cleland, "Understanding Project Authority," *Business Horizons* (Spring 1967), p. 66. Copyright 1967, by the Foundation for the School of Business at Indiana University. Reprinted by permission.

project budget (using it to "buy" people from the departments) and works with chief Jones to coordinate engineer Smith's time on the project and on other work. If manager Brown and chief Jones disagree about when and how much engineer Smith should work on Project X, the chief engineer settles the matter.

When to Use the Matrix Introduction of a matrix structure is not easy. As Stanley M. Davis and Paul R. Lawrence caution, "The change to a matrix cannot be accomplished by issuing a new organization chart."[17] The matrix organization involves changes in structure (dual chains of command), system (simultaneous operation along both product and functional lines), culture (the organizational spirit and character must be in harmony with the new form's requirements), behavior (working as part of a team rather than individually), and reward system (who will administer it?). For these reasons, any shift to a matrix form will probably take two or three years of hard effort.

As Jay R. Galbraith points out, organizational forms actually fall on a continuum between the pure functional organization and the pure product organization, with the matrix form being near the middle.[18] This continuum appears as Figure 5.9, with the

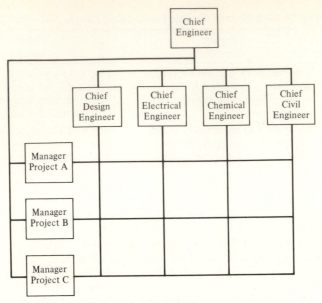

Figure 5.8 Typical matrix organization.

functional organization on the left and the product organization on the right. Galbraith offers several factors that may help an organization determine where it falls on the continuum.

Product Lines   If product lines are diverse and change rapidly, the organization should be on the right or "product" side of the continuum.

Interdependence   If organizational units are highly interdependent, with one unit's activities affecting another's, an organizational form on the product side of the continuum is appropriate. Tight schedules, strict coordination requirements, and interdependent decision making are facilitated by a product structure.

Technology   New, varied products and tight scheduling requirements lead to product-oriented organizational forms. But if the organization has a critical need for technologi-

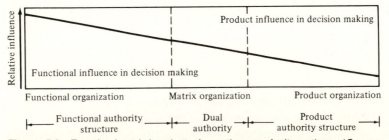

Figure 5.9 Function/matrix/product: A continuum of alternatives. (*Source:* After Jay R. Galbraith, "Matrix Organization Designs," *Business Horizons* 14 [February 1971], p. 37. Copyright 1971, by the Foundation for the School of Business at Indiana University. Reprinted by permission.)

cal expertise, the product form can not rapidly make that expertise available when and where needed. If the efficient use of technological expertise is critical to organizational success, the organization will be more toward the left or functional side of the alternatives continuum in Figure 5.9.

Economies of Scale   If manufacturing a product requires expensive equipment and facilities, the functional form will be more economical. The more important economies of scale are, the farther to the functional side the organizational structure will be.

Organizational Size   The larger the organization, the less it loses in economies of scale by adopting the product form. So for very large organizations, economies of scale become a less significant determinant of structure. According to Galbraith,

> Many organizations are experiencing pressures that force them to consider various forms of matrix designs. The most common pressure is increased volume of new products. Organizations facing this situation must either adopt some form of matrix organization, change to product forms of organization, or increase the time between start and introduction of the new product processes.
>
> For most organizations, the matrix design is the most effective alternative. Managers must be aware of the different kinds of matrix designs and develop some basis for choosing among them.[19]

Evolution to the Matrix

With so many departmentalization methods available, how does the organization choose the most appropriate one? The two major choices of earlier times were the centralized functional form and the decentralized product form whose differences were presented in Tables 5.1 and 5.2. The matrix form tries to achieve the advantages of both forms but carries with it the potentially serious disadvantage of dual authority relationships or diversity of command.

Harvey F. Kolodny perceives an evolutionary process beginning with functional organization and moving through project management to the matrix, the stages being determined by environmental conditions. The process begins as the functional organization finds itself unable to cope with the uncertainty, complexity, and technological change characteristic of the modern business environment. The vertical hierarchy of authority cannot respond to change rapidly enough, so tasks and activities are grouped as "projects," and authority is decentralized to project managers. Kolodny says,

> Project organization aims to complete a temporary task in a fixed amount of time, for a predetermined cost, and according to a tightly specified set of performance standards. In the end, project managers aim to put themselves out of business.[20]

Eventually the tasks that were once "projects" become permanent organizational activities, and the organization evolves toward the matrix form. Table 5.4 indicates the determinants that promote organizational evolution from the functional form to the matrix form.

Table 5.4   FUNCTION TO PROJECT TO MATRIX: DETERMINANTS OF ORGANIZATIONAL EVOLUTION

Form	Determinants
Function	1. Efficiency is a success criterion. 2. Competitive advantage is along a single parameter (technology, price, performance, or delivery). 3. Markets are relatively predictable. 4. Narrow range of products with long time horizons.
Project	1. Several simultaneous success criteria (performance, cost, price, schedule, technology, efficiency). 2. Moderate market change. 3. Differentiated clients and markets. 4. Moderate number of products (projects). 5. Specified time horizons for each client or project. 6. Interconnectedness between outside and focal organization.
Matrix	1. Innovation is a success criterion. 2. Differentiated products, markets, customers. 3. High variability and uncertainty in product-market mix. 4. Time horizons for product vary from medium to long.

Source: Adapted from Harvey F. Kolodny, "Evolution to a Matrix Organization," *Academy of Management Review* 4 (October 1979): 551.

The matrix form does not affect all organizational members equally. Stanley M. Davis and Paul R. Lawrence point out that only a few of the organization's people—usually middle-level and some upper-level managers and professionals—will ever be in a matrix, reporting to more than one supervisor or supervising people in more than one unit: "In an organization with 50,000 employees, only 500 to 1500 may be in the matrix; and in one with 500 people, only 50 may be in the matrix."[21]

Diversity of Command

The biggest problem in using project and matrix management structures is often said to be diversity of command. Many functional managers have difficulty in understanding and accepting partial loss of control and direction over an employee who has been assigned to a project. This difficulty is especially acute if employees work on special projects while sitting in their normal places. Functional managers face their own time pressures and deadlines but they must accept the fact that they are not entitled to assign more than a prescribed part of each subordinate's duties.

If the supervisor cannot accept the new situation, the project employee experiences the conflict, ambiguity, and stress of being caught in the middle. The supervisor makes pay, promotion, and other decisions, yet the employee is also responsible to the project manager. Top management must ensure that functional managers understand and accept the dual authority structure.

The project manager must often be a diplomat, skilled in smoothing out the difficulties that temporary assignments and relationships can create. Project managers are frequently on an organizational level equal—or even subordinate—to the level of functional managers from whom they must borrow personnel. Yet they must request employees, use them effectively to get the job done, and at the same time make sure that project members are not harassed or overworked.

SUMMARY

Departmentalization is the process of splitting the organization into subdivisions. Early organizations managed by the owner/entrepreneur had little need for departmentalization. As organizations grew larger and more complex, developing into mass-production industries, departmentalization became necessary.

The classical perspective was represented primarily by Lyndall Urwick's departmentalization categories. The six *unitary* methods—by person, product, area, customer, date or time, and number—use a single, common, mutually exclusive principle for grouping workers. The two *serial* methods—by process and machine—are often used when an organization's input must go through a series of stages before becoming the final product. The third classical departmental method is to group organization members according to the *functions* they perform. Although many departmentalization methods exist, the two most usual are departmentalization by product and by function. The mixing of methods at different organizational levels is common practice.

The classical school examined the formal organization, as embodied in the organization chart. The human relations school examined the informal organization as established by employees themselves. Human relations scholars consider organization members not so much as members of departments but as members of groups. Three types of groups exist within organizations: functional, task, and interest.

The need for a more flexible viewpoint developed largely because the past several decades have been more dynamic, complex, and turbulent than previous times. The modern perspective tries to account for instability and change when organizations departmentalize. A major point is that the organization must first have a clear understanding of its goals and priorities, then departmentalize in such a way as to achieve them.

Two forms for dealing with the modern era's uncertainty are project management and matrix management. The organization should consider several factors before selecting an appropriate design from the product/matrix/function continuum of design alternatives.

DISCUSSION QUESTIONS

1. Why is departmentalization a "differentiating strategy"?
2. What are the forms of unitary departmentalization, and how do they differ? What are the advantages and disadvantages of unitary departmentalization?
3. What is serial departmentalization?
4. What are functional departmentalization's benefits? Why is it so popular?
5. What are the major issues in the product versus function departmentalization debate?
6. Distinguish between formal and informal groups. Distinguish between functional, task, and interest groups.

7. What is the modern perspective on departmentalization?
8. According to Henry Mintzberg, what are the benefits of grouping? Can you suggest others?
9. What are some of the factors that organizations use to determine which departmentalization system they will use?
10. Differentiate between sequential, pooled, and reciprocal interdependence. Why are these differences important?
11. How do centralization and decentralization influence departmentalization?
12. Distinguish between project management and matrix management.
13. What problems does project management solve? What problems does it create?
14. What are the differences between the functional and project organizational structures?
15. The chapter presents the advantages of centralized project management at BellSouth. Can you think of any disadvantages?
16. Discuss the departmentalization systems in organizations of which you have been a member.
17. According to Jay R. Galbraith, the most common pressure forcing organizations to consider matrix designs is increased volume of new products. Why do you think this is so?
18. According to a popular book on excellent present-day organizations, most such organizations have either never used the matrix form or have used it and then abandoned it. Do you have any ideas on why that is so?

THE INDUSTRIAL DIVISION

Until recently, the Industrial Division of Hamilton Ross & Co.: Architects-Engineers-Planners, Inc., consisted of two engineering departments: the mechanical department and the electrical department. Morale and enthusiasm among the engineers and draftsmen were good, and product quality was high. The division's organization chart looked like Figure C.1.

Division manager Harriet Brown decided that the firm could achieve even better results by doing a little reorganizing. She thought that greater efficiency would be achieved by establishing drafting as a separate department. She explained the reorganization to the division staff and set up a time schedule for making the changes. After reorganization, the chart looked like Figure C.2.

Under the new arrangement, the two engineering departments continued to operate more or less as they had before—preparing detailed technical specifications and rough construction drawings. Formerly, draftsmen within each department did the finished drawings. Under the new organization, the engineers submitted rough sketches to the head of the drafting department, who assigned them to specific draftsmen.

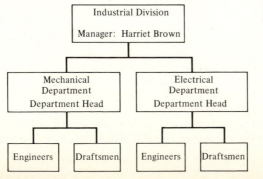

Figure C.1   The Industrial Division: Organization chart before reorganization.

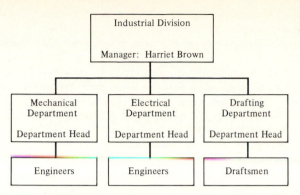

The written specifications and the final drawings, of course, had to match up. Before the reorganization, the heads of the mechanical and electrical departments were responsible for coordinating the writing and the drawing. But after the reorganization, division manager Brown noticed that the drawings were of lower quality than before and that discrepancies were beginning to appear between the specifications and the drawings.

Should Brown go back to the old form of organization or should she keep trying to make the new form work? If so, how?

THE ELECTRIC AUTHORITY

The Electric Authority is departmentalized by function. Close coordination among the functional units is essential to good customer service, but coordination is not always easy because the functional units are spread all over the county.

Before the simplest job can be completed, it must pass through four geographically separated departments. First, the engineering department designs the job. Then the construction department does the actual work. Third, the customer service department verifies the customer's records. Finally, the meter department installs the meter.

Many times the Authority must handle rush jobs. Under functional departmentalization, four managers must be convinced that the job needs to be done in a hurry. More than once, a job has been rushed through engineering, only to sit for two weeks on a desk in construction. Customers must often call several phone numbers in order to find out how far along their jobs are.

Recently, the number of complaints has become so large that the local newspaper has begun writing editorials about the Authority's inefficiency. What action should the Electric Authority board of directors now take?

NOTES

1. Lyndall Urwick, *Notes on the Theory of Organization* (New York: American Management Association, 1952), p. 25. The rest of the section on the classical perspective is indebted to this source, pp. 18–33.
2. James G. March and Herbert A. Simon, *Organizations* (New York: Wiley, 1958), pp. 25–26.
3. William F. Whyte, "The Social Structure of the Restaurant," *American Journal of Sociology* 54 (January 1949): 302–310.

4. Philip Selznick, "An Approach to a Theory of Bureaucracy," *American Sociological Review* 8 (February 1943): 47.

5. Chester I. Barnard, *The Functions of the Executive* (Cambridge, MA: Harvard University Press, 1938), p. 115.

6. For further explanation and discussion of group types, see Abraham Zaleznik and David Moment, *The Dynamics of Interpersonal Behavior* (New York: Wiley, 1964); and George C. Homans, *The Human Group* (New York: Harcourt Brace, 1950).

7. Henry Mintzberg, *The Structuring of Organizations: A Synthesis of Research* (Englewood Cliffs, NJ: Prentice-Hall, 1979), p. 106.

8. Lyndall Urwick, *Notes on the Theory of Organization,* pp. 31–32.

9. Arthur H. Walker and Jay W. Lorsch, "Organizational Choice: Product vs. Function," *Harvard Business Review* 46 (November/December 1968): 129–138.

10. Ibid., p. 137.

11. James D. Thompson, *Organizations in Action: Social Science Bases of Administrative Theory* (New York: McGraw-Hill, 1967), p. 57.

12. Paul R. Lawrence and Jay W. Lorsch, *Organization and Environment* (Cambridge, MA: Harvard University Press, 1967).

13. James D. Thompson, *Organizations in Action.*

14. Pradip N. Khandwalla, *The Design of Organizations* (New York: Harcourt Brace Jovanovich, 1977), p. 499.

15. Russell Robb, *Lectures on Organization* (Easton, PA: Hive Publishing Company, 1972), p. 7.

16. For further information on centralized project management at BellSouth, see James B. Dilworth et al., "Centralized Project Management," *Journal of Systems Management* 36 (August 1985): 30–35.

17. Stanley M. Davis and Paul R. Lawrence, *Matrix* (Reading, MA: Addison-Wesley, 1977), p. 19.

18. The following discussion is indebted to Jay R. Galbraith, "Matrix Organization Designs," *Business Horizons* 14 (February 1971): 29–40.

19. Ibid., p. 40.

20. Harvey F. Kolodny, "Evolution of a Matrix Organization," *Academy of Management Review* 4 (October 1979): 547.

21. Stanley M. Davis and Paul R. Lawrence, *Matrix,* p. 23.

ADDITIONAL READINGS

Blau, Peter M., Wolf V. Heydebrand, and Robert E. Staugger. "The Structure of Small Bureaucracies." *American Sociological Review* 31 (April 1966): 179–191.

Boyle, J. M. "Reorganization Reconsidered: An Empirical Approach to the Departmentalization Problem." *Public Administration Review* 29 (September 1979): 458–465.

Butler, A. "Project Management: A Study of Organizational Conflict." *Academy of Management Journal* 16 (March 1973): 84–102.

Comstock, Donald E., and Richard W. Scott. "Technology and the Structure of Subunits— Distinguishing Individual and Workgroup Effects." *Administrative Science Quarterly* 22 (June 1977): 177–202.

Daft, R.L., and P.J. Bradshaw. "The Process of Horizontal Differentiation: Two Models." *Administrative Science Quarterly* 25 (September 1980): 441–456.

Daniels, John D., Robert A. Pitts, and Marietta J. Tretter. "Strategy and Structure of U.S. Multinationals: An Exploratory Study." *Academy of Management Journal* 27 (June 1984): 292–307.

Dewar, R., and J. Hage. "Size, Technology and Structural Differentiation: Towards a Theoretical Synthesis." *Administrative Science Quarterly* 23 (March 1978): 111–134.

Donaldson, Lex. "Divisionalization and Diversification: A Longitudinal Study." *Academy of Management Journal* 25 (December 1982): 909–914.

Drucker, Peter F. *Management: Tasks, Practices, Responsibilities.* New York: Harper & Row, 1974.

Golembiewski, Robert T. "Small Groups and Large Organizations." *Handbook of Organizations.* Edited by J.G. March. Chicago: Rand McNally, 1965.

Joyce, William F. "Matrix Organization: A Social Experiment." *Academy of Management Journal* 29 (September 1986): 536–561.

Kingdon, Donald Ralph. *Matrix Organization.* London: Tavistock Publications, 1973.

Lawrence, Paul R., and Jay W. Lorsch. "Differentiation and Integration in Complex Organizations." *Administrative Science Quarterly* 12 (June 1967): 1–47.

Leatt, Peggy, and Rodney Schneck. "Criteria for Grouping Nursing Subunits in Hospitals." *Academy of Management Journal* 27 (March 1984): 150–165.

Reeser, C. "Some Potential Human Problems of the Project Organization," *Academy of Management Journal* 12 (December 1969): 459–467.

Telem, Moshe. "The Process Organizational Structure." *Journal of Management Studies* 22 (January 1985): 38–52.

Line and Staff

For many years, organizations have divided their work into line functions and staff functions. This division has often caused problems. The classical school tried to solve these problems by defining the three types of authority that line gives to staff. The human relations school explored the causes for line-staff conflict and found them to be more interpersonal than structural.

The modern perspective is that the relative importance and influence of staff should depend upon the specific situation. As the chapter will show, some recent developments in the structuring and managing of organizations have had the incidental benefit of reducing line-staff conflict.

THE NATURE OF LINE AND STAFF

Line-Staff Activities

Line personnel are *directly* engaged in tasks necessary to accomplish an organization's goals. These tasks are commonly referred to as "line activities" or "line operations." Staff personnel contribute *indirectly* to the attainment of organizational goals by supporting the line personnel—either by helping them perform their line functions (as an "assistant to the president" would do) or by giving them specialized advice or service (as a "staff accountant" would do). Lyndall Urwick's distinction between line and staff activities is helpful: "Line activities are those in the absence of which it is impossible to imagine the undertaking continuing even for a brief period. In a manufacturing business, they are usually *making* and *selling*." All other activities are staff activities because they "are not the basic things which the undertaking exists to do."[1] Employees who purchase the raw materials, run the cafeteria, and negotiate the contracts are staff people. Line relationships exist within both line and staff activities. The cafeteria cooks have a line relationship with the cafeteria manager, who heads up a staff activity.

Line-Staff Authority

The line-staff distinction is a differentiation of *function* (as shown in the OT-Model on the inside covers) because line and staff *do different things.* However, a differentiation of *authority* results from the differentiation of function. Line authority is the right to *take or demand action;* staff authority is the right to *advise.*

According to classicists James D. Mooney and Alan C. Reiley:

> The staff function in an organization means the service of *advice* or *counsel,* as distinguished from the function of authority or command. . . . The familiar expression, borrowed from the military terminology, is "line and staff." The almost invariable use of these terms in conjunction is intended simply to distinguish between the right of command and the function of counsel.[2]

In the traditional thinking of the classical writers, staff would not have formal authority over line. According to Urwick, authority "should always be expressed through the line activities of an undertaking; the chain of command, the central skeleton of authority and responsibility, should be built up around the delegation of responsibility for the line activities of that particular enterprise."[3]

In light of conditions prevailing when the classicists wrote, this position made sense. Many organizations observed by the classical theorists continued to be controlled by the entrepreneurs who had founded them. An entrepreneur would get a great idea for a product, start a business to manufacture it, and then continue to make all the major decisions concerning it. Those staff members hired to assist the owner/entrepreneur were advisers only, clearly not entitled to authority.

Line-Staff and the Chart

Figure 6.1 is a typical organization chart for a consumer products company. The arrangement of blocks in the chart does not necessarily indicate whether a function is line or staff. Marketing and production are line functions, because of their direct involvement in achieving organizational goals. Within the marketing area, research is a staff function. The research area helps the marketing personnel determine where the markets are for the company's products. Personnel is a staff activity that contains four functions: compensation, employment, training, and employee relations. On an *organizational* level, they are all staff functions, since they are part of a staff unit. On a *unit* level, they are line functions, because they are directly engaged in meeting the objectives of the personnel unit: to provide all areas of the organization with the best possible human resources.

Location of the Staff   Depending upon the firm's needs, staff may be located at just about any level in the organizational hierarchy. If the staff group offers service only to the president, it will appear high on the chart. If a staff department serves diverse organizational units, it may also be high up in the hierarchy. For example, such staff departments as public relations, personnel, and legal are often situated at an upper level because they serve many organizational units that branch out below them. If the staff

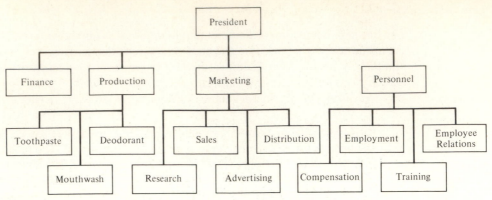

Figure 6.1   Personal Products, Inc.: Organization chart.

group's services are available primarily or solely to a single organizational function, it will appear as subordinate to that function on the organization chart.

Staff Parallelism   A large organization with many geographical or product divisions may establish parallel departments for the *same* staff function with some departments serving the divisions and some serving the organization as a whole. For instance, the centralized finance department staff would deal with organization-wide finance and accounting issues; a divisional accounting department would handle only the division's accounting requirements.

Figure 6.2 illustrates staff parallelism within the XYZ Manufacturing Corporation. This organization is decentralized; the plant managers have full responsibility and authority for plant activities. All instructions and other important communications from headquarters go through each plant manager's office, rather than directly to the plant departments. In addition, the plant personnel manager and the plant controller head up staff departments that are parallel to functional departments in the home office. Although the home-office vice presidents of personnel and finance do not have direct line authority over their plant counterparts, they do maintain functional or "dotted-line" relationships with the plant people. As we shall see later in the chapter, these dotted-line relationships can cause conflict.

How the Line-Staff Differentiation Develops

The definition and evolution of line and staff are logical responses to problems arising out of organizational growth and change. Here is how the process might have occurred at Paul Revere's silver bowl shop.

At first Paul carried out all functions necessary for making silver bowls. He obtained financing, secured raw materials, produced bowls, and sold them. As the demand for bowls grew, he could not perform all of the shop's tasks, so he hired employees. Since he was a master craftsman, he assigned to his unskilled assistants the boring, routine tasks that he disliked most: gathering the firewood, stoking the fires used

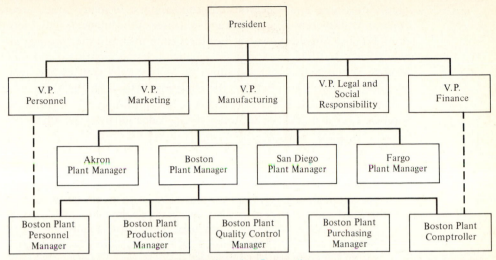

Figure 6.2   Staff parallelism at XYZ Manufacturing Corporation.

for melting silver, and sweeping the shop. Delegating these tasks allowed him more time for silversmithing.

All of these assistants were part of Paul Revere's general staff because they were employed to support the man who was making the bowls. As the business continued to thrive, Paul hired other bowl makers to produce alongside him. Paul and the bowl makers were the line people; the rest were staff people who did whatever the line people didn't want to bother with because they had more important things to do. This difference in importance of activities led to status differences. Indeed, in some of today's more traditional organizations (like the railroads), enormous status differences persist between those who produce the product or perform the service and all the other employees. In Paul Revere's time, this status difference was understandable. Making bowls was the reason for establishing the business in the first place.

The vast majority of early economic organizations that developed a need for organizational skills and techniques were started by an individual like Paul Revere who wanted to make something: bowls, muskets, textiles, and so on. Therefore, the natural tendency in these early organizations was to focus on the production function.

Additional "Line" Functions   This emphasis on the importance of production fit in well with the founder/producer/entrepreneur's orientation—as long as he was around. Not until the late 1940s and early 1950s was the definition of "line" expanded to include the marketing/distribution people. This expansion made sense as consumers became more selective, markets became saturated, and competition increased. By this time, Chevrolet had proven wrong Ford's strategy of letting customers have whatever color they wanted as long as it was black.

During the mid-twentieth century, the increased cost of money and the greater size and complexity of organizations led to intensified use of financial controls, cost-of-capital measures, and decentralized profit centers. In many large corporations, these developments increased the status and influence of the financial staff—termed the "bean counters" by Chrysler President Lee Iacocca in his best-seller *Iacocca: An Autobiography* (1984). In 1958 Frederick G. Donner became chairman and CEO of General Motors, the first time that a member of the financial staff rather than someone experienced in operations had led the company. Although the Donner administration seemed successful, achieving record sales and profits by 1965, former GM executive John De Lorean marks the beginning of GM's decline from the time when the financial managers gained control:

> What was happening was a predictable result, however, when the control of a consumer goods company moves into the hands of purely financial managers. Short-term profits are dramatically improved, but a lack of sensitivity for product, for markets and for customers also sets in, which is usually detrimental to the long-term strength of the corporation. Therefore, those lauding GM's management in the 1960s could not see the organizational fissures developing as they looked at the bright figures appearing on the corporate cash register.[4]

For our purposes, the point of these developments in the 1950s and 1960s is that as different issues become critical to the achievement of organizational goals, different areas (production, marketing) assume the driver's seat, further blurring the distinction between line and staff. The recent downturn in U.S. smokestack industries and the realization that the Japanese are outperforming American companies led by smart, MBA-trained financial managers have led to a resurgence of interest in *production*. This resurgence may once again cause many organizations to redefine who is line and who is staff.

Change Adds Staff   The early producer/entrepreneurs developed their own processes to produce their own products. This was followed by a period of rapid technological change. Even the best of producer/entrepreneurs found the technology in their fields outdistancing their ability to use it, and perhaps even to understand it. Consequently, technologically trained staff experts were hired to handle the new developments that owners either could not understand or would not take the time to understand. For instance, with the advent of computers and the development of management information systems, owners and managers either had to take time off from their first love— building cars, running railroads—or hire information-system managers to utilize this new technology.

Central Staff and Coordination   As a production organization grows, it needs more staff to support its expanded production and marketing activities. Adding more people in these areas will also add greater coordination problems. John De Lorean provides the following example.

   At GM the custom had been for the corporate management staff to make policy decisions, then assign responsibility for implementing them to one of the car divisions. However, in the case of the Vega, the car was developed by corporate engineering and design staffs, then turned over to Chevrolet for production and marketing. Central staff delivered the first prototype to Chevrolet and, after eight miles of driving at the GM test track, "the front of the Vega broke off. The front end of the car separated from the rest of the vehicle."[5] The central staff designers and engineers had not been sufficiently in touch with their divisional counterparts, who might have told them that the Vega as created on paper and in prototype would not be a satisfactory production automobile.

LINE AND STAFF STRUCTURE

The Military Model

The classical writers frequently used the military as a model for business and government organizations. Ever since Philip of Macedon, the line-staff distinction has perhaps been most clear in the military. A staff of officers is specifically assigned to assist every commander. The commander commands the staff, but the staff is directly supervised by a chief of staff or executive officer.

Staff Functions   The military staff has five functions: providing information, making estimates, making recommendations, preparing plans and orders, and supervising the execution of plans and orders. All staff actions are designed to help the unit carry out its mission and to help the commander fulfill his responsibilities.

Staff Structure   The military staff may include three different groups: coordinating, special, and personal. Each *coordinating* staff officer is concerned with one of these five fields: personnel, intelligence, operations, logistics, and civil-military operations. *Special* staff officers deal with technical and administrative matters. *Personal* staff officers assist the commander in personal matters and report directly to him, rather than to the chief of staff. Figure 6.3 shows a typical military staff structure. All of the 12 officers in the organization chart have one primary function: to help the commander do a better job as commander.

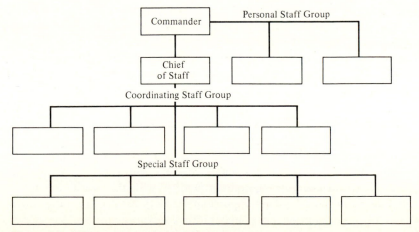

Figure 6.3   Military commander's staff structure.

The successful experience of the military with staff structures has led many other organizations to apply staff principles to their own situations.

Business Organizations

The use of staff people in modern business organizations is similar to their use in the military, though the categories of staff are not as specific and clear-cut.

Personal Staff   Personal staff members provide assistance to one manager.[6] These people are of two types: the staff assistant and the line assistant. The staff assistant provides administrative support to the manager, has no line or supervisory authority and is, in essence, the manager's personal aide, as in "assistant to the president." Owners, entrepreneurs, and managers want to maintain control over their growing domains. A direct solution to this problem is to hire an assistant, accountable only to them. Such assistants serve as the "eyes and ears" of their bosses; they considerably expand the ability of the boss to know what's going on. According to Urwick, the "assistant to" should

> never have or be allowed to imagine that he has any authority of his own. He is merely an extension of his chief's personality, expressing his chief's authority. This does not mean that he may not do a great deal of work for his chief. He may draft and issue over his own signature almost every instruction which emanates from his chief's headquarters. But he does so as the representative of his chief's authority. The instructions are his chief's instructions, not his.[7]

Line assistants also perform supportive tasks, assisting managers in carrying out their duties. But line assistants also act in a managerial fashion. The manager may give the line assistant responsibility for areas or projects that are essential to the unit's operation.

The distinction between the staff assistant and the line assistant can be clearly seen in higher education. Consider the staff in the office of the Dean of Business Administration. The staff assistant, who would be called something like "administrative assistant to the dean," performs all the clerical and administrative detail work that the dean doesn't have time for. The line assistant, probably called the "assistant dean," may have responsibility for graduate, undergraduate, or executive development programs. In addition, the assistant dean helps out with some of the dean's paperwork, such as compiling reports and preparing the annual budget.

Specialized Staff   Corporations hire specialized staff in such areas as data processing, personnel, finance, public relations, law, and control (audit, quality control). They allow line personnel to be free of activities which are important but are not directly concerned with producing and selling products and services. Rather than have line personnel spend their time becoming familiar with the specific details of affirmative action and equal employment opportunity (EEO), XYZ Corporation will hire specialists to file the appropriate government forms, recruit minorities, screen candidates, and so forth.

An organization's legal department is the clearest example of specialized staff. This group advises managers regarding the legal aspects of their actions and decisions. Managers must then decide whether to follow the advice or ignore it. If ignoring advice might lead to severe financial, moral, or legal consequences, then the legal staff usually has the right to inform top management that a lower-level manager is endangering the organization.

One possible danger of using specialized staff personnel is that the line may not stay on top of developments in certain areas because they feel "that is staff's responsibility." Seeing no need to be concerned about these secondary activities, the line may relinquish them completely. The result may be that important matters—for example, EEO, affirmative action, and other hiring policies and procedures—which should be every manager's concern, are relegated to an isolated area within the personnel department. When an organization has specialized expertise available in such areas, line managers sometimes tend to ignore their own responsibilities in these areas. An attitude of "let the experts handle it" replaces the sense of responsibility that line managers should always retain. Line personnel then run the danger of letting staff indirectly control them in important ways.

THE CLASSICAL PERSPECTIVE

Classical organization theory adhered closely to the line-staff distinction. The basic classical structure was a hierarchy of line authority, with staff people working mainly out of the general manager's office. According to Henri Fayol:

> The staff is a group of men equipped with the strength, knowledge and time which the general manager may lack and is an adjunct, reinforcement and sort of extension of the manager's personality. There are no levels of authority in it, and it takes orders only from the general manager. Such a group is known as general staff in the army, and I have kept this name for lack of any other which might have proved preferable.[8]

The Line-Staff Dilemma

The basic problem with the line-staff distinction is how to assign authority and responsibility. If you hire expertise, how do you make best use of it if at the same time line managers are told that they have ultimate authority and responsibility for organizational decisions? The staff is hired to help the line attain organizational objectives. Yet the line personnel may listen to the advice of these staff experts who were hired purposely for their special knowledge and training, and then ignore it.

Make Line Follow Staff Advice   A quick solution is to force line to follow staff's advice, within staff's area of expertise. In some organizations, the personnel department hires all new people and assigns them to supervisors; the legal department negotiates all contracts; and the purchasing department buys all the materials that the production people use. These practices may appear to make perfect sense, but in each instance the line has lost some authority over the processes used to attain organizational goals. Yet, the line is still *accountable* for achieving those goals. Imagine a line manager responsible for output, but with no authority to hire the people and buy the materials that can mean success or failure.

Let Line Disregard Staff Advice   On the other hand, if line managers can consistently disregard all staff advice, then the expensive experts are not being properly used. From the classical perspective, the answer to the dilemma is *defining authority properly.* Organizations need a structural mechanism that permits staff advice to be used *without* jeopardizing the line's authority.

Types of Staff Authority

The classical school decided to focus on and define how much and what kind of authority a staff person could have. The classicists divided "authority" into a number of types and degrees.

Advisory Authority   When staff members have advisory authority, they *must be consulted* if the decisions of line managers enter their areas of expertise. Line managers do not have to follow staff's advice, but they must consult with staff and consider the advice.

For example, line managers who make public statements on controversial issues may be required to check first with the legal staff, to be sure that their statements do not leave their organizations open to lawsuits. If the legal staff approves, the line manager can make the statement. If the legal staff disapproves, the line manager can still make the statement. Staff has had the opportunity to offer its expertise to the line decision maker. Line can then do what it chooses.

Whether or not to use the advice remains the line manager's choice, in theory. However, two factors encourage the manager to follow legal's advice. First, having expensive legal experts and not following their advice leaves the line manager's intelligence and managerial common sense open to question. The line manager's lack of knowledge in a certain area is the very reason for giving advisory authority to staff experts.

Second, as the human relations writers were quick to point out, the organization's informal communication system would quickly let the "right" people know that the line manager was making a mistake. The classical school tended to overlook the human element in such situations. They ignored the "grapevine" and failed to acknowledge how informal authority is really exercised. A cardinal classical principle was unity of command: A person should work for only one boss. The human relations school showed that introducing staff into the organizational structure also introduced informal authority relationships, which sometimes tend to invalidate the unity-of-command principle.

For instance, if you are the Ajax Roller Bearing foreman in the lower left portion of Figure 6.4 and Sam Scoville, a staff engineer in work methods, comes out of an air-conditioned office to offer advice, you will probably listen—not necessarily because you believe him but because he has a better line of communication to your top boss than you do. Since staff areas don't have as many reporting layers as line areas do, the path to the top is usually quicker and more direct. If you don't consider Sam's suggestions, you know that he will tell his boss, who will tell her boss (the chief engineer), who will tell the production vice president during a golf game that "some stubborn foreman in your area isn't being very reasonable by ignoring our advice." In this case, fear would be a powerful motivator to follow staff's advice.

Concurrent Authority   If line and staff managers have concurrent authority, they must both agree on certain actions that fall within the staff's area of expertise. For example, acts to discipline employees are often signed by a personnel officer and the employee's line manager. This process ensures that the organization has followed all relevant legal and administrative procedures. A line manager may be required to have a purchasing contract countersigned by the legal department. The second signature indicates that the legal department has not only exercised its advisory authority concerning the contract but also agrees that it is a good, solid contract. Requiring a second signature gives the legal department much more than advisory authority.

In effect, the *shared* authority in these examples requires manager and expert to meet, agree on a course of action, and verify their agreement with their signatures. This process works well only when manager and expert agree. As the human relations school pointed out, a problem arises when they don't agree. Then whoever has more power or a better bargaining position will win out.

Envision a situation in which a staff legal person repeatedly challenges a certain production manager's decisions and refuses to sign documents. The conflict will have

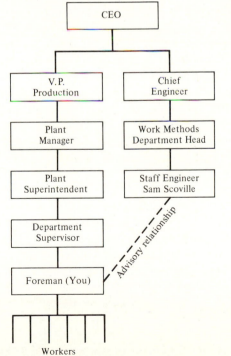

Figure 6.4 Ajax Roller Bearing: Communication lines to the top.

to be resolved by a high-level person to whom both legal and production ultimately report—probably the chief executive officer. For involving the CEO in the wrangle, somebody is going to have to pay some political costs. In many cases (especially those that the human relations school was observing), the CEO comes from a production-oriented background. After challenging the production manager a few times, the staff legal person will probably be told to find a more compatible organization within which to work. In such an instance, concurrent authority on paper would in reality be quite similar to advisory authority.

Full Functional Authority   This type of authority involves the freedom to exercise judgment and take action completely and freely. Staff are sometimes given full functional authority in areas such as maintenance, personnel recruiting, and purchasing that do not conflict with line. Three kinds of staff areas often have full functional authority. First are those activities in which the line has historically had no interest (such as running the cafeteria) because the activities are unrelated to the reasons for setting up the business in the first place. Second are those highly technical areas that may interest the line (such as labor law and engineering) but which the line cannot keep up with and still fulfill its production function. Third are those areas, like safety and quality control, so important to the achievement of organizational goals that they override the line's concern with production.

In this regard, classical theory once again imagines an ideal state that rarely exists, because few staff areas do not interact at all with the line. When they meet, conflict may result. For example, a quality control inspector (a staff position) may be given full functional authority to decide whether a building foundation is up to standard. The construction site foreman may imply that unless the inspector signs off on some recently completed (but obviously below-standard) work, the inspector may become part of the foundation. In their line-staff distinctions, the classical writers did not usually take such real-world possibilities into account.

The line-staff differentiation is a functional one because the line and the staff perform different types of activities for the organization. A result of the line-staff distinction is a differentiation of the organization's authority. Line must decide how much and what kinds of authority staff should have.

THE HUMAN RELATIONS PERSPECTIVE

As viewed by the classical school, the distinctions between line and staff were quite clear-cut. Line and staff each had their separate duties and areas of authority. The line-staff relationships were clearly defined on the organization chart for anyone to see. However, as examples in this chapter have already suggested, what looks good on paper doesn't always work in practice. The human relations school examined a problem that does not show up on the chart: conflict between line and staff.

Line-Staff Conflict

Conflict between line and staff is common in many organizations. Melville Dalton has described how line and staff often feel about each other:

Explaining the relatively few cases in which his staff has succeeded in "selling ideas" to the line, an assistant staff head remarked, "We're always in hot water with these old guys on the line. You can't tell them a damned thing. They're bull-headed as hell! Most of the time we offer a suggestion it's either laughed at or not considered at all. The same idea in the mouth of some old codger on the line'd get a round of applause. They treat us like kids."

Line officers in these plants often referred to staff personnel (especially members of the auditing, production planning, industrial engineering, and industrial relations staffs) as "college punks," "slide rules," "crackpots," "pretty boys," and "chair-warmers."[9]

Causes of Conflict   Here are some of Dalton's conclusions about the differences between line and staff:

1. Line and staff perform different functions.
2. Line people tend to be older and less educated than staff people.
3. Line people tend to have higher status than staff people.
4. Staff people have better career opportunities than line people.
5. Staff feels the need to justify its existence.
6. Line fears that staff will undermine its authority.

Many of these differences can lead to conflict. We might add to that list the difference in loyalty felt by the two groups. The line is loyal to the organization. Staff specialists are often loyal to a profession. These loyalty differences are a further source of conflict.

Different Backgrounds   Perhaps the largest contributor to line-staff conflict is the differences in backgrounds. Envision Joe Jenkins, a production superintendent in a traditional production organization, such as a steel mill. In the age-old Horatio Alger fashion, Joe has worked his way up the line—from worker to foreman to supervisor to superintendent. He is mature, street-wise, task oriented and, although without much formal education, a proven performer in his present job. Now imagine Chick Holden—young, bright, self-confident, with a master's degree in engineering. He has learned all the modern techniques in school. Put Joe and Chick in the same room to talk about production problems, and a line-staff conflict will probably result. They will have little in common to talk about and won't even speak the same language. True, these are stereotypes, but they illustrate a real problem.[10]

A Summary of Differences   The major differences between Joe and Chick are summarized in Table 6.1. The picture that emerges is of two entirely different types of people working in areas that have different goals, values, time frames, interpersonal styles, and loyalties. The staff person enters the organization filled with a missionary zeal to teach the uneducated how to do the job correctly. When the staff person offers advice, the line person wonders, "What does this kid know about the realities of running a business?"

The reluctance of production people to accept staff expertise, ideas, and suggestions frequently frustrates the staff. When that frustration is combined with the staff's

Table 6.1   A LINE SUPERINTENDENT AND A STAFF ENGINEER CONTRASTED

Issue	Line superintendent	Staff engineer
Commitment/loyalty	To organization	To profession/field/discipline
Time horizon	Short run	Longer run
Goal direction	Operational, measurable production goals	Nonoperational, nonquantifiable professional goals
Supervisory style	Task oriented	Relationship oriented
Education level	Lower	Higher
Age	Older	Younger

lack of a product to display and admire—because staff usually deal in ideas instead of physical products—we can readily see why staff persons are less likely than line managers to feel job satisfaction.[11]

Line-Staff Relationships: Two Models

Robert T. Golembiewski has presented two models which show how staff and line view staff's relationship to line.[12] One is called the *neutral-and-inferior-instrument (NII) model:* staff are instruments to be used by line; staff are inferior to line; and staff should remain neutral, simply supplying line with information to be used as line sees fit. The second is the *colleague model:* staff and line are joint participants in organizational ventures, equals in attempting to attain organizational goals. Although staff supports line, it is not inferior to line.

These models are extremes. Staff would prefer to be the colleagues of line. Some line members would prefer that the staff serve strictly as neutral, inferior instruments. In most organizations, the staff's role will be somewhere between these extremes.

Table 6.2 shows how ten questions relating to staff would be answered, depending on which model was in effect. The two answers to each question reflect widely differing attitudes about staff's function. From the classical perspective, these questions would simply not arise; they are irrelevant to how the organization should best be structured. From the human relations perspective, these questions reflect the kinds of problems that occur between people, even if they do not occur between blocks on a chart. From the systems/contingency perspective, neither the NII model nor the colleague model is "better." In some organizations, heartless though it may seem to staff, staff should serve as neutral, inferior instruments—much as typists and filing clerks do. In other organizations, soft-hearted though it may seem to line, goals are best achieved if line and staff are true colleagues.

Resistance to Change   Golembiewski contrasts the NII model and colleague model on three other criteria: resistance to change, authoritarianism, and job frustration/satisfaction. Under the NII model, line resists change and staff seeks change. Under the colleague model, both line and staff have low resistance to change. Both groups realize that change is necessary, helpful, and unavoidable. Line and staff work together as colleagues to maximize the benefits of change and minimize its costs.

Table 6.2 **THE NII MODEL AND THE COLLEAGUE MODEL: RESPONSES TO
10 QUESTIONS ABOUT STAFF**

NII model	Question asked about staff	Colleague model
Of little or no importance	In relation to line operations, how important do you feel top management thinks staff functions to be?	Very important
Usually punitive	How are staff reports viewed in your organization?	Always helpful
Not closely at all	How closely do you work with the line in developing a formal recommendation which your department will submit?	Very closely
None	How much voice do you have in implementing your recommendations?	Very much
Never	At *your* level, how often are line-staff differences reconciled without resorting to higher authority?	Always
Never	At *upper* levels, how often are line-staff differences reconciled without resorting to higher authority?	Always
Always	If staff people see an irregularity on the line, how often do they report it to their staff superior for reporting to a line superior?	Never
Never	If staff people see an irregularity on the line, how often do they report it directly to the appropriate line person?	Always
Far away	Where is your department located in relation to line operations?	Very near
Lower	How do line salaries compare with staff salaries at your level?	Equal or higher

Source: Adapted from Robert T. Golembiewski, "Personality and Organization Structure: Staff Models and Behavior Patterns," *Academy of Management Journal 9* (September 1966): 221. Used by permission.

Authoritarianism   Under the NII model, staff do not have any authority; it is monopolized by the line. In self-defense, staff may have to be more authoritarian than they would like, to avoid being pushed around. Under the colleague model, neither group particularly wants to exert authority or be subject to it. Neither group is on a "power trip."

Job Frustration and Satisfaction   Staff people are more frustrated and less satisfied, under the NII model. Being treated as inferior instruments has those understandable effects on people. Acting as colleagues with the line lowers frustration and increases satisfaction among the staff. They play a part in decision making and can see the fruits of their labors. Therefore, they feel good about their staff role.

Parallelism and Conflict

One final problem for staff arises out of the parallel staff departments that have in recent years become common within many large organizations. Look back at Figure 6.2 on page 137 for an example. The plant staff report on a line basis to the plant manager, but they also have an informal or dotted-line relationship with their functional home-office counterparts. The plant staffers must satisfy their line boss, the plant manager.

But, since such organizations typically offer advancement within function, rather than permitting employees to switch functions, the plant staff people must also satisfy their home-office counterparts, who have great influence in promotion decisions.

While these problems can perhaps be easily ironed out on paper, in reality employees in such situations must often choose to whom they will be loyal, with their careers on the line. The obvious stress created by this problem has not yet been addressed in detail.

Dual reporting patterns are difficult for line as well as staff. The Boston plant manager of XYZ Manufacturing Corporation in Figure 6.2, responsible for the plant's performance, is no happier about the possibility of being bypassed than the staff people are about having to please two bosses.[13]

Resistance to change, desire for authority, feelings of frustration and satisfaction, the problem of pleasing two superiors—these subjects do not enter at all into classical line-staff discussions. But they are important to line and staff *people,* and so they affect organizational performance.

THE MODERN PERSPECTIVE

The modern school has extended the discussion of line-staff conflicts begun by the human relations school. Although often scorned by the line, the staff would not continue to exist if it did not help in reaching organizational goals. The staff obviously has an important role to play. The job of both line and staff is to review that role continuously, in view of changing conditions.

Control of Resources

D. J. Hickson and his colleagues have developed a "strategic contingencies theory of organizational power" that helps explain the line-staff conflict.[14] According to this theory, the power of an organizational unit depends on the degree to which it has *essential organizational resources*—skills, materials, activities—that no other unit can supply. If I have something that you need, then I have power over you. Even if line and staff people have never heard of the strategic contingencies theory of intraorganizational power, they know its truth. Therefore, the line gives up essential resources to staff grudgingly, and the staff always wants more essential resources.

Acquiring Additional Staff Resources   Organizations sometimes join together to participate in joint programs and activities that the separate organizations could not sustain independently. Michael Aiken and Jerald Hage have examined the effects of such interorganizational efforts on the internal structure and behavior of the separate organizations.[15] They found that one reason for joint activities was one organization's need for the specialized skills that another organization could supply. Another benefit was the combined ability to add specialty skills, including staff-type expertise, that the organizations might not have been able to afford independently.

Combining organizational resources adds new occupational specializations to each participating organization, because "joint programs are likely to be of a highly specialized nature, providing services and activities that the focal organization cannot support alone."[16] Furthermore, the staff of each participating organization receives exposure to

> new ideas, new perspectives, and new techniques for solving organizational problems. The establishment of collegial relationships with comparable staff members of other organizations provides them with a comparative framework for understanding their own organizations. This is likely to affect their professional activities . . . as well as reinforce professional standards of excellence.[17]

Staff: An Ambiguous Role

The current ambiguity about the role of staff is in part a reflection of significant changes in corporate structures that have occurred in the 1970s and 1980s. Companies are decentralizing their operations and streamlining their managerial hierarchies, eliminating layers of middle management—among them many staff people. During the 1950s and 1960s, many companies grew in size and complexity through diversification, acquisition, and geographical expansion. Staff specialists helped organizations cope with the pressures of growth and prosperity. Many new government regulations of the 1970s required additional staff experts, to keep organizations within the rules. But in the 1980s, even though the earlier pressures that brought staff on board had been relieved, the staff remained.

Xerox serves as an example of what can happen in an overstaffed organization. According to *Business Week:*

> At Xerox, the proliferation of second-guessing staffers undercut the company's ability to adapt existing products to local markets and make the technological breakthroughs crucial to developing new ones. In turn, these failings allowed the Japanese to steal a march on it. The result: Xerox's share of the U.S. market for plain paper copiers and supplies plunged from 98% in 1970 to between 40% and 45% in 1982.[18]

According to frustrated Xerox managers, phases of product development that should have taken two weeks actually took two years. The staff specialists kept the company from making big mistakes, but they also stifled the innovation for which Xerox was known.

The Impact of Modern Developments

The line-staff issue is still awaiting systematic study. As Vivian Nossiter writes:

> There is a gap between the literature on line and staff and current conceptualizations about organizational realities. The terms mean different things to different people. Their current usage indicates they are valid in the sense of fulfilling a need, but the different meanings indicate a gap between theory and application.[19]

While we wait for the study and clarification that will close the gap referred to by Nossiter, some modern developments can be discussed. Three in particular have affected the staff function: decentralized profit centers, management by objectives, and the project management form.

Profit Centers   The managers of decentralized profit centers can often hire or not hire staff as they wish. Since their budgets are on the line, they add permanent staff only if they can make important contributions. The ROI manager can also "purchase" people from the central office staff group and pay for them out of the profit-center budget. Staff are often forced to "sell" themselves to profit-center managers. No longer can the staff hotshot walk in and say, "I'm smart, you're dumb; do it my way because I've got clout upstairs and you don't." The profit-center concept forces an attitude change on staff. They must add directly to profits, rather than wander around the operating units, doing little to justify their existence.

MBO   Under management by objectives (MBO), employee and manager discuss and agree on what the employee's job objectives and responsibilities shall be, and on how the employee will be evaluated. The widespread acceptance and use of MBO have reduced line-staff conflict. Once job roles and relationships are clarified and specific results are agreed upon, staff accountability becomes real rather than merely philosophical.

Project Teams   If a project team is formed to attain a goal, the dynamics of the situation tend to make the entire group feel accountable. All team members are experts in their fields, and all the expertise is presumably needed or members wouldn't be on the team. Under these conditions, the line-staff distinction may become obscure and the issue irrelevant.

Influences on Staff Size and Significance

Four other influences can determine the size and significance of staff: organizational technology, size, type, and life-cycle stage.

Technology   Joan Woodward proposed that the type of technology in a production organization determines whether extensive use of staff is appropriate.[20] She showed that organizations using mass production found staff especially valuable. In organizations manufacturing their products individually or in small batches *and* in organizations combining single-unit/small-batch production and mass production, simple line organization worked quite well. In these latter organizations, line personnel apparently performed such "staff" functions as quality control, thereby fulfilling more enlarged roles than their counterparts in line-staff organizations. Figure 6.5 depicts these relationships.

Size   Organizational size and staff size are related. As an organization's membership increases, the proportion of staff members increases at least as fast, sometimes faster. Once an organization reaches a certain size, its proportion of staff people levels off and may drop.[21] As the organization continues to grow, the staff handles the larger work

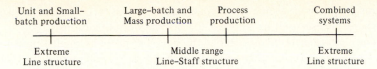

Figure 6.5 Woodward's technological continuum and line-staff structures. (*Source:* After Joan Woodward, *Industrial Organization: Theory and Practice* [London: Oxford University Press, 1965]. Used by permission.)

load by standardizing procedures and policies or improving communications, not by enlarging the staff.

Type Vivian Nossiter has observed that whether an organization regards staff highly may depend on the organization's business.[22] At Raytheon, which is in the high-tech business of electronics, employees value education and technical expertise, so they have a high regard for staff. At Gillette, in the more mechanical business of making razors and blades, employees have less regard for staff.

Life-Cycle Stage As the organization moves through the life cycle, its professional staff gradually acquires power. A glance back at Figure 3.2 (page 50) will show that organizations at Stage III of the typical life cycle tend to be dominated by professional staff with financial and legal backgrounds. As the organizational structure becomes larger and more bureaucratic, staff specialists are increasingly called on until they eventually become dominant in organizational affairs.

The Future

Line-staff conflict is most pronounced in stable, traditional, production-oriented industries. In these industries, especially those with a tradition of formal line-staff distinctions (like the steel and automobile industries), line-staff conflict is more likely than in the newer service-oriented industries.

Service-oriented firms have greater difficulty in separating line from staff. At a Holiday Inn, for instance, the "product" is a contented customer, and virtually all the organization's activities contribute directly to customer satisfaction.

The Holiday Inn example illustrates the fact that the historical conflict between line and staff will probably become less and less important in the future. Organizations must recognize the interdepartmental, interrelated nature of the activities necessary for achieving organizational goals. Obviously, no job exists in the organizational structure unless it contributes something toward achieving the organization's ends. As dynamic, social, systemwide relationships are increasingly recognized, the line-staff distinction must become increasingly blurred.

SUMMARY

Line personnel contribute directly to the attainment of organizational goals. Staff personnel contribute indirectly. The line-staff distinction came about in response to problems arising from growing and changing organizations. The military staff functions and structure were used as a model for business organizations.

The classical school approached the line-staff problem by distinguishing the three types of authority the line might give the staff: advisory, concurrent, and full functional. The human relations school showed that informal authority and relationships can greatly influence formal authority and the relationships appearing on the organization chart.

Robert T. Golembiewski has constructed two models embodying the extremes of staff involvement: the neutral-and-inferior-instrument model and the colleague model. A comparison of these models reveals that the staff role can be variously perceived and used. Many of the differences between the models center not on the structural concerns of the classicists but on human concerns.

The modern school has extended the study of line-staff conflict. Certain modern developments—the trend toward profit centers, management by objectives, and project teams—have blurred the line-staff division. Four other influences on staff size and significance are organizational technology, size, type, and life-cycle stage.

DISCUSSION QUESTIONS

1. What is the major difference between line and staff personnel?
2. What is the importance of *authority* in determining whether an organizational member is line or staff?
3. How does the line-staff differentiation come about?
4. Distinguish between personal and specialized staff.
5. What is "the line-staff dilemma"? Why is it a dilemma?
6. What are the types of staff authority? What does identifying these types contribute to solving the line-staff dilemma?
7. What is the human relations perspective on line-staff conflict? What is the human relations solution to the line-staff dilemma?
8. What causes conflict between line and staff?
9. What is the "strategic contingencies theory of organizational power"? How does it help to explain the line-staff conflict?
10. What is the "neutral-and-inferior-instrument model"? How does it help us to understand the nature of line-staff relationships?
11. How does the neutral-and-inferior-instrument model differ from the colleague model? What are the advantages of each model?
12. What is the modern perspective on line and staff?
13. How do organizational size, technology, and the nature of the business affect the line-staff relationship?
14. Can you make any predictions about future line-staff relationships? Will staff become even more influential, or will line reestablish its dominance?

■   PUTNAM PLASTICS CORPORATION

Dawn Sharp, a new member of Putnam Plastics Corporation's headquarters staff, thought she had found a way for Putnam to save many thousands of dollars per year: cut down on the number of clerk-typists. She found that the Eastern Division achieved satisfactory results with only 0.8 clerk-typists per manager. The statistic for the other divisions was: Southern Division, 1.2; Northern Division, 2.0; and Western Division 2.2. Sharp reported her findings to the divisional vice presidents, confident that she had performed a useful service.

The Eastern Division vice president concurred that Eastern used its clerk-typists efficiently. The other vice presidents disagreed with Sharp's findings—violently. The response to Sharp's boss from Waldo Olive, vice president of the Southern Division, was typical: "One person will decide how many typists we need in my division, and that one person is not Ms. Sharp, whoever she is. The tinkering of headquarters staff with line matters is usually harmless, but when you start telling line vice presidents how many people to hire in a certain function, that's where I call a halt."

To what extent is this a "typical line-staff conflict"? Are such conflicts inevitable? Do you see how this particular conflict could have been avoided? If you were Dawn Sharp's boss, how would you react?

■ ## *WHITNEY CONVERSION CORP.*

Steve Whitney, president of Whitney Conversion Corp., had long been fed up with the dissension between line and staff in his organization. Staff said line wouldn't follow their advice; line usually said the advice wasn't worth following.

Now Whitney read the report of a consulting firm that had spent two months reviewing line-staff relations at Whitney Conversion:

> We suggest that you abandon your present practice of giving separate, generous budgets to staff departments. Instead, make these departments pay their way by offering services to line departments on a negotiated-fee basis. In this way, line departments will receive only that staff assistance for which they are willing to pay, and staff departments will be motivated to trim down their activities to those that are truly useful. These changes should do much to reduce both your cost of doing business and the line-staff friction that has troubled you.

Sounds good to me, thought Steve Whitney.

What do you think the different reactions to this proposal will be around Whitney Conversion Corp.?

■ ## *STANDARD TIMES AT GAINESVILLE SUPPLY INC.*

The top management at Gainesville Supply Inc. had assigned its new Work Methods Department the task of establishing "standard times" within the Widget Packing Department. After some observation of the widget packers, but no conversation with them or their supervisor, Work Methods reported to management that a packer should be able to pack a box of widgets in 75 seconds, or 48 boxes per hour.

Laura Martin, head of the Widget Packing Department, got the memo about the new "standard time for widget packing" late one afternoon. A highly experienced widget packer herself and a respected manager, Martin just laughed at the proposed standard time and set the memo aside. It might look good on paper, but it just couldn't be done.

Next day at the morning meeting, Martin told her widget packers: "If you hear anything about a 'standard time' of 48 widget boxes per hour, just don't pay any attention to it. We've been averaging 35 for years. I'd say 40 boxes per hour is absolute tops, and I'll straighten Work Methods out on this in a hurry."

Later that morning, Martin went upstairs to explain that the new standard was entirely unrealistic. Her boss straightened her out in a hurry: "Laura, the new standard will go into effect tomorrow. Work Methods has improved the results in several other departments already. Sure, the departments resist at first, but they always find that they can meet standard with an extra effort."

"Maybe that's true elsewhere," said Laura, "but I know widget packing and I know we can't pack that many, even with these new methods that they want us to use."

"Martin, get back downstairs, explain that the new standard times will be met, teach your people the new methods, stick to widget packing, and leave methods and times to the Work Methods Department. That's what we pay you for, and that's what we pay them for."

Martin tried her best, but her department knew how she felt about the situation. The Widget Packing Department failed to meet the new work standards, and the head of the Work Standards Department blamed Laura Martin. He recommended that Martin be demoted to widget packer.

What are the line-staff issues here? What went wrong? What can be done now?

NOTES

1. Lyndall Urwick, *Notes on the Theory of Organization* (New York: American Management Association, 1952), p. 72.
2. James D. Mooney and Alan C. Reiley, *Onward Industry: The Principles of Organization and Their Significance to Modern Industry* (New York: Harper & Brothers, 1931), p. 60.
3. Lyndall Urwick, *Notes on the Theory of Organization,* p. 72.
4. In J. Patrick Wright, *On a Clear Day You Can See General Motors* (New York: Avon, 1979), p. 228.
5. Ibid., p. 190.
6. See Victor F. Phillips, *The Organizational Role of the Assistant-to* (New York: American Management Association, 1971).
7. Quoted in James D. Mooney and Alan C. Reiley, *Onward Industry,* p. 73.
8. Henri Fayol, *General and Industrial Management,* trans. Constance Storrs (London: Pitman, 1949), p. 63.
9. Melville Dalton, "Conflicts Between Staff and Line Managerial Officers," *American Sociological Review* 15 (June 1950): 345.
10. See Paul C. Nystrom, "Comparing Beliefs of Line and Technostructure Managers," *Academy of Management Journal* 29 (December 1986): 812–819.
11. For further discussion of these points, see L.W. Porter, "Job Attitudes in Management—III: Perceived Deficiencies in Need Fulfillment As a Function of Line Versus Staff Types of Jobs," *Journal of Applied Psychology* 47 (May 1963): 267–275; and L.W. Porter and E.E. Lawler, "Properties of Organization Structure in Relation to Job Attitudes and Job Behavior," *Psychological Bulletin* 64 (January 1965): 23–51.
12. Robert T. Golembiewski, "Personality and Organization Structure: Staff Models and Behavior Patterns," *Academy of Management Journal* 9 (September 1966): 217–232.
13. For further discussion of this point, see Max D. Richards and Paul S. Greenlaw, *Management: Decisions and Behavior* (Homewood, IL: Richard D. Irwin, 1972), pp. 286–287.

14. D.J. Hickson et al., "A Strategic Contingencies Theory of Intraorganizational Power," *Administrative Science Quarterly* 16 (June 1971): 216–229.
15. Michael Aiken and Jerald Hage, "Organizational Interdependence and Intraorganizational Structure," *American Sociological Review* 33 (December 1968): 912–930.
16. Ibid., p. 927.
17. Ibid.
18. *Business Week,* 25 April 1983, p. 54.
19. Vivian Nossiter, "A New Approach Toward Resolving the Line and Staff Dilemma," *Academy of Management Review* 4 (January 1979): 104.
20. Joan Woodward, *Industrial Organization: Theory and Practice* (London: Oxford University Press, 1965).
21. See Peter M. Blau and Richard A. Schoenherr, *The Structure of Organizations* (New York: Basic Books, 1971), pp. 82–110.
22. Vivian Nossiter, "A New Approach Toward Resolving the Line and Staff Dilemma," 103–106.

ADDITIONAL READINGS

Belasco, James A., and Joseph A. Alutto. "Line-Staff Conflicts: Some Empirical Insights." *Academy of Management Journal* 12 (December 1969): 469–477.
Browne, Philip J., and Robert T. Golembiewski. "The Line-Staff Concept Revisited—An Empirical Study of Organizational Images." *Academy of Management Journal* 17 (September 1974): 406–417.
Dale, Ernest, and Lyndall F. Urwick. *Staff and Organization.* New York: McGraw-Hill, 1960.
Dalton, M. "Changing Line-Staff Relations." *Personnel Administration* 29 (March/April 1966): 3–5.
Filley, Alan C. "Decisions and Research in Staff Utilization." *Academy of Management Journal* 6 (September 1973): 220–231.
Fisch, Gerald. "Line-Staff Is Obsolete." *Harvard Business Review* 39 (September/October 1961): 67–79.
Jennings, Ken. "Improving Line-Staff Relationships." *Personnel Administrator* 20 (October 1975): 47–51.
McConkey, Dale D. "Staff Objectives Are Different." *Personnel Journal* 51 (July 1972): 477–483, 537.
Myers, C.A., and J.G. Turnbull. "Line and Staff in Industrial Relations." *Harvard Business Review* 34 (July/August 1956): 113–124.
Stieglitz, Harold. "Staff-Staff Relationships." *Management Record* 24 (February 1962): 2–13.
Tomasko, Robert M. "Reducing the Girth of Corporate Headquarters Staff." *Management Review* 73 (January 1984): 26–28, 37–39.

Delegation

The preceding three chapters have covered three ways in which the organization differentiates its tasks: by jobs, by departments, and by line-and-staff functions. This chapter and the following one explore two ways in which the organization differentiates its formal decision-making authority: by delegation and by decentralization.

The OT-Model on the inside covers cannot show the real-life overlap of task differentiation and authority differentiation. Very few employees simply perform tasks, without having any authority. Very few executives simply have the authority to make decisions about what tasks other people should perform, without doing any tasks themselves. However, for purposes of explaining these differentiation strategies, we have separated them.

This chapter presents the delegation of formal authority from the classical, human relations, and modern perspectives. The classical tendency was to avoid delegating and to make decisions as far *up* the organization as possible. The human relations school encouraged delegation of authority and employee participation in decision making. The modern attitude, heavily influenced by the human relations school, is that while delegation is desirable in most situations, it may be undesirable in some. The characteristics of the situation, the task, the manager, and the subordinate all work together to determine whether or not delegation is likely to work well.

THE NATURE OF DELEGATION

Delegation and decentralization are related concepts in the organization theory literature. Both terms refer primarily to the disbursement of formal decision-making authority within the organization.

Delegation

Delegation occurs when a manager allocates duties and/or decision-making authority to a subordinate. For example, a bank manager in charge of loans might delegate to an assistant the authority to make loans below $10,000. For larger loans, the assistant would need to get the manager's approval. Likewise, a hospital chief of medical services may delegate to staff surgeons the authority to perform minor surgery without review. More difficult surgical cases would require collaboration among a team of surgeons, with final approval by the chief of medical services. In the loan office and in the hospital, a manager passed formal decision-making authority in specific task areas downward through the organization to subordinates.

Decentralization

Decentralization represents an organization-wide commitment to delegation. Decentralization and delegation are normally found together, but not necessarily. A manager with considerable decision-making authority in a decentralized organization may choose to delegate few decisions to subordinates. Conversely, a manager with little decision-making authority may share that small amount of authority with subordinates.

THE ASPECTS OF DELEGATION

The process of delegation from manager to subordinate contains two distinct aspects: assigning duties and granting decision-making authority.

Delegating Duties

Managers assign or delegate duties to subordinates. They specify what each subordinate's job is and (ideally) rank the components of the subordinate's work in importance. They turn subordinates loose to do the work and then evaluate them on their performance. Delegation and evaluation are obviously much easier when the duties of subordinates are operational and specific rather than vague.

National sales manager Marilyn Smith hires Harry Jones as Detroit regional sales manager. She tells Harry that he is accountable for maintaining the present sales volume of existing products as well as for increasing sales of the new product line by 20 percent. Marilyn advises Harry that his best strategy for reaching these goals is to devote more attention to the high-volume firms, but reminds him that the company will also gain from more sales to the low-volume firms. Marilyn has stipulated Harry's geographical area of responsibility, his formal authority, and his operationally defined goals. How he achieves those goals is left to his own initiative and managerial discretion.

Harry's formal authority may be defined by a budget, a company rule book on practices and procedures, and the sales code of ethics. Harry can take a wide variety of actions, so long as he doesn't overstep the constraints of the formal authority delegated to him.

Delegating Decision-making Authority

"Delegating decision-making authority" is a concept often complicated by the many definitions of decision making. Most narrowly, it means the act of making a choice. However, the concept is much broader as it is commonly used in conjunction with delegation and decentralization; it refers to any one or several parts of the decision-making *process* or to the process in its entirety. This process includes surveillance of the environment to spot potential problem situations requiring decisions, the actual specification of the particular problem to be solved, the search for alternative solutions, analyzing the pros and cons of those alternatives, making the choice, and implementing it. In the context of delegation, granting decision-making authority could involve one, several, or all of the steps in the decision-making process. The manager hands down to subordinates the formal authority to act in specific decision areas on the manager's behalf. The manager may withdraw this transferred authority at any time.

Responsibility and Authority   Many members of organizations complain that they have more responsibility than authority. This is usually caused by the lack of clear, operational goals. Subordinate managers, given ill-defined areas of responsibility and anxious to please by doing a good job, often feel the job's dimensions and responsibility to be much greater than their control over the variables affecting their success. If Harry is simply told, "Increase sales in Detroit or else"—without knowing how much to increase sales, or what additional resources he can have (e.g., more salespeople, market studies)—he will be frustrated. The relationship between formal decision authority and job responsibility is usually more clear in textbooks than it is in reality.

Duties and Authority   The granting of formal authority is logically coupled with the assignment of duties. They normally go hand in hand. Yet managers don't always do what seems logical and normal. For example, a boss may help out a relative or friend by creating a title—a formal position with formal authority, but with no duties. Or a firm may "kick someone upstairs" into a position of greater formal authority, on paper, but with nothing to do.

Bypassing the Manager   Another problem that sometimes arises is bypassing managers in the chain of command. Consider a hypothetical example: George Steinbrenner hires Billy Martin (again) to manage the New York Yankees, saying "I have full faith in you, so you run the ball club on the field, and I'll stay in the front office." After 17 close losses in a row, Steinbrenner begins to take a more active role. In one game, with a man on first, Martin tells the batter to perform a certain task: bunt. As he is about to leave the dugout, the batter gets a call from Steinbrenner ordering him to perform a different task: hit and run. The batter starts for the plate, shaking his head.

   The manager was bypassed, and the subordinate was ordered to do something by the manager's manager. Such bypassing destroys the superior-subordinate relationship essential for organizational effectiveness in general and delegation effectiveness in particular.

THE CLASSICAL PERSPECTIVE

Early Attitudes

Delegation of Tasks   The classical school believed that owners and managers could define tasks clearly and specifically, then assign them to other organizational members.

In the mechanistic organizations envisioned by the classicists, tasks were simple, highly specialized, and unchanging. Such tasks, and routine decisions about them, could easily be delegated to subordinates.

Delegation of Authority   In the days when organizations and their technology were stable and uncomplicated, delegation of authority was not very often seen as necessary for two reasons. First, the owner/entrepreneur had his own name on the door and capital at risk. Therefore he had the unchallenged right of private property to make all the decisions, define how jobs would be performed, and specify how subordinates must behave if they wanted to continue working. After all, it was the owner's organization, the owner's product, and the owner's method for producing it. Why shouldn't the owner have the right to make all the decisions? Who else could be as trusted as the owner himself to make decisions with the same concern for the owner's well-being?

Second, since the owner had developed the product or service in the first place, built the production or service organization from scratch, and understood it more thoroughly than anyone else could, why should any decision-making authority be given to people who could not possibly understand the organization as well as the owner did? Once early owners told employees what to do and how to do it, they saw no decisions remaining to be made. A shade tobacco farm exemplifies this kind of operation. The farm is generally run by the owner or a longtime employee who has grown up in tobacco. Since the process of growing tobacco has not changed for many years, the typical owner or manager is an expert who tells the rest of the people what to do and when to do it. The need or opportunity to delegate authority is minimal.

Much of the conflict within Apple Computer over the roles of Steven Jobs and Stephen Wosniack can be traced to their unwillingness or inability to delegate. They started Apple in a garage, then built it into a multimillion-dollar corporation. In the early days, the two entrepreneurs were able to run the organization by eyeball contact, without delegation. Since they knew more about Apple's workings and its products than anyone else, that method worked well—for a while. As time passed, Jobs and Wosniack tried to retain administrative control without much delegation, but found that this wasn't possible, because of Apple's explosive growth. They became frustrated and left Apple to set up new organizations in which they could once again (for a time) retain personal control.

Why Delegate?

Employees are usually promoted to managerial positions because they are the best performers of the tasks that they will be managing. This tendency to take task experts and make them managers stems from early classical thinking. If you want a manager of typists, salespeople, or computer programmers, you will probably promote the best, most capable typist, salesperson, or computer programmer. Once the promotion has occurred, why should the new manager delegate decision-making authority to less qualified, less motivated, less capable subordinates—the very people who were recently determined to be less deserving of promotion than the new manager?

In addition, the classicists believed that higher-level managers, by virtue of their elevated perspectives, had a better view of developments in the company, the industry, and the general economy. Therefore, they were better able to make decisions that would benefit the whole organization.

Delegate Only If Necessary

An overburdened administrator may have to allow subordinates to do certain routine jobs. Otherwise, the manager becomes swamped by the job, quality falls off, and performance declines. Classicists James D. Mooney and Alan C. Reiley commented that "one of the tragedies of business experience is the frequency with which men, always efficient in anything that they personally can do, will finally be crushed and fail under the weight of accumulated duties that they do not know and cannot learn how to delegate."[1] Managers must often take the risk that less qualified persons will do unsatisfactory work—with managers remaining accountable for the results.

Delegation of authority must eventually follow delegation of tasks. Mooney and Reiley observed:

> When an organization outgrows the possibility of universal face-to-face leadership, there must ensue that feature of organization which we may call sub-delegation. This means that the leader no longer delegates an authority to do certain specified things. He begins to delegate an authority similar to his own; in other words, he delegates the right of delegation itself.[2]

Lyndall Urwick agreed with the necessity of delegation: "Without delegation no organization can function effectively. Yet, lack of courage to delegate properly and of knowledge how to do it is one of the most general causes of failure in organization."[3]

THE HUMAN RELATIONS PERSPECTIVE

The classicists preferred control at the top; the human relations school sought greater democracy within the organization. Managers should encourage their subordinates to participate in decision making. The human relations movement sought to increase the practice of delegation by showing that *participative management* was to the benefit of workers, managers, and the organization. From the human relations perspective, this principle was valid whether applied to one-to-one delegation or organization-wide decentralization (discussed in the next chapter). In between these extremes was participation on a work-unit basis. The human relations writers encouraged unit managers to use participation throughout their units, regardless of organization-wide practice. From the human relations viewpoint, participative management would quite naturally increase the number and kinds of decisions delegated to subordinates.

In addition, delegation is designed to produce specialized training and increased competence in subordinates to whom authority is delegated. However, this increased expertise may result in too narrow a focus on the subunit's specialized goals, rather than on those of the entire organization. Although they were concerned about this "bifurcation of interests" to which delegation could lead, the human relations writers still believed that managers should delegate decision-making authority when possible.[4]

Degrees of Participation

As Figure 7.1 shows, employee participation in decision making can fall within a wide range—from tell and sell to decision making by the group rather than the manager.[5] Under the "tell" approach, employee participation is nonexistent; the manager makes the decision, then announces it. At the other end of the spectrum, the employee group identifies problems, evaluates alternatives, and makes choices. The problem-solving group's manager provides advice, moderates group discussions, informs the group about the needs and expectations of other groups within the organization, searches out information, and provides resources. The manager becomes the group's *facilitator* rather than its director—helping the group to make its own decisions.

Managers encourage different degrees of participation at different times. The manager may "sell" the idea of no smoking in committee meetings, "tell" the group that start time is being shifted from 8:30 to 9:00, and ask the group to decide how large the contributions to the flower-and-gift fund should be.

Some Early Evidence Favoring Participation

The Hawthorne Studies   The studies at Western Electric's Hawthorne Works were described in Chapter 1. The researchers initially intended to study the relationship between lighting levels and worker productivity. However, because of the "Hawthorne effect," productivity *rose* even when lighting level *dropped*. The workers were producing more and their morale was higher, not because lighting levels were increased or decreased, but because their supervisors and the experimenters were listening to what they said and paying attention to them as people.

Bavelas Study   Another early study of participation was conducted by Alex Bavelas in 1948. Bavelas chose a group of sewing machine operators who were averaging about

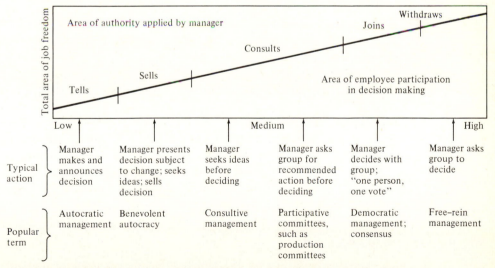

Figure 7.1 Employee participation in decision making: A continuum. (*Source:* After Keith Davis and John Newstrom, *Human Behavior at Work: Organizational Behavior* [New York: McGraw-Hill Book Company, 1985], p. 192. Used by permission.)

74 units per hour and asked them if they would like to set their own standard. They agreed to do so, decided on 84 units per hour, and soon exceeded that standard. After another discussion, they decided to attempt 95 units per hour, but failed. They finally decided on the more realistic, but still high, standard of 90 units per hour and almost met it over a period of several months. Participation in goal setting resulted in a productivity increase of about 22 percent.[6]

Coch and French Study   In the late 1940s, Lester Coch and John French, Jr., compared the output of factory workers under three different conditions for introducing change: no worker participation (control group), some participation (first experimental group), and total participation (second and third experimental groups).[7]

The control group (no participation) was simply told what the changes were (minor job modifications and a new piece rate) and why they were needed. Within 40 days of the changes, 17 percent quit and many of the remaining employees complained, held up production, refused to cooperate, and filed grievances. Output in units per hour remained about the same.

After hearing a dramatic explanation of the need for change, the first experimental group (some participation) was asked to help management develop the new work methods and pay rates. The group selected some operators for special training; these operators later trained the rest in the new methods. After two weeks of adjustment, the some-participation group began to exceed its previous output, and for the next two weeks the group's production curve trended upward. No workers quit, and attitude was good.

The next two experimental groups (total participation) also heard a persuasive explanation of why changes were needed. Since these groups were smaller, all operators (rather than a representative selection) helped design the new jobs. Performance in these two groups was best of all; improvement in units per hour was almost immediate, and the groups soon progressed to an output level 14 percent higher than the level before the introduction of change.

Two and a half months after the experiment, the remaining members of the no-participation control group were taught a new job using the total-participation technique. Under that technique, the group achieved high production levels, with no quits and with a generally good attitude.

Total participation and representative participation seemed in these experiments to encourage both high morale and increased production, compared to no participation.

Filley, House, and Kerr Review   A.C. Filley, R.J. House, and S. Kerr reviewed 38 studies on participation. These studies revealed that participative management is almost always associated with greater employee satisfaction, productivity, or both.[8] Katherine I. Miller and Peter R. Monge analyzed 47 studies and concluded that participation has a positive effect on both satisfaction and productivity, with a somewhat stronger effect on satisfaction.[9]

Why Participation Is Advocated

Some additional reasons for the human-relations advocacy of participation are presented on the following page.

It is philosophically satisfying. The notion of participation has considerable philosophical appeal in our society. Managers who use participation reflect their belief that their subordinates want to work, enjoy doing their work well, and are uniquely qualified to participate in decisions about how the work should be done—because they are the ones doing it. The manager who uses a participative approach is sending a message to employees: "I want you to participate in decisions because I value your opinions, your experience, and your desire to do a good job." Managers who discourage employee participation are sending quite a different message to employees.

Two heads are better than one. Group discussion is an effective method for generating alternative solutions to problems and then choosing the best one.[10] Synergy and brainstorming are two ideas based directly on this principle. The recent success of Japanese management techniques and quality circles has lent additional emphasis to this method in current management practices.

Participants in decisions understand them better. Many people object to decisions because they don't see any good reason for them. Participation enables employees to understand what the problems are, why solutions must be found, and the rationale underlying decisions which affect them. Authoritarian managers sometimes make decisions arbitrarily. Managers using participative techniques are forced to analyze the issues involved, so they can explain to employees how proposed decisions will affect them and the achievement of the organization's goals and objectives. In short, participation reduces unnecessary decisions and increases employee acceptance of necessary decisions and their willingness to implement them.

Participation clears the communication channels. In some cases, decisions that employees might view as acceptable and necessary are resisted because communication breaks down somewhere between manager and employees. Since participation ensures a two-way communication channel, any misunderstandings can be cleared up.

Participation reduces employee fears. Employees fear the unknown. Participation permits a full and frank discussion of the reasons for and the effects of decisions. Participating employees understand how the decision may affect their economic, personal, and social concerns.

Participation and motivation are interrelated. Rensis Likert points out that members must view their organization's mission as an important one:

> To be highly motivated, each member of the organization must feel that the organization's objectives are of significance and that his own particular task contributes in an indispensable manner to the organization's achievement of its objectives. He should see his role as difficult, important, and meaningful. This is necessary if the individual is to achieve and maintain a sense of personal worth and importance. When jobs do not meet this specification, they should be reorganized so that they do. This is likely to require the participation of those involved in the work. . . .[11]

Participation increases commitment. Employees who have been involved in decision making will be more committed to helping make the decisions work. Even if others eventually make the decisions, or even if the employees disagree with them, they have been involved in the process and have had the opportunity to express their opinions and influence others.[12]

THE MODERN PERSPECTIVE

The modern approach to delegation has been very much influenced by the arguments of the human relations school in favor of delegation and participation. Several other modern developments have made irrelevant the classical contention that, since senior managers have the expertise, they can and should make most decisions. The increasing complexity of the environment and the corresponding need to train and rely on able subordinates has led to delegation; these subordinates must be given some freedom of movement if they are to react quickly and appropriately to change. Today's worker also has an increased sense of professionalism, matched by an increased expectation of job autonomy.

The classicists assumed that the managerial ranks were filled by the people most expert in the tasks they now managed. These days, the manager is apt to be either someone who has never done the task (such as a college graduate engineer hired as a production supervisor) or someone whose on-the-job experience is now obsolete (such as a general manager trying to figure out how to operate a desk-top computer). Managers simply cannot keep track of all the new information and technology.

Furthermore, now that many highly routine tasks have become automated, the average supervisor must oversee a greater variety of tasks than ever before. The classical assumptions that (1) the manager's expertise is superior to that of employees, and (2) the manager should retain complete control of decision making if possible, have become ancient history. Delegation is no longer a necessary evil, but a necessary skill to master.

On the other hand, modern writers recognize that the success or failure of delegation and participation is very much influenced by the people involved and the situation. While managers must understand the many good reasons for delegating decisions through participation, they must be aware of the pitfalls as well. As M. Shaskin has pointed out, the manager must have the ability and resources to carry out the employee group's recommendation. Otherwise, the employees will feel that they have wasted time on a useless exercise.[13] Furthermore, the manager must really believe in the participative approach, rather than simply trying to manipulate the group into making those recommendations already favored by the manager. Employees are quick to sense a manager's lack of commitment to true participation.

When Delegation of Authority Works

The modern position is to identify situations in which delegation is desirable.[14] And as is so often true, delegation is desirable when its benefits outweigh its costs. In general, delegation works when both subordinates and managers are able and willing, and when performance can be monitored. These criteria are explained below.

Able Subordinates   Delegation can work when subordinates have (or can readily and economically get) training, ability, knowledge, experience, and information in specific decision areas. Subordinates with these characteristics can make good decisions within limited areas of responsibility.

This first criterion is obvious. Delegating decisions to a subordinate who doesn't know or understand the decision area is unreasonable. For example, asking a janitor to devise long-term corporate strategy is not reasonable because the janitor lacks the information and training needed to develop a beneficial organization-wide plan. Asking the president to decide what products do the best job of cleaning mahogany-chrome-glass executive desks is similarly unreasonable—though the president, of course, has the authority to make that decision.

Delegation demands an assessment of the capabilities of the people to whom the manager intends to delegate decisions. They may need training and experience in making decisions. The manager should initially allow decision responsibility in areas where mistakes are not costly and in which subordinates have knowledge and training. For instance, a maintenance manager may start by delegating to the janitorial staff the authority to decide which products should be used to clean executive desks. The costs of a poor decision are relatively small, the expertise of the deciding group is high, and the decision will probably be a good one.

The classical belief that employees shouldn't participate in making decisions about their work was derived from Frederick W. Taylor and the scientific management movement. The worker Schmidt had been loading pig iron for years. Then Taylor came along with scientific methods to determine how much Schmidt should work and how much he should rest. This caused an almost immediate huge increase in Schmidt's production. This scientific approach was applied to more and more jobs, with subsequent productivity gains. Taylor demonstrated the drawbacks of letting subordinates, untrained in "scientific" principles, choose their own work methods. Left on their own, they would choose the wrong method.

As the "manual" work force of Taylor's day became a more "mental" work force after World War II, application of scientific management principles became more difficult and delegation began to make more sense. Many of today's workers are paid for what they know as well as for what they do. The modern approach argues that authority should be delegated to these knowledgeable workers for their own and the organization's benefit.

Motivated Subordinates   If subordinates are motivated and committed, these qualities can compensate for many shortcomings. Highly committed people try harder; through sheer effort, they can often overcome a lack of knowledge, training, experience, and information. Such people willingly accept delegated authority, if their managers ask them to. On the other hand, all the knowledge and training in the world will do no good if an uncaring subordinate does not want to apply them. In earlier times, most managers felt that most subordinates were motivated by fear and greed, not by a commitment to the organization and its goals. Therefore, they delegated as little authority as possible. The modern manager realizes that this view of motivation is inadequate to explain the intense commitments of many people to their organizations.

Reasons for Avoiding Responsibility   Employees may hesitate to make commitments and to accept delegated authority for many reasons. Decision making requires hard thinking. Asking the boss what to do is often easier than deciding on your own what to do. Also, letting managers make all the decisions shifts responsibility to managers, who must shoulder the burden of unfortunate outcomes. After all, subordinates are not getting paid to make decisions, so why should they make them?

Other reasons for rejecting delegated authority are fear of criticism, lack of information and resources, and lack of self-confidence. Finally, subordinates may already be overworked, especially if they manage time poorly or have not delegated properly themselves. An overworked subordinate will naturally shy away from additional responsibilities.

Willing and Able Managers   Delegation will work only if managers want it to work and know how to make it work. Consider manager Nelson Baldwin. He is in charge of his department and knows that he will be held accountable for its performance. He feels that he is the boss because he is the best person for the job; clearly, he was made manager because he is smarter, more perceptive, loyal, and able than anyone else in his group. This attitude is reinforced by his title and high salary. Why should such an all-star manager pass decision making down to his subordinates?

And yet, Nelson Baldwin probably wants his own boss to delegate considerable decision-making authority down to him. Most managers are much more ready to accept delegation from above than they are to delegate downward. When managing others, they want to define the issues and fit the degree of delegation and participation to the situation. When being managed, they invariably want considerable delegation and full participation, no matter what the situation.[15]

Job security also affects delegation decisions. Some managers accept delegation as a desirable principle, but are so insecure about their own jobs that they don't dare let subordinates make decisions for which they themselves are ultimately responsible. Many managers worry about failing. They know the theoretical benefits of delegation, but feel the risk of poor decisions by subordinates is simply too high. Conversely, they don't want to take the chance of subordinates attracting the favorable attention of superiors by making great decisions.

Depending upon how they treat the results of delegation, organizations can easily reassure (or discourage) insecure delegators. Consider a sales manager who trusts the sales force to follow company policy. Then a salesperson violates the policy, and the company loses a customer as a result. The attitude of the organization's managers toward delegation will be affected by what action the upper administration takes. The sales manager may be either counseled and encouraged or reprimanded and perhaps fired; managerial interest in delegating will consequently either increase or diminish.

Performance Can Be Monitored   Finally, delegation works best when the performance of subordinates to whom authority has been delegated can be monitored. The delegating manager needs a feedback mechanism that indicates whether subordinates are making good or bad decisions. For some issues, the mechanism can be quite objective and easy to comprehend. Did the subordinate sell a certain number of trucks? Did the subordinate stay within the budget? In such cases, managers can establish norms, easily note deviations from them, and take prompt remedial action.

Writers on management by objectives have made one point abundantly clear: the boss, the subordinate, and the entire organization benefit greatly when goals, objectives, and tasks are made measurable. Whenever possible, managers who delegate decisions or tasks should make plain what constitutes a good decision or the successful completion of a task.

Two Monitoring Strategies: MBE and Budgets

Management by Exception   Selling a certain number of trucks and staying within a certain budget are two simple examples of management by exception (MBE): the delegating manager gets involved only if something goes exceptionally wrong.

Under MBE, measurable targets are established whenever possible. These targets or standards are based on averages of past performance or reasonable projections of future performance. When results achieved by subordinates are reasonably close to standard, managers do not need to oversee the job process directly. Instead, they can spend their time on long-range planning or researching new ways of doing the job. When a deviation (or exception) from the standard occurs, the manager gets a quick signal that managerial attention is needed. Since an "exception" is defined as a deviation from the goal or standard, management by exception can obviously occur only if goals have been developed and made known.

Budgets   Within large formal organizations, the most widely used performance monitor is the budget. A budget is a plan expressed in dollars and cents. The budget forecasts what the organization expects to happen within each budgeted area over a specified time period. Once the organization's financial plans are expressed in the form of budgets, they serve both as control devices and as performance standards. Actual performance is periodically measured against the expectations reflected in the budgets, to let managers know how the organization is doing.

The budgeting process is an opportunity to gain, in the areas of planning and control, the previously discussed advantages of employee participation. Budgets constructed with the help of employees are likely to be realistic financial plans. Also, employees are more likely to adhere to budgets that they help to prepare.

The preceding devices are ways of monitoring performance fairly precisely. Managers are usually more willing to delegate authority when they know that maintaining accountability for the delegated areas of responsibility is relatively easy, and that bad decisions will become evident before disaster strikes.

A Strategy for Delegation

An approach that has helped many managers accept delegation is considering the making of decisions as a process rather than as an act. The manager nervous about losing control over the ultimate choice can delegate the other steps in the decision-making process but reserve the right to make the final choice. Subordinates can: identify problem areas, generate their own alternative solutions, evaluate solutions derived by themselves or specified by the boss, choose from a list of alternatives satisfactory to the boss, develop means for implementing choices, follow up on choices, and so on. The manager uncomfortable with total delegation can delegate all these stages of the process except making the choice.

Managers unfamiliar with their subordinates or trying to train subordinates in new areas of decision responsibility can break the process down and delegate responsibility for decisions gradually. These managers simultaneously build the ability and confidence of subordinates to make decisions and reduce their own insecurity about delegation.

Some Situational Variables

The human relations school encouraged the sharing of authority with subordinates. Even if authority was not formally delegated, the human relations movement thought that employees should participate in making decisions that affected them.

Brownell's Variables   The modern approach is to determine *when and under what circumstances participative management works.* In his article "Participative Management: The State of the Art," Peter Brownell surveys those factors which should be analyzed to determine whether an organization, unit, or manager should encourage delegation through participation.[16] Here is an outline of variables identified by Brownell which can be considered when making that decision.

   I. Cultural Variables
      A. National, regional
      B. Political
      C. Social
  II. Organizational Variables
      A. Environmental stability
      B. Technology
      C. Task uncertainty
      D. Organizational structure
 III. Interpersonal Variables and Leadership Style
      A. Task characteristics
      B. Group characteristics
      C. Situational characteristics
  IV. Individual Variables
      A. Individual characteristics
      B. Personality variables
      C. Individual perceptions

Not only do each of these factors affect the success or failure of participative management; many of the factors also affect each other.

   The organization would first consider the cultural and organizational variables, to design an organizational structure that will succeed at a given place and time. The organization would consider answers to such questions as:

   Cultural: How will the culture in, let us say, our Birmingham, Alabama location affect us? What are the politics there? What are the local customs and mores? Can we use the same procedures we employ in our Bangor, Maine branch?

   Organizational: Is the market environment for making and selling widgets stable or rapidly changing? How complex is our widget-making technology? To what extent are the task requirements predictable and routine? Do we have all the information that we need to perform all our tasks, or are there gaps? What has our experience with centralization and decentralization been?

Answers to these questions enable the firm to determine *the desirable degree of participative management* in the Birmingham, Alabama unit.

Answers to the following questions will tell the firm *how to make that degree of participation succeed.*

Interpersonal Variables: What is the degree of "task pressure" in our organization? How interesting are our tasks? How large are our work groups? How skilled is the average group member compared to the supervisor? Are our employees ambitious? Hostile? Unionized?

Individual Variables: How old is our work force going to be? Will they accept formal authority readily?

Modern research in organization theory has supplied data relating many variables to the success of participative management. Firms should use a systems/contingency approach in establishing the degree of participation. They must first assess the organization's different parts and understand how they interrelate and interact. Then they must study earlier research reports that have shown the relationships between the many relevant variables and the success or failure of participative management. Finally, they must apply their findings to their own situations.

Vroom's Variables   Victor H. Vroom has presented several variables that the manager should consider before determining whether to permit no participation in decision making, complete participation, or some degree in between the extremes reflected in Figure 7.1 (page 161).[17]

1. How important is the quality of the decision? The more important the quality, the greater the need for complete information. More participants mean more information. If the decision merely needs to be workable but not of particularly high quality, the manager can make it.
2. How much of the information needed to make the decision does the manager already have? The less information the manager has, the greater the need for participation.
3. How clearly structured or defined is the problem? The clearer the problem, the less the need for participation.
4. How important to the decision's success is the acceptance/commitment of others? If it is important, they should participate in making the decision.
5. How probable is it that other members will accept the manager's decision? If chances of rejection are high, then others should participate to increase the likelihood of acceptance.
6. What is the probability that participation in decision making will provoke conflict among the participants? The greater the probability that working on the problem will create conflict, the less appropriate their participation is.

The Vroom-Yetton model in Figure 7.2 enables the modern organizational leader to determine *when* to share decision-making authority with subordinates. In effect, the model advocates a situationally driven approach to determining where on the leadership-behavior continuum in Figure 7.1 the leader's behavior should fall.

A. Does the problem possess a quality requirement?
B. Do I have sufficient information to make a high–quality decision?
C. Is the problem structured?
D. Is acceptance of the decision by subordinates important for effective implementation?
E. If I were to make the decision by myself, am I reasonably certain that it would be accepted
   by my subordinates?
F. Do subordinates share the organizational goals to be attained in solving this problem?
G. Is conflict among subordinates likely in preferred solutions?

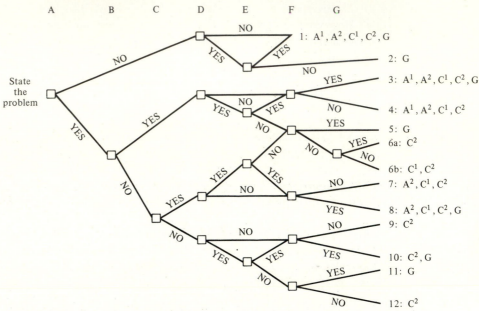

Figure 7.2 Decision process flowchart. (*Source:* Adapted from *Leadership and Decision-making* by Victor H. Vroom and Philip W. Yetton by permission of the University of Pittsburgh Press. © 1973 by University of Pittsburgh Press.)

The model provides for five degrees of shared decision making:

A^1: The A stands for "autocratic." In A^1, the manager makes the decision alone.

A^2: The manager gathers information from subordinates, then makes the decision.

C^1: The C stands for "consultative." In C^1, the manager tells individual subordinates what the problem is, gets their ideas and suggestions, and then makes the decision.

C^2: The consultation is not with individuals as in C^1 but with the group, at a meeting.

G: The G stands for "group." The manager chairs a meeting, at which the group arrives at a consensus decision.

In order to decide which approach to use in solving a given problem, the manager asks the series of questions at the top of Figure 7.2 and uses the "Yes" or "No" answers to move along the proper path to the right. The first three questions relate to the *quality* of the decision. The last four questions relate to *acceptance* of the decision by subordinates. At the far right in the figure, the problems are given numbers from 1 to 12, and the appropriate decision processes are indicated.

Consider the path through the chart that results from these responses:

A. Does the problem possess a quality requirement? YES.

B. Do I have sufficient information to make a high-quality decision? YES.

D. Is acceptance of the decision by subordinates important for effective implementation? NO.

F. Do subordinates share the organizational goals to be attained in solving this problem? YES.

The interesting result of this YES-YES-NO-YES response series is that the manager may use *any* of the five approaches to solve this problem. Certain other response series permit only one approach.

Fitting Strategy to People The days of one-on-one supervision, when an owner/manager could closely supervise all subordinates while they were doing their jobs, are long gone. Due to the complex and rapidly changing nature of many organizational tasks, managers must rely more and more on people working effectively without close supervision. In addition, the increasingly educated and professional work force demands job autonomy and is more capable of self-direction. The modern problem, then, is to fit the delegation strategy to the people in a particular task situation—to decide what, when, how, and to whom decision-making authority should be delegated.

SUMMARY

Delegation has two aspects: the assigning of duties and the granting of decision-making authority. From the perspective of the early classicists, delegation was seen as sometimes necessary but not particularly desirable. The human relations writers wanted to democratize organizations. Naturally they favored the delegation of authority and employee participation in decision making. The Hawthorne, Bavelas, and Coch and French studies presented some early evidence on the benefits of participation. The human relations theorists proposed both philosophical and practical benefits of subordinate participation.

The modern viewpoint on delegation falls somewhere between the classical and human relations positions. Delegation is appropriate and workable when subordinates are able and willing to accept it and when managers are able and willing to offer it. If either party has serious reservations, delegation will probably not work. Another requirement is that the performance of subordinates to whom authority and tasks are delegated should be subject to fairly precise monitoring.

Successful participation by employees in decision making, like successful delegation, also requires that both parties be able and willing. In addition, organizations must be aware that participation demands more time and money than authoritarian methods do.

When considered as a *process* rather than an *outcome,* decision making has several stages: identifying the problem, searching for alternative solutions, evaluating alternatives, choosing the best alternative, and implementing the chosen alternative. Managers can use delegation and participation at any stage, or at all stages. In almost every important decision situation, some delegation is possible and desirable during one or more decision steps. Only the most secure managers confidently delegate the last two decision steps to subordinates: choosing the best alternative and implementing it. Only the most egotistical managers completely exclude subordinates from involvement in the first three steps. Most good managers solicit input, ideas, and reactions, then close the office door, make the decision, and take responsibility for it.

DISCUSSION QUESTIONS

1. Why is delegation considered to be a specialization of authority rather than a specialization of task?

2. What is delegation? How does it differ from decentralization?

3. Describe delegation's two distinct aspects.

4. Why was the classical school unenthusiastic about delegation?

5. According to the classical school, what is the only good time to delegate?

6. Why did the human relations writers like delegation?

7. Figure 7.1 indicates the degrees of participation that can be accomplished through delegation. What kinds of decisions would you place in each "typical action" category if you were a manager?

8. What was the significance of the study by Coch and French?

9. Why does participation work? According to Peter Brownell and Victor H. Vroom, when does participation work?

10. According to Rensis Likert, what is the relationship between participation and motivation?

11. What are the two major influences on the modern approach to delegation?

12. When does delegation of authority work?

13. What is MBE? How does it help in the delegation process?

14. In the modern world, can a manager avoid delegation? Should the manager try to avoid it?

15. What relationship do you see between delegation and span of control?

16. Describe the Vroom-Yetton model. Construct a few hypothetical organizational problems and follow them through the flowchart in Figure 7.2.

■ *DICKERSON REALTY*

Dickerson Realty centers around Ms. Dickerson. She does the bookkeeping, controls the advertising, takes her turn at floor duty, and makes all the decisions about the firm's operations. She often works 12 hours a day, 7 days a week. She lives alone and usually takes paperwork home with her.

Some of the associate realtors at Dickerson Realty think the firm is in a real slump. Ever since last summer when Ms. Dickerson went out of town for a month, things seem to have changed.

The early summer is often the most active period of the real estate year. Many associates felt that while Ms. Dickerson was away not much could be accomplished. Even though she directed the office by long distance phone every day, many questions went unanswered and many decisions were not made. No sales meetings were held during her absence.

When Ms. Dickerson returned, she found that most associates were inactive. Some were much more involved in personal projects than they were in real estate. Listings were still coming in, but their level was far below last year's.

Ms. Dickerson seems to have too much to do. The associates often ask for her help in the field, but she gets "tied up at the office" and frequently shows up several hours late. Many associates feel that they have lost potential sales because of poor coordination at the office. Listings have been turned in promptly but not "worked" properly. Days often pass before Ms. Dickerson makes a file, then types, copies, and distributes the listing to other associates, and advertises the listing in the paper.

As a result, the sales force is very discouraged. Ms. Dickerson is discouraged, too. For the past two years, gross sales of Dickerson Realty averaged $1,500,000 a month. For the past several months, despite Ms. Dickerson's working harder than ever before, sales have averaged around $200,000 per month.

What seems to be the main problem at Dickerson Realty? If you were called in as a consultant, how would you go about solving it?

ADMINISTRATIVE SERVICES SUPERVISOR

Immediately after she accepted the promotion to administrative services supervisor, Kathy Cohen was called into the office of administrative services manager J. C. Hutchins.

During the interview Hutchins said, "I want you to take the bull by the horns, Kathy. You've been in administrative services for eight years, and you know what needs to be done. Don't be afraid to use your own judgment in supervising the work. As long as you're getting the job done, I won't bother you."

Hutchins concluded by saying, "Of course, my door is always open if you have any problems you can't solve."

Cohen was anxious to look good in her manager's eyes. She wanted to show management that they had made a good choice. So she determined to do everything she could to avoid bothering the boss with problems. She thought taking a problem to Hutchins would reflect weakness on her part.

One frequent problem was that the work was not completed on time. Rather than bother Hutchins or crack down on the person failing to do the work, Cohen found it faster to do the work herself.

Eventually, Cohen found that she could not keep up with all the demands upon her. She finally decided that she could not handle the pressure and was not cut out for supervisor, so she submitted her resignation. Administrative services manager J. C. Hutchins was shocked and amazed.

What happened? What went wrong?

ALL-AMERICAN CORPORATION

For ten years George Barker had been Northern Region manager of All-American Corporation. And for ten years he had made all the decisions about how to allocate inadequate resources within the region. He felt that only he had the appropriate knowledge and administrative perspective to make the tough decisions.

Within the region were six districts, each with a manager. Within each district were from six to ten offices, each with a manager. Every year the office managers complained to the district managers about inadequate budgets, and the district managers passed these complaints (along with many complaints of their own) to George Barker, who felt that he did the best he could with what he had.

Then Barker began working on a master of business administration degree. In several courses he studied the idea of increased delegation. He was intrigued by the thought that delegation might help him to avoid complaints about his budget decisions. In fact, delegation might even result in better decisions.

His professors had pointed out that delegation would make lower-level managers understand the problems of allocating scarce resources. They would also get some good experience in what it is like to make important management decisions.

Since resource allocation decisions had to be made soon, Barker was tempted to give greater delegation a try in his region. He liked the theoretical advantages that his professors had pointed out, but he was not totally convinced that he and the region were ready for increased delegation.

What should George Barker do?

NOTES

1. James D. Mooney and Alan C. Reiley, *Onward Industry: The Principles of Organization and Their Significance to Modern Industry* (New York: Harper & Brothers, 1931), p. 39.
2. Ibid., pp. 36–37.
3. Lyndall Urwick, *The Elements of Administration* (New York: Harper & Row, 1943), p. 51.
4. In their review of Philip Selznick's work, March and Simon discuss this bifurcation of interests. See James G. March and Herbert A. Simon, *Organizations* (New York: Wiley, 1958), pp. 41–42.
5. For further discussion, see Keith Davis and John Newstrom, *Human Behavior at Work: Organizational Behavior* (New York: McGraw-Hill, 1985), pp. 192–198.
6. Norman R.F. Maier, *Psychology in Industry* (Boston: Houghton Mifflin, 1946), pp. 264–266.
7. Lester Coch and J.T.P. French, Jr., "Overcoming Resistance to Change," *Human Relations* 1 (1948): 512–532.
8. A.C. Filley, R.J. House, and S. Kerr, *Managerial Process and Organizational Behavior* (Glenview, IL: Scott, Foresman, 1976). See also E.A. Locke et al., "The Relative Effectiveness of Four Methods of Motivating Employee Performance," in *Changes in Working Life*, ed. K.D. Duncan, M.M. Greenberg, and D. Wallis (New York: Wiley, 1980), pp. 363–387.
9. Katherine I. Miller and Peter R. Monge, "Participation, Satisfaction, and Productivity: A Meta-Analytic Review," *Academy of Management Journal* 29 (December 1986): 727–753. For an earlier review of over 50 empirical studies coming to essentially the same conclusion, see E.A. Locke and D.M. Schweiger, "Participation in Decision Making: One More Look," *Research in Organizational Behavior* 1 (1979): 265–339.
10. For further discussion of this point, see L.R. Hoffman and N.R.F. Maier, "Valence in the Adoption of Solutions by Problem Solving Groups: Quality and Acceptance As Goals of Leaders and Members," *Journal of Personality and Social Psychology* 6 (June 1967): 175–182.
11. Rensis Likert, *New Patterns of Management* (New York: McGraw-Hill, 1961), p. 103.
12. Richard Steers, "Antecedents and Outcomes of Organizational Commitment," *Administrative Science Quarterly* 22 (March 1977): 46–56.

13. M. Shaskin, "Changing Toward Participative Management Approaches: A Model and Methods," *Academy of Management Review* 1 (July 1976): 75–85.

14. For an examination of such situations, see Carrie R. Leana, "Predictors and Consequences of Delegation," *Academy of Management Journal* 29 (December 1986): 754–774.

15. R.E. Miles, *Theories of Management: Implications for Organizational Behavior and Development* (New York: McGraw-Hill, 1975), p. 83.

16. Peter Brownell, "Participative Management: The State of the Art," *Wharton Magazine* 7 (Fall 1982): 38–43.

17. Victor H. Vroom, "New Look at Managerial Decision Making," *Organizational Dynamics* 1 (Spring 1973): 66–80; Victor H. Vroom and Philip W. Yetton, *Leadership and Decision-making* (Pittsburgh: University of Pittsburgh Press, 1973); and Victor H. Vroom, "Can Leaders Learn to Lead?" *Organizational Dynamics* 4 (Winter 1976): 17–28.

ADDITIONAL READINGS

Arthur, Diane. "Guidelines for Effective Delegation." *Supervisory Management* 24 (October 1979): 9–13.

Baker, H. Kent, and Stevan H. Holmberg. "Stepping Up to Supervision: Mastering Delegation." *Supervisory Management* 26 (October 1981): 15–21.

Cosier, Richard A., and John C. Aplin. "Effects of Delegated Choice on Performance." *Personnel Psychology* 33 (Autumn 1980): 581–593.

Finney, Paul D. "Delegation and the Art of Accountability." *Management World* 10 (September 1981): 29–30.

Ford, Robert C. "Delegation Without Fear." *Supervisory Management* 28 (July 1983): 2–8.

Haynes, Marion E. "Delegation: There's More to It Than Letting Someone Else Do It!" *Supervisory Management* 25 (January 1980): 9–15.

Lagges, James G. "The Role of Delegation in Improving Productivity." *Personnel Journal* 58 (November 1979): 776–779.

Loban, Lawrence. "Delegation." *Supervision* 42 (October 1980): 5–7.

Michael, Stephen R. "Control, Contingency and Delegation in Decision-Making." *Training and Development Journal* 33 (February 1979): 36–42.

Montana, Patrick J., and Deborah F. Nash. "Delegation: The Art of Managing." *Personnel Journal* 60 (October 1981): 784–787.

Raudsepp, Eugene. "Why Managers Don't Delegate." *Journal of Applied Management* 4 (September/October 1979): 25–27.

Steinmetz, Lawrence L. *The Art and Skill of Delegation.* Reading, MA: Addison-Wesley, 1976.

Decentralization

The previous chapter presented the concept of delegation; the process of a boss releasing formal decision-making authority to a subordinate in a specified area. The major difference between delegation and decentralization is *degree of application.* Decentralization is, in effect, the adoption of delegation as an organization-wide philosophy and practice.

Delegation and decentralization usually go together, but not always. Within a decentralized organization, some managers may choose to delegate as little as possible. Within a centralized organization, some managers may delegate enthusiastically and extensively.

Since delegation and decentralization are similar in principle, the three major schools of organizational thought advance the same arguments for or against decentralization that they advanced for or against delegation. The classicists acknowledged that decentralization could have some practical benefits. The human relations school favored decentralization as a means of achieving greater employee participation in decision making. And the modern school recommends seeking a proper balance between centralization and decentralization.

CENTRALIZATION AND DECENTRALIZATION

As we use "centralization" and "decentralization," they are short terms for *centralization and decentralization of formal decision-making authority.* A centralized organization concentrates this authority at its very top levels. A decentralized organization releases much of this authority to lower organizational levels.

Different Meanings

Henry Mintzberg has pointed out that the term "decentralization" has three separate uses in organization theory literature.[1]

1. The dispersal of *formal* decision-making authority *down* through the hierarchy. In this sense of decentralization, it is synonymous with delegation in presuming that managers throughout the organization give decision-making authority in certain selected areas to subordinates. The organization becomes permeated with the philosophy of participation, which drives delegation.
2. The dispersal of *informal* decision-making authority *sideways*—away from the line managers in the hierarchy of authority and to the staff specialists and experts.
3. The dispersal of the organization's physical assets, services, and resources. This use of decentralization (or centralization) refers to geographic locations, not decision making. For example, a company may physically "decentralize" by placing warehouses all over the country, but a centralized computer network would permit all decisions affecting the warehouses to be made in the home office.

These three meanings for the same term sometimes lead to confusion. For our purposes, decentralization is the adoption of delegation as an organization-wide philosophy and practice.

How Decentralization Comes About

During the early stages of an organization's life, it will be highly centralized. The owner runs the basic activities—production, finance, sales—and hires specialists to handle functions like accounting, insurance, and advertising. As the organization expands, the owner adds other functions and hires people with expertise in such areas as personnel and marketing. At a certain point in this expansion, the owner must answer an important question: "Should I keep making all the decisions, or should I let subordinates make some of them?" In all likelihood, the owner will decide, at first, to let subordinates make certain routine operational decisions; later they may even be allowed to make some policy decisions as well. As this delegation process takes place throughout the organization, and especially when increasing size leads to geographic dispersion requiring remote control, the movement toward decentralization occurs.[2]

Implementing Decentralization   Both delegation and decentralization may occur for the same philosophical reason (the desire to involve subordinates in decisions that concern them) or the same practical reason (the need for greater decision-making participation due to larger size, increased complexity, or rapid change). But they differ considerably in implementation. Individual managers, in keeping with their own managerial styles and personal interests, can choose to delegate or not to delegate the authority to make certain decisions. In contrast, the decentralization process is *categorical:* decision making is pushed down through the organizational hierarchy, regardless of executive interests or preferences.

Decentralization and Control   Decentralization requires that formal authority to make operating decisions be given or assigned to organizational subunits. If the general course of these subunits is to be properly directed, the senior executive group needs a mechanism to control the subunits. If the operating units receive no direction from the CEO or executive group, they might (knowingly or unknowingly) engage in activities contrary to the interests of the organization as a whole.

For example, if GM's Delco subunit had complete decision-making autonomy without a GM review, what would prevent Delco from making nuclear reactors or toasters, rather than the batteries that GM needs? The federal nature of our government system causes similar problems for subdivisions that allow decentralized policy-making in certain areas while maintaining overall control. Whatever functions and authority are not specifically assigned to the national government are reserved to the states. Consequently, there are considerable variations in state laws, rules, and operational policies. Certain acts are crimes in one state but not in another, and the prison sentences for identical crimes vary widely from state to state—and in fact from judge to judge. These apparently unfair differences result from the decentralization of lawmaking in our country.

In the decentralized organization, control is usually achieved by means of either the holding-company concept or the profit-center concept, both pioneered at du Pont and broadened at General Motors. The specifics of control are achieved through information systems and formalized standards. Formalization—rules, job definitions, standard procedures, and specifications—promotes and enables decentralization. According to Peter M. Blau and Richard A. Schoenherr:

> Formalized standards that restrict the scope of discretion make decentralized decisions less precarious for effective management and coordination, which diminishes the reluctance of executives to delegate responsibilities way down the line to local managers far removed in space as well as in social distance from top management at the headquarters.[3]

To sum up, successful decentralization requires support throughout the organization for the philosophy of decentralization, as well as control mechanisms that guide the activities of subordinates and allow upper management to keep track of what the decentralized subunits are doing.

The Centralization/Decentralization Continuum

Discussions of centralization and decentralization tend to be in absolute terms. An observer may say, "That's a centralized company," or "The president changed over from a centralized organization to a decentralized one." As a matter of fact, both absolute centralization and absolute decentralization are virtually impossible.

Absolute Centralization   If an organization were absolutely centralized, subordinates would not have freedom of choice about anything and the top manager would make *every* decision. Can you imagine a top manager making decisions about the correct postage for every piece of mail, the size of brooms for maintenance, and the cafeteria menu as well as international expansion, a federal injunction, and a ten-state labor strike? Out of necessity, every organization is decentralized to some extent.

Until the 1980s, U.S. Steel was so highly centralized that, according to one production manager, even routine decisions "like starting up a blast furnace had to be approved on the 61st floor."[4] Partly as a result of this highly centralized structure, the company's share of the domestic steel market dropped drastically in 1982, and it lost $152 on every ton of steel shipped.

Absolute Decentralization   If authority in an organization were absolutely decentralized, anarchy would result as all employees, who had equal decision-making authority, took whatever actions they thought best. Under such circumstances, even if all employees tried sincerely to achieve their own job goals, overall effectiveness would probably be minimal and organizational goal achievement impossible.

In an attempt to turn its dismal 1982 performance around, U.S. Steel laid off staff people, eliminated layers of management, and turned its billion-dollar steel fabricating unit into a decentralized profit center. According to *Business Week,* "Its managers foundered. Everything from controlling labor costs and becoming marketers to managing their own balance sheet proved beyond their ken. The result: a $137 million operating loss in 1983."[5]

The members of the steel-fabricating profit center were sincerely *trying* to achieve the organization's goals by maximizing the performance of their own unit. Consider what chaos an organization would be in if its employees—all having great decision-making authority within their areas—were dishonest or just didn't care. The harmful possibilities increase dramatically. The organization can be hurt by decision makers who lack training, information, perspective, and intelligence, and also by decision makers who may be dishonest or apathetic.

In brief, we are looking at the *degree* to which lower organizational levels share in formal decision-making authority. Every organization must be centralized to some extent. Without a management staff to set goals and coordinate efforts toward their achievement, the organization's members and subunits might go their separate ways, with disastrous results.

The Continuum   The foregoing explanation suggests that we should speak about centralization and decentralization in *relative* terms. They are at opposite ends of a continuum. The relevant questions then become, "*How much* decentralization does ABC Company have?" or "*To what extent* has the president centralized XYZ Company?" or "Which decisions should be decentralized, and how far?"

Recentralization

A movement from less to more centralization is called *re*centralization: upper management takes back some of the authority that lower-level managers once had. Several factors can lead to recentralization.

Economic Distress   In times of economic distress or organizational decline, organizational leaders may feel a need to retrieve from lower-level managers and employees the authority to make important decisions. When the leaders are concerned about survival—of the organization and of themselves within it—they want to be able to make the decisions on which their fates depend.[6]

Dwindling Opportunities   A young, expanding organization tends to decentralize. Top managers face so many new challenges that they willingly pass down their old ones. As the growth rate levels off and new experiences decrease, managers begin taking back the responsibilities that they were once glad to get rid of. Everyone wants to look busy and useful to the organization so once the growth opportunities dwindle, people may stop delegating, start pulling authority back, and the organization moves into a recentralization phase.

Computer Networks

A technological development that has had great effect on centralization/decentralization decisions is the advent of inexpensive computer networks. These systems considerably diminish the communication gaps between the home office and field units. Upper-level managers can "control" many divisions and subunits via computer terminals.

As many firms grew and spread out geographically during the 1920s and 1930s, the return-on-investment decentralization method was a tremendous aid in controlling far-flung enterprises and keeping all organizational units heading toward the same goal. Now, desktop computer terminals allow the chief executive almost literally to look over the shoulders of all unit managers. As the enormous capacity of computers has provided more timely and accurate information, the top managers of large organizations see the possibility of reasserting their direct decision-making control over their entire enterprises.

The history of organizational development (and a look at your own experience) shows people's reluctance to share decision-making authority with others. Making the decisions yourself always seems better than trusting someone else to make them, especially if your boss is holding you accountable for results. When modern high-level managers can turn to terminals on their desks and punch up any information from any part of the organization at the same moment that unit managers can, those top managers may be strongly tempted to interject advice and make decisions for the unit managers. The lack of information technology made it imperative to give well-indoctrinated priests considerable decision-making autonomy as they travelled the ancient world doing the church's work. The availability of instant communications has made it highly tempting to reestablish centralized control from Rome.

The computer has made both centralization and decentralization easier to achieve. So decentralization, which was once necessary for control, may increasingly become a managerial expression of belief in the human relations philosophy. Even though technological advancements have made centralization easier, many organizations would do well to continue decentralizing. The young, well-educated managers entering business and industry today want to participate in decision making. Progressive firms will let them do so.

THE CLASSICAL PERSPECTIVE

The classical perspective on decentralization is probably predictable by now: Top managers are paid to make decisions and take responsibility for them; therefore, decentralization should be undertaken with caution. However, as organizations grew during the 1920s and 1930s, decentralization became necessary. The classicists accepted decentralization because they had to accept it as a method of retaining control over growing, widespread enterprises. As R.C. Davis has pointed out, "Decentralization usually is necessary for maximum economy and effectiveness when a wide geographical dispersion of activities requires remote control."[7] The managers of large organizations often decentralized *structurally*—into profit centers or subsidiary corporations, for example—and then did little further delegating or decentralizing within the newly created, semi-independent units.

Fayol's View   Henri Fayol recognized that centralization and decentralization are extremes on a continuum. He viewed centralization as a fact of nature, with some decentralization being necessary at times. He said:

> Like division of work, centralization belongs to the natural order; this turns on the fact that in every organism, animal or social, sensations converge towards the brain or directive part, and from the brain or directive part, orders are sent out which set all parts of the organism in movement. Centralization is not a system of management good or bad of itself, capable of being adopted or discarded at the whim of managers or of circumstances; it is always present to a greater or less extent. The question of centralization or decentralization is a simple question of proportion; it is a matter of finding the optimum degree for the particular concern.[8]

The problem posed in Fayol's last sentence continues to be the problem with which the systems/contingency theorists wrestle today.

Decentralization at General Motors

Perhaps no one organization is more responsible for developing, implementing, and popularizing the concept of structural decentralization than General Motors. Under the direction of President Alfred P. Sloan, Jr., and with the help of Donaldson Brown's financial wizardry, "decentralization" and "General Motors" became almost synonymous.

Sloan was a manager at Hyatt Roller Bearing when GM founder William Durant acquired that company. When the economic recession of 1918 hit the auto industry, Durant began getting stock market margin calls, and major GM stockholder Pierre du Pont forced him out and took control to save his own investment in GM stock. Sloan took that opportunity to write his now-famous memo to du Pont, showing him how to pull together the diverse pieces of the GM empire. The memo is a political masterpiece in that it promises to make the whole greater than the sum of its parts while at the same time it is not a threat to the autonomous managers of GM's divisions. It took the financial genius of Donaldson Brown to make it work. Brown had pioneered the return-on-investment concept discussed below at du Pont, and Sloan wanted to apply that concept at GM.

In the memo explaining the concept to Pierre du Pont in 1918, Sloan said:

The object of this study is to suggest an organization for the General Motors Corporation which will definitely place the line of authority throughout its extensive operations
as well as coordinate each branch of its service, at the same time destroying none
of the effectiveness with which its work has heretofore been conducted.

The basis upon which this study has been made is founded upon two principles, which
are stated as follows:

1. The responsibility attached to the chief executive of each operation shall in no way
   be limited. Each such organization headed by its chief executive shall be complete
   in every necessary function and enabled to exercise its full initiative and logical
   development.
2. Certain central organization functions are absolutely essential to the logical development and proper control of the Corporation's activities.[9]

These principles established the ideas of (1) independent operating divisions and (2) a
central office to coordinate and support the efforts of the independent divisions. Although Sloan recognized that these two principles contradict each other if taken
literally, he made the idea work.

In summing up that early study Sloan said, in 1972, that it

presented a specific structure for the corporation as it existed at that time. It recognized the form of the divisions, each of which was a self-contained group of functions
(engineering, production, sales). It grouped the divisions according to like activities
and . . . proposed to place an executive in charge of each group. The plan provided
for advisory staffs, which would be without line authority. It provided for a financial
staff. It distinguished policy from administration of policy and specified the location
of each in the structure. It expressed in its way the concept that was later to be
formulated as decentralized operations with coordinated control.[10]

Decentralization at General Motors served as a model for many other organizations
that saw the advantages of "decentralized operations with coordinated control."

In reviewing the history of organizations, the classicists saw that, despite some
theoretical disadvantages from their perspective, decentralization could succeed. The du
Pont and General Motors organizations had achieved so many benefits from decentralization that the concept had to become part of classical organization theory. Indeed, these
two organizations represented diametrically opposite uses of the concept. Du Pont used
it to decentralize a previously centralized organization; GM used it to organize and
recentralize, to some degree, an organization whose parts were so separate that it was
nearly off the decentralization continuum. So, the classicists conceded that when an
organization became very large, decentralization of the GM type could be appropriate.

Decentralization in Historical Perspective

As a major means for differentiating organizational authority, decentralization came
into its own following World War I. According to Alfred D. Chandler, Jr., who
published his administrative history of 50 large industrial firms in 1956, "This relatively
new type of decentralized, overall management structure has become a dominant
one."[11] Chandler goes on to explain that the growing complexity of operations during

the prosperous 1920s and 1940s—brought about by new product lines and markets, geographical expansion, and greater size—led to administrative problems best solved by decentralization. Companies retaining their tight, centralized structures tended to have little competition, grow slowly, and have one major product line.[12]

Decentralization and the Holding Company   Large organizations may contain complicated and varied, yet *unrelated,* major activities. Coordination requirements in such conglomerate forms of organization are typically only financial, much as a person might own a portfolio of different stocks. The various activities can be managed as independent operations, often as subsidiary companies, with the central coordinating headquarters being little more than a financial holding company—a company whose sole function is to hold or own other companies. Many modern conglomerates operate in this decentralized fashion, using financial performance measures such as profitability, return on investment, or deviation from budgets to evaluate both the management and each division's continued desirability in the portfolio.

The Profit-Center Approach

A common decentralization approach is to create profit centers, sometimes called ROI centers or budget centers. A profit center in effect functions as an independent company, except that it is part of a larger organization which establishes overall policy, allocates capital, hires, fires, and evaluates the profit center's top managers, and monitors the center's usefulness in reaching organizational goals. To house advertising, legal, public relations, and other specialists in the profit units might make little economic sense. Therefore, the larger parent organization frequently houses such support staff, providing them to the profit centers as needed.

Table 8.1 shows the effects of the profit-center decentralization approach on managers by contrasting the profit-center manager and the functional manager on several task dimensions.

General Motors Profit Centers   Two companies that pioneered in the use of profit centers are General Motors and du Pont. General Motors has long been made up of several product divisions. Top management determines what the market for each product is, what resources shall be allocated to each division, and what return they expect on those resources. They communicate these expectations to the product division managers.

Consider Bob Roberts, the hypothetical president of GM's Chevrolet division. He controls all of Chevrolet's assets and resources. He is expected to achieve a reasonable return on those divisional assets by selling automobiles in the lower-priced end of the automotive market. He has much autonomy. But—he cannot merge with Ford, make Oldsmobiles or Cadillacs, sell out to some wealthy Venezuelans, or donate Chevrolet's resources to the Salvation Army. The GM executive group holds Bob Roberts accountable for *making a profit by selling Chevrolets.*

du Pont's Profit Centers   As is true at GM, du Pont's profit centers have their own assets (and liabilities) and share general corporate resources, such as research laborato-

Table 8.1 PROFIT-CENTER MANAGERS AND FUNCTIONAL MANAGERS:
DIMENSIONS OF THE TASK

Dimensions	Profit-center manager	Functional manager
Strategic		
Orientation	Entrepreneurial	Professional
Relevant environment	External	Internal
Objective of task	Adaptability	Efficiency
Ambiguity of task	High	Low
Operational		
Responsibility	Broad, cross-functional	Specialized, single function
Authority	Less than responsibility	Equal to responsibility
Interdependence on others	May be high	Usually low
Performance evaluation		
Measurements	Profit, growth, return on investment	Costs, compared to standards or budgets
Quality of feedback	Slow, garbled	Rapid, accurate
Risks and rewards		
Risk of failure	Higher	Lower
Compensation potential	Higher	Lower

Source: Richard F. Vancil, *Decentralization: Managerial Ambiguity by Design* (Homewood, IL: Dow Jones-Irwin, 1978), p. 122. Used by permission.

ries and headquarters buildings, with other profit centers. The du Pont organization expects that each divisional manager will achieve a rate of return on allocated assets that is commensurate with the du Pont profit plan.

Du Pont measures profit center success in terms of *return on investment* (ROI). The du Pont system is diagrammed in Figure 8.1. If ROI falls below the targeted level, then the du Pont corporate staff and the profit-center staff work together to find out why the figure is off. Improving the unsatisfactory ROI figure may require marketing, managerial, and/or production changes.

Senior du Pont managers use target ROI as a basis for evaluating and rewarding profit-center managers. Upper management also uses ROI as a standard for allocating resources. Those profit centers with a high ROI this year will receive more resources next year. Profit-center managers are highly motivated to achieve or exceed their target ROI, for obvious reasons.

Strategic Business Units A recently developed subtype of the profit center is the *strategic business unit* (SBU). According to *Business Week,* these SBUs are

> self-contained businesses that meet three criteria: They have a set of clearly defined external competitors, their managers are responsible for developing and implementing their own strategies, and their profitability can be measured in real income, rather than in artificial dollars, posted as transfer payments between divisions.[13]

This new concept focuses attention on the large-scale potential of profit centers to fulfill the entrepreneurial instincts of highly achievement-oriented managers. SBUs are an opportunity for managers to feel that they are "running their own businesses" and to

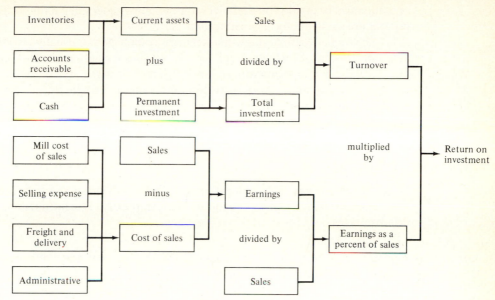

Figure 8.1   The du Pont system of financial control.

be evaluated on objective, market-based performance. Most corporations conjure up the image of a tepid organization man in a grey flannel suit. In contrast, the SBU notion suggests excitement and opportunity.

Decentralization and Unitary Organization

The history of organizations suggests that differentiating by a unitary departmentalization scheme (such as by product) makes decentralization relatively easy. If the firm does not base decentralization on product, customer, region, or other easily identifiable divisions, it will not have any logical basis for using ROI as a performance standard.

Usefulness of Return on Investment   ROI is a useful management tool. Since any profit center resembles a miniature company within the larger organization, the control/performance standard is that small company's ROI. If the profit center is responsible for its own product (rather than merely helping the larger organization make or sell its one product line), then the competitive marketplace will determine whether the profit center is performing well.

For instance, if one Burger King store is more profitable than another or than a McDonald's in the same area, then the first Burger King manager is probably doing a better job than the other managers. Since Burger King is a division of General Mills, the performance of the Burger King division manager can be similarly measured by comparing that division's performance with the ROI of other General Mills divisions or competing burger franchises. Decentralization is made easy because (1) the entire operation can be divided into relatively autonomous geographic units, and (2) objective criteria are available for evaluating unit performance.

The single-location, single-market organization cannot usually be subdivided into autonomous units for which an objective performance measure (such as ROI) is available. All units at the location must work together to make and sell their products. If the french-fry, hamburger, and soft-drink functions at a single Burger King store were all ROI centers competing for the same customers, imagine the chaos, conflict, and confusion that would result.

Benefits and Disadvantages

Decentralization has philosophical appeal. Decentralization can help keep managers from being overwhelmed by organizational complexity. Decentralization also has its disadvantages.

Benefits   According to Peter Drucker, GM executives in the 1940s reported several primary benefits of decentralization:

1. Fast decisions, and common knowledge of who makes them and the policies on which they are based, all preceded by discussion. No "edict management."
2. Absence of conflict between divisional and GM interests.
3. Fair dealing, appreciation of good work, and reduction of personality issues, intrigues, and factionalism.
4. Democratic, informal management. People speak freely before decisions are made, then support them.
5. No gap in executive group between the privileged few and the others. President and associates all have the same rights.
6. Large management group; many experienced people available to take on top responsibilities.
7. Accountability for all; weak divisions and managers can't hide.[14]

Considering the arguments favoring decentralization in general and profit centers in particular, how can any multiproduct, humanistic organization decline to decentralize?

Costs   Several costs are often associated with decentralization:

1. Decentralization often requires more managers, with possible cost duplication.
2. Decentralization requires more elaborate information systems, so that top managers can effectively monitor the decentralized operations.
3. Since fewer decisions are made at the top (where experience in decision making is greatest), the chances of costly, bad decisions increase.
4. Equipping lower-level personnel to make decisions means additional training costs and subsequently higher-quality, more expensive employees.

Short-Run Profit-making Myopia   Another disadvantage of decentralization is short-run profit-making myopia. Profit-center managers tend, perhaps naturally, to focus on immediate rather than long-range results. Top management expects each profit-center manager to maintain or increase profits; therefore, managers try to make short-run ROI look good. Yet, an emphasis on short-run profits at the expense of the firm's long-run welfare can cause irreparable harm.

John Dearden offers four common situations that can lead to an overemphasis on short-run results:

1. A company decentralizes in order to increase profits. The profit-center managers know that a quick way to increase profits is to cut costs, so they may let the research and development group go—sacrificing important long-term needs in order to improve the next period's ROI.
2. Top management replaces a division manager because the division has not achieved its target ROI. The new manager thinks strictly in terms of a quick fix, which may not benefit the overall organization.
3. A divisional manager hears a rumor that she is "on the skids." She figures that she has nothing to lose and so adopts an attitude of "Damn the torpedoes; full speed ahead!" Her strategy is to show immediate results, to think "Don't worry about tomorrow because I may not be here." Improper planning and resource allocation may result.
4. A profit center has been meeting its targets, but the new manager wants to make a name for himself. He therefore takes any means available to do so. Such managers are dangerous; they place their own egos and personal success above the well-being of the organization and fellow workers.[15]

Adjustments for New Products   Problems may arise using ROI as a strict criterion for evaluation and reward. As one example, introducing a new product line will make some subjective adjustment of the target ROI necessary, to account for unusual expenses and inadequate return in the early stages of bringing a new product to market. Seldom will the new product's ROI match the ROI of a well-established, successful product because of the associated start-up costs and initial investment costs. If new products are compared with established products, the inclination will be to withdraw from new products since their initial ROIs will be low.

Allocating Costs and Resources   Even if an organization establishes profit centers, allocating costs and resources can still be a problem. Consider a department store that arranges its products into miniature boutiques. These boutiques compete against each other on a profit-center basis. They should share certain overhead expenses: the store manager's salary, light bill, rent, fire insurance, and so on. But how is the overhead to be divided up? If it is apportioned by profit-center sales volume, then a section like jewelry, with high dollar volume but small floor space, may be asked to pay a disproportionate part of the store's lighting costs. On the other hand, if overhead is partitioned by floor space, a department like children's clothes with large floor space may overpay (relative to the jewelry section) for overhead costs. GM and du Pont have these same difficulties in allocating costs.

Allocating resources can also cause problems. Consider a drugstore with a camera department. The camera department may take up less floor space than the drug section; yet in a given period, the sales volume of cameras may be higher than the sales volume of drugs. Based on sales volume, the camera manager might argue for a larger allocation of an important resource: floor space. If the camera department gets more and more floor space, and uses it to sell more and more cameras, the eventual result might be a drugstore with no drugs.

Transfer Pricing   The preceding discussion illustrates how difficult the allocation of costs and resources to profit centers can become. There is also a potential tendency for profit-center goals to obscure overall organizational goals. This problem can occur in transfer pricing.

Transfer pricing is the process of establishing the price for a product that one organizational subunit makes and then sells (or transfers) to another subunit of the same organization. Buick needs batteries for its cars. GM has decided that its Buick division must buy batteries from its Delco division. Determining what price Buick pays can be a sticky issue. Buick and Delco must negotiate a battery price. Buick wants to buy the batteries as cheaply as possible. Delco wants to sell at the highest price. Success or failure at battery price negotiation will be reflected in profit-center performance—and perhaps in the better negotiator's bonus check.

Perhaps GM should let Buick request competitive bids from all battery manufacturers. Imagine that Sears offers to supply Die-Hard's at a cheaper price than Delco's. Sears will increase its profits, Buick will decrease its costs, and the experience will provide discipline for Delco's management. But GM's annual profits may decline if Delco's battery-making facilities are idle because of lower demand.

Lack of a Reference Market   A "reference market" for batteries exists, a market with which GM, Delco, and Buick can compare Delco's battery prices. Even so, as we just saw, establishing a fair transfer price is not easy. When no reference market exists, the problem is that much more difficult.

One group at Buick assembles engines, and another group uses those engines in the assembly of complete cars. How much should the car assembly group pay the engine assembly group for each engine? The engine represents the cost of its parts (paid for by the engine assembly group to the various parts groups) plus the value of the engine assembly group's labor, so the fair engine price would include both costs. If the engine assembly group paid "too much" for parts because of high transfer prices, then the transfer price it charges the car assembly group will be higher than it ought to be—which will affect the performance of the car assembly "profit center." Many other complications may be out of the car assembly group's control but still affect the price it pays for engines: the engine assembly group may be stuck with an unfavorable labor agreement, the engine assemblers may be inexperienced, the physical facilities for engine assembly may be dilapidated, and so on.

Cost Plus   One solution to these difficulties is to use a "cost plus" system: the engine assembly group would simply calculate its cost to assemble an engine and charge that price plus a "fair" profit to the automobile assembly group. However, this offers no incentive for the engine assemblers to be efficient. There is also no objective measure on which to evaluate the engine assembly group managers. Since the group can pass along all of its costs, so what if it pays $3, $10, or even $30 for a piston rod? Group managers know they are going to get profits anyway since they merely total up their costs and add on the gravy.

Standard Cost   Another solution to the transfer pricing problem is to use a standard cost. GM industrial engineers would examine machine costs, labor costs, capital costs, administrative costs and would then establish a "standard cost" for making a specific engine in a specific plant. Upper management would evaluate the engine assembly manager on how close actual cost was to standard cost.

All of these solutions to the transfer pricing problem can work. But no one yet has seriously suggested that the cooks in GM's cafeterias should "sell" their output to the serving people on a transfer price basis. At some point, attempts to determine the costs involved at each stage of interdependent operations become ridiculous.

Top managers do not get to be top managers by being ignorant of the disadvantages inherent in decentralizing by setting up profit centers. They know the dangers and must be astute enough managerially to achieve decentralization's benefits while avoiding its pitfalls.

GM, Decentralization, and the Modern Era

General Motors pioneered the use of decentralization as a way of maintaining control and accountability. Despite the difficulties in allocating costs and resources, the GM model of decentralization has been widely imitated. But how applicable is this "classical" model to the modern organization?

According to Peter Drucker, not very applicable. By far the largest revenue source for GM is the making of cars that differ only in details. Drucker says:

> By contrast, the typical businesses today are multiproduct, multitechnology, and multimarket. They may not be conglomerates, but they are diversified. And their central problem is a problem General Motors did not have: the organization of complexity and diversity.
>
> There is, moreover, an even more difficult situation to which the GM pattern cannot be applied: the large single-product, single-technology business that, unlike GM, cannot be subdivided into distinct and yet comparable parts. Typical are the "materials" businesses such as steel and aluminum companies. Here belong, also, the larger transportation businesses, such as railroads, airlines, and the large commercial banks. These businesses are too big for a functional structure; it ceases to be a skeleton and becomes a straitjacket. They are also incapable of being genuinely decentralized; no one part on its own is a genuine "business." Yet as we are shifting from mechanical to process technologies, and from making goods to pro-

ducing knowledge and services, these large, complex, but integrated businesses are becoming more important than the multidivisional businesses of the 1920s and 1930s.[16]

Drucker sums up his account of the GM model's disadvantages by saying: "Today's organizer is challenged by an increasing demand to organize entrepreneurship and innovation. But for this undertaking, the General Motors model offers no guidance."[17]

THE HUMAN RELATIONS PERSPECTIVE

True Participation

Like delegation, decentralization involves the downward movement of formal decision-making authority within the organization. Since the human relations school strongly favored the delegation of authority from one individual to another, they of course favored the organization-wide practice of delegation that organizational decentralization encourages.

The human relations school approved of decentralization for the same reasons (expressed in Chapter 7) that they approved of delegation. They argued for as much employee participation in decision making, and therefore as much decentralization of authority, as possible. And, decentralization of authority must be *genuine,* not simply cosmetic. Real decision-making power must reside in lower employee levels, not just in the profit-center managers. True, policy decisions must remain with top management. But operational decisions should be made as close to their point of impact as possible, in the view of the human relations proponents.

Criticisms of the Human Relations Perspective

Among the criticisms leveled at the human relations theorists on decentralization, two stand out.

Costs   First, the costs of participation in the decentralized organization may outweigh its benefits. Three costs are:

1. Programs needed to train supervisory personnel in newly decentralized, participative organizations are expensive.
2. Decentralized, participatory decision making can lead to costly time lags in the decision-making process.
3. In a participatory organization, secrecy is minimal; "leaks" may give competitors expensive advantages.

Desire for Authority   From the human relations perspective, managers in decentralized organizations should willingly relinquish authority to subordinates and to lower organizational levels. Opponents say that giving up authority willingly is contrary to the typical manager's nature. Indeed, one reason for wanting to be a manager is often a desire for authority and responsibility. If such managers are forced to give up authority through decentralization, they may be dissatisfied and ineffective. They may also quit.

These criticisms need to be addressed before attempting participative management throughout a decentralized organization.

THE MODERN PERSPECTIVE

The classical school favored centralization of authority but eventually accepted structural decentralization into product divisions and profit centers. The human relations school favored decentralization of decision-making authority for the benefit of both the organization and its people. As usual, the modern perspective is that "it all depends."

The systems/contingency proponents leave themselves open to charges of indecisiveness, but they are just being realistic. Each organizational system is unique and ever-changing; each organizational system operates in a unique, ever-changing environment. Therefore, trying to apply *general* principles of centralization/decentralization to *particular* organizations is unwise and can even be harmful.

Decentralization Guidelines: Major Factors

We are not dealing with absolutes but with a centralization/decentralization continuum. The organization's problem is to find its own best balance between centralization and decentralization. Several factors influence whether an organization can, or must, decentralize. Among them are organizational size, technology, and environment—three major subjects to be covered later in separate chapters.

Size   As an organization becomes larger by adding personnel, top management's ability to control activities becomes strained. Simply knowing what's going on becomes more difficult, as does making decisions based on that knowledge. In order to solve the communication and decision-making problems that accompany increasing size, top management is likely to let go of some decision-making authority. If most of the new people are specialists or skilled workers, or if the new people are merely added to existing functions, management may simply *delegate* some authority downward. But if new people also mean new functions, units, departments, and divisions, then an organization-wide push toward *decentralization* may be called for.[18]

Technology   Technological advances often result, more or less naturally, in decentralization. An organization's technological requirements may become so complex that they are beyond management's ability to comprehend them. Nuclear engineers, research and development scientists, pioneering doctors, or other experts, depending on the organization, must be hired to design, create, and operate the new technologies. These experts must have enough freedom to design their new products, create their new inventions, or perform the latest surgical marvels. Since higher-level managers can not possibly keep up with the specialized expertise of these subordinates, some decentralization is inevitable.

Environment   If the middle and lower levels of an organization operate in a rapidly changing, complex, competitive, hostile, or crisis environment, they must have the authority to adapt to conditions. A hospital's board of directors does not have meetings to discuss steps that emergency room personnel should take on a particular Saturday night; the board allows its medical specialists in the emergency room to make these life-and-death decisions. Likewise, a corporation trying to sell products in a highly competitive area may realize that centralized pricing decisions are too slow. Therefore, salespeople in the field may be granted the authority (within limits) to adjust prices quickly if competitors make price changes.

Some organizations operate in more stable environments. When change takes place slowly, upper management has time to identify problems, consider many alternatives, gather information, and analyze thoroughly before acting. In this type of environment, a centralized organization can work well. Colleges and universities are examples of organizations whose environments are usually stable. Decisions about whether to add a school of law, raise tuition, or change to the trimester system can be made slowly and carefully.

According to Henry Mintzberg, the nature of the environment—whether it is simple or complex, stable or dynamic—has major importance in centralization/decentralization decisions.[19] If the environment is *simple and stable,* a centralized bureaucracy may work best. The simplicity of the work, often unskilled manufacturing work, and the standardization of products and processes make coordination at the top of the hierarchy possible. The environment's stability permits a bureaucratic structure to work well. If the environment is *complex and stable,* a decentralized bureaucracy may be called for. The work is predictable, so work processes can be standardized. But, the work is highly skilled and difficult, so decision-making authority must be decentralized. Typical decentralized bureaucracies are hospitals and universities, both with many professional employees.

If the environment is *simple and dynamic,* a centralized organic form—like an entrepreneurship—may be appropriate. Environmental simplicity permits tight control and direct supervision by the entrepreneur. The dynamic aspect of the environment demands a flexible, organic form rather than a slow-reacting bureaucracy. Finally, a *complex and dynamic* environment usually requires a decentralized, organic structure. NASA used such an organizational structure to put a man on the moon.

Further Guidelines

The organization trying to decide where it should fall on the centralization/decentralization continuum can consider several further guidelines.[20] They are, of course, similar to the delegation guidelines discussed in the previous chapter.

Measurability of Results   The profit-center approach to decentralization is so attractive because it simultaneously (1) gives decision-making power to subordinate levels of the organization and (2) maintains upper-management control. Busy senior executives perceive that they can get relief from their hectic work pace without losing control over what's going on.

Bosses recognize that they are responsible and accountable for the performance of subordinate units. They are more comfortable about delegating authority if they have a mechanism to ensure that they can effectively monitor the performance of subordinates. The divisionalized profit-center approach facilitates the decentralization of decision-making power without sacrificing control. If the standard ROI criterion is unavailable or inappropriate as a measure of results, then decentralization is more difficult.

Even if clear-cut performance measures are not available, decentralization can work—if employees fully understand organizational goals, identify with them, and are willing to work hard to achieve them. Just because results cannot be measured in dollar terms is no reason for an organization to remain highly centralized.

Availability of Information   Who has the information necessary for making a decision? How long will it take and how much will it cost to communicate that information to other potential decision makers, as decentralization would require? Authority should not be forced on people to whom necessary decision-making information is not customarily available. As a matter of fact, studies show that decentralized authority will tend to stop at that level where the needed information *can* be accumulated. People below that level simply will not accept authority because they don't feel that they know enough, or can find out enough, to make good decisions.

Ability of Decision Makers   Who has the ability—the training, knowledge, experience, and personal qualities—to make the decision? Although computer operators have their preferences, they may know nothing about electronics or cost/benefit analysis and should probably not decide which computing equipment to buy. On the other hand, the general manager would be foolish *not* to let the MIS director make the decision about the computing equipment, because that person does have the required expertise.

Timeliness of Decisions   How fast must decisions be made? Especially in retail businesses, changes in market conditions or social trends require rapid responses. Decentralization lends itself to quick decision making at lower levels, where it may be essential. A decentralized retail organization can capitalize on a trend while the lower-level managers of its centralized competitor are still consolidating and analyzing data, before forwarding it up the chain of command to the senior-level policymakers.

Consistency Required   How important is consistency in organizational decision making? If Mr. or Ms. Big makes all of the decisions, they will probably be more consistent than if numerous people make decisions. The more decision makers an organization has, the less likely it is that decisions will be consistent and uniform.

Coordination Required   At what level must decisions be made for the organization to function at its best? An organization whose activities or departments require the coordination of many elements cannot readily decentralize authority. For example, GM cannot let each group on the Buick assembly line decide when to come to work. When an organization's tasks and activities are interdependent, authority must be largely centralized. When tasks are independent and autonomous, decentralization may be appropriate.

Significance of Decisions   How significant is the decision to the organization's long-term welfare? Will it affect only a small part of the operation, or will it have impact on the whole organization? Top managers must learn to distinguish between levels of decision significance. The U.S. State Department may have little decentralization of decision-making authority, while the Department of Transportation may have a lot. Further, some types of decisions at State—such as policy toward Greenland—may be decentralized while other types are tightly centralized.

Effect on Morale   What effect will decentralization have on morale and on-the-job initiative? The organization should not damage managerial morale by giving managers more authority than they feel equipped to exercise effectively.

On the other hand, most people like to participate in making decisions that affect their jobs. As many high-technology companies have learned, decentralization of decision making often improves morale and initiative. Centralization can have the opposite effect. In J. Patrick Wright's *On a Clear Day You Can See General Motors,* John De Lorean explains what happened in 1969 when top management overruled the engineering staff's suggestions for a small car. The result was that nobody in the Chevrolet division cared about the Vega that top management actually decided to build.

> We were to start building the car in little more than a year, and nobody wanted anything to do with it. The Vega was an orphan. Chevy's engineering staff was disgruntled because it felt it had proposed a much better car (and it had) than the one it was given by the corporate management. It was going through the motions of preparing the car for production, and that was all. Engineers are a very proud group. They take immense interest and pride in their creations, but they are very disinclined to accept the work of somebody else. This was not their car, so they did not want to work on it.[21]

Management Philosophy   Some people feel the need to be in control of everything all the time. Managers who don't trust or won't depend on others have their favorite expressions: "If you want a job done right, you've got to do it yourself" or "You just can't get good help anymore." Decentralization can work only in an atmosphere of trust. Authoritarian managers decentralize only out of necessity. Even if all indicators suggest that an organization could benefit from decentralization, its prevailing management philosophy may cause it to remain centralized. The move to decentralization may have to wait until the retirement of domineering, authoritarian managers.

For many years, Eastman Kodak Co. was highly centralized. Although a leader in the photography business, its slow way of operating enabled competitors to take and maintain the lead in instant photography, 35mm cameras, and videocassette recorders. Finally, in 1985 the company reorganized its photography business into 17 entrepreneurial units. The old functional structure gave way to one in which unit managers oversee all aspects of the unit's products. Top management in Rochester, N.Y. has adopted a management style that encourages unit managers and management teams of subsidiary ventures to take more risks. Kodak hopes that these structural changes will enable the company's profit levels to bounce back.[22]

With training and encouragement, management styles and organizational structures *can* change. Managers can learn the benefits of decentralization and of having more confidence in subordinates.

The New Entrepreneurship   Kodak's 17 product groups typify an emerging trend: the creation within large organizations of decentralized, relatively autonomous units that capture one primary human-relations advantage of decentralized decision-making structures. The term used is *intrapreneurship,* an attempt to create entrepreneurial flair, creativity, and excitement within a large organization.

Although the intense interest in entrepreneurship is new, the concept is not. Organizations have frequently established special groups as vehicles for creating products and services. Indeed, Peter Drucker argued years ago for this basic idea. Drucker recognized that innovative units needed to be set up as separate "businesses," rather than as "functions" within the larger organization. He said:

> One way to organize innovative units within a large business might well be to group them together into an innovative group, which reports to one member of top management who has no other function but to guide, help, advise, review, and direct the innovating team at work. This is, in effect, what the DuPont Development Department is. Innovation has its own logic, which is different from the logic of an ongoing business. No matter how much the innovative units may themselves differ in their technologies, their markets, their products, or their services, they all have in common that they are innovative.
>
> Even such autonomous team organization may be too restricted for the kind of innovation that will increasingly be needed, innovation in fields that are quite different from anything that business has done so far. We may need to set up the innovating unit as a genuine entrepreneur.[23]

Large organizations, troubled by their lack of quick, flexible responses to new ideas, markets, and technologies have begun to encourage such entrepreneurship from within. They see these entrepreneurial units as a way to develop their own future rather than paying a high price for a fledgling organization founded by a creative entrepreneur on the outside. By funding their own entrepreneurial efforts, large organizations can encourage new ideas and can participate fully in the profits of success.

Decentralization and Performance   The various decentralization guidelines, principles, and models need to be considered together, since they may contradict each other. The desire for consistency and speed, for instance, may best be met by centralized decision making. Yet decentralized decision making or the formation of an entrepreneurial unit may vastly improve the morale of lower-level managers and would-be entrepreneurs. Once again, organizations must consider both the *dollar* costs and benefits and the *human* costs and benefits in determining the proper centralization/ decentralization balance.

The human relations benefits of decentralization are plain. Emerging evidence suggests that decentralization also has bottom-line benefits. After reviewing the literature on structure and performance, Dan R. Dalton and associates conclude tentatively that "centralization is negatively associated with performance." Although performance data from varied organizational groups are scarce, "the limited evidence tends to support a negative relationship between centralization and performance for managers and professionals in studies using hard performance criteria."[24]

Two Sets of Findings

We conclude this chapter by examining the sets of findings about decentralization by two scholars. Based on their studies, they have drawn some conclusions about when to decentralize.

In *The Fundamentals of Top Management* (1951), R.C. Davis concluded that decentralization is most effective and economical in large, stable, functionally complex, physically dispersed organizations with competent decentralized managers and operators of high morale. Decentralization is less necessary if communication is fast and reliable, and if standardization is high. Decentralization is less desirable if emergencies are frequent.[25]

Writing 25 years later, Pradip N. Khandwalla drew quite similar conclusions. Khandwalla also viewed decentralization as appropriate in large organizations with variable, nonstandard tasks. Additionally, he maintained that a competitive environment and a top management interested in employee morale and decision-making participation as well as in efficiency would encourage decentralization and promote its success.

R.C. Davis thought that the effective and economical degree of decentralization would vary inversely with communication capabilities; faster and more accurate communication would make decentralization less necessary. Khandwalla saw not an inverse relationship but a direct one. He said, "The more comprehensive and sophisticated the control and information system, the more decentralized is decision making in the organization."[26]

SUMMARY

Decentralization of organizational authority often comes about simply because the organization becomes so large that control by one owner/entrepreneur is impossible. Although philosophically opposed to the downward movement of authority, the classicists eventually accepted structural decentralization as a helpful way of simultaneously differentiating authority and maintaining upper-management control. Profit centers of the sort set up by General Motors and du Pont served as models for classical thinkers.

Decentralization in organizations departmentalized on some unitary basis, such as by product, customer, or region, is relatively simple. Even so, organizations will want to weigh the advantages and disadvantages carefully before decentralizing.

The human relations school was as philosophically in favor of decentralization as the classical school was philosophically opposed. From the human relations perspective, involving employees in making decisions that affect them has both human and organizational benefits.

From the modern perspective, neither centralization nor decentralization is inherently desirable or undesirable. The organizational system must consider such elements of its unique situation as its size, technology, environment, measurability of results, availability of information, ability of decision makers, timeliness and significance of decisions, the organization's need for consistency and coordination, the state of organizational morale, and management philosophy—all of which vary from organization to organization, and, in fact, from day to day within each organization. Deciding how much or how little to decentralize is difficult. But no one ever claimed that making major organizational decisions is easy.

DISCUSSION QUESTIONS

1. Is delegation possible without decentralization? Is decentralization possible without delegation?
2. What is decentralization? How is it related to authority?
3. What is the relationship between technology (particularly the computer) and decentralization?
4. What is recentralization? What factors lead to it?
5. What is the classical perspective on decentralization?
6. What is the role of the profit-center approach in decentralization?
7. Why is decentralization relatively easy to achieve in an organization that uses a unitary departmentalization scheme?
8. What are some of decentralization's disadvantages? How can they be overcome?
9. From the human relations viewpoint, why are the arguments in favor of delegation and decentralization essentially the same?
10. What are the criticisms of the human relations perspective on decentralization?
11. What are the major guidelines for using decentralization?
12. What is decentralization's customary effect on morale?
13. As organizations move to centralized data bases, what will the effect on decentralization be?
14. How do a profit-center manager and a functional manager differ? Which would you rather be?
15. Decentralization's effectiveness tends to vary directly with what factors? With what factors does it tend to vary inversely?

■ MULTIPRODUCTS CORPORATION

MultiProducts Corporation is an enormous, highly diversified company with 18 operating divisions, each set up as a profit center. The vice presidents in charge of the divisions have great autonomy; subject to the broad policies established at company headquarters, they run their divisions as they see fit. The target ROI of each profit center is 12 percent.

The divisional vice presidents are paid a low base salary but can receive large bonuses under the company's incentive compensation plan. Bonuses in the $100,000 to $200,000 range are not unusual for successful vice presidents. After the company's annual profits are known, the "excess contributions to profits" of the vice presidents—contributions of each division over and above the 12 percent target—are calculated and used as the basis for annual bonuses. Vice presidents regularly achieving no more than the targeted 12 percent do not stick around long.

Discuss the short-term and long-term advantages and disadvantages of the incentive compensation plan to MultiProducts Corporation. Should the company consider abandoning the plan and paying the vice presidents a substantial straight salary with no bonus? How far down the organization do you think such profit-center and bonus arrangements should go?

THE MARTIN GIBSON COMPANY

The Martin Gibson Company is the nation's largest producer and seller of stringed musical instruments and supplies. The company is vertically integrated; it owns the forests that supply the wood for musical instruments, makes the products, and handles their wholesale distribution. Instruments are made at 11 plants located throughout the East and Southeast. Each plant manufactures a different product.

Reporting directly to President Gibson are the vice presidents of four areas: marketing, production, finance, and employee relations. The plant managers report to the vice president of production, and the people in charge of marketing, finance, and employee relations report to their counterpart vice presidents in the home office.

The Martin Gibson board of directors is considering a reorganization to improve operating efficiency. A few directors want to leave things as they are. Some directors want all plant personnel to report to the plant managers, who in turn would report to a new executive vice president. All communications to and from the plants would pass through the plant manager. Other directors want a different vice president to be responsible for each product line. One director has said, "I'm not sure yet exactly how we should reorganize; I just know that we've got to decentralize."

Evaluate the various ideas about reorganization. Recommend a reorganization plan for the Martin Gibson Company, with accompanying organization chart.

AT THE COUNTRY CLUB

While waiting to tee off at the country club, Lillian Hollowell and Sarah Dinsmore were arguing about computers. Hollowell, president of Conglomerate Industries, spoke this way:

"Sarah, I don't know what I did before I got my desktop computer. Now I can combine company info with outside data bases. I can convert reams of numbers into colorful charts and graphs that my managers can easily understand. I can use my computer as an electronic mailbox to send reports, memos, and drafts simultaneously to many people. To sum up, the computer has enabled me to decentralize and delegate, *and* have more time for golf. I don't have to depend any longer on summary reports from my finance department. I have instant access to my company's data base, so I can call up info on current and past performance of any of my subsidiaries, along with comparative industry and economic information from outside data bases. If I see something out of the ordinary, I can get right to the subsidiary president responsible and check it out, or hold a teleconference with several managers."

Sarah Dinsmore, president of International Financial Group, wasn't persuaded. "I want no part of the computer. The blasted things churn out a ton of information, but I still can't get immediate, pertinent views and facts. I've tried three different systems and I despised them all. If you want to do anything beyond the simplest operation, you need to be very familiar with the machine. I don't have the time to gain that familiarity, so I've turned my link in our current system over to my executive assistant. She knows how to run it and so I don't think I'll ever need to learn."

Will Sarah Dinsmore be able to function effectively for very long with this attitude, or will she eventually have to learn how to use the computer as a means to decentralize and delegate?

COMPUTEX INTERNATIONAL

After a decade of centralized operations, Computex International decentralized. The company's basic profit-and-loss unit was redefined to encompass a complete business, and the manager of each business was given control of all resources—people, capital, and facilities—needed to take its products from conception to sales.

After decentralization, CI's managers were measured on two separate profit lines: operating profit (the raw profit generated from operations) and organization profit (the bottom line after subtracting research and development expenses). Under this arrangement, managers could not solve their day-to-day financial problems by cutting back on R&D.

Gloria Forgan, president of Computex International, explained her philosophy this way: "At CI, we have firm financial controls at the top. We don't try to make product decisions; that's for the group managers. The only thing we control tightly is resource allocations. If a business is running well, I leave it alone. But if a group gets into trouble, I step in."

In an off-the-record comment, group manager Warren Hodges expressed a contrary perspective: "Yeah, Forgan leaves us alone if profits stick close to the 20 percent growth curve, but if you slip, she's all over you. I just can't make great things happen in my group if I have to review every little item with Forgan. She's an A-1 second-guesser. You do best around here if you tell her what she wants to hear. She comes into your office like a holy terror. She'll give you 30 seconds for your side, then she'll totally change your group's direction in an instant. This morning, without my knowledge, she approved a multimillion-dollar production equipment purchase that's going to cause me to throw out my whole manufacturing strategy and start over. Sure, my operating results over the past year aren't what I wish they had been, but is that any reason for her to storm in here and take over everything?"

Evaluate decentralization at Computex International. Does Gloria Forgan seem to be interfering in the activities of the profit-and-loss units, or is she simply exercising her responsibility as company president to correct a group's problems?

NOTES

1. Henry Mintzberg, *The Structuring of Organizations: A Synthesis of Research* (Englewood Cliffs, NJ: Prentice-Hall, 1979), pp. 185–186.
2. For further discussion of how increasing size tends to stimulate decentralization, see James D. Mooney and Alan C. Reiley, *Onward Industry: The Principles of Organization and Their Significance to Modern Industry* (New York: Harper & Brothers, 1931), pp. 514–515; see also Alfred D. Chandler, Jr., "Management Decentralization: An Historical Analysis," *Business History Review* 30 (June 1956): 281–282.
3. Peter M. Blau and Richard A. Schoenherr, *The Structure of Organizations* (New York: Basic Books, 1971), p. 121.
4. *Business Week,* 25 February 1985, p. 51.

5. Ibid., p. 54.

6. Henry Mintzberg, *The Structuring of Organizations,* pp. 185–186.

7. R.C. Davis, *The Fundamentals of Top Management* (New York: Harper & Brothers, 1951), p. 304.

8. Henri Fayol, *General and Industrial Management,* trans. Constance Storrs (London: Pitman, 1949), p. 33.

9. Alfred P. Sloan, Jr., *My Years with General Motors* (Garden City, NY: Doubleday, 1972), p. 57.

10. Ibid., pp. 59–60.

11. Alfred D. Chandler, Jr., "Management Decentralization: An Historical Analysis," p. 170.

12. Ibid., pp. 170–171.

13. *Business Week,* 1 March 1982, p. 112.

14. Peter Drucker, *The Concept of the Corporation* (New York: New American Library, 1964), p. 51. (Originally published in 1946.)

15. John Dearden, "Limits on Decentralized Profit Responsibility," *Harvard Business Review* 40 (July/August 1962): 87–88.

16. Peter F. Drucker, *People and Performance: The Best of Peter Drucker on Management* (New York: Harper's College Press, 1977), p. 167.

17. Ibid., p. 168.

18. For discussion of the relationship between decentralization, size, and diversification, see Peter H. Grinyer and Masoud Yasai-Ardekani, "Strategy, Structure, Size and Bureaucracy," *Academy of Management Journal* 24 (September 1981): 471–486.

19. Henry Mintzberg, *The Structuring of Organizations,* pp. 276–283.

20. For a classic discussion of guidelines for decentralizing, see R.C. Davis, *The Fundamentals of Top Management,* pp. 306–316.

21. J. Patrick Wright, *On a Clear Day You Can See General Motors* (New York: Avon, 1979), p. 190.

22. "Kodak Is Trying to Break Out of Its Shell," *Business Week,* 10 June 1985, pp. 93–95.

23. Peter F. Drucker, *People and Performance: The Best of Peter Drucker on Management,* pp. 161–162.

24. Dan R. Dalton et al., "Organization Structure and Performance: A Critical Review," *Academy of Management Review* 5 (March 1980): 49–64.

25. R.C. Davis, *The Fundamentals of Top Management,* p. 315.

26. Pradip N. Khandwalla, *The Design of Organizations* (New York: Harcourt Brace Jovanovich, 1977), p. 511.

ADDITIONAL READINGS

Boseman, F. Glenn, and Robert E. Jones. "Marketing Conditions, Decentralization, and Organizational Effectiveness." *Human Relations* 27 (September 1974): 665–676.

Brooke, M.Z. *Centralization and Autonomy.* New York: Praeger, 1984.

———. "Autonomy and Centralization in Multinational Firms." *International Studies of Management and Organization* 14 (Spring 1984): 3–22.

Cordiner, Ralph. "The Implications of Industrial Decentralization." General Management Series, no. 133. New York: American Management Association, 1945.

———. "Problems of Management in a Large Decentralized Organization." General Management Series, no. 159. New York: American Management Association, 1952, 3–17.

Dale, Ernest. *Planning and Developing the Company Organization Structure.* New York: American Management Association, 1952.

Greenwood, Ronald. *Managerial Decentralization.* 2d rev. ed. Easton, PA: Hive Publishing Company, 1982.

Hage, Jerald, and Michael Aiken. "The Relationship of Centralization to Other Structural Properties." *Administrative Science Quarterly* 12 (June 1967): 72–92.

Harrigan, Kathryn Rudie. "Vertical Integration and Corporate Strategy." *Academy of Management Journal* 28 (June 1985): 397–425.

———. "Formulating Vertical Integration Strategies." *Academy of Management Review* 9 (October 1984): 638–652.

Levinson, Robert E. *Making the Most of Entrepreneurial Management: Decentralizing America's Corporations.* New York: AMACOM, 1986.

Moch, Michael K. "Structure and Organizational Resource Allocation." *Administrative Science Quarterly* 21 (December 1976): 661–674.

Murphy, David Charles. "On Entropy As a Measure of Decentralization." *Decision Sciences* 7 (October 1976): 675–676.

Negandhi, Anant R., and Bernard C. Reimann. "Correlates of Decentralization: Closed- and Open-Systems Perspectives." *Academy of Management Journal* 16 (August 1973): 509–513.

Solomons, David S. *Divisional Performance: Measurement and Control.* 2d ed. New York: Wiener Publishing, 1983.

Staiger, John G. "What Cannot Be Decentralized." *Management Record* 25 (January 1963): 19–21.

Vancil, Richard F. *Decentralization.* Homewood, IL: Dow Jones-Irwin, 1979.

COMPREHENSIVE CASES

PART 2

■

NATIONAL BUSINESS MACHINES

National Business Machines branch office number 120 is a marketing and service organization consisting of nearly 200 employees. The data-processing division is divided into four sections: two marketing units and two systems engineering units. This arrangement is depicted in the organization chart in Figure C2.1

The two marketing units sell new hardware. Each marketing unit has ten salespersons. The two systems engineering (SE) units provide technical assistance to the marketing units. They help in selecting hardware, systems design, computer programming, operator training, installed systems review, computer application development, and many other functions associated with selling and installing computer systems. Each SE unit has ten systems engineers.

The SE units are independent of each other. One unit supports marketing unit A, and the other unit supports marketing unit B.

Systems engineering includes three types of skills and knowledge: those associated with small, medium, and large computer systems. Small systems are usually purchased by the brand-new data-processing user getting first exposure to the world of automation. Systems engineers in this area must of course be skilled systems analysts and programmers, but they must also be educators and psychologists. New data-processing users know only as much about the machines as the marketing representatives have told them. They are often unsure about whether they can deal

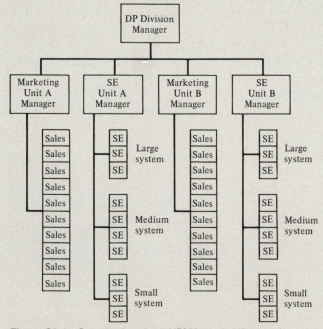

Figure C2.1   Organization chart: NBM branch office number 120.

with the machines. The small-system SE's must expand their knowledge and help them build confidence.

The medium-system SE works with a larger, higher-priced machine that has probably been installed for a few years. Users have their own data-processing staffs. Instead of being concerned with programming and operator training, the medium-system SE spends time looking for more advanced applications, such as installing terminals in different user departments.

The large-system SE deals with sophisticated data-processing installations. Large-system users are data-processing professionals with high standards, internal education programs and staffs of 50 or more.

The small-system SE may be working on five or six accounts per day, while the large-system SE may spend a week at one location.

In NBM branch office number 120, both SE units have systems engineers of all three types. This organizational structure has several advantages, but it also causes several problems.

The first problem occurs because the three data-processing system types— small, medium, and large—represent three quite different technologies. The effective SE manager must be well-versed in the latest trends of three separate disciplines. Both SE managers do a good job, but communications problems sometimes arise because they do not have experience in working on data-processing systems of all three kinds.

For example, both current SE managers have backgrounds in medium and large systems. The common misconception is that they should thoroughly understand small computer installations because small systems must be easier to install than large systems. However, in addition to designing the system and writing the programs, the small-system SE performs tasks that the SE's working on medium and large systems never perform. The small-system SE has to explain why the new user must spell the customer's name in exactly the same way every time, or why a diskette created on one type of personal computer cannot be compatible with another. Mistakes in these details can cause unbelievable delays in an installation and can be very difficult to locate.

Another problem is the division's sales quota. Since NBM makes more money when installing large machines, the manager naturally meets the quota faster by installing large machines. Of course, everyone realizes the advantages of selling small machines to many customers in the expectation that they will later graduate to medium and large machines. However, the short-run emphasis always seems to be on the large systems.

This situation causes a morale problem among the small-system SE's. They see the large-system people getting the bonuses and the recognition at branch office meetings. The small-system SE's also think that their compensation is not proportionate to the compensation of the large-system SE's. Actually, most large-system SE's have worked longer for NBM and have developed more skills, so their average compensation is justifiably higher. However, the small-system SE's tend to overlook this fact.

Having two SE managers each control three SE classifications may be inherently inefficient. For instance, imagine this situation. Manager A needs a small-system

(continued)

SE and does not have one available. Manager B has an available SE with the proper talents. Manager A asks to borrow the SE. If manager B allows the borrowing, the borrowed SE may be needed by manager B but unavailable the very next day. On the other hand, NBM is a service organization, so manager B probably allows manager A to borrow the SE.

Consider the borrowed SE. Once assigned to the project, the SE will probably have to stay with it until it is finished, even if an SE from unit A becomes available. Once the borrowed SE gets to know the people and situation at the new installation and begins to design systems and develop programs, manager B will be reluctant to make a change. So the borrowed SE will be working for a manager who does not appraise performance or make salary recommendations. The borrowed SE may work 60 to 80 hours a week on a crash project, and manager B may never hear about it.

How has the data-processing division differentiated its work? What problems have arisen from the division's differentiation strategies? For each problem, what alternative solutions do you see? What are their advantages and disadvantages? Which solutions would you recommend? Do you foresee any difficulties in implementing them? How might the introduction of the even smaller personal computer affect this organizational structure?

HENDRICKS NUCLEAR PLANT

Hendricks Nuclear Plant is owned and operated by Ohio Power Company (OPCO). After its completion in 1986, Unit 1 was released from OPCO's Construction Department (where I work) to the Nuclear Generation Department. At present, Unit 1 is operating, and Unit 2 is nearing completion.

Unit 2 is being built by the Hopkins Construction Company. OPCO has assigned design responsibility to Design Services, Inc., which in turn has assigned a major portion of the design work to the Bardo Corporation. Design Services has assigned the pipe-support design to Pipe Support Services, Inc.

The OPCO Construction Department maintains a staff on site whose primary personnel are the project manager, the Quality Control supervisor, and the Construction Services Group supervisor. This staff administers the contracts, mainly with Hopkins Construction Company, but also with Design Services, Pipe Support Services, and others.

The sequence of events in building a plant is as follows (see Figure C2.2). To all contractors, Ohio Power issues specifications approved by the Nuclear Regulatory Commission. Bardo Corporation and Pipe Support Services issue design drawings to Design Services, which reviews and approves them. Hopkins Construction takes the approved design drawings and constructs the plant.

Plant construction proceeds on a "system-by-system" basis. Upon completing a system, Hopkins Construction releases control of it to the OPCO Construction Department. The Construction Services Group supervisor and the Quality Control supervisor review the system and, when satisfied, release it to the Nuclear Generation Department, whose Start-up supervisor reviews and tests the system from the standpoint of how well it will operate and function. The Start-up supervisor then turns the system over to the Plant Superintendent, who in turn releases it to the Operations

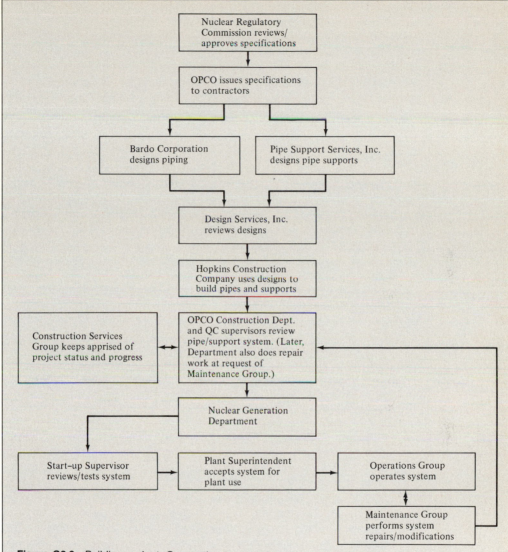

Figure C2.2   Building a plant: Conception to operation.

Group for use. The Operations Group can release it as necessary to the Maintenance Group for repairs or modifications. The Maintenance Group can perform the work themselves, or they can assign the work to the Construction Department.

   The purpose of the Construction Department's Construction Services Group is "to know what's going on." This group holds regular meetings to discuss the status and progress on design, materials, construction, and responsibility turnover. My job

(continued)

is to report to the Construction Services Group on the mechanical areas, especially piping and pipe supports.

Pipe supports are considered *safety related* when they support piping required for the safe operation of the plant. The safety of these supports recently became a critical issue because at London Nuclear Plant a pipe support failed last month, leaving the plant in jeopardy. Consequently, the Nuclear Regulatory Commission issued Bulletin 86-02, requiring all nuclear plants to review their safety-related pipe supports and to verify the review's completeness. Unit 1 at Hendricks Nuclear Plant has been shut down and construction of Unit 2 has been suspended until the review has been completed.

For plants under construction (like Unit 2), such a review is handled through the design process or by modification of the construction methods. For an operating plant (like Unit 1), a bulletin like 86-02 is accommodated procedurally through the Operations Group (if an operational change) or through the Maintenance Group (if a modification or repair). Because this is not an operational change, it has been assigned to the Maintenance Group. The NRC bulletin requires (1) *that the pipe supports be visually inspected* to see if they were installed as specified in the design drawings, and (2) *that the pipe support fasteners (bolts) be tested.*

These bolts are used to hold the supports to the floor or to the wall. How deep the bolts are driven determines how much load a support can carry. The Maintenance Group has discovered that the drawings do not give the installation details of the bolts. Therefore the Maintenance Group can not test the bolts because they do not know the design requirements for embedding the bolts.

Because I often work closely with Jerry Jenkins of Pipe Support Services, I was asked to get this information from him, so we could undertake and conclude the review, restart Unit 1, and resume work on Unit 2. He said he would have to discuss the request with his vice president and then come to the job site to discuss it with us.

When I met with our Construction Department project manager, he told me bolt embedding was considered "craftsmanship," not governed by design criteria. That was why the drawings did not give installation requirements. He and his staff had calculated how deeply the bolts should be embedded, but as a result of high employee turnover, the analysis had somehow been lost.

In addition, a review of the project manager's drawings revealed that, because of a misunderstanding between Hopkins Construction and the project staff, the drawings had not been revised to show weld sizes or construction deviations from design. This failure to revise now means that the original drawings must be redrawn based on field inspection of the supports, a new analysis must be made, and the bolts must be tested to see if they were installed as the analysis required. The upshot is that all safety-related hangers (and there are hundreds, if not thousands) must be tested.

After this meeting, I realized that what had started as a small inspection-and-testing program had turned into a massive program that was going to delay restarting Unit 1 indefinitely. I made upper management aware of these complications, so that organizational changes could be made to accommodate this vastly enlarged program.

Management's problem is how best to assign resources to the tasks of (1) inspecting the supports, (2) performing the analyses, and (3) testing the bolts. Their resources are Bardo Corporation, Pipe Support Services, Inc., Design Services, Inc.,

Hopkins Construction Company, and, within OPCO itself, Quality Control, Start-up, Construction Services Group, and Maintenance Group.

The hardest decision is choosing *who is to be responsible for inspecting the supports.* Although this stage sounds trivial, an inspector must look at each support with drawing in hand, mark the corrections needed, supply any missing information, and return the drawing to the designer for analysis.

Maintenance Group started the inspection program but lacked the personnel to inspect all the supports. Pipe Support Services was considered for continuing the inspection because they knew what information would be required for the analysis. Hopkins Construction was also considered; they were intimately familiar with the supports because they had built them. Start-up was considered because they are part of the Nuclear Generation Department and could act on behalf of the Maintenance Group. Also, because the support inspection was the first part of the program, Start-up could assist Nuclear Generation in maintaining better control over the entire program through early involvement.

The next decision to be made is *who will perform the analysis.* Pipe Support Services has the contract to do this; hence they are an obvious consideration. Design Services has review responsibility of all design and also has a staff of engineers and managers, so they are a good possibility. Bardo Corporation has a similar staff, but they are not being seriously considered except possibly to assist Design Services.

The easiest decision choice seems to be *who will test the bolts.* Testing will involve a lot of labor, which falls under the pipefitters' jurisdiction. Since Hopkins Construction holds the pipefitters' union contract, it perhaps seems only natural that Hopkins do the testing. However, OPCO wants someone to oversee Hopkins Construction. Maintenance Group and Construction Services Group are too small for this function. Operations Group has too many other plant responsibilities to be involved in this program. OPCO is left with Start-up and Quality Control. QC has worked closely with Hopkins Construction in the past and is accustomed to performing verification.

Who should be given responsibility for (1) inspecting the supports, (2) analyzing the results, and (3) testing the bolts? Should OPCO be reconstructed for greater effectiveness?

FINANCIAL GROUP, INC.

Financial Group, Inc., a multibank holding company with headquarters in Newark, New Jersey, owns 33 banks and 9 bank-related affiliates. The banks serve their customers from 173 banking offices located throughout New Jersey. The company's consolidated total assets of $6.4 billion rank it as the third largest bank holding company in New Jersey and one of the major bank holding companies in the Northeast. The company's lead bank is the $2.7 billion Financial Bank of Newark.

Financial Group's organization differs from those of its competing bank holding companies in that it has not merged its affiliates and acquisitions into one single bank. Each acquired Financial Group bank operates independently, within holding company guidelines. Each bank has its own president/chief executive officer (usually the for-

(continued)

mer president/CEO of the acquired bank), and its own board of directors and operating staff. Under this decentralized structure, each affiliate is responsible for its own financial bottom line.

The holding company's board of directors sees three advantages to maintaining the autonomy of the affiliate banks. First, each affiliate knows its region best and can determine customer needs and preferences better than a group of directors in Newark can. Second, requiring each affiliate to be accountable for its own growth and profits, and remunerating affiliate personnel based on that performance, gives incentive to the affiliates to operate as efficiently and effectively as possible. Third, the holding company feels that even though the overall structure is decentralized, economies of scale can still be realized by centralizing certain functions—for example, investments.

The holding company maintains a centralized investment portfolio for three reasons. First, the nature of investments calls for careful orchestration due to tax laws and market risk. Second, purchasing and selling securities in large blocks often results in better prices; therefore, small affiliates can pool their resources to their mutual benefit. Finally, a centralized investment portfolio can best be managed by an expert in the field, who is up-to-date and knowledgeable concerning the financial markets.

In operation, each of the 33 affiliates has a separate investment portfolio. That is, each affiliate has its own securities which it buys out of affiliate funds and owns as liquidity, growth, and profit vehicles. The 33 portfolios are managed by a single portfolio manager, who works for and operates out of the lead bank's investment division in Newark. The manager speaks with many financial institutions in an effort to predict market trends and make wise investments for the affiliate banks. The manager talks to the CEO of most affiliates at least once a week, relaying financial information and suggesting investment opportunities. In theory, the actual investment decision regarding type of security and maturity is left up to the affiliate CEO. In reality, the portfolio manager sets the parameters of investment decisions based on holding company policy. She can veto any investment decision made by a CEO.

The present portfolio manager is a young woman who has only recently completed an investment management training program. Although she is somewhat new to the job, she is quickly gaining the confidence and knowledge necessary to run an $800 million portfolio. The portfolio manager is evaluated based on her performance record: the growth, profit, and ingenuity of investments, which must be made within company guidelines.

The relationship between the portfolio manager and most of the affiliates is strong. They appear to respect each other's knowledge and expertise. At the portfolio manager's suggestion, some of the affiliates have purchased computer programs to help them determine their liquidity needs and asset-and-liability sensitivity.

Some of the affiliates, however, have been less than cooperative with the portfolio manager. Certain conflicts have come to the attention of executive holding company management by way of apparent poor management of affiliate investment funds. The holding company would like the conflicts to be resolved at the portfolio manager's level, but the corporation is willing to intervene if necessary. The banks presenting the most problems are Financial Bank of Madison, Financial Bank of Summit, and Financial Bank of Dover.

Financial Bank of Madison was one of the original banks in the Financial Group corporation. A large percentage of the present bank executives worked in its forerunner, the Madison Bank. The CEO of Financial Bank of Madison is a rather conservative man who regularly meets growth goals but has recently lagged in profit margins. The CEO does not handle the daily investment transactions; instead a young Madison investment officer is the contact person for the portfolio manager. This Madison officer rarely follows the portfolio manager's advice. His general attitude on the phone is belligerent and rude. He sometimes makes uncomplimentary references about the portfolio manager's youth and gender. Most recently, the Madison bank lost a considerable amount of money by paying more interest on a customer's certificate of deposit than it could offset in an investment security. Had the Madison bank followed the procedure suggested by the portfolio manager, the situation could have been avoided.

Financial Bank of Summit is a relatively stable affiliate with marginal growth potential and marginal profit results. Like Financial Bank of Madison, Summit's daily investment transactions are conducted by an investment officer under the CEO's supervision. The Summit investment officer would like to rely on the portfolio manager's advice. However, the Summit officer relays the information to the CEO and waits for him to make the investment decision. Because the CEO takes a relaxed approach to these decisions, it can take the Summit investment officer anywhere from an hour to several days to get the Summit CEO's decision back to the portfolio manager. Given the volatile nature of the securities markets, many investment opportunities are missed during this lag time.

Financial Bank of Dover was acquired in 1987 as a result of a hostile takeover. At the time of acquisition, its loan and investment portfolios were in bad shape. The corporation sent Newark officers to Dover for a short period to rectify the situation. Even so, the portfolios are still below growth potentials and profit goals. The Dover Bank evidently resents Newark's involvement in its affairs. As a result, the Dover CEO refuses to contact the centrally located portfolio manager and routinely ignores her investment advice.

What has brought about the problem between the portfolio manager and the three affiliates? Is it a line-staff problem? A decentralization problem? Another kind of problem? How would you solve it? What can be done to improve the relationships between the holding company and the three problem affiliates?

Integrating

Strategies

*P*art 2, "Differentiating Strategies," examined how organizations break down their work. Part 3, "Integrating Strategies," presents the ways in which the organization combines the differentiated efforts of its members into a unified whole.

As the OT-Model on the inside covers shows, the five broad integrating strategies are coordination by hierarchy of authority, formalization, committees, span of control, and communication. Again we have attempted to present this material in a roughly developmental sequence. The oldest, most widely used integrating mechanism is, of course, the owner/founder/entrepreneur who creates an organization and then supervises, directs, and leads it. That person's formal authority to issue coordinating commands is obvious. Eventually the formal authority of the growing organization's owner/founder spreads throughout the organization to other managers and supervisors, who coordinate the work of their subordinates.

As work force size and geographical spread of the organization's units increase, other coordinating mechanisms become necessary. One response to this need is the development of formal rules and procedures. Another is greater attention to span of control, to ensure that lower-level managers in the hierarchy can efficiently supervise their subordinates and keep them heading toward the organization's goals.

Committees also serve to coordinate by bringing together representatives of diverse organizational parts in a structured, routine way. Finally, the topic of communication may well represent the essence of all coordinating mechanisms. All integrating devices involve communication, but its importance for ensuring effective integration of all organizational effort is so great that it warrants a separate chapter. Part 3's five chapters—the hierarchy of authority, formalization, committees, span of control, and communication—describe the integrating devices that tie the organization back together. In a sense, every differentiating strategy requires a counterbalancing integrating strategy. No one person in a modern, complex organization can do and know everything, so tasks must be divided up and assigned. The organization must coordinate these many divided-up tasks or it will become ineffective and chaotic. Striking a balance between these opposites—differentiation and integration—is a critical management task.

CHAPTER 9

The Hierarchy of Authority

The previous section of the book explained the differentiating strategies that split up the organization's efforts. This chapter is the first of five that show how the differentiated efforts are integrated—that is, brought back together in a unified attempt to reach organizational goals.

Among the integrating strategies, the hierarchy of authority is an obvious starting point. It focuses on the ways in which the owner/entrepreneur—or top management, in the large modern corporation or bureaucracy—gets people throughout the organization to expend effort, to work toward the achievement of certain goals. As we explained in Chapter 3 on goals, someone must somehow articulate the organization's goals in such a way that others can see, understand, and relate to them. This process allows organizational members to balance the costs of exerting effort on the organization's behalf with the benefits to be derived from organizational membership.

Perfect and automatic congruence between these costs and benefits is seldom achieved (except perhaps among religious or political fanatics who completely give up self-identity for the faith or cause). Therefore, the role of the leader is critical in forging the links between organizationally derived rewards or benefits and individual needs for those rewards or benefits. Indeed, even among fanatics, a complete relinquishment of the self is often brought about by a charismatic leader who is able to persuade converts that their interests and the organization's are identical.

This chapter describes the hierarchy of authority and presents a variety of viewpoints on the division of authority and its exercise through leadership, particularly the perspectives of the classical, human relations, and modern schools.

The classicists favored a strict hierarchy of authority. The human relations school was interested in the interrelationships of authority, power, and leadership. A major concern of the modern school is to find ways of determining what kind of leader is best suited to hold each position within the hierarchy of authority.

THE NATURE OF AUTHORITY

What Is Authority?

All organizational members have a *responsibility* to carry out, to the best of their abilities, the duties that their superiors assign to them and the functions of their positions. *Authority* is the set of rights that enables members to discharge their responsibilities. R.C. Davis defines managerial authority this way:

> Managerial authority is the right to exercise executive leadership. It is the right to plan, organize, and control the organization's activities for which the executive is responsible. It consists principally of the rights of decision and command.[1]

Within the scope of their responsibilities, managers have the right—the formal authority—to decide what should be done and how it should be done, and the additional right to give the necessary orders to subordinates that will get the job done, thereby fulfilling the responsibilities of the unit members and their managers to the organization.

Authority and Leadership

The hierarchy of authority—the situating of authority at the different organizational levels—allows leadership to secure the cooperation of members in reaching organizational goals.

The Small Organization   In the small, simple entrepreneurial organization, the hierarchy is short, perhaps consisting of one person with ten helpers. The exercise of authority will probably be based on:

> The entrepreneur's knowledge of the production process—the entrepreneur's expertise;
>
> The entrepreneur's ownership of the right (perhaps by means of a patent) to produce the product and the equipment with which to produce it;
>
> The entrepreneur's control of organizational human resources—the right to hire and fire, to reward and punish.

These attributes obviously give the small entrepreneur a great deal of authority and power over the organization's people and processes. In this simple world without governmental oversight, union relations, or special interest groups, and with competitive markets for both the supplies purchased and the products sold, the major choices related to running the business are entirely *the entrepreneur's*.

The entrepreneur's control methods will probably be a combination of eyeball contact plus simple measures of product quantity and quality. The hierarchy is short, the leadership style focuses on production, the authority is based on the right of private property plus the owner's ability to control organizational resources completely without interference, and the concurrence of employees that the owner's authority, power, and rights are legitimate. If we add several hundred employees and a few layers to the hierarchy, we arrive at the typical organization for which the classical writers were trying to find techniques for integrating the efforts of members.

The Right of Private Property   The authority of entrepreneurs and business managers is ultimately based on the right of private property. According to R.C. Davis, the continued existence of a capitalistic society's values requires

> the utilization of the physical and human resources of the particular society. The right of the private business organization to use these resources depends on the delegation, to the owners of the business, of private property rights by organized society through its elected representatives. The right of the executive to plan, organize, and control their use by the business organization is a right that is delegated by the ownership. . . . People have fought for the right of private property for centuries. It is a basic requisite for the existence of personal liberties.[2]

The Large Organization   We have looked briefly at the small entrepreneur-directed organization in its relatively simple environment. In contrast, picture a large corporation with thousands of employees and many organizational levels operating in a less-than-freely-competitive environment. The corporation's stock is publicly owned and widely held, so the top managers are no longer the "owners" of the business as was the small entrepreneur. The corporation has high social visibility; governments, unions, and special interest groups are all trying to influence it. In this situation, which is diametrically opposite to the entrepreneur situation, the dominant coalition at the top of the organizational pyramid must exert its influence through the skillful use of authority, power, and leadership. These interrelated topics will be discussed at length presently. Chapter 10, Formalization, expands these ideas by discussing the *structural* techniques used by top managers to control and direct employee effort. Additionally, the literature of organizational behavior (OB) includes many *motivational* techniques for achieving these same ends. The interested student might want to examine some OB texts to become familiar with the full range of strategies managers may use to secure compliance with organizational requirements and to obtain motivated effort toward achieving organizational goals.

THE CLASSICAL PERSPECTIVE

The classical school maintained that organizational efforts could be best coordinated by means of a rigidly enforced chain of command. The owner/entrepreneur at the top of the hierarchy hired people, told them what to do and how to do it, and disciplined those who did not comply. The logic of this situation was simple: The entrepreneur owned the means of production, had capital at risk, and had the rights associated with private property. His name and reputation were bound up with the quality of the product or service. Why shouldn't he have the right to choose the workers and tell these hired hands how to do the task?

The Pyramidal Organization

As the number of employees, tasks, units, departments, and managerial levels increased, the traditional organization studied by the classical writers took on the shape of a pyramid when depicted on a chart. Each box on the organization chart had other boxes beneath it. The person in the higher-level box or position—and only this person—

had the formal authority and responsibility to coordinate the efforts of those in lower-level boxes or positions. This single reporting relationship ensured that every subordinate had one and only one boss. *Unity of command* became a fundamental principle of organizing, a sure way to avoid confusion over who was in charge and who was responsible for specific organizational tasks. A chain of command could be established even in relatively large organizations to permit the top manager to control and coordinate the differentiated efforts of the entire organization. The principle of unity of command enabled both subordinates and their superiors to know who was in charge of whom.

Organizational authority is divided and spread throughout the organizational hierarchy represented on the pyramid-shaped chart. Different positions, responsible for particular functions, are allocated the appropriate authority for fulfilling their responsibilities. Authority is allocated to positions, not persons. Although the persons may change, each position's responsibility and authority stay the same.

The Scalar Process

To the classicists, the following terms had the same meaning: hierarchy of authority, scalar chain, chain of command, scalar process, scalar principle. One of Henri Fayol's 14 universal management principles involved the scalar chain. According to Fayol, all employees should be aware of the organizational hierarchy, the different levels in the chain of command. Communications should generally flow through the formal chain of command. Here is how classicists James D. Mooney and Alan C. Reiley described the scalar process:

> The supreme co-ordinating authority must rest somewhere and in some form in every organization. . . . It is equally essential to the very idea and concept of organization that there must be a process, formal in character, through which this co-ordinating authority operates from the top throughout the entire structure of the organized body.[3]

Workers Become Supervisors

In the days of uncomplicated tasks and environments, with relatively slow rates of change, persons at or near the top of the hierarchy were apt to be owner/entrepreneurs and family members (in smaller organizations) or exceptionally skilled workers worthy of advancement (in larger organizations). The owner/entrepreneur would most likely choose lower-level managers on the basis of their technical skill (although sometimes they were selected because they were the owner's relatives). After all, who but the best worker would logically be appointed as a supervisor in the hierarchy?

A Sensible Position   In many respects, the classical position made sense. Take the best workers and give them titles, a little extra money, and the authority to hire and fire. The best workers would then supervise the efforts of other workers, leading by their own good example and having the power and rights bestowed upon them by organizational owners. These owners could stake their claims on the right of private property. The supervisors appointed at subordinate levels had to stake their right to direct the behavior of their subordinates on a derivative claim. Their power to act on behalf of the owner, commonly termed formal or legitimate authority, was based on the powers granted to them by the owner to hire, fire, promote, pay, reward, and punish subordinates. The owner also tried to clarify for supervisors the scope of the decisions they could make without the owner's review.

Degrees of Authority In the past and today, managers and supervisors are granted varying degrees of authority. A manager who can hire and fire subordinates at will and who has total control of the production process (such as a plant manager in a highly decentralized organization) has a great deal of formal authority. Conversely, managers who have to call in the personnel department about every employee matter and who are totally controlled in their utilization of departmental resources (such as assembly-line foremen in a unionized plant) have relatively little decision-making power. The modern ideas of leadership discussed later in this chapter take on real significance for these relatively powerless individuals as they seek to find non-organizationally derived bases of power to influence their subordinates.

THE HUMAN RELATIONS PERSPECTIVE

Classical/Human Relations Differences

The classical and human relations perspectives on the hierarchy of authority were different for some very good reasons. The earlier organizations studied by the classicists could easily trace their heritage back to the owner/entrepreneur and see the dominant presence of the person or family who had capital at risk and a reputation at stake. From this perspective, the right of private property and the legitimacy of the structured authority patterns made considerable sense.

On the other hand, the human relations writers could not see these relationships so clearly. Talking theoretically about "the right of private property" was one thing when you could actually see and know the owner (your boss), quite another thing when working for the telephone company and wondering who the "owner" actually was and what rights your boss had to tell you what to do. Further confusion might result if you held common stock and were therefore a part owner and your boss owned no stock. The newer attitude toward authority had several sources, among them:

1. The increasingly widespread ownership of common stock;
2. The divorcing of ownership from management;
3. The lack of a dominant group overseeing management;
4. The recognition that people bought stock in a company not for the satisfactions of ownership but as a form of investment similar to buying gold, paintings, or putting money into savings accounts.

Under these conditions the argument could reasonably be put forth: If top management has no significant ownership position, where do they get the right to direct the behavior of subordinates in an authoritarian relationship? Why should subordinates accept that direction?

Authority-Acceptance Theory

The human relations school wanted to understand how authority and power influence subordinate behavior. Chester I. Barnard presented a good answer to this problem in his classic book *The Functions of the Executive.*[4] According to Barnard, authority is *the quality of an order that causes someone else to accept it and to do as ordered.* So whether an order has authority or not is determined by the order *receiver,* not by the sender or "person in authority."

This position is considerably different from the classical notion that authority was derived from the right of private property in ownership and was properly traced from the top down through the organization. Barnard would trace it from the bottom up, as each level of members accepts the authority of progressively higher-level managers whose right to lead is, in effect, granted by the led.

The factors influencing the acceptance of authority lie in the nature of the sender and receiver, their relationships to the organization and to each other, and in the nature of the communication itself. Just as many governments must rely on the consent of the governed, so must organizational leaders.

Preconditions for Accepting Authority   According to Barnard, four preconditions must be met before an employee will accept an order that is meant to be authoritative. The employee may not accept the order even if the preconditions are met. But if they are not, the employee either will not or cannot accept the order.

1. *The employee must understand the order.* A manager who inadequately communicates orders has not exercised authority, because employees cannot comply with orders that they do not understand.

2. *The employee must believe that the order is consistent with the organization's goals.* If an order appears to conflict with an organizational goal or with past practice, the manager must explain why it is different this time. If employees believe that "management couldn't really want us to do that" because the order makes no sense in terms of the organizational goals as employees understand them, they won't do it or they will twist it in such a way that it does make sense. In either event, the order was not followed, and authority was lost.

3. *The employee must believe that the order is consistent with the employee's own goals.* This precondition is related to whatever reasons the employee had for affiliating with the organization in the first place. If carrying out the order will result in the organization's becoming less attractive to the employee, the order will be disobeyed or (more usually) evaded. If the order is totally inconsistent with goals or principles that are important to the employee, and the order cannot be disobeyed or avoided, the employee will probably resign.

4. *The employee must be physically and mentally able to carry out the order.* This precondition is so obvious that mentioning it seems absurd. Yet we are sometimes asked to do the impossible. Managers who give orders without knowing each employee's

capabilities soon find out that if it can't be done, it won't be—and whatever authority they thought they had, they didn't have.

Securing Compliance   Once the preconditions to the acceptance of authority have been met, how do managers actually secure compliance? The compliance necessary for a smoothly functioning organization comes about for three reasons.

1. *Effective managers issue orders that comply with the four preconditions.* The effective executive issues orders that are *accepted.* Orders that do not comply with the preconditions are not obeyed, and the manager who issues them causes big problems. Of such a person it is said, "She abuses her authority" or "He doesn't know how to use his authority." If managers meet the preconditions, employees in most organizational cultures—realizing that someone has to give the orders—will allow them to be authoritarian and autocratic. Once the manager begins to ignore the preconditions, employees begin to ignore the orders. Instead of recognizing the failure as their own, such managers complain, "You just can't get good help any more."

2. *People joining an organization expect to be given commands regarding certain aspects of their behavior in the organization. They obey orders within these "zones of acceptance" without question.* Here is how Daniel Katz and Robert L. Kahn describe that situation:

> To say that the occupant of one role has authority over the occupant of another on organizational matters means that the influence of the one over the other is a matter of organizational law; it is legitimate and is so accepted. Compliance with authoritative requests thus becomes a generalized role expectation in organizations; each member of the organization is expected by all others to so comply, and relevant persons and agencies outside the organization agree and on occasion reinforce this view.
>
> Such acceptance of authority is in effect a key clause in the psychological contract (and sometimes, the legal contract) in terms of which each new member accepts membership and enters the organization. He understands these terms at the time of entry; his supervisor assumes the same terms and assumes the new employee's understanding and acceptance of them. His peers agree, and by their agreement reinforce the contractual obligations.[5]

Orders can be divided into three classes: clearly acceptable, clearly unacceptable, and doubtful. The clearly acceptable are those areas that Katz and Kahn describe; they represent requests to do something consistent with the job description. Unacceptable are those that greatly exceed any reasonable bounds of the job description or the employee's psychological contract with the organization. Doubtful orders are by far the most interesting, as these commands—in areas not completely inside or outside reasonable job expectations—require the subordinate to consider whether or not to comply. In this situation, the pros and cons of the job and one's continued success in it—or in extreme cases, even continued employment in that job—will determine the decision to accept the order, not accept it, or interpret it to make it acceptable.

3. *Most group members want "their" organization to run smoothly so they can gain the benefits that they anticipated when they joined. Therefore, group members will bring social pressure to bear on any member unwilling to accept authority.* People joining

organizations realize that they cannot achieve their own personal goals if the organization fails. An organization will have great difficulty in succeeding if its members do not accept authority and take orders. Therefore, those members who identify with and work toward organizational goals for their own reasons will often exert pressure to conform on uncooperative members.

Power

In Chester I. Barnard's view, *authority* comes from those over whom the manager exercises it. If employees do not accept authority, it does not exist. Yet, the formal organization can do more than simply watch to see whether employees accept authority; the organization can take steps to encourage or influence authority acceptance. True, authority-acceptance theory redirected managerial attention away from the classical emphasis on formal authority derived from ownership and toward thinking about ways to secure acceptance of authority. Nevertheless, the human relations writers recognized that a manager's *power* can certainly enhance the likelihood that the manager's authority will be accepted.

David Mechanic defines power as "any force that results in behavior that would not have occurred if the force had not been present."[6] Therefore, power can influence behavior whether people accept it or not.[7]

Walter Buckley uses *the organizational group* to distinguish between authority and power.[8] If the group leadership is taking the group toward the group's goals, then the leaders are exercising authority. If the leaders are taking the group toward the leaders' goals, then they are exercising power and the group, rather than *accepting* authority, is complying with the leadership's exercise of power. Figure 9.1 presents Buckley's authority system and power system.

The idea of power became an additional focus of the human relations writers as they sought to understand how organizations gain member compliance even in situations where authority-acceptance theory would seem to point toward noncompliance.

Physical Power   Power is of three types: physical, material, and symbolic.[9] In some organizations, the power base for securing cooperation is a loaded gun, a whip, or steel bars. Physical power influences behavior in such organizations as street gangs, concentration camps, prisons, and prisoner-of-war camps. Group members behave in a manner not so much designed to acquire a physical reward as to avoid physical punishment.

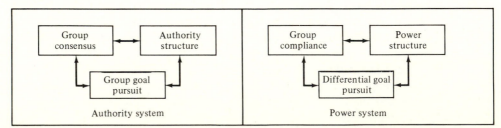

Figure 9.1   Authority and power systems. (*Source:* From Walter Buckley, *Sociology and Modern Systems Theory,* © 1967, p. 178. Reprinted by permission of Prentice-Hall, Inc., Englewood Cliffs, NJ)

In the public and private organizations that concern us, physical power hardly ever comes into use, although the physical force of organized society serves to back up the exercise of authority in organizations.

Material Power The base of material power is money, which can be used to buy goods and services. Most incentive systems, including the power to hire, pay, promote, lay off, and fire, are based on material power.

Symbolic Power Physical power and material power enable the power-holder to control the extent to which persons over whom power is wielded can fulfill their physiological needs and safety-security needs. Symbolic power is the ability to offer or withhold the symbolic rewards that are required to fulfill people's needs for social recognition, esteem, status, and self-fulfillment. Although symbolic power is exercised in most organizations, it is the sole power available to managers in such organizations as churches, social groups, political clubs, and voluntary associations. Three subtypes of symbolic power are referent power, expert power, and legitimate power.

Referent power If person A admires, identifies with, and wants to be like person B, then person B serves as a reference point or role model for person A. Person B commands A's respect and has a measure of power over A. This power relationship can exist, for example, between daughter and mother, scout and scoutmaster, subordinate and superior. Groups may also exert referent power over their members. If a group member identifies closely with the group, then the group has the power to reward or punish the member symbolically by approval, disapproval, or in other nonmaterial ways.

Expert power Knowledge is power. Organizations are filled with experts, wielding the power of their knowledge. In fact, many organizational members hold their positions and exercise influence over others because they know more about their specialties than anyone else does.

Legitimate power The final type of symbolic power is known as legitimate power. This notion assumes that certain people in some situations have an inherent right to power over other people. Legitimate power is closely related to what we referred to earlier as formal authority. Employees accept the exercise of legitimate power. People working for the classical owner/entrepreneur acknowledged the property owner's right to direct their behavior. Similarly, today's workers know when they enter an organization that persons above them in the organizational hierarchy have the power to give them orders simply by virtue of the organizational positions held. Most managerial decisions are implemented readily because employees recognize the decision maker's legitimate power to order their implementation.

Leadership

Authority and Leadership An organization's hierarchy of authority reflects how organizational authority to give orders and make decisions is divided and where it is located. Leadership refers to the ways in which organizational managers and supervisors use their power and authority. The hierarchy describes the "what" and "where" of authority; leadership refers to the "who" and "how." James D. Mooney expressed the distinction this way:

> Here we come to what I conceive to be a vital distinction; that between authority as such, and the form of authority that projects itself through *leadership*. The difference may be seen in their relation to the organization itself. It takes supreme co-ordinating authority to create an organization; leadership, on the other hand, always presupposes the organization. I would define leadership as the form in organization through which authority enters into the process; which means, of course, that there must be leadership as the necessary directive of the entire organized movement.[10]

Trait Theory   Early studies of leadership paralleled the classical approach to organizational structure. After all, the classical writers thought they could observe successful organizations, then deduce principles from these observations to build a body of knowledge. Why shouldn't the same approach work in observing successful leaders to derive their common traits and characteristics? So, early work in leadership, following the classical thought process, sought to find these commonalities.

Stogdill's Review   In his major review of leadership studies from the early 1900s to 1948, R.M. Stogdill identified a number of traits that, according to researchers, seemed to differentiate between leaders and nonleaders.[11] These traits were intelligence, alertness to the needs of others, understanding of the task, initiative and persistence in dealing with problems, self-confidence, and the desire to accept responsibility and occupy a position of dominance and control.

Despite these general results, Stogdill concluded that the traits important or essential to successful leadership often varied from situation to situation. A person does not become a leader simply by virtue of possessing a specific combination of traits. Instead, the successful pattern of leader characteristics must bear some relevant relationship to the characteristics, goals, and activities of *the followers*.[12]

The basic premise of the trait approach was that certain traits are necessary for effective leadership. In effect, Stogdill found in 1948 that previous studies had failed to support that premise. Such assessments sent researchers in new directions to discover what distinguished successful leaders from unsuccessful ones. Although many then focused on behavioral research, some industrial psychologists seeking better ways of selecting potential managers continued to conduct trait research.

Twenty-Five Years Later   In 1974 Stogdill again reviewed the trait literature.[13] He found that the research effort had broadened to include managerial *skills* as well as traits. Table 9.1 presents Gary A. Yukl's lists of the traits and skills which often seem to be associated with successful leaders. These characteristics may increase the *likelihood* that a leader will be effective, but they do not *guarantee* effectiveness. The relative importance of the different traits and skills depends on the nature of the leadership situation.

Table 9.1   TRAITS AND SKILLS OFTEN ASSOCIATED WITH SUCCESSFUL LEADERS

Traits	Skills
Adaptable to situations	Clever and intelligent
Alert to social environment	Conceptually skilled
Ambitious and achievement oriented	Creative
Assertive	Diplomatic and tactful
Cooperative	Fluent in speaking
Decisive	Knowledgeable about group task
Dependable	Organized: has administrative ability
Dominant: wants to influence others	Persuasive
Energetic: high activity level	Socially skilled
Persistent	
Self-confident	
Tolerant of stress	
Willing to assume responsibility	

Source: Gary A. Yukl, *Leadership in Organizations,* © 1981, p. 70. Reprinted by permission of Prentice-Hall, Inc., Englewood Cliffs, NJ.

Leader Behavior: Ohio State Studies

The trait approach failed as a predictor of leadership success and as a guide to identifying those characteristics that, if developed, would result in effective leaders. Therefore, the emphasis of research on leadership shifted to the behavioral orientation emerging from the post-World War II human relations movement. Researchers changed over from the study of leadership *traits* to leadership *behaviors*.

Most studies of leadership behavior have used questionnaires to find out what leaders *do*. Research of this type has been dominated by the Ohio State University leadership studies begun in the late 1940s. This research focused on identifying leader behavior which is instrumental in attaining group and organizational goals.

A questionnaire was developed to measure 150 items which the researchers agreed represented good examples of leader functions. The questionnaire was administered in a variety of situations. Analysis of the results indicated that subordinates perceived the leader's behavior primarily in terms of two distinct behavior categories, labeled "consideration" and "initiating structure."[14]

Consideration   Consideration includes behavior concerned with leader supportiveness, friendliness, openness in communication, willingness to consult with subordinates, and recognition of subordinate contributions. These behaviors are all important in establishing and maintaining good relationships with subordinates.

Initiating Structure   The leader provides structure for group activities by directing subordinates, clarifying subordinate roles, planning, coordinating, problem solving, and pressing subordinates to perform better. These task-oriented behaviors are important for making the best use of people and resources to attain group goals.

These two dimensions of leadership are independent. A person may score high on both, low on both, or high on one and low on the other.

Inconclusive Results   Since the Ohio State research, many other studies have explored the relationship of "consideration" and "initiating structure" to various other measures of leadership effectiveness. The results are inconclusive.[15]

University of Michigan Studies

Another set of studies on leadership behavior was carried out by University of Michigan researchers at about the same time as the Ohio State studies.[16] The focus of the Michigan research was identifying the relationships among three elements: leader behavior, group processes, and group performance. As was true of the Ohio State work, one objective of the Michigan studies was to identify patterns of leadership behavior that led to effective group performance. Data were gathered in a variety of settings: insurance companies, manufacturing firms, utilities, railroads, and so on.

The Michigan researchers found that successful leaders demonstrated skills in planning and scheduling the work, coordinating subordinate activities, and providing necessary resources for task accomplishment. The researchers used the term *production orientation* to refer to this aspect of the leader's job.

However, the successful leaders were also concerned for human relations. They were considerate, helpful, and supportive. They tended to use general supervision rather than close supervision. They established goals and guidelines, then allowed subordinates some autonomy in deciding how to do the work. The term *employee orientation* was used for this aspect of leadership.

Production orientation and employee orientation parallel the two Ohio State leadership dimensions: initiating structure and consideration. The fact that the Michigan results and Ohio State results are similar should not be surprising. One significant finding at Michigan was that such nonproductivity criteria as job dissatisfaction, turnover, and absenteeism increased under production-oriented managers and decreased under employee-oriented managers. The Ohio State and Michigan studies imply that the manager should concentrate on the "people part" of the organization. The continuum in Figure 9.2 spans the different leadership behaviors. At the far left is boss-centered leadership in which the manager makes decisions, then informs employees of them. At the other end is subordinate-centered leadership. According to the Michigan and Ohio State results, managers should move as far to the right side of the continuum as they comfortably can.

The Ohio State and Michigan studies demonstrated that what the manager *does* is more important than what the manager *is*. Of course, in reality, traits and behavior cannot be totally separated; people with certain traits do tend to behave in certain ways.

The Leader as Integrator

Daniel Katz and Robert L. Kahn provide an excellent summary statement of effective leader behavior from the human relations perspective:

> . . . the most effective leader in a pivotal organizational role is not the perfect bureaucrat (rational, role-actuated, heedless of primary bonds), but rather the successful integra-

tor of primary and secondary relationships in the organizational situation. This means not only that the successful leader mediates and tempers the organizational requirements to the needs of persons; he does so in ways which are not organizationally damaging and, indeed, are organization-enhancing. He promotes group loyalty and personal ties. He demonstrates care for persons as persons. He relies on referent power rather than on the power of legitimacy and sanctions alone. He encourages the development of positive identification with the organization and creates among his peers and subordinates a degree of personal commitment and identification. He does these things by developing a relationship with others in the organization in which he introduces what might be termed primary variations on the secondary requirements of organization. Within limits he adapts his own interpersonal style to the needs of other persons. In so doing, he generates among members of his group a resultant strength of motivation for the achievement of group and organizational goals which more than compensates for occasional bureaucratic irregularities.[17]

Based as it is on an effort to gain willing acceptance of authority, this attitude is a long way from the classical owner's exercise of formal power and authority.

THE MODERN PERSPECTIVE

Most human relations writers send this message: participatory, employee-centered leadership is good and should be developed throughout the organizational hierarchy. Since the research on this point is ambiguous, the message is founded more on faith than on data.

The lack of empirical support for the human relations approach to leadership and

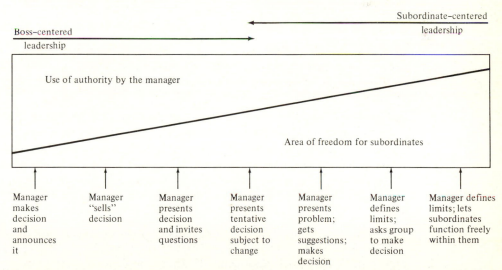

Figure 9.2 The continuum of leadership behavior. (Reprinted by permission of the *Harvard Business Review*. Exhibit 1 of "How to Choose a Leadership Pattern" by Robert Tannenbaum and Warren H. Schmidt [May/June 1973]. Copyright © 1973 by the President and Fellows of Harvard College; all rights reserved.)

authority led to the systems/contingency line of reasoning. The contingency theorists concluded that universally accurate answers to the classical organizational questions did not exist. Instead, the "best" organizational approach varied from industry to industry, department to department, and person to person. Thinking of the organization as a system led to the conclusion that the answer to a particular question was contingent upon the best fusion of the forces and factors in a particular setting at a particular time.

Leader Characteristics

The preceding discussion suggests that, from the modern viewpoint, the appropriate leadership style in a given situation depends on the forces operating on the *leader,* the *subordinates,* the *organization,* and the *environment.*

Two important characteristics are the leader's *personality* and *style.* They can significantly influence the leader-subordinate interaction.

Personality   What are the leader's values, attitudes, and traits? Is the leader aggressive, altruistic, moody, composed, trusting? Are the leader's personality characteristics (which can probably not be changed) conducive to effective leadership in *this* situation?

Style   Is the leader authoritarian or participative, autocratic or democratic, theory X or Y? Is the leader a delegator or a "decision hoarder"? Job-centered or employee-centered? If leaders are motivated to change, they can—up to a point. However, personality is a determinant of style, so certain aspects of a given leader's style are probably set.

Subordinate Characteristics

A leader may possess many fine characteristics, but they will not be fully effective if they clash with subordinate characteristics.

Personality   Like their leaders, subordinates have their distinguishing values, attitudes, and traits. A subordinate can be aggressive or passive, altruistic or selfish, moody or friendly, composed or nervous, trusting or suspicious. If a "personality conflict" develops between a leader and a subordinate, part of the leader's job is to encourage its resolution, if only in an "agreement to disagree." People of distinctly different personality types can still work together to get the job done.

Expectations   What do subordinates expect of their leader, and are these expectations realistic? At what point will the efficiency of subordinates decrease, because their expectations have been disappointed? Many employee expectations are reasonable; subordinates expect fair treatment, recognition for good work, satisfactory working conditions, a reasonable work load. The good leader stays aware of employee expectations, tries to meet those that are reasonable, and resolves disagreements about those that seem unreasonable.

Organization Characteristics

Certain organizational characteristics affect both leaders and subordinates.

Structure   Is the organization bureaucratic, or is it flexible, open, and adaptive? Is decision making centralized or decentralized? Is the span of control wide, or is it narrow to encourage close supervision of employees by their leaders? Are the tasks routine or creative? Is the communication system open, or is it filled with barriers? Ideally, the organization achieves a compatible blend of structure, leaders, and subordinates.

Groups   How effective are the organization's groups, and how are they structured? What are the rules and norms for group behavior? What is the group's self-image? Is the group cohesive? Is it in the early or later stages of development? Answers to such questions will affect whether a given person can lead a particular group effectively, and whether a given employee—with certain personality traits and expectations—can function well within a particular group.

Time   What is the normal time cycle for completing routine daily operations? Does the organization experience frequent emergencies and crises? Is the pace frantic and hectic, or steady and relaxed? Some leaders and subordinates can't stand time pressure; others thrive on it.

The Environment

The environment within which leadership is exercised affects the appropriateness of different leadership styles. Time and again, those styles that seem to work in a controlled "laboratory" environment fail when transplanted into the real world. When the environment is changed, the findings may also change. These truths are frustrating, but it is important to recognize that no two leadership situations are identical.

Each organization is a unique and complex system of interrelated parts. No easy answers exist as to how those parts can be encouraged to function most effectively. The organization's leadership must be aware of the many factors that can affect leaders, subordinates, and the organization itself and then try to meld the different organizational elements into a productive, satisfying whole. Using slightly different terminology, Figure 9.3 reflects the interacting forces which, in the opinion of Y.K. Shetty, shape the manager's leadership style.

Fred E. Fiedler's Work

Exercising authority through leadership is a complex process. The many situationally based factors affecting successful leadership add to that complexity. The pioneering studies by Fred E. Fiedler tried to answer the question: What kind of situation requires what kind of leader? Fiedler discusses two leadership styles with which we are already familiar: job-centered and people-centered. Whether a given situation calls for a job-

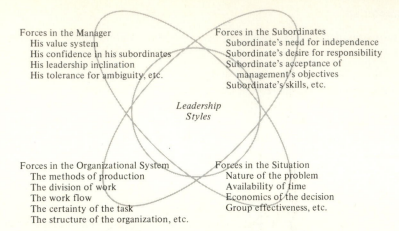

Forces in the Manager
   His value system
   His confidence in his subordinates
   His leadership inclination
   His tolerance for ambiguity, etc.

Forces in the Subordinates
   Subordinate's need for independence
   Subordinate's desire for responsibility
   Subordinate's acceptance of
      management's objectives
   Subordinate's skills, etc.

*Leadership
Styles*

Forces in the Organizational System
   The methods of production
   The division of work
   The work flow
   The certainty of the task
   The structure of the organization, etc.

Forces in the Situation
   Nature of the problem
   Availability of time
   Economics of the decision
   Group effectiveness, etc.

Figure 9.3   Interacting forces which shape the manager's leadership style.
(*Source:* From Y. K. Shetty, "Leadership and Organization Character," *Personnel Administration* 33 [July/August 1970], p. 19. Used by permission.)

centered style or a people-centered style depends on the influences of three variables found in every leadership situation: leader-member relations, task structure, and the leader's position power.

Appropriate Leadership Style   After studying 800 groups, Fiedler determined which situations called for job-centered leadership and which called for people-centered leadership. The results appear in Figure 9.4. Leader characteristics ranging from job-centered to people-centered appear on the vertical axis, and job-situation characteristics ranging from favorable to unfavorable for the leader appear on the horizontal axis. As an example of how to read the graph, Situation IV (horizontal axis: good leader-member relations, unstructured task, and weak leader position power) seems to call for a people-centered leader. Surprisingly, the job-centered style seems appropriate at the extremes. Situation I (highly favorable for the leader) and Situation VIII (highly unfavorable) *both* seem to call for a job-centered leader.

Limitations   The Fiedler model describes only eight situations made up of only three different variables. It offers only two leadership-style possibilities. It is static, not dynamic. It also assumes that in each situation, the leader has the same relationship with each group member: good or moderately poor. These simplifications and generalities obviously limit the model's real-life applications.

   Nevertheless, Fiedler made an important contribution in suggesting that we cannot legitimately point to "good leaders" and "bad leaders." We must specify the situation in which leadership is exercised.

Path-Goal Theory

The path-goal leadership theory appeared in the early 1970s.[18] According to this theory, good leaders behave in the following ways: (1) they make rewards available to subordi-

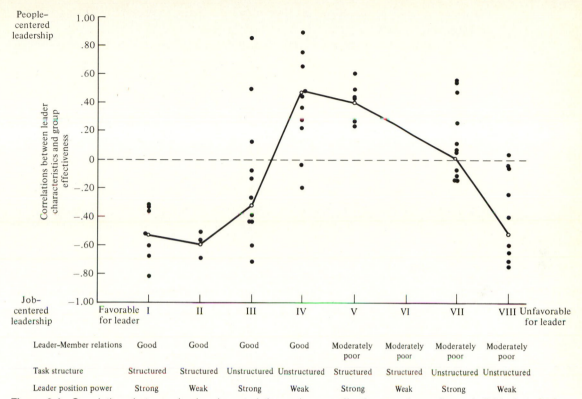

Figure 9.4 Correlations between leader characteristics and group effectiveness. *Legend:* • = Individual study / ○ = Average of all studies (*Source:* After Fred E. Fiedler, *A Theory of Leadership Effectiveness* [New York: McGraw-Hill, 1967], p. 148. Used by permission.)

nates, (2) they make sure that these rewards are tied to the accomplishment of specific goals, and (3) they continually clarify for employees what kind of behavior (or "path") will lead to accomplishing the specific goals and to receiving the rewards for goal accomplishment. The leader behaving in these ways will have motivated, satisfied employees who accept the manager's leadership.

Leadership Behaviors The effective path-goal leader provides four kinds of leadership: directive, achievement-oriented, supportive, and participative. *Directive* leadership provides guidance to subordinates by explaining formal procedures, rules, guidelines, performance standards, and generally communicating organizational expectations. *Achievement-oriented* leadership establishes challenging, yet achievable goals in order to improve subordinate performance. *Supportive* leadership demonstrates concern for the needs and general welfare of subordinates. Leaders nurture and show that they care about subordinates. *Participative* leadership calls for the involvement of subordinates with managers in decision making. The emphasis is on consultation and information sharing.

　　To sum up, the leader identifies goals and the rewards associated with their achievement, identifies and clears the paths to their achievement, and tries to satisfy the interim needs of employees as they travel the paths to accomplish the goals and achieve the rewards.

These four leader behaviors do not automatically ensure effective employee performance. Such situational factors as subordinate characteristics and work environment characteristics will also have bearing on employee effectiveness and satisfaction.

Trait Theory Again?

While substantial efforts have been made to match up appropriate leader characteristics with different situations, the task is difficult and the results still inconclusive. Perhaps that is why some popular books on leadership seem to have reverted to a form of trait theory. For example, in his Pulitzer Prize-winning book *Leadership* (1978), James MacGregor Burns identifies two broad leadership categories and five characteristics of leadership.[19] The two categories are transactional leadership and transforming leadership.

Transactional A transaction occurs when two or more people exchange goods or services to achieve their respective objectives. If the people engaged in the transaction are representing others, then they are practicing one kind of transactional leadership. Most negotiations involving elected or appointed representatives are of the transactional form. The negotiating leaders act not in the best interests of all but on behalf of their groups. Transactional leaders are more concerned with "means values" (fairness, responsibility, honesty) than with "end values." At upper organizational levels, collective bargaining between management and labor exemplifies transactional leadership.

Transactional leadership also takes place throughout the leader's normal workday, and in fact takes up most of the day, as the leader engages in activities, interactions, and exchanges with followers. Here is how Thomas J. Peters and Robert H. Waterman, Jr., describe leadership; most of the leader activities in the following passage are transactional:

> Leadership is many things. It is patient, usually boring coalition building. It is the purposeful seeding of cabals that one hopes will result in the appropriate ferment in the bowels of the organization. It is meticulously shifting the attention of the institution through the mundane language of management systems. It is altering agendas so that new priorities get enough attention. It is being visible when things are going awry, and invisible when they are working well. It's building a loyal team at the top that speaks more or less with one voice. It's listening carefully much of the time, frequently speaking with encouragement, and reinforcing words with believable action. It's being tough when necessary, and it's the occasional naked use of power—or the "subtle accumulation of nuances, a hundred things done a little better," as Henry Kissinger once put it.[20]

Transforming Transforming leaders are concerned with such "end values" as liberty, justice, and equality. Over relatively long periods of time, these leaders transform, teach, shape, alter, and elevate the goals and values of their followers and sometimes of society. During the 1960s, Martin Luther King, Jr., provided transforming leadership. He spearheaded the civil rights movement and helped Americans to learn the true meaning of equality.

Within the business organization, the transforming leader helps followers to find meaning and value in work. By means of the day's many transactions, the leader assists followers in getting the work done. In a transforming capacity, the leader helps followers to see a purpose, often an uplifting one, in what they are doing. Such leadership is described in terms like elevating, mobilizing, inspiring, exalting, uplifting, exhorting, and evangelizing. According to Peters and Waterman, "transforming leadership . . . raises the level of human conduct and ethical aspiration of both the leader and the led, and thus has a transforming effect on both."[21]

Characteristics of Leadership

James MacGregor Burns offers five characteristics that mark the relationship of the good leader to the group.

Collective   Leadership is collective; a leader must have at least one follower, more often a collection of followers. When followers respond to their leader, a mutually sustaining relationship develops that binds leader and followers into a collective group. This group establishes a hierarchy, determines acceptable norms and roles, and identifies group goals.

Dissensual   Leadership is dissensual; it involves disagreement and often arises out of disagreement. Total agreement makes organizations complacent, so many organizations build some potential for disagreement and conflict into their structures. Conflict produces leaders; leaders seek to attract followers who will help them expand their power. Conflict also causes groups to unite; a group threatened by another group becomes more cohesive. The aware leader understands the relationship between disagreement and leadership.

Causative   Leaders and followers interact in a way that causes things to happen. Leaders cause change and are themselves changed as they exercise leadership.

Morally Purposeful   Burns views the proper leader as guiding the group toward morally acceptable goals. He does not consider persons who take groups down barren paths or toward unethical or immoral goals to be true leaders. Since Adolf Hitler's aims and methods flew in the face of freedom, dignity, and equality, they were not moral and so Burns does not consider him a leader in the true sense.

Elevating   The proper interaction between leader and followers elevates everyone to a higher level of morality. The whole becomes greater than the sum of its parts. Occasionally, a truly exceptional leader will already have achieved a high moral plateau. That leader then helps followers who aspire to the leader's higher level. Gandhi and Martin Luther King, Jr., might serve as examples.

Current Directions in Compliance

The modern viewpoint is that the authority relationship between the organization's representative (the boss) and the individual employee is transactional. People come to the organization *expecting* order, structure, and hierarchical relationships; indeed they prefer an orderly situation to chaos. Consequently, subordinates accept or at least tolerate the exercise of considerable authority by their superiors.

In addition, employees realize that nonacceptance by the group can have negative results such as loss of income, loss of friends, and so on. Therefore, the ability of the organizational hierarchy to direct behavior becomes considerable, even without the traditional argument of the right of private property.

Because today's subordinates accept authority quite readily, discussions of authority and power that formerly stressed the superior-subordinate relationship have broadened to include the power that *groups*—organizations themselves and units within organizations—acquire and exert. The modern focus has shifted from vertical to horizontal relationships. How and why does one organization or department exert influence on another?

Reducing Uncertainty   In a well-known study representing this modern focus, D.J. Hickson and his colleagues advance a "strategic contingency" theory of power to point up the power accruing to those organizational units or members able to *reduce organizational uncertainty.*[22] Organizations do not like uncertainty, so any unit or member who can reduce uncertainty is able to acquire power. The more critical the uncertainty is to organizational success, and the less replaceable the unit/member is, the greater will be the unit/member's power and influence.

Solving Problems   Gerald R. Salancik and Jeffrey Pfeffer have elaborated on strategic-contingency theory by maintaining that power accrues to those units and people who can *solve critical organizational problems* (a type of organizational uncertainty).[23] If the organization is fighting serious lawsuits, the legal department has power; if gaining a greater share of the market is a critical problem, the marketing department acquires power; if production problems are threatening the organization's existence, the powerful group is the engineers. The groups with power soon begin exercising it in areas other than their own. In time, the company president may come from the group that has faced and solved the organization's critical problems.

Power in the older sense accrued to individuals. In this newer sense, power accrues to *activities* that are important to organizational success and survival (though of course individuals head up and represent these activities).

Individual Resource Exchanges   The ability to give or withhold resources necessary for job accomplishment and personal satisfaction is also a source of power for individuals within organizations. Your need for my resources, both in kind and quantity, drives my ability to direct your behavior in the organizational setting. The more important the resource is to you, the greater is my power to influence your behavior. If I, as a manager, want to influence your behavior, then it behooves me to identify which resources under my control are important to you and then make them available as payoffs for your complying with my authority.

Any organizational member's control over resources, coupled with an awareness of which resources are important to which people, will add up to that member's organizational power. This approach to leadership and the use of authority and power broadens these issues considerably.

Three Levels of Interdependence   Modern scholars study organizational power relationships from a systems perspective. At one level, departmental units within the organizational system struggle for power. Those units able to reduce uncertainty and solve problems acquire the most power. At another level, the modern school studies power relationships between organizations and the structural responses of organizations to those relationships. The third level involves identifying environmental factors other than specific organizations, to determine how they affect organizational design choices. Such influences as government intervention, foreign developments, and even changing social norms may call for structural responses, to cope with the power relationships and mutual interdependencies which these relevant forces represent. These factors will be the focus of Chapter 16, Environment.

SUMMARY

The hierarchy of authority is a natural outcome of organizational growth. As employee numbers and tasks increase, coordination needs demand that the organization chart expand upward as well as outward.

The classicists were firm believers in the hierarchy of authority, keeping authority as close to upper organizational levels as possible. The human relations school studied the concepts of authority, power, and leadership. To be effective leaders, managers must know how and why employees react to authority and power. Authority-acceptance theory explains why organization members accept the use of authority by their leaders. In addition to authority, members of the hierarchy have varying degrees of power, primarily the power to reward and punish. The three power types are physical, material, and symbolic (with its three subtypes: referent, expert, and legitimate power).

Trait theory—the idea that certain traits can result in effective leadership—was found to be of limited utility. The human relations school maintained that what a leader *does* is more important than what a leader *is*. The emphasis shifted from the study of traits to the study of behaviors. The Ohio State studies resulted in a leadership theory based on two factors: *consideration* for workers and *initiating structure* for the work. Researchers at the University of Michigan identified two leadership styles—employee-oriented and production-oriented—that paralleled the two Ohio State factors.

The modern school continues to try to determine what kind of situation requires what kind of leader. Fred E. Fiedler's pioneering work defined the situations that called for job-centered leadership or for people-centered leadership. Path-goal theory proposes three behaviors for successful leadership—and four types of leadership (directive, achievement-oriented, supportive, and participative). The modern conclusion is that *characteristics of specific leaders, subordinates, and organizations join together to cause a particular leader in a particular position within the hierarchy of authority to be an effective or ineffective integrator of organizational effort in a given situation.* The modern manager may well look back with nostalgia to an earlier time when leadership simply meant telling people below you in the organizational hierarchy what to do and making sure that they did it.

Within the organization, those persons directing activities which reduce uncertainty and solve problems acquire organizational power. In relationships between organizations and individuals, the control of important resources affecting inputs, outputs, and satisfaction is a power source increasingly studied by the modern school.

DISCUSSION QUESTIONS

1. What is the hierarchy of authority?
2. What does the right of private property have to do with authority?
3. How and why did the human relations perspective on authority differ from the classical perspective?
4. According to Chester I. Barnard, what four preconditions are necessary before employees will accept authority? Do you believe they are necessary?
5. What is power? What is its source? How does it differ from authority?
6. Why do you suppose organizational members want to acquire power, assume leadership roles, and exercise authority?
7. Describe the hierarchy of authority in an organization of which you have been a member. How did the hierarchy serve to coordinate the organization's activities?
8. What is the trait theory of leadership? What does it contribute to our understanding of leadership?
9. What is a transactional leader? A transforming leader? If you led an organization, which type would you try to be?
10. What were the contributions of the leadership studies at the University of Michigan and at Ohio State University? Are their findings relevant today?
11. How are leadership and authority related?
12. Discuss Fred E. Fiedler's contribution to our understanding of leadership. What are the components of his leadership model? Why is he viewed as a pioneer of the modern attitude toward leadership?
13. What is path-goal theory? Contrast it with the Fiedler model in terms of advantages and disadvantages.
14. What leader characteristics contribute to leader effectiveness? What subordinate characteristics? What organizational characteristics?
15. Can organizational Unit A have power over Unit B even if they are not in a supervisor-subordinate linkage? If so, what might give Unit A this power?
16. If you were hiring someone for a managerial position, how would you try to predict that person's leadership potential? How confident would you be in your prediction?

■ ### WITTBERG & SMITH INVESTMENTS

John Seaber had a problem. One of his account representatives just wasn't cutting the mustard. Chuck had gone through the New York training program, passed all of his exams, and was now back in the Miami office of Wittberg & Smith Investments. Seaber had hoped to turn Chuck into an outstanding account rep, but it just wasn't working out: eight months in a row under his quota.

He looked out the large window of his office into the boardroom. The market had just opened and the other representatives were either on the phone or rushing to place buy and sell orders. Chuck was over at the water fountain laughing and talking with a couple of the clerks.

John Seaber gave Chuck the news that afternoon, concluding this way:

"We've carried you for eight months, Chuck, and I'm at the end of the line. You'll get one month's draw as severance pay. You are to have your desk cleaned out by Friday at five."

Chuck didn't seem upset. He just smiled as he left and said, "Maybe so, John, maybe so."

Chuck went back to his desk and dialed the private New York number of the firm's managing partner, Arthur Smith.

"Hello, Dad? This is Chuck. . . . Yeah, I've got a little problem down here. I didn't quite make quota so Seaber told me to hit the road. Can you give me a hand?"

"Must be some misunderstanding, Chuck. Don't you worry. I'll call John and straighten it out."

If Mr. Smith can get Chuck Smith reinstated with a phone call, does that reflect an organizational problem? Or is helping out his son simply a privilege of a managing partner? Once this situation becomes common knowledge, what will be the effect in the Miami branch office? How can John Seaber best deal with "the Chuck Smith situation"?

■ MONSTER EQUIPMENT INC.

The first time Linda Shaughnessy used a Monster multistation weight machine, she was hooked. She was so enthusiastic about Monster Equipment that she eventually went to work for the company as a sales representative. With the help and guidance of her supervisor, marketing manager Arnold Franco, she soon led the company in her specialty: sales and installation of Monster Equipment in health spas for women.

One day she got the following memo:

To: Linda Shaughnessy, Sales
From: Hobart Newhouse, Vice President Public Relations
Subject: Superstar Endorsements

Ms. Shaughnessy, I am very familiar with your success as a representative of Monster Equipment. Because you are so highly regarded among the nation's female bodybuilding superstars, I want to propose the following.

I would like for you to spend approximately 25 percent of your time on the road to try to sign up the bodybuilding superstars as endorsers of Monster Equipment. For this aspect of your responsibilities, you would report to me at the vice-presidential level. For your sales responsibilities, you would of course continue to report to Arnold Franco.

I believe we can offer you a salary supplement and bonus plan that will make this new division of your time extremely attractive to you. If you accept this proposal, I shall inform Mr. Franco and get the paperwork moving.

Shaughnessy saw a terrific opportunity in Newhouse's offer, but she also saw some potential problems. What were these problems? Should Shaughnessy accept the offer immediately? Only after talking with Arnold Franco? Should Newhouse have spoken to Franco first, or do you feel that a vice president doesn't have to clear such matters with a marketing manager?

NOTES

1. R.C. Davis, *The Fundamentals of Top Management* (New York: Harper & Brothers, 1951), p. 281.
2. Ibid., pp. 284, 286.
3. James D. Mooney and Alan C. Reiley, *Onward Industry: The Principles of Organization and Their Significance to Modern Industry* (New York: Harper & Brothers, 1931), p. 19.
4. Chester I. Barnard, *The Functions of the Executive* (Cambridge, MA.: Harvard University Press, 1938), Chapter 12.
5. Daniel Katz and Robert L. Kahn, *The Social Psychology of Organizations* (New York: Wiley, 1966), p. 204.
6. David Mechanic, "Sources of Power of Lower Participants in Complex Organizations," *Administrative Science Quarterly* 7 (December 1962): 350.
7. For a review of the differences between potential and real use of power, see Keith G. Provan, "Recognizing, Measuring, and Interpreting the Potential/Enacted Power Distinction in Organizational Research," *Academy of Management Review* 5 (October 1980): 549–559.
8. Walter Buckley, *Sociology and Modern Systems Theory* (Englewood Cliffs, NJ: Prentice-Hall, 1967), p. 178. For a more elaborate discussion of how power operates in specific situations, see Anthony T. Cobb, "An Episodic Model of Power: Toward an Integration of Theory and Research," *Academy of Management Review* 9 (July 1984): 482–493; and W. Graham Astley and Paramjit S. Sachdeva, "Structural Sources of Intraorganizational Power: A Theoretical Synthesis," *Academy of Management Review* 9 (January 1984): 104–113.
9. For further discussion of these power types, see John R.P. French, Jr., and Bertram Raven, "The Bases of Social Power," in *Group Dynamics: Research and Theory,* ed. D. Cartwright and A. Zander (Evanston, IL: Row, Peterson, 1960), pp. 607–623. These *power* types and subtypes are similar to Max Weber's *authority* types: personal or charismatic, traditional, rational-legal, technical, and formal.
10. James D. Mooney, "The Principles of Organization," in *Papers on the Science of Administration,* ed. Luther Gulick and Lyndall Urwick (1937; reprint ed., Clifton, NJ: Augustus M. Kelly, 1973), p. 93.
11. R.M. Stogdill, "Personal Factors Associated with Leadership: A Survey of the Literature," *Journal of Psychology* 25 (March 1948): 35–71.
12. Ibid., p. 64.
13. R.M. Stogdill, *Handbook of Leadership: A Survey of Theory and Research* (New York: The Free Press, 1974).
14. J.K. Hemphill and A.E. Coons, "Development of the Leader Behavior Description Questionnaire," in *Leader Behavior: Its Description and Measurement,* ed. R.M. Stogdill and A.E. Coons (Columbus: Bureau of Business Research, Ohio State University, 1957).
15. R.M. Stogdill, *Handbook of Leadership.*
16. Representative publications of the Michigan group include D. Katz and R.L. Kahn, "Human Organization and Worker Motivation," in *Industrial Productivity,* ed. L. Reed Tripp (Madison, WI: Industrial Relations Research Association, 1951), pp. 146–171; and D. Katz et al., *Productivity, Supervision and Morale in an Office Situation* (Ann Arbor, MI: Institute for Social Research, 1950).

17. Daniel Katz and Robert L. Kahn, *The Social Psychology of Organizations,* pp. 325–326.
18. See Robert J. House, "A Path-Goal Theory of Leader Effectiveness," *Administrative Science Quarterly* 16 (September 1971): 321-328; and Charles N. Greene, "Questions of Causation in the Path-Goal Theory of Leadership," *Academy of Management Journal* 22 (March 1979): 22–41.
19. James MacGregor Burns, *Leadership* (New York: Harper Colophon Books, 1978).
20. Thomas J. Peters and Robert H. Waterman, Jr., *In Search of Excellence: Lessons from America's Best-Run Companies* (New York: Harper & Row, 1982), p. 82.
21. Ibid., p. 83.
22. D.J. Hickson, C.R. Hinings, C.A. Lee, R.E. Schneck, and J.M. Pennings, "A Strategic Contingencies Theory of Intraorganizational Power," *Administrative Science Quarterly* 16 (June 1971): 216–229.
23. Gerald R. Salancik and Jeffrey Pfeffer, "Who Gets Power and How They Hold On to It: A Strategic-Contingency Model of Power," *Organizational Dynamics* 5 (Winter 1977): 3–21.

ADDITIONAL READINGS

Bass, Bernard M. "Leadership: Good, Better, Best." *Organizational Dynamics* 13 (Winter 1985): 26–40.

Behling, Orlando, and Charles F. Rauch, Jr. "A Functional Perspective on Improving Leadership Effectiveness." *Organizational Dynamics* 13 (Spring 1985): 51–61.

Benfari, Robert C., Harry E. Wilkinson, and Charles D. Orth. "The Effective Use of Power." *Business Horizons* 29 (May/June 1986): 12–16.

Bennis, W., and B. Nanus. *Leaders: The Strategies for Taking Charge.* New York: Harper & Row, 1985.

Child, John, and Bruce Partridge. *Lost Managers: Supervisors in Industry and Society.* Cambridge, MA: Harvard University Press, 1982.

Dalton, M. *Men Who Manage.* New York: Wiley, 1959.

Dubin, Robert. *Leadership and Productivity.* San Francisco: Chandler Publishing Company, 1965.

Fiedler, Fred E., and Martin M. Chemers. *Leadership and Effective Management.* Glenview, IL: Scott, Foresman, 1974.

Fleishman, E.A. *"Leadership Climate" and Supervisory Behavior.* Columbus, OH: Personnel Research Board, Ohio State University Press, 1951.

Graef, Claude L. "The Situational Leadership Theory: A Critical View." *Academy of Management Review* 8 (April 1983): 285–291.

House, R.J., and M.L. Baetz. "Leadership: Some Empirical Generalizations and New Research Directions." In *Research in Organizational Behavior,* vol. 1. Edited by B.M. Staw, pp. 341–423. Greenwich, CT: JAI Press, 1979.

Hunt, J.G., U. Sekaran, and C.A. Schriesheim, eds. *Leadership: Beyond Establishment Views.* Carbondale, IL: Southern Illinois University Press, 1981.

Jacobs, T.O. *Leadership and Exchange in Formal Organizations.* Alexandria, VA: Human Resources Research Organization, 1971.

Jones, Gareth R. "Forms of Control and Leader Behavior." *Journal of Management* 9 (Fall/Winter 1983): 159–172.

Kotter, John P. *Power and Influence: Beyond Formal Authority.* New York: Macmillan, 1985.

Maccoby, Michael. *The Leader: A New Face for American Management.* New York: Ballantine Books, 1983.

Mackenzie, Kenneth D. "Virtual Positions and Power." *Management Science* 32 (May 1986): 622–642.

Mintzberg, Henry. *Power in and Around Organizations.* Englewood Cliffs, NJ: Prentice-Hall, 1983.

Misumi, Jyuji, and Mark F. Peterson. "The Performance-Maintenance (PM) Theory of Leadership: Review of a Japanese Research Program." *Administrative Science Quarterly* 30 (June 1985): 198–223.

Pfeffer, Jeffrey. *Power in Organizations.* Marshfield, MA: Pitman Publishing Inc., 1981.

Schein, Edgar H. *Organizational Culture and Leadership: A Dynamic View.* San Francisco: Jossey-Bass, 1985.

Schriesheim, Chester A. "The Great High Consideration—High Initiating Structure Leadership Myth: Evidence on its Generalizability." *Journal of Social Psychology* 116 (April 1982): 221–228.

Shukla, Ramesh K. "Influence of Power Bases in Organizational Decision Making: A Contingency Model." *Decision Sciences* 13 (July 1982): 450–470.

Skinner, E.W. "Relationships Between Leadership Behavior Patterns and Organizational-Situational Variables." *Personnel Psychology* 22 (Autumn 1969): 489–494.

Smith, Jonathan E., Kenneth P. Carson, and Ralph A. Alexander. "Leadership: It Can Make a Difference." *Academy of Management Journal* 27 (December 1984): 765–776.

Vroom, Victor H. "Leadership." In *Handbook of Industrial and Organizational Psychology.* Edited by Marvin Dunnette. Chicago: Rand McNally, 1976.

Yukl, G.A. *Leadership in Organizations.* Englewood Cliffs, NJ: Prentice-Hall, 1981.

Zaleznik, A. "Managers and Leaders: Are They Different?" *Harvard Business Review* 55 (May/June 1977): 67–78.

Formalization

The last chapter explored a basic integrating mechanism of any organization: leadership. In its most direct form, owner/entrepreneurs oversee the activities of people they have employed to help them reach their goals. Both the employees and society at large grant that business owners have a legitimate right to direct employee behavior within the organizational setting; they own the means of production and, within our society, are supported by the right of private property. In other societies, leadership may come about in other ways—for example, by divine right or brute force. The legitimate right to lead becomes real in our society through authority-acceptance theory.

This chapter takes as its beginning premise the general willingness of subordinates in an organization to accept authority. It takes for granted that mechanisms of leadership, power, and authority have been developed and put into place. What organizational strategies are then available to ensure that employees comply with management's wishes when direct managerial oversight is impossible because *management is not physically present?*

When the organization grows beyond a certain size, top managers obviously cannot oversee all activities of all subordinates. Also, size often brings geographical spread, which makes direct supervision even more difficult.

Another relevant factor is the limitations on top-manager expertise that come with organizational growth. Like everyone else, managers have what Nobel Laureate Herbert A. Simon called "bounded rationality": limitations on their ability to know everything that ideally they would like to know. Managers try to make rational decisions, within the boundaries of their incomplete knowledge. Large organizations often have highly complex production processes. They may also be surrounded by concerned, possibly hostile, constituencies, for instance, a pesticide manufacturer surrounded by a concerned community and subject to the attentions of an inquisitive government monitoring agency. The operation of many modern organizations requires an overwhelming knowledge of law, local customs, health and safety standards, production techniques, and labor relations—more knowledge than any one person, no matter how intelligent and hardworking, could hope to master in a lifetime.

Yet, even though managers and their subordinates cannot know everything, they are still responsible for complying with laws, customs, and standards; with using effective production techniques; with maintaining suitable labor relations. The oversight problem does not go away just because the task seems huge, if not impossible. Managers remain responsible for achieving organizational goals. In such a complex environment, where constant direct supervision is impossible, managerial abilities to guide subordinates will be severely taxed. So organizations must find mechanisms that ensure employee compliance.

Two mechanisms already discussed in Part 2, Differentiating Strategies, are decentralization and delegation. Under decentralization, top managers set up units as profit centers, then hold subordinate managers responsible for reaching targeted return-on-investment criteria. Under delegation, top managers make their subordinate managers accountable for rather formal sets of tasks. Both of these mechanisms were designed in part to solve the oversight problem.

A third approach, favored during the classical era and still used in all organizations to coordinate activities, is *formalization*—of rules, standards, policies, methods, procedures. This chapter covers the origins of formalization as organizations grew during the classical era, the human relations reaction against classical formalization, and the more moderate modern approach to the issue.

CATEGORIES OF FORMALIZATION

In *The Structure of Organizations: A Synthesis of Research* (1979), Henry Mintzberg divides the mechanisms of formalization into three classes: performance control, action planning, and behavior formalization.[1]

Performance Control

Some formalization devices are standards for *general performance,* without reference to any of the specific actions that add up to this general performance. A performance control standard would be, "Increase sales by 10 percent this year."

Action Planning

This mechanism tells employees more specifically what to do: "In order to increase sales by 10 percent this year, introduce a line of blue widgets."

Behavior Formalization

At its extreme, action planning becomes behavior formalization, in which employees are told what to do and how to do it in minute detail. Their job behavior is thoroughly formalized into specifics. According to Mintzberg,

> Action planning emerges as the means by which the nonroutine decisions and actions of an entire organization, typically structured on a functional basis, can be designed as an integrated system. All of this is accomplished in advance, on the drawing board

so to speak. Behavior formalization designs the organization as an integrated system, too, but only for its routine activities. Action planning is its counterpart for the nonroutine activities, for the changes. It specifies who will do what, when, and where, so that the change will take place as desired.[2]

Training and Indoctrination   Later in his book, Mintzberg discusses training and indoctrination, which can be considered special cases of behavior formalization. The organization uses training and indoctrination to introduce new employees into vital parts of the organization, doing organizational jobs in the way that the organization wants them done. If John Doe is hired to be an auto tire-tread maker, he will typically be brought into a tire plant training room where someone will show him how to put treads on tires, tell him what level of job performance is expected of him, give him the rules and regulations governing his behavior while on the job, explain the terms of the union contract, and make him aware of people with whom he will be expected to cooperate. When the training program is over, John Doe will have a good idea of what behavior and activity the organization expects from him.

Training and indoctrination programs build the formal relationships of employees with their organizations. The material can be presented both orally and in such written documents as a policy manual, handbook for new employees, copy of the union contract, and so on. Basic training for army recruits, internships and residencies for medical professionals, and preprofessional training for accountants all serve the same primary purpose: to build the job-related behaviors and skills necessary to perform at levels expected by the organization.

Process Control

Process-control methods are those formal standards placed on an operating process that an organizational member is performing. For example, a heart monitor may ring to signal a nurse that she must attend to a patient; an automatic weighing machine may tell an operator that cans of coffee are coming out of the fill unit with insufficient weight.

Other types of process control also monitor the job behavior of organizational members. Data-entry clerks using modern computer terminals are automatically asked to respond to a preprogrammed sequence of questions that, when answered, give the information necessary for paying an insurance claim, approving a bank loan, or some other transaction. The computer program will typically have yet a further control over the input clerk which tests the information typed in against appropriate boundaries. For instance, if the computer clerk attempts to overpay an insurance claim by thousands of dollars, the computer tests the amount being typed in and challenges it as incorrect or unacceptable. The entry clerk then has to check the work and correct the figure.

In such cases, a top manager has created a formal standard against which all responses are tested while a transaction is taking place. Employees are monitored continuously to prevent them from making mistakes. Employee performance in many organizations is similarly monitored or controlled while processes are underway. Cars are brought to the assembly-line worker at a predetermined rate of speed; the worker must perform an operation before the work flows past that station. The machinery paces and controls the worker's job, and deviation is possible only if the worker rebels against the system. The rebellion can't last long because the worker at the next station can't do his job if the previous worker did not do her job. Machine pacing and the interdependence of steps in the process in effect introduce two separate controls on employees.

The moving assembly line is the typical example of process control. Here is how spot welder Phil Stallings describes his work on the line.

> I start the automobile, the first welds. From there it goes to another line, where the floor's put on, the roof, the trunk hood, the doors. Then it's put on a frame. There is hundreds of lines. . . . I stand in one spot, about two- or three-feet area, all night. [The line] don't stop. It just goes and goes and goes. I bet there's men who have lived and died out there, never seen the end of that line. And they never will—because it's endless. . . . Should I leave this job to go to the bathroom I risk being fired. The line moves all the time.[3]

Similarly, a truck driver's speedometer serves as a process control over the rate of travel; a teacher uses test scores to measure student progress in the learning process; and a plant manager's evaluation of a supervisor's managerial skills is based partly on how many grievances the supervisor's subordinates have filed. These measures are different from Mintzberg's in that they monitor performance while it is going on rather than before or after the fact. As such, they formalize the work behavior of the people whose performance is being monitored.

Steven Kerr and John W. Slocum, Jr., point out that the task itself sometimes stimulates the worker to carry out a predetermined part in the process:

> For example, a stimulus—the sounding of an alarm or the appearance of a patron at a bar—will often evoke some response, simple or elaborate, which is automatic in that it has developed over time and been found by the task's performer to constitute an appropriate reaction. Thus, the arrival of an undercoated automobile in front of a paint station may trigger an automatic response on the part of a worker who picks up a piece of sandpaper in his or her left hand and an air sander in the right. The worker follows a performance program—a set of codified responses—in a routine manner evoked each time the same stimulus is presented.[4]

When task uncertainty and interdependence are low, organizational leaders can provide members with formalized written policies and procedures that tell them, in advance, how to respond to routine stimuli. Organizational members can then make appropriate, predetermined responses, even if their supervisors are not present.

THE CLASSICAL PERSPECTIVE

Max Weber and Bureaucracy

Max Weber's detailed investigation into bureaucracy's nature, characteristics, and advantages serves to illustrate the merits of formalization from the classical perspective.

As discussed in Chapter 2, Weber saw the characteristics of large-scale twentieth-century bureaucracies as: hierarchical organization, rational job structures, separation of owners and managers, impersonal rules for all, selection by competence, and written formalization. This last principle means that the rules, decisions, and actions of the bureaucracy are formalized in writing. Weber says:

> Administrative acts, decisions, and rules are formulated and recorded in writing, even in cases where oral discussion is the rule or is even mandatory. This applies at least to preliminary discussions and proposals, to final decisions, and to all sorts of orders and rules. The combination of written documents and a continuous organization of official functions constitutes the "office" which is the central focus of all types of modern corporate action.[5]

The Purposes of Formalization

In general, formalization is designed to take the place of direct personal oversight and to avoid having to solve recurring problems over and over again. According to Jerald Hage:

> Organizations learn from past experiences and employ rules as a repository of that experience. Some organizations carefully codify each job, describing the specific details, and then ensure conformity to the job prescription. Other organizations have loosely defined jobs and do not carefully control work behavior. *Formalization,* or standardization, is measured by the proportion of codified jobs and the range of variation that is tolerated within the rules defining the jobs. The higher the proportion of codified jobs and the less the range of variation allowed, the more formalized the organization.[6]

From the classical perspective, formalization had several more purposes that made the specific statement of policies, methods, and procedures desirable.

Unwilling, Unable Subordinates   Although many organizational members are willing and able to work toward organizational goals without direct supervision, some are not. The former are willing to acknowledge the organization's right or authority to tell them what to do; the latter employees rebel some of the time, or all the time, until their rebellion is discovered and they are dismissed from the organization.

The degree of control exerted will vary. A white-collar, out-of-office salesperson may have to submit a monthly record of sales calls made; a blue-collar assembly-line employee may have to meet a daily production quota. The sales-call record and the production quota are both formal reporting mechanisms designed to monitor the behavior of subordinate employees with different job types and work cycles. The monthly versus daily requirement may reflect the organization's different expectations of the two employees and different degrees of trust in them.

Even more important, the organization needs to know—before it is too late—if its employees are, intentionally or unintentionally, doing something contrary to organizational wishes. Whether the undesirable behavior results from rebellion, ignorance, or inattention, it must be stopped before it harms the organization.

Ensuring Efficiency   A second reason for the development of formalization techniques during the classical era was to ensure efficiency. Organizations spend much time, effort, and money trying to determine the one best way to conduct an operation, handle paperwork, or close a sale on the phone. Policies, procedures, and training programs then ensure that persons performing these carefully studied functions perform them in the single best way.

Efficiency was the issue of concern to Frederick W. Taylor (1856–1915) in his classic studies of production processes. At Bethlehem Steel Works in 1899, Taylor experimented with men loading pig iron onto freight cars. When he began, they were loading an average of 12.5 long tons per day (2240 pounds to the long ton). Taylor specially selected and trained a worker whom he called "Schmidt." Through scientific investigation and analysis of the job, Taylor concluded that Schmidt should work 43 percent of the time and rest 57 percent of the time. On the first day using this schedule, Schmidt loaded 47.5 long tons.

As a common illustration of scientific management principles, Taylor used an American baseball team. On such a team,

> You will see that the science of doing every little act that is done by every player on the baseball field has been developed. Every single element of the game of baseball has been the subject of the most intimate, the closest study of many men, and finally, the best way of doing each act that takes place on the baseball field has been fairly well agreed upon and established as a standard throughout the country. The players have not only been told the best way of making each important motion or play, but they have been taught, coached and trained to it through months of drilling. And I think that every man who has watched first-class play, or who knows anything of the management of the modern baseball team, realizes fully the utter impossibility of winning with the best team of individual players that was ever gotten together unless every man on the team obeys the signals or orders of the coach and obeys them at once when the coach gives those orders; that is, without the intimate cooperation between all members of the team and the management, which is characteristic of scientific management.[7]

Frank Gilbreth (1868–1924) also achieved impressive production gains by applying scientific management principles. Gilbreth first directed his attention to the ancient craft of bricklaying. By carefully observing bricklayers at work, thinking about the job scientifically, and then planning and implementing the best way to do it, Gilbreth quickly improved a craft that had been performed inefficiently for hundreds of years. Gilbreth and his wife Lillian studied time and motion by taking moving pictures of people working with a clock in the background to measure the time required for each motion. Using this information, they developed methods for increasing industrial production efficiency.

Once Taylor, Gilbreth, and their industrial engineering descendants established the most efficient production methods, mechanisms had to be devised to ensure that workmen actually used the methods. Production quotas have been the most widely used compliance device for stimulating the continued use by workmen of the one best, most efficient way.

Consistency of Behavior   A third related, but slightly different, purpose of formalization is to ensure consistency of employee behavior. Organizations, particularly during the classical era, wanted their jobs done the same way regardless of which employee was doing the job. If an organization stresses fair treatment of its clients, then the organization wants every clerk handling returned merchandise to treat every customer in just about the same way. Employees of politically oriented organizations—for example, employees in a congressional office, handlers of complaints in a publicly regulated utility, and teachers in a school system—are expected to follow prescribed rules and regulations to ensure that all clients are dealt with in the same manner. An organization not doing so may find itself featured in an exposé on the nightly news, accused of favoritism and other unfair practices.

Since all organizations, particularly in the modern period, must to one degree or another be sensitive to external needs and pressures, potentially inconsistent employee behavior demands top-management control even though top managers cannot observe every organizational transaction with the public. Certain organizations that are very sensitive to public opinion establish policies, explain them thoroughly to employees, then build in multiple check mechanisms to prohibit inequity or dishonesty by organizational members. How large is a state employee's expense account to be? How does a welfare agency determine who gets how much assistance? These and similar questions are precisely answered "by the book," with follow-up audits to ensure that organizational members are complying.

The classicists saw little merit in giving employees discretion and little need to make jobs challenging by permitting flexibility of employee response. They wanted to guarantee consistency of employee behavior as far as humanly possible.

Clarifying Job Expectations   Formalization is a means of clarifying employee job expectations. Organizations give job descriptions to employees, indicate their job scopes, and delineate their responsibilities and authority. Organizations have rules and regulations that govern day-to-day job performance. Organizations have performance appraisal systems that compare expected performance with actual performance. All of these formalized elements *clarify what the organization expects from employees* in return for the organizational payoffs that employees derive in exchange for exerting effort on the organization's behalf.

For example, if I am supposed to produce 78 units per hour, sell 55 cases of candy bars per day, contact 15 new customers per week, or give 50 speeches per year, then I have a basis for understanding how my performance relates to the overall organizational goal. I also understand what an employee who wishes to remain in my organizational position is supposed to do. Part of a minister's job description may be "to visit the sick in the hospital." If he does not visit the sick, he is just as subject to dismissal as the assembly-line worker unable to meet the production quota. Through formal means, both know what the organization expects of them; both know that they will be judged against formalized standards.

Organizational Benefits of Clarity From the organization's viewpoint, formal standards result in beneficial clear-cut definitions of functions and responsibilities. Managers cannot always directly supervise the behavior or activity of subordinates. Well-defined job roles ensure that organizational members do not perform the wrong tasks or overlook the right ones, and that two people are not doing the same job. Too many people have had the experience of doing a great job, then finding out that the job was unnecessary or had already been done by someone else. Some organizations introduce double work to be sure that errors are not made or that dishonest employees are caught. However, the organization does not usually want to waste the time of its people in duplicated work efforts. Formalized methods serve to avoid this situation.

The Incomplete Planning Process No organization can plan for every future eventuality. As employees perform their tasks, situations not specifically covered by policies, procedures, or decision rules will arise. To prepare employees for such occasions, organizations must thoroughly train members in the organizational mission, purpose, values, goals, and methods. In new and unfamiliar situations, the thoroughly trained organizational member can be trusted to think and act as top managers would—without checking back with headquarters. Formalized training fills the holes in the organizational planning process.

Consider the early missionaries of the Catholic Church. The Church could not possibly plan for all the diverse situations these distant carriers of the faith would encounter. To be certain that these missionaries made decisions in congruence with Church principles, they were trained thoroughly before being sent off throughout the world. Once they were gone, they were on their own; they could not telephone or telegraph back to Rome for instructions about how to handle an unfamiliar issue. Only if a missionary had been completely trained and indoctrinated could the missionary be sent out alone. So the training and indoctrination process serves, in essence, to clone the organization's top managers. In new situations, the organizational representatives will ideally make the same decisions that top managers would.

The ethical codes and norms of many professional societies (such as the American Medical Association, American Bar Association, American Management Association) provide a current illustration of this point. These societies seek to train their members in generally accepted principles or ethical codes. When organization members face unfamiliar situations, their decisions—based on a common professional value system—should reflect the viewpoint of the profession.

The Organizational Memory Formalization creates an organizational memory about what works and what does not, what past precedents will affect future occurrences. Some parts of this memory are never written down; they become part of organizational myth, folklore, and culture that members pass along through rituals, behavior patterns, tales, and habitual ways of doing things. However, much of the organizational memory is written down and becomes the basis of policies, procedures, and practices in the formal organizational literature, or less formally in the correspondence, memos, and reports in the organization's file cabinets. Supreme Court decisions are published and circulated, on the assumption that they will affect future cases. In the same way, the organization's union grievances, personnel policies, and organizational procedures also create a base of expectations about how the organizational past will affect the future.

The organizational memory has lasting effects, not all of them beneficial from the organization's perspective. For instance, management always has a hard time during union negotiations in dropping a benefit agreed to in a former contract. Not only does the institutional memory build habits and sanctioned behavior patterns; it also creates employee expectations about what is and is not part of their jobs and about organizational rewards. During the 1980s, the American Telephone & Telegraph Company struggled to learn new behaviors necessary to succeed in a competitive environment rather than in its previous regulated environment. The company's considerable organizational memory influenced its ability to change. Employees of the old "Ma Bell" had grown accustomed to job security and above-average wages; these employees now work for a new AT&T, fighting for its share of a highly competitive telecommunications market. The U.S. Postal Service is also beginning to feel the heat of competition, and its institutional memory will likewise be a considerable tempering influence on its ability to respond.

On the plus side, the institutional memory provides guidance in unforeseen areas where clear rules and regulations do not apply or are not readily available. Here the organizational memory—or, in a broader sense, the *culture* (to be discussed later in detail)—allows people to evaluate situations in terms of "I wonder how old Harry would have handled this one?" This part of the organizational memory can be kept accessible by means of an organizational history which extolls old Harry's values and beliefs, or in company files of past decisions that employees can refer to and apply to present situations. In these ways, values and beliefs of former top managers can be kept alive to influence the behavior of today's employees.

Identification with the Organization   A final reason for formalization is to reinforce employee identification with the organization and its overall goals. Continued compliance with top management's directives can be encouraged by mechanisms which reinforce and remind the membership of their reasons for joining together to achieve a common, conscious purpose—why they are working cooperatively to achieve the organization's aims. In a less formal way, the institutional memory and the organizational culture help to serve these purposes by reinforcing the positive organizational values and pointing out deviance from them.

The organization's assurances of what it will and won't do for employees are contained in formal policy statements. Employees reading those statements are reminded of why they joined the organization in the first place and why they stay with it. If formal policy and reality disagree, then the policy statements may provide the mechanism whereby employees can challenge bad decisions by their bosses. As a result, employees in formalized organizations may have *more* discretion and independence than employees in less formalized settings. According to W. Richard Scott:

> Because obedience is owed not to a person—whether a traditional chief or a charismatic leader—but to a set of impersonal principles, subordinates in bureaucratic systems have a stronger basis for independent action, guided by their interpretation of the principles.[8]

Most organizations are aware of the morale and effectiveness problems that can arise when what the organization *says* it will do differs from what the organization actually does. Organizations do not want to lose credibility with their members, because a loss of credibility in one area carries over into all organizational promises.

The managers of the classical era made many efforts to formalize and standardize employee behavior. They thought formalization could enhance their ability to reach organizational goals in a rational, predictable, totally controllable way. They could best meet their responsibilities and eliminate subordinate decision-making opportunities through tightly defined rules, procedures, and guidelines.

The Elements of Formalization

The basic elements for implementing the objectives of top management through formalization originated with the classicists and persist into the present. They are policies, standard methods, procedures, and rules.

Policies   A policy is a statement of organizational intent. It is designed as a *guide* to making decisions about recurring organizational problems or avoiding potential problems. "No ticket, no wash," "Satisfaction guaranteed or your money back," and "No checks cashed" are organizational policy statements designed to guide employees in dealing with customers. If a longstanding customer comes in with no ticket, or a frequent buyer asks to cash a check, employees know the organization's position on the issue but also know that they have the flexibility and discretion to make an exception to the policy.

Organizations may also have many internal policies, similarly designed to solve and avoid problems. "We promote from within" and "No husband and wife shall work in the same department" are illustrations of internal policies.

Policies may be broad or narrow, general or specific, depending on the degree to which the organization's leaders feel the need and have the ability to constrain the decision-making flexibility of the organization's members. If an important organizational goal is to keep the customer happy, then the "satisfaction guaranteed" policy strongly encourages employees to comply with all but the most outrageous customer requests. Indeed, customer satisfaction is so important to some retail stores that even this flexibility has been removed and the policy has become an organizational rule.

Since policies are a guide to how employees should think about problems, managers should be sure that the policies they establish give employees the kind and amount of guidance they need.

Methods   The difference between a policy and a standard method is not clear-cut. Both guide employees in the solution of recurring problems. Policies tend to tell employees *what* to do (or not to do); standard methods give more specific instruction in *how* to carry out an activity.

The best known use of standard methods is the automobile assembly line. The parts on which the employee works are standardized, as are the employee's tools. It follows that the method of using the tools to assemble the parts should be standardized for greater overall efficiency.

If an organization is going to standardize a method, it obviously wants the chosen method to be the best one possible. Industrial engineers may have to spend many hours in determining the best way to carry out one organizational operation, and the organization may have hundreds of operations. Therefore, determining the "one best way" to perform every function may be too costly.

However, once standard methods have been worked out, they can be useful to managers trying to plan the work flow. Standard methods often take a standard length of time to perform and are accompanied by a standard cost. Therefore, the manager can easily plan how long a job is going to take and how much it will cost.

Procedures   The main difference between a standard method and a standard operating procedure (SOP) is that a procedure usually involves *several people* carrying out a *sequence of activities.* Each organizational member gives specialized attention to one function that needs to be done. Then, these functions must be coordinated to accomplish the organization's day-to-day activities. Procedures tie all the organization's working parts together. Most organizations have dozens or even hundreds of standard operating procedures. If they did not, they would have to determine new routines and standards every time a problem recurred. Standard operating procedures make it unnecessary to reinvent the wheel continually. An example of a standard operating procedure is described in the box on page 250.

Procedures are essential to the smooth running of the organization. Yet they can overwhelm employees and customers if they become too elaborate (as anyone knows who has tried to cut through government red tape). The efficient organization will establish only those procedures that facilitate achievement of organizational objectives.

Rules   Rules are specific statements of *what may and may not be done.* Rules tell the organizational membership exactly what boundaries the leadership has placed on stipulated behavior areas. "No smoking," "No conference football team may practice before July 31," and "Hard hats must be worn in this area" are examples of organizational rules.

Guides or Rules?   Organizations must know how flexible they intend the elements of formalization to be and must communicate the degree of flexibility to subordinates. In particular, they must let subordinates know whether their instructions are *rules* or *guides.* When possible, instructions should be expressed as guides. People and circumstances change over time. A rule that seemed sensible in the past may be useless today. The people who implement a plan are often in a better position than the planner to determine how the plan should be applied.

Sometimes, however, rules are preferable to guides. The classicists thought that rules were *usually* preferable. If personnel lack the judgment necessary to use flexible guidelines, strict rules may be needed. Or if a procedure involves the interaction of several people, rules may be necessary so that the steps in the procedure can be coordinated.

To sum up the classical attitude toward formalization: Managers—from the top person on down through the hierarchy—can't be everyplace at once. Therefore, organizations need formalized rules, policies, and procedures to keep employees moving

---

Welding Permit Procedure

In light of the serious fire hazards involved in welding and cutting with acetylene gas torch or electric arc equipment, a Welding Permit Procedure has been established. No work of this nature—by the Maintenance Department or by outside contractors—may be done without this permit. The *only* exception is in the maintenance shop where adequate welding space and protection have been provided.

No compressed gas cylinders are to be left either on transport carts or on the floor unless they are securely supported by chains to prevent them from falling.

Specific Instructions

1. The Fire Chief is responsible for administering this procedure.
2. Permits are to be issued by Watchmen, who must keep a log of all permits issued. Permits are good for *one day only.*
3. Permits may be obtained by Maintenance Foremen or Project Engineers (or Tower Foremen when the Maintenance Foremen are not available). The permit must be signed by the person obtaining it after indicating by check mark that all precautions listed on the back of the card have been taken.
4. Permits must also be signed by the Department Head, Operating Supervisor, or Foreman of the department where work is to be carried out, indicating that the person in charge is aware of such work going on.
5. A helper *must* be present to act as a fire watch while the work is being carried out.
6. When work covered by the permit is completed for that day, the permit must again be signed by the person obtaining the permit, signifying that the work area was inspected for fire hazards.
7. The permit must then be returned to the Watchman for recording completion of the work in the log.
8. The Watchmen will inspect all areas where welding equipment has been used, on all plant tours on the second and third shifts. A record of inspections must be kept in the log.
9. Should a permit not be returned at the end of the day, the Watchman will try to locate it at the earliest opportunity.

---

toward organizational goals even when managers cannot supervise them directly. Employees following strict organizational standards have no need of discretion or independence. The less opportunity for independent thinking and decision making that employees have, the fewer mistakes they will make.

As we shall see next, the human relations school was able to moderate this position. Even so, modern organizations still regularly employ the formalized principles and devices favored by the classicists, if not as rigidly.

THE HUMAN RELATIONS PERSPECTIVE

The classical position came to be called "the machine school" or the "mechanistic approach" to organization. Both Alvin W. Gouldner and James Worthy used the former term frequently, and Tom Burns and G.M. Stalker used the term "mechanistic" in a widely cited book.[9]

Willing Cooperation

The human relations writers believed that organizations should not be built on bureaucratic, mechanistic, formalized models. A general reason for their opposition arose out of why people join organizations in the first place. In the effective organization, people join and cooperate *willingly*—not because they are made to follow a formal standard. According to Chester I. Barnard:

> By definition there can be no organization without persons. However, as . . . it is not persons, but the services or acts or action or influences of persons, which should be treated as constituting organizations, it is clear that *willingness* of persons to contribute efforts to the cooperative system is indispensable.[10]

If people willingly join an organization and cooperate with a leadership that offers appropriate inducements, then strict formalization and mechanistic controls are not necessary. At the same time, if organizational members are dissatisfied and unwilling to cooperate, then a formalized set of rules, regulations, and standards can probably not force them to be fully cooperative and productive.

The mechanistic approach is best exemplified by bureaucracies, as studied by Max Weber. The *efficiency* of both machines and bureaucracies is self-evident. However, bureaucratic organizations gain control of members at too great an expense, according to some writers.

The Consequences of Control

James G. March and Herbert A. Simon have summed up the work of three writers on the subject of control: Robert K. Merton, Philip Selznick, and Alvin W. Gouldner.[11] Briefly, the argument is that bureaucratic organizations use a "machine" model as a control device. The consequences, both anticipated and unanticipated, of using that model serve to *reinforce and intensify* the tendency to use control devices. The machine model—designed to control when necessary—leads to ever greater control.

Figure 10.1 presents Merton's model of bureaucracy's undesirable outcomes. In the Merton model, top management's demand for control leads to an emphasis on *reliability* of behavior; top management wants employees to be predictable and accountable, so standard operating procedures are instituted and constantly checked. Control by SOP has three predictable outcomes, all desired by management. One is a *reduction in the number of personalized relationships* between organizational members. Relationships should be between offices, roles, or positions—not people. A second is *internalization of the organization's rules.* The rules were originally designed to help achieve organizational goals. Once internalized, they take on a positive value of their own. Finally, the organization increasingly uses *categorization* as a decision-making technique. Situations are placed into the first category (of a relatively small number of

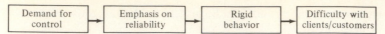

Figure 10.1 Consequences of bureaucratic demand for control (simplification of Merton Model). (*Source:* After James G. March and Herbert A. Simon, *Organizations* [New York: John Wiley & Sons, Inc., 1958], p. 41.)

categories) that seems to apply. A relatively narrow range of alternative solutions to problems is the result.

Rigidity and Resistance

Rigid Behavior One likely result of formal bureaucratic rules and procedures is *rigid behavior* by organizational members. The worst consequence of rigid behavior is *difficulty in dealing with clients and customers*. Clients and situations are dealt with by applying rules to general categories, instead of to individual and unique persons or circumstances.

Resistance to Change Another consequence of the mechanistic model and the rigid behavior it promotes is *organizational resistance to change*. Bureaucracy thrives on the status quo. When nothing changes and everything is routine, formal rules and procedures supply the answers to most employee questions about how they should behave and handle situations. But the modern era is characterized by change—scientific, technical, and social. Integration of effort through formalized control mechanisms will always have a place in organizations, but bureaucracies held together primarily through formalization may eventually become too rigid to cope with an everchanging environment.

Goal Displacement

An overemphasis on form rather than substance ultimately leads to goal displacement. Following the organization's rules and regulations becomes so important to members—because their evaluations are based on how well they follow them—that they focus their behavior on complying with the rules rather than striving to reach organizational goals. The organizational desire for conformity leads to overconformity. As Robert K. Merton puts it, "Adherence to the rules, originally conceived as a means, becomes transformed into an end in itself."[12]

If the organization can plan for every possible eventuality and formulate a rule to cover it, then organizational goals can be achieved merely through compliance with the rules and regulations. However, the human relations writers recognized that few organizational functions are predictable enough to allow such heavy reliance on rules. When organizations emphatically stress compliance with the rules, employees learn to follow them even if they conflict with reason and common sense. The relief efforts to aid starving people in Africa during the middle 1980s were said to have been considerably slowed, even thwarted, by bureaucratic reliance on rules that made no sense in that situation.

Bureaupathic Behavior   Victor A. Thompson has called the tendency of organizational members to follow the rules for their own sake "bureaupathic" behavior, caused by an insecurity which is itself caused by

> the growing gap between the rights of authority (to review, to veto, to affirm) and the specialized ability or skill required to solve most organizational problems. The intellectual, problem-solving content of executive offices is being increasingly diverted to specialists, leaving hierarchical rights (and duties) as the principal components of executive posts. Persons in hierarchical positions are therefore increasingly dependent upon subordinate and non-subordinate specialists for the achievement of organizational (or unit) goals.[13]

These pressures and insecurities lead managers to create more and more rules to protect themselves and subordinates from making bad decisions. The creation of rules also results in rigid resistance to change.

The Effects of Professionalization

The increasing specialization and professionalization of the people performing organizational functions have another implication for mechanistic, formalized bureaucracies. Formalization is designed to provide guides and standards of behavior for organizational employees. Professionals, employed in increasing numbers of organizations, bring their own behavior standards with them. According to Richard H. Hall, "The presence of organizational guidelines (formalization) is thus a duplication and probably perceived as less valid than are the norms of the profession involved. For professionals, therefore, the greater the degree of formalization in the organization, the greater the likelihood of alienation from work."[14]

After summarizing the research, Hall says: "All the studies . . . have concluded that professionalization and formalization are incompatible. The more professionalized the work force, the more likely that formalization will lead to conflict and alienation."[15]

Criticisms of Bureaucratic Formalization

Since "bureaucracy" is the best-known term for organizational patterns that stress formalization, the human relations school has frequently attacked bureaucracy as typifying the emphasis of the classicists on formalization. In his essay *The Death of Bureaucracy,* Warren Bennis summarized the human relations criticisms of formalized methods, rules, and regulations. Although he focuses on bureaucracy, the criticisms apply to any organization that places heavy emphasis on formalization.

1. Bureaucracy does not adequately allow for personal growth and the development of mature personalities.
2. It develops conformity and "group-think."
3. It does not take into account the "informal organization" and the emergent and unanticipated problems.
4. Its systems of control and authority are hopelessly outdated.
5. It has no adequate juridical process.

6. It does not possess adequate means for resolving differences and conflicts among ranks and, most particularly, among functional groups.
7. Communication (and innovative ideas) are thwarted or distorted because of hierarchical divisions.
8. The full human resources of bureaucracy are not being utilized because of mistrust, fear of reprisals, etc.
9. It cannot assimilate the influx of new technology or scientists entering the organization.
10. It will modify the personality structure such that employees will become and reflect the dull, gray, conditioned "organization man."[16]

Writing in 1966, Warren Bennis made this forecast:

[A] major shock to bureaucracy has been caused by scientific and technical revolution. It is the requirement of adaptability to the environment which leads to the predicted demise of bureaucracy and to the collapse of management as we know it now.[17]

Yet, bureaucracies continue to survive, and management as we know it now is not strikingly different from management as Bennis knew it then. Even so, the rigidly bureaucratic structure does not adapt to environmental change as well as some other structures do. Whether bureaucracies will some day pay the price predicted by Bennis, only time will tell.

Further Criticisms

Many organizations rely extensively on rules, regulations, and other formalization devices. Daniel Katz and Robert L. Kahn have termed such organizations "machine-like," with their employees representing smaller machines within the larger organization machine. Katz and Kahn recognized the limitations of such organizations in dealing with the internal issues raised by Bennis, primarily human relationships within the organization. In addition, they stressed the limitations of machine theory in dealing with the external environment. Specifically, machine theory "neglected many types of input-output exchange with the environment. It restricted input to raw materials and labor power" and ignored such inputs as people's values and needs, and the organization's need for social and public support. On the output side, machine theory excluded "all outcomes besides the physical product exported."[18]

The criticisms put forth by Bennis, Katz, and Kahn can be summarized this way: Formalization is harmful when it inhibits human development and interaction. Formalization is potentially dangerous to organizational survival when it locks the organization so rigidly into rules and regulations that it cannot respond appropriately to changes in the world around it.

THE MODERN PERSPECTIVE

The modern approach is to base the degree of organizational formalization on the organization's circumstances. In 1966 Tom Burns and G.M. Stalker described the differences between mechanistic and organic organizations as well as the circumstances in which each form works best. Following the machine theory of Katz and Kahn, they identified the key characteristics of the mechanistic organizational form and concluded that the form works best in a *stable* environment. Once the organization has been designed, each job has been specialized into its "one best way," people have been hired and trained, rules have been written, and relationships have been formalized, the mechanistic organization should run smoothly, *if* the environment remains stable.

However, the human relations writers had pointed out the inadequacies of the mechanistic model within a rapidly changing environment. Under such circumstances, according to Burns and Stalker, the organic organization is most appropriate.[19] The classicists favored formalized, mechanistic organizations; the human relations writers favored more flexible, organic organizations. The modern position, as expressed by Burns and Stalker, is that the appropriate form depends upon the situation.

Table 10.1 contrasts the formalized, mechanistic form and the flexible, organic form in terms of several organizational aspects. Of course, all organizations fall somewhere between these theoretical extremes in real life.

Table 10.1   MECHANISTIC AND ORGANIC ORGANIZATIONS CONTRASTED

Formalized—mechanistic	Flexible—organic
1. Tasks are highly differentiated and specialized. The relationship between tasks and organizational objectives is often not clear to those doing the tasks.	1. Tasks are more interrelated. The relevance of tasks to organizational objectives is emphasized.
2. Tasks tend to remain rigidly defined unless top management sees a need to redefine them.	2. Tasks are continually readjusted and redefined as organizational members interact.
3. Roles are specifically defined. Each member's rights, obligations, and technical methods are prescribed.	3. Roles are generally defined. Members accept general responsibility for task accomplishment beyond their own tasks.
4. The structures of control, authority, and communication are hierarchic. Sanctions derive from an employment contract between employees and the organization.	4. The structures of control, authority, and communication comprise a network. Sanctions derive from a community of interest.
5. The chief executive knows best.	5. The best knowledge may be located anywhere in the network. This location becomes the center of authority.
6. Communication is primarily vertical, between superior and subordinate.	6. Communication is both vertical and horizontal.
7. Communication consists primarily of instructions and decisions by superiors, and information and requests for decisions by subordinates.	7. The content of communications is primarily advice and information.
8. Loyalty to the organization and obedience to superiors are conditions of membership.	8. Commitment to the organization's tasks and goals is more highly valued than loyalty and obedience.
9. Importance and prestige are attached to identification with the organization and its members.	9. Importance and prestige are attached to affiliations and expertise in the external environment.

Source: Adapted from Richard M. Steers, *Organizational Effectiveness: A Behavioral View* (Santa Monica, CA: Goodyear Publishing Co., 1977), p. 90. See also Tom Burns and G.M. Stalker, *The Management of Innovation* (London: Tavistock Publications Inc., 1966), pp. 117–122.

Toward Measuring Formalization

Formalization has been used as a variable in a number of modern studies on organization. Previous studies often applied general meanings of formalization without being concerned about measuring it. But more precise measurement is needed to permit studies of when formalization is or is not useful. One thrust of modern research efforts has been to define formalization in terms that can be measured within specific organizations.

Subjective Reports   With that end in mind, Jerald Hage and Michael Aiken have broken formalization down into two components: *job codification* and *rule observation*. These two terms represent the answers to two questions: *How many* rules is an organizational member asked to follow? *How closely* must the member follow them? Hage and Aiken gauged the subjective perceptions of organizational members regarding these two criteria by asking them specific questions and analyzing their answers.[20]

Put It in Writing   Derek S. Pugh and his Aston group limited formalization to "the extent to which rules, procedures, instructions, and communications are written down."[21] They studied official documents and records of organizations to assess the degree of formalization and then gave the organizations scores on a formalization scale—a high score signifying a great reliance on written communication.

The two standard methods of determining organizational formalization, then, are to assess member perceptions and to look at organizational records. The advantage of the former method is that it can also assess member perceptions about informal, unwritten procedures. The disadvantage is that those perceptions may be inaccurate.

Formalization and Other Characteristics

Using the preceding two methods, modern writers have tried to assess the relationship between formalization and other organizational characteristics.

Centralization   Hage and Aiken found a negative relationship between formalization and centralization; centralized organizations tend to need fewer rules and regulations than decentralized organizations because top managers are on hand to make most decisions.[22]

Organizations with a few people at the top who make all the decisions are inclined to formalize rules and regulations, to ensure that their decisions are carried out in a consistent manner. Such organizations also tend to have relatively few professional staff people. The presence of professional staff permits less formalization since professional expertise substitutes for rules as a means of control. Furthermore, as discussed previously, professionals prefer to rely on their professional standards and expertise rather than on extensive rules and regulations applied to their work behavior; therefore, they may discourage the general use of rules within the organization.

Technology   Hage and Aiken contrasted social agencies with routine and nonroutine activities. They concluded, as one would expect, that the organizations with routine activities (for instance, the patterns used in all client interviews are quite similar) experienced greater formalization of organizational roles than organizations with more varied activities.[23] Pugh and associates, examining a greater variety of organizations, came to similar conclusions: Technological complexity tends to be accompanied by a formalized structuring of employee work-flow activities.[24] In diverse organizations ranging from a football team to a Roman Catholic archdiocese, Sanford M. Dornbusch and W. Richard Scott observed similar patterns: The more routine (less "technical") the organization's activities, the more likely that employees will follow formalized procedural specifications.[25]

Size   The Aston measure of formalization was the extent to which organizations write down their procedures and policies. A major finding of this group was that increasing size tends to result in formalization as they define it. As organizations hire more people, activities become more structured and less personal. More formal written documents are one result. The Aston group concluded that size has a greater effect on formalization than technology does. Robert M. Marsh and Hiroshi Mannari also found that formalization is more closely related to size than to technology.[26]

Technical Specificity   One effort to measure and study formalization and relate it to "technical specificity" was made by Edward Harvey, who used the term *program specification:* "Programs are defined as a mechanism or rules in terms of which an attempt is made to give directions to organizational activity. Specification refers to the variable extent to which such programs are detailed or spelled out."[27] Harvey presents three types of organizational programs:

1. Role programming: The formalization of duties and responsibilities as a sense of job specification.
2. Output programming: The formal delineation of steps through which raw materials pass in the course of becoming the organization's outputs.
3. Communication programming: The formal specification of the structure, content, and timing of communication within the organization.[28]

A plant with technical diffuseness uses many technical processes to produce many products. A plant with technical specificity produces a few products with a few processes. A major finding of Harvey's was that as technical specificity increases, organizational *program specification increases.* In other words, formalization will be more prevalent in organizations which use few processes to produce few products.

Performance   Too much formalization should presumably lead to boredom, dissatisfaction, hostility—and subsequent poor performance. With too little formalization, employees will not know exactly what they are to do, also resulting in poor performance. Will some optimal degree of formalization lead to optimal performance? Are formalization and performance related? Dan R. Dalton and his colleagues have examined the research findings of seven studies on this subject. They conclude "that an association between levels of formalization and performance has not been convincingly demonstrated."[29]

A Broader Framework

Formalization is an essential control device for integrating the efforts of organizational members. While many studies have examined it, questions remain as to how much and what kinds of formalization lead to the best results. Kathleen M. Eisenhardt offers several options to this problem that deserve further exploration.[30]

Eisenhardt first considers a job that is simple, routine, highly formalized, and precisely defined. The worker's job behaviors are easily observed and measured, and the worker is rewarded based on how closely the actual job behaviors match the job design. This combination of job/behaviors/reward is convenient for the organization but not very motivating for the worker.

Another possibility is a job with complex, interesting, and flexible content, but with job behaviors that are not easily observed and measured. Organizations have two basic choices here. First, they can assess whether workers are engaging in appropriate behaviors by using elaborate (and expensive) information systems with many formal measures, such as budgeting systems or multiple layers of management. Rewards are then based on how well actual employee behaviors match desired behaviors. A second approach is essentially to ignore behaviors and to reward employees based on performance or results, for instance, profitability or revenues. Some employees may prefer such a reward system; many others will view it as too variable and risky. Furthermore, in some nonquantitative areas like morale improvement and problem prevention, results are difficult to measure.

If the costs of formalization are simply too great with certain jobs, or if workers in those jobs customarily rebel against formalization (as most professionals do), the organization can focus not on job design, behavior assessment, or reward schemes, but on employing and training people whose goals, objectives, and preferences coincide with management's.

Which of these approaches an organization takes, each with its different degree of formalization, will depend on such circumstances as the nature of the job and the worker doing it, and the availability of information systems.

SUMMARY

Formalization of rules, standards, policies, methods, and procedures is a primary means of integrating organizational effort. Five classes of formalization mechanisms are performance control, action planning, behavior formalization, training and indoctrination, and process control.

Max Weber observed that a characteristic of modern bureaucracies is the formalization of rules, decisions, and actions in writing. In general, formalization is designed to take the place of direct personal oversight by managers and supervisors, and to avoid having continually to solve recurring problems. In addition, the classicists viewed formalization as a means of (1) controlling unwilling or unable subordinates, (2) ensuring efficiency, (3) ensuring consistency of employee behavior, (4) clarifying employee job expectations, (5) filling the inevitable holes in the organizational planning process, (6) creating an organizational memory, and (7) reinforcing employee identification with the organization and its goals. The primary elements of formalization are policies (statements of organizational intent, and guides as to *what* employees are or are not to do), methods (specific instructions for employees telling *how* to do what they do), procedures (telling several people how to carry out a sequence of activities), and rules (specific statements of what employees may and may not do). Although organizations can view the elements of formalization as either guides or rules, the classicists thought that rules were usually preferable.

The human relations writers tried to moderate the classical position that organizations should be built on mechanistic, formalized models because such models, designed for control, led to ever greater control. Robert K. Merton maintained that the organization's demand for control of employee behavior led eventually to employee difficulty in dealing with clients and customers. According to the human relations position, employees in highly formalized organizations become resistant to change and place following the rules ahead of achieving organizational goals; the means become the end, and the result is what Victor A. Thompson calls bureaupathic behavior. Warren Bennis proposed ten criticisms of bureaucracy, dealing primarily with unsatisfactory human relationships in the formalized organization. Daniel Katz and Robert L. Kahn pointed out that formalization can actually threaten organizational survival if it restricts the organization's ability to respond to change.

The modern approach has been to determine how much and what kinds of formalization can benefit different organizational situations. Tom Burns and G.M. Stalker have contrasted the formalized, mechanistic organization with the flexible, organic organization, suggesting that formalization can be useful when the environment is stable. One modern effort has been to define and measure formalization. Jerald Hage and Michael Aiken break formalization down into job codification and rule observation. The Aston group limited formalization to those rules and procedures specified *in writing*. Hage and Aiken found a slight positive relationship between formalization and centralization, and between formalization and the routineness of activities in social agencies. The Aston group determined that increasing organizational size leads to more procedures and policies expressed in writing (their measure of formalization). Edward Harvey concluded that as technical specificity increases, organizational program specification increases. That is, plants producing few products with a few specific technical processes tend to spell out the mechanisms or rules that workers must employ or follow.

Kathleen M. Eisenhardt offered a series of formalization options. Which option an organization chooses will depend on its goals and its unique circumstances.

DISCUSSION QUESTIONS

1. What is formalization?
2. Explain Henry Mintzberg's three classes of formalization mechanisms.
3. What is process control?
4. Describe some of formalization's major purposes, from the classical perspective. How many of them still seem relevant today?
5. What is the relationship between formalization and the organization's planning process?
6. Discuss the "institutional memory" of an organization of which you have been a member. How is that memory preserved?
7. Differentiate between policies, methods, procedures, and rules.

8. Briefly contrast the classical and human relations perspectives on formalization.

9. How can formalization lead to rigidity of behavior and resistance to change? Do you think these negative effects can be avoided, while retaining formalization's advantages?

10. Describe an organization with which you are familiar in which goal displacement—the tendency for "following the rules" to become a goal—has occurred.

11. According to Richard H. Hall, professionalism and formalization are incompatible. Why is that?

12. Warren Bennis offers ten criticisms of bureaucracy. With which do you agree? Disagree?

13. Formalized, mechanistic organizations and flexible, organic organizations are contrasted in Table 10.1. Which type would you rather work for as a top manager? As a lower-level white-collar employee?

14. To what extent can formalization be measured?

15. What is the relationship between formalization and some other organizational characteristics?

16. Why is formalization viewed as an integrating strategy?

■ WIDGET SHIPPING

Mary Ammerman, manager of the widget shipping department, had to leave town for a week. She didn't really trust her new shipping foreman, Bob Pinner, to use his discretion about prioritizing widget shipping orders, so she wrote him a memo including these statements: "While I'm gone, I want you to ship widgets strictly as you receive the orders. First order in, first order out; second order in, second order out; no exceptions."

Bob Pinner was satisfied with these instructions. He was just learning this new job and wasn't interested in making decisions on his own.

Quitting time in the shipping department was 5 P.M. At 4:45 P.M. on the day Mary Ammerman left, shipping had two orders for two widgets each to get out. Since fulfilling each order took about seven minutes, these two shipments were going to be it for the day. Then Pinner got a phone call from Eloise Crystal, administrative assistant to Paul Green, the vice president for sales. "Hold everything, Mr. Pinner. Mr. Green wants a rush order for 20,000 widgets to go out by special truck today to Acme Manufacturing."

"But gosh, Ms. Crystal, I have two orders ahead of that one, and Ms. Ammerman said to handle the orders as placed, no exceptions."

After a moment of murmuring in the background, Bob Pinner heard a voice that could only be Mr. Green's: "Look, Pinner, you get this order out or your head will roll. Is that clear?"

Pinner took a deep breath: "I'm sorry, Mr. Green, but Ms. Ammerman runs the shipping department, and orders are orders."

Should Bob Pinner have done anything differently? Should *anyone* have done anything differently?

■ PIP'S DRY CLEANERS

Regina Lane, an old-timer at Pip's Dry Cleaners, had explained to new employee Bruce Swift that customers were not supposed to pick up dry cleaning without a receipt. Customers who forgot or lost their receipts had to show a driver's license and sign a statement that they had picked up their clothes.

Anna Curtin came into the store and apologized for not bringing her receipt. Regina

Lane just laughed and said: "Ms. Curtin, in all the years I've been here, you haven't brought your receipt yet." She didn't ask for identification or have Curtin sign the customary statement. After Ms. Curtin went out, Lane said to Bruce Swift, "She's a good customer; she's just forgetful. No harm done."

The next time Ms. Curtin came in, both Bruce Swift and Regina Lane were behind the counter. Swift handed the dry cleaning to Ms. Curtin and did not ask her to produce identification or sign a statement. Regina Lane observed the incident without comment. The next "customer" in line, an inspector out of Pip's corporate headquarters, reported the incident. Lane was strongly censured and Swift was fired for "violation of company policies."

Should the company have censured Lane and fired Swift? Should Swift have gone "by the book" no matter what Lane said? What suggestions would you make to Pip's about how to handle these situations?

SOME WORK TO DO

In A.D. 27, Augustus called his comitatus together and said, "Gentlemen, we have some work to do. I want an empire, so I have decided to expand the Roman Republic. I want Spain, Gaul, and Rhaetia; I want Mauretania, Numidia, and Cyrenaica; and I want Macedonia, Thrace, Dacia, Egypt, and Syria. Each will be headed up by a regional vice president.

"Gaius, you handle the conquering; that's the easy part. Catullus, you have the tough part. We need to send our people into all parts of my Empire. They'll be thousands of miles from Rome, with no telephones, telegraphs, or satellite communications. The Postal Service is disgracefully slow. How are we going to keep track of our regional vice presidents and other far-flung organizational members? How are we going to ensure that they behave, independently and autonomously, just as they would if they were here under my direct supervision?"

What advice would you give Catullus?

TERMINAL ILLNESS

Sol Farmer was a computer terminal operator. The machine monitored his productivity constantly and kept a record of how fast he entered data. Farmer had to work at a certain pace—and the machine made sure that he did.

One day Sol Farmer got fed up and shouted: "I'm tired of having a blasted machine tell me what to do!" But nobody heard him; he was alone in a small room with his machine.

What is the problem at the computer terminal, and how would you solve it?

NOTES

1. Henry Mintzberg, *The Structuring of Organizations: A Synthesis of Research* (Englewood Cliffs, NJ: Prentice-Hall, 1979), p. 154.
2. Ibid.
3. Studs Terkel, *Working* (New York: Avon Books, 1974), pp. 221–222.
4. Steven Kerr and John W. Slocum, Jr., "Controlling the Performances of People in Organiza-

tions," in *Handbook of Organizational Design,* vol. 2, ed. Paul C. Nystrom and William H. Starbuck (New York: Oxford University Press, 1981), p. 124.

5. Max Weber, *The Theory of Social and Economic Organization,* trans. A.M. Henderson and Talcott Parsons; ed. Talcott Parsons (New York: The Free Press, 1947), p. 331.

6. Jerald Hage, "An Axiomatic Theory of Organizations," *Administrative Science Quarterly* 10 (December 1965): 295.

7. Frederick W. Taylor, "The Management of Organizations," in *Organization Theory: Selected Readings,* ed. D.S. Pugh (Hammondsworth, England: Penguin Books, 1971), pp. 128–129.

8. W. Richard Scott, *Organizations: Rational, Natural, and Open Systems* (Englewood Cliffs, NJ: Prentice-Hall, 1981), p. 70.

9. Tom Burns and G.M. Stalker, *The Management of Innovation* (London: Tavistock Publications, 1966).

10. Chester I. Barnard, *The Functions of the Executive* (Cambridge, MA: Harvard University Press, 1938), p. 83.

11. James G. March and Herbert A. Simon, *Organizations* (New York: Wiley, 1958), pp. 37–47.

12. Robert K. Merton, *Social Theory and Social Structure* (New York: The Free Press, 1957), p. 199.

13. Victor A. Thompson, *Modern Organizations* (New York: Knopf, 1961), pp. 156–157.

14. Richard H. Hall, *Organizations: Structure and Process* (Englewood Cliffs, NJ: Prentice-Hall, 1982), p. 108. See also James E. Sorensen and Thomas L. Sorensen, "The Conflict of Professionals in Bureaucratic Organizations," *Administrative Science Quarterly* 19 (March 1974): 98–106.

15. Ibid., p. 110.

16. Warren Bennis, *Beyond Bureaucracy* (New York: McGraw-Hill, 1966), p. 6.

17. Ibid., p. 10.

18. Daniel Katz and Robert L. Kahn, *The Social Psychology of Organizations* (New York: Wiley, 1966), p. 73.

19. Tom Burns and G.M. Stalker, *The Management of Innovation,* pp. 117–122.

20. Jerald Hage and Michael Aiken, "The Relationship of Centralization to Other Structural Properties," *Administrative Science Quarterly* 11 (June 1967): 79.

21. Derek S. Pugh, David J. Hickson, C.R. Hinings, and C. Turner, "Dimensions of Organization Structure," *Administrative Science Quarterly* 13 (March 1968): 75.

22. Jerald Hage and Michael Aiken, "The Relationship of Centralization to Other Structural Properties," pp. 72–91.

23. Jerald Hage and Michael Aiken, "Routine Technology, Social Structure and Organizational Goals," *Administrative Science Quarterly* 14 (September 1969): 366–377.

24. Derek S. Pugh, D.J. Hickson, C.R. Hinings, and C. Turner, "The Context of Organizational Structures," *Administrative Science Quarterly* 14 (March 1969): 91–114.

25. Sanford M. Dornbusch and W. Richard Scott, *Evaluation and the Exercise of Authority* (New York: Basic Books, 1975), cited in *Organizations: Rational, Natural, and Open Systems,* W. Richard Scott, p. 227.

26. Derek S. Pugh, D.J. Hickson, C.R. Hinings, and C. Turner, "The Context of Organizational Structures," pp. 91–114; D.J. Hickson, D.S. Pugh, and Diana Pheysey, "Operational Technology and Organizational Structure: An Empirical Reappraisal," *Administrative Science Quarterly* 14 (September 1969): 378–397; Robert M. Marsh and Hiroshi Mannari, "Technology and Size as Determinants of the Organizational Structure of Japanese Factories," *Administrative Science Quarterly* 26 (March 1981): 33. Further confirmation of the positive relationship between size and formalization appears in Peter M. Blau and Richard Schoenherr, *The Structure of Organizations* (New York: Basic Books, 1971); John Child, "Predicting and Understanding Organization Structure," *Administrative Science Quarterly* 18 (June

1973): 168–185; and J.H.K. Inkson, D.S. Pugh, and D.J. Hickson, "Organizational Context and Structure: An Abbreviated Replication," *Administrative Science Quarterly* 15 (June 1970): 318–329.

27. Edward Harvey, "Technology and the Structure of Organizations," *American Sociological Review* 33 (April 1968): 247–259.

28. Ibid., p. 256.

29. Dan R. Dalton et al., "Organization Structure and Performance: A Critical Review," *Academy of Management Review* 5 (January 1980): 58. This lack of a definite relationship is confirmed in a later review by Louis W. Fry, "Technology-Structure Research: Three Critical Issues," *Academy of Management Journal* 25 (September 1982): 532–552.

30. Kathleen M. Eisenhardt, "Control: Organizational and Economic Approaches," *Management Science* 31 (February 1985): 147–148.

ADDITIONAL READINGS

Biggart, Nicole Woolsey, and Gary G. Hamilton. "The Power of Obedience." *Administrative Science Quarterly* 29 (December 1984): 540–549.

Flamholtz, Eric. "Organizational Control Systems as a Managerial Tool." *California Management Review* 22 (Winter 1979): 50–59.

Gouldner, Alvin W. *Patterns of Industrial Bureaucracy.* Glencoe, IL.: The Free Press, 1954.

Hardy, Cynthia. "The Nature of Unobtrusive Power." *Journal of Management Studies* 22 (July 1985): 384–399.

Merchant, Kenneth A., and William J. Bruns, Jr. "Measurements to Cure Management Myopia." *Business Horizons* 29 (May/June 1986): 56–64.

Wiewel, Wim, and Albert Hunter. "The Interorganizational Network As a Resource: A Comparative Case Study on Organizational Genesis." *Administrative Science Quarterly* 30 (December 1985): 482–496.

Committees

The concept of achieving coordination through groups of all kinds is well established. Most organizations of any size have a formalized committee process to perform differentiated tasks and to integrate organizational effort. Although committees are the subject of many jokes and complaints, modern organizations rely increasingly on them.

As the saying goes, a camel is a horse created by a committee. True, committees can be misused. Managers sometimes form committees to avoid responsibility, to gain endorsement for decisions already made, or to delay arriving at decisions. However, committees also have many benefits.

Our major task in this chapter is to examine the nature and roles of committees and similar groups, as seen by the classical, human relations, and modern schools of thought.

THE NATURE AND COMPOSITION OF COMMITTEES

A committee is a group of organizational members who come together for a period of time in order to achieve a purpose or fulfill a mandate. The committee is accountable to the person or group that caused the committee to be formed. It may consist of specialists, nonspecialists, or both. These committee members spend only part of their time doing committee work and the rest of their time performing their normal duties. The task assigned to the committee may be to exchange views and information, recommend action, generate ideas, give advice, or make choices. The committee may have a long life or a short life. It may be big or small and may deal with issues broad or narrow. It may consist of company senior-level managers or even outsiders, as on a board of directors. Its members may be top-level managers trying to solve problems of finance allocation or long-range planning for the entire organization, or they may be production-level employees in a quality circle, work-improvement group, or United Way solicitation team. In fact, a committee may be made up of members from any organizational level or combination of levels.

Although an organization's coordinating groups may be referred to by various terms—board, team, council, or task force—we shall refer to them all simply as committees.

Functional Types

One way to categorize committees is by the functional activities in which they engage. Using this premise, Table 11.1 reports Rollie Tillman's survey of committee types in organizations with more than 10,000 members. A similar survey today would probably reflect even more committee activity, because all organizations have more information to handle.

The "general management" committee was most frequently found, followed by "labor and personnel" and "finance and control." The average number of members was eight for all committee types. The number of meetings was higher for nonspecialty areas (general management, marketing, and production) than for areas more apt to require specific expertise (labor and personnel, research and development, and public relations). These latter committees don't meet as often because individual experts are supposed to know how to solve most problems in their specialized areas. Committees in more general areas need to draw upon different departments for information and to keep members up to date on broader developments, so they meet more often.

The Integrating Function

For convenience of discussion, we have categorized ten major organizational strategies in terms of differentiation and integration. Nevertheless, each strategy has elements of both differentiation and integration, and committees illustrate this fact very well. If a committee is given an organizational task to perform, then we have seen differentiation in action. In fact, such a committee may be called a "task force." That committee

Table 11.1 SURVEY OF COMMITTEE ACTIVITIES

Type of committee	% of Total committee types surveyed	% of Surveyed members serving on each type*	Average number of members	Average number of meetings per year
General management	30.3	77.4	8.6	27
Labor and personnel	15.4	39.4	7.1	14
Finance and control	14.8	37.7	6.7	23
Production	9.9	25.2	8.9	28
Research and development and new products	9.8	24.9	8.2	18
Marketing	9.3	23.9	7.4	24
Public relations	2.2	5.5	7.4	9
Others	8.3	21.1	8.3	14

*Total adds up to more than 100% because many members serve on more than one committee.

Source: Reprinted by permission of the *Harvard Business Review.* Exhibit from "Problems in Review: Committees on Trial" by Rollie Tillman, Jr. (May/June 1960): 6–12, 162–172. Copyright © 1960 by the President and Fellows of Harvard College; all rights reserved.

itself may serve as a broadly based device for integrating the expertise and opinions of its members into a unified task-force proposal.

On the other hand, the typical purpose of the president's executive committee is to assure the participation of representatives from the various differentiated units in top-level decision making and policy formulation. As the senior coordinating/integrating official, President Smith may call together the executive committee for such purposes as:

> to share Smith's vision of the overall organizational goal, so that each unit reporting to the president can see how that unit fits into the big picture;
>
> to present a specific issue to the committee, then solicit information and reactions from members representing the functional units, so that units will understand each other's problems and prospects regarding the issue;
>
> to hammer out compromise solutions to problems that affect all represented units.

The president's executive committee can evaluate proposals for new acquisitions or capital outlays by discussing with the president and with each other what impact each proposal will have on the units. Committee members learn about the concerns and constraints of other units that cause certain decisions to be made. They can then go back to their subordinates and explain why things did or did not go the way their units wanted them to.

The president's executive committee members perform a truly integrative function similar to that of city council members, whose duty it is to represent the interests of their constituents to the whole council. Committee or council members cannot be hardheaded and unyielding. They must be like the petroleum-producing state's senator who expresses the state's concerns in the national debate over petroleum issues but may eventually have to compromise the state's interests for the nation's good. So too must the production manager strongly express the production unit's interests and concerns to the committee and the president. After all committee members have offered advice and information, the president integrates their findings, weighs the costs and benefits, then makes the final decision—which may or may not be favorable to the production unit.

Committees at lower organizational levels follow a similar process. They are formed to integrate the efforts, concerns, and information of people who might not otherwise communicate with each other and therefore might not be aware of what impact their actions could have on other organizational units. The proliferation of committees in organizations may also be based partly on the old adage that it's better to be safe than sorry. It's better to form a committee so that all units can have their say in advance than to listen to complaints later.

Coordinating by Committee at GM An early master of using committees to integrate the interests, information, and concerns of different units was Alfred P. Sloan, Jr., of General Motors. Sloan felt that the best way to balance the interests and coordinate the activities of GM's separate operations and the corporation itself was to call representatives of the different operations together and give them the power to resolve problems and make decisions. Here is Sloan's expression of the General Technical Committee's functions:

> The committee would deal in problems which would be of interest to all divisions and would in dealing with such matters largely formulate the general engineering policies of the corporation.
>
> The committee would not, as to principle, deal with the specific problems of any individual operation. Each function of that operation would be under the absolute control of the general manager of that division.[1]

The four key elements of any committee are its mandate or purpose, life span, people, and accountability. These elements will now be discussed in turn.

The Mandate

Need for Clarity   Committees don't usually create themselves. Whoever creates the committee should have a clear idea of its purpose or goal and should express that purpose—along with any necessary instructions for achieving it, as well as the limits of the committee's authority and its life span and deadlines—in the committee's mandate or formal charge. The mandate spells out the committee's role and scope. A clear statement of the committee's purpose lets members know why the committee exists and why its work is important. Examples of committee goals are to establish a corporation's annual budget, to recommend three candidates for a vacant university presidency, to decide which new computer system to buy, and to propose congressional legislation on foreign policy.

Committee goal statements range from the specific to the general. A specific goal would be for an ad hoc committee to solve a critical production or quality problem. A general, nonoperational goal would be for a university's academic program review committee: "To review courses and curricula to ensure that the university offers its students a responsible, high-quality academic experience." A committee mandate may well contain more than one goal or purpose, and these multiple goals may also range from general to specific.

An unclear mandate leaves the committee to figure out what it is supposed to do, how to do it, and when to announce success or quit trying. In such circumstances, committee members are frustrated by not knowing whether their efforts are useful or appropriate. Neither the committee chair nor the members know when or if the mandate has been fulfilled. For that reason, many committees continue to exist long beyond the time when they were useful, merely because the mandate was not specific enough to indicate clearly when the committees had concluded their work.

Some mandates are purposely vague. An unclear mandate can disguise a manager's desire to limit meaningful employee participation in the decision-making process. Citizens committees appointed by a city council are common examples of groups with ill-defined mandates. By appointing committees to "study" park beautification, street improvement needs, rezoning matters, or other community-wide issues, a council appears to be encouraging broad-based participation. In reality, however, the council may make final decisions on these issues in a closed session, sometimes before the appointed committees have completed their deliberations.

Since the need for clarity is so critical, the founder of the committee should provide a written document so that the committee members will have no doubt about their goals, tasks, time schedule, and authority limits. The mandate can then serve as a continuing reference source to anchor the committee's efforts.

Importance of Mandate   Within the organization itself, *goals* determine which strategies and activities are to be undertaken. The same is true of a committee. Its mandate determines such characteristics as its life span, which organizational members shall serve, how many shall serve, the nature of their involvement, and perhaps even who the leader shall be.

Life Span

Another way to categorize committees is in terms of their duration or life span. Some organizations have committees that last indefinitely. Committees with long lives might be, for example, the executive committee of U.S. Steel's board of directors or the U.S. Senate's Foreign Relations Committee. Other committees may have a deadline for completing their work. The committee members know the group's life span—when it will start and end. An example would be a committee investigating whether to begin an urban renewal project. The two broad categories of committees, in terms of life span, are permanent (or standing) committees and temporary (ad hoc or special) committees.

Permanent   The permanent or standing committee is designed and expected to have a long life. Unless the organizational structure changes, the committee may exist as long as the organization itself does. Permanent committees bring a consistency of organizational knowledge and perspective to a variety of applications over time. Standing committees play vital organizational roles; management relies on them to perform important tasks. Standing committees have stable membership and a purpose (or "charge") so general that the committee's activities will be quite varied. For instance, the House Ethics Committee meets to investigate alleged improprieties of state representatives. Although all committee business deals with "ethics," each allegation and investigation will be different. Another example would be a grievance committee. Rarely are two grievances exactly alike; they must all be handled differently.

Temporary   Temporary or ad hoc committees are formed to complete specific jobs. They apply a variety of knowledge and perspectives to a specific situation. Once the job is done, the committee disbands. A corporation's executive committee may appoint an ad hoc subcommittee to investigate a wage-and-salary package for employees; a city council may appoint a citizens group to investigate crime in the community; or the United Nations may appoint staff members and outside experts to make recommendations for dealing with a conflict between Iran and Iraq.

The People

The "people" aspects of the committee are: a *specific collection* of organizational members; a *predetermined number* of organizational members; and a *leader*.

Specific Collection   Committee members are selected for various reasons. Some members may serve because of their expertise. For example, a given committee may need the expert advice of a doctor, a lawyer, and an accountant. Members may be selected for political reasons. Certain government committee memberships carrying high prestige and salary, for instance, are alloted to supporters of the political party in control. Some members may be at key organizational information points, able to collect information for the committee and make sure that the committee's deliberations and findings are reported throughout the organization. For example, a university's long-range planning committee may include all of the university's deans.[2]

Number   The size of a committee is related to its goals and to its reason for existing. A small group may not have the expertise or political representation needed to accomplish its task efficiently. A large group may have uninterested or continually absent members, or may make the hearing of each member's questions, answers, and other contributions impossible. Also, less aggressive members may be afraid to participate.

Leader   The formal, designated leader usually sets the agenda, calls and runs the meetings, provides information, distributes data, and performs other activities that support and coordinate the committee's efforts. The discussion on leadership in Chapter 9 applies directly to committee leadership.

Accountability

All committees are accountable to some other group or person. That group or person is ultimately responsible for what the committee does, how efficiently it is done, and for disbanding the committee when its work is finished. Just as the committee is accountable to its creator, so too is the creator responsible to a boss for performance and results.

Problems can arise because one party assigns the work, another party does the work, and the first party must then make appropriate use of the results or implement the recommendation. All too frequently, the implementer is placed in the difficult position of trying to explain and justify the committee's recommendation to those affected by it, because the committee has disbanded. The implementer and affected persons have no one to go to for clarification or appeal. More importantly, the person who formed the committee originally may not follow through on the recommendation, and problems may remain unaddressed or unresolved.

THE CLASSICAL PERSPECTIVE

General Opposition

The classicists were generally hostile to committees. They viewed the typical committee as someone's attempt to avoid decision responsibility.

Lyndall Urwick says, "A committee is that form in an organization in which responsibility is assigned to a group of individuals acting in a corporate capacity. A committee is always an alternative to assigning the same responsibility or responsibilities to an individual."[3] The classical writers preferred that individual managers assume those responsibilities called for by their organizational positions. Since the classical school favored well-defined assignment and maintenance of organizational authority relationships, they were opposed to giving very important decisions to committees.

The classical school had great faith in the ability of well-chosen managers to integrate the activities and people for whom they were responsible. Committees were often seen as a means to avoid that responsibility.

Negative Aspects

The classicists resisted committees because they perceived numerous negative aspects. They believed these disadvantages outweighed any potential benefits. The human relations school, of course, concluded just the opposite.

Self-Interest   According to the classicists, committees cannot make good decisions on matters affecting the whole organization because of the self-interest, group loyalties, conflicting commitments, and departmental identifications of committee members. For example, consider a committee made up of division managers who are asked to allocate new capital spending among their divisions. If they don't come to a stalemate, they are likely to set up coalitions or hand out equal shares to all members in order to reach agreement. Because of self-interest, the committee's decision will probably not be to the organization's best benefit.

At the national level, congressional committees are hard pressed to make objective decisions about matters of great concern to states represented by committee members. If a committee is debating whether to tax either cigarettes or lobsters, we shouldn't expect the congresswoman from Maine to agree with the congressman from North Carolina—unless one or the other has no interest in reelection.

A benefit of committees is that they bring a variety of perspectives together. Their corresponding disadvantage is that members may not be able to put those perspectives aside and be impartial when their own sectional interests are at stake.

Inadequate Knowledge   Sometimes, the members don't know what the committee's goals are and don't have the necessary information, skill, training, or experience to solve problems or make decisions. The person told to form the committee may not know (or may know but not want to reveal) the committee's objectives, authority, and scope of inquiry. A committee without the knowledge or expertise necessary to achieve its stated goal will resent the time and energy required by committee work. To ask a committee of automotive assembly-line supervisors to analyze the technical aspects of different data processing systems can only breed frustration in the name of participation.

Inadequate Authority   Committees may be asked to make recommendations in areas over which they have no authority. Consider a committee formed to find out why customers are not buying a firm's TV sets. The committee's investigation reveals that the boss's spouse has demanded a wedge-shaped TV set that fits into a corner of the bedroom. The committee's deliberations and findings are only going to cause frustration because the committee has inadequate authority to remedy the situation. The boss is not going to change TV shapes and get into an argument with the spouse.

Imagine a committee brought together to reduce the large turnover among computer operators. The committee finds that the turnover is caused by the company's abysmally low wages. Unless the company changes its wage policy (which it probably won't), the committee members may well become irritated and hostile.

Irrelevant Issues   From time to time, committees are established to address issues, solve problems, or offer advice on matters of absolutely no interest to committee members. Company XYZ's middle managers are asked to allocate parking lot spaces to employees; a company's engineers are asked to recommend color schemes for the cafeteria; college professors are asked to determine the date for a student spring frolic. These are familiar examples of committees being formed to deal with matters in which members have little interest.

Irresponsible Decisions   A major disadvantage of committees is that the responsibility for decisions can be divided up. If a decision is bad, no one person can be held accountable for it. If the committee voted secretly, each committee member has a ready-made alibi for an unpopular decision.

The classicists wanted a clearly delineated authority structure, to pin down the responsibility for good and bad decisions. When this authority structure is modified by decision-making committees, the relationship between authority and responsibility becomes unclear. Rather than being held thoroughly and unquestionably accountable for a bad decision, a manager can say, "I favored the other alternative, but the committee all opposed me, so I had to go along."

Actually, the manager is enjoying a no-lose situation: the opportunity to avoid responsibility for bad decisions and the opportunity to share the applause for good ones. The organization must ask itself this question: If our managers accept the praise for good decisions and avoid the blame for bad ones, what are we paying them for?

Mediocre Decisions   Another major criticism of committees is that, rather than finding the best decision, they tend to compromise to reach a decision that is no one's first choice but that everyone can live with. Since committees are typically designed to represent various interests, concerns, and personal values, arriving at a decision that every member favors equally is difficult. This difficulty is compounded if the problem to be solved is vague or poorly defined or if hard data are not available, making it necessary to rely on value judgments.

The classic disagreement between the sales manager and the finance manager illustrates this problem. If credit is extended to more customers, the sales manager is happy because sales will increase; the finance manager is unhappy because the firm's financial stability may be endangered. If credit is restricted, the sales manager is unhappy and the finance manager is satisfied. Now picture a committee discussing this problem. Both managers sit on the committee. The group may decide on a compromise that does not best serve organizational goals. Even worse, the committee may decide in favor of the manager who talks louder or more smoothly, or has more political clout.

Group decision making may be better than the decision making of the average group member. It may *not* be better than the decision making of the group's most informed, insightful, experienced member. If the other committee members do not recognize or acknowledge that person's superior decision-making qualifications, the committee may make less-than-desirable decisions.

Poor Personnel Decisions   Committees are inclined to be bad employers. As Urwick puts it, "The decisions of a group on a personnel issue nearly always tend to follow 'the letter of the law' and, too often, to represent the lowest common factor of generosity and flexibility of the members."[4] Since the committee members may not know the employees who are involved, they may use impersonal and objective data, and apply the pertinent personnel policies strictly rather than taking individual circumstances into account. Employees on the receiving end of negative committee decisions cannot go to any one person to get the committee's rationale or to find out what might be done to modify or change the negative decision. Finally, by placing personnel matters in a committee's hands, the organization weakens the ability of managers to perform their supervisory responsibilities.

Failure to Reach Consensus   Many of the preceding ailments afflicting committees lead to frustration. No outcome is more aggravating than failure to reach consensus. Some committees are doomed to fail. A group that has no possible basis for agreement is sometimes asked to reach one. This approach can be used to buy time, during which a controversial issue might cool down or go away. However, the cost in committee member frustration may be quite high.

The committee may fail even if it is not designed to fail. Hung juries are not uncommon, because people will draw different conclusions from the same testimony and hard facts.

Hasty Consensus   The opposite problem is the committee's tendency to agree on *any* decision as soon as possible, because disagreement is uncomfortable. A problem-solving group that values comfort above frank and open discussion will minimize dissent, avoid controversial topics, superficially explore only a few safe alternatives, and then agree on one. The group will stick with that choice even if drawbacks and risks are later brought up, the attitude being "We've made up our minds—don't confuse us with facts." The modern term for this tendency to avoid unpleasant disagreement by arriving at a hasty consensus is *groupthink*.[5]

Lack of Follow-up   Follow-up and control procedures are usually accomplished not by the committee but by individual managers at the point of implementation. Of course, a decision-making group can keep watch over decision implementation, and perhaps it should. Still, the direct responsibility to ensure an outcome that will meet the original mandate often lies with the individual manager, who may or may not follow up effectively.

Cost   The final negative aspect of committees from the classical perspective is that they usually cost more—in time and money—than they are worth. Bringing the committee's members together is expensive. The cost of a one-hour meeting is not merely the total salaries of the members for one hour but also includes the cost of their *not* doing their normal tasks during that hour.

In addition, committees are formed and meetings are called to handle topics that require a sharing of different viewpoints. Much time will be required to hear all these views. Discussing an issue in an open forum takes more time than if each person reads a concise, well-constructed position paper. Furthermore, variations in comprehension ability, background, preparation, and communication skills make it unlikely that committee meetings will ever be as *efficient* a communication device as the written word.

Legitimate Uses

The classicists were not totally opposed to committees and granted that they could serve limited informational and advisory functions.

Disseminating Information The classicists viewed information dissemination as a legitimate committee function. The Monday morning executive committee meeting gave the president a chance to tell the committee members what they were supposed to do that week. The classical school could easily accept such a committee meeting because the president was assigning duties and passing out information, not delegating authority. Instead, the meeting reinforced the existing responsibility/authority relationships. Actually, such a committee meeting was less "committee" than "meeting."

The meeting might proceed to a sharing of information and opinions. The president could restate and clarify goals and objectives, to show subordinates how their activities contributed to the common purpose. The classicists viewed such group meetings as no more than a face-to-face technique for (1) preserving the existing authority structure and (2) enabling the boss to give employees immediate feedback about whether or not they were on the right track.

Advising Lyndall Urwick granted that committees could sometimes perform a useful advisory function. The chief executive could convene an ad hoc group to offer insight or advice on a specific issue, or could maintain a general policy advisory group. Hearing diverse opinions from a managerial or staff group would enable executives to make better decisions about integrating the efforts of those responsible to them. But the classical executive always retained the right to make the final decision.

Except for these few limited uses, the committee was not a part of classical thinking. The classicists believed that people were hired to perform specific tasks, exercise specific responsibilities, and fill specific slots in the authority relationship structure. What, then, is the purpose of committee deliberations? They simply take people away from the jobs they were hired to do, and the enterprise suffers because committee members can't spend their full time doing what they are paid for. If the organization's members have time to attend committee meetings, then the organization isn't utilizing their time efficiently. Either essential jobs are not being performed, or people who shouldn't have been hired in the first place are using their time to call and attend meetings, and should be laid off.

The classical school would have expressed surprise upon finding that the camel resembles the horse as closely as it does.

THE HUMAN RELATIONS PERSPECTIVE

The human relations school had little to say about committees as such. Instead, they considered committees as *groups* and applied their theories of group behavior and group process to committees as they did to other organizational groups, such as departments. The human relations school viewed participative decision making and face-to-face information sharing as positive, desirable activities, with benefits for both the individual and the organization. The committee, then, was seen as an appropriate and progressive device for encouraging employee participation in organizational coordination and decision making.

The Nature of Groups

Since committees are formally sponsored, formally organized groups, the nature and process of group activity became an important focus of the human relations writers. A group is a collection of people who interact over a period of time to achieve common goals. We have all been exposed to countless numbers of groups—in business, education, government, and so forth. Our families are groups; our friendship circles are groups. Many groups have an impact on us, and we in turn affect our own groups.

Formal and Informal Groups

One of the many ways to categorize groups is according to whether they are formal or informal.

Formal   Many types of formal groups appear on organization charts. Divisions, departments, and task forces are all formal groups. An organizational committee is a formal body and should have formalized structure, membership, procedures, and authority.

The organization needs some permanent formal groups to carry on its day-to-day operations. Departmental groupings typically are such permanent groups. IBM could not survive if it did not have production groups and sales groups, nor could Stanford University without its departmental faculty groups, nor the Internal Revenue Service without its agent groups. The *positions* within a formal group do not change very often, but the *people* holding them may change frequently.

The organization establishes temporary formal groups whenever certain nonroutine tasks or problems need attention. These groups exist for a short time to perform specific activities. The matrix departmentalization strategies discussed in Chapter 5 fall into this class, as do most committees. If management feels that the temporary group is especially productive, it may continue to refer tasks to the group and may convert it into a permanent group. Although almost every committee has some characteristic that limits its life span—a particular project, issue, or due date—some committees do continue indefinitely as important permanent design features.

Informal An informal group comes into being without official organizational encouragement or approval, to satisfy certain needs of organizational members. For example, all members need friendly companionship. If organizational jobs tend to isolate workers, they will seek each other out and establish informal groups.

These groups can have a social purpose or they can perform tasks. Cliques, bowling teams, and the water-fountain gang are social groups. Members get together because they share common values, interests, and attitudes. In a task-oriented informal group, people voluntarily get together to solve problems or complete projects. Workers may have informal group discussions, for instance, then confer with management about their concerns.

Formal and Informal Overlap In sponsored formal groups, the organization decides what the relationships of group members shall be. Those relationships are structured in such a way as to achieve organizational goals. In the self-sponsored informal group, the members structure their own interpersonal relationships in order to achieve the group's goals. Organizational grouping may encourage or destroy informal groupings. For example, if the organization transfers 15 people to a new out-of-state branch office, they will form new informal groups to replace the ones they left behind.

The organization's formal and informal groups will rarely be the same, but they will usually overlap. As informal groups within and across formal groups try to achieve their goals, they can either reinforce or thwart the attainment of organizational goals. The organization should encourage those informal groups whose goals seem to support or be congruent with those of the organization.

McGregor's Good Group

In *The Human Side of Enterprise*, human relations exponent Douglas McGregor offered several characteristics of the well-functioning, effective, creative group.[6]

1. The atmosphere tends to be informal, comfortable, relaxed.
2. There is a lot of discussion in which virtually everyone participates, but it remains pertinent to the group's task.
3. The group members understand and accept their task or objective. They freely discuss their objective until they have formulated it in such a way that they can commit themselves to it.
4. The chairperson of the group does not dominate it, nor does the group defer unduly to the chair. In fact, the leadership shifts from time to time depending on the circumstances. Members don't struggle for power. The issue is not who controls but how to get the job done.
5. The group is self-conscious of its own operation.
6. The members listen to each other! Every idea is given a hearing. People do not seem to be afraid of appearing foolish by putting forth a creative thought even if it seems fairly extreme.
7. There is disagreement. Disagreements are not suppressed or overridden by premature group action. The reasons for disagreement are carefully examined, and the group seeks to resolve them rather than to dominate dissenters.

8. Criticism is frequent, frank, and relatively comfortable. Members do not attack each other personally; they deal with each other's ideas.
9. People freely express their feelings and ideas, both on the problem and on the group's operation.
10. Most decisions are reached by a kind of consensus; everyone is in general agreement and willing to go along. Formal voting is at a minimum; the group does not accept a simple majority as a proper basis for action.
11. When action is taken, clear assignments are made and accepted.

The human relations school would want all groups, including committees, to function in such a fashion.

Now that we know what a good group is from a human relations perspective, let us examine some findings and insights of researchers with a human relations orientation that might offer guidance in the development of good groups.

Human Relations Research

The volumes of work on small-group behavior produced by the human relations scholars are important for our understanding of committees and how they work. The human relations writers do not necessarily condemn or support committee use in any particular or specific way (other than their endorsement of any organizational device that encourages the participation of subordinate-level managers in decision making). Instead, the human relations writers have provided knowledge about several significant aspects of committee and other small-group operations. Rather than being concerned about mandates, time spans, and accountability, the human relations writers focused on the *people part*—the committee members themselves. More specifically:

1. Spatial arrangement: How can the committee members be most effectively arranged within their work/discussion space?
2. Size: How large should the group be in order to fulfill its mandate promptly and effectively?
3. Group dynamics: What forces come to bear on members in the committee situation? What techniques can help members to interact most satisfactorily and productively?
4. Leadership: What is effective committee leadership, and how can it be encouraged?

Spatial Arrangement

Although how the committee members are arranged is not an element of the committee itself, it is an important factor in the committee's performance. Different arrangements affect committee behavior differently. For example, sitting in a circle encourages committee members to participate; sitting in rows discourages participation.

Robert Sommer has studied the arrangement of people in face-to-face groups.[7] A group's initial physical arrangement depends on the group's task, the relationships and personalities of the group members, and how much and what kind of space is available. The resulting spatial arrangement will affect the group's communication, productivity, and social relationships. The position of persons within the overall arrangement is significant. The leader often sits at "the head of the table." Jury members at the ends of jury tables are more participative and influential in deliberations than members along the sides.

Size

The successful committee is made up of the right number of members. The committee's size will influence its effectiveness. Each additional member contributes some information and insight, but the additional members probably replicate information and skills already represented.

The most common guidelines for committee size are (1) how many people can reasonably interact, (2) who has important expertise to offer the group, and (3) which groups must be represented. If every affected group is represented, the committee may be too large. Yet, not representing all groups may leave the committee's decision open to criticism. Actually, the matter of "representation" is often stressed too much. If the members of a small committee are objective and cooperative, they will accomplish more than a large committee consisting of persons determined to represent their special interests.

Over 30 years ago, R.F. Bales and E.F. Borgatta concluded that groups of two to four persons were more anxious, sought opinions and information rather than offering them, and were more desirous of coming to agreement than were groups of five to seven persons. Bales and Borgatta believed that the smaller group size promoted a desire or need for harmony. In the larger group, people were more direct about offering their thoughts and opinions because it was harder to "get a word in edgewise."[8]

Estimates of appropriate sizes made by small-group researchers range from 5 to 15, with groups near 5 tending to be more effective than groups near 15. According to A.C. Filley:

> The typical committee should be, and is, relatively small. Recommended sizes range from three to nine members, and surveys of actual practice seldom miss these prescriptions by much. Of the 1,658 committees recorded in the *Harvard Business Review* survey [see Table 11.1 on p. 265], the average membership was eight. When asked for their preference, the 79 percent who answered suggested an ideal committee size that averaged 4.6 members.[9]

Group members must keep track both of the group as a whole and the individuals in it. This double task limits the membership of the effective group. According to A. Paul Hare, "The ability of the observing individual to perceive, keep track of, and judge each member separately in a social interaction situation may not extend much beyond the size of six or seven."[10]

Edwin J. Thomas and Clinton F. Fink reviewed 31 studies of group size. They concluded that "as size increases, there will be decreasing group cohesiveness and increasing organization and division of labor in the group, along with the development of cliques and possibly of factions."[11]

In addition, research suggests a direct relationship between group size and satisfaction (small group/large satisfaction; large group/small satisfaction)[12] but no clear relationship between size and group productivity.[13] In order to detect such a relationship, the group's *task* would probably have to be considered. As T.R. Mitchell explains, on some group tasks (for example, some piece-rate jobs), each new member will add a fixed amount to productivity. On group tasks where all work together and pool their resources, a limit will eventually be reached beyond which new members add coordination and motivation problems, and detract from productivity.[14] This explanation of the relationship between group size and productivity suggests the need to develop a contingency approach toward making such decisions as what size the committee will be. This approach will be discussed later in the chapter when we look at committees from the modern perspective.

Although picking any one number as ideal for all committees would be foolish, five-member problem-solving groups are often viewed as neither too small nor too large. In a study by P. Slater, group members viewed the best size for collecting, exchanging, analyzing, and evaluating information, then making a group decision about action, to be five members.[15]

Group Dynamics

Dorwin Cartwright points out how great an effect the groups to which we belong have on us:

> . . . the behavior, attitudes, beliefs, and values of the individual are all firmly grounded in the groups to which he belongs. How aggressive or cooperative a person is, how much self-respect and self-confidence he has, how energetic and productive his work is, what he aspires to, what he believes to be true and good, whom he loves or hates, and what beliefs and prejudices he holds—all these characteristics are highly determined by the individual's group memberships. . . . Attempts to change them must be concerned with the dynamics of groups.[16]

Several principles of group dynamics have arisen out of studies by human relations researchers. They can foster the productive use of organizational groups.

1. For a group to make changes effectively, the people who are going to be changed and the people who want the changes should both be represented in the group and should have a strong sense of belonging to it.
2. The more attractive a group is to its members, the more influence the group can have on them.
3. The higher a group member's prestige, the more influence that member can exert.
4. The group will strongly resist efforts to change members which, if successful, would cause these members to deviate from group norms.
5. Changes in one part of a group sometimes strain other parts. The group can reduce the strain only by eliminating the change or readjusting the related parts.

Analyzing Interaction: The Bales Technique   Robert F. Bales has developed a technique for analyzing and understanding the process of group interaction.[17] The method is best used over a long period of time that includes a variety of group activities.

Table 11.2 presents the Bales system. The first five behaviors help the group to accomplish its task. The second five behaviors relate mainly to housekeeping, to helping the group be a good group regardless of the task at hand. The last five behaviors, all harmful, are seen frequently in noncohesive groups and occasionally in all groups.

Any of the 15 behaviors can occur at any stage of group development: initiation, housekeeping, growth, feedback. Some behaviors are, of course, more frequent at different stages. For instance, the maintenance behaviors are always appropriate but are essential as the group does its housekeeping. The group, and especially its leader, can observe which behavior types are occurring and assess the stage of group development and what action seems needed. If the group is informing, clarifying, and summarizing, for example, it is working productively during the growth stage. If members are being aggressive and dominating, then the group needs to back up and do some housekeeping.

Table 11.2   ANALYZING GROUP INTERACTION

Group task behavior: conduct that advances the work of the group

1. *Initiating:* Proposes aims, ideas, action, tasks, goals, or procedures. Has new ideas or suggestions. Starts the discussion, defines the problem, suggests procedures.
2. *Informing or opining:* Asks for or offers facts, ideas, feelings, or opinions. Asks for or gives information.
3. *Clarifying or elaborating:* Illuminates or builds upon ideas or suggestions. Helps to explain. Gives examples, illustrations, interpretations, clears up confusion.
4. *Summarizing or coordinating:* Pulls data together, so group may consider where it is. Pulls ideas together. Shows relationships. Restates info, opinions, suggestions concisely after group has discussed. Offers decision or conclusion for group to accept or reject.
5. *Consensus testing:* Explores whether group may be nearing a decision. Prevents premature decision making. Finds out if group is ready to decide what to do.

Group maintenance behavior: conduct that helps the group function productively

6. *Harmonizing:* Reconciles disagreements, relieves tension, helps people explore differences. Helps people get together. Oil on troubled waters.
7. *Gate Keeping:* Brings other people in, suggests facilitating procedures, keeps communication channels open.
8. *Encouraging:* Is warm, friendly, and responsive. Indicates with words or facial expression that the contributions of others are accepted. Shows interest, kindness. Praises, agrees.
9. *Compromising:* Modifies position so group may move ahead. Admits error. Is willing to change own ideas to help the group.
10. *Giving feedback:* Tells others, in helpful ways, how their behavior is received, how they are coming across.

Personal or self-oriented behavior: conduct that interferes with group work

11. *Aggressing:* Attacks, deflates, uses sarcasm. Criticizes, blames others.
12. *Blocking:* Resists beyond reason, prevents group movement, won't go along with other people's suggestions. Argues, rejects.
13. *Dominating:* Interrupts, asserts authority, overparticipates to the point of interfering with others' participation. Talks too much.
14. *Avoiding:* Prevents group from facing controversy. Stays off subject to avoid commitment. Keeps people from discussing because dislikes arguments.
15. *Abandoning:* Makes an obvious display of lack of involvement. Shows that does not care about what is happening. Daydreams, doodles, whispers to others.

Source: Robert F. Bales, *Interaction Process Analysis: A Method for the Study of Small Groups* (Chicago, IL: University of Chicago Press, 1950). Used by permission.

Brainstorming   One device for getting everyone on the committee involved is brainstorming. A committee can generate more ideas and possibilities than any one member can, but members are sometimes hesitant to express their thoughts. Often occurring without a leader, brainstorming sessions are designed to get *all* notions out in the open, no matter how ridiculous or profound. A prohibition against evaluation enables all members to contribute fully and creatively, without the inhibiting fear of social censure or peer ridicule. Committee members say whatever comes into their heads. Instead of criticizing each other's ideas, members build on them. A recorder jots down all suggestions and comments for later evaluation.

After the spontaneous creativity has subsided, a single manager or the committee itself can examine the ideas coolly and rationally, in light of the organization's goals and resources.

People enjoy brainstorming sessions because they encourage a contagious enthusiasm and an uninhibited atmosphere for producing and building on ideas. However, five disadvantages sometimes occur:

1. *Boredom:* The novelty of brainstorming is initially exciting. People get a thrill out of dropping their inhibitions at the office. After a while, though, they tire of the "game," lose interest, and stop generating ideas.
2. *Ego involvement:* Group members sometimes have difficulty in maintaining a positive, nonevaluative attitude once their egos get involved. When we hear an idea that we think is absurd, our tendency is to criticize it. Even if everyone follows the "no-criticism" rule, group members may suspect or conclude that other members are being silently critical. Also, people may get attached to their own ideas, rather than trying to help the group come up with the group's best idea.
3. *Aimlessness:* Since a wide variety of ideas is encouraged—from the practical to the wildly bizarre—the group tends to wander randomly through the universe of ideas. The group may free-associate for hours along a train of thought which later proves to have been a total waste of time and effort.
4. *Time consumed:* If the problem is complex, brainstorming may take so long that the group becomes frustrated and less creative.
5. *Status problems:* Brainstormers are encouraged to offer all ideas, however "wild." Even so, if a high-status manager is present, the generation and expression of ideas may be inhibited.

The Gordon Technique   William J.J. Gordon tried to remedy some of these problems in brainstorming.[18] A major change was to introduce a discussion leader into the leaderless brainstorming format. The leader presents a target topic, related to the committee's purpose, and then encourages the group to explore its different aspects.

For example, assume that the organization is trying to develop a new toy. Instead of discussing toys, the Gordon-type group might be encouraged to discuss "play" or "childhood enjoyment." Since group members free-associate without limiting their thoughts to "new kind of toy," they may come up with new approaches to conceiving, building, or using toys.

The Gordon technique minimizes ego involvement and aimlessness. Ego involvement is minimal because group members do not know how their ideas are going to be used. Consequently, they do not know whose ideas are outrageous and whose ideas are conservative. Aimless discussion is discouraged by the group leader, who permits "free" association but only along certain lines.

The strengths of brainstorming (anything goes, say whatever you want, no criticism, no leader or boss, spontaneity, creativity) result naturally in its weaknesses (lack of control, aimless discussion, wasted time). For the Gordon method to achieve its advantages (some control, no aimless discussion, little wasted time), some spontaneity and creativity must be sacrificed. However, if the leader can provide just the right amount of control to avoid aimlessness but not stifle creativity, the Gordon technique can blend creativity with efficiency.

The Nominal Group Technique   In a nominal group, the generation and discussion of ideas are very orderly. Here are the steps:

1. Without discussion, all group members write down their thoughts on the problem.
2. Each member presents *one* idea per round to the group, again without discussion. This step continues through as many rounds as are needed for the presentation of all ideas.
3. All ideas are listed on a chalkboard or flip chart.
4. The group discusses the merits of each idea in turn.
5. The group votes on the ideas. The idea receiving the most votes is the group's choice.

The nominal group technique permits both independent thinking and group interaction. Every person's ideas are heard and discussed.

The Delphi Technique   The main difference between the nominal group technique and the Delphi technique is that Delphi group members *do not normally meet.* The leader sends a questionnaire to each group member, receives the results, summarizes them, then sends another copy of the questionnaire to group members along with the summary. The group members can then see how other members voted, before filling out the questionnaire again. The process can continue through an indefinite number of rounds. Results on the final questionnaire determine the group's decision.

Like other techniques, this one has several drawbacks:

1. Unless questions are carefully worded, a bias toward answering in a certain way may be introduced. Since the group members do not usually meet, that bias cannot be discussed and corrected.
2. The technique takes time. It is not suitable for problems needing quick solutions.
3. Interaction among members is minimal or nonexistent. Therefore, not much opportunity is offered for the mutual stimulation of ideas, opinions, and suggestions.

Leadership

In addition to their solid contributions on committee spatial arrangement, size, and interaction, human relations researchers have enlarged our understanding of small-group leadership. Much of the general information on leadership in Chapter 9 is relevant to chairing a committee. The following material is more specifically related to the special requirements of effective committee leadership.

The most important determinant of a committee's effectiveness is its chairperson. The chair must know and clearly express the committee's goal, scope, and authority. The chair must ensure that committee disagreement is constructive, not destructive.

In hopes of encouraging everyone to talk, the chairperson may be tempted to let the discussion wander. Part of the chairperson's art lies in knowing when this wandering stops being productive and starts wasting time. Most committee members do not like to waste time or have their time wasted. The more productive they are, the more they resent wasting time. Since productive people are important to a productive group, the chairperson must maintain the enthusiasm of the group's productive members by running the committee efficiently.[19]

Leading Discussions   Discussion leaders must have many skills. They must remember what has already been said in order to provide helpful summaries and reviews. They must pay attention to what is being said at the moment. They must be aware of nonverbal communication signals by persons other than the present speaker. They must perceive the direction of the committee. They must keep an eye on the clock. They must keep the gates of communication open, give everyone an equal chance to participate, and maintain impartiality by accepting rather than judging the opinions expressed. People are usually appointed committee chairs because they have higher rank or status than other committee members do. Therefore, to gain the benefits that can come out of open discussion, they must do everything possible to see that their higher status does not inhibit the free flow of ideas.

Some committee leaders seem to feel that their main task is to set the meeting time and place. Actually, the leadership position is crucial to group success. Enormous skill and effort are required to ensure that each committee member's time and energy are used productively.

Shared Achievement   According to Antony Jay, a committee chairmanship has only one legitimate source of pleasure:

> Pleasure in the achievements of the meeting—and to be legitimate, it must be shared by all those present. Meetings are *necessary* for all sorts of basic and primitive human reasons, but they are *useful* only if they are seen by all present to be getting somewhere—and somewhere they know they could not have gotten to individually.[20]

Social Relations   If the committee's mandate is clear, the group understands its purpose or task. The importance of the leader in moving the committee toward its goal is self-evident. A contribution of the human relations school has been its emphasis on the importance of the group's social relations (what R.F. Bales referred to as "maintenance behaviors") and on the leader's responsibility for them.

A.C. Filley reviewed practice and opinion regarding the committee leader's role. Filley confirmed that leaders have both a task role and a social role to play. Members want and expect the leader to take charge of the group's proceedings. But the group must also be built and maintained *as a group.* Perhaps the group chairperson has the time and ability to perform both the task and social roles. If not, one or more other members must perform the social-leadership role. Both are necessary.[21]

Group Assets and Liabilities

When compared to problem solving by individuals, problem solving by groups has both assets and liabilities. Norman R.F. Maier has summed up these plus and minus features.[22]

Group Assets   Group problem solving has the following advantages.

1. *More knowledge and information.* The group has more knowledge and information than any one of its members.
2. *More approaches.* Group members bring different approaches to problem solving and keep each other's thinking from getting into ruts.
3. *Greater acceptance of solution.* When people work together to arrive at a solution, they take a personal interest in that solution and feel responsible for making it work.
4. *Better understanding of decisions.* Employees seem to think that many management decisions are arrived at arbitrarily. Group members who participate in decision making understand why one alternative was accepted and others rejected.

Group Liabilities   The group approach does have some liabilities.

1. *Social pressure.* People want to be good group members. They want to be accepted by the group. Therefore, social pressure can lead to consensus solutions that may not be of the highest quality.
2. *Vocal members may determine outcomes.* Studies have shown that sheer repetition of statements in favor of a solution can help to achieve it. When a solution has had enough positive comments made in its favor, the group tends to adopt it regardless of its quality.
3. *Individual domination.* A persuasive, stubborn, persistent group member may influence the group to adopt a solution of lower quality.
4. *Desire to win arguments.* Some group members would rather argue successfully for their own pet solutions than help the others to reach the best group solution.

Assets or Liabilities   Maier maintains that some group factors can be good or bad, depending on the group leader's skill.

1. *Disagreement.* The good group leader encourages creative disagreement that leads to an airing of all viewpoints. Excessive disagreement leads to hard feelings and a reluctance on the part of some group members to support group solutions.
2. *Conflicting interests versus mutual interests.* The good group leader can help the group establish its mutual interests. The less effective group leader is unable to keep group members from dwelling on conflicting interests.

3. *Risk taking.* Research has shown that groups are more willing to make riskier decisions than are individuals. The leader must encourage the group to be brave and innovative, but not foolhardy.

4. *Time requirements.* Individuals can usually make decisions faster than groups can, so some problems requiring immediate action must be solved by individuals. Within a group, the leader must be sure that the group members have time to offer ideas from their different perspectives; otherwise the diverse talents represented by the group are wasted. On the other hand, the leader cannot let the discussion go on and on until group members are willing to agree on *any* solution, just so they can leave the meeting.

5. *Performing in front of others.* Being in a group affects all members differently, but it does have an effect. Some people perform better when others are watching. They are more motivated and work harder when they are "on stage." Other group members get "stage fright"; they freeze up and cannot make their contributions. The good group leader is able to bring out the best of both types.

Many contributions of the human relations school have improved the abilities of committees to fulfill their mandates and perform their tasks. However, the major human relations efforts have been directed toward improving the social aspects that can help or hinder a committee as it goes about its work.

THE MODERN PERSPECTIVE

The Situation

The modern school has not yet developed a clear position on coordination by committee. What modern writers have sought to do, however, is to distinguish those situations which encourage the positive aspects of committees from those which seem to stimulate mainly the disadvantages. In other words, the trend is to find the driving forces that make committee benefits outweigh the costs. Today's writers recognize that committee benefits outweigh costs *in certain situations* and that costs outweigh benefits *in certain situations.* These researchers seek to create models and offer guidelines that can enable managers to recognize when to use committees and when to avoid them.

Managers must understand the disadvantages and limitations of committees, as spelled out by the classical school. If forming a committee will create frustration or conflict because participants do not know or care about the issues to be examined, then the manager should just go ahead and make the decisions. If the manager's mind is already made up on an issue, forming a committee to investigate and make recommendations will serve no purpose. Finally, if committee members have too much at stake personally or cannot resist taking a departmental perspective rather than an organizational perspective, the committee will be characterized by compromise and mediocre decisions.

The Leader

When to use or not to use a particular committee depends on the situation but also on *the leader.* These two elements are equally important. If the situation calls for a committee and the organizational unit leader can't or won't work with a committee, the organization had better not form one. Chief executives who don't want advice don't want advisory committees. If the leader typically wants a committee in order to avoid making decisions in situations demanding immediate action, the organization had better consider finding new leadership. The pilot of a hijacked airplane should not convene a committee whose purpose is to decide whether to cooperate with the hijacker.

In general, if committees can be structured and led so that potential disadvantages are avoided and inherent advantages are utilized, organizations should form them.

Further Guidelines

The following guidelines can help determine whether a committee or a manager should be used in a certain organizational situation.

Time Available   An information-sharing committee will usually save organizational time by enabling face-to-face interaction and discussion. Problem-solving committees that must interact as they go through the problem-solving steps may take too much time. If time is short, a manager should come up with a solution and have it implemented.

Knowledge Available   The combined knowledge, skills, training, and experience of a committee can profitably be brought to bear on many problems. If committee members don't have the requisite background, however, and a single executive does, then that executive should make the decision. If *no one* in the organization has the background to handle a problem, a committee that brainstorms the problem thoroughly may come to a better decision than any individual organizational member could.

Organizational Importance of Problem   If the problem is important to the organization, the benefits of the time members spend on the problem-solving committee may outweigh the costs. If the problem is unimportant, committee time should not be spent on it. For the top management group at General Motors to evaluate paper clip waste would be absurd.

Individual Importance of Problem   If people don't care at all about a problem, they should not serve on a committee that is trying to solve it. If their concerns about the problem are deeply personal—if they care *too much* about the problem—they should not serve. The committee should consist of people who care about the outcome but don't care so much that they are unable to put aside their own interests or those of their departments.

The Leader's Preferences   Managers forming committees must honestly ask themselves whether they want group input. Committee members quickly recognize whether their work is used and appreciated, then react accordingly. If managers have reputations for accepting only those recommendations that agree with what they have already decided to do, the committee will probably try to save time and effort by determining the position of the boss, then agreeing with it.

Different Problems, Different Groups

Andre L. Delbecq suggests that appropriate problem-solving groups and their processes are contingent upon the problems they are attempting to solve and should be varied accordingly.[23]

Routine Decision Making   Delbecq describes as routine those decisions made when (1) the group agrees on the desired goal and (2) the group possesses the skills, methods, and technologies to achieve it.

Creative Decision Making   Creative decision making occurs when groups do not have an agreed-upon method for solving a problem, perhaps because they don't know what caused it or have never before encountered a similar problem.

Negotiated Decision Making   When opposing factions come together and try to agree, the decision must be negotiated. Depending upon the type of decision to be made, the decision-making group will vary in five ways: structure, roles, process, style, and norms. Table 11.3 presents the characteristics that Delbecq sees as appropriate for making the three types of decisions.

According to Delbecq, the modern manager must teach subordinates the differences between decision-making situations and instruct them in the appropriate behavior within each situation. He concludes his contingency approach to group decision making by maintaining that "creative" and "negotiated" strategies can also play a part in "routine" decision-making situations.

SUMMARY

Organizations often establish committees to perform organizational duties, so committee work might at first appear to be a differentiation function. However, that work is usually coordinative—leaders of several departments or supervisors of several units get together to coordinate the efforts of their groups. Organizations must select committee members and leaders carefully, then state committee objectives clearly.

Rollie Tillman examined large organizations and found seven major committee types, averaging about eight members and twenty meetings a year. Such committees are either standing (relatively permanent) or ad hoc (temporary). They solve problems, share information, and generate ideas. Four key elements of any committee are its mandate, life span, people, and accountability.

The classical school preferred to rely on the decisions of individual managers, not committees. They viewed committees as adversely affected by the self-interest of members as well as by the frequent absence of interest, inadequate knowledge and authority, irresponsible and mediocre decisions, lack of accountability, and lack of follow-up.

The human relations school commented more often on groups generally than on committees in particular. They felt that the principles of good group behavior were applicable to that special type of group called the committee. Groups are formal (like committees) or informal (like street-corner gangs). Human relations research has added to our understanding of committee spatial arrangement, size, group dynamics, and leadership. Committee interaction is promoted by sitting in a circle. A committee size

Table 11.3   DECISION TYPES AND GROUP CHARACTERISTICS

Decision type	Structure	Roles	Group characteristic		
			Process	Style	Norms
Routine	Specialists with coordinator as leader	Independent effort by specialists; leader coordinates efforts	Occasional full-group meetings; many one-on-one sessions between specialists	High stress, time pressure, commitment, decentralization	Professionalism, commitment, economy, efficiency
Creative	Heterogeneous members with different frames of reference; leader is a facilitator	Each member explores all ideas with the group, no matter how intuitive or roughly formed the ideas are	Spontaneity, full participation, suspension of judgment, analyze fully, don't use standard idea-gathering & problem-solving processes	Relaxed, nonstressful, supportive	Support originality, allow eccentricity, nonauthoritarian, open communication, seek consensus
Negotiated	Proportionate representation of factions, impartial formal chairperson	Each person represents a faction, protects its concerns while trying for acceptable compromise	Orderly, formalized procedures, votes; each faction has veto power	Frankness and candor, respect for due process, open to moderation, avoid open hostility and aggression	Desire to reach agreement, acceptance of conflict and disagreement as healthy and natural, willing to accept partial agreement

Source: Adapted from Andre L. Delbecq, "The Management of Decision-Making Within the Firm: Three Strategies for Three Types of Decision-Making," *Academy of Management Journal* 10 (December 1967): 329–339. Used by permission.

of five members or so often seems effective. Techniques relevant to the improvement of group dynamics are the Bales system for measuring interaction, brainstorming, the Gordon technique (adding a leader and a key concept to brainstorming), the nominal group technique (adding the silent generation of ideas), and the Delphi technique (the group that never meets.) The committee's chairperson is vitally important, both to the accomplishment of the committee's job and to its social relations.

Norman R.F. Maier has proposed four potential assets of problem-solving groups (more information, more approaches, greater acceptance of the solution, and better understanding of decisions), four potential liabilities (adverse effects of social pressure, overly vocal members, individual domination, and the desire to win arguments instead of arrive at solutions), and five factors that may be assets or liabilities, depending upon how effective the group leader is: disagreement, conflicting versus mutual interests, risk taking, time requirements, and performing in front of others.

The modern school has stressed that when or how to use a committee usually depends upon the situation and upon both the potential committee leader and the unit leader or manager to whom the committee will report. Managers must understand the potential disadvantages of committees (as stressed by the classicists), the advantages (as stressed by the human relations school), and then use committees for those coordinating efforts in which the benefits of the form can outweigh its drawbacks. The organization must find a match between the situation calling for a committee and the leader capable of working with a committee or accepting its findings.

Five guidelines can help to determine whether to use a committee rather than an individual manager: the time and knowledge available, the organizational and individual importance of the problem, and the manager's preferences.

Andre L. Delbecq's contingency-based approach shows how five characteristics of groups (structure, member roles, process, style, and norms) vary with three decision situations: routine, creative, and negotiated.

DISCUSSION QUESTIONS

1. What is a committee? What are its two major purposes?
2. What were Rollie Tillman's major findings regarding committees?
3. How should the membership of the committee be determined?
4. Why is the committee's mandate or charge so important?
5. What is the classical position on committee use?
6. What is the human relations position on committee use?
7. According to Douglas MacGregor, what is a good group? Have you ever been in a group like that?
8. Ideally, how many people should serve on a committee? Why?
9. When and why is brainstorming an appropriate committee activity? What problems can be involved in the use of brainstorming?
10. What are the characteristics of an effective committee chairperson?
11. What are the advantages and disadvantages of turning organizational problems over to groups such as committees?
12. What is the modern perspective on committee use?
13. How should a manager decide when to use a problem-solving committee?
14. Describe the best and worst committee on which you have ever served. What made the one good and the other bad?

THE PRESIDENT'S ADVISORY COUNCIL

Soon after founding the Smith Company, President Homer Smith set up an advisory council of seven members, to be elected by employees in the company's seven departments. At first, the employee representatives had a lot to complain about. The new company did have problems, the employees were often dissatisfied, and the President's Advisory Council frequently engaged in heated discussions with Smith.

Over time the company's routines were established, and the committee worked out its problem-solving approaches. Difficulties were resolved calmly and rationally. The employees gave credit to the advisory council and President Smith for the improvements at Smith Company.

President Smith eventually concluded that the advisory council might have outlived its usefulness. A two-hour meeting last week consisted of the pros and cons of a new reporting form that a committee member had proposed. At the end of two hours, when President Smith said he didn't really care whether the company used the new form or not, the advisers confessed that they didn't care either; they were simply trying to have a "productive meeting."

What different functions did the council serve over the years? What functions is it serving now? Should Smith disband the President's Advisory Council?

THE BOARD OF DEACONS

Every Thursday afternoon, Senior Deacon James Schaub conducted a meeting of the Board of Deacons. In addition to leading the group through an agenda of church-related items, he made announcements, accepted suggestions, and sometimes offered inspirational messages. During these very informal meetings, the deacons drank coffee and tea, ate snacks, and sometimes engaged in good-humored banter. Most deacons seemed to enjoy mixing church business with pleasure, as did Senior Deacon Schaub. However, several often got restless and seemed to want to finish the business promptly and go home.

Late one Wednesday afternoon, Schaub realized that for the first time in many months, he had absolutely nothing to put on the board's agenda. If a deacon were to ask him "Why are we meeting?" he might have to say "Because it's Thursday afternoon." He was behind in his work at his regular job; perhaps he should cancel the meeting. "No," he decided, "let's meet anyway."

The deacons showed up promptly. They drank, ate, and chatted as usual. A couple of deacons looked at their watches occasionally. No one asked for an agenda. As the deacons were leaving, one said, "Good get-together today, Brother Jim." Schaub was relieved; he guessed holding the meeting was the right thing to do after all.

Over the next few days, he received notes from three deacons, of which the following was typical:

Jim, I'm a busy person. Some of the others seem interested in endless socializing. I have other responsibilities. While I am glad to serve my church, I don't appreciate leaving my work to attend meetings with no purpose. The next time you plan to hold a meeting without an agenda, kindly let me know.

Should James Schaub have cancelled the board meeting? What does his holding the meeting say about his committee leadership style? What are the advantages and disadvantages of that style?

■ *ELITE ELECTRIC COMPANY: THE DAILY OPERATIONS MEETING*

CAST OF CHARACTERS

Plant Operations Manager	Peter Johnson
Safety Manager	Martin Massell
Engineering Manager	David Arato
Production Manager	Brian Campbell
Customer Service	Michael St. John
Purchasing Manager	Paul Barbato
Personnel Manager	Jane Wieder
Accounting Representative	Harvey Jones
Quality Control Manager	Elizabeth Schultz

Peter Johnson (Plant Operations Manager): O.K., everybody, it's 9:00 so let's get started. You all have a copy of the agenda so you know we're going to start with safety first.

Martin Massell (Safety Manager): Well, Peter, I have a number of things to go over. First, we should look into whether the right people are getting proper feedback from Maintenance. Yesterday while the maintenance crew was washing down the walls, water leaked into the electrical wiring. They didn't tell anybody what they'd done, so we had some smoke develop. We were lucky we didn't have a fire.

Peter Johnson: O.K., Martin, we'll have Irving (Maintenance Manager) look into it, and he'll get back to you. What else?

Martin Massell: I recently found out that the forklift operators are driving the lifts too fast in the plant. I'm sending out a memo telling them to slow down.

David Arato (Engineering Manager): Why don't we just put some bumps in the floor so they can't speed over them?

Martin Massell: David, we are looking at that. We may decide to use the speed bumps, but we have to get some cost estimates, and we have to see how Maintenance will feel about it.

Peter Johnson: By the way, where is the representative from Maintenance? [Pause] Well, I'll have to contact Irving on that. Anything else, Martin?

Martin Massell: Oh, yeah, I forgot to tell you yesterday. The entire loading dock has been cleaned, so we shouldn't be having any more problems. By the way, Brian, make sure you contact Irving about the spill in that area.

Brian Campbell (Production Manager): Oh, I forgot to tell you, Peter, but Irving said that we'd have to close down machines #1 and #6 to fix the leak that's causing the oil spill. I've already gone ahead and done that.

Peter Johnson: Gee, Brian, I wish you'd clear things like that with me first. How badly will the shutdown affect our production?

Brian Campbell: Oh, not too badly; we should be able to get away with a minimum of overtime this weekend.

Peter Johnson: O.K., but in the future let me know before you shut any machines down. Mike, Customer Service is next. How are we doing with our parent company?

Michael St. John (Customer Service): Oh, fairly well. We're starting to get some flak for not taking that Japanese order, but the folks at the parent company understand. They may not like it, but they can deal with it. Oh, Paul, are you going to have enough transistors on hand to complete the Canadian order by next Tuesday?

Paul Barbato (Purchasing Manager): Sure, Mike, I sent you a memo on that yesterday. Didn't you get it?

Michael St. John: Sorry, but I haven't had a chance to get to my morning mail yet. I was too busy with some visitors from Europe.

Peter Johnson: Are our visitors being taken care of, Mike? Can we do anything else to make their stay here more comfortable?

Michael St. John: No, Peter, everything's fine.

Peter Johnson: O.K., then let's move on to Employee Relations. Jane?

Jane Wieder (Personnel Manager): First, I would like to introduce two guests from Training Programs, Inc. As you know, they'll soon begin offering us a series of programs. Second, Al Janow's grievance has been resolved. Third, at the Management/Employee Meeting yesterday, we agreed that a representative from each department would attend in the future. Fourth, the Interview Workshop memo is done, Peter, and here it is [gives memo to Peter]. Fifth, we have to work out the date for our Annual Family Get-Together. How does July look?

Michael St. John: July looks terrible, Jane. We'll probably be putting in a lot of overtime then, because the Australian order has to be out in the beginning of August. Can we push it up to June?

Harvey Jones (Accounting Representative): Don't forget that revised budgets are due in June. [For another 15 minutes, the group continues to discuss the best date for the Annual Family Get-Together.]

Jane Wieder: Sixth, please notify us of any changes in your marital status, address, and so forth. We need to keep our records up to date. Seventh, older company cars can now be purchased by employees. We'll soon be instituting a lottery system to decide who can buy the cars.

David Arato: Jane, will we get a memo on that?

Jane Wieder: Yes, David, I'll have one out by the end of the week.

Peter Johnson: We need to move on to Quality Control. Elizabeth?

Elizabeth Schultz (Quality Control Manager): Our #2 and #8 machines have been throwing out bent transistor leads, so those two machines will be down over the weekend. Irving [Maintenance Manager] and Brian [Production Manager] are aware of the problem. We have to straighten that mess out before we do the order from IBM. I also noticed that the last gold shipment had some other metals in it. Paul, can you check that out to see what went wrong?

Paul Barbato: How much extraneous metal was present?

Elizabeth Schultz: We didn't do complete tests but it looked like about 5 ounces per 100 pounds.

Paul Barbato: Heck, that's not much.

Elizabeth Schultz: Well, we think it is, and we'd like it checked out.

Peter Johnson: O.K., Elizabeth, Paul will look into it. Now let's turn to Production.

Brian Campbell: Yes, here's the most recent production summary. Last Monday we manufactured 3000 transistors. Machines #1, #2, and #8 did 300, machines #3 and #4 were down, and the rest of the output was achieved by the remaining machines. On Tuesday, we had to change over to produce the larger integrated circuits that Control Data needed. That resulted in two hours of downtime. Machines #6 and #7 did 20 percent of the production run of 5000 boards. Machine #1 continued to manufacture the small transistorized chips, with machines #2 and #5 completing the rest of the circuit-board runs. [At about this time, two people get up and leave the room.] Wednesday we switched back to transistor runs on all machines. Unfortunately, machine #2 went down for the entire day, and machine #7 was scheduled for preventive maintenance. Even so, we manufactured 2700 transistors. Machines #4, #5, and #8 did approximately 60 percent of the work. [Several people are yawning now.] Thursday, I regret to report, we produced only 100 transistors and had to ship part of our run to the cathode ray tube production group for Digital Equipment Corporation. We produced [shuffles through his papers] 500 units for Digital. Machines #3, #4, and #5 were used for the DEC run, and machines #1, #2, and #6 were kept on transistor production. Machine #7 was down. On Friday we had half a day, and in the morning we had that blackout, so we were only able to get 100 transistors and 22 CRT's out.

Peter Johnson: Brian, do you think you'll be able to make up the rest of the orders this week without much overtime?

Brian Campbell: I don't know, Peter. I think we need to talk to Harry Brown (Union Representative).

Peter Johnson: That may be difficult since Harry's on vacation, but I'll try to get in touch with him. If I can't, let's go ahead as planned and just take the consequences. O.K., time's about up so let's go around the room and see what else anybody has to say.

Paul Barbato: Nothing.

Brian Campbell: Dave (Engineering Manager), I need to talk to you about the machine changeover and also about designing a better ramp. Does anybody have any questions about my production report? [No one has a question.]

Elizabeth Schultz: Peter, can I see you after the meeting to discuss a personal matter? [Peter shakes his head.]

David Arato: Nothing; I pass.

Martin Massell: I just want to let everyone know that we had a problem in one of the machine wells. While they were pouring concrete around the well, some slipped in and it took us a couple of days to get it cleaned up.

Jane Wieder: Paul, I need to see you on Mary Bernstein's problem.

Michael St. John: We may be getting a very big order from Grumman.

Harvey Jones: The following people have not reported their exempt status to payroll. [He lists 12 names.] Remember, Jane's memo three weeks ago made it clear that we need this information.

Peter Johnson: Brian, I want to take a couple of people from the university on a tour next week. I'll call you and set something up. Good meeting, everybody. See you tomorrow—same time, same place.

What seems to have been the purpose of this meeting? Which items do you think should have been handled through some means other than a meeting? What is your overall evaluation of the meeting? What advantages and disadvantages of committees are reflected here? If you conclude that the meeting was not satisfactory, how would you portion out the responsibility for its shortcomings?

This case is adapted from Barry R. Armandi, "Elite Electric Company," *Journal of Management Case Studies,* in press. Used by permission.

NOTES

1. Alfred P. Sloan, Jr., *My Years with General Motors* (Garden City, NY: Doubleday, 1972), pp. 121–122.
2. For an interesting article on how university administrators assemble the committee members depending on which of seven authority-task problems they ask the committee to solve, see Mary Lippitt Nichols, "An Exploratory Study of Committee Composition As an Administrative Problem-Solving Tool," *Decision Sciences* 12 (April 1981): 338–351.

3. Lyndall Urwick, *Notes on the Theory of Organization* (New York: American Management Association, 1952), pp. 61–62.

4. Ibid., pp. 64–65.

5. Irving L. Janis attributes four of our nation's greatest fiascoes to groupthink at the top policymaking level. These four "hardheaded actions by softheaded groups" were our unpreparedness at Pearl Harbor, the invasion of North Korea, the Bay of Pigs invasion, and the escalation of the Vietnam war. See Irving L. Janis, *Victims of Groupthink* (Boston: Houghton Mifflin, 1972).

6. Douglas McGregor, *The Human Side of Enterprise* (New York: McGraw-Hill, 1960), pp. 232–235.

7. Robert Sommer, "Small Group Ecology," *Psychological Bulletin* 67 (February 1967): 145–152.

8. R.F. Bales and E.F. Borgatta, "Size of Group As a Factor in the Interaction Profile," in *Small Groups,* ed. A.P. Hare, E.F. Borgatta, and R.F. Bales (New York: Knopf, 1955), pp. 396–413.

9. A.C. Filley, "Committee Management: Guidelines from Social Science Research," *California Management Review* 13 (Fall 1970): 14.

10. A. Paul Hare, *Handbook of Small Group Research* (New York: The Free Press of Glencoe, 1962), p. 227.

11. Edwin J. Thomas and Clinton F. Fink, "Effects of Group Size," *Psychological Bulletin* 60 (June 1963): 375.

12. L.W. Porter and E.E. Lawler, *Managerial Attitudes and Performance* (Homewood, IL.: Richard D. Irwin, 1968).

13. L.L. Cummings and C.J. Berger, "Organization Structure: How Does It Influence Attitudes and Performance?" *Organizational Dynamics* 5 (Autumn 1976): 34–49.

14. See T.R. Mitchell, *People in Organizations* (New York: McGraw-Hill, 1978), p. 188.

15. P. Slater, "Contrasting Correlates of Group Size," *Sociometry* 21 (June 1958): 137.

16. Dorwin Cartwright, "Achieving Change in People: Some Applications of Group Dynamics Theory," *Human Relations* 4 (October 1951): 387.

17. Robert F. Bales, *Interaction Process Analysis: A Method for the Study of Small Groups* (Cambridge, MA: Addison-Wesley, 1950).

18. See William J.J. Gordon, *Synectics: The Development of Creative Capacity* (New York: Harper & Row, 1961).

19. For an interesting case study of interaction between a committee and its chair, see Peter C. Gronn, "Committee Talk: Negotiating 'Personnel Development' at a Training College," *Journal of Management Studies* 22 (May 1985): 245–268.

20. Antony Jay, "How to Run a Meeting," *Harvard Business Review* 54 (March/April 1976): 52.

21. A.C. Filley, "Committee Management," p. 17.

22. Norman R.F. Maier, "Assets and Liabilities in Group Problem Solving: The Need for an Integrative Function," *Psychological Review* 74 (July 1967): 239–249.

23. Andre L. Delbecq, "The Management of Decision-Making Within the Firm: Three Strategies for Three Types of Decision Making," *Academy of Management Journal* 10 (December 1967): 329–339.

ADDITIONAL READINGS

Bormann, Ernest G. *Discussion and Group Methods—Theory and Practice.* New York: Harper & Row, 1969.

Chitayat, Gideon. "The Organization and Effectiveness of Boards of Directors." *Journal of General Management* 6 (Winter 1980/81): 42–52.

Ford, Robert C., and M. Gene Newport, "Strategic Steps for Resolving the Committee Dilemma." *Advanced Management Journal* 51 (Spring 1986): 9–14.

Gilsdorf, J.W., and M.H. Rader. "Bringing Out the Best in Committee Members." *Supervisory Management* 26 (November 1981): 6–11.

Gladstein, Deborah L. "Groups in Context: A Model of Task Group Effectiveness." *Administrative Science Quarterly* 29 (December 1984): 499–517.

Hader, John J. *Committees: Their Purposes, Functions and Administration.* New York: American Management Association, 1929.

Klumpf, Ned. "Effective Meetings—A Management Must." *Supervisory Management* 29 (December 1984): 28–32.

Lagges, James G. "The Board of Directors: Boon or Bane for Stockholders and Management?" *Business Horizons* 25 (March/April 1982): 43–50.

Shenoy, Prakash. "On Committee Decision Making: A Game Theoretical Approach." *Management Science* 26 (April 1980): 387–400.

Soden, Glenn W. "Avoid Meetings or Make Them Work." *Business Horizons* 27 (March/April 1984): 47–49.

Sulzner, George T. "The Impact of Labor-Management Cooperation Committees on Personnel Policies and Practices at Twenty Federal Bargaining Units." *Journal of Collective Negotiations in the Public Sector* 11:1 (1982): 37–45.

Tasklanganos, Angelos A. "The Committee in Business: Asset or Liability?" *Personnel Journal* 54 (February 1975): 90–92.

Tropman, John E. *The Essentials of Committee Management.* Chicago: Nelson-Hall, 1979.

Vancil, R.F., and C.H. Green. "How CEOs Use Top Management Committees." *Harvard Business Review* 62 (January/February 1984): 65–73.

Zander, Alvin. *The Purposes of Groups and Organizations.* San Francisco: Jossey-Bass, 1985.

Span of Control

The first three integrating strategies in the OT-Model are coordination by hierarchy, by formal rules, and by committee. The fourth way of integrating the organization's tasks, energies, and efforts is through selecting an appropriate span of control (sometimes called span of management or span of supervision), a term referring to the number of people directly supervised by one manager. However, the issue of concern is not the absolute number of persons reflected on the organization chart as reporting to a manager, but the number that a manager can supervise *effectively.* Span of control can be determined merely by counting people. *Effective* span of control is a more complex issue.

The classical school favored a narrow span of control, to enhance close supervision and conform to the unity-of-command principle. Their rule of thumb was that a manager can effectively supervise no more than five to seven subordinates. The human relations school had no direct interest in the quantity of subordinates supervised; they were concerned about the quality of supervisor-subordinate relationships and in the job satisfaction of each. To encourage trust and participative management, they favored wider spans of control.

In addition, they saw the communications difficulties of growing firms with narrow spans of control. If absolute organizational size increases and span of control remains the same, the organization's height (or number of levels between the CEO and the shop floor) must increase. More links in a communications chain lead to greater distortion of messages; each link has the potential for misunderstanding or distorting the message before passing it along. Therefore, more organizational levels mean more possibilities for vertical miscommunication.

The modern school has examined the many factors that must be considered in order to establish the optimum span of control in each organizational setting and even at each organizational level.

David D. Van Fleet and Arthur G. Bedeian have searched the organization theory literature for statements about span of control at different points over the past

200 years. Table 12.1 presents some of those statements. Until about 1955, organization theorists seemed quite ready to discuss span of control in terms of specific numbers. The 1955 statement by Harold Koontz and Cyril O'Donnell includes no numbers and foreshadows the modern position that no ideal number exists.

THE CLASSICAL PERSPECTIVE

Of all the differentiating and integrating strategies, span of control most readily lends itself to *counting*. And count the classical school did. The counting tradition is as old as the Biblical Book of Exodus. Finding that he could not respond directly to Israel's needs, concerns, and conflicts, Moses organized the government into rulers of thousands, rulers of hundreds, of fifties, and of tens (Exodus 18:25). The belief that an optimal span of supervision could be found seemed to hold for thousands of years.

The issue continues to be important. Too much supervision, reflected in narrow control spans, costs money and leads to communication delays. Not enough supervision can lead to employee deviance from the organizational goal. Therefore, much energy has been expended over the ages to find the right balance. Several statements in Table 12.1 are by military men for whom the right balance could make the difference between defeat and victory.

The Direct Approach

For these reasons, early classical writers spent a great deal of time and effort determining what spans had been successful throughout history and observing what spans seemed to work in successful organizations. Existing successful organizations were examined, the numbers of subordinates supervised by managers were counted, and the results were taken to be ideal spans of control. This drive to find a specific number tied in well with the "principles" approach to management. Derive and apply the right principles and numbers, and everything will fall into place.

The difficulty with this approach is that successful organizations vary greatly in their spans of control. Although the mean number at higher organizational levels might be 4, spans of control in successful organizations might range from 2 to 20.

Urwick's Position

Lyndall Urwick and other classical writers often looked to the military model for solutions to organizational problems. General Ian Hamilton, to whose writing Urwick refers, supported a narrow span of control in the military. Since managing soldiers of industry was not viewed very differently from managing their military cousins, the narrow span was carried over into industry.

Urwick's 1938 comment on span of control is well known: "No superior can supervise directly the work of more than five or, at the most, six subordinates whose work interlocks."[1] Later writers presented research evidence showing larger spans of control to be equally effective. But as recently as 1956, Urwick defended his principle by stressing its key phrase: *whose work interlocks.*[2] The Pope can "supervise" hundreds of Cardinals only because their work does not interlock. When the efforts of organiza-

Table 12.1 A CHRONOLOGICAL COLLECTION OF STATEMENTS ON THE SPAN OF MANAGEMENT

Approximate date	Author	Statement
1800	Eli Whitney	"I find it vain to think of employing a great number of hands . . . unless I can actually be present in many places at the same time."
1810	Napoleon I	"No man can command more than five distinct bodies in the same theatre of war."
1830	Karl von Clausewitz	"Plainly . . . one person can only exercise direct command over a limited number. If there are more than ten parts, a difficulty arises in transmitting orders with the necessary rapidity and exactitude."
1916	Henri Fayol	"Whatever his level of authority, one head only has direct command over a small number of subordinates, less than six normally. Only the . . . foreman or his equivalent . . . is in direct command of twenty or thirty men, when the work is simple."
1921	Ian Hamilton	"The average human brain finds its effective scope in handling from three to six other brains."
1931	Henry S. Dennison	"If a man is really to lead men . . . there will be some maximum number of them to whom he can give his fullest service . . . for anything more exacting than the direction of simple or uniform mechanical work it seldom runs beyond six to twelve people."
1933	V.A. Graicunas	". . . in the vast majority of cases the 'span of attention' is limited to six digits."
1937	Luther Gulick	"Just as the hand of man can span only a limited number of notes on the piano, so the mind and will of man can span but a limited number of managerial contacts."
1938	Lyndall Urwick	"No superior can supervise directly the work of more than five or, at the most, six subordinates whose work interlocks."
1947	R.C. Davis	(a) "The range of the optimum unit of operative supervision extends probably from a minimum of 10 operatives to a maximum of 30 for most concerns." (b) "The unit of executive supervision appears . . . to range from 3 to 8 or 9 subordinates."
1951	William Newman	"Empirical studies suggest that executives in higher echelons should have a span of three to seven operating subordinates, whereas the optimum range for first-line supervisors of routine activities is usually from fifteen to twenty employees."
1955	Harold Koontz and Cyril O'Donnell	"There is a limit to the number of persons an individual can effectively manage, even though that limit is not finite for every case but will vary with the complexity of the relationship supervised and the ability of managers and subordinates."

Source: Adapted from David D. Van Fleet and Arthur G. Bedeian, "A History of the Span of Management," *Academy of Management Review* 2 (July 1977): 358. Used by permission.

tional people are interdependent, their immediate superior can supervise no more than five or six of them, according to Urwick.

Graicunas's Position

V.A. Graicunas published his famous work on span of control in 1933.[3] Graicunas recognized that all superiors must communicate with their subordinates *as individuals*. In addition, since the tasks of many subordinates interrelate, superiors must often supervise the *relationships* and *joint efforts* of subordinates. The purely classical assumption was that a superior merely had to convey instructions to subordinates who would, in machinelike fashion, carry them out. Graicunas saw that, in reality, subordinates seek each other's advice, assistance, and cooperation—leaving open the possibility of misinterpretation and misunderstanding, unless the superior closely supervises the relationships as well as the individuals.

Types of Contacts   Graicunas noted that the contacts between managers and subordinates can be of three types:

1. *Direct single contacts* between one manager and one subordinate.
2. *Direct group contacts* between one manager and two or more subordinates.
3. *Cross contacts* between subordinates in the manager's absence.

Numbers of Contacts   Graicunas came up with a formula for determining how many contacts a given manager supervises: $C = N(2^N/2 + N - 1)$, where C equals the total number of different contacts and N equals the number of the manager's direct subordinates.[4]

Table 12.2 presents Graicunas's results: how many relationships a manager must supervise, given a certain number of subordinates. The table shows how adding subordinates to a manager's span of control quickly complicates the manager's ability to maintain control. Consider a manager with two subordinates. According to Graicunas, that manager is involved in six supervisory relationships. First, the manager supervises subordinate A and also supervises subordinate B. The manager may also supervise AB as a pair and may supervise the relationship between A and B as well. Here are the relationships. The manager may:

Supervise A ⎤
Supervise B ⎦ Direct Single Contacts

Supervise A with B in attendance ⎤
Supervise B with A in attendance ⎦ Direct Group Contacts

Supervise A when A consults with B ⎤
Supervise B when B consults with A ⎦ Cross Contacts

According to the formula, the Pope would be responsible for many *trillions* of contacts if all the Cardinals interacted.

Although some of the relationships reflected in Table 12.2 may seem more similar

Table 12.2   RESULTS OF GRAICUNAS FORMULA

Number of manager's subordinates	Number of relationships manager must supervise
1	1
2	6
3	18
4	44
5	100
6	222
7	490
8	1,080
9	2,376
10	5,210
11	11,374
12	24,708
18	2,359,602

Source: V.A. Graicunas, "Relationship in Organization," in *Papers on the Science of Administration,* ed. Luther Gulick and Lyndall Urwick (1937; reprint ed., Clifton, NJ: Augustus M. Kelley, 1973), p. 186. Used by permission.

than different, Graicunas maintained that each relationship has different psychological shadings.

Quality of Contacts   Of course, as Graicunas acknowledged, the formula and table do not take the *quality* of subordinates into account. Managers with four independent, intelligent, interacting subordinates formally reporting to them (44 relationships) may not spend as much time in supervision as managers with three barely competent subordinates (18 relationships), each performing functions vital to organizational success.

The Graicunas results and the classical attempts to find an ideal number are interesting but not very instructive. Variation in organizational circumstances makes it unrealistic to expect that the effective span of control will be the same for a surgery team, a group of telephone operators, a prison farm, and U.S. Steel's long-range planning committee.

To sum up, the classical school assumed that subordinates needed careful supervision to ensure that they used production methods that management deemed best and to keep them busy. Close supervision allowed the organization's managerial brains to keep the corporate body's other parts working toward the organizational goal. A narrow span of control made such supervision possible. Smaller spans also limited the decision making of subordinates. In the classical view, limited spans of control resulted in better organizational decision making and greater organizational success.

THE HUMAN RELATIONS PERSPECTIVE

Forced Delegation

The human relations school favored a wider span of control. They saw the most obvious organizational and personal benefit as automatic delegation of authority. The more people a boss must supervise, the less time that boss has to dictate and check up on job performance. Managers who supervise many subordinates tend, out of necessity, to state the results they expect, then leave subordinates alone to accomplish their tasks however they wish.

Furthermore, giving managers wide spans of control *and* making them account-able for achieving specific results strongly encourages managers to hire good people and train them well. If you can't watch over your subordinates and yet must rely on them to keep your job, you'd better make sure that they know how to do their jobs. Robert E. Wood used such a method when he reorganized Sears, Roebuck in the mid-1930s. He hired the best people, trained them well, provided them with a stimulating work environment, and—contrary to the conventional wisdom of the organization theorists of his day—widened the span of control. According to James C. Worthy:

> At Sears, key executives in both the field organization and the parent merchandising organization were deliberately spread thin and given more subordinates than they could possibly control closely. This effectively compelled the maximum decentraliza-tion of authority and relegated responsibility to successively lower levels within the organization.[5]

The Sears, Roebuck Study   Worthy's 1950 study of Sears, Roebuck is perhaps the most famous and influential work reflecting the human relations perspective on span of control.[6] At the time of the study, Sears continued to practice Robert E. Wood's philosophy of forced delegation. Worthy's study covered two groups of Sears stores. One group had only two management levels (the store manager and approximately 30 department managers); another group had three levels. Worthy found that the stores with two levels had higher sales volume, profits, and morale. He concluded that this wide span resulted in better attitudes among subordinates, more effective supervision, and more individual initiative. The store managers *had* to delegate. Therefore, they recruited people carefully and trained them well.

For their part, the subordinates at the two-level Sears stores were forced to accept their delegated duties and decision-making authority. Because they couldn't run to the store manager with every little problem, they had to become more independent. The results? Effective performance and high morale among second-level managers. A final benefit to Sears was faster vertical communication, because of fewer management levels.

Lyndall Urwick's response to this study was that the activities of the subordinate managers did not significantly interlock; they were responsible only for their own areas and could act autonomously within them. Therefore, Urwick did not feel that the Sears study contradicted his span-of-control principle.

Spans and Levels

Another, more subtle argument for widening the span is to reduce the number of managerial levels, which improves vertical communication within the organization. Organizational levels and span of control are directly related. The wider the span of control, the fewer the organizational levels—when there are a fixed number of em-ployees. If span of control is increased, the number of managers and the number of

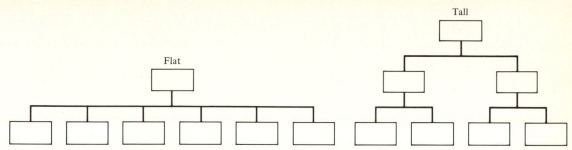

Figure 12.1   Flat and tall organizations.

levels on the chart will both be reduced. Organizations with many levels and relatively few employees reporting to each manager are called *tall* organizations, because their organization charts look tall. Organizations with relatively few levels and many employees reporting to each manager are called *flat* organizations. Figure 12.1 presents simplified organization charts for a flat organization and a tall organization, each with seven members.

Harold Koontz points out that "the difference between an average management span of, say, four, and one of eight in a company of 4000 nonmanagerial employees can make a difference of two entire levels of management and of nearly 800 managers!"[7] Fewer levels means fewer impediments to the flow of up-and-down communications.

Herbert A. Simon recognized the conflict between a limited span of control and a rapid flow of information and decisions:

> Administrative efficiency is enhanced by keeping at a minimum the number of organizational levels through which a matter must pass before it is acted upon.
>
> This latter proverb is one of the fundamental criteria that guide administrative analysts in simplifying procedures. Yet in many situations the results to which this principle leads are in direct contradiction to the requirements of the principle of span of control. . . .[8]

To illustrate Simon's point, imagine Company A and Company B, each with 4096 nonmanagerial employees. Company A has a four-person span of control, and Company B has an eight-person span. As seen in Figure 12.2, Company A will have seven levels and Company B will have five levels. Company A's span permits closer supervision of employees, but Company B's span enables information to flow more rapidly.

Another drawback of the tall hierarchy is that it can inhibit prompt decisions if the authority for deciding a given issue is far removed from the level at which the issue arises. For example, a manager finds out that a customer needs a certain special service. The manager does not have the authority to provide the service and so refers the request up through the hierarchy. In the tall hierarchy, the request may have to make its way slowly upward through numerous organizational levels. By the time approval comes back down to the manager, the customer may have decided to do business with a competitor who can supply the service more promptly.

The tall hierarchy may increase supervisory costs as it requires more managers

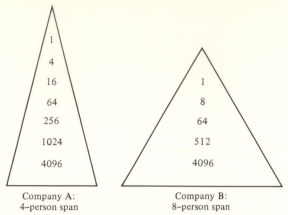

Company A: Company B:
4–person span   8–person span

Figure 12.2   Contrasting control spans.

than a flat structure. Since the salaries of managers are usually higher than the salaries of subordinates, then having more levels is more expensive for the organization, other things being equal. In fact, one of C. Northcote Parkinson's tongue-in-cheek recommendations (*Parkinson's Law,* 1957) to aspiring bureaucrats is to find a way to gather subordinates, in order to build more levels or layers. The more levels below you, the greater your worth to the organization and the larger your salary.

The flat hierarchy enables the different levels to take advantage of opportunities more quickly. Going up through channels presents few problems because the organization has so few levels. The corresponding disadvantage is that decisions may not be well considered by affected units, and important aspects of a problem may be overlooked. The flat hierarchy may lose in thoroughness what it gains in speed.

Levels, Span, and Performance   R. Carzo, Jr., and J.N. Yanouzas gave an identical task to two groups, both with 15 members.[9] The different structures—a two-level hierarchy and a four-level hierarchy—appear in Figure 12.3. Both groups accomplished the task in about the same time, the interruptions in the up-and-down communications of the tall structure apparently being offset by the difficulties the 14 people at the same level within the flat structure had in communicating horizontally. The group in the tall structure performed the task more successfully than the group in the flat structure, in terms of the established performance criteria. Carzo and Yanouzas explained this outcome in two ways:

1. The decisions made within the tall structure were repeatedly analyzed at the different supervisory levels, not just the single supervisory level in the flat structure;
2. Since the supervisors in the tall structure did not have to spend all their time in direct supervision of subordinates, they had more time to think about the task, understand it, and make better decisions about it.

Levels, Span, and Psychological Aspects   L.W. Porter and E.E. Lawler found that tall structures enable some employees to feel more secure, because the supervisor is usually

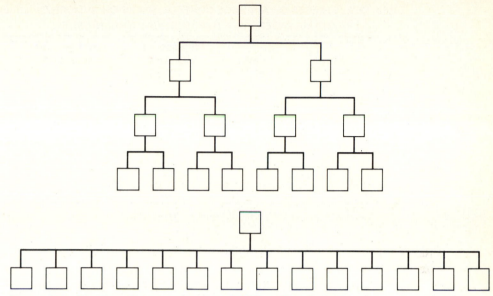

Figure 12.3   The Carzo-Yanouzas experiment: Tall and flat structures.

available to give advice and assistance.[10] On the other hand, considerable research suggests that tall structures result in more attentive supervision than subordinates really want.

L.L. Cummings and C.J. Berger found that top managers prefer tall structures and lower-level managers prefer flat structures.[11] Top managers apparently feel that they can control the organization's activities more effectively if relatively few subordinates report directly to them. Lower-level managers apparently prefer the flatter structures that permit them more independence and freedom from the close supervision of top managers. This preference of lower-level managers embodies the major advantage of wider control spans from a human relations viewpoint: Such spans encourage job autonomy and a personal sense of accomplishment throughout the organization—as any delegation/decentralization movement would.

A Hypothetical Organization's Spans and Levels   Table 12.3 presents the relationship between number of organizational levels and span of control in a hypothetical organization. This organization has 3600 workers and 200 supervisors, each with an 18-worker average span of control. The table shows that with an average control span of 3 per manager, the organization will require 5 managerial levels: the president (level 1) supervises 3 vice presidents (level 2); they each supervise 2 or 3 subordinates at managerial level 3, and so on, down to the fifth-level managers who each supervise 3 first-line supervisors.

If the organization increases the average span of control from 3 to 4, it can drop one managerial level. If it further increases span of control from 4 to 6, it can drop another managerial level.

With similar results, we can also think in terms of dropping managerial levels to cause a wider span of control. If top management decides to release some middle

Table 12.3   EFFECTS OF AVERAGE CONTROL SPANS ON NUMBER OF LEVELS AND MANAGERS IN A HYPOTHETICAL ORGANIZATION

	Level	With average span of 3	With average span of 4	With average span of 6
Number of	1	1	1	1
managers	2	3	4	6
required	3	8	13	34
at each	4	23	50	
level	5	67		
Total Managers		102	68	41
First-line Supervisors		200	200	200
Workers		3600	3600	3600

Source: Adapted from C.W. Barkdull, "Span of Control: A Method of Evaluation," *Michigan Business Review* 15 (May 1963): 25–32. Used by permission.

managers during financially difficult times, the average control span of the remaining managers will broaden.

Although Table 12.3 presents a hypothetical situation, it reflects real life; empirical research has shown a negative relationship between levels and span of control: as one goes up, the other goes down.[12]

THE MODERN PERSPECTIVE

The classical school favored close supervision and a narrow span of control. The human relations school favored more independent action by subordinates and a wider span of control. The modern contingency school is perhaps nowhere more fully developed than in its approach to the span-of-control issue. The modern school maintains that the effective span for a given organizational situation can be determined not by looking at a general theory or principle but by discovering and examining the factors that may affect the optimum span in that particular situation. A discussion of factors that may affect span of control follows.

Technology: Woodward's Work

Throughout the 1950s, Joan Woodward studied the relationship between structure and technology in 100 British industrial firms. She found technology of three types: unit or small-batch production (such as tailor-made clothes), mass production (such as assembly lines), and continuous-process production (such as oil refineries).[13] Unit production is technologically simplest, and continuous-process production is most complex.

Woodward looked at spans of control within the three technology types and found that the degree of technological complexity affected span of control differently at different managerial levels.

The Chief Executive   As organizational technology became more complex, the chief executive's span of control *increased*. Woodward found these average control spans:

unit production, 4; mass production, 7; process production, 10. The busy chief executive in the technologically complex organization must delegate, encourage lower-level decision making, rely on staff aides, and use committees—all of which widen the span of control at the very top.

The Middle Managers   In contrast, increased technological complexity caused span of control at the middle-manager level to *decrease.* As an organization becomes more technologically advanced, the jobs of its middle managers become more complex. If they are to function efficiently and effectively, these managers must supervise fewer lower-level managers.

The Supervisors   For supervisory-level managers, the span of control varied from narrow to wide and back to narrow, with increasing technological complexity. Unit or small-batch and continuous-process production had narrow spans of control, while the middle technological category, mass production, had a wide span. The span of control for mass production can be larger without impeding organizational effectiveness because there are alternative control devices to help monitor the work. Consider an automobile assembly line with a machine-paced work flow that brings the work to the worker and gives that person a fixed amount of time to perform the task before the line carries it on to another work station. This machine pacing partially supervises the worker and expands the number of subordinates a supervisor can effectively oversee. This assistance is less frequently found in the small-batch or continuous-flow production processes. The nature of the technology in both of these cases prevents the use of machine assistance and calls for greater reliance on the supervisor to supervise and, consequently, a narrow span of control.

Two general conclusions might be that increased technological complexity:

1. Makes a *wider* span *necessary* at the top and *possible* at the bottom;
2. Makes a *narrower* span necessary in the *middle.*

These conclusions conveniently ignore all other factors affecting the organizational system. If other influences are more significant, they can easily outweigh the influence of technology on span of control.[14]

Importance to the Contingency Approach   Although Woodward's intent was to draw some generalizations about span of control in the spirit of the classical tradition, her data were meaningless until they were classified according to complexity of the technological process used. Upon seeing the relationship between technological complexity and span of control, other scholars had an incentive to search for further factors that might have a bearing on effective spans.

The modern perspective began to evolve. Empirical studies had been unable to supply universal answers to the span-of-control question. Organization theorists recognized that the effective span of control would be determined by an organization's technological complexity *plus* many other factors. They began their quest to identify those factors.

Although the available results are mixed, researchers have identified four factors whose characteristics can lead to larger or smaller spans in particular situations: the manager, the subordinate, the task, and the organizational environment.

Managerial Characteristics

Span of control is related to the manager's style, ability, and available time. These characteristics will be discussed in turn.

Style   Managerial style can influence effective span of control. Consider the authoritarian Theory X manager who must have complete control, know what everybody is doing, check all the work, and make all the decisions personally. Such a managerial style limits the number of subordinates that the manager can supervise effectively to the range favored by the classicists: roughly 5 to 7. On the other hand, consider the Theory Y manager who trusts, trains, delegates, manages by exception, and is more concerned with results than with ego. This manager can effectively supervise more people than the first manager can. Chapter 9 presented Fred E. Fiedler's contention that the organization can to an extent match the manager's job to the manager's leadership style. Similarly, the organization can match span of control with the managerial style. The manager's philosophy and attitude toward workers will result in a managerial style that works best with wider or more narrow spans of control.

Ability   The manager's ability is another important determinant of the optimum supervisory span. If managers have inadequate leadership skills or job knowledge, faulty understanding of organizational resource location and availability, an inability to communicate with superiors and subordinates, or are just new to the job, they will have difficulty with a broad span of control. In his study of hypotheses about span of control, Jon G. Udell looked for a relationship between span of control and managerial ability, using level of formal education and years of experience in present position as ability criteria.[15] Although these are modest measures of ability, they are probably adequate proxies for intellectual and work capabilities. In Udell's sample of 67 marketing CEO's, he found no such relationship. Nevertheless, the intuitive appeal of a relationship between ability and span of control suggests that further research on this point is warranted.

Available Time   The manager typically has many job-related obligations and responsibilities in addition to supervising. She may serve on committees, interact with her own boss, and handle other internal and external responsibilities that take time away from supervision. On the other hand, she may have supervisory helpers who enable her to supervise more employees. William G. Ouchi and John B. Dowling maintain that the *number* of subordinates supervised is not the most descriptive span-of-control measure. A properly adjusted measure would incorporate (1) what percentage of the manager's time is devoted to direct supervision, and (2) how many supervisory helpers the manager has.[16]

Subordinate Characteristics

The most important factor governing effective span of control is the ability and characteristics of subordinates. If subordinates are trained, competent, and job-involved, a manager can effectively supervise more of them than if subordinates are untrained, incompetent, and uninterested.[17] Consider the job of managing highly trained, dedicated research scientists. Their manager might casually oversee their activities, but the main managerial task is not to supervise the scientists; it is to connect them with the organizational resources they need to do their jobs. Rather than "manage," the group's manager should coordinate and facilitate, seeking organizational solutions to the group's problems. If the group's work is largely self-paced and independent, the manager may supervise several dozen subordinates effectively and comfortably.

On the other hand, consider a manager responsible for teaching entry-level employees a new and complex task. The employees have little knowledge and limited ability, so the manager must spend much instruction and coordination time with them. To do the job properly, the manager must have a small span of control.

Task Characteristics

Complexity   Another important factor in determining the optimum span of control is the complexity of the tasks being supervised. Supervising a professional football team is more difficult than supervising switchboard operators or ditch diggers. From the standpoint of task complexity, the potential for coordination problems is much greater with the football team than with the operators or diggers. When more things can go wrong, the manager is less able to coordinate a large number of people effectively.

Complexity can be due to the repetitiveness, similarity, change rate, measurability, and interdependence of tasks. The *repetitiveness* of the tasks performed by subordinates affects span of control. If the same activities must be done repeatedly, the supervisor can easily monitor results. The same is true at the managerial level. If supervisors face recurring problems and situations, their managers can structure methods, policies, and standard operating procedures for the supervisors to use in solving them. If problems are more varied, subordinates will have to refer more decisions upward to the manager.

Not all available research fully supports this intuitively appealing point. For example, Robert D. Dewar and Donald P. Simet were unable to find a relationship, at any organizational level, between task routineness of subordinates and control spans of their superiors—perhaps because they studied quasi-professional organizations rather than manufacturing organizations.[18]

The *similarity* of tasks performed by different subordinates affects span of control.[19] If each subordinate is doing a different task, the manager's coordination problems may be great and span of control must therefore be narrow.

The greater the *rate of change* in a task, the narrower must be the management span for the supervisor of that task, because a rapid rate of change increases the demands on the supervisor as teacher. The manager is always doing some teaching in the ongoing process of developing subordinates. When the group is experiencing rapid job change, the manager must spend time keeping up with change and teaching subordinates new tasks, which cuts into the time available for overseeing and coordinating, thereby reducing the manager's effective span of control. Because of relatively constant technology, a salt mine supervisor can supervise more workers than can a manager in a video-game plant.

Another important aspect of task complexity that affects span of control is the degree to which job results can be *measured*. If the output of subordinates can be measured precisely, the supervisor will have less need to observe *how* subordinates reach their goals.

If you tell your sales force that they must sell 30 elephants by the end of the month, you probably turn them loose to sell the elephants in any way they can. You then spend your time in familiarizing new salespeople with the product; reviewing corporate goals, methods, and policies with the present sales force; and counting order tickets at the end of the month. If the sales tickets total at least 30, you need not change your style. On the other hand, to supervise a group of reference librarians, a head reference librarian would have to watch them locate materials, listen to them advise library patrons, and so on. In other words, the supervision focus would be on observing the *process* rather than the *output,* because the reference librarian's output is so intangible.

As the classical school realized, the degree to which tasks *interlock* is indeed an influence on the ideal span of control. Departmental tasks which must be tightly coordinated with other tasks will obviously require more supervisory time for resolving inevitable problems. When the outputs of employees must mesh, there will be many points of friction within their interactions. The rapidity with which employees interface and the degree of control they have over the interaction will also influence the degree and amount of supervisory time required to mediate disputes, coordinate tasks, and resolve conflict. A highly interdependent, piece-work assembly operation such as assembling dolls or building a home will require more supervisory time than would the hand-making of clay pots or the work of a bank teller.[20]

Importance of Task   The importance of the task being supervised to the organization's goals will also affect the span of control. A critically important task will probably be tightly supervised; a less important task will not be. The span of control for supervisors of nuclear power plant operators will probably be narrower than the span for the supervisors of the power plant's grounds crew, because the tasks of the operators are so much more critical to the achievement of organizational goals.

Organizational Characteristics

Size   As an organization grows larger by adding employees, span of control at all levels will tend to increase. As more people are added, existing managers have more people to supervise. At some point, though, the organization must reduce span of control by hiring more managers to supervise the additional subordinates. (Of course, reducing the span at one level by hiring more managers will *increase* the span at the next-higher level.) If organizational growth continues, the expansion and contraction of control spans will also continue.

Gerald G. Fisch explains the positive relationship between organizational size and span of control this way: "The larger the company, the greater is the likelihood of diversification; and the greater the degree of diversification, the larger the size of the span of management."[21] Fisch offers du Pont as an example. Reporting directly to the president are 12 industrial departments and 11 auxiliary departments. Rather than try to directly supervise the top people in these diverse product areas, the president relies on formalized policies and procedures established by top management and enforced by high-level committees. Since these policies are in place, and since the president could not keep up with so many and such diverse product areas if he wanted to, the span of control at the top is quite wide.

The relationship of organizational size to the other organizational elements is the subject of Chapter 14.

Group Size   R.J. House and J.B. Miner have suggested that the proven relationship between group size and group consensus and cohesiveness is relevant to span-of-control discussions.[22] Increasing group size (and span of control) tends to decrease cohesiveness and consensus. If the organization values these qualities highly, and if the people in the organization's groups need to work together, then it will try to keep span of control within conventional limits. If consensus and cohesiveness are unnecessary, undesirable, or achievable only at a high cost in managerial time, then the organization may allow control spans to widen.

Interdependence of Units   Supervisors coordinating the activities of their units with the activities of other units cannot effectively control many subordinates. On an assembly line, each unit in the interlocking work sequence works relatively independently. Therefore, the supervisor of any given unit on the line can support, coordinate, and direct that unit's activities almost exclusively. Such a situation makes supervising a fairly large number of workers possible, even though the interlocking nature of the work may be a source of friction.

In contrast, consider training director Shirley Jones, trying to secure the support of several departments for a training program she wants to offer next month. Jones must spend time away from her own department. Her absence reduces her time available for supervising her own people and, therefore, her effective span of control.

Geographical Spread   Geographical distance separating units and activities may influence the number of subordinates a manager can direct effectively. Scattered activities are harder to coordinate than activities that are close together, so one might suspect that managers of such activities will have relatively narrow control spans.

However, the Udell study found a *positive* relationship between geographical spread and span of control.[23] One possible explanation is that managers far removed from subordinates have to delegate more authority than managers in the same location. Such delegation naturally leads to wider control spans. Furthermore, improvements in communications technology have reduced the impact of geographical dispersion on span of control. Today, such twentieth-century developments as television, computers, word processing equipment, and all other aspects of telecommunications have made possible nearly instantaneous communication with anybody anywhere. This new technology allows managers to supervise more people spread out over a larger geographical area.

The Lockheed Study

The preceding discussion demonstrates that the optimum span of control depends on many variables. How do these variables influence the span—from industry to industry, organization to organization, and department to department? During the early 1960s, Lockheed Missiles and Space Company attempted to answer some of these questions.[24]

Influences on Span of Control   Lockheed identified six important influences on span of control: similarity of functions, geographical nearness, complexity of functions, direction and control (how much supervision and training do subordinates need), coordination, and planning. The company then divided each influence up into five levels of difficulty and assigned weights to each level of difficulty to reflect the relative importance of each influence. (See Table 12.4.) After each managerial position was analyzed in these terms, the results were adjusted to take into account how much assistance each manager had.

Comparison with Standard   Results were then compared with a standard. This standard, developed by observing the spans of control in well-managed units, appears in

Table 12.4   LOCKHEED STUDY: FACTORS INFLUENCING SPAN OF CONTROL, LEVEL OF DIFFICULTY, AND FACTOR WEIGHT

Factor influencing span of control	Level of difficulty plus factor weight				
Similarity of functions	Identical 1	Almost alike 2	Similar 3	Different 4	Totally different 5
Geographical nearness	All together 1	All in one building 2	Separate buildings, one plant location 3	Separate locations, one geographical area 4	Different geographical areas 5
Complexity of functions	Simple and repetitive 2	Routine 4	Slightly complex 6	Complex 8	Very complex 10
Direction and control	Minimum supervision and training 3	Limited supervision 6	Moderate periodic supervision 9	Frequent continuing supervision 12	Constant close supervision 15
Coordination	Minimum relationships with others 2	Some relationships with others 4	Moderate relationships, easily controlled 6	Considerable close relationships 8	Extensive relationships 10
Planning	Minimum scope and complexity 2	Limited scope and complexity 4	Moderate scope and complexity 6	Much scope and complexity 8	Very large scope and complexity 10

Source: Adapted from C.W. Barkdull, "Span of Control—A Method of Evaluation," *Michigan Business Review* 15 (May 1963): 23–28. Used by permission.

Table 12.5. A manager supervising subordinates whose characteristics are, let us say, those described in column 2 of Table 12.4 would receive a span factor weighting of 22 (arrived at by adding up the weights in that column). According to Table 12.5, that manager should be able to supervise from 8 to 11 people effectively.

As a result of this study, Lockheed increased its average span of control and eliminated one level of management.

Other Approaches

Although the Lockheed study provides an interesting contingency approach, further work must be done to resolve the span-of-control controversy. Approaches to the problem have been varied. Michael Keren and David Levhari offer a mathematical model for computing "the optimum span of control of each level of a hierarchy," using wage costs and time costs as criteria.[25] Rolla Edward Park's approach, based on the economic ideas of diminishing returns and marginal profit-wage analysis, uses as a criterion the value of additional product contributed by each additional subordinate.[26] These subordinates contribute less to product largely because the increased span of control makes the manager's job more difficult. Beyond some optimum point, an additional subordinate will add less to product than the subordinate's wages. Here is economist Park's span-of-control principle: "There is an *optimum* span of control for any management situation, and that optimum will in general depend on the complexity of the relationships supervised, the ability of the managers and subordinates, and the wages of the managers and subordinates."[27]

The quest continues for a method of establishing control spans that are not so narrow as to be overly expensive and injurious to the morale of overmanaged subordinates, and not so broad as to reduce coordination and productivity. If the theorists ever do come to agreement on this issue, real-life organizations may not conform to their precepts anyway. As David D. Van Fleet reminds us, organization structure

> tends to evolve under the influence of personnel decisions, budget and contract constraints, and historical trends. In personnel actions, the factors that receive attention are not likely to be the ones usually conceived of as affecting the span. It may well be that existing spans in ongoing organizations are more the result of . . . personnel decisions rather than organizational design decisions.[28]

Table 12.5 LOCKHEED STUDY: FACTOR WEIGHTING TOTALS AND SUGGESTED SPAN OF CONTROL

Total of factor weightings	Suggested span of control
40–42	4–5
37–39	4–6
34–36	4–7
31–33	5–8
28–30	6–9
25–27	7–10
22–24	8–11

Source: Adapted from C.W. Barkdull, "Span of Control—A Method of Evaluation," *Michigan Business Review* 15 (May 1963): 23–28. Used by permission.

So regardless of how the span should ideally or theoretically be determined, it may actually result from the manager's personnel philosophy or the type of worker available. The organization theorist can only recommend what might work or ought to work. Organizational management will apply those recommendations, taking actual available personnel into account.

SUMMARY

The earliest classical approach to the span-of-control issue was quite direct: study the spans at successful companies and try these spans elsewhere. Lyndall Urwick represented the typical classical opinion when he established a maximum span of five or six employees whose work interlocked. Graicunas contributed a simple formula to show how rapidly an increase in span of control can complicate a manager's job.

The human relations school favored a wide span of control which fit in with all of their ideas about humanizing the workplace through delegation and participative management. James Worthy's study of Sears, Roebuck added some data in support of the human relations position, which was largely intuitive rather than based on specific cases. The number of organizational levels is related to spans of control. Narrow spans result in "tall" organizations and can also result in vertical communication difficulties as instructions, decisions, and feedback pass through numerous levels in the organizational hierarchy. Wide spans of control result in "flat" organizations with fewer managerial levels in the hierarchy. Employees cannot be supervised as closely, but up-and-down communications are facilitated by having fewer levels between the bottom and the top.

The modern perspective on span of control is easy to express—proper span depends on the situation—and hard to implement, because "the situation" is always affected by a large array of changing influences. Joan Woodward noted the effects of technological complexity on the control spans that emerged in 100 British industrial firms.

Effective span of control is also affected by the characteristics of managers, subordinates, tasks, and the organizational environment. A narrow span suits certain managerial styles; in fact, some authoritarian styles demand a narrow span. A more democratic managerial style does not necessarily demand a wider span of control but can readily encourage and adjust to the wider span. Managerial ability also affects effective control spans. An able, experienced manager can handle a wider control span than a new manager can. Finally, some managers simply have more time available for managing than others do. That time makes wider spans of control possible.

Two primary task characteristics can affect span of control: complexity (comprised of repetitiveness, similarity to tasks of other workers, rate of change, measurability of results, and task interdependence) and importance. Span of control usually must be narrower if tasks supervised have these characteristics: nonrepetitive, varied, fast changing, nonmeasurable, highly interdependent, and critically important. If tasks supervised have the following characteristics, span of control can usually be wider: repetitive, similar, unchanging, measurable, not interdependent, and not vitally important. In the real world, tasks often fall into unfortunate combinations of "narrow-span" and "wider-span" characteristics. For example, worker tasks may be repetitive, varied on a given day, unchanging from day to day, measurable, not interdependent, and critically important. All the organization can do is consider the mixture of task characteristics and then arrive at a span of control that fits the mixture.

Increasing organizational size tends to lead to wider control spans, up to a point. If organizational work units are interdependent, they may need supervision by a manager with a rather narrow span of control. Widespread operations tend to require narrower control spans, though communications advances have made wider spans possible.

Lockheed has provided an example of the modern contingency approach in action: The company determined what variables influenced their specific spans of control, assigned weights to reflect each variable's importance, and used the study's results to increase the average managerial span of control and reduce the number of managerial levels.

Mathematical models and relationships of economic variables are two of the approaches offered by modern writers on span of control.

DISCUSSION QUESTIONS

1. What is "the span-of-control problem"? Is it really a problem?
2. What solutions to the span-of-control problem are available?
3. What is the classical position on span of control?
4. What is the key phrase in Lyndall Urwick's statement about maximum span of control? Do you think that key phrase is always applicable?
5. Give a critique of the Graicunas approach to span of control.
6. What is the human relations position on span of control?
7. How is span of control related to organizational information flow and decision making?
8. What did the Sears, Roebuck study tell us about span of control?
9. According to Joan Woodward's work, how is technology related to span of control? Do you agree?
10. When determining span of control, what managerial characteristics are important? Subordinate characteristics? Task characteristics?
11. What is meant by "tall" and "flat" organizations? How does span of control enter into whether an organization is tall or flat?
12. Would you prefer to be president of a tall organization or a flat one? Which would you prefer to work for?
13. What are the Lockheed study's implications for span of control? Do you agree with the weighting of the factors in that study?
14. Do you think span of control should be determined in advance, or should an organization simply allow it to happen as developments occur?
15. If you were a manager, what is the widest span that you would want to control? If you were an employee reporting to a manager, what is the widest span of which you would want to be a member? If the two numbers are different, why?

■ ### THE HAPPY FEET SHOE COMPANY

The Happy Feet Shoe Company is a large producer of such shoe accessories as shoe polish, boot cream, suede spray, and shoe dye. The largest of the company's ten plants is located in Brunswick, Georgia. That plant employs 2500 people. The company's headquarters is in Charleston, South Carolina.

The Brunswick plant has grown steadily and this growth has brought problems. It seems that every time the formal organization structure is defined and charted, new changes occur that necessitate a reexamination of the relationship between the plant manager and the department heads reporting directly to him.

When the Brunswick plant opened in 1975, the plant manager had one assistant (who acted primarily as a staff person) and 12 department heads. Figure C.1 depicts this situation.

In 1985 staff activities were added, and the number of departments was increased to 16. The assistant plant manager gradually became an operating person, to whom six department heads reported directly. The others continued reporting to the plant manager. Figure C.2 depicts these new relationships.

The company's continued growth put increasing pressure on the plant manager, since his office was a channel through which flowed a growing number of communications from Charleston to the different departments. The 1985 additions of staff helped to relieve some pressure, but the plant manager still had to be kept informed about home office/plant dealings. As a result of the position's pressures and responsibilities, the plant has had eight managers in the past ten years. Although the Brunswick plant remains very profitable, the high turnover of plant managers has undoubtedly had a negative effect on profitability and management morale.

Fred Johnson took over as plant manager three months ago. He consolidated accounting and finance under one supervisor and combined industrial relations with plant services. These changes helped a little, but they did not decrease the number of decisions that Johnson must make.

Johnson struggled to deal with ever-increasing communications. His problems seemed to be compounding. To a lesser extent, the department heads have recently begun

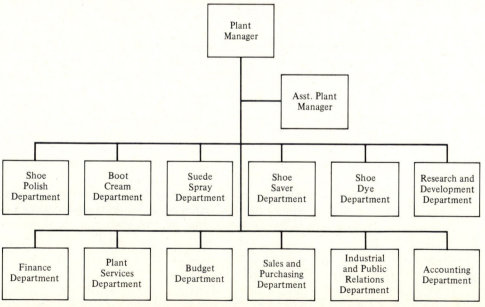

Figure C.1   Happy Feet organization chart: 1975.

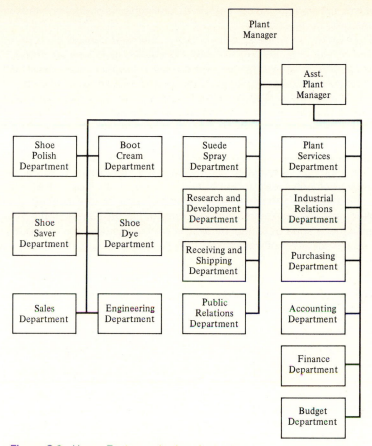

Figure C.2   Happy Feet organization chart: 1985.

feeling the same pressures, so several have quit. Now not only is Johnson faced with a pyramid of decisions and projects that need coordinating; he also has some inexperienced subordinates. Johnson cannot seem to keep in touch with what is going on.

What is Fred Johnson's main problem? To solve it, what steps would you advise him to take?

CUNNINGHAM COMPANY

New Cunningham Company President Amory Cleveland inherited a top-heavy organization during a time of industrial downturn. Although earnings in the first quarter of 1988 were only two-thirds of what they had been in 1987, corporate overhead remained constant at $28 million a year. Cunningham had 12 layers of management, while its leading Japanese competitor had only 6.

In the past, Cunningham Company had hired numerous MBAs into high-level slots and had allowed them to exercise authority based on their financial analyses rather than on their knowledge of the business. Cunningham executives really didn't trust their subordinates, so they added layers of staff to check on line operations. In their struggle for even more power, the staff people often ignored Cunningham's problems in their drive to achieve what was best for themselves.

After looking over the situation, Amory Cleveland concluded, "The excessive overhead costs of our unwieldy organization have caused us to lose our competitive edge. We need to operate with fewer people who are given broader responsibilities."

Cunningham Company had formerly reacted to downturns by laying off workers and cutting back on advertising and public relations. During really bad times, departments were asked to cut 10 percent of their people. Cuts were based on seniority; product quality and operational efficiency did not enter in. During these cutbacks the corporate staff was usually left intact, so the ratio of managers to workers became even higher. This time, Amory Cleveland decided, things would be different.

Cleveland quickly chopped his headquarters staff from 240 to 75. He pushed decision-making authority down to the operating units, even though that sometimes meant adding operating staff. He encouraged the use of participatory management techniques to let workers and line managers figure out ways to increase productivity. And he increased every manager's span of control by eliminating excess divisionalization. For example, he abolished district sales offices and let regional sales managers oversee local offices directly.

What might Cunningham Company gain as a result of Amory Cleveland's changes? What will the company lose?

NOTES

1. Lyndall F. Urwick, *Scientific Principles and Organization* (New York: American Management Association, 1938), p. 8.
2. Lyndall F. Urwick, "The Manager's Span of Control," *Harvard Business Review* 34 (May/June 1956): 39–47.
3. V.A. Graicunas, "Relationship in Organization," in *Papers on the Science of Administration,* ed. Luther Gulick and Lyndall Urwick (1937; reprint ed., Clifton, NJ: Augustus M. Kelley, 1973), pp. 181–188.
4. Ibid., p. 186.
5. James C. Worthy, *Shaping an American Institution: Robert E. Wood and Sears, Roebuck* (Urbana: University of Illinois Press, 1984), p. 122.
6. James C. Worthy, "Organization Structure and Employee Morale," *American Sociological Review* 15 (April 1950): 169–179. See also Lyndall F. Urwick, "The Manager's Span of Control," p. 45.
7. Harold Koontz, "Making Theory Operational: The Span of Management," *Journal of Management Studies* 3 (October 1966): 229.
8. Herbert A. Simon, *Administrative Behavior* (New York: Macmillan, 1947), p. 26.
9. R. Carzo, Jr., and J. N. Yanouzas, "Effects of Flat and Tall Organization Structure," *Administrative Science Quarterly* 14 (March 1969): 178–191.
10. L. W. Porter and E. E. Lawler, "The Effects of 'Tall' vs. 'Flat' Organizations on Managerial Job Satisfaction," *Personnel Psychology* 17 (Spring 1964): 135–148.
11. L. L. Cummings and C. J. Berger, "Organization Structure: How Does It Influence Attitudes and Performance?" *Organizational Dynamics* 5 (Autumn 1976): 34–49.
12. For an interesting approach to determining the optimum number of levels, see Elliott Jaques, "Too Many Management Levels," *California Management Review* 8 (Fall 1965): 13–20.

13. Joan Woodward, *Industrial Organization: Theory and Practice* (New York: Oxford University Press, 1965).

14. For some evidence that Woodward's findings may not hold true in all cultures, see Robert M. Marsh and Hiroshi Mannari, "Technology and Size as Determinants of the Organizational Structure of Japanese Factories," *Administrative Science Quarterly* 26 (March 1981): 47–49.

15. Jon G. Udell, "An Empirical Test of Hypotheses Relating to Span of Control," *Administrative Science Quarterly* 12 (December 1967): 420–439.

16. William G. Ouchi and John B. Dowling, "Defining the Span of Control," *Administrative Science Quarterly* 19 (September 1974): 357–365.

17. For substantiation of this point, see Jon G. Udell, "An Empirical Test of Hypotheses Relating to Span of Control," pp. 433–435. Udell noted that the more years of experience employees have, the larger is their supervisor's span of control.

18. Robert D. Dewar and Donald P. Simet, "A Level Specific Prediction of Spans of Control Examining the Effects of Size, Technology, and Specialization," *Academy of Management Journal* 24 (March 1981): 5–24.

19. Ibid. See also Udell, "An Empirical Test of Hypotheses Relating to Span of Control."

20. A point supported empirically by Gerald D. Bell, "Determinants of Span of Control," *American Journal of Sociology* 73 (July 1967): 100–109.

21. Gerald G. Fisch, "Stretching the Span of Management," *Harvard Business Review* 41 (September/October 1963): 81.

22. R. J. House and J. B. Miner, "Merging Management and Behavioral Theory: The Interaction Between Span of Control and Group Size," *Administrative Science Quarterly* 14 (September 1969): 451–464.

23. Jon G. Udell, "An Empirical Test of Hypotheses Relating to Span of Control," pp. 426–427.

24. C. W. Barkdull, "Span of Control—A Method of Evaluation," *Michigan Business Review* 15 (May 1963): 23–28.

25. Michael Keren and David Levhari, "The Optimum Span of Control in a Pure Hierarchy," *Management Science* 25 (November 1979): 1162–1172.

26. Rolla Edward Park, "The Span of Control: An Economist's View of the Facts and Fables," *Advanced Management Journal* 30 (October 1965): 47–51.

27. Ibid. See also David D. Van Fleet, "A Tentative Approach to Optimizing Span of Management," *Akron Business and Economic Review* 5 (Spring 1974): 39–43. Rather than seek an optimum, Robert Granford Wright uses a contingency approach to achieving a realistic and proper control span in his "An Approach to Find Realistic Spans of Management," *Arizona Business Bulletin* 17 (November 1970): 20–28.

28. David D. Van Fleet, "Span of Management Research and Issues," *Academy of Management Journal* 26 (September 1983): 551.

ADDITIONAL READINGS

Collins, Paul D., and Frank Hull. "Technology and Span of Control: Woodward Revisited." *Journal of Management Studies* 23 (March 1986): 143–164.

Entwisle, Doris R., and John Walton. "Observations on the Span of Control." *Administrative Science Quarterly* 6 (March 1961): 522–533.

Janger, Allen. "Analyzing the Span of Control." *Management Record* 22 (June 1960): 7–10.

Neumann, Paul. "What Speed of Communication Is Doing to Span of Control." *Administrative Management* 39 (November 1978): 30–31, 46.

Simon, Herbert. "The Span of Control: A Reply." *Advanced Management Journal* 22 (April 1957): 14.

Stieglitz, Harold. "Optimizing Span of Control." *Management Record* 24 (September 1962): 25–29.

Urwick, Lyndall F. "The Span of Control—Some Facts About the Fables." *Advanced Management Journal* 21 (November 1956): 5–15.

Van Fleet, D. D. "Span of Control: A Review and Restatement." *Akron Business and Economic Review* 5 (Winter 1974): 34–42.

Communication

Of all the integrating devices, communication may be the most important. It is the glue that holds organizations together. And like glue, it comes in different mixtures with different qualities, and works better in some situations than others.

"Communication" is a somewhat fuzzy term, with diverse meanings in the organizational context. It can signify information, or data, or even gossip. It can refer to the systems used to pass information throughout the organization. What it is and why it is so important are the topics of this chapter.

We are using communication to conclude the "Integrating" section of this book for two principal reasons. First, many writers consider communication to be the broadest, most pervasive, most important of all integrating mechanisms—a super, overriding mechanism that encompasses the other four. The second reason is that communication is the organizational integrating device most recently to have been determined worthy of separate study. The classical writers considered communication similar to bicycle riding; once you learn how to do it, there's no more to say about it. Indeed, in the index of James D. Mooney and Alan C. Reiley's *Onward Industry: The Principles of Organization and Their Significance to Modern Industry* (1931), entries under the "Communication" heading refer readers to discussions of the telegraph and the mail service. The adequacy of organizational information flows and the ability of managers and other employees to transmit, obtain, and use relevant information were seemingly taken for granted.

The human relations writers were almost entirely responsible for recognizing and writing about the importance of communication to effective organizational functioning. In extending that recognition, the modern writers have studied how information travels through organizations, especially in computerized systems. As high-speed computer networks were introduced, organizations and their members began to ask themselves, "What do we really need to know in order to do our jobs, and how can we get what we need reliably, quickly, and understandably?" The dangers of the "information explosion" are that information may be inaccurate, distorted, too plentiful, late, or lost. Therefore, modern writers are investigating the issue of how to set up informational networks that provide the right information in the right form at the right time, so that users can do effective work and make the right decisions in their jobs.

The modern emphasis is on the design and structuring of information systems, in light of the belief that the entire organization should be viewed as a mechanism for efficient information processing. In this view, the necessary information system would *dictate the organization's design.* Those scholars and practitioners following this thought process may well represent the future course of organizational design. Going beyond the idea of providing information to *a person* at the right time and place, they are studying the possibility of *the computer itself* using the information to make decisions in such routine areas as inventory ordering and machine-use scheduling. The next step is the study of artificial intelligence, which may someday enable computers to make even nonquantified decisions that only humans can now make.

THE NATURE OF COMMUNICATIONS

Humans differ from other animals in their ability to represent and share their experiences symbolically, primarily through language. We can discover facts and develop ideas, theories, concepts, and opinions, and then pass this information on to other people, in the present and the future. Similarly, organizations develop procedures for sharing information. As organizations grow beyond the capability of one person to tell all others what to do and how, systems of communication must be designed to ensure that organization members get the information they need to make decisions consistent with organizational goals. The design of such systems really has two sides: getting useful, accurate, timely information to the people who require it, and screening out useless, inaccurate information.

Communication Flows

Down, Up, Horizontal   Organizational communication can flow in three directions: downward, upward, and horizontally. Downward communication consists of information flowing from higher levels to lower levels in the hierarchy, as when a manager gives instructions to a subordinate. Some downward communication types and devices are instructional or informative memos, policy statements, procedures, manuals, oral job instructions, staff meetings, the public address system, and performance feedback.

Upward communication flows from lower levels to higher levels, as when a subordinate sends a report to a manager. Common upward communication types and devices are budget reports, suggestion boxes, grievances, and attitude survey responses.

Horizontal communications flow from one side of the hierarchy to the other, most frequently from peer to peer at the same organizational level and within the same unit. Horizontal communication can also occur between people at similar levels but in different areas, sections, or departments.

Formal Channels An organization's leadership wants most communication to go through the channels explicit in the organization chart for two reasons. First, this procedure ensures the preservation of the boss's authority; "Going through channels" lets the boss know what is happening at subordinate levels and makes it reasonable for the boss to be held accountable for the actions of subordinates. For the manager of the stock brokerage office to say "I didn't know my employees were churning the accounts of elderly investors" is not typically a legitimate defense. As the motto on Harry S Truman's desk said, "The buck stops here." Having the organization's main communication channels contained within the hierarchy structure ensures that sufficient information accompanies "the buck."

Second, the formal channels of communication are designed to make certain that *only enough* information goes to the specific decision makers who need it. Every organization is overloaded with information. Using the formal channels expressed in the organization chart to screen out the irrelevant reduces that information to a workable quantity. Top managers cannot personally confront and sift through all available data. Lower levels need to compress and summarize, then select what goes up to the next level. This selection process leaves open the possibility that important information may be left out. All organizations must somehow cope with this double bind: Top managers can't possibly deal personally with all of the information system's output, yet valuable information may be filtered out as data passes up through the formal hierarchy.

Informal Channels Most formal communications follow the up-and-down pattern expressed in the organization chart, but many informal communications are horizontal. For instance, Mary Jones of Department X may need some information from Joe Smith in Department Y. She can follow the hierarchy and go through her boss and Joe's boss, either or both of whom may also want to know about the information requested. Or Mary may avoid formal channels and converse directly with Joe. This approach saves time and avoids distortions that the bosses may introduce. The potential disadvantages of their informal conversation are that their bosses may not become aware of information they should know about, and that Joe's information may be inaccurate or incomplete.

THE CLASSICAL PERSPECTIVE

Taking Communication for Granted

Most classical writers and managers took effective communication for granted. The organization chart spelled out organizational relationships and communication channels. The top manager was intelligent, wise, and skilled in the organization's technology, as were lesser managers to a lesser degree. Communication was viewed primarily as the process whereby upper organizational levels told lower levels what to do and how to do it.

The net result of the classical position was a belief that communication could be naturally and competently handled by downward messages from superiors to subordinates, as depicted on the organization chart. Managers communicated downward, had no need for receiving information or feedback from below, and could either handle problems themselves or with help from their own immediate superiors.

The typical classical organization was a simple one, without interpersonal problems, large size, environmental restraints, technological complexity, concern about life-cycle stage, or rapid change. Owner/managers knew the entire job because they had created it in creating the organization. Other managers mastered the job over time, through the experience of growing up in the organization. In those days of slowly changing technology, the senior plant manager could still go down on the shop floor and take a turn on the job.

Fayol's Viewpoint

Unlike most of the other classicists, Henri Fayol wrote about the nature and significance of communication in coordinating organizational activities. In his famous *General and Industrial Management* (1916), within the discussion of principles of organizational spirit and the scalar chain, Fayol spoke of how important communication is to effective management.

Fayol agreed with the other classicists that communications should generally flow up and down the hierarchy or scalar chain. But he also said, "When an employee is obliged to choose between two practices, and it is impossible for him to take advice from his superior, he should be courageous enough and feel free enough to adopt the line dictated by the general interest."[1] If the boss is not around and something has to be done immediately, the employee should acquire needed information from whatever source and then take action.

Fayol's communication "bridge" or "gangplank" is depicted in Figure 13.1. In many organizations, persons F and P often have to communicate. For their communications invariably to have to travel up and down through nine other people wastes time and resources. If F and P can cut across organizational lines by using a "bridge," they can save time and probably increase communication accuracy.

Fayol sums up his position this way: "It is an error to depart needlessly from the line of authority, but it is an even greater one to keep to it when detriment to the business ensues."[2]

Except for Fayol and a few others, the classicists did not think of communication

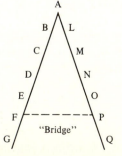

Figure 13.1 Henri Fayol's communication "bridge."

as a potential organizational problem. They took communication for granted or, at best, viewed it as a top-down activity. They felt that the worker could easily be told how to do a simple task that didn't change much from the first day on the job until retirement. Once a coal miner learned how to work a mine, or a steelworker learned the furnace, or the engineer learned how to run the train, not much was left except to discipline deviant behavior or correct improper performance of the task. Engaging in give-and-take sessions, quality-circle programs, or participative management procedures did not fit in with the attitude of the early organizational leaders: "I am the boss; you do as I say."

THE HUMAN RELATIONS PERSPECTIVE

Human Relations and Hawthorne

The human relations writers contributed significantly to our understanding of communication. Several discoveries of the Hawthorne researchers were that:

1. Employees listened but did not always hear or understand.
2. Employees had ideas about how to do their jobs that were often better than the methods determined by their "scientific" managers.
3. Employees thought about their jobs and were willing to talk about them with others.

Since the human relations school recognized that "employees are people too," they were of course interested in the "people aspects" of organizational communications. These aspects became clear during the Hawthorne studies. The human relations school began to study the grapevine and communication networks, and to construct models of how communication takes place. They moved from verbal to nonverbal communications and stressed the value of listening. Perhaps most importantly, they studied the many barriers to effective communication, barriers caused mainly by variations in people's needs, interests, and attitudes—none of which were of much concern to the classical designers of organizations.

The early human relations scholars also learned that formal communication channels do *not* transmit sufficient information for optimum job performance. Adequate communication is *not* guaranteed by the classical reliance on the organizational hierarchy. These insights led to an intensified study of communication as a process.

Once these discoveries were made, communication could be looked at as a two-part, even a two-way, process. Realizing that *the receiver* played a major role in communication was a major development that spawned numerous studies of several issues. The logic of these issues flows for the most part out of the two-way communications model. The model led to an understanding of how messages get from boss to subordinate. This understanding became the first step in the "authority-acceptance" work of Chester I. Barnard and others. Consequently, how the communication process worked became an important issue for the human relations school to explain.

The Two-Way Communication Process Model

The human relations researchers tried to describe their developing comprehension of the communication process symbolically. Figure 13.2 presents a typical two-way communication picture or model. One value of such models was that they enabled researchers to identify and focus on the places in the communication process where communication might break down. Once the idea of barriers to effective communication became prevalent, researchers began examining all of the many impediments to interpersonal communication.

Communication begins with ideation: a sender has an idea to transmit to a receiver. The idea can be a fact, a command, an observation, or anything else that the sender wants to communicate. The idea is developed by the sender into a symbolic representation, transmitted through an appropriate channel, and interpreted by the receiver. Finally, the receiver responds to the message, and this response may stimulate further communication from the original sender. Let us look more closely at the elements in the communication process.

Sender The sender is someone with a reason for communicating. The sender could be a sales representative with an idea for a prospective buyer or an executive with an idea that could improve the productive efficiency of a plant.

Encoding The sender cannot send the idea itself. Encoding involves converting the sender's original idea into a symbolic form (words, pictures, gestures, numbers) or code that will be meaningful to the receiver.

Message The product of the encoding process is the message, a set of symbols designed to transfer meaning from the sender to the receiver. The effectiveness of communication depends upon the sender's ability to build verbal or nonverbal messages.

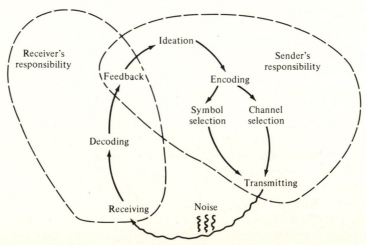

Figure 13.2 The communication process.

Channel   The channel is the medium through which the message travels. It carries the message. It may be a sound wave, a touch, or a written note. Although the channel has a simple function—carrying the message from the source to the receiver—it has been given much attention in studies of communication. For example, Marshall McLuhan suggests that the channel *is* the message, that the communication medium itself determines how a receiver envisions the sender's idea.

Receiver   The sender encodes a message and transmits it along a communication channel. At the other end of the channel, the physical stimuli that make up the message (such as sounds or words on a page) must be received by the receiver's sensory apparatus.

Decoding   The received message is converted into nervous impulses that are sent to the brain. In a way that is not fully understood, the central nervous system converts these impulses into ideas that have meaning for the receiver. This process is called decoding.

Feedback   The last step in the communication process is really the first step in a new communication sequence: physical or verbal reaction to a message. The inclusion of feedback in the model emphasizes the importance of *what happens to a message after it is sent.* If a sender gets no feedback or feedback indicating faulty message reception, why so? *What went wrong* can then become a focus of study, leading to investigations of (1) people's ability to receive over different channels, (2) why receivers do not "hear" some messages and "mis-hear" others, and (3) what barriers exist to effective communication.

Communication Networks

The basic sender-receiver model was expanded to include the study of how multiple senders and receivers process information. The famous experimental studies of Alex Bavelas compared the effectiveness of four communication networks: the circle, the chain, the wheel, and the star. Figure 13.3 presents these networks, each representing a different type of interpersonal communication structure. At the bottom of the figure, the networks are compared on the basis of six characteristics: speed, accuracy, morale, leadership stability, organization, and flexibility.

Network Effectiveness   The organization uses its formal communication networks to integrate its tasks. The typical organization chart resembles the "chain" network. Organizational leaders can benefit by knowing that such a network is usually fast and accurate, but is not very flexible and does not promote high morale.

Later researchers using the Bavelas networks found that groups working on rather simple tasks in the more centralized networks (chain and wheel) performed better than groups working in the more decentralized networks (circle and star).[3] In the former, information is sent to the center (rather than having all participants share the information) where the problem is solved or a decision made and the results sent

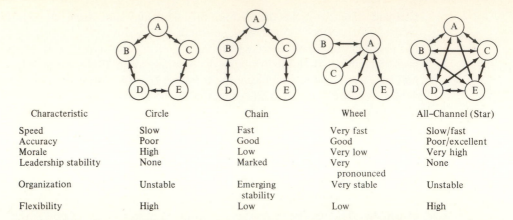

Characteristic	Circle	Chain	Wheel	All–Channel (Star)
Speed	Slow	Fast	Very fast	Slow/fast
Accuracy	Poor	Good	Good	Poor/excellent
Morale	High	Low	Very low	Very high
Leadership stability	None	Marked	Very pronounced	None
Organization	Unstable	Emerging stability	Very stable	Unstable
Flexibility	High	Low	Low	High

Figure 13.3   Four network types and their communications characteristics. (*Source:* Phillip V. Lewis, *Organizational Communication: The Essence of Effective Management* [New York: John Wiley & Sons, 1986], p. 51, as adapted from Alex Bavelas and Dermot Barrett, "An Experimental Approach to Organizational Communication," *Personnel* 27 [March 1951], pp. 370–371. Used by permission.)

to the participants. However, other researchers found that groups working on complex or ambiguous tasks performed better in decentralized networks.[4]

The Grapevine

As they gained familiarity with the human aspects of organizations, researchers realized that the formal communications channels and networks do not do all the work. They began to examine the informal channels, particularly the organizational grapevine. Keith Davis has identified four types of grapevine chain.[5] They appear in Figure 13.4.

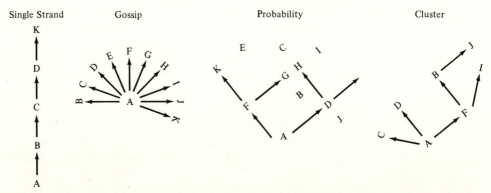

Figure 13.4   Types of grapevine chains. (*Source:* Reprinted by permission of the *Harvard Business Review*. Exhibit from "Management Communication and the Grapevine" by Keith Davis [September/ October 1953], p. 45. Copyright © 1953 by the President and Fellows of Harvard College; all rights reserved.)

Single Strand   In the single-strand grapevine, one person passes information to another who passes it to another, and so forth. The same people usually serve repeatedly as links in the communication chain.

Gossip   In the gossip chain, person A hears something and passes it along to anyone who will listen. Information not directly related to the jobs of grapevine participants is often spread quickly in this way—for instance, "Mr. Jones has just been fired" or "Ms. Smith dated Mr. Green last night."

Probability   In the probability chain, person A communicates randomly with other people, in accordance with the laws of probability. Persons F and D pass the word along in the same fashion.

Cluster   In this grapevine type, person A sends information to a select cluster of people, usually trusted members of a clique. They convey the information to other trusted people. Since most employees belong to trusted clusters or cliques, this form of grapevine transmission is frequently found in organizations.

Accuracy   The human relations writers found not only that informal channels exist but that they tend to be quite accurate. Keith Davis maintained that the grapevine is 75 to 95 percent accurate.[6] Its bad reputation is often due to the incompleteness of the information it transmits, the occasional rumor that has no basis in fact, and management's generally hostile attitude toward an unofficial communication channel which often seems faster and more accurate than the formal channels established by management.

Nonverbal Communication

Although most significant organizational communications use words, communication can be nonverbal as well as verbal. In fact, nonverbal messages account for at least half of the total meaning produced in face-to-face communication.

Space Usage   The arrangement of buildings at a plant site and of the rooms within the buildings affects the ways in which communicators interact. Dividing up a large room into small cubicles affects the communication between employees working in the room.

Within a room, different seating patterns influence communication. A committee chairperson who wants to encourage interaction among members will place seats in a circle. A manager who wants to do all the talking will place the chairs in a rectangle of rows. Such aspects of the physical setting as temperature, lighting, drapes, carpeting, and room color also have their effect.

Territoriality is one aspect of space usage. We all have an invisible personal space surrounding ourselves, and we allow that space to be entered only under certain conditions. We also consider the space within which we work to be "ours."[7]

Body Language   We communicate nonverbally by moving our bodies in certain ways. To communicate various ideas you may wave your hand, shake your finger, nod, cross your arms, stamp your foot, point, wipe your forehead, smile, look away, and so on.[8]

Appearance   Appearance also communicates nonverbally. The clothes we wear, the jewelry with which we ornament ourselves, and the way we arrange our hair say something about us. Organizations often have formal dress and appearance codes (for example, suit, white shirt, solid tie, hat, no facial hair) or informal expectations about how people should dress, all designed to convey a certain organizational image. An IBM typewriter salesperson would not make calls wearing a UCLA sweatshirt and Adidas jogging shoes.

Physical Barriers to Communication

Once the communication process had been expressed in models like the one in Figure 13.2, researchers could identify the points in the process where communication became distorted or ineffectual, or broke down altogether.

Noise   One barrier to communication that appears in Figure 13.2 is noise. Noise is any unplanned interruption of the communication process, and it can occur at any point in the process. Although noise can be internal (like anxiety or stress within the sender or receiver), it is usually an external physical barrier to communication that disrupts the fidelity of messages. Examples might include a change in temperature, the presence of an attractive person of the opposite sex, a disturbing sound, or a competing message.

The sender's responsibility is to select the communication channel that minimizes the chance of noise. The sender can also use techniques designed to keep the receiver's attention in the presence of distracting noise, such as unusual phrases and short, concise messages.

Information Overload   A special type of physical barrier to communication is information overload: too many messages coming in at once on one channel. Modern technology has created an information explosion that can either enhance organizational performance or overwhelm the organization's people, depending on the appropriateness of the reaction. J. G. Miller has presented several possible reactions to information overload:

1. Omission—failing to notice and process some of the information;
2. Error—processing information incorrectly;
3. Queuing—delaying during peak load periods, hoping to catch up later;
4. Filtering—setting up a priority system that omits the processing of some information;
5. Approximation—responding to information in a general rather than a precise way;
6. Escape—ignoring the processing task and leaving the information behind.[9]

The organization must do what it can to ensure appropriate responses to information overload. In certain situations, not doing the work at all might be better than doing it incorrectly. In other situations, responding to the information approximately might be preferable to not processing the information at all, even if the approximation involves some error.

The management-information-systems approach to information overload will be discussed later in the chapter.

Personal Barriers

The classicists thought that communications from sender to receiver were more or less automatic and problem-free. The human relations school realized that, because people are not machines, both the sender and the receiver can, knowingly and unknowingly, create barriers to communication.

Distortion by the Sender   In order to attain personal objectives, senders sometimes falsify or withhold information. Employees may not be completely candid with their supervisors. Company public relations officials may distort information transmitted to the public. Middle managers may filter facts before relaying them to top management. When employees are communicating with superiors who have the power to dispense promotions, pink slips, favorable assignments, and job transfers, they may be inclined to filter out information that may be personally damaging or that supervisors may not want to hear.

If frequently practiced, manipulation of information by the sender causes receiver skepticism concerning message accuracy. The information system becomes inefficient because the receiver does not always get accurate information and therefore does not trust or act on the information, even if it happens to be accurate.

Semantic Barriers   Because reality itself cannot usually be sent along communication channels, senders send symbolic representations of reality. If sender and receiver have different meanings for the same symbols, communication problems result.

The complex, elaborate terminology and jargon of data processing are useful to people within the EDP group but have little meaning to people outside the group. Data-processing managers who want to explain the computer system to production foremen must use verbal symbols that have meaning to the foremen, even if those symbols are not as precise as the terminology of data processing.

When the sender and the receiver miss each other with their meanings, William V. Haney says that *bypassing* occurs.[10] Bypassing comes about when both parties use the same word with different meanings or different words with the same meaning. To illustrate the same-word/different-meaning miscommunication pattern, let us say that production has been stopped because a machine has broken down. The manager tells the line supervisor, "Get rid of that trouble on the Number Three line." The supervisor scraps the machine and replaces it with a new one, and the manager hits the ceiling because, under pressure from her boss to economize, she wanted the machine fixed, not replaced. The manager and the supervisor apparently had different meanings for the verbal symbols "Get rid of that trouble."

Filtering by the Receiver   The classicists assumed that subordinates receiving instructions and information understood and accepted them without complication. In contrast, the human relations scholars, working with models of the communications process, focused intense attention on the message receiver's role, what the receiver is doing as the message comes in. They learned that personal filtering systems screen out much incoming information.

While personal filters are very useful in protecting receivers from information overload, they may cause receivers to distort incoming messages. For example, cultural precepts produce filters called *attitudinal barriers* that cause stereotyping: filtering out differences while allowing similarities to come through. The receiver who thinks in stereotypes does not have as efficient a decoding process as the receiver who avoids stereotyping.

Personal Barriers and the Organization   The preceding barriers and filters, along with many others, affect the everyday communication situations that occur in all organizations. The contribution of the human relations writers was to call attention to the filters and other factors that inhibit or distort the flow of information to organizational members as they work toward achieving organizational goals.

Personal communication barriers are a problem with no quick and easy solution. Being personal, they are subject to the many aspects of interpersonal relationships. The human relations writers have helped us to realize their existence and to understand how they occur.

The human relations school has stimulated most modern organizations to take a strong interest in communication and the barriers to communication. The classicists were not much concerned about organizational communication. The position of human relations exponents is at the opposite extreme; they believe that most organizational problems can be solved and most organizational functions improved by developing more effective communication channels.

THE MODERN PERSPECTIVE

If the organization is a system, then communication is the means for letting each part of the system know what the other parts are doing. If every organizational member, group, and situation is unique, a contingency perspective suggests that the skilled organizational communicator will plan a bit differently for each unique communication situation—a true systems/contingency approach to communication. Although modern organization theorists recognize these truths, a comprehensive systems/contingency perspective on communication has yet to evolve.

Perhaps the nearest thing to a modern position would be to consider organizations as information-processing systems. This view has led to two groups of writings on (1) management information systems (MIS), and (2) organizational design as an information-processing problem. These two approaches to the *mechanics* of modern organizational communication must be blended with and tempered by the *human* communication concerns of organizational members.

Management Information Systems

Increasing organizational concern with the communication barriers and gaps of formal communication systems has led to the evolution of *management information systems* (MIS), or, more recently, *management information and decision systems* (MIDS). A management information system can be defined as any *systematic* procedure for providing appropriate *information* to a *manager* at the time that information is needed. Although an MIS can be represented by something as simple as a memorandum containing information that helps to facilitate decision making, the term has come to be synonymous with *computerized data retrieval systems.*

Management information systems have resulted directly from the computerization of data. As computers have become more widely available, organizations have had to answer such questions as: What information do we need to put in the data base? How should it be arranged, catalogued, kept confidential, and distributed? Managers trained in the human relations tradition may think they have an "intuitive feel" for solving communication problems. But once these managers actually try to deal with computers and their programmers, they will find that data acquisition, verification, and storage become more complex issues than they at first appear to be.

Accessibility versus Quality   The importance of the management information system's quality becomes even greater when research on how organizational members get information is considered. Charles A. O'Reilly III examined the use that social workers made of four information sources: (1) files (handbooks and procedures); (2) updates (memos and newsletters); (3) peers and supervisor; and (4) external sources. O'Reilly found a preference for *readily accessible* information over *high-quality* information. The social workers had heavy case loads, time pressures, and many distractions. Therefore, they were willing to forego hard-to-get, high-quality information in favor of more accessible, lower-quality information.[11]

Busy people use the information at hand, rather than seeking out better, hard-to-find information. The responsibility of the MIS, then, is to make the accessible information of the highest possible quality.

Since most MIS applications are at the operational level, problems have most often occurred there. These problems are of four kinds: information overload, numeric myopia, the language barrier, and inadequate cost-benefit analysis.

Information Overload   Too much information can be as bad as no information at all, and MIS operations may cause information overload. Most managers have an inadequate idea about exactly what information they need in decision settings. Rather than requesting specific, essential information, they may ask the systems designer for *all* data that might be relevant. The common assumption is that the more information, the better the decision. Therefore, the systems designer provides a wealth of information in the form of a computer printout. The printout may say so much that it actually tells the manager nothing, because the useful data are hidden among the useless.

Humans use psychological filters to prevent information overload. Organizations must set up similar filters to screen out unimportant information. And this is not so easy, especially if, as Aaron Wildavsky suggests, data-processing people try to increase the demand for their output whether it is useful or not. He says:

> In almost all private and public organizations, data are treated as overhead, like light bulbs or lavatory paper. An allocation is made to a data-processing center, whose purpose is to produce data. Not surprisingly, it gets to be very good at improving its performance; every year it produces more data. On what is its budget based? The work it has performed in the past and the backlog of requests it cannot fill. The more unfulfilled requests it generates, therefore, the better its chance for more money. So producers suggest all sorts of data they would provide if only potential users would make their needs known.[12]

Martha S. Feldman and James G. March provide two other reasons for information overload.[13] First, organizational members soon learn that the penalties for not having enough information are greater than the penalties for having too much. Therefore, they typically request more information than they need, so as not to be caught short. Second, abundant and conspicuous information requests symbolize the manager's commitment to making rational decisions. These requests give evidence to observers that the manager seeks out all relevant information before making a decision. These two motivations lead to an overloading of the information system, the photocopy machine, and the manager's briefcase.

Numeric Myopia   Myopia is nearsightedness. Numeric myopia refers to the tendency to focus on the numbers close at hand, rather than trying to understand how the numbers came about. Organizations have a tendency to believe that the computer output is exact, even though the input information was approximate. Although most organization members are familiar with the "garbage-in, garbage-out" principle, they often have difficulty identifying garbage on the printout.

The organization design issue here is broader than overload and myopia. A major discussion item on senior managerial agendas is the emerging trend for each manager to have a personal computer with personal data files on personal floppy diskettes. Imagine a meeting of ten managers, each with a printout analysis based on each manager's assumptions and data base—and *all different*. Breaking the tunnel vision and false sense of precision which numbers carried to three decimal places engender is difficult enough without having *ten* such numbers under discussion at once. The distribution of personal computers and data bases has become an increasingly important organizational issue.[14]

Language Barrier   A third problem area is the language barrier—for instance, between the data-processing and operational people. The operations people tell the systems people what they think they want, and the data-processing equipment is directed to provide what the systems people think the operations people want. However, both groups use terminology peculiar to themselves, and they do not always speak the same language. As a result, anyone involved with computer-based management information systems can tell many tales of forms generated that no one used, information disseminated that no one wanted, and data requested that no one could find.

Language barriers between people using different computer systems are increasing. For example, the IBM PC user has difficulty in communicating with the Apple user (and neither understands the main-frame people), since they employ unique languages, programs, and methods of addressing the information systems constructed on their personal computers.

Cost-Benefit Analysis   The final problem area is inadequate cost-benefit analysis. When MIS is installed, it is sometimes regarded as a new toy that can be used to play with pet projects. This attitude can hurt any organization, both in selecting equipment and in applying it to operational problems. Management information systems can be expensive. Any MIS project should be carefully analyzed in terms of its costs versus its benefits.

An emerging variant of this problem is how the MIS operation fits into the organizational reporting structure. As MIS has increased in cost and importance, it has gradually risen up the organizational hierarchy. Not long ago, the management information system was typically a subordinate unit in the accounting department. Now, MIS may be directed by a vice president reporting directly to the president. The typical MIS unit has rapidly grown in visibility, number-crunching capability, staff programming support, and proportion of organizational resources allocated to it.

A parallel development is that user groups—demanding more and more time and effort from the MIS unit as they become more comfortable with computer assistance in decision making—become impatient waiting for their turn on the organization's

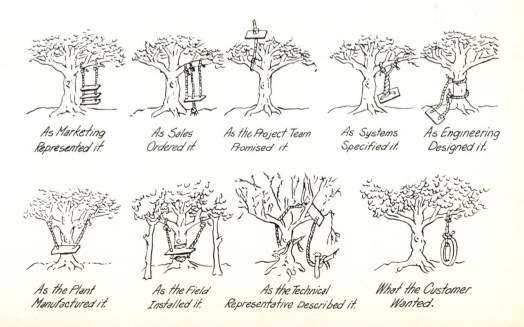

As Marketing Represented it.   As Sales Ordered it.   As the Project Team Promised it.   As Systems Specified it.   As Engineering Designed it.

As the Plant Manufactured it.   As the Field Installed it.   As the Technical Representative Described it.   What the Customer Wanted.

computers. They have also become more capable of doing the work on their own personal computers. The net results are a bypassing of the organization's expensive computer hardware, the proliferation of different systems, and an increasing organizational concern about just how to manage its information.

Structural Solutions   As organizations wrestle with these problems, they look to organizational designers for solutions. Robert W. Zmud has proposed a structural strategy for fitting the MIS subunit to the organizational need. Table 13.1 presents Zmud's design alternatives for organizing the information systems function. For example, Zmud suggests that the nature of MIS research and development lends itself to a product form of structure (with the subunit organized about end products), while MIS internal auditing should perhaps take a functional form best suited to achieve economies of scale and work specialization. Zmud cautions that other factors—such as the organization's overall structural form, leadership styles of key managers, organizational priorities and strategies—may affect these structural choices.

The Chief Information Officer   Some organizations have established a new upper-level administrator to manage the organization's information. Among the titles being used are vice president for information services, information resources manager, and chief information officer, or CIO. These CIO's try to eliminate the communications gap between the organization's nontechnical people and the MIS staff. They must know MIS technology and they must also understand the organization's business. They oversee the data processing and other communications technology, often report to the CEO or board chairman, and concentrate on long-term strategy and planning rather than day-to-day computer operations. In a 1986 survey of 120 large corporations, 40 percent were found to have a CIO.[15]

Other Factors   The cost-benefit analysis of the MIS operation should not be confined to financial considerations. Other factors, such as effects on morale, must be assessed when determining an MIS operation's costs and benefits. These cost-benefit problems will be overcome as organizations become more aware of the strengths and the limitations of electronic equipment and as designers become more oriented toward organizational applications.

Table 13.1   DESIGN ALTERNATIVES FOR ORGANIZING THE INFORMATION SYSTEMS FUNCTION

Information systems subunit	Appropriate structure
Data processing	Product, with some functional
Systems development	Functional
Systems analysts	Matrix
Research and development	Product
Planning	Functional, with some product
Internal auditing	Functional
Administration	Functional

Source: Adapted from Robert W. Zmud, "Design Alternatives for Organizing Information Systems Activities," *MIS Quarterly* 8 (June 1984): 88. Used by permission.

The Information-Processing Approach

The second avenue of modern investigation into organizational communication is based on the principles suggested by Jay Galbraith's information-processing approach.[16] Galbraith's idea, since elaborated upon by others, is that what the organization does, how it is done, and the environment within which it is done, all influence the way in which information should be processed. In particular, Galbraith saw a relationship between organizational *uncertainty* and organizational information-processing requirements.

Uncertainty and Information   Following up on Galbraith's work, Michael L. Tushman and David A. Nadler have focused on the relationship between the uncertainty facing an organizational subunit and that subunit's information-processing requirements.[17] Uncertainty arises out of subunit task characteristics (primarily task complexity), subunit task environment (whether stable or changing), and inter-unit task dependence (if a subunit depends on other units, uncertainty increases).[18] Since Tushman and Nadler define uncertainty as "the difference between information possessed and information required to complete a task,"[19] it follows that the greater a subunit's uncertainty, the greater will be its need for information delivered by an effective MIS.

In his early work, Galbraith made two general suggestions for processing information. First, try to *reduce the need* for processing. Next, try to *increase the processing capacity.*

Reducing the Need   One way to reduce the need for processing information is *coordination by rules and programs.* Rules and programs tell employees exactly what to do about recurring problems and how to perform routine tasks. They minimize the need for information exchange between superiors and subordinates or between managers of different units working on related projects. *Coordination by targets and goals* serves a similar purpose. Managers and employees are given targets and goals to shoot for. They can make their own decisions about how to achieve them. Their superiors enter in only if goals are not met. If the organization finds that it cannot process its information adequately, it can extend its target times. Extending a deadline from 10 to 20 days doubles the amount of time within which the same amount of information must be processed. However, this increased ease of processing information has its costs: more expense to achieve the same output, more inventory, and greater delay to customers.

Environmental management can reduce the need for information processing. Instead of relying on a tire manufacturer, an automobile company can "manage its environment" by buying out the tire company or manufacturing its own tires. The resulting "vertical integration" will cut down on the information that must be processed or exchanged. Decentralizing by establishing product divisions serves a similar purpose.

Increasing the Capacity   The organization can increase its capacity to process information by formalizing the language in which the information is transmitted. The formalized language of accounting serves such a purpose; it enables the transmittal of information in a compact, logical, consistent form. The capacity of the individual manager to process this formalized language may be enhanced by computers or other machinery, assistants-to, clerks, and secretaries. Again, these enhancements are not without cost.

The use of formalized language and computers facilitates processing of the information flow *up* to the decision maker. Creating lateral, cross-department communication channels and working relationships may move the decision point *down* to where the information exists. If two managers share a problem, for example, they can work it out between them, rather than referring it to their mutual superior. If interdependent departments share enough problems, one organizational member can be assigned to serve in a liaison role between them. If several departments are engaged in interdependent activities, each affected department may have a member on a coordinating task force. Direct contact, liaison, and the task force are devices for solving problems at the level where they arise, rather than referring them up the hierarchy. Therefore, information-processing activities of managers farther up the hierarchy are reduced.

Information Processing in Work Units   Charles Perrow categorized job tasks along two dimensions—analyzability and variety—that represent two types of task uncertainty. *Analyzability* refers to uncertainty concerning the work process itself. The work of an assembly line is high in analyzability (and low in uncertainty). The process is predictable and repeatable. The work of a master chef is less analyzable (more uncertain) because the processes vary from day to day. The nature of a work unit's process is related to its problems and how they are solved when they occur. Most problems on the assembly line have occurred many times before, and their solutions can usually be found by using an objective, predetermined, step-by-step problem-solving procedure. If something doesn't smell or taste right in the kitchen, the chef may have to spend time brainstorming, pondering, and otherwise thinking creatively about what action to take.

Variety refers to uncertainty concerning the *frequency* of unexpected events, activities, and problems associated with a task. Surprises are infrequent on the assembly line, and problems are predictable. In contrast, the activities and problems of engineers and accountants are highly varied and unpredictable.

Perrow's two dimensions, along with examples of the four different work-unit types, appear in Figure 13.5. In terms of problem solving, the horizontal axis reflects *how frequently* problems occur and the vertical axis reflects *how problems are solved* when they *do* occur. Work units engaged in nonroutine technology (R&D, strategic planning) experience many problems that are not readily susceptible to analysis and solution using standard, predetermined problem-solving techniques. Work units engaging in routine technology (clerks, assembly-line workers) don't have many problems, and when problems occur, they can usually be handled by means of standard, step-by-step, usually computational problem-solving procedures.

Richard L. Daft and Norman B. Macintosh wanted to know *how much* and *what kind* of information is typically processed in each of the classic Perrow work-unit types.[20] Their results appear in Figure 13.5. Daft and Macintosh found, not surprisingly, that work units with a high variety of activities and problems—R&D, strategic planning, engineers, accountants, computer programmers—process large amounts of information. Work units with fewer activities and problems spend more time on direct production activities and less time on information processing. So, task variety and amount of information processed seem to be positively related.

Daft and Macintosh expected a negative relationship between task analyzability and the amount of information processed. They expected that the low-analyzability work units in the top two squares of the figure would need to process more information

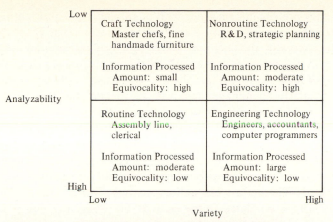

Figure 13.5 Daft-Macintosh information-processing model.
(*Source:* Adapted from "A Tentative Exploration into the Amount and
Equivocality of Information Processing in Organizational Work Units"
by Richard L. Daft and Norman B. Macintosh, published in *Administrative Science Quarterly* 26 [March 1981] by permission of *Administrative Science Quarterly.* Copyright © 1981 Cornell University. All
rights reserved.)

than the high-analyzability work units in the bottom of the figure. They thought that
participants in less well-defined situations might seek and process more data, to clarify
their situations. In fact, task analyzability and amount of information processed appeared to be positively, not negatively, related. Work-unit participants apparently
sought *less* information when their tasks were intangible and poorly understood. They
may have learned the difficulty of developing and sharing relevant problem-solving
information. Rather than spend time defining the low-analyzability task well enough
to ask for, process, and share the appropriate information, participants in these situations did not bother to ask or even know who to ask; they used their own creative
thought processes.

Organization theorists tend to assume a close relationship between uncertainty
and the amount of information processed. According to Daft and Macintosh, that
relationship does seem to hold when task variety is the measure of uncertainty. It does
not hold as well when task analyzability is the measure of uncertainty.

Daft and Macintosh used a measure they called "equivocality" to reflect *what
kind* of information the work units processed. Information is unequivocal to the extent
that users know just what it means. A measurement made with a micrometer is
unequivocal; a supervisor's verbal explanation is more equivocal, more subject to
interpretation. Equivocality is the basis for the expression, "A picture is worth ten
thousand words." Figure 13.5 shows that as uncertainty about the task process and
indefiniteness of problem-solving procedures increase (that is, as we move from high
analyzability to low analyzability), the equivocality or ambiguity of the information
processed also increases. The information processed by chefs as they try to solve their
problems is more equivocal, less precise than the information processed by clerks as
they engage in problem solving. The clerks know just how to respond to the information
they get and process; the chefs and builders of handmade furniture are not as certain
of how to respond.

A chef may process information small in amount and equivocal in nature either because that is the only information available or because that is the information he chooses to use. Actually, the chef may prefer equivocal information. Rather than run a chemical analysis on a sauce to know whether the proportions of ingredients are correct, the chef may dip in a finger, lick it, and trust to the equivocal sensation he experiences. Similarly, a manager may view a precise, unequivocal message as an oversimplification of a complex situation and may therefore decide to ignore it.

Daft and Macintosh found that the high-analyzability work units (those with clearly defined work processes, procedures, and problem-solving methods) tended to process information of low equivocality. Low-analyzability work units processed information of high equivocality. So task analyzability and information equivocality seem negatively related. Whether a work unit experienced low or high variety of activities and problems seemed unrelated to the equivocality of information processed.

Participants in high-analyzability work units are more apt to benefit from computer-generated quantitative data than are participants in low-analyzability work units. Computer-assisted information processing may benefit the work of clerks; it may not be of any help in the kitchen of a master chef. In such nonroutine technology activities as R&D and strategic planning, according to Daft and Macintosh, "computer processing would not solve the information problem because computers deal with unequivocal, standardized information. . . . Other mechanisms, such as adding more personnel or restructuring the hierarchy, would be more likely to provide information with adequate equivocality,"[21] again suggesting that equivocality is not necessarily an undesirable quality in information.

One might predict that if information is equivocal, a work unit would need to process more of it, to compensate for its equivocality. Daft and Macintosh found a somewhat surprising negative relationship between the amount and equivocality of information. When available information was equivocal, less of it was processed. When information was precise, more of it was processed. Daft and Macintosh suggested that, in some work activities, a small amount of equivocal and ambiguous information may convey more meaning and content to experienced interpreters than precise, concise information.

The M-Form Hypothesis   Oliver E. Williamson examined the impact of growing organizational size on information processing and organizational design.[22] The typical unitary (U-form) firm is organized into three functional divisions: manufacturing, sales, and finance. Williamson argued that greater size leads to two major information-processing problems in the U-form organization: (1) more information is generated than top managers can process, and (2) transmission errors (for example, unintentional distortion and inappropriate filtering) increase as more managers try to collect more information and pass it up through more levels to top managers. As a result, top managers have excessive information, much of which may be unreliable.

Williamson maintains that organizations can overcome these information-processing limitations through restructuring into a multidivisional form (M-form) in which divisions—organized along product, brand, or geographic lines—operate somewhat autonomously. Richard M. Burton and Børge Obel tested Williamson's hypothesis by computer simulation and found the M-form superior to the U-form.[23]

The information-processing difficulties of top business managers are matched, if not exceeded, by those of persons in high public office. In *The M-Form Society* (1984), William G. Ouchi claimed that the M-form is such a good solution to information-processing and other problems that it can serve as a model for governing society itself.

Strategy and Structure   William G. Egelhoff examined a multinational corporation with subsidiaries structured into divisions of four different kinds: functional, international, product, and geographical. He investigated the relationships between organizational structures, strategies, and information-processing requirements. Egelhoff found a definite relationship or "fit" between an organization's structure and its overall strategy. Furthermore, the information-processing requirements of each structure/strategy combination provided an explanation of why that fit had evolved and why it worked. Egelhoff concluded: "The argument presented here has been that this general fit [between strategies and structures] can be accurately represented by the fit between the information-processing capacities of an organization's structure and the information processing required to implement its strategy or cope with its environment."[24]

The Modern Synthesis

The two modern approaches to organizational communication—management information systems and information processing—are not at odds with each other. Rather, they are developing in similar fashion and are fusing together. The MIS writers are focusing on the hardware side of MIS development: (1) seeking to link decision makers with the accurate, secure data bases they need, (2) installing common computers that can "talk" to each other, and (3) organizing the MIS function within the overall organizational structure. The information-processing writers look to the setting within which the organization and its units operate, to determine what information the organizational structure must be designed to accommodate.

Environment and Information   If the organization operates in a hostile, ever-changing setting, the organization's information-processing mechanisms must be designed to sense environmental changes rapidly and communicate them to the organization's decision makers so they can react appropriately. In a combat situation, a forward fire controller communicates back to combat headquarters by walkie-talkie. Not much different in principle are the attempts of XYZ Corporation's marketing research consultants to find out whether any new ABC Corporation products will create adverse consequences for XYZ Corporation's detergent. If the Wisk detergent makers learn from their forward observers in the marketplace that a New Improved Liquid Tide is coming out soon, Wisk can take countermeasures to protect its market position. On the other hand, the environment of a regulated utility does not change rapidly, so there is less need for a major resource commitment at the organizational boundary to gather and process information.

The dovetailing of the information-processing and MIS writers will take place, as they both struggle with the problem of getting the right information to the right person at the right time, so that the right decision—the one that will lead to the achievement of organizational goals—will be made.

SUMMARY

Of all the integrating strategies and activities, organizational communication poses the most problems—and offers the most opportunities for organizational improvement. The classicists concentrated on communication as information exchange and behavior control. From the classical perspective, communication was straightforward and uncomplicated. The job of employees was to get the product out; the job of managers was to tell them how to do it. Henri Fayol did recognize the occasional need to communicate across organizational lines.

The human relations school was more concerned with the quality of communication than with its quantity or direction. After realizing the importance of informal groups, demonstrated by the Hawthorne research, they began to study the informal communication grapevines within organizations, along with the more formal communication networks. They constructed communication models that enabled isolation of the many points in the process where communication can break down.

The heart of the human relations approach is to improve formal and informal human relationships within the organization, as a means of increasing worker satisfaction and organizational success. Communication is obviously basic to these goals.

The human side of communication stressed by the human relations school continues to be of great concern to organizations. Of equally great concern is the mechanical side of communication. Thanks to computers and other technological developments, organizations have more information available and more means for communicating that information rapidly than ever before. The problem for the modern organization is to keep the human aspect in view while making the most efficient use of progress on the mechanical side.

How to get the right information to the right person at the right time has become an enormous problem for modern organizations. Its very name suggests that the management information system (MIS) is a systems approach to solving that problem. There are four kinds of difficulties related to MIS: information overload, numeric myopia, the language barrier, and inadequate cost-benefit analysis.

The information-processing writers take a somewhat broader view of the organization as an information-processing system trying to cope with uncertainty by getting information to the decision point where it is needed. Richard L. Daft and Norman B. Macintosh showed that the amount and type of information processed vary with the analyzability and variety of organizational tasks. Oliver E. Williamson maintained that the M-form organization provides a solution to two major information-processing problems of large modern organizations. In their computerized simulation designed to test Williamson's M-form hypothesis, Richard M. Burton and Børge Obel found that the multidivisional form of organization is superior to the unitary form. William G. Egelhoff showed the relationship between structure, strategy, and information-processing requirements in a multinational corporation's foreign subsidiaries.

DISCUSSION QUESTIONS

1. Why is communication viewed as an integrating strategy within organizations?

2. Why was the classical school so unconcerned with the topic of communication?

3. Why do top managers want employees to use the formal communications channels reflected in the organization chart?

4. What is Fayol's bridge? If you were a manager, would you permit your subordinates to use such bridges?

5. Why was communication so much more important to the human relations school than to the classical school?

6. What are the steps in the communication process?

7. What are the different kinds of communication networks? Under what circumstances is each most effective?

8. What is the grapevine? Why must an organization's managers understand it? Describe a grapevine of which you are a member.

9. What is nonverbal communication? Why must organizational members be aware of it?

10. What barriers can interfere with communication?

11. Why is feedback so important in the communication process?

12. What is bypassing? How can it be avoided?

13. What is the modern perspective on communication?

14. What is MIS? What are its problems? How can they be overcome?

15. What is the information-processing approach to communication?

16. What is the relationship between information processing and environmental uncertainty?

17. Do you think structure is determined more by the organization's technology or its information-processing requirements?

■   ## *SOUTHERN INSURANCE HOTLINE*

Jackie Davitt is one of several program directors for Southern Insurance Company. She receives information, regulation changes, and legal interpretations about the program for which she is responsible. She then sends the information to the people responsible for implementing the program.

As a staff person, Davitt must be careful not to assume authority within Southern's administrative structure. She must send any changes or new regulations through the service delivery manager, who in turn transmits the information down through two or three more levels. Figure C.1 is an organization chart that reflects the situation.

Because information must pass through several levels, the process of implementing change in Davitt's program can be quite slow. Furthermore, Davitt must often wait a long time to see if her instructions have been clearly understood or correctly interpreted, because this feedback must come up to Davitt through several organizational levels. The same is true of any information requests addressed to Davitt. Her expertise cannot be obtained directly. Units having a problem must ask for Davitt's help through channels.

One day, while thinking about the problems caused by these delays, Davitt had an idea. Why not a "hot line"? The hot line phone would have no dial, to remind everyone symbolically that the chain of command must be followed if an organization is to run smoothly. Any unit supervisor picking up a hot line phone would be immediately connected to a central switchboard operator. The unit supervisor would state the problem or ask the question, and then the switchboard operator would direct the question to the appropriate program director. That person would handle the problem as quickly as possible by sending a standard reply memo to the inquiring supervisor, with copies to all higher levels of supervisory authority. Davitt thought that this method would encourage fast, easy use of staff expertise without endangering the authority of line supervisors.

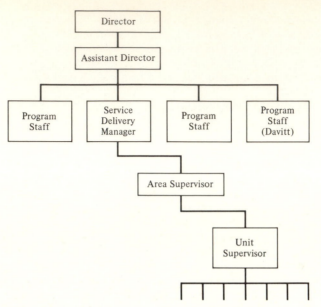

Figure C.1   Southern Insurance organization chart.

What are the pros and cons of this hotline solution? Can you suggest other organizational strategies that might solve this problem more effectively?

■ THE PLAN

The atmosphere in the war room of the Pacific Grand Command was always intense. Today the level of urgency was even higher than usual. The meeting had been abruptly called to discuss a letter to the Command from Lt. Marvin Grey, commander of an advanced observation post on a remote atoll. Grey's unit had been operating for some time without any telephone or wireless communication with headquarters.

The time was late in World War II, and the place was a Pacific island designed to serve as the forward high-command post for the invasion of mainland Japan, about to get underway. Only five persons were supposed to know about the invasion plan: the two generals and one admiral making up the Pacific Grand Command, the commander of the allied forces, and the president of the United States. Nevertheless, the letter from Lt. Marvin Grey, commander of a remote outpost, reflected a fairly complete knowledge of the invasion plan. Grey was writing to get clarification of some details.

As the discussion began behind closed doors, the clerks outside the meeting room reflected on the obvious deep concern on the faces of the Grand Command as they had hustled into the room.

Clerk: I wonder what's got those guys so stirred up.
Typist: I don't know. Forget it. Whatever it is, we'll wind up typing it. By the way, I suppose we'll all get together as usual tonight at the club for a few beers. What do you think of that new guy Harry? It must be fun to have his job, driving the mail boat and getting to see what's going on all over.

Meanwhile, on a lonely atoll, the following conversation was taking place:

Lt. Marvin Grey: Brad, when's the mail boat due?

Brad: Tomorrow, sir. Mail from home—and scuttlebutt from HQ. I like to hear it, even though some of it's pretty wild.

Lt. Grey: Well, Brad, just don't talk about any of that stuff with anybody but me. Remember: a slip of the lip can sink a ship.

Discuss the communication phenomenon illustrated in this account. Should generals and admirals perhaps learn to type?

■   ## THE PILE

After Sally's promotion, Fred took over as production manager at Andy Monroe Company, a middle-sized business with a few hundred employees. As Fred attempted to figure out the sources and types of information he would need to make the production decisions, he sifted through the material spilling out of his in-basket. He came across a large pile of computer paper covered with numbers and called in his secretary to ask for further information about it.

The secretary explained that a pile of paper like this was delivered daily by the MIS department but said she had no idea what was in it or how it was used. Fred called Sally at her new job and asked for help. After she hemmed and hawed a bit, Sally admitted that she didn't have any notion of what use Fred could make of the daily pile of paper. When Fred asked her why the pile was put together, she said it had started showing up just after she had a conversation with the newly hired MIS director. Eager to help, he had come around to top managers and had asked what information they needed in order to make decisions. Sally had thoughtfully responded in detail. She included all the factors that she ever considered in her decisions, even those that she used only infrequently. The new MIS director promptly sent her a daily supply of information pertaining to all those factors.

Fred looked at the pile and sighed.

What problem does this incident reflect? What can be done now?

■   ## WHO'S IN CHARGE?

The Barksdale Bank was an industry leader in converting to computers. Over 20 years ago, Barksdale purchased a GE computer, hired programmers, and wrote a unique program to handle the heavy volume of records on loans and related financial transactions. The Barksdale system was widely acclaimed; visitors from far and near came to observe the system and talk to the man in charge, Dave Clayton.

As was typical at that time, Clayton was an accountant who became fascinated by what he was reading about computers, dug into the topic, learned enough to see the potential of computers, and convinced his chief financial officer that a computer could save time and money for the Barksdale Bank.

Even the skeptics in management soon became excited about computer applications and asked Clayton to add more and more functions. Eventually the number of jobs increased far beyond the original function—servicing loans—to cover a broad range of applications, from payroll to providing computer support to bank clients through an in-house client consulting service department. The number of employees in Dave Clayton's department increased considerably, as did the number and size of the computers used. Clayton was consuming a considerable amount of the organization's resources.

Clayton is now reaching the end of his career, and the executive committee is meeting today to discuss his replacement. The more they talk, the more they realize how dramatically the function, nature, and responsibility of Clayton's department have changed. It becomes clear that the computer operation might need reorganization. Soon the argument is raging, between the chief financial officer (who has grown accustomed to having direction of the computers) and everyone else (who feels it is time to do things differently).

How should this dilemma at the Barksdale Bank be resolved?

NOTES

1. Henri Fayol, *General and Industrial Management,* trans. Constance Storrs (London: Pitman, 1949), p. 36.

2. Ibid.

3. Harold Guetzkow and Herbert A. Simon, "The Impact of Certain Communication Nets upon Organization and Performance in Task-Oriented Groups," *Management Science* 1 (April/July 1955): 233–250.

4. Reported in W. Richard Scott, *Organizations: Rational, Natural, and Open Systems* (Englewood Cliffs, NJ: Prentice-Hall, 1981), p. 149.

5. Keith Davis, "Management Communication and the Grapevine," *Harvard Business Review* 31 (September/October 1953): 45.

6. Keith Davis, "The Care and Cultivation of the Corporate Grapevine," *Dun's Review* 102 (1973): 44–47.

7. For further examples, see Michael Korda, *Power! How to Get It, How to Use It* (New York: Random House, 1975).

8. For further examples, see Julius Fast, *The Body Language of Sex, Power, and Aggression* (Philadelphia: Lippincott, 1977).

9. J. G. Miller, "Information Input, Overload, and Psychopathology," *American Journal of Psychiatry* 116 (February 1960): 695–704.

10. William V. Haney, *Communication and Interpersonal Relations* (Homewood, IL.: Richard D. Irwin, 1979), pp. 284–337.

11. Charles A. O'Reilly III, "Variations in Decision Makers' Use of Information Sources: The Impact of Quality and Accessibility of Information," *Academy of Management Journal* 25 (December 1982): 767.

12. Aaron Wildavsky, "Information as an Organizational Problem," *Journal of Management Studies* 20 (January 1983): 35.

13. Martha S. Feldman and James G. March, "Information in Organizations as Signal and Symbol," *Administrative Science Quarterly* 26 (June 1981): 171–186.

14. For discussion of this issue, and some solutions, see Robert W. Zmud, "Design Alternatives for Organizing Information Systems Activities," *MIS Quarterly* 8 (June 1984): 79–93.

15. "Management's Newest Star: Meet the Chief Information Officer," *Business Week,* 13 October 1986, pp. 160–172.

16. See Jay Galbraith, "Organizational Design: An Information Processing View," *Interfaces* 4 (May 1974): 28–36; and *Organizational Design* (Reading, MA: Addison-Wesley, 1977).

17. Michael L. Tushman and David A. Nadler, "Information Processing as an Integrating Concept in Organizational Design," *Academy of Management Review* 3 (July 1978): 613–624.

18. For a discussion of how complexity, centralization, and formalization are related to organizational communications, see Jerald Hage, Michael Aiken, and Cora Bagley Marrett, "Organi-

zation Structure and Communications," *American Sociological Review* 36 (October 1971): 860–871.

19. Tushman and Nadler, "Information Processing as an Integrating Concept in Organizational Design," p. 615.

20. Richard L. Daft and Norman B. Macintosh, "A Tentative Exploration into the Amount and Equivocality of Information Processing in Organizational Work Units, *Administrative Science Quarterly* 26 (March 1981): 207–224.

21. Ibid., p. 221.

22. Oliver E. Williamson, *Corporate Control and Business Behavior* (Englewood Cliffs, NJ: Prentice-Hall, 1970). See especially Chapter 8.

23. Richard M. Burton and Børge Obel, "A Computer Simulation Test of the M-Form Hypothesis," *Administrative Science Quarterly* 25 (September 1980): 457–466.

24. William G. Egelhoff, "Strategy and Structure in Multinational Corporations: An Information-Processing Approach," *Administrative Science Quarterly* 27 (September 1982): 454.

ADDITIONAL READINGS

Athanassiades, John C. "The Distortion of Upward Communication in Hierarchical Organizations." *Academy of Management Journal* 16 (June 1973): 207–226.

Brilhart, John K. *Effective Group Discussion.* 4th ed. Dubuque, IA: William Brown, 1982.

Cummings, H. Wayland, Larry W. Long, and Michael L. Lewis. *Managing Communication in Organizations.* Dubuque, IA: Gorsuch Scarisbrick, 1982.

Daft, Richard L., and Robert H. Lengel. "Organizational Information Requirements, Media Richness and Structural Design." *Management Science* 32 (May 1986): 554–571.

Davis, Keith. "A Method of Studying Communication Patterns in Organizations." *Personnel Psychology* 6 (Autumn 1953): 301–312.

Dollinger, Marc J. "Environmental Boundary Spanning and Information Processing Effects on Organizational Performance." *Academy of Management Journal* 27 (June 1984): 351–368.

Fisher, Dalmar. *Communication in Organizations.* St. Paul, MN: West Publishing, 1980.

Gardener, Edward P.M. "A Systems Approach to Bank Prudential Management and Supervision: The Utilization of Feedforward Control." *Journal of Management Studies* 22 (January 1985): 1–24.

Goldhaber, Gerald M. *Organizational Communication.* 3rd ed. Dubuque, IA: William C. Brown, 1983.

Harriman, Bruce. "Up and Down the Communications Ladder." *Harvard Business Review* 52 (September/October 1974): 143–151.

Hayakawa, S.I., et al. *Language in Thought and Action.* 4th ed. New York: Harcourt, Brace & World, 1978.

Knapp, Mark. *Nonverbal Communication in Human Interaction.* 2d ed. New York: Holt, Rinehart & Winston, 1978.

Phillips, Gerald M. *Communication and Communication Systems.* Homewood, IL: Richard D. Irwin, 1968.

Shaw, James B. "An Information-Processing Approach to the Study of Job Design." *Academy of Management Review* 5 (January 1980): 41–48.

Strassmann, Paul A. *Information Payoff: The Transformation of Work in the Electronic Age.* New York: Free Press, 1985.

Thayer, Lee. *Communication and Communication Systems.* Homewood, IL: Richard D. Irwin, 1968.

COMPREHENSIVE CASES

201st MISSILE MAINTENANCE FACILITY

The 201st Missile Maintenance Facility is located at a remote air base on the coast of South Korea. Its job is the assembly and maintenance of air-to-air guided missiles carried by the supersonic fighter-bombers assigned to the air base.

The maintenance and assembly of these missiles require the handling and check-out of highly explosive warheads, moderately explosive solid fuel rocket motors, and complex guidance and control units ranging from radar-guided to heat-seeking types.

Successful performance of maintenance and assembly procedures requires careful handling and intense concentration, because a mistake can result in serious injury or death, and damage to thousands of dollars worth of equipment. The men working in this facility have undergone extensive training in the Air Force missile school, have several years of practical experience, and are well above average in intelligence. They know their difficult jobs, and they do them well.

The minimum work schedule at the facility is specified as 10 hours per day, 6 days per week, with a very rare half-day off on Saturday. The long hours and difficult work put great stress upon the workers. In addition, the 13-month tour of duty is designed as "unaccompanied"—that is, no families—and most of the men assigned to the maintenance facility have families back home. The already difficult working conditions are compounded by periodic alerts. These exercises begin with a siren blast at about 4:30 A.M., and last 2 or 3 days. During these alerts, the munitions facilities operate 24 hours a day, with the workers on 12-hour shifts.

Major Parker, the supervisor of the missile maintenance facility, has tried to give the workers as much free time as possible in order to make conditions more bearable. He realistically schedules the day's objectives and, if they are accomplished before the end of the formal workday, he lets most of the workers leave early. Major Parker and the men feel that this time off is an honestly derived benefit of their efficiency in performing their tasks.

The maintenance facility runs smoothly, and the workers are fairly satisfied. They require very little supervision and make most of the decisions concerning routine maintenance. They report these decisions and the resulting status of the missile inventory to Major Parker, who relays the information to the central munitions control section. Being allowed to handle maintenance as they think best indicates to the men that their judgment and experience are respected. The occasional shortening of their working hours indicates to them that Major Parker trusts them to meet their objectives. They feel that as long as they can produce, they can avoid constant 10-hour workdays.

Higher base officials sometimes conduct inspection tours. During one of these tours, on the afternoon of an average workday, the inspecting official (a logistics officer knowing little about munitions) noticed that fewer workers were present than the number listed on the duty roster. When asked about this difference, Major Parker replied that his practice was to let some of the men go if they had completed all their assigned tasks for the day.

Shortly thereafter the squadron commander (who had been to the missile maintenance facility only twice in the previous year) issued a directive stating that all workers would work a full 10-hour day every day unless they were sick or had to attend to a genuine emergency. Major Parker relayed this news to the workers. After some initial expression of discontent, they did not seem to be too upset.

However, in the past 3 or 4 weeks, Major Parker has noticed a significant drop in the unit's performance level. The men are accomplishing less work in a 10-hour day than they had previously accomplished when working only 7, 8, or 9 hours a day. When he confronted the workers with this fact, they asked why they should work at top speed and finish a project early when all they had to look forward to was meaningless work designed to keep them busy until the end of the workday. That work often consists of sweeping, mopping, painting, or cutting grass. On those occasions, their friends never seem to tire of commenting on how far their highly specialized technical training has gotten them.

Other unfortunate signs have also appeared. Workers now go to rather lengthy "emergency" appointments during the workday, and production is decreasing still further. Three or four men often go on an errand that actually requires only one person. And no one seems to think of reordering needed maintenance materials until the facility is completely out of them. The lack of materials occasionally makes it necessary to withdraw missiles from an operationally ready status.

Major Parker understands what is going on. He realizes that the men sincerely disagree with the new policy for good reasons and that they are letting their disagreement be known. They view the new policy as a penalty for their initiative in improving the overall performance of the squadron. They therefore have decided to perform no better than any other unit, even though they know that the squadron's performance and rating will be hurt.

Major Parker has discussed the situation with several of his fellow officers. They have offered possible solutions ranging from punishment to weekly beer parties for relieving tension. Major Parker does not feel that most of these suggestions would have a definite positive effect. If they did, he thinks the effect would be short-lived. However, something has to be done, or there will soon be serious consequences for all concerned.

What design issues are contributing to the problem? After considering alternative strategies, how should Parker proceed?

GALLAGHER CONSTRUCTION COMPANY

Gallagher Construction Company is a small commercial contractor. The company's yearly volume is around $3 million, with an average of six jobs in progress at any one time.

Partners Mike and Paddy Gallagher have recently hired Dick Smith as a project manager. In addition to such activities as keeping job records, writing contracts for subcontractors, selecting suppliers, producing shop drawings, and approving pur-

(continued)

chase orders, one of Smith's important functions is to serve as the link between the Gallagher brothers and the job superintendents. Before Smith was hired, the superintendents dealt directly with the Gallaghers.

The Gallagher Construction superintendents have a great deal of independence in handling a job. They schedule and coordinate the subcontractors selected by the project manager, keep the job on schedule and according to specifications, hire the general labor, keep time records for payroll purposes, and order supplies. The Gallagher brothers always tried to treat the superintendents as equal partners in charge of field operations, making decisions by consensus instead of direct order. Dick Smith uses this same approach. However, in the event of disagreement, the project manager is supposed to have the final word.

A conflict has developed between Dick Smith and one of the superintendents, Bill Brownell. In his early fifties, Brownell has been a superintendent with Gallagher Construction for five years. He has not gladly accepted Smith's authority as project manager and at times takes his problems directly to "the boss," as he refers to senior partner Mike Gallagher. The senior partner has tried to discourage Brownell from jumping the lines of authority, because the most important reason for hiring project manager Smith was to relieve the Gallaghers from the pressures of handling day-to-day problems. However, the relationship between Brownell and Gallagher developed over the years, and Gallagher finds changing it difficult.

Brownell is a competent, cost-conscious superintendent. He can be trusted to keep a job going on schedule without pressure from the office. He is proud of his work crew, and they are extremely loyal to him. Smith has observed that from time to time, when no more work on the job is available, Brownell lets the men loaf around or leave for the day, without reporting the fact to the office. This practice is one way of reinforcing their loyalty to him.

Brownell wants to run his crew without any interference from the managerial level. If Smith so much as asks one of Brownell's men a casual question, Brownell objects that Smith is not using the proper line of authority. Brownell's particular quirk is that he clearly sees the line of authority below him but does not see it above him. However, he is always fairly polite to Smith, and he does get results.

At project manager Smith's recommendation, the Gallaghers have decided to collect daily data from each job, showing the number of hours worked by laborers, mechanics, and foremen, and the specific types and quantities of work completed. These reports are designed to establish unit costs for specific parts of a job so that future bids on jobs will be more accurate. Before requiring these reports, the company had simply relied on experience to make bids. As bidding became more competitive, the Gallaghers recognized the need for cost figures when Smith pointed that need out to them. Now, Brownell has refused to keep daily reports of labor and material used on the jobs he supervises.

When Smith questioned Brownell about the lack of reports, Brownell did not reply directly. Instead he said, "In order for me to know where I can save the company money, I need to get from you a breakdown of how much you estimated each operation was going to cost when you submitted the bid for a job. That's the only way I know where we can save some money."

Smith regarded this request as highly unusual. He replied, "Bill, we don't have the data in that form, but I suppose we could do some calculations for the next couple of days and come up with the numbers. But I can't drop everything to do that. Anyway, you've always done a good job of holding down field costs without that information. And you've got to be just as cost-conscious about each operation on the job, no matter what we estimated that operation would cost when we made the bid."

Brownell said, "I don't see that as a very helpful answer, and if I can't get a cost breakdown, you'll get no daily reports from me."

Smith took the problem to Mike Gallagher, who said that the request was unreasonable and that he would get Brownell to produce the reports. Gallagher spoke to Brownell and then got back with Smith: "You will get reports from Brownell, and if you don't, start looking for another superintendent."

Smith did not get the reports, submitted some names of possible replacements for Brownell, waited—and heard nothing. Smith felt that the Gallaghers were not supporting him, so he stopped asking Brownell for reports.

Two months went by. The company began bidding for more and more jobs, and the Gallaghers realized that they simply had to get reports from all superintendents. Paddy Gallagher went to see Brownell and, as a result of their conference, Brownell began submitting reports. They were not in good order. They usually gave about half of the information needed. In addition, Brownell usually penciled in an unpleasant comment or two. One day he included among the penciled notes the fact that his resignation would be effective in three months, when the current project ended.

The Gallaghers do not know what to do. Good construction superintendents are scarce, and Brownell is good. Many companies advertise widely in major cities hoping to attract capable superintendents. The Gallaghers do not want to lose Brownell, but they do not want to put up with his insubordination any longer because they see how useful timely reports can be.

What should the Gallaghers do?

FLINT HILL SECURITIES

Flint Hill Securities operates seven branch offices that conduct a general brokerage business in stocks, bonds, and commodities. Annual commission business has increased from $4 million to $73 million over the past 15 years, and the partners plan to continue opening branches as population and investment interest in greater Flint Hill increase.

Two years ago, senior partner Smith Hammett noted with alarm a sharp increase in the firm's operating and overhead costs. He was determined to study ways in which the firm might lower these costs, or at least hold the line. Hammett began by taking inspection trips to the branch offices. He quickly saw that much branch office space was being wasted, primarily because the firm's registered representatives had gradually acquired large, expensive pieces of furniture and equipment. Hammett knew that a brokerage firm must keep up a prestigious public appearance, but he felt that the branches had gone too far. In addition, some brokers with large

(continued)

and profitable accounts had insisted on private offices, and managing partners had acceeded to these demands by constructing walls and partitions.

Shortly thereafter Smith Hammett called in his special assistant Tom McKinney and discussed the cost increases with him. He went on, "Tom, Flint Hill Securities has grown so large that we obviously need someone to work full time on our operating methods and facilities. I've talked this situation over with the partners, and we've decided that you are the man to run our new Personnel and Equipment Planning Department. I've recently toured the branches and have concluded that we could save many thousands of dollars a year if we do two things: standardize the furniture and equipment in the branches, and reserve private offices strictly for the managing partners.

"Although I'm pretty sure of some steps that ought to be taken, I don't want to ram anything down the throats of the branches. I want to get their help and participation, not arouse their resentment. So, you'll have a permanent advisory committee made up of one person from each branch. You and that group can be really effective in deciding how we can use our buildings, equipment, and employees more efficiently. Each branch managing partner will appoint a delegate to the committee. When you get your recommendations together, you'll report back to the partners." And so the Operations Advisory Committee was born.

For the next two years, the committee met regularly and worked seriously and enthusiastically. Committee members tried hard to keep their managing partners informed about the committee's activities. Henry Murphy, representative from the Boiling Springs branch, reported back to the committee that he spent at least an hour a week with his boss telling him what the committee was doing and asking for his ideas. His boss was interested not only in the committee's broader recommendations but in the details of committee activities. Other members reported that they too were able to keep their managers informed, and that the managers seemed quite interested in the committee's work. In all branches except Boiling Springs, however, the managing partners did not seem to have the time to hear about the committee's activities to any great extent.

As the committee arrived at its various recommendations, the delegates from the branches reported the recommendations back to their managing partners. Although the partners were willing to listen, they rarely got around to implementing the committee's recommendations.

After two years of work, the committee had compiled hundreds of pages of data and had arrived at 23 recommendations for improving the brokerage firm's operations. The 23 committee recommendations ranged from uniform salary scales and schedules, limited days off for personal business, and centralized purchase of specified typing and dictating equipment for the branches, to a policy on the purchase of janitorial supplies.

The committee members were proud of their work and had obvious high regard for Tom McKinney's leadership. Yet they were concerned that their recommendations were not being implemented in the branches. The committee talked about the best way to get the recommendations adopted. Henry Murphy claimed that his managing partner was ready to put many of them into effect immediately and maintained that it was up to committee members to convince their own managing partners. All the others said that senior partner Smith Hammett should issue the recommendations as directives over his signature. June Carter summed up their reasoning: "We know that the recommendations are best for the firm, but the managing partners have done things in their own way for so long that they don't want to make any changes that they haven't come up with on their own. The only way to get them to cooperate is for Mr. Hammett to say these recommendations are now the firm's official policy and *they are going to go into effect.*"

In his next weekly meeting with Smith Hammett, Tom McKinney reported the committee's strong opinion that Hammett himself should sponsor the recommendations. Mr. Hammett was not thoroughly convinced: "Tom, I know that you and I have discussed the committee's work briefly each week, but even so, I'm a little hazy on the recommendations. I'll tell you what. Let's hold a joint meeting of the committee and the firm's partners so that we can all go over the recommendations together. By the way, whatever happened to my suggestion that we standardize the equipment and furniture in the branches and dismantle the private offices that those registered reps wangled for themselves?"

McKinney said, "To tell you the truth, Mr. Hammett, the committee had so many issues to deal with that it didn't tackle those problems."

Hammett expressed his disappointment: "Tom, your committee could have done some really useful work on those questions. I hope you'll get them on your agenda as soon as possible. The branches simply do not need all that fancy equipment and furniture. And a broker needs to be accessible to the client, not hidden away in an office reading the *Wall Street Journal.*" McKinney assured Hammett that those two issues would be on an upcoming committee agenda.

Hammett sent out a notice of the meeting to the members of the partnership and to the committee members, including a list of the 23 recommendations.

Just before the meeting began, Hammett called Tom McKinney into his office for a brief review of the final recommendations. McKinney explained to Hammett the reasons for each recommendation and indicated how it would help the bank to reduce costs.

While Hammett and McKinney were engaged in that review, two members of the Flint Hill Securities partnership were having lunch at a nearby restaurant. They discussed the committee's recommendations informally as they ate.

Bob Higginbotham: Well, Polly, what do you think about the recommendations?
Polly Johnson: Bob, I have a problem with several of them. For starters, I've got several Wharton MBAs who have just about decided to come in as registered rep trainees, but under this proposed salary schedule, I'm going to lose them.
Bob: Yeah, I think we'll lose more than we gain from a lot of these policy changes. Look at the new days-off policy. My best young commodities broker spends more time out of the office than in it. When she came on board, I told her to get out into the community and meet people; join the tennis club; get involved in United Way. That's where you get the clients, not sitting in the office waiting for walk-in business. But under this new policy, I'll have to charge her with a day off whenever she's not in the office for a certain number of hours.

(continued)

Polly: Actually, Bob, you have a problem with the very policy change I like. If days off are limited and our people know it, they won't keep coming up with these stories about sitting with a sick friend, when I know they're out sailing on the bay. I don't see why we can't go on just as we have for many years—let the branch partners make the decisions on these matters as they see fit, considering local conditions and preferences.

Bob: Say, Polly, do you remember a couple of years ago how hot the old man got about the rosewood desks I ordered for all my staff, and the private offices we set up for some of the high-production brokers? Did the committee have anything to say about that? I don't see any reference in the recommendations.

Polly: I guess they didn't get around to it. But I notice that they got around to deciding on a policy for buying janitorial supplies. This mop or that one; it doesn't really matter to me.

Bob: I wonder what's behind these recommendations, Polly. Don't they trust us out in the branches? After all, we're partners in this firm. It's our own money we're dealing with. And I treat the money that way.

Polly: Besides, things are going great for the firm. Commission business has gone up steadily. I'm afraid that if we start skimping on furniture and concentrating on janitorial soap powder, we'll lose track of what we're here for: to be the best brokerage firm in the greater Flint Hill area. Well, we'd better get on over to the meeting. Maybe once I hear the committee's reasoning on some of these things, I'll be able to accept them.

Senior partner Smith Hammett started the meeting promptly. He asked Tom McKinney to read the 23 recommendations rapidly and then opened the floor for discussion. The first two recommendations dealt with uniform salary schedules and days off with pay. The general reaction of the partners was that the recommendations—in the abstract—would be beneficial to the firm: with uniform salary schedules, all employees in all branches would be treated the same; with a strict days-off policy, all employees would know just where they stood on this issue. However, the partners seemed to feel that their own branch offices would be damaged more than helped by implementation of these two proposed policies. The meeting was scheduled for two hours. It lasted three hours, the participants discussed only these 2 of the 23 recommendations, and they came to no agreement on those 2.

After the meeting, Hammett asked Tom McKinney to stay for a conference. Hammett spoke: "Tom, you know that I have confidence in you. That's why I asked you to head up the Personnel and Equipment Planning Department; that's why I asked you to lead the Operations Advisory Committee. But I must say that the partners impressed me with their objections to your recommendations on this salary thing. And you didn't fare any better with your days-off policy. I know you've done a lot of work on these matters, Tom, but did the committee really think through these policy changes before bringing them to the partnership? If so, why couldn't you convince the partners? Maybe you need to go back to the drawing board and research these problems more thoroughly."

"Mr. Hammett, I can understand why you feel that way, and I'm not sure what went wrong in there. These are good recommendations; they will save the firm money, without any loss of dignity or appearance. Maybe it's like some committee members said—the partners have been used to doing things in the same old way for so long that they aren't going to learn any new tricks unless you put on the pressure."

Though neither would admit it aloud, Tom McKinney and Smith Hammett were both thoroughly discouraged. They sat silently, each with the same thought in mind: The committee had been in existence for two years without a single one of its recommendations being implemented.

What went wrong? What now?

Contingency Factors

in Organization

Theory

PART

4

*T*he OT-Model on the inside covers contains five differentiating concepts and five integrating concepts—most of them contributed originally by the classical school. Up to this point, we have developed these ten concepts from the classical, human relations, and modern perspectives.

An organization's uses of these concepts reflect internal decisions made by the organization's dominant coalition, seeking to reach its goals. This coalition has a great deal of freedom in making decisions about centralization versus decentralization, participative management versus authoritarian management, proportion of line versus staff, and so on. Thus far, we have considered only one major constraint upon the dominant group's freedom: the need to attract members to the organization by offering them inducements to join. In the discussion of the modern approach to each of these structural dimensions, forces other than the demands and desires of organization members were occasionally noted, but they were not discussed specifically and fully.

In Part 4, we open up the discussion to those other significant influences upon organizational design. As the OT-Model reflects, these influences—sometimes called contingency factors—are the organization's *size, technology, environment,* and *life-cycle stage.* Most of the material falling under these four headings could perhaps be placed in one huge category called "everything beyond the immediate control of the organizational designer," because the four topics are definitionally imprecise and, to an extent, arbitrary. Nonetheless, these categories have arisen in the modern era as ways to pigeonhole knowledge, classify hypotheses, and narrow research efforts down into less-than-lifelong undertakings. Chapters 14 through 17 are devoted to these four topics.

Size, technology, environment, and life-cycle stage each represent part of the organizational uncertainty that moderates the ability of the dominant coalition to reach its goals. The faster these influences change, the more uncertainty with which the organization will have to cope.

Consider the design of an organization intended to be a self-perpetuating space colony. The designers can think through all of the factors involved: they can determine the organization's size (in view of reproduction and mortality rates, and the limited area in the spacecraft), they can supply its technology, they can predict the environment (outer space) with certainty, and they can estimate or control the organization's life span. Once the factors are analyzed, the designers can develop a design strategy, implement it, and shoot the rocket into space for its trip lasting, say, two centuries.

Now consider the design of an organization that makes cosmetics. The designers know very little about what will happen next in the cosmetics market or what new strategies they will have to adopt in order to cope with change and uncertainty. Social forces may cause people to abandon cosmetics; the government may control or seize cosmetics; researchers may find that lipstick and rouge cause obesity; the competition may introduce a superior, less expensive cosmetic; the organization's most creative people may quit. If any one or a combination of these developments occurs, the organization will have to respond in some way.

Of course, organizations and their designers are not totally at the mercy of changes in organizational size, technology, environment, or life-cycle stage. Understanding and keeping track of these factors allow the development of coping strategies. If an organization experiences frequent government interference, for example, it can establish an Office of Government Interference Prediction and Control to anticipate and cope with this factor.

Size

Size is an important characteristic of all organizations. By examining the relationship between size and other organizational components, we can more fully understand different organizational structures and problems. Even the most casual observer perceives that organizations of different sizes have different structures. The local bakery and the Wonder Bread division of Continental Baking are structured differently. This chapter's focus is to examine differences in structure that are due to size alone.

The analogy between human and organizational systems and structures can help us to perceive the relationship between size and structure. As the human grows from infancy to adulthood, changes in absolute size are accompanied by structural changes—the arms and legs become longer, the trunk expands. Once the human system has matured, increases or decreases in size or bulk are not so directly accompanied by structural changes.

We will again use Paul Revere and his silver bowl shop—this time to illustrate some effects of increasing size on the organization—and then discuss several ways of defining and measuring size. The rest of the chapter presents results of numerous research studies exploring the relationship between organizational size and structure. In particular, size is seen to affect the number of levels in the organizational hierarchy, degree of centralization/decentralization, formality of organizational procedures, percentage of administrators to nonadministrators, and stress levels of the organization's members.

HOW ORGANIZATIONS GROW

Paul Revere and his silver bowl manufacturing operation can once more illustrate principles of how organizations develop. We shall use it to examine how growth from small size to large size affects the developing organization's structure. Let us assume that the demand for Paul's silver bowls increases rapidly—so much so that he cannot meet the demand by working alone. Paul could decide that his one-man operation should grow no more; he could manufacture bowls at his own pace and sell them to customers willing to wait. On the other hand, he could choose to grow by adding personnel, equipment, or both.

If he adds more people or new machines, he must now *differentiate* the tasks to be performed. Previously, he did everything himself. Now he must either instruct and supervise a helper, or introduce a helper-machine somewhere within the total bowl-making task sequence. Because bowl-making equipment was nonexistent, not available, or too hard to devise, Paul would probably have hired a helper. With the new person comes a new problem for Paul: coordination. Paul doubles his staff but he may not double the organization's productivity because he must give up some of his own bowl-making time to instruct, direct, and control his helper.

As Paul hires more people in response to a growing market for bowls, he must further differentiate bowl-making tasks and responsibilities into smaller and more specialized units or functions. He may hire a bowl seller, a silver buyer, a firewood gatherer, and so on, as he passes along the unskilled and uninteresting tasks to others and retains the skilled aspects of bowl production for himself. Eventually, Paul (and many others who set up small businesses) will realize that he is spending more time in supervising and controlling, differentiating and integrating, than he is spending on personal production. At that point he must decide whether he is going to be a crafts-man, or a manager, or stop growing.

If Paul decides to grow, then he must either hire skilled craftsmen to make bowls under his supervision or break up bowl production into highly specialized, easily learned tasks and hire less skilled people to do those tasks. His next step will be determined by his own preferences, the availability of craftsmen, how readily bowl making can be broken down into specialized subunits, and the volume of demand for finished bowls.

As the bowl shop grows, Paul will need to coordinate and integrate increasing numbers of people and tasks. Larger size will also bring potential communication problems, competition for resources among the organization's units, interpersonal conflicts, and other related difficulties. Communications channels, delegation, decentralization, committee use, and many other organizational aspects will be affected by increasing size.

The point of this silversmithing example is that no matter what other factors affect organizational design and shape, sheer size (or lack of it) exerts pressure that causes large organizations and small organizations to structure themselves differently. And this result is true for churches, sophisticated electronics manufacturers, governments, and silver bowl factories.

DEFINING AND MEASURING SIZE

In the Paul Revere example, we used the term "size" rather loosely. For more serious discussion, we need a more precise definition, and arriving at one is more difficult than it might at first appear. What is large or small size? Is IBM larger than the Baptist Church? Is Mary's Deli smaller than Sam's Dry Cleaning?

The Size Continuum

One way to illustrate largeness and smallness is to place similar organizations on a continuum. Figure 14.1 presents a simplified continuum of six computer organizations arranged by size. As the figure shows, IBM is acknowledged to be the largest of the six computer manufacturers. Aser Technologies, a relative newcomer to the field, is much smaller than the others. The remaining organizations fall somewhere in between. Even though persons familiar with the computer industry would probably agree about where the six companies fall on the continuum, we have not answered this basic question: *How* is IBM larger than the rest? Is the measure of largeness gross revenues? Assets? The number of units sold last year? The number of full-time employees?

Financial Measures

Some researchers use financial measures of size, such as assets, profits, or dollar sales. The arrangement in Figure 14.1 is based on gross sales in dollars. These financial measures can be helpful when undertaking *economic* investigations of organizations. Investment analysis, for instance, properly places more emphasis on financial measures than on others. But when we study an organization's internal structural components, the financial measures lose their usefulness. Enormous financial resources could be tied up in a very small, simple organization (like a diamond dealership) with few activities. On the other hand, some very large organizations with many activities (like the Boy Scouts) require only moderate financial resources. Using financial measures to reflect size leads to "apples-and-oranges" comparisons that do not help us to study organizational design or to develop a theory of organizations.

Social Measures

For our purposes, the human aspects of an organization are more meaningful than the financial aspects, because we are focusing on the social components of organizational structure. As a matter of fact, many studies have found a high degree of association between the financial and social measures. D.S. Pugh and his colleagues, collectively known as the "Aston group," discovered high positive relationships between three organizational characteristics: number of employees, assets, and sales. Since the three are closely related, perhaps we could use any one of them. Yet, the social indicators are more meaningful in organization theory work than the financial measures, since as a rule the more employees there are, the more different activities there are to organize.

Full-time Employees   For the preceding reasons, most researchers in the organization theory field use the term "size" to refer to *how many people work full time for an*

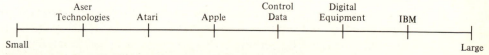

Figure 14.1 Organizational size continuum: Computer companies.

organization. Size in this sense has the greatest effect on the concerns and problems examined by organization theorists.

A word of caution: Because "size" has more than one meaning, we must know how size is defined in order to understand any study purporting to show a relationship between size and other organizational characteristics. In her study of different size measures, Nina Gupta makes this observation:

> A potential explanation for the contradictory evidence with respect to the size effect may rest with the appropriateness of the definition of size to the other variables of interest. For example, number of employees may be related to organizational climate, energic input to perceived task characteristics, and activity cycles to organizational technology. Obviously, it is impossible to isolate these differential relationships with the use of only one definition of size.[1]

SIZE AND STRUCTURE

Durkheim: Population and the Division of Labor

Emile Durkheim was among the first to propose a relationship between size and structure.[2] He pointed out that as a society's total population increases, so does the division of labor into specialties. Although these changes accompany each other, the relationship is not always linear. The society or other organization eventually reaches a saturation point (what economists call the point of diminishing returns) after which further size increases do *not* lead to further increases in the division of labor.

Blau: Size Affects Structure

Peter Blau has developed the principle that size affects structure in some detail. His theory advances the following major ideas.[3]

1. An *increase* in organizational size will lead to an *increase* in the differentiation of organizational effort (further specialization of labor, more spatial dispersion of work sites, new departments and divisions, more levels in the organizational hierarchy of authority), although at a *declining* rate. This proposition points out, first, that larger size usually affords the opportunity to subdivide activities into smaller component parts. Working by himself, Paul Revere had to perform all silver bowl manufacturing activities. As his market grew and his business volume increased, he hired more workers and assigned them to new subdivisions or subcomponents of the total manufacturing process. If demand for bowls increased even more, those subcomponents would become further specialized; rather than the one wood chopper he initially hired to help him out, he would employ a Wood Procurement Unit—with a Tree Identification Specialist, a Chopper Specialist, a Branch Trimmer, a Wood Shavings Remover, and so on. Booming business might lead Paul to create 10, 20, or 50 more Wood Procurement Units all performing the same functions, but within each unit a point would be reached beyond which labor could no longer be sensibly specialized. For example, it would be absurd for Paul to hire different specialists to remove the large, medium, and small wood shavings.

2. Blau's first proposition suggested that an increase in organizational size leads to more organizational subunits. An increase in size will also lead to larger size of the individual subunits and to a wider managerial span of control. Rather than adding more managers, a growing organization will at first allow each manager's span of control to widen. But a manager's span of control cannot continue to widen indefinitely. Eventually, the organization will have to reorganize its structure by adding a new management layer, to accommodate the new employees and to reduce span of managerial control back to a more desirable level.

3. Blau also proposed that as larger size leads to more structural differentiation, the ratio of administrators to nonadministrators becomes larger. This point will be developed later in the chapter.

A Curvilinear Relationship   In essence, Blau is saying that increasing size produces increases in structural differentiation—more different specialties, more different departments, more different administrative ranks. But at some point, size continues *to increase* while structural differentiation *levels off.* Figure 14.2 presents a simplified model of Blau's theory. As we go up the curve, size increases and so does structural differentiation, but at a declining rate. At point *x,* structure has become constant and stable; it will stay that way even if size increases further. Blau's basic hypothesis is that *changes in size cause changes in structure.*

The Aston Group

D.S. Pugh's "Aston group" proposed seven primary influences on organizations (including size) and used them to predict three dimensions of organizational structure: structuring of activities, concentration of authority, and line control of workflow.[4] Their research showed that size was *the major predictor* of structure.

Inkson's Ratchet

J.H.K. Inkson cautioned that changes in size and structure might not always occur simultaneously.[5] Long-run structural changes may occur with changes in size. But in the short run, a "ratchet mechanism" may be at work. Although adding new people is often associated with new departments, new specialties, or new branch offices, a

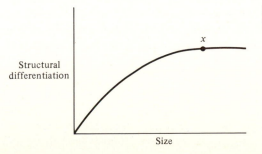

Figure 14.2 A simplified model of Blau's theory.

reduction in the number of employees may not lead to abandoning the newer specialties or closing the newer departments or branches. The "ratchet mechanism" holds the structure constant while the work force declines.

Meyer's Study over Time

Most studies in the 1960s and 1970s proposed that a certain size *causes* a certain structure even though the size and structure were examined at the same time. Marshall Meyer's work is important because it examines changes in size and structure over a five-year period.[6] Meyer studied 194 municipal finance departments in 1966 and again in 1971. Finding a positive relationship between size in 1966 and number of divisions in 1971, he concluded that organizational size at one point predicts number of organizational divisions at a later point. He tested for the reverse—present number of divisions can predict future size—and found no supporting evidence.

The National Study

John Child's "National Study" of 82 diverse organizations, replicating the Aston group's research, also found size and structural complexity to be related.[7] In his own study, the Aston study, and the Blau/Schoenherr study, Child found high correlations between size and (1) functional specialization (number of divisions or departments) and (2) role specialization (number of job specialties). The National and Aston samples were mixed, containing both manufacturing and nonmanufacturing organizations; the Blau/Schoenherr study used only government agencies.

Hall: A Weak Association

Richard H. Hall and his colleagues came to a different conclusion: If a size-structure relationship does exist, it is at best a weak one:

> Blau et al. have indicated that structural differentiation is a *consequence* of expanding size. Our study suggests that it is relatively rare that the two factors are even associated and thus the temporal sequence or causality (expanding size produces greater differentiation) posited by Blau and his colleagues is open to question.[8]

Within 75 organizations, Hall examined the relationship between size and three measures of organizational complexity: horizontal differentiation, hierarchical differentiation, and spatial dispersion. Because the associations were so weak, though positive, Hall concluded that a relationship between size and structural complexity had not been demonstrated.

Armandi: A Linear Relationship

In a study of 104 New York savings and loan associations, Barry Armandi found support for Blau's general proposition that size changes lead to structural changes.[9]

Blau, however, suggested that as new people are added, new specialties will also be added but at a *declining* rate. Armandi found that new people and new specialties increased *at about the same rate.* The two sets of findings are reflected in Figure 14.3.

Explaining the Differences   Differences in the Blau and Armandi samples may have caused the different results. The 50 government agencies studied by Blau averaged 1194 employees. The 104 associations studied by Armandi averaged 53 employees. The organizations in the Blau study were mature, stable, and no longer growing. Also, being federal agencies, these organizations could expand only if granted more money. Armandi's savings and loan associations were growing, and their growth rates could change drastically with increases in savings activity. These findings suggest that smaller organizations in the earlier stages of the life cycle and more mature organizations change structurally at different rates.

Aldrich: Structure Affects Size

The Aston studies indicated that size is an independent variable: size changes *lead to* structural changes. Howard E. Aldrich reexamined the Aston data and proposed that *technology* is the *independent* variable and *size* the *dependent* variable.[10] According to Aldrich, "Structuring of activities is presumed to have a positive impact on size because the more highly structured firms, with their greater degree of specialization, formalization, and monitoring of role performance, simply need to employ a larger work force than less structured firms."[11] Aldrich's point is that organizations don't hire people and then say, "Let's increase the number of departments and divisions, and find new, special jobs for these new employees." Rather, the organization first decides to have new tasks, or departments, or divisions, and then finds the qualified people it needs.

The hypothesis of Blau and the Aston group is that *changes in size cause changes in structure.* Aldrich's hypothesis is that *changes in structure* (often brought about by changes in technology) *cause changes in size.*

Explaining the Differences   These apparently contradictory hypotheses can perhaps be reconciled. *Small* organizations seem to expand horizontally—adding new jobs,

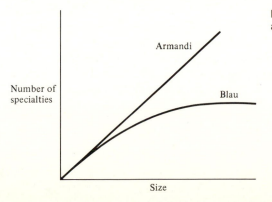

Figure 14.3 Size and specialties: Blau and Armandi.

departments, or divisions, then hiring the personnel to fill them. After small organizations become large and achieve a certain stable structure, they add new people to staff *vertical* expansion (new layers of management in the hierarchy of authority). Small organizations expand outward; large organizations expand upward.

During recessions, organizations will usually decrease size (cut personnel) first, leading to newspaper stories on the high unemployment rate. If business worsens, organizations follow up these personnel cuts with structural changes—eliminating jobs, departments, divisions, and/or levels.

We might oversimplify these size-structure findings this way:

1. In bad times, decreases in size may eventually lead to structural changes for large and small organizations.
2. In good times:
    a. Large organizations increase their size, then change the structure by increasing the number of managerial levels.
    b. Small organizations expand structure horizontally, then increase size to fill up the structure.
3. At some point, as Blau maintains, increasing size has no further effect on structure.

SIZE AND THE HIERARCHY

Parkinson's Law

One of the earliest principles relating organizational size to structure can be credited to C. Northcote Parkinson. His now-famous "Parkinson's Law" states that "Work expands so as to fill the time available for its completion."[12] Since work (especially paperwork) is so expandable, "there need be little or no relationship between the work to be done and the size of the staff to which it may be assigned."[13]

Parkinson evolved his law by observing the English bureaucracy and examining British Navy and Colonial Office statistics from 1914 to 1954. Parkinson noted that over the 1914–1928 period, the number of British warships dropped from 62 to 20, and yet the number of admiralty officials rose by more than 75 percent. For the purposes of our discussion, Parkinson's most important point is that "administrators are more or less bound to multiply,"[14] no matter how much work (if any) needs to be done.

Consider administrator Tom Brown, whose work has expanded to fill his workday. For whatever reason—perhaps because middle age has decreased his energy but his work to be done remains the same—he believes himself to be overworked. Rather than resign or share the work with a colleague of equal rank, Brown demands at least two assistants, Jones and Smith (never just one, for reasons that Parkinson makes clear). When Assistant Smith inevitably complains of being overworked, as her work expands to fill her available time, Administrator Brown advises that Smith should have two assistants. To keep the peace, Assistant Jones also gets additional help from two assistants. These seven people are now doing the work that Administrator Brown used to do, and furthermore they make so much work for each other—in the form of memos, reports, and files to be written and read—that they, and their proliferating counterparts in the organization's other units, keep busy all day long.

In this fashion, according to Parkinson, the administrative staff of most organizations increases from 5.17 to 6.56 percent per year, regardless of the work (if any) to be done. We can easily see why Parkinson subtitled his law "The Rising Pyramid."

More People, More Levels   Many researchers have tested Parkinson's findings and have supported his conclusion: more people mean more levels.[15] To illustrate: XYZ Corporation foresees increasing demand for its product and begins adding employees. Existing managers become overburdened as their spans of control widen. They request and receive permission to subdivide their duties and appoint assistant managers to help them. These assistant managers become a new level in the hierarchy.

Conversely, in difficult times the organization reduces its size by eliminating jobs, divisions, departments, and branches. Personnel cuts mean shrinking spans of control. After the shifting and combining of units and responsibilities are over, some managers—having no one left to manage—are transferred or laid off. The result may well be fewer managers and fewer management levels.

In either case, the relationship between size and number of levels in the hierarchy is positive: size increases are accompanied by more levels; size decreases are accompanied by fewer levels.

SIZE AND CENTRALIZATION

Numerous studies have shown a *negative* relationship between *increasing* size and *increasing* centralization of decision making.[16] Larger size gives rise to conditions that encourage organization-wide delegation of authority.

The Organization Itself

This negative relationship is understandable. As more employees are hired, personalized supervision becomes increasingly difficult and so the overall organization becomes more difficult to control. In order to coordinate work activities more effectively, management systematically delegates decision-making authority to lower levels. Such organization-wide delegation of authority is one type of decentralization.

The Organization's Units

The negative relationship between size and centralization holds true not only for the organization as a whole but for the units within it as well. For instance, an increased demand for its services leads a branch of a bank to hire more people. Swamped with new banking business and new personnel, the branch manager appoints the head teller to act with managerial authority in opening new accounts and granting credit up to a reasonable level. This delegation of authority releases the manager to concentrate on more important customers.

SIZE AND FORMALIZATION

Most researchers agree that as organizational size increases, so do formal procedures.[17] No matter what kinds of organizations are studied—government agencies, savings and loan associations, British and American manufacturing companies, or service organizations—the same conclusion emerges.

As an organization adds people, control and communication become more difficult. Standardization becomes the solution. To control the behavior of so many members, the organization issues formal written policies, procedures, rules, and regulations. The lines of communication are also formalized. "You must go through the proper channels" is an admonition frequently heard in organizations, especially bureaucracies.

In large organizations this formal, impersonalized, "big-brother" atmosphere is necessary to help coordinate employee activities. If formal standards exist, deviations can be easily perceived and corrective action quickly taken.

Smaller organizations also need to control employees and communicate with them, but with fewer people, control and consistency are more easily achieved. Managers can communicate with employees one-on-one, face-to-face—rather than issuing manuals of rules and policies.

Size and Structure Summarized

The organization theory literature contains understandable and consistent findings on the size-structure relationship. Larger size does lead to more substructures within the overall organizational structure. Furthermore, larger organizations have more complex structural dimensions (such as division of labor, horizontal and vertical differentiation, and spatial dispersion), are more decentralized, and are more formal.

SIZE AND ADMINISTRATORS

More Administrators

Size increases lead eventually to more administrators and more administrative levels. But do size increases lead to a higher or a lower *percentage* of administrators?

Some of the earliest work on this relationship was done by Frederic W. Terrien and Donald L. Mills.[18] In their study of 428 California school districts, they found that *larger* districts had a *higher* percentage of administrators. These districts reacted to growth by adding administrators who either served as subordinates of existing administrators or headed up new divisions and departments. The result of these actions was a larger percentage of administrators as size increased.

Fewer Administrators

Theodore R. Anderson and Seymour Warkov tested the conclusion reached by Terrien and Mills.[19] In their study of 49 Veterans Administration hospitals, they came up with quite unexpected results: the larger hospitals had a *smaller* percentage of administrators.

Explaining the Differences   Anderson and Warkov presented the following propositions to explain the different results.

1. Same Job, Same Place: The percentage of administrators *decreases* as the number of persons performing *identical tasks* in the *same place* increases (as was true at the VA hospitals).
2. Same Job, Different Place: The percentage of administrators *increases* as the number of *different work locations* increases (as was true in the school districts).
3. Same Place, Different Tasks: The percentage of administrators *increases* as the number of *tasks* performed at the same place increases (or as roles become increasingly specialized and differentiated).

According to Terrien and Mills, larger size means a larger percentage of administrators. According to Anderson and Warkov, *if* larger size means more tasks done in more places, then the percentage of administrators in the organization will rise.

Decreasing Size

Do decreases in size lead to a smaller percentage of administrators? Apparently not. As numbers of employees decrease, numbers of administrators also decrease—but *not as rapidly.* This lag results in a higher percentage of administrators no matter what the organization's size before the decrease.

When organizations cut back on nonadministrators in severe times, they do not cut back as much on administrators. Perhaps they view the bad times as a temporary quirk—to be followed by good times when they will need experienced administrators. Or perhaps they feel the need for creative administrative talent to get through the bad times. For whatever reason, size-administrator relationships are different in good and bad times.

Freeman and Hannan: Growth and Decline   John Freeman and Michael T. Hannan studied size-administrator relationships in 769 California school districts between 1968 and 1972, a period of both economic good times and bad times.[20] They found that the school districts added people in all categories during growth periods but were reluctant to shed excess employees, administrators in particular, during periods of decline.

Long Island Lighting: The Wrong Cutbacks?   The dangers of cutting back on the wrong groups are illustrated in the experience of Long Island Lighting over a 25-year period. During 1960 to 1975 the company added people at all levels, a disproportionately large number of them at supervisory and administrative levels. When controversy over the company's Shoreham nuclear reactor led to a decline in profits, the company began cutting back on personnel. Most cuts were made in positions that were at lower organizational levels but were important to smooth organizational functioning: linemen, tree cutters, electricians, and so on. The company's reluctance to fire managers was apparent.

In September 1985 when Hurricane Gloria devastated Long Island, the company could not respond; it did not have enough field personnel. Many areas were without electricity for 7 to 12 days. To get the system back together, Long Island Lighting had to hire crews from Pennsylvania, New Jersey, and Virginia. Long Island Lighting's cutbacks seem to have been in the wrong areas.

Cullen et al.: Size in Universities   In a sample of 134 Ph.D.-granting universities, John B. Cullen and his associates found, as Blau had theorized, that increasing size led to increasing structural differentiation.[21] Yet in times of decline, a mixed result occurred. Differentiation decreased as size declined, but at a lower rate. And administrative size did not decline in numbers or percentage. In fact, many universities added *more* administrators, "perhaps to reform their organizations and stem the loss of students."[22]

Type of Organization

Studies relating size to administration may be affected by the type of organization being examined. Is the organization a school, a government, a corporation? The answer may affect the study's outcome.

If an organization is in decline and its size is decreasing, a reduction in number of administrators might be expected. In his study of school districts, however, Jeffrey D. Ford found that as school district enrollments decreased, administrators tended to be *added,* not reduced as we might expect.[23] How do the school districts justify large numbers of administrators when times are bad?

Two facts account for this surprising trend. First, school districts are experienced and ingenious at finding funds, especially federal monies, with which to pay administrative salaries and other expenses. According to Ford, revenues from all sources actually increased in the declining school districts studied. Second, school districts are often locked into long-term collective bargaining agreements and tenure policies that protect the jobs of teachers even in hard times. As enrollments decline, surplus teachers are often given administrative jobs.

The effect of alternative public funding sources and long-term retention contracts and policies is to retain and even add to "administrative fat" despite declining enrollments. In contrast, private businesses concerned about profits would quickly identify and cut loose the excess administrative baggage.

Especially when examining declining organizations, we need to keep organizational type constantly in mind to avoid drawing conclusions that may not have general application.

SIZE AND STRESS

Kahn: Size Affects Stress

Does organizational size affect the stress levels of organizational members? Robert L. Kahn and his associates showed in 1964 that larger organizations are more stressful to members than smaller organizations.[24] The stress level stays more or less constant as organizational size grows to 50 employees, begins to increase as organizational size reaches 50 to 100 employees, and continues rising up to about 5000 employees, where the stress curve levels off.

Positive Stress?   The attitude today is that stress does have some positive benefits. A certain amount of stress keeps the human system alert and motivates organizational members to be productive. Of course, too much stress is harmful.

Stress Reduction

Certain developments of the last (and perhaps the next) 20 years are capable of reducing harmful stress levels in organizations. A major cause of stress in large organizations is the difficulty of coordinating so many people. Giving organizational subunits more independence through decentralization can reduce coordination requirements and the stress levels of some employees—though the unit head, with consequently greater responsibility, may well be more highly stressed.

Another relevant development is the computer revolution. Personal computers, inexpensive microcomputers, and terminals make working at home more convenient than ever before. The near future may see more and more employees of large organizations working at home—away from much organizational stress. Likewise, the rebirth of "cottage industries" and the trend toward a service-oriented economy may make working for large organizations less stressful in the future.[25] Working at home is more comfortable. Workers can take breaks, do different tasks to break the monotony, and interact with family members if they desire. In short, the worker controls the environment, thereby reducing stress and anxiety.

SUMMARY

Organizational size and structure appear to be related. The nature of that relationship has been of continuing interest to modern organization theorists. They usually define and measure an organization's size as the number of full-time employees.

Emile Durkheim observed that a growing society divides its labor activities into specialties up to the point of diminishing returns. Using that principle as a base, Peter Blau maintained that structural differentiation increases within growing organizations, at a declining rate. Blau's basic hypothesis is that size changes cause structural changes. The Aston group concurred that size is the major predictor of structure. However, Howard E. Aldrich reexamined the Aston data and concluded that technology affects structure, which then affects size. J.H.K. Inkson observed that a "ratchet mechanism" keeps declining size from having as great an effect on structure as increasing size does. Marshall Meyer's study of size and structure at five-year intervals demonstrated the effect of size on structure (number of organizational divisions) over time. John Child's "National Study" also found size and structural complexity to be related.

Richard H. Hall's study of 75 organizations is one of the few to doubt the positive relationship between size and structural complexity. Barry Armandi found that as the size of savings and loan associations increased, so did structural differentiation (new job specialties)—at about the same rate. Blau had noted that such specialties were added at a declining rate to the government agencies that he studied. The different results were probably caused by differences in average organizational size (53 for the S&L's and 1194 for the government agencies), funding sources (private versus public), and life-cycle stage (growing versus mature).

C. Northcote Parkinson and others have shown that size increases are accompanied by more levels in the organizational hierarchy and size decreases by fewer levels. Larger size seems to go hand in hand with increased decentralization, formalization, and stress levels. Increases or decreases in size lead to more or fewer administrators, but the relationship between size and *percentage* of administrators is not clear-cut; it apparently depends on such factors as organization type and whether total size is increasing or decreasing.

DISCUSSION QUESTIONS

1. How is organizational size best measured?
2. According to Peter Blau, how does organizational size affect structure?
3. What is "Inkson's ratchet"?
4. What is the significance of Meyer's work on size and structure?
5. According to the National Study, what is the relationship between size and structure? What structural aspects does size affect?
6. What were Howard Aldrich's findings regarding the size-structure relationship?
7. What is Parkinson's Law?
8. Are Parkinson's findings true in the organizations with which you are familiar?
9. Do large and small organizations necessarily have different structures?
10. Consider the five differentiating functions. How do you think each is related to organizational size?
11. Consider the five integrating functions. How do you think each is related to organizational size?
12. Do you think most organizations would be more effective if organizational leaders gave more thought to the size-structure relationship, or should the relationship simply be allowed to develop naturally?
13. Without having read Chapter 15 on technology, do you think that an organization's size or its technology has a greater impact on its structure?

MAXI-TECH COMPUTER

During his time as CEO, Maxi-Tech Computer President Fisher Weber concentrated on conceiving broad marketing strategies and allowed his managers great leeway in executing those plans. Over the firm's most successful four-year period, sales growth averaged a compound rate of 75 percent.

Investors then concluded correctly that Maxi-Tech's go-go years were at an end; the stock plunged from 98½ to 34 in a few months. The company had grown rapidly and successfully; sales for the current year would still be in the $530 million range. Yet Maxi-Tech was no longer the industry trend setter it had been. The board of directors summarily ousted Fisher Weber, at least in part because of "his failure to institute more systematic controls."

Harry Mitchell, the new CEO, moved quickly to bring more management discipline to

Maxi-Tech through long-term planning and stringent management controls. In his first address to top management, he said, "At this point in our history, we need a stronger effort to improve software quality and reliability; closer relationships with third-party systems houses that buy our computers for resale as part of larger systems; development of a national account program; and more efficient manufacturing and order flow. Further, we've got to spend more on research and development. We have traditionally spent only 8 percent of revenues on R&D; that's why our bottom line has been so good. Now we have to spend more on R&D, to compete against the larger companies entering our market. Let me emphasize one final point: When a company reaches the size of Maxi-Tech Computer, it needs lots of structure, discipline, and planning. I intend to introduce and stress those characteristics."

Does Harry Mitchell sound like he's on the right track? What other steps do you think he should take? What kinds of functions should he add?

ADVENTURES IN VENTURES

Ken Bogan, president of Xorex Corp., called Executive Vice President Annette Adler into his office. "Annette," he said, "as you know, we've got a $1.7 billion research budget, so we're capable of undertaking any product development project internally. But I'm impressed by the entrepreneurial environment that smaller companies are able to create. Do you think we could develop such an environment here at Xorex?"

"Ken, we might try to encourage a start-up atmosphere within the company. We could rebuild our product organizations around a series of strategic business units in which small engineering teams compete for the opportunity to take an idea from the concept stage to a feasibility model. We could reward successful project leaders with bonuses, banquets, stock options, personal computers, things like that. The recession has shown how vulnerable some of our existing product lines are. If we don't try something to pick up the slack, we may be in trouble. But to tell you the truth, Ken, I think we're just too big for any internal entrepreneurship."

"Well, Annette, what do you recommend? I still think we can do it internally, but I'm willing to listen to your ideas."

Annette was excited. "I think we should set up a venture-investing operation to tap into innovations outside Xorex. We'll make money *and* speed the process of product development. Our internal development efforts have always been too slow. I think we should buy ourselves some equity—in the 20 to 40 percent range—in smaller technology companies. That way we can use their expertise without acquiring them."

"No, Annette," said Ken, "I'm not comfortable unless we have more control than that. I think outright acquisition is the way to go. I'm for taking over a few entrepreneurial companies. The brilliant, independent individuals in such organizations will benefit from our management control procedures and the organizational structures that have been so successful for us. We'll supply them with reporting procedures, benefit plans, and our own management people. That will leave them free to be creative and innovative, under our supervision of course. What do you think?"

If you were Annette Adler, how would you tactfully explain what the effect of imposing Xorex's organizational strategies on smaller entrepreneurial firms will probably be? Would you continue to recommend venture investing, or would you return to Ken's original idea: internal entrepreneurship?

■ ***ROBEY PAPER COMPANY***

Experienced managers at Robey Paper Company always requested budgets well in excess of what they really needed, in the expectation that their requests would be cut. They always spent slightly more than they were budgeted; they were willing to accept a hand slap for exceeding their budgets in order to make their case for larger budgets next year.

These experienced managers knew that to have fully staffed departments when they needed them, they had to try to hire more people than they might need at a given moment. During the frequent slack times, these extras were given make-work assignments. But during busy periods, the departments used all employees fully.

Dot Rauscher, who came to Robey Paper from a competitor about two years ago, hadn't learned these games yet. She was honest in her budget requests and used company resources wisely. If some of her people seemed not to have enough to do, she allowed other departments to take them. Over her first two years, her department budget and personnel size remained steady.

Unexpected bad times brought a belt-tightening memo from Morris Robey: Every department had to reduce its costs by 15 percent within 90 days.

What could Morris Robey have done to avoid or minimize the problem brought on by hard times? How should Dot Rauscher respond to Robey's directive? Should Rauscher begin dealing with her personnel and resource requests differently? It is said that "every organization has some fat in it." How does that "fat" affect "size" as a "contingency factor"?

NOTES

1. Nina Gupta, "Some Alternative Definitions of Size," *Academy of Management Journal* 23 (December 1980): 764–765.
2. Emile Durkheim, *The Division of Labor in Society,* trans. George Simpson (New York: The Free Press, 1933).
3. Peter Blau, "A Formal Theory of Differentiation in Organizations," *American Sociological Review* 35 (April 1970): 201–208.
4. D.S. Pugh, D.J. Hickson, C.R. Hinings, and C. Turner, "The Context of Organization Structures," *Administrative Science Quarterly* 14 (March 1969): 91–114.
5. J.H.K. Inkson, D.S. Pugh, and D.J. Hickson, "Organizational Context and Structure: An Abbreviated Replication," *Administrative Science Quarterly* 15 (September 1970): 318–329.
6. Marshall Meyer, "Size and the Structure of Organizations: A Causal Analysis," *American Sociological Review* 37 (August 1972): 434–440.
7. John Child, "Predicting and Understanding Organization Structure," *Administrative Science Quarterly* 18 (June 1973): 168–185.
8. Richard H. Hall, J. Eugene Haas, and Norman J. Johnson, "Organizational Size, Complexity and Formalization," *American Sociological Review* 32 (December 1967): 903–912.
9. Barry Armandi, *Organizational Structure and Efficiency* (Washington, DC: University Press of America, 1981).
10. Howard E. Aldrich, "Technology and Organizational Structures: A Re-examination of the Findings of the Aston Group," *Administrative Science Quarterly* 17 (March 1972): 26–43.
11. Ibid., p. 38.
12. C. Northcote Parkinson, *Parkinson's Law* (Boston: Houghton Mifflin, 1957), p. 2.
13. Ibid.

14. Ibid., p. 7.

15. For example, Richard H. Hall, "The Concept of Bureaucracy: An Empirical Assessment," *American Journal of Sociology* 69 (July 1963): 32–40; Peter M. Blau, "The Hierarchy of Authority in Organizations," *American Journal of Sociology* 73 (January 1968): 453–467; Peter M. Blau and Richard A. Schoenherr, *The Structure of Organizations* (New York: Basic Books, 1971); Barry Armandi, *Organizational Structure and Efficiency*; Peter M. Blau, "Interdependence and Hierarchy in Organization," *Social Science Research* 1 (1972): 1–24; D.S. Pugh et al., "The Context of Organization Structures"; C.R. Hinings and G.L. Lee, "Dimensions of Organization Structure and Their Context: A Replication," *Sociology* 5 (January 1971): 83–93; John Child, "Predicting and Understanding Organization Structure."

16. For example, David J. Hickson, D.S. Pugh, and Diana C. Pheysey, "Operations Technology and Organization Structure: An Empirical Reappraisal," *Administrative Science Quarterly* 14 (September 1969): 378–397; C.R. Hinings and G.L. Lee, "Dimensions of Organization Structure and Their Context: A Replication"; Peter Blau and Richard A. Schoenherr, *The Structure of Organizations*; Barry Armandi, *Organizational Structure and Efficiency*; Pradip N. Khandwalla, "Mass Output Orientation of Operations Technology and Organizational Structure," *Administrative Science Quarterly* 19 (March 1974): 74–97.

17. For example, Richard H. Hall, "The Concept of Bureaucracy: An Empirical Assessment"; Richard H. Hall, J. Eugene Haas, and Norman J. Johnson, "Organizational Size, Complexity and Formalization"; David J. Hickson, D.S. Pugh, and Diana C. Pheysey, "Operations Technology and Organization Structure: An Empirical Reappraisal"; C.R. Hinings and G.L. Lee, "Dimensions of Organization Structure and Their Context: A Replication"; John Child, "Predicting and Understanding Organization Structure"; Barry Armandi, *Organizational Structure and Efficiency*.

18. Frederic W. Terrien and Donald L. Mills, "The Effects of Changing Size upon the Internal Structure of Organizations," *American Sociological Review* 20 (February 1955): 11–14.

19. Theodore R. Anderson and Seymour Warkov, "Organizational Size and Functional Complexity: A Study of Administration in Hospitals," *American Sociological Review* 26 (February 1961): 23–28.

20. John Freeman and Michael T. Hannan, "Growth and Decline Processes in Organizations," *American Sociological Review* 40 (April 1975): 215–228.

21. John B. Cullen, Kenneth S. Anderson, and Douglas D. Baker, "Blau's Theory of Structural Differentiation Revisited: A Theory of Structural Change or Scale," *Academy of Management Journal* 29 (June 1986): 203–229.

22. Ibid., p. 223.

23. Jeffrey D. Ford, "The Administrative Component in Growing and Declining Organizations: A Longitudinal Analysis," *Academy of Management Journal* 23 (December 1980): 615–630.

24. Robert L. Kahn et al., *Organizational Stress: Studies in Role Conflict and Ambiguity* (New York: Wiley, 1964).

25. Alvin Toffler aptly noted the potential effects of this phenomenon in his book *The Third Wave* (New York: William Morrow, 1980).

ADDITIONAL READINGS

Beyer, Janice M., and Harrison M. Trice. "A Reexamination of the Relations Between Size and Various Components of Organizational Complexity." *Administrative Science Quarterly* 24 (March 1979): 48–64.

Caplow, Theodore. "Organizational Size." *Administrative Science Quarterly* 2 (March 1957): 484–505.

Gooding, Richard Z., and John A. Wagner III. "A Meta-Analytic Review of the Relationship Between Size and Performance: The Productivity and Efficiency of Organizations and Their Subunits." *Administrative Science Quarterly* 30 (December 1985): 462–481.

Indik, Bernard P. "The Relationship Between Organization Size and Supervision Ratio." *Administrative Science Quarterly* 9 (December 1964): 301–312.

Klatzky, S.R. "Automation, Size, and the Locus of Decision Making: The Cascade Effect." *Journal of Business* 43 (April 1970): 141–151.

——— "The Relationship of Organizational Size to Complexity and Coordination." *Administrative Science Quarterly* 15 (December 1970): 428–438.

Noell, James J. "On the Administrative Sector of Social Systems: An Analysis of the Size and Complexity of Government Bureaucracies in the American States." *Social Forces* 52 (June 1974): 549–558.

Pondy, Louis R. "Effects of Size, Complexity, and Ownership on Administrative Intensity." *Administrative Science Quarterly* 14 (March 1969): 47–61.

Pryor, Frederic L. "Size of Production Establishments in Manufacturing." *The Economic Journal* 82 (June 1972): 547–566.

Rees, R.D. "Optimum Plant Size in United Kingdom Industries: Some Survivor Estimates." *Economica* 40 (November 1973): 394–401.

Rushing, William A. "The Effects of Industry Size and Division of Labor on Administration." *Administrative Science Quarterly* 12 (September 1967): 273–295.

Wittnebert, Fred R. "Bigness Versus Profitability." *Harvard Business Review* 48 (January/February 1970): 158–166.

Technology

Size is one major factor that contributes to the differences in organizational structures. Another major factor is technology. The argument continues as to which is the more important influence. To those favoring technology, the nature of the task is much more significant in determining structure than the size of the organization; small scientific laboratories and big scientific laboratories are structurally much more similar than big laboratories and big banks are.

This chapter will first define "technology" and trace its evolution. Three major systems of describing and categorizing technology will then be explained: those of Joan Woodward, James D. Thompson, and Charles Perrow. Finally, we will examine several studies that explore the link between technology and structure.

THE NATURE OF TECHNOLOGY

Defining Technology

"Technology" has many meanings. This diversity of definitions has led to difficulty in comparing studies of the relationship between technology and structure. To many researchers (and managers), technology refers to an organization's physical capabilities and attributes—its machinery, tools, and equipment. Others insist on considering an organization's knowledge—its know-how—as a part of its technology. Here are some ways in which a number of authors have defined or described technology:

- The knowledge and the methods that are used in transforming materials and other inputs into finished products and services. (N.B. Brown and D.J. Moberg)
- The set of man-machine activities which together produce a desired good or service. (J.D. Thompson and F.L. Bates)
- The tools used and the specialized ideas needed in getting particular kinds of work done. (R. Dubin)

- The actions that an individual performs upon an object, with or without the aid of tools or mechanical devices, in order to make some change in that object. (Charles Perrow)
- The techniques and science of production and distribution of goods and services found in a given society. (B.J. Hodge and W.P. Anthony)
- The methods and processes of manufacture. (Joan Woodward)
- The sequence of physical techniques of the organization, even if the physical techniques involve only pen, ink, and paper. (D.S. Pugh, D.J. Hickson, C.R. Hinings, and C. Turner)
- The substitution of mechanical equipment for human labor. (Peter Blau)
- The work done in organizations. (Charles Perrow)

These many different viewpoints reflect the fact that technology can be examined at various levels. At the individual level, technology is made up of the tools and knowledge needed to accomplish a given task. At the organizational level, other categorization schemes have been put forth. Some writers subdivide technology into the technologies of operations, materials, and knowledge. Other writers refer to the technology of the inputs, the technology of the transformation process, and the technology of the outputs. At the level of society itself, technology might mean the entire science of production and distribution.

In Systems Terms   The most all-encompassing definition might be arrived at by using systems terms: an organization's technology is its set of techniques (both material and mental) used to transform the system's inputs into its outputs. The system can be any type of organization—a manufacturing corporation, a government agency, a hospital, or a political party. The inputs can be knowledge, energy, raw materials, or money. The outputs can be goods or services.

Evolution of Technology

The Crafts   In the early stages of man's organizational life, the craftsmanship of skilled artisans was the basic, elementary form of technology. The tools of these workers—hammer, knife, pen, awl, and other instruments—are simple and easy to use. But using them masterfully requires both knowledge and experience, usually acquired through a training program called an apprenticeship. In different crafts, the duration of training may vary from a couple of years to a couple of decades. Workers acquire skill in using tools under the careful supervision of an experienced master craftsman. Once the master has certified the apprentice's expertise, the apprentice can begin producing items independently. The technology of such a system results in products high in quality (and price) but relatively few in number.

Increasing Mechanization   With the Industrial Revolution came increased mechanization. Society rapidly moved from agrarian to industrial economies. Thanks to numerous inventions, organizational technology took a great leap forward. No longer did a consumer have to wait for a skilled master to create a product, nor did the consumer have to be well off to afford it. Products of reasonable quality could now be manufactured quickly, in standardized forms at affordable prices.

The new technology also changed the tasks that people performed. Rather than independently using crude instruments and hand tools, workers now became members of organizations and operated machines with many moving parts. These machines increased worker productivity. Some workers became important elements of the production process, because of their ability to operate complicated pieces of equipment. Others became unimportant and easily replaceable parts of large assembly lines.

Automation   The era of automation is gradually developing, as mass production becomes more necessary, as machines become more efficient, and as workers increasingly resist doing repetitive, unchallenging jobs. In this most recent stage of technological evolution, the essential elements are computers and robotics. These high-speed machines can perform countless tasks countless numbers of times, without tiring and without making many mistakes. The emergence of these electronic devices has moved mechanical technology to its highest level yet.

Although computers and robotics have freed workers from routine jobs, they have also made it difficult for many low-level, unskilled people to find jobs. Until educational and skill levels increase, automation may continue to depress certain segments of the labor force.

Biological and Chemical Technology   The next great advances in technology may well be biological and chemical. Recent developments in genetic engineering have led to new agricultural processes and to higher-quality products. The ability to grow food staples without dirt, using liquified nutrient mixtures and aquafarms, will have far-reaching benefits—especially for developing and third-world countries. The end of this century may see the disappearance of food shortages, undernourishment, and starvation.

Technophiles and Technophobes   Sterling McMurrin divides people into two types—technophiles and technophobes.[1] Technophiles feel that the world is better off today because of technology. They respect and admire the technologists who have given us so many material advantages. But technological advancements are not without their disadvantages. Technophobes fear technology because of its problems and potential dangers. Technology has contributed to wars, pollution, dehumanization, and the erosion of natural resources. Because technological discoveries can be abused and misused, we live in constant danger of annihilation and extinction.

Both sides can present impressive evidence. From the first perspective, technology may be our salvation; from the second perspective, technology may be the death of us.

TYPES OF TECHNOLOGY

To explain the relationship between technology and structure, organization theorists have come up with various ways of describing the types of technology. This section will explain the categorization schemes of Joan Woodward, James D. Thompson, and Charles Perrow.

Joan Woodward

Classical Principles in Practice   Perhaps the best-known researcher into the technology question is Joan Woodward.[2] During the 1950s and 1960s, Woodward and her associates investigated 100 manufacturing firms in South Essex, England. These studies were designed to answer two questions: (1) Are the managers in these firms following classical management principles? (2) What effect does following or not following classical principles have on the performance of firms? Preliminary results showed that managers generally ignored classical principles—and often violated them outright. Furthermore, for the most part, following or not following classical principles was unrelated to whether or not a firm was successful.

Classifying Technology   In their search for other factors that might explain performance differences, the researchers turned to the production processes of firms—their "technology." They classified firms into three groups, according to their production systems:

1. Unit and small-batch production
2. Large-batch and mass production
3. Continuous-process production

The characteristics of these technology types appear in Table 15.1.

Unit and Small-Batch Production   This type involves the production of custom-ordered, custom-tailored items, as single units or in small batches. Production runs are usually limited to a small quantity. Custom work is the firm's objective, and the production process (especially in single-unit production) is not mechanized. Examples

Table 15.1   JOAN WOODWARD'S TECHNOLOGY TYPES

Unit and small-batch production
1. Production of simple units to customer order
2. Production of technically complex units
3. Fabrication of large equipment, in stages or units
4. Production of small batches
Large-batch and mass production
5. Production of large batches—assembly-line type
6. Mass production
Process production
7. Process production of chemicals in batches
8. Continuous-flow production of liquids, gases, and solid shapes
Combined systems
9. Production of components in large batches, subsequently assembled diversely
10. Process production combined with the preparation of a product for sale by large-batch or mass-production methods

Source: Joan Woodward, *Management and Technology* (London: Her Majesty's Stationery Office, 1958), p. 8. Used by permission of the Controller of Her Britannic Majesty's Stationery Office.

of items produced in this way are custom-tailored clothes, specialized components for space vehicles, and custom-made construction equipment.

Large-Batch and Mass Production   Systems in this category produce large quantities of items, often on assembly lines. Production runs are long, and products are uniform. Finished products are usually kept in an inventory, from which the firm fills customer orders. These systems produce such items as automobiles, television sets, home computers, toasters, and other standardized, mass-produced goods.

Continuous-Process Production   Products manufactured by complex equipment in a continuous process, then sold by weight or volume, come under this third category. The process is different from the assembly line in that once it begins, it does not stop and re-start. Continuous-process production is used for such outputs as gases, chemicals, oil refining, photographic film, and beer.

Woodward went on to show the relationships between the production processes and the organizational structures of these English manufacturing firms. Those results will be presented later in this chapter.

Woodward's categorization system is obviously somewhat narrow, primarily because she was studying *only manufacturing firms.* According to Charles Perrow, her classifications are not really "technology" categories but a mixture of production type, production-run size, layout of work, and type of customer order.

James D. Thompson

Woodward's work was largely empirical; she looked at real firms and compared their production processes and organizational structures. James D. Thompson's approach was more theoretical, conceptual, and deductive.[3] Furthermore, he tried to cover the technology of *all* organizations, not just manufacturers.

His technology types are three: long-linked, mediating, and intensive.

Long-Linked Technology   Long-linked technology is sequential; Task A must be completed before Task B which must be completed before Task C. On a large scale, a mass-production assembly line is the most obvious example of long-linked technology. However, any assembled product requires this technology type. For instance, a parent assembling a Christmas toy for a child uses long-linked technology. *All* of Joan Woodward's production processes are long-linked.

Mediating Technology   Some organizations mediate or act as go-betweens, bringing two or more clients or customers together. Organizations employing this technology are mainly in *service* industries. Examples are stockbrokers, who execute buy and sell orders for customers; real estate agents, who aid in the transfer of buildings and land; commercial bankers, who link borrowers and depositors; employment agencies, which help match employers and employees; and the phone company and post office, which can link just about all of us. Any organization whose function is brokering or acting as an agent or representative falls under this technology category.

Intensive Technology   Organizations with intensive technology use a variety of specialized technologies and tasks to help one client at a time. The organization serves as a pool or common place for different specialties to come together and serve the customer in the best possible way. Examples of intensive technology users are hospitals, in which different experts come together to improve the patient's condition; universities, in which various specialists attempt to increase each student's knowledge; and "financial supermarkets," which provide various kinds of financial expertise designed to increase the wealth of clients.

Thompson's three technology types are illustrated in Figure 15.1.

Charles Perrow

According to Charles Perrow, *technology* is *the work that the organization does,* the actions that organizational members perform—whether on people, objects, raw materials, or symbols. *Structure* is *the way the organization's people are arranged to get the work done.*[4] Since Perrow's is a problem-solving approach to technology, his categorization scheme can be applied to any organization.

Perrow classifies organizational technologies by asking two questions about the problems, the exceptional cases that organizations encounter as they perform their work.

1. *How frequently* do problems or exceptional cases occur? Organizational technologies can be placed on a continuum, with "few problems" at one end and "many problems" at the other. For instance, an experienced banjo maker runs into few problems, few exceptional cases. A newspaper editor runs into many problems, many exceptions, and makes many varied decisions.

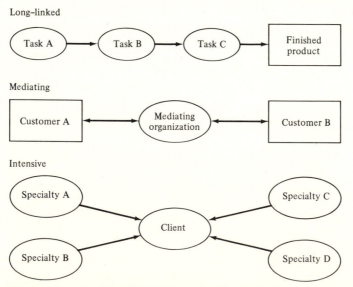

Figure 15.1   James D. Thompson's technology types.

2. Once a problem develops, *how does the organization go about searching for a solution?* Typical problems of certain organizations are highly "analyzable" and can be solved logically. Typical problems of other organizations are highly "unanalyzable" and must be solved intuitively. In Perrow's scheme, problems fall on a continuum ranging from analyzable/logical to unanalyzable/intuitive.

Figure 15.2 reflects the answers to these two questions, when placed on a few-exceptions/many-exceptions continuum and a logical-solutions/intuitive-solutions continuum. The result is a matrix of four technology types that Perrow names craft, nonroutine, routine, and engineering.[5]

Craft Technology In craft technology, the worker's tasks involve few exceptional cases or problems. Craftsmen know their skills and apply them with precision. If a problem occurs, the craftsman solves it by calling upon experience and intuition rather than systematic analysis. If a craftsman of banjo necks discovers that a banjo string buzzes against a fret, the craftsman cannot go to a handbook or program to solve the problem. The craftsman may hammer in the fret a little deeper, raise the bridge, adjust the tension rod in the neck, change to a string of heavier gauge, or may take all of these trial-and-error steps until the string stops buzzing.

Routine Technology When an organization's technology involves few exceptional cases, which can be solved logically and systematically, Perrow calls the technology routine. Newspaper production (as opposed to newspaper editing), the life insurance industry, automobile assembly lines, and clerk-typist pools illustrate routine technology. Because it has few problems and predictable solutions, most organizations try to achieve this technology type.

Nonroutine Technology If problems are many and solutions are arrived at intuitively rather than logically, Perrow calls the technology nonroutine. The technology of the aerospace industry is largely nonroutine.

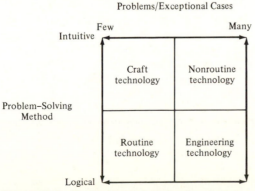

Figure 15.2 Charles Perrow's technology types.

Engineering Technology   Engineering typifies a technology presenting many problems that can generally be solved analytically and logically. The technology is complex; yet problems can usually be solved by using time-tested formulas and techniques. Problems falling into this class are those of lawyers, accountants, doctors, and, of course, engineers.

Different Technology, Different Structure   Perrow's point is that these four different technologies require different organizational structures. An agency issuing license plates uses routine technology and may be best served by a bureaucratic structure. An aerospace company working on a series of innovative, unique projects may use a matrix form of organization.

TECHNOLOGY AND STRUCTURE

The classical scholars believed that sound organizational principles and management principles were more or less universal. The modern view is that an organization's structure and management depend on that organization's unique situation. According to this "contingency" attitude, organizational technology is one determinant of appropriate organizational structure. This section will present the results of several researchers or research groups that have tried to show the relationship between technology and structure.

Joan Woodward and the Technological Imperative

As described earlier in the chapter, Joan Woodward divided 100 manufacturing firms into three groups according to the nature of their production processes: unit and small-batch production, large-batch and mass production, and continuous-process production. She believed that production processes become technologically more complex as organizations move from unit to mass to continuous-process production. Table 15.2 displays her findings.

Woodward's results demonstrated some interesting organizational relationships.

1. *As technological complexity increases, the number of managers per worker and managerial levels in the hierarchy also increase.* Organizations specializing in unit and small-batch production tend to be flat; organizations using continuous-process production tend to be tall. In the advanced and complex technologies, organizations have a greater need to supervise and coordinate the task activities of subordinates. They therefore have more managers and levels.
2. *In mass production, supervisory span of control is wider than in unit or continuous production.* The nature of unit and process work dictates smaller work groups, supervised by a leader. The mass-production assembly line contains many routine, unskilled tasks, permitting one leader to supervise many workers.
3. *Increased technological complexity requires a larger staff (nonworker, nonmanager) component,* primarily because the complex plant and machinery require a trained maintenance staff, but also because such firms need more

Table 15.2   WOODWARD'S FINDINGS ON THE RELATIONSHIP BETWEEN TECHNOLOGY AND STRUCTURE

	Unit & small-batch	Large-batch & mass production	Continuous-process
Median levels of management	3	4	6
Median ratio of nonmanagers to managers	23:1	16:1	8:1
Median span of control: CEO	4 (Range: 2–9)	7 (Range: 4–13)	10 (Range: 5–19)
Median span of control: Supervisors	23	49	13
Median ratio of workers to staff	8:1	6:1	2:1
Clarity of line-staff distinctions	Low	High	Low
Formalization of duties/responsibilities	Low	High	Low
Centralization	Low	High	Low
Participative management	High	Low	High
Written communication (paperwork)	Low	High	Low
Spoken communication	High	Low	High

Source: Adapted from Joan Woodward, *Industrial Organization: Theory and Practice* (London: Oxford University Press, 1965). Used by permission.

people in personnel, accounting, quality control, research and development, and other support services.

Woodward made two additional observations.

1. Within each of the three technological categories, the more successful firms were nearer the medians than were the less successful firms, suggesting that a particular production process requires certain structural characteristics of firms using it. Firms employing other structural characteristics pay for their individuality in lower profits.
2. Organizational size seemed *unrelated* to production system. Both large and small organizations appeared in each of the three technology groups. This finding has proven to be particularly controversial.

Although Woodward herself did not claim that technology in and of itself *determines* structure, her work became the basis for an attitude known as "the technological imperative"—the belief that technology is the primary determinant of organizational structure.

Challenging the Technological Imperative: The Aston Studies

Woodward's findings had suggested a relationship between technology and structure. Later on in the 1960s, a group of researchers based at the University of Aston in Birmingham, England sought to test the so-called technological imperative.[6] Woodward had studied only manufacturing firms. The Aston group examined both manufacturing and nonmanufacturing firms. Of the 46 organizations, 26 were autonomous and 20 were branches of parent organizations.

Workflow Integration   As usual in these studies, a major decision was choosing just what technology to measure and compare. The Aston researchers ignored "materials" technology and "knowledge" technology to concentrate on operations technology. The composite measure they arrived at contained five elements. One element was *automation of equipment.* On the automation scale, organizations received scores according to the following basis:

ITEM	SCORE
Hand tools and machines	0
Power tools and machines	1
Single-cycle automatics and self-feeding machines	2
Automatic, repeating machines	3
Self-measuring, self-adjusting machines	4

Put together, the five elements made up a measure called *workflow integration.* Organizations with high workflow-integration scores were technologically complex; organizations with low scores were technologically simple. The highest scores were received by a vehicle manufacturer, a brewery, and three food manufacturers. The lowest scores were received by a retail store chain, a government inspection department, a department store, and an education department.

Two other phases of the Aston work were important:

1. They related structure and workflow integration to organizational *size.*
2. They redefined Woodward's categories into a measure called *production continuity* so that the Woodward and Aston firms and results could be compared.

The Aston Results   Table 15.3 presents some of the Aston results concerning the relationships between technology, size, and structure. The first two columns are results for all 46 organizations studied, both manufacturing and nonmanufacturing. The last three columns are Aston and Woodward results for the 31 manufacturing firms only. "Aston tech" means workflow integration, and "Woodward tech" means production continuity. The "tech" columns reflect moderately positive correlations between structure and technology. In general, the more complex the technology, the greater the organization's specialization, standardization, and formalization.

But even more significant are the correlations in the "size" columns; they are invariably higher than the "tech" correlations. In the organizations studied, size was a more important predictor of structure than technology was. Woodward had found "no significant relationship" between production system and size.

In trying to reconcile their results with Woodward's, the Aston group concluded that (1) operations technology variables primarily affect the *production-linked,* workflow aspects of administrative structure, and (2) technology exerts more influence on the structures of smaller firms, like those Woodward studied. In a smaller firm, everyone's activities are closer to the shop floor, to the work flow itself. Size brings with it

Table 15.3   THE ASTON CORRELATIONS: TECHNOLOGY, SIZE, AND STRUCTURE

Structural element	All 46 organizations		31 Manufacturing organizations		
	Aston tech	Size	Aston tech	Woodward tech	Size
Degree to which activities are structured	.34	.69	.17	.41	.78
Role of specialization	.38	.75	.25	.52	.83
Functional specialization	.44	.67	.19	.34	.75
Standardization of procedures	.46	.56	.19	.35	.65
Formalization (documentation)	.17	.55	.04	.27	.67
CEO's span of control	.06	.32	−.09	.08	.29

Source: Adapted from "Operations Technology and Organization Structure: An Empirical Reappraisal" by David J. Hickson, D.S. Pugh, and Diana C. Pheysey, published in *Administrative Science Quarterly* 14 (September 1969) by permission of *Administrative Science Quarterly.* Copyright © 1969 Cornell University. All rights reserved.

staff and specialist departments, standard procedures, formal documentation, and centralized authority that are unrelated to the organization's technology.

The National Study

In the late 1960s, John Child tried to replicate the Aston studies.[7] Child's work has come to be called the "National Study" because the 82 firms examined were located throughout England and Scotland. The Aston study included branches and departments of organizations; the National Study included only autonomous organizations.

Child's findings regarding technology supported the Aston results. The degree of workflow integration (the Aston technology measure) was related to degree of specialization, standardization, and formalization. Furthermore, Child confirmed that size was a better predictor of structure than technology was, particularly in manufacturing firms.

The Blau Study

In the mid-1970s, Peter Blau and his associates investigated 110 New Jersey manufacturing firms, to study the relationship between technology and structure.[8] In addition to the technological complexity of the production side, they were interested in the mechanization and automation of administrative work. Were such new developments as computers having effects on organizational structure? For his purpose, Blau considered technology to be "the substitution of mechanical equipment for human labor."[9] He thought that such a definition would enable comparison of his results with earlier research.

Blau's Results   Blau's findings are generally, but not wholly, consistent with those of the Aston school and the National Study: technological complexity does *not* have a major effect on such structural elements as number of organizational levels, CEO span of control, ratio of managers/supervisors to workers, and staff positions relative to line positions. Again unlike Woodward, Blau found that size *does* influence structure in manufacturing organizations.

The Aston study had suggested that an organization's technology might affect those structural elements directly linked to production. Blau's results did not confirm that suggestion. The Aston study further suggested that technology may exert greater influence on the structures of smaller firms. Again, Blau could not confirm any such relationship.

Curvilinear Relationships   Blau did support one of Woodward's findings: advances in production technology (from unit to mass production to process production) do have a *curvilinear* (U-shaped or inverted U-shaped) relationship to some structural aspects. Table 15.1 (on p. 378) presented Woodward's findings. Several structural aspects in that table move at first in one direction (as we go from unit to mass production) and then *reverse* themselves (as we go from mass to process production). Blau pointed out that even though the Aston and National studies perceived similar movements, they did not fully appreciate the significance because their techniques indicated only linear relationships.

Technology and Coordination: The Van de Ven Study

In the mid-1970s, Andrew H. Van de Ven and his colleagues examined the relationship between technology and coordination within 197 work units of a large employment security agency.[10] They investigated two aspects of each unit's technology (task nonroutineness and task interdependence) and three modes of coordination (impersonal, personal, and group).

Nonroutineness and Interdependence of Tasks   Task nonroutineness is composed of task variability and task difficulty. These task dimensions are similar to Charles Perrow's, shown in Figure 15.2 on page 381. Routine tasks are unchanging and simple. Nonroutine tasks are variable and/or difficult. Task interdependence, an aspect based on James D. Thompson's work, refers to how dependent the units are upon each other in order to complete their tasks. The four categories of task interdependence are pooled, sequential, reciprocal, and team.

Pooled interdependence refers to the task activity of a unit that requires no interaction with any other unit in order to do its job. *Sequential* interdependence refers to units that cannot complete their work until they get another unit's output. *Reciprocal* interdependence refers to units that exchange work back and forth. *Team* interdependence refers to the situation in which several units must work together to complete a task.

Modes of Coordination   Van de Ven's three modes of coordination are impersonal, personal, and group. *Impersonal* coordination is achieved through plans, rules, policies, manuals, and other standardized, formalized systems. *Personal* coordination refers to coordination achieved by person-to-person communication. *Group* coordination involves the communication of unit representatives, who report results or give instructions to their units. Table 15.4 summarizes Van de Ven's categories.

Table 15.4   VAN DE VEN'S MEASURES OF TECHNOLOGY AND COORDINATION

Technology measures

1. *Task Nonroutineness*

   a. Task variability | Highly variable, difficult, nonroutine tasks are viewed as

   b. Task difficulty | "technologically" complex. Unchanging, simple, routine tasks are
viewed as "technologically" simple.

2. *Task Interdependence*

   a. Pooled interdependence—Independent, self-contained units.

               Example: A nightclub hat-check service. Least technologically complex.

   b. Sequential interdependence—Each unit relies on output of the previous unit.

               Example: Production unit uses output of raw materials unit. More technologically complex.

   c. Reciprocal interdependence—Units exchange output back and forth.

               Example: An airline's serviced planes and planes needing servicing go back and forth from operations units to maintenance units. Quite technologically complex.

   d. Team interdependence—Several units concentrate on one task.

               Example: Project teams work together to build a lunar module. Most technologically complex.

Coordination modes

1. *Impersonal*—Coordination is achieved by means other than people: plans, rules, manuals.
2. *Personal*—People doing different parts of the work, in different units or in the same unit, coordinate by communicating with each other.
3. *Group*—Unit representatives have a meeting, then report back to their units.

Source: Adapted from Andrew H. Van de Ven, Andre L. Delbecq, and Richard Koenig, Jr., "Determinants of Coordination Modes within Organizations," *American Sociological Review* 41 (April 1976): 322–338. Used by permission.

Conclusions   Van de Ven drew several conclusions from his study.

1. *Routine* (technologically simple) tasks can usually be coordinated by *impersonal* modes.
2. *Nonroutine* (technologically complex) tasks are best coordinated through *group* meetings.
3. The more *interdependent* the tasks, the less likely that they can be coordinated impersonally. *Group* or *personal* modes are usually required.
4. Larger unit *size* leads to coordination by *impersonal* means. Larger units made greater use of rules, plans, policies, and other formal communication and control devices.

One aspect of an organization's structure is how it coordinates its work. Van de Ven's study shows that both the technology and the size of one large organization's units affected that organization's coordination methods.

Structure in Another Culture: The Marsh and Mannari Study

Researchers have also explored how size and technology are related to organizational structure in other cultures. Robert M. Marsh and Hiroshi Mannari investigated such effects in 50 Japanese factories.[11] Their results confirm the findings of some of the studies previously mentioned, but not all of them. In the Japanese factories, the following findings were generally consistent with previous research on American and British companies:

1. Size has a greater effect on structural differentiation (for instance, specialization of labor) than technology does.
2. Variations in such labor inputs as dollars and personnel are due more to differences in technology (automation) than to size.
3. The complexity and sophistication of an organization's composite knowledge (as measured by number of university graduates employed) is more related to technology than to size.
4. In most organizations, the original owner/manager individual or group eventually evolves into two groups: owners and managers. Increasing technological sophistication contributes more to this evolution than does increasing organizational size.
5. The chief executive's span of control is influenced more by technology than by size. As technological sophistication increases, so does the CEO's span of control. In technologically advanced factories, team management is employed rather than sole governance of a powerful CEO.
6. Formalization is more influenced by size than by technology. As the organization grows larger, it experiences a greater need to control activities through documentation.

The Marsh and Mannari findings differ from those of the Aston group, Blau, and Woodward in several important respects. The Aston studies showed a negative relationship between size and centralization, and Woodward reported a negative relationship between technology and centralization. Marsh and Mannari found a *random* relationship between size, technology, and centralization. A stable and dependable understanding of the relationship between these three variables seems not yet to have been achieved.

Blau and others have reported that when the effects of organizational complexity are eliminated, the CEO's span of control will increase as the organization adds people. Marsh and Mannari report that adding people has *no effect* on the Japanese CEO's span of control—regardless of whether or not the researcher eliminates the effects of complexity. Yet, technology *does* affect the CEO's span of control in the Japanese factories, increasingly sophisticated technology leading to wider control spans.

The Marsh and Mannari study is important because it transcends European and American cultures. In addition, these authors argue strongly for a causal system in which technology takes precedence over both size and structure as a determinant of organizational variations.

A Final Caution

Researchers continue to disagree about the relationship between technology and structure.[12] One reason is that researchers sometimes study different organizational levels. In his examination of 20 manufacturing plants, B.C. Reimann demonstrated that results will be different at two different levels of analysis: overall organizational structure and work flow.[13] At the organizational level, Reimann found only one structural variable related to technology: number of levels in the hierarchy. At the work-flow level, an entirely different variable was related to technology: decentralization of operating decisions.

Another reason for disagreement about technology-structure relationships is the difficulty of defining terms. In the study just cited, Reimann defined technology as "degree of mass production," but other definitions are possible, and they might lead to different results. Donald Gerwin questions whether the terms "technology" and "structure" are different at all.[14] He contends that such structural variables as formalization, span of control, and hierarchical levels can be viewed as "administrative technologies" that aid in efficiently converting inputs into outputs.

Likewise, the centralization or decentralization of organizational decision making is critically affected by the degree of computerized technology. By having fast access to information and with sophisticated, easy-to-use simulations, upper management can effectively and efficiently make decisions formerly delegated to middle levels of management.

Gerwin suggests a close conceptual link between technology and formalization—the use of rules and procedures. Referring to Perrow's work, he gives the following example:

> Perrow's . . . second technological dimension . . . is associated with whether problems are solved by logical means or intuition. However, logical means imply standardized rules which are aspects of formalization.[15]

So formalization, too, may be just one more dimension of technology, rather than being a distinct structural feature.

Are technology and structure separate terms, or do they overlap? The lack of a definite answer does much to explain current disagreement on technology-structure relationships.

SUMMARY

Technology has several definitions and descriptions. Since the term can properly be used in many ways, no one definition of technology is "correct."

Technology has evolved in stages—from the craftsmanship of independent workers using hand tools to today's computers and robots. Joan Woodward classified manufacturing organization technologies into three types: unit and small-batch production, large-batch and mass production, and continuous-process production. James D. Thompson's three technology types, applicable to all organizations and not just manufacturers, are long-linked, mediating, and intensive. Long-linked technology involves sequential tasks; each must be completed before the next can begin. Brokers and other go-betweens use mediating technology. Intensive technology describes the work of such organizations as hospitals, in which one client benefits from the sequential or simultaneous application of several specialty skills. Charles Perrow breaks technology down into four categories: craft, routine, nonroutine, and engineering. Where a particular organization's technology falls depends on whether it has few or many problems to solve and whether these problems are solved by logical or intuitive means.

Joan Woodward found that certain aspects of structure were to an extent dependent on the kind of technology. She noted some interesting similarities between the structural aspects of the simplest and the most complex technologies; they often resembled each other more than they resembled the moderately complex mass-production technology.

Using a technology measure called workflow integration, the Aston researchers studied 46 manufacturing and nonmanufacturing firms. Although they found some positive correlations between technology and structure, these relationships were nearly overwhelmed by the relationship between *size* and structure. The Aston results were generally confirmed by John Child's National Study.

Peter Blau's study of 110 New Jersey manufacturing firms was largely consistent with the Aston and National results. Blau also found some curvilinear relationships between structure and technological complexity, as had Woodward: as technological complexity increases, certain structural elements shift in one direction; as technological complexity continues to increase, these structural elements shift back in the other direction.

Andrew H. Van de Ven determined that both technology and size can affect an organization's coordination methods.

Robert M. Marsh and Hiroshi Mannari showed that technology/size/structure relationships may differ in organizations within different cultures. Donald Gerwin made the provocative suggestion that "technology" and "structure" may be two different terms for describing the same organizational characteristics.

The bulk of the evidence suggests that technology and structure are related, even though the relationship may not be as strong as that between size and structure.

DISCUSSION QUESTIONS

1. For the purposes of the organization theorist, what is technology?
2. Which of the chapter's definitions of technology makes the most sense to you?
3. Are you a technophile or a technophobe?
4. What are the different types of technology?
5. What are unit, large-batch, and continuous-process production?
6. What are long-linked, mediating, and intensive technology?
7. How does Charles Perrow define technology? How does his definition help us to understand the relationship between structure and technology?
8. According to Joan Woodward, what is the relationship between technology and structure?
9. According to the Aston group, what is the relationship between technology and structure?
10. Are the Aston results and the Woodward results incompatible?
11. What do you think the relationship between technology and structure is?
12. Do you think size or technology is more important in organizational design?
13. Consider the five differentiating functions. How do you think each is related to organizational technology?
14. Consider the five integrating functions. How do you think each is related to organizational technology?
15. Donald Gerwin suggests that an organization's structure may simply be different aspects or manifestations of its technology. Of which structural aspects might that suggestion be true? Not true?

■ ### *FINE FAMILY MOTELS*

The reservation clerks at the 105 units of the Fine Family Motel chain worked hard, but the chain's occupancy rate seemed to keep drifting lower. When that rate hit 58 percent, management realized that something had to be done.

While most locations had an acceptable vacancy rate, a few high-vacancy locations pulled down the overall rate. Unfortunately, the high-vacancy locations seemed to shift around from month to month. The local reservation clerks, travel agents, and airline reservation networks weren't aware of the high-vacancy areas until the problem became acute. The company was willing to offer discounts of up to 50 percent in the high-vacancy areas to fill rooms, if it could identify them promptly and get the information out to tour brokers, travel wholesalers, and other client sources.

What technological changes would benefit Fine Family Motels? What structural changes would they necessitate?

■ ### *TOYOTA VERSUS GM*

Sakichi Toyoda's textile machine and the factory based on it were the origins of the Toyoda family's empire. His son founded Toyota Motor before World War II. By the mid-eighties Toyota was the world's third-largest car company. Today a third generation of Toyodas is committed to overtaking General Motors and becoming number one.

Toyota encourages intense worker loyalty. "Every employee is a brother," goes one Toyota slogan. To bind workers together, the company provides recreational programs and clubs. Company stores in Toyota City offer low-cost goods, and low-interest home loans are available. In the past 35 years, Toyota employees have submitted 10 million suggestions to cut costs and improve efficiency.

Toyota exerts strong influence on its several hundred parts suppliers. They must open their books to Toyota, which then sets parts prices.

Technologically, the company has come a long way from Sakichi Toyoda's textile machine. Toyota's flexible production line can switch from four-cylinder to six-cylinder engines in minutes. The heart of Toyota's production success is the *kanban* just-in-time inventory system. Based on the speed of the production line, that system delivers parts only a few hours before they are used. Thanks to worker loyalty, management strength, control over suppliers, technological sophistication, and attention to the tiniest manufacturing details, Toyota is the world's lowest-cost auto producer.

In the mid-eighties, Toyota began making plans to bring the battle to GM's home ground; Toyota was going to build a $500 million U.S. plant to produce 200,000 Camry automobiles a year.

What problems may Toyota have as it tries to bring its sophisticated just-in-time production system to the United States, and how should the company try to avoid or solve them? How should GM respond to the Toyota threat?

NOTES

1. Sterling McMurrin, "The Quality of Life in a Quantitative Society," *Conference Board Record* 5 (January 1968): 22–24.

2. See Joan Woodward, *Industrial Organization: Theory and Practice* (London: Oxford University Press, 1965); *Management and Technology* (London: Her Majesty's Stationery Office), 1958.

3. James D. Thompson, *Organizations in Action: Social Science Bases of Administrative Theory* (New York: McGraw-Hill, 1967).

4. Charles Perrow, "A Framework for the Comparative Analysis of Organizations," *American Sociological Review* 32 (April 1967): 194–208.

5. For an in-depth test of Perrow's technology dimensions and a refined scale for measuring them, see Michael Withey et al., "Measures of Perrow's Work Unit Technology: An Empirical Assessment and a New Scale," *Academy of Management Journal* 26 (March 1983): 45–63.

6. David J. Hickson, D.S. Pugh, and Diana C. Pheysey, "Operations Technology and Organization Structure: An Empirical Reappraisal," *Administrative Science Quarterly* 14 (September 1969): 378–397.

7. John Child and Roger Mansfield, "Technology, Size and Organization Structure," *Sociology* 6 (September 1972): 369–393.

8. Peter Blau et al., "Technology and Organization in Manufacturing," *Administrative Science Quarterly* 21 (March 1976): 20–40.

9. Ibid., p. 21.

10. Andrew H. Van de Ven, Andre L. Delbecq, and Richard Koenig, Jr., "Determinants of Coordination Modes Within Organizations," *American Sociological Review* 41 (April 1976): 322–338.

11. Robert M. Marsh and Hiroshi Mannari, "Technology and Size as Determinants of the Organizational Structure of Japanese Factories," *Administrative Science Quarterly* 26 (March 1981): 33–57.

12. For an excellent summary of the enormous number of research studies on technology and structure, see Louis W. Fry, "Technology-Structure Research: Three Critical Issues," *Academy of Management Journal* 23 (March 1980): 61–77.

13. B.C. Reimann, "Organization Structure and Technology in Manufacturing: System Versus Work Flow Level Perspectives," *Academy of Management Journal* 23 (March 1980): 61–77.

14. Donald Gerwin, "The Comparative Analysis of Structure and Technology: A Critical Appraisal," *Academy of Management Review* 4 (January 1979): 41–51.

15. Ibid., p. 45.

ADDITIONAL READINGS

Aldrich, Howard E. "Technology and Organizational Structure: A Reexamination of the Findings of the Aston Group." *Administrative Science Quarterly* 17 (March 1972): 26–43.

Alexander, Judith W., and W. Alan Randolph. "The Fit Between Technology and Structure as a Predictor of Performance in Nursing Subunits." *Academy of Management Journal* 28 (December 1985): 844–859.

Burns, Tom, and G.M. Stalker. *The Management of Innovation.* London: Tavistock Publications, 1961.

Carter, Nancy M. "Computerization as a Predominate Technology: Its Influence on the Structure of Newspaper Organizations." *Academy of Management Journal* 27 (June 1984): 247–270.

Dess, Gregory G., and Donald W. Beard. "Dimensions of Organizational Task Environments." *Administrative Science Quarterly* 29 (March 1984): 52–73.

Dewar, Robert D., and Jerald Hage. "Size, Technology, Complexity, and Structural Differentiation: Toward a Theoretical Synthesis." *Administrative Science Quarterly* 23 (March 1978): 111–136.

Donaldson, Lex. "Woodward, Technology, Organizational Structure and Performance—A Critique of the Universal Generalization." *Journal of Management Studies* 13 (October 1976): 255–273.

Fry, Louis W., and John W. Slocum, Jr. "Technology, Structure, and Workgroup Effectiveness: A Test of a Contingency Model." *Academy of Management Journal* 27 (June 1984): 221–246.

Gerwin, Donald. "Relationships Between Structure and Technology at the Organizational and Job Levels." *Journal of Management Studies* 16 (February 1979): 70–79.

Gillespie, David F., and Dennis S. Mileti. "Technology and the Study of Organizations: An Overview and Appraisal." *Academy of Management Review* 2 (January 1977): 7–16.

Grimes, A.J., and S.M. Klein. "The Technological Imperative: The Relative Impact of Task Unit, Model Technology, and Hierarchy on Structure." *Academy of Management Journal* 16 (December 1973): 583–597.

Hage, Jerald, and Michael Aiken. "Routine Technology, Social Structure, and Organizational Goals." *Administrative Science Quarterly* 14 (September 1969): 366–376.

Khandwalla, Pradip N. "Mass Output Orientation of Operations Technology and Organizational Structure." *Administrative Science Quarterly* 19 (March 1974): 74–97.

Mohr, Lawrence. "Operations Technology and Organizational Structure." *Administrative Science Quarterly* 16 (December 1971): 444–459.

Perrow, Charles. *Normal Accidents: Living with High-Risk Technologies.* New York: Basic Books, 1984.

Rousseau, Denise M., and Robert A. Cooke. "Technology and Structure: The Concrete, Abstract, and Activity Systems of Organizations." *Journal of Management* 10 (Fall/Winter 1984): 345–361.

Environment

Technology has shrunk the world. Computers, transmission satellites, high-speed jets, missiles, and other modern developments have caused us to reconsider our planet's magnitude: formerly huge, it is now tiny. Countries realize that their once-sacred boundaries are no longer safe. Societies recognize that they need each other for friendship, protection, even survival. The social systems that we call nations see their environments exploding and becoming more complex.

Smaller systems like business organizations view the world similarly. Their environments contain new elements, many of them unexpected. In order to survive and coexist with competitors, an organization must identify and interpret its environment.

This chapter first explains several important concepts: the organization's general and specific environments, the boundary, and the domain. Four broad environmental influences on the organization are then presented: social/cultural, economic, physical, and technological. The number and nature of these influences result in an organizational environment with four properties: complexity, diversity, change, and uncertainty. Next, we explore several environmental theories from which the preceding terms and concepts have emerged. Finally, the chapter shows how organizations try to deal successfully with the other organizations in the environment.

DEFINITIONS AND CONCEPTS

In an oversimplified sense, everything not a part of the organization is its environment. But that description is too broad to be useful.

Environment: General and Specific

The *general environment* is that set of conditions which may *eventually* have an impact on the organization. An environmental element may be so hidden or obscure that the organization does not at first recognize its significance. For instance, a small

American trucking concern would have known in the early 1970s that its petroleum suppliers were part of its specific environment but might not have recognized that OPEC, half a world away, was a part of its general environment. The oil embargo established by OPEC had an immediate effect on some organizations, but the effect on others lagged for months and years. Much later, the small trucking company may have noticed gas price increases and long lines at the gas pumps, perhaps without understanding the reasons. By reading magazines and newspapers, and watching TV, most people eventually perceived the impact of OPEC on their own lives and businesses. OPEC is an element in the general environment of any organization that uses petroleum products.

The *specific environment* is that set of conditions having a *direct* and immediate impact on the organization. When organization theorists say "environment," they usually mean specific environment. The world's timber forests, for example, are within the specific environment of book publishers, who need paper to manufacture their products. If a massive forest fire decreases paper production by 10 percent, demand for paper will exceed supply, and prices of paper products to book publishers will rise. Book publishers may absorb the increased cost of publishing, they may try to pass the cost on to customers, or both parties may share in the extra cost. Although timber reserves may be far away from New York City's book publishers, these reserves are part of each publisher's specific environment.

Relevance and Control

The organization is of course a system. C. West Churchman suggests that in order to determine whether an element or influence is a part of the organizational system, its environment, or neither, we can ask two questions:

1. *Relevance:* Is the element in question relevant to the accomplishment of the system's goals and objectives?
2. *Control:* Can the system control the element?

If the answers are *yes/yes,* then the element is part of the *system.* A *yes/no* combination means that the element is a part of either the *specific* or *general environment.* Any other element is not a part of the system *nor* the environment.[1]

Figure 16.1 sums up the foregoing discussion. In the figure, the organization's environment is seen to be *the set of factors having some impact on or relevance to the organization but beyond the organization's absolute control.*

BOUNDARY AND DOMAIN

The Organizational System

Figure 16.2 displays the components of the organizational system. *Inputs* are the resources necessary to keep the system operating. *Process* is the transformation of the inputs into the outputs. *Outputs* are the results of the system's processing; they are the reasons for the system's existence. *Feedback* means using some output as further input,

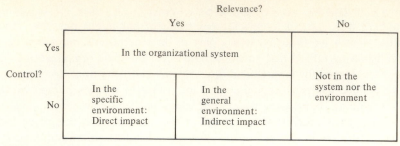

Figure 16.1   Environmental clarification.

often in the form of information about the output, to check on the process and ensure that it is reliable.

The Boundary

The boundary is an imaginary, flexible limit separating the system from its environment. It is imaginary because it resides only in the minds of people within the system or investigating the system. It is flexible because it expands or contracts as the organizational system becomes larger or smaller, taking on more or fewer activities. The boundary is a theoretical concept used to designate which factors are within the system itself (over which the organization has great control) or within the environment (over which it does not have absolute control).

Flexibility: An Example   The car rental company Avis can serve to illustrate the boundary's flexibility. Avis had its beginnings at airport counters. Since Avis did all its business in airport terminals, they were the boundaries of each Avis operation. With the expansion of the economy, Avis set up rental counters in urban areas, and then in suburban and rural areas, greatly expanding the company's boundary. To avoid being overly affected by the economy's cyclical swings and to provide another outlet for its services, Avis entered into the car leasing business, enlarging the Avis system's boundary again. Finally, Avis began to sell the used cars from their rental and leasing operations. An organization that began by renting cars at airports has become a

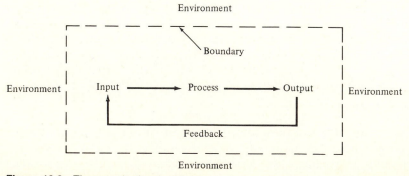

Figure 16.2   The organizational system.

full-service car transportation company, expanding its boundary at each step along the way.

The Domain

The boundary is an invisible line separating the organizational system from its environment. The domain is the part of the environment which the organization views as its "territory." It consists of those environmental segments with which the organization wishes to deal, such as its vendors and its customers. The organization depends on those segments to supply its inputs and purchase its outputs.

According to James D. Thompson, the organization must develop strategies for dealing with this dependency.[2] Three common strategies are contracting, co-opting, and coalescing. *Contracting* means formalizing the relationship with an environmental element by entering into an agreement to supply the organization with inputs or purchase its outputs. *Co-opting* means making the environmental element a part of the system. *Coalescing* means forming another organization, a coalition, out of the organization and its environmental elements. These three strategies will be discussed in a later section of this chapter devoted to interorganizational relations.

The organization can form and change its domain. Occasionally, the domain can change without the organization's agreement. For example, many years ago the government caused the du Pont Chemical Company to get rid of its controlling interest in General Motors. More recently, the government ordered the break-up of the American Telephone & Telegraph Company. In both cases an environmental element caused the company to alter its domain unwillingly.

ENVIRONMENTAL ELEMENTS

The elements in the environments of most organizations are of four general kinds: social/cultural, economic, physical, and technological. Each kind has several subdivisions.

Social/Cultural Elements

The social and cultural elements are the other systems with which the organization has relationships: governmental, educational, legal/political, and the general public.

Government The government imposes restrictions on all organizations. Government monetary and fiscal policies affect inflation and unemployment rates, the prices of goods and services, and the organization's cost of doing business. Government regulations affect the treatment of organizational members; for example, organizations can no longer hire and fire at will.

Education The values taught within both the home and our educational institutions are brought by members to their organizations. For instance, many years ago our educational leaders (and leaders in other business, social, and cultural institutions) often used an authoritarian style. Students were taught not to question authority, to do what they were told—attitudes that carried over into the workplace. The social revolution of the sixties brought about a questioning of those values. The notions of team play, loyalty, and devotion to duty were replaced in the "I/Me" generation of the seventies by a "what's-in-it-for-me" attitude. Our educational system often reinforced such behavior. Students may not have been required to do their homework, for example, as long as they passed the exam. Pretty soon, many didn't do their homework, and the number of failures and illiterates increased. All the organizations of which these students became members were affected by the newer attitudes and lack of basic skills. Of course, the brighter side of the relationship between educational institutions and business organizations is the continued high standards of many business and professional schools which are training the organizational leaders of the future.

Legal/Political   Changes in the law obviously affect the operations of many organizations. Since the late 1950s, these changes have often come so rapidly and are so complex that organizations have had to hire armies of lawyers to cope with them. On the political side, organizations hire professional lobbyists to "help inform the judgment" of influential politicians. To survive and grow, the organization is forced to deal successfully with the political system.

General Public   Major organizations have had "public relations" departments for many decades. More recently, the demands of the general public have caused organizations to reexamine their activities and priorities. Since about 1970, the concept of corporate social responsibility has emerged dramatically. Each organization must now satisfy its own set of constituents—members, employees, stockholders, customers, suppliers.

Economic Elements

In addition to cultural and social relationships, the typical organization has financial relationships with other systems in its environment. Most notable of these other systems are the capital and money markets, customers, labor, suppliers, and competitors.

Capital and Money Markets   Corporations, governments, and other organizations go to the capital and money markets to obtain needed funds. The rates of interest on these funds will depend on the supply of available money and the demand for it in the general economy. Interest rates influence a corporation's costs, prices, profits, and dividends. "Wall Street" is an environmental element affecting any organization that borrows or lends money, or sells securities of any kind to the public.

Customers   An organization's customers buy its goods or services—its output. Therefore, the organization must be continually aware of customer needs. Radical changes in customer preferences can cause radical changes in the organization. For example, following the oil embargo of the early 1970s, the American public's preference shifted rather quickly away from gas-guzzling cars. U.S. auto manufacturers did not read these changes in preference very well and continued to manufacture the large, less energy-efficient cars. People began buying the gas-saving cars offered by Japanese and German manufacturers. The impact on American auto manufacturers was severe: plummeting profits for all, losses for some, and near bankruptcy for Chrysler. Failure to notice a change in a relevant, uncontrollable element beyond the system's boundary nearly caused the collapse of a once-insulated industry.

Labor   The effects of the organization's relationships with labor are seen most clearly in unionization. Some say that unions have affected organizations positively, by encouraging higher pay, better working conditions, and more benefits. Others point to lower productivity, featherbedding, goldbricking, closed shops, and resistance to merit pay. The labor force is a system that provides the organization's human resources. Such changes in the system as strikes, slowdowns, and turnover can affect organizational productivity. Labor demands can increase the organization's costs. To avoid unionization, strike threats, and other costly demands, some northeastern companies have relocated to "right-to-work" states with more favorable business climates.

Suppliers   Just as the capital and money markets supply financial inputs and the labor markets supply human inputs, suppliers provide their outputs to other organizations as raw-material inputs. Since an unreliable supplier or industry-wide disaster could be so costly, organizations strive to keep back-up supply sources available. Relying on one vendor places the organization at that vendor's mercy.

Competitors   Competitors providing the same output—the same goods or services—give an organization's customers a choice. The organization tries to take some business away from its competitors, but not too much. If the organization becomes too big and monopolizes its market, the government can use the legal system to break up the monopoly, as happened in the mid-1980s to American Telephone & Telegraph. Competitors engaging in price wars, like those occurring from time to time in the gasoline and personal computer industries, cause decreasing prices and narrow profit margins.

Physical Elements

Several organizational inputs and outputs involve interaction with the natural physical world. Many organizations are dependent on natural resources for such inputs as minerals, metals, water, and electricity. A company wishing to start a solar-powered utility, for example, will locate its generating plant in the sun belt rather than in Alaska. Another case in point is the paper mill industry. Many years ago, paper mills were operated at the edge of forests. As forests became depleted because mill operators did not replant tree seedlings, the mills became inoperable—all their input had been used up. Today, paper manufacturers work hard to replenish their most important natural resource.

The organization's processing of its inputs can create undesirable outputs, such as waste and other pollutants. Air, water, and noise pollution created by smoke-bellowing, chemical-dumping, ear-piercing plants spoil the surrounding environment for all living members of the ecological system. The government has often stepped in, passing stringent legislation to preserve the physical environment.

Technological Elements

Organizations are affected by new and improved processes, machinery, equipment, computers, and other devices that reduce costs and increase productivity and comfort. Companies must develop or invent new processes and keep up with technological changes or find their products obsolete, of lower quality, or too costly. The importance of technology can be illustrated by developments in the fields of personal computers, robotics, and genetic engineering.

Computers   In effect, Apple created a new market for computers by producing an affordable personal computer. Its competitors like Commodore were excited about this surge in personal computer buying since they were already in the small-computer market and could easily capture some of the new buyers. Once Apple and Commodore became solidly entrenched, such computer giants as IBM and Digital Equipment had to move quickly to enter this new arena or be left behind.

Robotics   With advances in integrated circuits and miniaturization, robots for industrial purposes can now be manufactured at reasonable prices. Major car manufacturers like GM, Ford, and Chrysler have used robots to increase productivity, standardize quality, and reduce costs. Robotics has enabled American car manufacturers to compete more successfully with the Japanese.

Genetic Engineering   Genetic engineering has encouraged some organizations to explore which of their products might be synthesized biologically. Drug companies can now cheaply produce drugs that used to be rare and costly. For example, Interferon, a drug that may have great potential in the fight against cancer, was previously too costly to market on a grand scale; thanks to advances in genetics, most patients can now afford it. New technology is developing geometrically, and affected organizations must respond quickly and positively.

ENVIRONMENTAL PROPERTIES

For a given organization, the environmental elements just discussed result in an environment that, according to Stephen M. Shortell, has four properties: complexity, diversity, change, and uncertainty.[3]

Complexity

Complexity refers to the sheer *number* of elements in the organization's specific environment. A simple environment has few elements; a complex environment has many elements. The number of elements and their interactions with the organization can affect the organization's structure. An organization operating within a complex environment may have to hire staff experts to manage the many elements. A company like General Motors operates in a highly complex environment; various consumer, governmental, and political elements make demands upon GM. To handle these demands, GM maintains staffs of lawyers, accountants, training and development specialists, personnel experts, and strategic planners. Therefore, GM's ratio of line employees to staff employees will differ from that of a small organization in a simple environment. A mom-and-pop store deals only with local customers and a few suppliers. The store does not need full-time lawyers, accountants, or other staff professionals.

Diversity

Complexity refers to *how many* elements are within the organization's specific environment. Diversity refers to how many *different* elements there are—the *variety* of elements. A *homogeneous* environment contains few different elements; a *heterogeneous* environment contains many. Before the break-up of AT&T, organizations had only one supplier of phone service within their environments. Now, other companies supply a variety of phone equipment and service, adding to both the complexity and diversity of environmental elements for all organizations using telephones. The Environmental Protection Agency operates in a complex environment, dealing with numerous organizations producing diverse types of pollutant chemicals, waste, radioactive materials, sewage, and so forth. In contrast, the average community must cope with relatively few kinds of polluters.

Change

Change is of course inevitable, but some environments change more, faster, and less predictably than others. The environmental change continuum ranges from stable to dynamic. A stable environment remains relatively unchanged for months or years. Elements in a dynamic environment shift often and in unexpected ways.

Stable Environments   The environments of regulated electric utilities are typically stable. Demands for power may change, but they are predictable in light of projected changes in the population and the weather. Likewise, such elements as government restrictions and suppliers remain relatively constant.

Dynamic Environments   Most organizations, however, must function within a dynamic or turbulent environment. Consider the computer industry. As technology advances, the industry changes rapidly. The recent explosion of demand for personal computers has caused many computer companies to reorient themselves in order to supply this new, exciting instrument. Dramatic changes in this industry occur semiannually or annually, rather than every five or ten years. Organizations using computers are being bombarded with smaller and faster computers, with larger memories, advanced optics, and revolutionary peripherals that make last year's computers obsolete.

Uncertainty

Uncertainty refers to *how predictable* the changes (whether few or many) in the organization's environment are. James D. Thompson has stressed the importance of uncertainty to organizations: "Uncertainty appears as the fundamental problem for complex organizations, and coping with uncertainty is the essence of the administrative process."[4] Every organization experiences uncertainty. No organization can predict with absolute surety what will happen in its environment.

Relevant information reduces uncertainty, so organizations try to acquire a reasonable amount of knowledge pertinent to their activities. The cost of acquiring information rises faster than the usefulness of the information obtained, so organizations acquire and absorb just enough information to operate effectively and efficiently. They accept some uncertainty, rather than trying to acquire the last few—very expensive— pieces of information.

The oil embargo of the early 1970s caused much organizational uncertainty. Some organizations were prepared for it when it began, but many were not. As the embargo progressed, affected organizations—primarily car manufacturers—were increasingly uncertain about when it would end, what the price of oil would be, and whether enough oil would be available at any price. Governments were uncertain about the embargo's impact on inflation, energy sources, and international relations: Would the oil-consuming nations fight back? As usually happens when global uncertainty is high, economic and social chaos resulted.

Structure and Uncertainty   Lawrence G. Hrebiniak and Charles C. Snow examined 88 companies in four industries to determine if organizational structure and environmental uncertainty are related.[5] They discovered a positive association between decentralization and uncertainty in the air transportation industry; and a negative association in the semiconductor industry. These findings suggest that industry type should perhaps be incorporated into any explanation of structural response to environmental uncertainty.

The Duncan Model

Robert B. Duncan's model, depicted in Figure 16.3, integrates three environmental properties: change, complexity, and uncertainty.[6] The static environment of low uncertainty described in Cell 1 has elements that are few, similar, and unchanging. The dynamic environment of high uncertainty described in Cell 4 has many different, constantly changing elements. Cells 2 and 3 fall in between.

The model also indicates the appropriate organizational structures within the four environments. Cells 1 and 2, characterized by low uncertainty, permit more fixed, mechanistic structures, the major difference being the degree of centralization. Because of their uncertain environments, organizations falling in Cells 3 and 4 require more flexible, organic structures. Again, the degree of centralization is different, depending on environmental complexity. Organizations with more complex environments must allow lower-level managers—closer to the environment—to make decisions so as to avoid costly blunders and missed opportunities arising out of rapid environmental changes.

ENVIRONMENTAL MODELS

The preceding sections of this chapter explored various concepts related to organizational environment. This section examines the rich theories and studies that have given rise to many of the foregoing concepts.

	Simple environment	Complex environment
Static environment	**Cell 1** Low uncertainty 1. Few elements in the environment 2. Elements are similar 3. Elements are unchanging Appropriate structure: Complexity, formalization, and centralization all high	**Cell 2** Moderately low uncertainty 1. Many elements in the environment 2. Elements are dissimilar 3. Elements are unchanging Appropriate structure: Complexity and formalization high, centralization low
Dynamic environment	**Cell 3** Moderately high uncertainty 1. Few elements in the environment 2. Elements are similar 3. Elements change continuously Appropriate structure: Complexity and formalization low, centralization high	**Cell 4** High uncertainty 1. Many elements in the environment 2. Elements are dissimilar 3. Elements change continuously Appropriate structure: Complexity, formalization, and centralization all low

Figure 16.3 Duncan's model of environmental properties and structures. (*Source:* Adapted from "The Characteristics of Organizational Environments and Perceived Environmental Uncertainty" by Robert B. Duncan, published in *Administrative Science Quarterly* 17 [September 1972] by permission of *Administrative Science Quarterly*. Copyright © 1972 Cornell University. All rights reserved.)

Burns and Stalker: Structure and Environment Related

In their study of 20 United Kingdom industrial firms, Tom Burns and G.M. Stalker identified organizational environments as either dynamic/changing or static/stable.[7] They discovered a relationship between each organization's environment and its structure. Stable environments evoked rigid, mechanistic structures; dynamic environments produced flexible, organic structures.

Mechanistic and Organic Structures According to Burns and Stalker, the organization in a stable environment has a mechanistic structure and a classical management system with rules, procedures, a clear hierarchy of authority, specified techniques, and set duties. Most activities are closely controlled by superiors, and communications tend to go up and down rather than side to side. The organization in a dynamic environment has an organic structure and a freer-flowing management style. Rules, procedures, regulations, and other specifications are not as formalized. The hierarchy of authority is not always clear, authority is decentralized, and interaction is both horizontal and vertical.

Table 10.1 (p. 255) in Chapter 10, Formalization, presented a detailed comparison of mechanistic and organic organizations.

Lawrence and Lorsch: Plastics, Foods, Containers

Paul R. Lawrence and Jay W. Lorsch supported and extended Burns and Stalker's work.[8] Lawrence and Lorsch studied ten companies in three industries with environments of widely differing uncertainty and diversity: plastics, foods, and containers. Products and demands in the plastics industry shift constantly. Changes in the container industry's environment are small and predictable. The food industry falls in between.

Subsystems   Lawrence and Lorsch tested two major hypotheses. First, the structures of organizational subsystems (for example, departments) are affected by the certainty or uncertainty of their subenvironments. When examining three departments within firms—research and development, manufacturing, and sales—they found support for their hypothesis. The more certain the environment, the more formalized the departments became. For instance, the manufacturing departments had a relatively certain subenvironment; therefore, production workers existed in a formal structure and were short-run oriented. Operating in a less certain environment, the R&D units were less formal, more professional, and more concerned with the long run. Table 16.1 presents Lawrence and Lorsch's findings.

Lawrence and Lorsch also found that the successful firms in these industries placed more stress on integrating the work than did the less successful firms—in both stable and dynamic environments. The successful firms used committees and task forces to achieve cooperation and coordination.

James D. Thompson: Buffering and Adapting

In 1967 James D. Thompson published his famous work on organizations, technology, and environment.[9] Two of Thompson's important concepts were organizational buffers and organizational adaptation to the environment.

Protective Buffers   Thompson envisioned the organization as a *technical core* (the means for getting the organization's job done) surrounded by buffers. These buffers absorb environmental uncertainty and protect the core from the environment, so that the core can do its work unmolested. The goal of the buffers is to allow the core to

Table 16.1   DEPARTMENTAL DIFFERENCES DUE TO ENVIRONMENTAL UNCERTAINTY

Aspect	R&D dept.: dynamic environment	Mfg. dept.: stable environment	Sales dept.: moderate environment
Goal	Quality and development	Efficiency	Customer satisfaction
Time horizon	Long	Short	Short
Interpersonal orientation	Mostly task	Task	Social
Formalization	Low	High	High
Differentiation	High	Low	Medium

Source: Adapted from Paul R. Lawrence and Jay W. Lorsch, *Organization and Environment* (Homewood, IL: Richard D. Irwin, 1969), pp. 23–39. Copyright © 1967, 1986 by the President and Fellows of Harvard College. Republished as a Harvard Business School Classic: Boston: Harvard Business School Press, 1986. Used with permission.

operate as a closed system. The buffers filter environmental influences, warding off the harmful, distracting ones.

Production is the technical core of a manufacturing firm. Such departments as industrial relations, customer service, R&D, finance, and purchasing even out the system's inputs and outputs to permit a steady, continuous flow. Because the technical core needs raw materials to convert into output, purchasing is responsible for keeping them on hand. If one supplier runs out, purchasing will usually have a back-up source so that the technical core can keep producing. The production function is buffered by the purchasing function from concern about whether sufficient raw materials will be available.

Adaptability to the Environment Thompson also demonstrated that organizations adapt their structures and strategies to their environments. Figure 16.4 shows how organizations react to environments of differing stability and diversity. Organizations in Cell 1 (stable, low-diversity environment) have only the few functional divisions necessary to do the work. Members adapt to the few changes in the environment's few elements by following the rules. In addition to their functional divisions, organizations in Cell 4 need other divisions, contingency planning, and protective buffers to cope with the frequent changes in the environment's many elements.

	Stable environment	Unstable environment
Low-diversity environment	**Cell 1** Few functional divisions Use rules to adapt to environment Example: Corner grocery store	**Cell 3** Moderate number of functional divisions Decentralized authority; geographical decentralization Use contingency planning to adapt to environment Example: EDP systems
High-diversity environment	**Cell 2** Many functional divisions, to master the environment's diverse elements Use rules to adapt to environment Example: Large department store	**Cell 4** Many functional divisions, to master the environment's diverse elements Use contingency planning to adapt to environment and buffers to absorb environmental uncertainty Example: Large, complex corporations

Figure 16.4 Organizational adaptation to the environment. (*Source:* After James D. Thompson, *Organizations in Action: Social Science Bases of Administrative Theory* [New York: McGraw-Hill, 1967], pp. 68–74.)

McDonough and Leifer: Multiple Structures

According to Thompson, organizations change their structures to accommodate changes in their environments. Edward F. McDonough III and Richard Leifer have shown that within 21 manufacturing and insurance work groups, supervisors varied the groups' positions along three structural dimensions—centralization of decision making, specialization of labor, and formalization of procedures—according to whether group members were undertaking (1) routine tasks in a certain environment or (2) nonroutine tasks in an uncertain environment.[10] "Environment" here means both internal influences (such as the behavior of other work units) and external influences (such as government regulations, suppliers, and technological changes).

Significantly, since some group members engaged in routine tasks/certain environment while others engaged in nonroutine tasks/uncertain environment, the work units were in effect employing *different structures at the same time.* For example, group members working on nonroutine tasks in an uncertain environment experienced greater centralization (the supervisor made more decisions) and greater division of labor (each member performed fewer tasks). Group members working on routine tasks in a certain environment had the opposite experience. According to McDonough and Leifer:

> In general, supervisors evidently rely on multiple structures in order to carry out the different tasks of the work unit and to cope with the different environments they face . . . but the supervisor's use of a particular structure may depend on his personal preference for a particular structure or his perception of the fitness of his subordinates to make decisions, operate with loosely defined rules, or work on larger, more complex tasks.[11]

Emery and Trist: Classifying the Environment

Fred E. Emery and Eric L. Trist have identified four types of organizational environments: placid/randomized, placid/clustered, disturbed/reactive, and turbulent.[12]

Placid/Randomized   In the placid/randomized environment, elements change slowly and randomly. The organization in this environment has enough buyers for its output, but it cannot greatly affect its environment in general or its market in particular. A typical organization operating in a placid/randomized environment would be a small retail clothing store.

Placid/Clustered   Elements in the placid/clustered environment change slowly but more predictably because, rather than being random, they are clustered together into patterns. Organizations in such environments need to make forecasts and plans. These organizations are usually large, centralized, and hierarchical. A public utility like an electric power company would be an example.

Disturbed/Reactive   Within this environment, large organizations are themselves the major environmental influences upon each other. Any one organization can have a resounding impact on the others and can disturb their common environment. Changes are not random, but predicting them is difficult. Therefore, organizations do more *reacting* to change than planning for it. To survive in an environment so easily disturbed, an organization must be flexible and decentralized so it can react rapidly and appropriately. A typical example would be a tobacco company.

Turbulent   The turbulent environment is the most uncertain of all. Its many fast-changing elements are interrelated, producing "ripple effects" when any change occurs. Predicting and responding to these changes are difficult because other organizations, society, and the economy are so intermixed. Organizations in turbulent environments do little planning and forecasting; they do rely heavily on research and development. These organizations survive by being flexible and adaptable. A manufacturer of computer hardware and software would be an example.

The Partitioned Environment

Joseph E. McCann and John Selsky have extended the Emery-Trist model to include a fifth type: the partitioned environment.[13] Emery and Trist's turbulent environment contains an extreme degree of uncertainty called hyperturbulence. In a hyperturbulent environment, changes are so frequent and uncertain that the environment is *totally* unpredictable and unmanageable. In essence, utter chaos occurs.

According to McCann and Selsky, the organization that foresees hyperturbulence will try to manage and protect particularly important organizational resources by partitioning the environment. Among medical personnel in the military, the term "triage" means to use scarce medical resources according to a system of priorities: urgency, chance for survival, etc. McCann and Selsky use the term "social triage" to describe the organization's efforts to protect parts of the organization by managing parts of the turbulent environment. The organization tries to do so by either *shutting out* the turbulence or *containing* it.

The Social Enclave   Within an organization that has experienced social triage, two types of domains may exist within a single environment: social enclaves (which shut out turbulence) and social vortices (which contain turbulence). A social enclave in a turbulent environment is an area made relatively calm by members who resist external demands. An example would be a clan—a group of people who band together to survive within a troubled environment. Another illustration would be a monastery that walls itself off from the outside world.

Hyperturbulence accelerates the formation of organizational enclaves. Today, many corporations—beset by unfriendly takeover attempts or straining to survive within uncertain environments—are willing to be acquired or absorbed by other organizations just to find relief in a relatively calm, safe haven. Likewise, to counter the uncertainties of the 1973 oil embargo, many oil-consuming nations banded together to develop new technologies and conservation methods. In brief, the members of an enclave try to isolate themselves from the turbulent environment.

The Social Vortex   The social vortex is just the opposite; it is an attempt to partition or isolate turbulent environmental elements within manageable boundaries. Organization members, or groups of organizations, defend those boundaries to make certain that the turbulence remains contained within and will not escape to contaminate the rest of the environment. In the mid-1980s, for instance, various world powers tried to keep violent conflicts within the geographical boundaries of Lebanon, to prevent trouble from spreading to neighboring countries. A university experiencing faculty unrest may decide to restructure itself so that the dissenting "troublemakers" are isolated within controllable units. Figure 16.5 illustrates the difference between social enclaves and vortices.

Organizations cannot protect themselves from all turbulent environmental elements. The idea behind partitioning the environment is that organizations can create enclaves and vortices to protect themselves from the most harmful influences of the most turbulent environmental elements.

Niche Theory: The Ecological Perspective

Ecology is the study of how organisms relate to their environments. Most ecological theories take a *selective* perspective; that is, the environment selects for survival those organisms that are the fittest. In an environment whose only vegetation consists of tall trees, giraffes will survive and short-necked animals will not. The giraffe did not *adapt* to the environment by analyzing it and deciding to grow a long neck. According to this perspective, the resources and other characteristics of an environment determine which organisms will survive in it.

The Ecology of Organizations   Most theories of how organizational structures relate to organizational environments take an *adaptive* perspective. The organization looks over the environment, then adapts to it by establishing the structure that will lead to organizational survival, growth, and profit. Although an adaptive perspective dominates the management literature, the sociological literature on organizations, decision-making theories of organization, and systems approaches to organization, Michael T. Hannan and John Freeman see "no reason to presume that the great structural variability among organizations reflects only or even primarily adaptation."[14]

Hannan and Freeman point out numerous limitations on the organization's ability to change its structure at will. These limitations are both internal (large investments

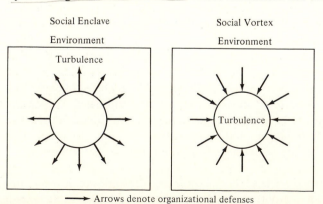

Arrows denote organizational defenses

Figure 16.5 Social enclaves and vortices contrasted.

in fixed assets, inadequate internal information flows to organizational decision makers, political objections of subunits to structural reorganization, and the difficulty and costliness of changing the status quo) and external (legal and financial barriers, inadequate information flows from the environment, external concerns about what changes the organization may legitimately make, and the "collective rationality problem": An organization may see a change in the environment and may make a structural change which would be a successful adaptation except that competing organizations may simultaneously adopt the same strategy and no one knows what the collective result of all these structural changes will be). For these reasons, Hannan and Freeman conclude that a selective perspective may be more valid than an adaptive perspective in explaining the relationships between organizations and their environments.

Using the Niche's Resources   Hannan and Freeman propose a "niche theory" borrowed from biology. Within different subsections or "niches" of the general environment, those organisms survive which best use the niche's particular resources. Polar bears make use of the resources in the Arctic niche; boa constrictors make use of the resources in the jungle niche. Similarly, those organizations succeed which make best use of the resources in a particular environmental setting. The more precisely the environmental niche can be defined, the more precisely can be defined the unique features of the organization surviving in that niche.

How Wide a Niche?   A problem for organizations is defining the niche into which they want to fit. If the niche is narrow, a "specialist" organization with highly specific characteristics may best fit the niche. If the niche is broad, a "generalist" organization may fit best. But generalist organizations are more costly since they must maintain excess capacity and expertise to accommodate the great variations in the broad niche within which they operate.

The Rate of Change   Of importance to all organizations is *the rate of environmental change.* In stable environments, specialist organizations are more effective than generalist organizations. For example, the environment for salt mining is highly stable. Consequently, United Salt Mining Company can spend time and money developing highly specialized skills and equipment devoted exclusively to the mining of salt, because the environment changes so slowly. On the other hand, the environment within which a clothing manufacturer operates changes quickly as fashion styles and preferences change. Clothing manufacturers must therefore take a generalist approach, hiring people with a broader range of skills and allocating organizational resources to maintain a proper fit with an ever-changing environment.

   A problem for any organization, then, is to what extent it should develop the capacity to adapt to change. If an organization develops a vast capacity but the environment remains stable, the organizational performance level will not be as high as it would be if the organization had assumed a stable environment and focused its efforts on making the best use of the resources within its niche.

The Extent of Change   If the environment is unstable, of great importance to organizations is *how long* a new, unfamiliar environmental state may last. If environmental changes tend to be brief, then the specialist organization may be able to "weather the storm" until normal conditions return. If new environmental states tend to occur quite frequently and be long-lasting, the generalist organization can use its reserve capacity to shift direction appropriately.

Flipping the Environmental Coin   Hannan and Freeman say that, from the perspective of ecological adaptation, organizations are engaged in a game of chance. First, organizations choose a strategy: to specialize or to generalize, to fit in a narrow niche or a broad one. Then the organizations flip an environmental coin with "stable" on one side and "unstable" on the other. In the stable environment, the specialist organizations win; in the unstable environment, the generalist organizations win. If the game consists of one flip and the environmental coin comes up "unstable," the specialist organization may eventually go out of business. If the game consists of many flips—frequent environmental changes—organizations experience the environment as an average.

An Example from the Construction Industry   Let's consider the construction industry. When demand is stable and high, a large firm specializing in modular homes will do very well. However, when demand for houses drops off, that firm will do poorly because its specialized employees don't know anything about construction except how to build modular homes. Smaller, craft-oriented construction firms that built houses when demand for them was high can now use their more flexible resource base—generalist craftsmen—to build swimming pools or office buildings or do landscaping work. They can easily adapt to the specific requirements of various niches within the construction industry.

INTERORGANIZATIONAL RELATIONS

The Resource Dependency Perspective

No organization is self-sufficient and all-powerful. Any organization is susceptible to influence from other organizations in its environment. Jeffrey Pfeffer and Gerald R. Salancik's *The External Control of Organizations: A Resource-Dependence Perspective* discusses the effects of environmental demands and constraints on organizations and their resources.[15]

According to these authors, every organization depends on "resource exchanges" with other organizations. The organization is affected by the *size* and *importance* (for reasons other than size) of resource exchanges. These exchanges involve both inputs and outputs. A company asks, "How much of our wood do we get from XYZ supplier?" The answer is the size of the resource exchanges with that supplier. The company asks, "How crucial is electricity to our operation?" The answer is the importance of the resource exchanges with the company's electrical power supplier. If the company does not pay its electricity bills, the electric utility will cut off the power supply. A company employing mountain whittlers can perhaps do without electricity, while a company using power machinery to make furniture will go broke.

Every organization is affected by the size and importance of its resource exchanges with other organizations. If size or importance is large, then the external organizations have potential power over the organization in question.

This view, sometimes called the strategic-constituencies perspective, reflects the fact that the organization is not concerned with all environmental influences on it. The organization *must* satisfy those constituencies which can threaten its survival—and *may* wish to satisfy some others as well.

For instance, General Motors can list numerous institutions and groups important for GM's continuing operation—government regulatory agencies, unions, consumers, banks, and suppliers among them. GM can rank these groups in order of importance, then concentrate on satisfying the more crucial ones. To sum up, this strategy acknowledges that the organization is dependent on its resources and must focus on the key resources to be effective.

The environment influences the organization. Any organization must develop strategies to deal with the other organizations that are always part of its environment. These other organizations are sometimes called the *organizational set.* Figure 16.6 arranges the organizational set of a car rental company into input organizations and output organizations.

In the area of interorganizational relations, five strategies for reducing uncertainty are common. They are buffering and smoothing, rationing and stockpiling, contracting, co-opting, and coalescing.

Buffering and Smoothing

Buffering   James D. Thompson's concept of buffering means the protection of the technical core from the environment. The buffers handle those interorganizational relationships that might interfere with the technical core's activities. For example, the federal government may demand certain financial information from XYZ company. The XYZ accounting staff fills out the forms so that line people can concentrate on producing, selling, and servicing XYZ's products.

Smoothing   Smoothing on the system's output side corresponds to buffering on the input side. If the demand for an organization's output is much higher at certain times than at others, the organization may try to smooth out the demand by encouraging customers to use other time periods. During regular business hours, the demand for electricity is heavy. Electric utilities try to smooth out this demand by offering lower rates before 8:00 A.M. and after 8:00 P.M. Similarly, many restaurants offer "early-bird specials" as an incentive for diners to come in before peak demand periods start.

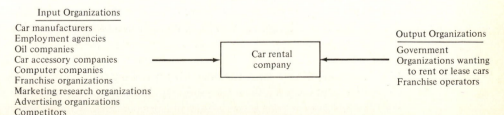

Figure 16.6   Example of organizational set: Car rental company.

Rationing and Stockpiling

To compensate for irregularities in materials supplied by other organizations, many firms engage in rationing when times are bad and stockpiling when times are better. An organization with a stockpile of resources can use those reserves, perhaps rationing them, during severe times such as embargoes, strikes, or disasters.

For example, a manufacturing company dependent on steel as a major resource may foresee a domestic steel strike. Before the strike, the company will stockpile steel. If the strike actually occurs, the company may ration its use of steel while it tries to obtain steel from an alternate source or tries to substitute other metals in its production process.

Contracting

Organizations frequently enter into long-term agreements with the input and output firms in their environments. These formal contracts are a major device for stabilizing interorganizational relations. The organization will normally have contracts with suppliers, to assure the constant availability of raw materials. It may also contract with organizations that want to buy its products.

Local and state governments often entice corporations to operate in their areas by offering long-term leases and other contractual arrangements on favorable terms. The corporations lower their costs of doing business, the communities benefit from the new jobs (which lead to more saving and spending), and the governments benefit from the additional tax revenues.

Co-opting

When an organization absorbs other organizations or individuals, the process is called co-opting. This strategy is often invoked when the organization is threatened with severe change or extinction by another organization. To stop the organizing efforts of union activists, for example, a nonunion organization may make them supervisors or managers. Similarly, though not exactly a co-opt, a crisis situation at Chrysler caused the company to offer the head of the autoworkers union a seat on the corporation's board of directors.

Here is another example. Small company ABC develops a wonder product: a cheap match that can be struck repeatedly. Rather than allowing its own products to become obsolete or undertaking massive R&D expenditures, mammoth company XYZ may make the struggling young owners of company ABC an offer they can't refuse. Company XYZ co-opts the competition by absorbing company ABC.

Coalescing

When an organization joins together with other organizations in its environment for a specific purpose—usually to take some unified action—the process is called coalescing. One motive for coalescing is to avoid price-cutting wars in which all competing organizations lose. To make sure that this situation doesn't occur, the competing organizations band together, agree on an output level and a price range, and stick to them. They may meet regularly to review any violations or to set new levels and prices. The OPEC cartel of oil producers is a vivid illustration of the coalescing strategy. Although OPEC is only as strong as its weakest link, it has often been able to control the oil market and affect the economies of many countries.

BOUNDARY SPANNING

Organizational concern with monitoring the environment has led to the concept of boundary spanning.[16] Every organization has a boundary—an imaginary line separating the organizational system from its environment. Modern organizations place some of their members in boundary-spanning positions. These members interact regularly with members of other organizations. Boundary spanners link the organization to important elements in its environment.

Information Transfer

Working in buffer departments, boundary spanners concentrate not on materials and other physical resources but on *the transfer of information* between the organization and its environment. The work of organizational members in the following positions often spans the organization's boundary: public relations, personnel, marketing research, sales, advertising, purchasing, legal, lobbying, and labor negotiations. Boundary spanners monitor environmental changes, process incoming information, and modify outgoing information. They buffer the organization from harmful information and try to influence the environment by sending out favorable organizational information.

Boundary spanners are important because they are the *sensors* of the organizational system: the advanced guard. In times of great uncertainty, the organization expands these positions in order to accumulate enough information to make effective decisions. The boundary-spanning sensors scan the environment to detect developments in technology, the law, politics, economics, and consumer expectations. The acquired information helps the organization adjust its plans, avoid pitfalls, and capture opportunities.

Misreading the Environment If the boundary spanners misread the environment, bad information may flow into or out of the organization. Bad information can sometimes cause disaster. For example, the White House sensors shrugged off the Watergate break-in as petty theft, of no real significance. Yet the efforts of another organization— the *Washington Post*—caused further organizations (like the FBI and Congress) to investigate the break-in more thoroughly. Inaccurate monitoring by White House boundary spanners contributed to the development of a great political scandal.

Disadvantages for Spanners

People in boundary-spanning positions often operate under several disadvantages, among them role conflict, inadequate authority, and high visibility.

Role Conflict   Role conflict occurs for boundary spanners because the organizations they serve and the environment they deal with may have different goals, values, and attitudes. Boundary spanners are often caught in the middle. Consider a customer who wants to buy products of higher quality. A salesperson wants to meet the customer's demand and make the sale but realizes that the high cost to the company of providing high quality to the customer will reduce company profits. Another example would be the personnel department member caught between conflicting demands: line managers want their friends and relatives hired, and the federal government wants affirmative action guidelines followed.

Lack of Authority   Boundary spanners are mainly in sensing positions, so little authority is delegated to them. Because they are in unique positions and usually have good information, boundary spanners often know what decisions should be made but lack the authority to make them. The result may be lost sales and poor public relations.

For example, a manager wishes to purchase a photocopy machine with special features. The manager presents the organization's needs to three photocopy representatives, two from major companies and one from a small, upstart company. While the major-company representatives are contacting their managers for clearance, the small-company representative says "Done!" and whips out a contract. The small-company representative obviously had the authority to agree to special features (or had the courage to make the sale and worry about the consequences later).

High Visibility   Because boundary spanners are in positions of high visibility as links between the organization and the environment, they can get both the glory for successes and the blame for failures. Each side of the boundary comes to depend on the spanners and attributes both successes and failures to them. Recall that when a messenger brought an ancient king the information that the battle had been lost, the king had the messenger killed. Boundary spanners also have considerable power as the major channels of information about the outside to the inside and vice versa. Both the organization and the environmental elements must therefore view the spanner as a significant, responsible liaison.

SUMMARY

The definition of such terms as general environment, specific environment, boundary, and domain are necessary to understand and identify an organization's environment. The environment of most organizations contains elements of four general kinds. The *social/cultural* elements consist of governmental, educational, and legal/political organizations, as well as the general public itself. The *economic* elements are the capital and money markets, customers, the labor force, suppliers, and competitors. The final two elements are the *physical world* and the many *technological changes* occurring so rapidly today.

The preceding four elements result in an organizational environment that has varying degrees of four properties: complexity (the *number* of environmental elements), diversity (the number of *different* elements), change, and uncertainty (the unpredictability of change). Robert B. Duncan's model indicates which organizational structures are appropriate to the different combinations of three environmental properties: change, complexity, and uncertainty.

The standard terminology of environmental studies has arisen from several important theories. Tom Burns and G.M. Stalker suggested that changing environments are associated with flexible organizational structures just as stable environments are associated with rigid, mechanistic structures. Paul R. Lawrence and Jay W. Lorsch have extended those findings to the departmental level. Departments with a more certain environment tend to be more formalized than departments operating in an uncertain environment. James D. Thompson contributed the notion of buffers to protect the organization's technical core. He also confirmed that organizational structures vary in reaction to environmental stability and diversity.

Edward F. McDonough III and Richard Leifer showed that supervisors of work groups sometimes employ different structures at the same time. Fred E. Emery and Eric L. Trist categorized organizational environments into four types: placid/randomized, placid/clustered, disturbed/reactive, and turbulent. Like other researchers, they concluded that the organization's environment affects its structure. Michael T. Hannan and John Freeman applied ecological theory to organizations and showed that organizations, like organisms, survive if they use the resources of their environmental niches more effectively than competitors do.

Organizations have developed several approaches and techniques for dealing with other organizations in the environment. As James D. Thompson has pointed out, organizations buffer the technical core against distractions on the input side and attempt to smooth out the customer's use of a product or service on the output side. Other common techniques for improving interorganizational relations are rationing and stockpiling, contracting, co-opting, and coalescing.

In order to monitor and positively affect its relationship with the environment, an organization may place some members in boundary-spanning positions. Boundary spanners deal with interorganizational information transfer; they filter incoming messages and modify outgoing messages to the organization's benefit. Three potential disadvantages for boundary spanners are role conflict, lack of authority, and high visibility.

DISCUSSION QUESTIONS

1. What is meant by an organization's "environment"?

2. Is "technology" a part of "environment"?

3. According to C. West Churchman, what questions must we ask in order to determine whether an element is part of a given organizational system? Can you think of any other, better questions to ask?

4. What are the elements of an organization's environment? Which is the most important?

5. How does uncertainty influence the design of organizations?

6. The Duncan model includes three environmental properties: change, uncertainty, and complexity. How are they related? What is their relative importance in determining organizational structure?

7. According to Burns and Stalker, what is the relationship between structure and environment?

8. How does the buffering concept relate to organizational structure and design?

9. What were the contributions of Emery and Trist to our understanding of organizational environments?

10. Offer an example of a contemporary organization operating in each type of Emery-Trist environment.
11. How do interorganizational relations contribute to organizational uncertainty? What strategies are available for reducing that uncertainty?
12. What is boundary spanning? In what types of organizations is it most important?
13. Would a modern organization have a greater need for boundary spanners than an organization operating in 1900?
14. What formal organizational position would a typical boundary spanner hold? At what level on the chart would the boundary spanner appear? To whom would the boundary spanner report? What would the boundary spanner's job description be?

■ THE WILTON STEEL COMPANY

The Wilton Steel Company is a large, multidivison iron and steel manufacturer, incorporated in the early 1900s. As the demand for steel increased in the growing nation, Wilton continuously built new plants when and where they were needed. As the population moved westward, so did the company.

The technology of steel manufacture changed little over the years, so many of the plants resembled each other. The major difference was that the original eastern plants had a firmly entrenched union, a higher paid labor force, higher cost land and facilities, and less efficient equipment. Indeed, some of the older plants were not only fully depreciated (so they represented little tax advantage) but were also the physical structures most needing repairs.

One prime example was Wilton's Belden smelter, located on the banks of Lake Erie. The plant had brought in 600 employees when it was built in 1925, and Wilton had created the company town of Belden, Pennsylvania. As time passed, the company turned the town over to individual ownership. The town's population is now about 25,000, most of whom directly or indirectly get their living from the smelter payroll.

In the late 1980s, the Environmental Protection Agency told the Wilton Steel Company that its Belden smelter was polluting the air and water. Wilton Steel either had to clean up the smelter quickly or close down. The demand for Wilton steel had leveled off because of a recession, and Wilton's price had not been competitive with the price of Japanese steel for some time. Therefore, Wilton had excess steel production capacity at that time. Wilton management estimated that the cost of cleaning up the old plant would be roughly equal to the cost of building a new plant (at which labor costs would probably be lower). However, Wilton management realized that if the plant closed down, the entire town of Belden, Pennsylvania would close down too.

After hearing about the clean-up order, union officials offered to settle for an extremely reasonable union contract, just to help the company stay. Belden city officials offered to reduce Wilton's property taxes to the minimum. Yet, these measures were not nearly enough to offset the high cost of cleaning up the smelter.

What should Wilton Steel do now?

■ METROPOLITAN CITY UNIVERSITY

Metropolitan City, with its population of 750,000, is a major center for manufacturing, insurance, transportation, and finance. It is one of the busiest port, trucking, and rail centers in the southeast. Metropolitan City offers a variety of entertainment, sports, and recreational opportunities. It has a wealth of cultural assets; the city has museums, art galleries, a symphony orchestra, an opera company, and theatre and ballet groups.

The area is rich in history. Minutes from downtown are numerous historic forts, settlements, and sites. One of the nation's oldest cities, with a handsomely restored old quarter and an imposing fort, is less than an hour's drive away.

In addition to its advantages, Metropolitan City also has its share of urban blight, crime, and unemployment. Wages are well below the national average.

The state already has several major public and private universities. The State Board of Control wants to establish Metropolitan City University in downtown Metropolitan City. The new university will have upper-level undergraduate programs and some master's programs. According to the Board, the primary mission of the new university shall be "to meet the needs of the region."

How might the new university's environment—the metropolitan region in which it is located—affect its structure? How might that structure be different from the structure of a major doctorate-granting, residential, state university? To what extent are these structural differences related to the different environments?

BELLSOUTH INTERNATIONAL?

Prior to the breakup of American Telephone & Telegraph Co., its subsidiary companies enjoyed large profits in a regulated industry. After the breakup, regional subsidiary BellSouth Corp. realized that, while most of its revenue would continue to come from local telephone customers, it would have to expand beyond its traditional telephone monopoly in order to grow and prosper.

Like the other regional Bell companies, BellSouth turned aggressive. The company began a program of acquisitions, start-ups, and joint ventures. BellSouth even attempted to participate in the modernization of the Chinese telephone system. Other regional Bell companies purchased retail computer stores, commercial real estate, and many other businesses ranging from publishing to paging services.

No one was more surprised by the aggressive behavior of BellSouth Corp. and the other Bell companies than U.S. District Judge Harold H. Greene, who presided over the AT&T breakup. He complained, "There is a strange gap between the public desire to have good local telephone service at reasonable rates and the almost frenzied efforts of the regional holding companies to diversify. No one dreamed at the time the decree was written that the regional companies would be spreading out all over the globe."

Should an astute observer have been able to "dream" that BellSouth would make such a response to environmental change? How would you evaluate that response? How would you evaluate Judge Greene's reaction? If it is in fact a "complaint," is it a reasonable one?

HECK, NO—WE WON'T GO

In an address to the National Association of Merchandisers, management consultant Sally Norton stated:

"One of your top challenges in the 1990s will be to deal with the effects of a major environmental change: *work force immobility.* People used to move every five or so years, on average. Now they are staying put. They are tied down by two-career marriages, housing costs, and an increasing emphasis on the quality of life. Most Americans will opt to remain in place, rather than shoot for fast-track career success. The old incentives that your companies used to offer are not going to be enough to offset the disadvantages of moving around. You are all going to face major problems in recruiting, training, motivating, and promoting employees—especially managers, technicians, and professionals, who will refuse in growing numbers to relocate. You will have to run your businesses effectively with fewer transfers. People used to move to the job; you will soon have to take the job to them.''

Do you agree with Sally Norton's predictions of environmental change? If Norton is correct, what steps should organizations take to prepare, particularly with regard to their structures?

NOTES

1. C. West Churchman, *The Systems Approach* (New York: Delacorte Press, 1968), Chapter 3.
2. James D. Thompson, *Organizations in Action: Social Science Bases of Administrative Theory* (New York: McGraw-Hill, 1967).
3. These four properties have been attributed to organizational environments by Stephen M. Shortell in "The Role of Environment in a Configurational Theory of Organizations," *Human Relations* 30 (March 1977): 275–302. Other categorization schemes are those of Pradip N. Khandwalla (five categories: turbulence, hostility, diversity, technical complexity, and restrictiveness) and Robert B. Duncan (two basic dimensions: change and complexity). See Pradip N. Khandwalla, *The Design of Organizations* (New York: Harcourt Brace Jovanovich, 1977); and Robert B. Duncan, "The Characteristics of Organizational Environments and Perceived Environmental Uncertainty," *Administrative Science Quarterly* 17 (September 1972): 313–327.
4. James D. Thompson, *Organizations in Action: Social Science Bases of Administrative Theory,* p. 159.
5. Lawrence G. Hrebiniak and Charles C. Snow, "Industry Differences in Environmental Uncertainty," *Academy of Management Journal* 23 (December 1980): 750–759.
6. Robert B. Duncan, "The Characteristics of Organizational Environments and Perceived Environmental Uncertainty," pp. 313–327.
7. Tom Burns and G.M. Stalker, *The Management of Innovation* (London: Tavistock Publications, 1961). Burns and Stalker's work was described briefly in Chapter 10 on Formalization.
8. Paul R. Lawrence and Jay W. Lorsch, *Organization and Environment: Managing Differentiation and Integration* (Boston: Harvard University, Graduate School of Business Administration, 1967).
9. James D. Thompson, *Organizations in Action: Social Science Bases of Administrative Theory.*
10. Edward F. McDonough III and Richard Leifer, "Using Simultaneous Structures to Cope with Uncertainty," *Academy of Management Journal* 26 (December 1983): 727–735.
11. Ibid., p. 733.
12. Fred E. Emery and Eric L. Trist, "Causal Texture of Organizational Environments, *Human Relations* 18 (February 1965): 21–32.
13. Joseph E. McCann and John Selsky, "Hyperturbulence and the Emergence of Type 5 Environments," *Academy of Management Review* 9 (July 1984): 460–470.

14. Michael T. Hannan and John Freeman, "The Population Ecology of Organizations," *American Journal of Sociology* 82 (March 1977): 930.

15. Jeffrey Pfeffer and Gerald R. Salancik, *The External Control of Organizations: A Resource-Dependence Perspective* (New York: Harper & Row, 1978).

16. See Howard Aldrich and Diane Herker, "Boundary-Spanning Roles and Organizational Structure," *Academy of Management Review* 2 (April 1977): 217–230.

ADDITIONAL READINGS

Adizes, Ichak. "Organizational Passages: Diagnosing and Treating Lifecycle Problems of Organizations." *Organizational Dynamics* 8 (Summer 1979): 3–25.

Aldrich, Howard, and Jeffrey Pfeffer. "Environments of Organizations." *Annual Review of Sociology.* Edited by I.A. Inkeles. Palo Alto, CA: Annual Reviews, 1976.

Boulton, William R., et al. "Strategic Planning: Determining the Impact of Environmental Characteristics and Uncertainty." *Academy of Management Journal* 25 (September 1982): 500–509.

Bourgeois, L.J., III. "Strategy and Environment: A Conceptual Integration." *Academy of Management Review* 5 (January 1980): 25–39.

Cobb, Anthony T. "An Episodic Model of Power: Toward an Integration of Theory and Research." *Academy of Management Review* 9 (July 1984): 482–493.

Dess, Gregory G., and Donald W. Beard. "Dimensions of Organizational Task Environments." *Administrative Science Quarterly* 29 (January 1984): 52–73.

Dill, W.R. "Environment As an Influence on Managerial Autonomy." *Administrative Science Quarterly* 2 (March 1958): 409–443.

Downey, H.K., Donn Hellriegel, and John Slocum. "Environmental Uncertainty: The Construct and Its Application." *Administrative Science Quarterly* 20 (December 1975): 613–629.

Hrebiniak, Lawrence G., and William F. Joyce. "Organizational Adaptation: Strategic Choice and Environmental Determinism." *Administrative Science Quarterly* 30 (September 1985): 336–349.

Kimberly, John R. "Environmental Constraints and Organizational Structure." *Administrative Science Quarterly* 20 (March 1975): 1–8.

Lenz, R.T., and Jack L. Engledow. "Environmental Analysis Units and Strategic Decision Making: A Field Study of Selected 'Leading Edge' Corporations." *Strategic Management Journal* 7 (January/February 1986): 69–89.

Miller, Danny. "Evolution and Revolution: A Quantum View of Structural Change in Organizations." *Journal of Management Studies* 19 (April 1982): 131–151.

Negandhi, Anant R. *Interorganizational Theory.* Kent, OH: Kent State University Press, 1980.

Romanelli, Elaine, and Michael L. Tushman. "Inertia, Environments and Strategic Choice: A Quasi-Experimental Design for Comparative-Longitudinal Research." *Management Science* 32 (May 1986): 608–621.

Schmidt, Stuart M., and Larry L. Cummings. "Organizational Environment, Differentiation and Perceived Environmental Uncertainty." *Decision Sciences* 7 (July 1976): 447–467.

Terreberry, Shirley. "The Evolution of Organizational Environments." *Administrative Science Quarterly* 12 (March 1968): 590–613.

Thompson, James D., and William J. McEwen. "Organizational Goals and Environment: Goal-Setting As an Interaction Process." *American Sociological Review* 23 (February 1958): 23–31.

Turkovich, R. "A Core Typology of Organizational Environments." *Administrative Science Quarterly* 19 (September 1974): 380–394.

Ulrich, David, and Jay B. Barney. "Perspectives in Organizations: Resource Dependence, Efficiency, and Population." *Academy of Management Review* 9 (July 1984): 471–481.

Yasai-Ardekani, Masoud. "Structural Adaptations to Environments." *Academy of Management Review* 11 (January 1986): 9–21.

The Life Cycle

In 1950 Kenneth Boulding first suggested the concept of organizational life cycles. Since that time, discussions of the organizational life cycle have taken place within many disciplines, including management, public administration, education, sociology, psychology, and marketing.

This chapter presents a general life-cycle model and several variations on it, discusses certain weaknesses of life-cycle theory, and answers two major questions about life cycles.

THE GENERAL MODEL: BIRTH, YOUTH, MATURITY/DECLINE

In the most general model, the organizational life cycle has three stages: birth, youth, and maturity/decline. These stages, briefly outlined in Chapter 3, will be amplified here. The more complex models will be presented later in this chapter.

Stage I: Birth

A merger or a joint venture may occasionally lead to the creation of a new organization. However, an organization is more often born in one of two ways: either a single-person craft expands, or an aggressive entrepreneur assembles people to help promote a new idea, product, or service. The motive in both cases is usually the desire for profits.

Importance of Origins   The time, place, and circumstances of the organization's birth are very important in determining its long-term success. In his investigation of organizational birth frequencies, Johannes M. Pennings says the following about the significance of the organization's creation:

> The act of creation itself may be contingent on the attributes of the socioeconomic setting from which the organization emerges. Furthermore, the entrepreneurial act involves a commitment to a location that constrains the organization geographically.

Other decisions at the time of creation imply a selection of markets or domains, the acquisition of equipment and other resources, and the recruitment of members, which impart a distinct and enduring posture toward the organization's environment. Organizational viability might be a function of those inert and early-acquired characteristics and their compatibility with environmental conditions. Although it is true that an organization can change and display flexibility to environmental modifications, it is cast into an initial mold that is discernible during the rest of its life. An understanding of its creation could, therefore, foster deeper insights into the subsequent relationship between the organization and its environment.[1]

Who and Where   Who sets the organization up and where it is set up will have lasting influence. Original owners tend to hire people similar to themselves; they, in turn, will later tend to do the same thing. Where the organization is established may well encourage or limit growth. The entrepreneur or craftsman interested in growth will take care not to locate in an area with geographical limitations or labor restrictions.

Expanding a Craft   An organization born from a craft has a natural division of labor, based on craft skills, in which jobs are easily interchanged. Most of the coordination is achieved, according to Henry Mintzberg, "by the standardization of skills—the result of apprenticeship training—with whatever independencies remain coordinated by mutual adjustment among the craftsmen."[2] The craft organization does not really need detailed coordination. The work group is small, and the entrepreneur/manager works alongside or near the employees. Goals are usually product oriented (for example, "we must make six pairs of shoes today"), and each worker has a clear role in achieving those goals. The unsophisticated technology allows a specialization of tasks, which makes coordination simple.

The Entrepreneur's Young Organization   In an organization set up by an entrepreneur, coordination also takes the form of direct supervision. The entrepreneur makes the important decisions and coordinates their execution by direct supervision. The entrepreneur can operate in this manner because the organization is small, with an informal, organic structure.

Enter the Family   Master craftsmen and entrepreneurs rarely wish to delegate decision-making authority. As organizational growth makes delegation necessary, the owners tend to rely on their families. Because they have monetary and emotional investments in the organization, family members have the most to gain or lose. They should therefore be concerned and responsible.

Family members must also be competent. If they insist on their "birthright" and, regardless of their competence, hold senior posts while their subordinates do the work they should be doing and make the decisions they should be making, the firm's success and even survival are in danger.

Exit the Family   Eventually, an expanding family business faces a management crisis: the need to formalize the process of administering the organization. According to Theodore Cohn and Roy A. Lindberg, that need arises when three kinds of organizational effort first occur together:

When (1) primary work, such as making and selling, and (2) supportive work, such as financing and inventory management are joined by (3) connecting work, such as is performed by foremen and other supervisors, an organization can no longer put off establishing a formal administrative process if it wishes to keep its gains or continue to grow.[3]

Further Growth   The organization may ultimately strain the capabilities of the entrepreneur's family. At that point, according to Bernard Barry, four courses of action are available:[4]

1. *To continue under family ownership and management.* Families may continue to own their firms and accept responsibility for their management, generation after generation. A family operation might be appropriate if the organization requires a high degree of trust. An organization using a secret manufacturing process may want to "keep it in the family." For the traditional family concern to survive, it must generally choose a business with two characteristics: (1) the technology is rather simple, and (2) the quality of service can compensate for other deficiencies. Even under these conditions, success is still uncertain.

2. *To continue under family ownership but not management.* A family may decide to abandon the day-to-day operation of its business and set up a holding company or investment trust to protect and manage its investments. In such firms, the separation of ownership and management is more or less complete. Some family members may remain interested in the firm, sitting on its board of directors or playing minor roles in its affairs.

The family holding company usually retains ultimate control of the business. This holding company may resist progressive suggestions from top management—for example, that the firm should diversify, expand, or decentralize. If disagreements on such matters cause able managers to resign, the organization may stagnate.

3. *To abandon total ownership but retain control.* A family can continue to control a company without complete ownership of the company's stock. A 51 percent ownership share can control any corporation, and a much smaller percentage of ownership can control many corporations, provided the rest of the stock is widely dispersed. Abandoning total ownership enables the family to acquire the capital that permits organizational growth. Family members can continue to be involved by representing the firm to its customers and playing prominent roles in the community.

If the firm does well and the nonfamily managers can achieve their career goals, this arrangement may work. If bad times come along, family members with a controlling interest may feel considerable pressure from shareholders and employees.

4. *To evolve into a formal concern.* If the firm is not doing well, then family members must join employees and other shareholders in questioning the wisdom of continued family control. Once the organization has professional management and a broad ownership base, it has entered its second stage: youth.

Stage II: Youth

When professional management takes over, unencumbered by a family with a controlling interest, the organization's primary goal often shifts from profit to growth. The new management team wants to demonstrate its competence, and growth is the most obvious way to do so. Growth means status; a manager of a large company is respected—even if the company's return on investment is low.

This new concern with growth has several results. First, goals become less specific, less measurable. Second, the organization places increasing emphasis on marketing, hoping for the increased sales that will justify the expansion of plant and acquisition of new, more efficient tools and equipment.

Stage III: Maturity/Decline

As an organization matures and starts to decline, a desire to *survive* overshadows the organization's earlier goals: profit and growth. Organizations at this stage are in many ways the opposite of Stage I organizations. The Stage III organization is large; its technology is complex; its structure is bureaucratic; it is financially oriented; it is greatly affected by market and social forces; and, because it is so complex and feels endangered, it emphasizes the integration of member efforts. A Stage III organization often tries to reverse its decline by looking closely at its structure and operations, then "revitalizing" them.

Organizations do not have to grow old before they decline or die. John Freeman and his colleagues have demonstrated what they call "a liability of newness" for three types of organizations: national labor unions, newspapers, and semiconductor manufacturers.[5] Newness is apparently a liability for such organizations because more younger firms die than older firms. Therefore, the older that organizations of these types become, the better in general are their chances for longer life.

Characteristics of the Stages

Structures and strategies change as organizations move through their life cycles. Table 17.1 presents some characteristics of organizations at each of three life-cycle stages. For instance, as an organization moves from inception to maturity, it tends to shift from a lack of formal structure, to formal centralization, to formal decentralization. During the three phases, its top managers are at first generalists, then specialists, then strategists and planners. Its communication processes begin informally and eventually become very formal.

The Life Cycle of Subunits

Just as the organization itself has a life cycle, so too do its subunits. A prime example is the stages in the lives of an organization's plants or factories. Interest in the social responsibility of organizations to the community has intensified; therefore, factory closings—which often affect communities drastically—have received increased attention over the past decade. Perhaps an understanding of factory life cycles can enable organizations to use their factories more effectively.

Roger W. Schmenner suggests that companies should gear their long-term plans for factories to normal factory life cycles.[6] He suggests that life-cycle plans can easily be implemented from the outset for new factories. Managers must study the history of

Table 17.1   CHARACTERISTICS AT DIFFERENT ORGANIZATIONAL LIFE-CYCLE STAGES

Characteristics	Inception stage	High-growth stage	Maturity stage
Type of structure	No formal structure	Centralized; Formal	Decentralized; Formal
Age and size	Young and small	Older and larger	Oldest and largest (or once large)
Growth rate	Inconsistent but improving	Rapid	Slowing or declining
Communication and planning	Informal; Face to face; Little planning	Moderately formal; Budgets	Very formal; Five-year plans; Rules and regulations
Decision-making method	Individual judgment; Entrepreneurial	Professional mgmt.; Analytical tools	Professional mgmt.; Bargaining
Make-up of top-level management staff	Generalists	Specialists	Strategists; Planners
Reward system	Personal and subjective	Impersonal and systematic	Impersonal, formal, and totally objective

Source: Adapted from Ken G. Smith, Terence R. Mitchell, and Charles E. Summer, "Top Level Management Priorities in Different Stages of the Organizational Life Cycle," *Academy of Management Journal* 28 (December 1985): 802. Used by permission.

existing plants, to understand where they have been and at what life-cycle stage they may presently be.

Managers establishing plans for factories will have the best chance for success if they focus on the following aspects of plant operations at different life-cycle stages.

I. *The Start-up and Early Years*
  A. Plant engineering: Work flow, materials handling, equipment choice.
  B. Work force: The number of workers, age balance, skill levels, wage schemes, and quality-of-work-life programs.
  C. Overhead functions: Raw materials purchasing, production planning, industrial engineering. Should the new factory perform these functions or share with the parent?
  D. Control systems: Production, inventory, and quality control systems.
  E. Contingency planning: This area involves such considerations as conditions for on-site expansion, products and processes that would/would not be consistent with the factory's capabilities, and conditions that might make closing the plant necessary.
II. *The Mature Years*
  A. Maintain "focused" manufacturing: Keep the product line small and manageable. Expand gradually.
  B. Make adjustments in light of the factory's changing role within the organization: Consider increased vertical integration, adding overhead functions, grouping factories geographically, and site-sharing by different divisions of the company.
  C. Keep the factory productive as it ages: Remain abreast of long-term industry trends; develop new programs to tap the thinking of workers and supervisors.

III. *The Failing Years*
   A. Try to save the plant: Replace equipment, make different products, change the layout, institute new work-force policies.
   B. Be ready to move quickly: If the factory must be closed, do it swiftly. A lingering death may cause lower morale, even sabotage.

LIFE-CYCLE MODELS

Over the past two decades, numerous variations on the basic life-cycle model have appeared. Five categories of models will be presented here.

Resources Models

The Social Resources Model In 1965 Arthur Stinchcombe attempted to show that the era during which an organization is founded has lasting effects on its later structure.[7] For example, textile organizations and automobile manufacturing organizations of the modern era are structured differently partly because they were founded during different time periods—the textiles during the nineteenth century and the automotives during the twentieth century. In textile companies of the mid-1960s, one could still find work being done by unpaid family members; this was not the case in automobile manufacturing companies.

Another interesting difference is that most industries founded in the twentieth century have staff departments of professionally trained people; organizations founded earlier tend not to have elaborate staff departments.

According to Stinchcombe, the social resources available at the time of an organization's founding largely determine its structure. The organization forms itself to take advantage of economic, technical, and environmental conditions. And not all structures are possible under all conditions.

But why do these structures persist over the years? Stinchcombe gives three reasons:

1. The original structure may continue to be the most effective for achieving the organization's purposes.
2. Tradition, vested interests, and persisting ideologies may tend to preserve the structure.
3. The organization may not be in the highly competitive environment that would require it to adapt alternate organizational forms in order to survive.[8]

The Slack-Structure Model The model of Frank Tuzzolino and Barry Armandi suggests that the organizational life cycle has five developmental stages, each associated with a certain organizational structure.[9] The stages and structures are:

STAGE	STRUCTURE
Creation	Ad hoc
Growth	Organic
Stabilization	Bureaucratic

Decline	Recentralization
Dissolution	(Absence of structure)

The dissolved organization can be reborn; it can be recreated, with a new, ad hoc structure. Figure 17.1 presents this model.

Tuzzolino and Armandi introduce into the model the concept of *organizational slack,* defined as payments to organizational members *in excess of* what the organization absolutely must pay them in order to have them function adequately to maintain the organization. The slack curve is roughly bell-shaped. The newly created and the dissolving organizations have hardly any slack; the growing and declining organizations have some slack; and the stable, bureaucratic organization has considerable slack.

Crisis Models

The Situational Confrontation Model   Gordon Lippitt's model maintains that crises requiring concentrated organizational attention in a sense define the stages of life-cycle growth.[10] The organization's place in its life cycle is determined not so much by size, market share, age, or management sophistication but—in true modern contingency fashion—by what key issues the organization is facing and how it confronts them. The organization must successfully and appropriately cope with one phases's crisis if it is to move on to the next phase. Lippitt identified six critical situations or confrontations. They are most likely to occur in the following order.

1. *Launching the venture.* What and how much are we willing to risk, personally and financially, to get this venture going?
2. *Survival and sacrifice.* How much are we willing to sacrifice, personally and financially, to keep this organization going?
3. *Achieving stability.* Are we willing to be formally organized? Are we willing to accept and enforce discipline?
4. *Pride and reputation.* Are we willing to engage in candid self-examination? Will we combat outside threats to the organization's reputation?
5. *Developing uniqueness.* Are we willing to put into effect the changes that will make us unique?

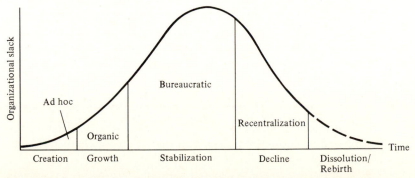

Figure 17.1   Tuzzolino and Armandi's slack-structure life-cycle model. (*Source:* Frank Tuzzolino and Barry Armandi, "Organizational Design, Slack, and the Life Cycle," *Academy of Management Proceedings* [1982], p. 261. Used by permission.)

6. *Contributing to society.* Are we willing to help our employees, our community, our society, our nation to fulfill themselves, without expecting a direct return? Will we use our resources to improve the quality of human life?

The first two crises would most often occur in the "birth" phase, the second two in the "youth" phase, and the third two in the "maturity" phase. Lippitt believed that organizations decline because of drastic changes in the external environment or because they fail to recognize and confront the six significant crises.

The Evolution-Revolution Model   Larry Greiner envisions the organization as developing through evolutionary periods, each concluded by a revolution.[11] During the evolutionary periods, the organization enjoys growth without major economic setbacks or severe internal disruption. The revolutionary phases usually occur as the managerial procedures designed for a smaller size and an earlier time become ineffective. During each revolutionary period, management's critical task is to discover new practices with which to manage the organization during the next evolutionary period.

The length of these time periods varies from industry to industry. Evolutionary periods often range from four to eight years. For a fast-growing industry they may be shorter, and for a mature, slow-growing industry they may be longer.

Growth phase 1: creation   During its first phase, the organization creates its product and its market. The creative-evolution stage has several characteristics:

- Being technically or entrepreneurially oriented, the company's founders disdain management activities. Their energies are entirely absorbed in making and selling a new product.
- Communication among employees is frequent and informal.
- Salaries are modest. Long hours of work are rewarded primarily by the promise of future benefits.
- Control of activities comes from immediate marketplace feedback; the management reacts to customer behavior.

The leadership crisis   As the company grows, its increasingly large-scale production requires more knowledge about the efficiencies of manufacturing. Effectively managing the larger number of employees through informal communication becomes impossible. Unlike the original employees, these new employees are not motivated by an intense dedication to the product or organization. These developments combine to bring about the first revolution: the leadership crisis. The solution is to locate and install a strong business manager, acceptable to the organization's founders, who can use effective management principles and techniques to lead the organization onward.

Growth phase 2: direction   Under the new, able leadership, the organization enters a second evolutionary period with the following characteristics:

- Manufacturing and marketing activities are separated, and all jobs become more specialized.

- The organization adopts work standards, incentives, budgets, and accounting systems.
- Communication becomes more formal and impersonal.
- The new manager and a few key associates direct organizational effort. Lower-level supervisors act as functional specialists rather than as autonomous decision makers.

The autonomy crisis   Although these new techniques channel employee efforts more efficiently into growth, they eventually become inadequate as the organization becomes even larger, more complex, and more diverse. Lower-level managers and supervisors find themselves restricted by the cumbersome, centralized hierarchy. They are torn between following established procedures and taking initiative. The autonomy crisis develops as lower-level managers demand more freedom to make decisions. The result of this "revolution" is greater delegation of authority.

Growth phase 3: delegation   This growth phase evolves from successful application of a decentralized organizational structure. Some of its characteristics are:

- Managers of plants and market territories acquire greater responsibility and authority.
- Profit centers and bonuses stimulate motivation.
- Top executives use periodic field reports to manage by exception.
- Management adds new acquisitions to the organization's other decentralized units.
- Communication from the top is infrequent and is usually by correspondence, telephone, or brief visits to field locations.

Expansion in this phase comes about primarily through motivation at lower levels. Managers at these levels have the authority and the incentives to penetrate larger markets, respond rapidly to customers, and develop new products.

The control crisis   Top executives eventually sense that they are losing control over the highly diversified field operations. The autonomous field managers have had much freedom, and freedom sometimes breeds a narrow, self-serving attitude. A crisis occurs as top management seeks to regain control over the whole company. That control is achieved by the use of special coordination techniques.

Growth phase 4: coordination   Top management initiates and administers new, formal control systems. Here are some of the new arrangement's characteristics:

- Formal planning procedures are established and intensely reviewed.
- Decentralized units are merged into product groups.
- Capital expenditures are carefully evaluated and parceled out across the organization.
- Certain technical functions, such as data processing, are centralized at headquarters, while many daily operating decisions remain decentralized.

The red-tape crisis   Eventually a lack of confidence builds between line and staff, and between headquarters and the field. The number of new systems and programs begins to exceed their usefulness. As procedures take precedence over problem solving and as innovation is dampened, a fourth revolutionary "red-tape" crisis occurs. The organization overcomes the crisis by placing a new emphasis on strong interpersonal collaboration.

Growth phase 5: collaboration   In this new phase, the organization stresses greater spontaneity in management action, teamwork, and the skillful confrontation and resolution of interpersonal differences. The collaborative stage has several characteristics, including the following:

- The focus is on team action to solve problems quickly.
- Key managers frequently discuss major problems in conference.
- Matrix-type structures are often used, to assemble the appropriate problem-solving teams.
- Economic rewards are geared more to team performance than to individual achievement.

The next, nameless crisis   Many large U.S. companies are now in the collaborative evolutionary stage. Although we must wait to see what revolutionary crisis these companies must face, Greiner suggests that the next major revolution may be emotional and physical exhaustion of employees, caused by intense collaborative teamwork and stressful pressure for innovative solutions to organizational problems. This crisis will require new structures and programs, to help employees rest, reflect, and become renewed. Greiner suggests that dual organizational structures may result—one structure for work and another for rest and reflection—with employees moving back and forth between them.

Greiner's conception of how an organization evolves from birth to maturity is depicted in Figure 17.2. At every stage of the organization's life history, different structures and procedures appear to be appropriate. The figure also shows the organization to be getting larger as it evolves. Whether the appropriate structures are determined by life-cycle stage or organizational size is open to question.

Decline and Inertia Models

The Whetten Model   Most organization theorists are inclined to concentrate on the earlier stages of the general life-cycle model. Since the early 1980s, the decline phase has been receiving more attention. Two notable contributors are David A. Whetten and Jeffrey D. Ford.

The organizational decline that concerns Whetten is marked by reductions in such significant measures as number of employees, profits, assets, customers and so on.[12] The decline results in increased stress on organizational members, more interpersonal conflict, low morale, and high turnover. The decline leads to across-the-board cutbacks in all departments, even those that have proven themselves efficient and effective. Whetten indicates four sources of organizational decline: atrophy, vulnerability, loss of legitimacy, and environmental entropy.

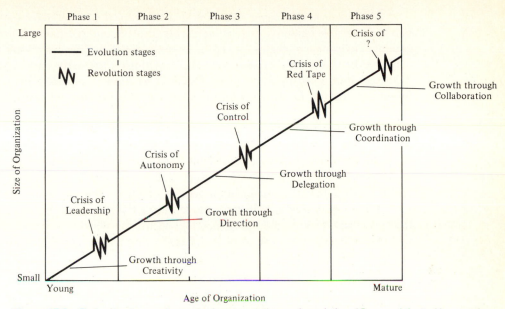

Figure 17.2   Greiner's stages of organizational evolution and revolution. (*Source:* Adapted by permission of the *Harvard Business Review*. Exhibit from "Evolution and Revolution as Organizations Grow" by Larry Greiner [July/August 1972], pp. 37–46. Copyright © 1972 by the President and Fellows of Harvard College; all rights reserved.)

Atrophy   Organizations can lose their edge and fail to adjust to changing times. Decline caused by lack of responsiveness to change can occur at any life-cycle stage, in both young and old organizations.

A notable feature of the decline stage, and a partial cause of it, is the organization's delusion of invulnerability. The organization is so large and successful that top management overlooks opportunities or glosses over danger signs. The organization has become fat and content. It has lost its "eye-of-the-tiger" look; it is no longer hungry for advancement.

Vulnerability   Young organizations, particularly those in their infancy, are highly susceptible to failure. Organizations that decline before they really get going are often started by people with strong technical backgrounds but without knowledge in other important areas, such as marketing and finance.

The U.S. Commerce Department indicates that almost 70 percent of new businesses decline and fail before they are three years old. These organizations do not have the experience to recognize and deal with the dangers in their environments. Their inexperience makes them vulnerable to all the difficulties that organizations must face.

Loss of legitimacy   Why does our organization exist? If the organization cannot give a credible answer to that question, it has lost its societal legitimacy and may soon die. David A. Whetten presents the case of the Federal Metal and Non-Metallic Mine Safety Board of Review. Although it had no work to do, it managed to survive until the head of the board indicated in an interview that the board was serving no function and had no reason to exist.

Environmental entropy   Entropy is a theoretical concept referring to any system's irreversible tendency toward increasing disorder and inertness. When an organization's environment begins to erode, organizational decline may soon follow. For instance, horse-drawn carriages were the rage during the early part of this century. Those organizations supplying materials for horse-drawn transportation were successful and important. However, with the advent of the gasoline combustion engine, the environment of these organizations began to change. Many organizations either did not recognize the significance of the change or refused to do anything about it. These organizations no longer exist.

Whetten describes several possible organizational responses to decline, among them defending, responding, preventing, and generating. The response chosen will depend on whether the organization accepts or rejects the impending change.

Figure 17.3 depicts Whetten's model. Proactive responses are those initiated by the organization before the change actually occurs but when it seems imminent. Reactive responses are not made until the change occurs. The model indicates that if the organization's attitude toward a change is positive, it will either generate (encourage the impending change) or respond (embrace the change after it occurs). If the organization's attitude is negative, it will first try to prevent the change from occurring, then defend itself against the change if it does occur.

The Ford Model   Jeffrey D. Ford has noted several characteristics of organizations in decline.[13]

1. The increase in number of administrators may be greater during decline than during the growth stages of the life cycle.
2. For a given size level, declining organizations are more highly structured than growing organizations.
3. Structural changes occur more rapidly during growth than during decline.
4. Size-structure relationships during growth periods are not the same after a decline period as they were before the decline period.
5. Decline causes structural changes. Reestablishing the original structure after the decline has ended is difficult. Ford calls this phenomenon "structural hysteresis."

The Inertia Model   Michael T. Hannan and John Freeman have theorized that as organizations move through the life cycle, they have an increasing tendency toward

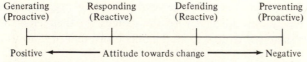

Figure 17.3   Management's responses to environmentally induced change. (*Source:* David A. Whetten, "Sources, Responses, and Effects of Organizational Decline," in *The Organizational Life Cycle: Issues in the Creation, Transformation and Decline of Organizations,* ed. John R. Kimberly and Robert H. Miles [San Francisco: Jossey-Bass Publications, 1980], p. 363. Used by permission.)

inertia—an unwillingness or inability to change.[14] Smaller, newer organizations respond more rapidly to threats and opportunities than larger, older organizations.

In the initial stages of the life cycle, the organization experiments with different routines, programs, and structures—trying to find a successful combination. Once the organization succeeds, it tends to retain and repeat successful patterns. As the organization moves through its life cycle, inertia sets in as it reproduces the successful structures of the past.

The Power Model

The relationship of power to the life cycle has been receiving attention in recent years. Henry Mintzberg has created a model showing the relationship between life-cycle stages and various configurations of organizational power.[15] The model includes six power types, each with a different balance of internal and external power.

Autocracy   High levels of power are tightly controlled in a very personal way by one individual. External groups with a stake in organizational activities have hardly any power. (Example: an entrepreneurial firm.)

Instrument   An external group or person exerts a high degree of control, while the internal members operate bureaucratically as an instrument for pursuing the external group's objectives. (Example: a prison.)

Missionary   An internal group or person—with a strong system of beliefs, developed from the organization's mission—exerts a high degree of control. The external group passively allows this dedicated internal group's missionary zeal and ideology to govern. (Example: The Foundation for Infantile Paralysis.)

Closed System   Internal control is bureaucratic; external control is passive or impotent. The organizational administrators in power want to increase their support base among the membership and maintain their power. (Examples: labor unions and political parties.)

Meritocracy   The internal group is professional and has extensive technical expertise. Their special knowledge is their source of power. The external group has little influence. The internal experts are primarily loyal to their professions rather than to the organization. (Example: a university.)

Political Arena   The central area of power is neither external nor internal. The external group is diffused, while the internal groups are highly politicized. Conflict is widespread, and identifying a controlling group is difficult. (Example: the U.S. Congress.)

These six power types or situations combine with four life-cycle stages to make up the Mintzberg life-cycle/power model depicted in Figure 17.4.

Stage I: Formation   During its formative stage, the organization is an autocracy with one person controlling the direction, elaborating goals, and acquiring the means for

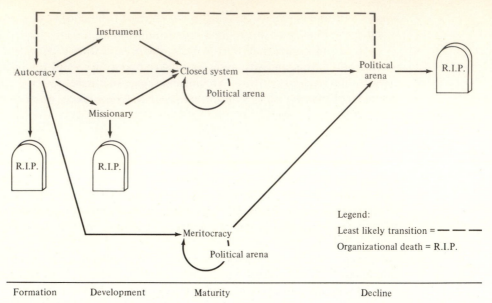

Figure 17.4   Mintzberg model: Organizational life cycle and power. (*Source:* After Henry Mintzberg, "Power and Organizational Life Cycles," *Academy of Management Review* 9 [April 1984], p. 213. Used by permission.)

achieving them. The autocracy may be brief, if the experts hired to help out subsequently "overthrow" the founder. Or the autocracy may exist until the founder retires or dies.

Stage II: Development   The young organization may expire during its formative years. If, however, it does grow and develop, its power arrangement may become a closed system but will more probably become missionary, instrument, or (for high-tech organizations) meritocracy.

The move from autocracy to missionary most often occurs after a charismatic leader departs. This type of leader has usually instilled a strong ideology in the organization which is perpetuated by lasting traditions, values, and norms. The autocracy may become an instrument form if the founder's departure leaves the organization vulnerable. An unfriendly takeover may ensue, or the founder's successors may sell out to an external group.

If the organization depends on technical expertise (a group of doctors, for example), the autocracy may swiftly become a mature meritocracy in which the experts assume the founder's power. The "development" stage is simply skipped.

Stage III: Maturity   Eventually both instruments and missionaries develop into closed systems, becoming more formalized as they grow. Formal control mechanisms enable a few leaders to exert power over lower levels in the hierarchy. Administrators take steps to consolidate their power and to remain firmly entrenched. In 1915 Robert Michels, convinced that such a power shift to a few administrators was inevitable, labeled this transition "the iron law of oligarchy."

Stage IV: Decline   In their maturity, organizations are either closed-system bureau-cracies or professionally dominated meritocracies. If, as has been said, "Absolute power tends to corrupt absolutely," then the decline of both organizational types may be inevitable. In the closed system, deviant groups may challenge the existing power group because the organization is no longer seeking to achieve its original goals. These challenging groups may be external (like consumer advocates) or internal (like disgrun-tled line workers). The organization becomes a political arena as various groups strug-gle for dominance.

In meritocracies the experts may become more interested in using their power than practicing their disciplines. Internal power struggles may ensue, followed by attempts of external groups to exert their influence. Again, the organizational environ-ment becomes politicized and filled with conflict. The organization may not survive the chaos, or a strong autocratic leader may reestablish order and begin the life/power cycle anew but with a more complex organization than the original.

The Management Components Model

Some life-cycle models include only the stages of growth or evolution. The very detailed PAEI model of Ichak Adizes, presented in Figure 17.5, also defines the stages of decline.[16]

According to Adizes, organizational effort has four primary components: *Pro-duction, Administration, Entrepreneurship,* and *Integration.* Those components make up the PAEI of his model. Successful organizations must *produce;* they must effectively achieve the results for which they were created. Organizations must be *administered;* the sequence, timing, and intensity of decisions must be right. Organizations must have a spirit of *entrepreneurship;* they must be creative, take risks, and adapt. Finally, the

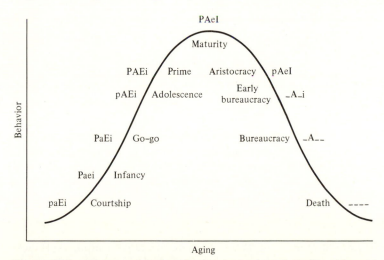

Figure 17.5   Adizes model: Organizational growth and decline. (*Source:* Adapted, by permission of the publisher, from "Organizational Passages: Diag-nosing and Treating Lifecycle Problems of Organizations," Ichak Adizes, *Or-ganizational Dynamics* 8 [Summer 1979], p. 8, © 1979 American Management Association, New York. All rights reserved.)

organization must be *integrated;* the parts must function as a whole. Adizes specifies ten life-cycle phases. As the organization passes from one phase to the next, it emphasizes different PAEI components or component combinations.

The Courtship Stage: paEi   During the courtship stage, entrepreneurship is dominant, with the other three components playing minor roles. An entrepreneur is excitedly trying to transform an imaginative idea into an organization. The entrepreneur courts supporters and sells them on the idea's possibilities.

The Infant Organization: Paei   Once the entrepreneur acquires the support to get the organization going, the focus shifts to production. Risks are involved, and expenses must be paid. Beset by short-term pressures, the organization thinks about little other than making and selling products, to justify the risks and to pay the bills. The organization has few policies, systems, procedures, or budgets. It is highly centralized; the entrepreneur usually runs everything. If the organization continues to focus on short-run market opportunities, it may enter its Go-Go Stage.

The Go-Go Stage: PaEi   During this stage, the production-oriented organization tries to take advantage of *every* opportunity. The organization may become endangered by spreading itself too thin; it may run out of capital. At this stage, the "founder's trap" may occur. The founder may insist on continuing to make all the decisions, refusing to establish workable systems, procedures, and policies that do not require the entrepreneur's personal decisions and judgments. To avoid this trap, the organization must give its administrative component more attention.

The Adolescent Organization: pAEi   As the administrative role rises in importance, the organization spends more time in meetings, to plan and coordinate. Computers are installed, training programs are developed, and labor policies are established. These efforts cost money, so the organization continues to look for new profit-making opportunities.

The Prime Organization: PAEi   During this stage, sales and profits grow at a stable, predictable rate. The organization has dependable plans and procedures. It is successful and in the prime of its life.

     What happens now may depend on the changing aspirations of top management. If these aspirations are fulfilled, the organization may continue its steady, successful growth. If managerial aspirations are frustrated, the entrepreneurial drive will eventually decline, along with the sense of urgency and the desire to grow and change. The organization may start to enjoy the fruits of yesterday's efforts instead of looking toward tomorrow's challenges.

The Mature Organization: PAeI   The mature organization continues to achieve satisfactory production results, has adequate administrative procedures and policies, and has an institutionalized system of coordination. The climate is friendly, yet formal. The organization spends less and less on research and development. The budget allocation for change and adaptation decreases. Eventually, as the entrepreneurial eagerness to excel dwindles, production results are adversely affected.

The Autocratic Organization: pAeI   The climate in the autocratic organization, with its emphasis on administration, is relatively stable. The concern is not so much with what you did and why you did it, but *how* you did it. Organizational members tend to lie low, to avoid making waves, to survive rather than succeed.

To maintain revenue growth, the organization raises prices rather than generate new products or penetrate new markets. Customers eventually refuse to pay the higher prices, sales drop, and total revenue declines.

The Early Bureaucracy: _A_i   During this next stage, the organization's unsatisfactory results become apparent to all. Instead of fighting competitors, the organization's executives begin fighting each other. The creative capabilities of managers are not directed toward production results, marketing strategies, or other constructive organizational projects; instead they are engaged in a struggle to survive by discrediting and eliminating their fellow administrators.

Bureaucracy: _A__   Very little gets done in the bureaucracy. The atmosphere is agreeable and peaceful, as everyone fills out the proper forms and adheres to systems, rules, and procedures. No one wants to change. Teamwork has disappeared—and so have results.

Death: ____   Ultimately, maintaining the empty forms of administration is not enough. The organization has no production results, a meaningless administrative system, no entrepreneurial drive, and no sense of integrative teamwork. The organization stops functioning and is dissolved.

Mintzberg's Review

Henry Mintzberg reviewed the literature and found that most life-cycle models include the same stages: craft, entrepreneurial, bureaucratic, divisionalized, and matrix.[17] The middle three stages are common to many organizations. Depending on the nature of their work, some organizations begin with a craft stage while others begin with entrepreneurship. Only a few organizations have reached the matrix stage. Here are Mintzberg's summary remarks:

> Organizations generally begin their lives with nonelaborated, organic structures. Some begin in the *craft* stage and then shift to the *entrepreneurial* stage as they begin to grow, although more seem to begin in the entrepreneurial stage. As organizations in the entrepreneurial stage age and grow, they begin to formalize their structure and eventually make the transition to a new stage, that of *bureaucratic* structure. Further growth and aging often drive stage-two bureaucracies to superimpose market-based grouping on their functional structure, thus bringing them into the new stage: *divisionalized* structure. Finally, some recent evidence suggests that there may be a final stage, that of *matrix* structure, which transcends divisionalization and causes a reversion to organic structure. Of course, not all organizations need to pass through all these stages, but many seem to pass through a number of them in the sequence presented.[18]

LIFE-CYCLE THEORY: SOME PROBLEMS

Although the different life-cycle theories have been expressed with confidence, several problems remain. After discussing them, we shall try to answer two questions:

1. Does the life cycle of an organization have predictable stages of development?
2. How similar is the organizational life cycle to the biological life cycle?

Problem 1: Separating the Stages

One main reason for examining the life-cycle process at all is to enable organizations to maximize their effectiveness by matching organizational structure and management practices to life-cycle stage. Managers of companies in obvious and sustained growth phases, for example, could design systems to cope with growth. Unfortunately, determining when one stage is ending and another is beginning is not easy. *Understanding* the life-cycle models is easier than *applying* them.

Problem 2: Counting the Stages

No one knows how many stages the life cycle has. There may be two (growth and decline), three (birth, growth, and decline), four (birth, growth, maturity, and decline), several researchers say five, and Adizes says ten. Perhaps the study of life-cycle models can give us no more than simply a feel for what some organizations look like at some few phases of their development.

Problem 3: Ignoring the Departments

Most models consider the organization as a single functioning unit. They seem to assume that all of an organization's parts move through the stages of growth and decline at the same rate. But perhaps the organization's departments are in different stages. One product division may be growing as the others decline. A decline in sales and production may spur the growth of the research and development department. Rather than being concerned about the organization's life-cycle stage, managers should perhaps concentrate on the developmental stages of the organizational components for which they are responsible.

Problem 4: An Unproven Theory

Most life-cycle models are armchair notions. They look good on paper, but little real-world research has been done to see whether any life-cycle theory explains anything about organizational structures and processes in reality.

Problem 5: Organization Life and Product Life

Life-cycle theory suggests that the organization changes its structure to meet the new demands of each life-cycle stage. This theory tends to ignore the effects on structure of another variable: product success or failure. Organizations exist to provide society with products and services. If the public stops buying, the organization may undergo wholesale structural changes—regardless of what life-cycle stage it may be in.

Problem 6: Assuming Identical Organizations

Most life-cycle models speak only of "the organization"; they treat all organizational types as identical equals—even though all organizations display qualities peculiar to themselves. Since organizations are unique, how can they all possibly react the same as they pass through the life-cycle phases? Future life-cycle research should probably focus on particular organizational types.

These six problems, and others, suggest that life-cycle theory may be of limited practical use.

We are now ready to answer two key questions about organizational life cycles.

LIFE-CYCLE THEORY: TWO QUESTIONS

Does the Life of an Organization Have Predictable Stages of Development?

A review of the life-cycle models suggests that the answer is "yes." Two common themes in these models support this answer: (1) Choices made at early stages in the organization's life shape the organization's enduring character and limit the options available later in organizational life; (2) The models suggest that different phases are accompanied by certain problems or crises demanding organizational decisions or responses. If the organization does not confront these difficulties and deal with them, it may perish—at any life-cycle phase.

Although the models were constructed independently, they are roughly similar. If Model A has more stages than Model T, it has probably subdivided a stage that Model T has left intact.

How Similar Is the Organizational Life Cycle to the Biological Life Cycle?

Some writers feel that using the language of biological life-cycle evolution in organization theory can be misleading. Organizations are not "born" in the biological sense. A new organization does not inherit traits as a new biological organism may. At a late stage in its life cycle, the biological organism's structure rapidly and irreversibly disintegrates. The organization undergoes no equivalent process; theoretically, it can have perpetual life.

On the other hand, the two life cycles do have similarities. The formative years of both the child and the organization are most critical. And perhaps the healthy, mature organization can "reproduce," passing its values and ideals along to successive generations of organizational members.

The biological metaphor does not fit organizations exactly. However, it offers enough parallels in discussions of organizational growth and development that its continued use is probable. Systems theorists, in particular, support the metaphor's use, since they feel that all systems have the same characteristics.

SUMMARY

Organizations are born and they die. Between these two points, they undergo many changes. This sequence of changes is often labeled the "life cycle." Understanding the life cycle and its stages may help the organization to adopt appropriate programs, routines, and structures.

For organizations and their subunits, the general life-cycle model encompasses the three stages of birth, youth, and maturity gradually blending into decline. Arthur Stinchcombe suggests that new organizations are founded partly in order to take advantage of social resources available at the time of their founding. These resources and the structures to which they give rise have lasting effects on the organization.

The life-cycle model advanced by Frank Tuzzolino and Barry Armandi has five stages, each associated with a different organizational structure: creation (ad hoc), growth (organic), stabilization (bureaucratic), decline (recentralization), and dissolution (no structure remaining). During the various stages, the organization has different amounts of slack (excess payments to organizational members). The new and dissolving organizations have the least slack; the stable, bureaucratic organization has the most.

Gordon Lippitt maintains that the life cycle comprises a series of six situations which the organization must confront successfully: launching the venture, survival and sacrifice, achieving stability, pride and reputation, developing uniqueness, and contributing to society.

Larry Greiner perceives five evolutionary stages for organizations, each concluded by a revolution. The evolutionary stages and culminating revolutions are: creation (concluded by the leadership crisis), direction (the autonomy crisis), delegation (the control crisis), coordination (the red-tape crisis), and collaboration (concluded by a crisis as yet not experienced or named).

David A. Whetten indicates four sources of organizational decline: atrophy, vulnerability, loss of legitimacy, and environmental entropy. If the organization perceives environmental changes (some of which may lead to decline), it has available two proactive responses (generating and preventing) and two reactive responses (responding and defending). Jeffrey D. Ford contrasts growing and declining organizations. The latter have an increasing proportion of administrators, are more highly structured, and tend to make fewer structural changes. But the structural changes made during decline tend to persist once the decline is arrested (if it is).

Michael T. Hannan and John Freeman propose that as the organization moves through its life cycle, the tendency toward inertia increases. If the organization is able to travel through its life cycle without declining, it keeps the structures and routines that have enabled it to continue.

Henry Mintzberg has suggested that internal/external power balances are related to the life cycle. He has also identified a sequence of five structures that many organizations seem to adopt naturally as they grow and mature: craft, entrepreneurial, bureaucratic, divisionalized, and matrix.

Ichak Adizes specifies ten life-cycle phases. Each phase is characterized by a varying degree of emphasis on one or more of four organizational components: production, administration, entrepreneurship, and integration (PAEI). For example, during the initial courtship stage, entrepreneurship dominates the other three components.

During the go-go stage, the organization emphasizes production and entrepreneurship at the expense of administration and integration.

Six problems arise out of the life-cycle concept: separating the stages, counting the stages, ignoring departments, using unproven theories, ignoring product influence, and assuming identical organizations. Two questions were answered: (1) Does the organization's life cycle have predictable stages of development? and (2) Is the organizational life cycle comparable to the biological life cycle?

The life-cycle model captures the dynamic flow of the process between organizational birth and death. From a theoretical perspective, referring to an organization's developmental stages as a life cycle seems valid and advantageous. From a practical perspective, organizations can better understand their history, deal with the present, and plan for the future if they have a basic understanding of the life cycle.

DISCUSSION QUESTIONS

1. Describe the general life-cycle model.
2. Table 17.1 presents seven types of changes that occur within organizations as they move from birth to maturity. Pick several of these changes and tell why you think they occur.
3. What are the advantages and disadvantages to young organizations of family participation in management?
4. Why does the primary organizational goal often eventually shift from profit to growth?
5. Summarize the importance of the organization's time, place, and circumstances of founding, according to Arthur Stinchcombe.
6. Explain the concept of organizational slack. Why do bureaucratic organizations have so much slack?
7. Try to think of real-life organizations that are facing the key issues specified in Lippitt's Situational Confrontation Model.
8. Present a critique of Larry Greiner's Evolution-Revolution Model. Do the "revolutions" seem inevitable to you?
9. According to David A. Whetten, the organization's delusion of invulnerability characterizes and partly causes decline. Give some real-life examples of this point.
10. According to Jeffrey Ford, structural changes occur more rapidly during growth than during decline. Why do you think that is so?
11. Why is inertia a constant threat for organizations?
12. According to Henry Mintzberg, how is organizational power distributed at different life-cycle stages?
13. Explain the four components of Ichak Adizes's PAEI Model. How might an actual organization make practical use of this model?
14. Describe several failing or defunct organizations with which you are familiar. Why did they fail? At what stage in the life cycle did they fail?
15. Which has the greater impact on organizational structure: environment or life-cycle stage?

■   *DOUG'S FRIED CHICKEN*

Within four years of assuming the presidency, Judy Hart brought Doug's Fried Chicken from a 2 percent market share to 20 percent. She was a risk-taking, innovative entrepreneur. She increased the chain from 400 outlets to 1743 and rapidly expanded into 27 countries. "I've got to be involved in a continual go-go growth cycle. Because of my successful track record, the franchisees and the board go along with any programs I propose," Hart believed.

Hart was flamboyant and sensational. She shifted the annual franchisee convention from Des Moines, Iowa to Disneyland. She moved headquarters from a converted post office into a new $5.8 million building.

Then Doug's board of directors dismissed Hart from the presidency. "Judy," said chairman Doug Jones, "for a while we liked your 'full-steam-ahead' attitude. But you can't seem to slow down. You're trying to change too many things, too fast."

The board elevated vice president for finance, John Davis, to the position of president. Davis was a conservative, accommodating executive who watched budgets closely and believed in rigorously controlled expansion. He emphasized fiscal responsibility. Davis set up a centralized purchasing system (which Judy Hart had always opposed). Board Chairman Doug Jones was pleased; he considered Davis to be "in tune with the mood of the board and the franchisees at this point in time."

Judy Hart was unemployed for three days. Then she was enthusiastically hired by Berger's Burgers, a company that had achieved financial stability only in the last couple of years. Now they were in a strong cash position. "Judy," said Horace Berger, chairman of the board, "we think we're ready to take off. We want to triple the number of Berger's Burgers outlets within three years. Can you do it?"

"Can do, Mr. Berger," said Judy happily. "But first we've got to refurbish this tacky headquarters building and change the site of the annual convention. I envision a truly spectacular party for the franchisees at Disney World. . . ."

How do you explain Judy Hart's unceremonious dumping from Doug's and her warm welcome at Berger's?

■   ACME FOOD SERVICE COMPANY

Acme Food Service Company is having trouble handling success. Acme has been in business for 25 years. Starting as a small family operation, Acme has enjoyed a growth in sales every year. The facilities have been expanded several times. The company was incorporated several years ago. Mr. Acme and his family own a controlling interest.

Even though business has increased annually, the organizational structure and operating procedures are basically the same as they were when the firm was started. The company has developed a few key personnel but does not really have any depth in first-line supervisors. As sales volume continues to increase, the supervisors are stretched to their limits.

The Acme family and other members of operating management have always been personally involved in supervision. However, in recent years the Acmes have moved farther away from direct supervision, although still participating in the business. As a result, other members of operating management have had to take on additional supervisory responsibilities.

To handle the steady annual improvements in sales, Acme has increased the number of operating personnel and has improved production methods. Yet the organizational structure continues to be strained as managers and supervisors are responsible for larger numbers of employees.

By most standards, Acme is a successful business. The company has achieved what all companies want: steady annual increases in sales and profits. Yet the company's personnel and facilities are barely able to handle each year's volume of business.

In terms of organizational life cycles, how would you analyze the Acme situation? What structural or other changes would you recommend?

■   ### GOOD-TIME CHUCKY'S

Good-Time Chucky's had for several years been a successful family restaurant business specializing in Cajun food. The New Orleans atmosphere, Cajun music, and spicy cooking appealed to a varied clientele. Over the past few years, the business had expanded fairly rapidly to its present size of 16 restaurants.

The business was organized as a partnership, with brothers Herman and Louis Thibodeaux as major owners. After realizing that Good-Time Chucky's restaurants were successful just about anywhere that they were located, the Thibodeaux family partnership began to wonder if the business ought to become a public corporation to finance expansion, primarily through a franchising program.

Their accountant gave them a report including the following advantages and disadvantages of "going public":

ADVANTAGES	DISADVANTAGES
Acquire expansion capital	Share decision making with investors
Protect personal assets	Share profits with investors
Easier access to credit	More government control
Stability	More paperwork
Retain majority stock interest	Greater social responsibility

How should Good-Time Chucky's decide whether now is the time in its organizational life cycle to go public?

■   ### OZYMANDIAS
(Percy Bysshe Shelley)

> I met a traveler from an antique land
> Who said: "Two vast and trunkless legs of stone
> Stand in the desert. Near them, on the sand,
> Half sunk, a shattered visage lies, whose frown,
> And wrinkled lip, and sneer of cold command,
> Tell that its sculptor well those passions read
> Which yet survive, stamped on these lifeless things,
> The hand that mocked them, and the heart that fed:
> And on the pedestal these words appear:
> 'My name is Ozymandias, king of kings:
> Look on my works, ye Mighty, and despair!'
> Nothing beside remains. Round the decay
> Of that colossal wreck, boundless and bare
> The lone and level sands stretch far away."

To what primary cause do you attribute the disappearance of the Ozymandian organization: managerial deficiencies, environmental factors, or the normal organizational life-cycle process?

■ *ECONOMY AIRLINES*

Minor Hamblin had a humanistic dream: to found a company in which every employee would be an owner/manager, a company in which people really would work together. Hamblin started the revolutionary low-fare, no-frills Economy Airlines. Within a few years, Economy was the fifth-largest U.S. passenger carrier. The company had no unions. New employees had to buy and hold 100 shares of Economy stock, offered at a 70 percent discount. Profit sharing regularly added substantial amounts to their paychecks. Hamblin believed that participatory management was the style that best suited contemporary employees. A Harvard professor called Economy Airlines "the most comprehensive and self-conscious effort to fit a business to the capabilities and attitudes of today's work force. Economy Airlines is doing everything right."

Economy had a flat structure with only three management levels. In terms of the organization chart, pilots and flight attendants were on the same level and had the same clout. The company had no secretaries; managers did their own typing and answered their own phones.

The company rapidly expanded its routes and schedules. Unfortunately, traffic growth failed to keep up with expansion. Other airlines adopted the low-fare, no-frills approach and even attacked Economy directly in their advertising campaigns. Economy's stock plunged from over 100 to 8. One employee observed, "When stock prices were high, profit sharing and stock ownership were great. Now they aren't so great." The Air Line Pilots Association began a drive to unionize Economy's pilots. New government regulations made Minor Hamblin wonder if he could even keep Economy's flying certificate.

Hamblin had a renewed realization that a company can't always control its own destiny. "The Harvard professor said I was doing everything right. Now I'm in danger of going belly-up." He wondered if he should convert Economy over to a more traditional structure, with more management layers, a clearly defined chain of command, and specialized employee tasks. Or perhaps he should sell out.

Can you tell where Economy Airlines is in its life cycle? What caused Economy's problems? Would a knowledge of life-cycle theory have helped Economy to avoid those problems? What steps should Economy Airlines take now?

NOTES

1. Johannes M. Pennings, "Organizational Birth Frequencies: An Empirical Investigation," *Administrative Science Quarterly* 27 (March 1982): 120.
2. Henry Mintzberg, *The Structuring of Organizations: A Synthesis of Research* (Englewood Cliffs, NJ: Prentice-Hall, 1979), p. 242.
3. Theodore Cohn and Roy A. Lindberg, *Survival and Growth* (New York: AMACOM, 1974), p. 5.
4. Bernard Barry, "Organizational Design in the Smaller Enterprise," in *Manpower Planning and Organizational Design,* ed. Donald T. Bryant and Richard J. Niehaus (New York: Plenum Press, 1977).
5. John Freeman, Glenn R. Carroll, and Michael T. Hannan, "The Liability of Newness: Age Dependence in Organizational Death Rates," *American Sociological Review* 48 (October 1983): 692–710.
6. Roger W. Schmenner, "Every Factory Has a Life Cycle," *Harvard Business Review* 61 (March/April 1983): 121–129.

7. Arthur Stinchcombe, "Social Structure and Organizations," in *Handbook of Organizations,* ed. James G. March (Chicago: Rand McNally College Publishing Co., 1965), pp. 142–193.

8. Ibid., p. 169.

9. Frank Tuzzolino and Barry Armandi, "Organizational Design, Slack, and the Life Cycle," *Academy of Management Proceedings* (1982): 15–18.

10. Gordon Lippitt, *Growth Stages in Organizations* (New York: Appleton-Century-Crofts, 1969).

11. Larry Greiner, "Evolution and Revolution as Organizations Grow," *Harvard Business Review* 50 (July/August 1972): 37–46.

12. David A. Whetten, "Sources, Responses, and Effects of Organizational Decline," in *The Organizational Life Cycle: Issues in the Creation, Transformation and Decline of Organizations,* ed. John R. Kimberly and Robert H. Miles (San Francisco: Jossey-Bass, 1980), pp. 342–374.

13. Jeffrey D. Ford, "The Occurrence of Structural Hysteresis in Declining Organizations," *Academy of Management Review* 5 (April 1980): 589–598.

14. Michael T. Hannan and John Freeman, "Structural Inertia and Organizational Change," *American Sociological Review* 49 (April 1984): 149–164.

15. Henry Mintzberg, "Power and Organizational Life Cycles," *Academy of Management Review* 9 (April 1984): 207–224.

16. Ichak Adizes, "Organizational Passages: Diagnosing and Treating Lifecycle Problems of Organizations," *Organizational Dynamics* 8 (Summer 1979): 3–25.

17. Henry Mintzberg, *The Structuring of Organizations: A Synthesis of Research.*

18. Ibid., p. 241.

ADDITIONAL READINGS

Beckard, R., and Harris, R.T. *Organizational Transitions: Managing Complex Change.* Reading, MA: Addison-Wesley, 1977.

Boswell, J. *The Rise and Decline of Small Firms.* London: Allen & Unwin, 1973.

Freeman, J., and M.T. Hannan. "Growth and Decline Processes in Organizations." *American Sociological Review* 40 (April 1975): 215–228.

Gray, Barbara, and Sonny S. Ariss. "Politics and Strategic Change Across Organizational Life Cycles." *Academy of Management Review* 10 (October 1985): 707–723.

Harris, Stanley G., and Robert I. Sutton. "Functions of Parting Ceremonies in Dying Organizations." *Academy of Management Journal* 29 (March 1986): 5–30.

Kimberly, J.R. "Issues in the Creation of Organizations: Initiation, Innovation, and Institutionalization." *Academy of Management Journal* 22 (September 1979): 437–457.

McKelvey, B. "Comment on the Biological Analogue in Organizational Science." *Administrative Science Quarterly* 24 (September 1979): 488–493.

Quinn, Robert E., and Kim Cameron. "Organization Life Cycles and Shifting Criteria of Effectiveness: Some Preliminary Evidence." *Management Science* 29 (January 1983): 33–51.

Smith, Ken G., Terence R. Mitchell, and Charles E. Summer. "Top Level Management Priorities in Different Stages of the Organizational Life Cycle." *Academy of Management Journal* 28 (December 1985): 799–820.

Stinchcombe, A.L. "Bureaucratic and Craft Administration of Production: A Comparative Study." *Administrative Science Quarterly* 4 (September 1959): 168–187.

Organization Theory and the Future

Although researchers in organization theory have supplied a large body of knowledge and various approaches and frameworks for arranging it, much is left to be done. After reviewing the OT-Model as a starting point, this chapter will discuss some of the difficulties involved in creating the "ideal" organization. By means of an extended analogy, we suggest how the "one best way" to organize might be approached.

Modern organization theory has its shortcomings. Its terms and concepts are often vague and difficult to measure. The chapter discusses these shortcomings.

After examining the characteristics of several so-called "excellent" present-day organizations, we indicate certain trends and make some projections about what major factors will influence future organizations.

THE OT-MODEL REVIEWED

The Organizing Methods

The OT-Model on the inside covers reflects the two primary organizing methods for achieving organizational goals: differentiation and integration. Both must be done well for an organization to succeed.

Differentiation   Differentiation has two dimensions. First is the specialization of *activity,* including the division of labor and departmentalization. Second is the specialization of *authority,* including delegation, decentralization, and the line-staff distinction. The organization uses the preceding five strategies to divide up its work.

Integration   Next are the five integrating strategies: the hierarchy of authority, formalization, committees, span of control, and communication. The organization uses these strategies to coordinate its activities and authority relationships, as it attempts to achieve organizational goals.

The Three Perspectives

Classical We have examined each differentiating and integrating strategy from three perspectives: classical, human relations, and modern. The classicists wanted to find the "one best way" to do the work. They sought to discover the optimum organizational design and the optimum system of organizational relationships, and then to apply their findings to all organizations. One result of this approach was a set of principles to guide practicing managers. Only if they adhered to the classical "rules" could managers be most effective.

An obvious shortcoming of this approach was its disregard for the social, human aspects of organization. The human relations school filled this void.

Human Relations The human relations perspective extended classical thought by including *the worker* and *the work group* as critical variables in the organizational equation. These behavioral scientists sought to show that human relationships were important to organizational performance. Studies of individual and group behavior aided organization theorists by demonstrating the value of the human component.

Yet, something was still missing. Why didn't the combined theories and techniques of the classicists and the behaviorists apply in all situations? The modern school's systems/contingency perspective sought to provide the missing link.

Modern Modern researchers have shown that concentration on the *task* and the *worker* is not enough. We must also pay close attention to the *situation*. This situational or contingency approach opened an enormous box of interesting speculations and began to cast doubts upon the "one-best-method" approach. The modern organization must consider the individual worker and task in combination with other workers and tasks. Each of these worker-task relationships and combinations is in some way unique, so no "one best way" is going to apply to all of them. In addition, the organization must make its decisions in light of its size, technology, environment, and life-cycle stage. The old equation for organizational effectiveness was something like:

$$\text{Best worker} + \text{Best tools} + \text{Best method} = \text{Organizational effectiveness}$$

Because of the interactions among so many relevant factors and influences, modern organization theorists no longer believe that any single equation for organizational effectiveness can be expressed.

The Contingency Variables

The modern school sees size, technology, environment, and life-cycle stage as the major "contingency variables" in any equation or other expression of how the organization should structure itself. These four components have far-reaching impact on the organization. In determining which differentiating and integrating strategies to use, the organization must consider its size (large or small?), technology (simple or complex?), environment (calm or turbulent?), and life-cycle stage (young or old?). These variables, of little or no concern to the classical or human relations theorists, have now become prominent in the analysis of organizations.

CREATING THE IDEAL ORGANIZATION?

One Best Way

A Closed Organizational System   The classical school had a closed-system perspective on organizations. Classical scholars and practitioners viewed organizations as reasonably homogeneous entities. The classicists believed that diligent study could reveal universally applicable answers to questions about structuring organizational tasks, authority relationships, and information flows. In retrospect, this approach was not unreasonable. Frederick W. Taylor and others of the scientific management movement were often able to find the "one best way" to perform *individual* tasks. Why couldn't the same rigorous scientific approach be used to design constellations or aggregations of tasks? Why couldn't there be one best way of organizing?

Simple Organizations and Theories   Organizations at the time were relatively small and homogeneous. The four so-called contingency variables were not yet exerting a variety of influences on organizations. Perhaps the classical school had reason to be optimistic about finding the one best organization theory. If we want to develop a theory of transportation when the only major form of transport is the train, then logic suggests that a theory of trains and a theory of transportation will be the same. In a similar sense, the classical school developed a theory of organizations when organizations were small, dominated by entrepreneurs, engaged in manufacturing, and operating in a stable environment. The reasonably certain world of the classical writers called forth a model that may still be quite appropriate for those modern organizations operating under these same conditions.

Complications

Theorizing about transportation becomes more difficult when forms of transport other than trains appear. Similarly, organization theory became more complicated as conditions other than those familiar to the classicists began to have an obvious impact. While the exact dynamics of that impact remain unclear, big organizations *do* differ from small ones, high-tech and low-tech companies *are* different, and the organizational structures of firms in a turbulent, hostile environment are *not* the same as structures of firms in a placid, friendly situation.

Scratching the Surface   Organization theorists and researchers need to answer this question: What should the ideal organization look like? An entrepreneur with an idea for a new organization should ideally be able to walk into an organization theorist's office and ask: What should my organization look like—now and in the future—to be effective? As the number of business failures suggests, we are far from achieving that ideal; the modern school is just beginning to scratch the surface.

Modern Assumptions

A Heterogeneous World   The classical and modern schools are in fair agreement on the issues needing answers. Like the classicists, modern writers want to know how

specialized the labor force should be, which decisions to delegate, when decentralization becomes appropriate, how wide the span of control should be, and so on. The
modern writers differ in the *assumptions* on which their studies are based. A fundamental modern assumption is that the world within which organizations operate is not
homogeneous and simple but heterogeneous, complex, and diverse.

Diversity and Similarity   This environmental diversity calls for diverse organizational
structures. It also leads logically to a problem for modern theorists. On the one hand,
if every different and unique environment calls for a different and unique structure, then
organization theory becomes irrelevant. If we cannot categorize organizations for
purposes of study, understanding, and modeling, then we have nothing to offer entrepreneurs or managers seeking answers to real issues of organizational structure. The
systems perspective leads us to say to the inquiring entrepreneur: "Everything is related
to everything else, so your organization must be structured to match its unique environmental context." The entrepreneur moves rapidly away from us, muttering about
ivory-tower eggheads.

On the other hand, to say that all organizations ought to have the same structural
characteristics offers no sense of reality. At the one extreme, all organizations are
different so they must be structured differently. At the the other extreme, all organizations are essentially similar and therefore may be structured similarly. We must search
for the answers somewhere between these two extremes.

The Design Question   We need a classification scheme general enough for application
to many organizations but specific enough to make relevant, useful recommendations
to these organizations. Such a scheme would serve as a method for investigating and
helping organizations. If validated by further research and study, the scheme could
provide an answer to the organizational design question.

Two Classification Schemes

People like to categorize things. Categorizing aids us in understanding and predicting.
If a friend tells us that Sam Jones is "an extrovert," for example, we understand Sam
to an extent and have an idea of how Sam will probably behave at the party tonight.
So too with organizations. If we can classify organizations, then we can better understand their internal workings and predict their actions. Before presenting our own
classification scheme, here are two that have proven useful.

The Etzioni Typology   Amitai Etzioni's typology of organizations is based on "compliance"—the way in which lower-level organizational members react to authority
within the organization.[1] Three types of authority have three corresponding types of
compliance:

AUTHORITY TYPE	COMPLIANCE TYPE
The use of force	Alienative or unfriendly compliance
The use of rewards	Utilitarian or calculative compliance
The use of persuasion	Moral or just compliance

Effective organizations have a congruent fit between authority and compliance; the authority and compliance systems match. If an organization finds itself in an incongruent state, it will move toward congruence by adjusting the compliance system or, more rarely, the authority system.

The Blau-Scott Typology   Peter Blau and W. Richard Scott based their classification scheme on the simple question: Who benefits? Who are the major beneficiaries of the organization's activities? The different answers to that question comprise the four organizational classes.[2]

In *mutual benefit associations,* the *organization's members* are the prime beneficiaries of the organization's actions. Examples are political parties, unions, street gangs, sororities, clubs, professional associations, and religious organizations. The major problem facing these associations is maintaining control of the voluntary membership.

The prime beneficiaries of *business concerns* are their *owners.* Examples are manufacturing organizations, wholesale and retail stores, banks, insurance companies, and other organizations operated for profit. The most pressing issue for this organizational type is operating efficiency: maximum return for minimum cost. These organizations can survive and grow only if they make a profit.

The prime beneficiaries of *service organizations* are their *clients.* Examples are hospitals, social welfare agencies, schools, and mental health clinics. The major problem in service organizations is maintaining a high level of professionalism so that the welfare of clients is enhanced.

Commonweal organizations have as their prime beneficiary *the public at large.* Examples are the military, the Department of State, and the police and fire departments. The crucial issue for these organizations is that they are ultimately under external control, by the public. Such organizations must establish efficient bureaucratic systems that satisfy the public's needs.

The Etzioni and Blau-Scott models allow us to view organizations from different perspectives. The Etzioni model uses compliance and authority as classifying criteria. The Blau-Scott model uses the prime beneficiary as the major criterion. Both models attempt to generalize to all organizations, to understand them by classifying them.

THE URN ANALOGY

The classification approach that we propose is explicitly based on the contingency framework demanded by systems thinking.

In a classic statistics exercise, students are presented with a jar or urn filled with balls or marbles of different colors. The students grab a sample handful of marbles and use the sample to predict the color mixture of the urn's entire marble population.

We would like to create urns full of organizations. We would pull out organizations by the handful, examine them, and draw conclusions about organizational similarities and differences—within one urn and from one urn to another. How many urns should we use, and how do we assign organizations to the separate urns?

Filling the Urns: The Variables in Combination

We propose using 16 urns. Each urn will represent a different combination of the four major contingency variables: size (small or large), age (young or old), technology (simple or complex), and environment (placid or turbulent). The 16 urns appear in Figure 18.1. Into each urn, we drop the organizations having that urn's unique combination of characteristics. For example, Paul Revere's newly formed silver shop would go in the first urn because the shop was small and young, its technology was simple, and its environment was placid. The huge and long-lived General Motors Corporation, with complex technology and a turbulent environment, would be dropped into urn 16.

Classifying Organizations This organizational classification approach is coherent and defensible. It recognizes not only the influence of each major contingency factor but also their relationships with each other. The research literature has often left us with ambiguous insights about the influence of a single contingency variable. Combining and considering them jointly in "urns" allows assessment and understanding of their simultaneous influence.

The Practitioner: One Best Way This approach should also be useful to the practitioner. Paul Revere would merely identify the contingency variables affecting his organization, ride to the proper urn, and look inside to see what organizations similar to his might look like. Indeed, if we go one step further and classify each urn's organizations as successful and unsuccessful, then we have achieved the ultimate goal of organization theory: the one best way to structure a given organization.

Structural Characteristics

Thus far, we have gone through three steps: (1) develop 16 categories of organizations, (2) put real organizations into them, and (3) determine the successful and unsuccessful

Legend: Size = Small (S) or Large (L)
Age = Young (Y) or Old (O)
Technology = Simple (S) or Complex (C)
Environment = Placid (P) or Turbulent (T)

Figure 18.1 The urn analogy.

organizations in each category. The next step would be to examine the structural characteristics of the successful organizations. To do so, we can use the classical features of organizational design covered in Chapters 4 through 13 of this book. For example, if the president of a slumping category-16 firm asks how the successful category-16 firms differentiate and integrate their work, we can give that information. We can show how the successful firms divide up the labor, departmentalize, delegate, communicate, and so on.

In their quest to arrive at the foregoing answers, modern organization theorists face huge obstacles. The largest is defining the terms that will permit setting boundaries between the classes or categories.

SHORTCOMINGS OF MODERN ORGANIZATION THEORY

When does an organization stop being young and start getting old? When does a small organization start becoming large, a simple one complex? When does the relatively stable environment become uncertain? We must answer these questions if we are to drop organizations into the right urns. An obvious complication is that we cannot give either-or answers; we are dealing with continuums: young-old, simple-complex, small-large, placid-turbulent. At this point in the history of organization theory, many of our definitions and concepts are vague.

Vague Definitions and Concepts

Effectiveness   All organizations strive to be effective. But what is effectiveness? The quick and easy answer is: the degree to which the organization attains its goals. As Chapter 3 showed, defining organizational goals in the first place is difficult. Once they are defined, many more questions remain: Which goals do we want most to attain—all of them? Does goal attainment have to equal 100 percent, or can an organization achieving nine goals out of ten, or 90 percent each of all ten goals, be labeled "effective"? Who decides?

Structure   We have used the term "structure" freely and often. Yet, organization theorists are far from agreeing on what an organization's structure is. Is structure comprised solely of horizontal and vertical differentiation, division of labor, span of control, and spatial dispersion? Or do we include formalization, decentralization, and delegation, which are more philosophically oriented processes than they are structures? Does structure include the social and economic aspects of an organization? We have achieved little agreement on the answers to these questions. Yet organization theory cannot mature into a true social science unless it can answer them.

Measurement Problems

In addition to definitional and conceptual problems, organization theory continues to be plagued by measurement problems. Indeed, the two sets of problems are related; we cannot measure something that we cannot define.

Division of Labor   How do we measure an organization's division of labor? A pretty good quick answer is to count the number of different jobs in the organization. But this answer raises other questions: Do we count part-time jobs or just full-time jobs? How do we handle new job titles for old jobs? We cannot measure division of labor until we can define it.

Measuring division of labor is difficult enough. Measuring centralization, delegation, formalization and other standard terms in organization theory is even harder.

No Absolute Scale   Another difficulty is that we lack an absolute scale of measures. For example, how small is small? What seems small to a steel company, a government agency, or an auto company may seem enormous to a pizza parlor, a mortuary, or a candle shop. Similarly, most of us would view a 4K byte RAM computer chip manufacturer as a technologically complex firm. To a chip manufacturer working on 128K RAM chips, the 4K RAM chip is child's play. Complexity, uncertainty, size, age, and other such terms are defined in the eye of the beholder, trite though it is to say so. Consistency requires that organization theory achieve some agreement about its measurement scales.

Categorization Problems

A final confounding problem is the difficulty in categorizing organizations for study. How do we categorize a steel mill with three major units of totally different character: a traditional blast furnace operation, a fully automated specialty steel mill, and a research laboratory? Or consider the Bell System before the break-up; it comprised a regulated monopoly, a competitive long-distance unit, a manufacturing facility, and a research laboratory featuring Nobel Prize winners.

Is the environment of the steel mill or of the Bell System stable or unstable? Is the organization large or small? Bureaucratic or nonbureaucratic? Should each organizational element be studied separately, or should they be combined—in the same "urn"? Theorists wanting to comment on organizational design must answer such questions.

TRENDS AND PROJECTIONS

No one knows what the future holds for organizations, but some strong current trends enable us to make a few projections. Organizations must consider such trends and projections as they prepare for the future. First, let us examine some trends among today's excellent organizations.

The Excellent Present-Day Organizations

In their best-selling book *In Search of Excellence: Lessons from America's Best-Run Companies,* which explores why some present-day corporations are more successful than others, Thomas J. Peters and Robert H. Waterman, Jr., listed the following eight criteria.[3]

A Bias for Action   First, the excellent corporations get things done. They don't become bogged down in bureaucracy or committee decision making. Companies like Digital Equipment, Data General, and National Semiconductor are movers, not waiters. To get things done, employees often interact directly with customers or bypass the corporate hierarchy.

Close to the Customer   "Give the customers what they want" is the motto of these highly effective organizations. They provide top quality, fast service, and dependability. Today's customer wants these features and is willing to pay for them. Commodity producers in particular—like Frito-Lay, Maytag, and Tupperware—listen to what their customers want. But so does IBM, which takes pride in its quick service.

Autonomy and Entrepreneurship   Innovative companies produce "champions"— originators of ideas that work. These champions are permitted free rein, to encourage their creativity. The 3M Corporation in particular has created an intense atmosphere of innovation by establishing "a loose network of laboratories and cubbyholes populated by feverish inventors and dauntless entrepreneurs who let their imaginations fly in all directions."[4]

Productivity Through People   Excellent companies realize that *employees* are the key to improved quality and increased production. These companies are not antagonistic to the work force. IBM and Texas Instruments are only two of many companies that claim to have "respect for the individual" and prove that claim by relying on employee input (through quality circles, for instance).

Close Contact with Employees   Peters and Waterman have coined the phrase Management by Walking Around. By practicing MBWA, the excellent managers find out what is really going on and make all employees feel important. As an example, the late Ray Kroc of McDonald's regularly visited stores and personally judged them on the company's four criteria: quality, service, cleanliness, and value.

Stick to the Knitting   Most excellent companies stay close to the business they know best. Not many of them are conglomerates. Procter & Gamble and Johnson & Johnson do not enter fields alien to their basic commodity lines. They wouldn't know the market or how to operate within it—so they don't even consider it.

Simple Form, Lean Staff   None of the excellent companies use a matrix form of organization. Those that once did use it abandoned it quickly. Their structures are simple, and their staffs are lean. Some multimillion-dollar companies are run by a top staff of seven.

Loose and Tight Control   The excellent companies mix centralization and decentralization. Decision making is decentralized, and lower-level managers have a great deal of authority. Yet these companies cling fanatically to their core values. Digital and 3M thrive on organized chaos, with many people and units working autonomously. But every employee strives for reliability and innovation. These values persist within the chaos.

Peters and Waterman conclude that *people*—customers and employees—are the key to excellence in the successful companies. The successful corporations have coped with modern trends and developments in these eight ways. Most firms like to copy the "stars." Using these eight criteria, combined with an overall orientation toward people, may enable organizations to do so.

Organizational Culture

The major focus of organization theory is on the structural variables. Also important is the culture of the organization—the human patterns of interaction, behavior, and relationships, how it feels to work for XYZ Corporation. An organization's culture is a system of behavior in which everything is socially learned and shared by the organization's members. Organization theorists are giving increasing attention to this culture.

One group of authors has defined culture as:

> the shared philosophies, ideologies, values, assumptions, beliefs, expectations, attitudes, and norms that knit a community together. All of these interrelated psychological qualities reveal a group's agreement, implicit or explicit, on how to approach decisions and problems: "the way things are done around here."[5]

In fact, a good short definition of culture might be "the way things are done around here." Culture consists of norms, folkways, mores, laws, language, symbols, and rituals. Let's look at each of these components.

Norms   Norms are standards of behavior, how people are expected to act. The typical organization has an intricate set of norms. Some are obvious; others require the advice and counsel of veteran organization members. As an illustration of a norm, in most organizations each member must use and respect the chain of command. An employee does not go over a supervisor's head.

Folkways   The customary, habitual ways in which organizational members act or think, without reflecting about them, comprise the organization's folkways. Shaking hands (or not shaking hands), wearing or not wearing a tie, and arriving and leaving at certain times (before or after the boss) are examples of folkways.

Mores   An organization's mores are a class of folkways that must be followed not because they are polite, but because they are essential to the organization's efficient operation and survival. Mores require certain acts and forbid others. By indicating what is right and wrong, they form the base of the organization's code of ethics. For instance, the mores of some organizations forbid disloyalty and backstabbing. The mores of most organizations require that employees follow the directions of the boss.

Laws   The laws of an organization are its rules and regulations. They are a special class of mores—those that have been written down rather than passed along through oral tradition. For example, an organizational rule may state that any employee claiming to be sick for three or more days must submit a doctor's note.

Language In addition to the common language of the larger culture, each organization has its own special language, its vehicle of communications. The language may be incomprehensible to outsiders. Consider this note that a manufacturing company consultant received from the president's assistant:

> The POD-FJT will show you the alley. The PM-ATS and the PD-RLO will accompany. D & T—9/7; 10:00. If unable, contact KM.

Only someone familiar with the company's cryptic language would understand the note.

Symbols Cultural symbols are evident in every organization. A symbol is a physical object that has a significance beyond itself, a sign that communicates an unspoken message. For example, having a corner office, more than one window, an office on the top floor, or a desk of a certain size may symbolize having a certain status, prestige, and power within an organization.

Rituals Rituals are symbolic acts that people perform to gain and maintain membership in an organization or one of its groups. For instance, your receiving an invitation to the annual costume party of the president and spouse may ritualistically signify your acceptance into the select corporate elite.

All of these components determine an organization's culture. The cultures of government agencies differ from the cultures of religious institutions and business corporations. And the cultures of the organizations within these general classes differ from each other.

Culture Categories

In their trend-setting work on corporate cultures, Terrence E. Deal and Allan A. Kennedy identify four culture types.[6] To categorize hundreds of corporations, they used two criteria: the degree of *risk* that the company and its employees were willing to take, and the speed at which the company and its employees got *feedback on decision outcomes*. Figure 18.2 displays the four culture types.

Tough-Guy, Macho Culture This high-risk/quick-feedback culture, the epitome of the "gambling syndrome," takes high risks in hopes of high returns. Organizations with this type of culture tend to be young in the life cycle. This all-or-nothing culture burns people up very quickly. It is fast paced, with a live-for-today type of value system. This culture encourages those internal entrepreneurs called "intrapreneurs."

Work-Hard, Play-Hard Culture In this culture, employees take few risks and get quick feedback on whether their decisions have paid off. Fun and action are important aspects of this culture. The company has a customer orientation, and the primary value is trying to satisfy customer needs. Persistence is a key virtue. Members of this culture will call on a customer five or six times to get the sale, rather than trying to get the big sale on the first call as would a member of a tough-guy culture.

Choosing a New Leader: A Tribal Society and a Corporate Society

We learnt that the paramount chief, His Excellency Duodu Kepi II, had died of cirrhosis of the liver five days before. News of his death had not reached the outside world because the telegraph line from Ngonga, erected soon after independence as part of a World Bank rural telecommunications project, had been stolen and sold as fencing material some years ago.

There were rumours in the village that fourteen of Duodu's eighteen wives and most of his personal servants were being strangled—a skewer pierced through their tongues first, so that they could not curse their executioners—to keep him company and wait upon him in the next world. Far more interesting to the villagers, however, was the question of the succession.

The official procedure for selecting a new paramount chief was straightforward. When the period of mourning ended, the Council of tribal elders were to meet in formal session. Names of candidates were to be put forward, their merits discussed and the decision reached on a vote.

The actual procedure was rather different. When Duodu Kepi II had been told by his witch doctor that he was dying, he called Chief Kyema, a trusted deputy who was too old to have any hope of winning the position for himself, and issued to him his last command. He told Kyema to see to it personally that the succession was resolved peacefully, without dividing the elders, and a worthy man chosen. He urged him to begin his task without delay. Kyema retired to his hut, and immediately sent his messenger to summon the elders to him secretly, one after another.

Receiving each alone, he informed them of the impending death of the Father of the Akwaaba people and, excepting present company, asked who would be the most suitable successor.

The names of eight of the available princes recurred in the course of these private sessions, so having completed the first round of talks, he embarked on a second aimed at narrowing down the list. When it had been reduced to three, he suggested to each of the elders that they should discuss the names with each other.

So by the time they all met together in formal session they all knew that Prince Ponsu would win, so they voted for him unanimously. Thus any subsequent unpleasantness that could have arisen as a result of some of them having publicly backed a loser was neatly avoided.

Not long before, in the vast London head office of one of the world's largest industrial concerns, ICI, the chairman, Sir Peter Allen, retired. He has prepared an account of how he arranged a smooth succession.

Official procedure is for the board of directors to meet in formal session, discuss the available candidates and reach their decision on a vote.

The actual procedure described by Sir Peter was somewhat different and designed, he said, to "leave no sour or unhappy consequences." He reported that the unwritten ICI custom is for a retiring chairman to "select a member of the board with no axe to grind, that is one who is about to retire . . . to take soundings."

Sir Peter, as he was determined not to seek re-election himself, acted as his own chairman-maker. "The first step was to see each of the directors in turn and alone," he said. ". . . I asked each director this question: 'Present company excepted, who would you like to see as the next chairman of ICI? . . .'

(continued)

> "Resuming after the holidays, I had a second round with all the directors, all in turn and in private . . . and asked if he had changed his mind."
>
> Sir Peter suggested to each: "You are, of course, perfectly free to discuss this among your colleagues and to change your mind between now and then" (the time when the election would take place).
>
> Soon, he was able to report that "the feelings of the board came down to a very short list." And he called them to a formal meeting. "I said that I thought, as everybody had had a chance of discussion with me fully and frankly on what he thought was the best choice . . . we should not have a public debate. . . . This was agreed without dissent, so that it seemed to me therefore that we should have a secret ballot without further ado."
>
> The pre-selected winner was then duly elected.
>
> *Source:* Excerpt from *The Yam Factor* by Martin Page. Copyright © 1972 by Martin Page. Reprinted by permission of Doubleday & Company, Inc.

Organizations of this cultural type get a lot of work done. They know how to make and sell a product. However, high sales volume can lead to lower quality, if a proper work-hard/play-hard mix is not achieved among employees.

Bet-Your-Company Culture   High risk and slow feedback dominate in this culture type. Companies make large investments whose payoffs may not occur for years, if ever. For example, oil companies spend millions for exploration and may come up "dry" many times before finding any oil. Because risks are large and payoffs distant, thoroughness and deliberation in management's decision making are the rule, and quick decisions are frowned upon.

Process Culture   The process culture is characterized by low risk and slow feedback. Organizational types with this sort of culture might be insurance companies, governments, utilities, and other bureaucratic, heavily regulated organizations. No one decision will make or break the company or an employee. The process culture and the work-hard/play-hard culture are both low risk, but employees in the process culture

Degree of Risk

		High	Low
Speed of Feedback	Quick	Tough–guy, macho culture	Work–hard/play–hard culture
	Slow	Bet-your–company culture	Process culture

Figure 18.2 Deal-Kennedy typology of corporate cultures. (*Source:* Terrence E. Deal and Allan A. Kennedy, *Corporate Cultures: The Rites and Rituals of Corporate Life,* © 1982, Addison-Wesley Publishing Company, Inc., Reading, MA. Adapted material. Reprinted with permission.)

rarely get positive official feedback. Only if something goes wrong do they hear about it and get blamed. This lack of feedback causes employees to concentrate on the process, on *how* they do their jobs, not on what they do or what the organization is trying to achieve. The means become more important than the ends.

In this culture, the key value is getting the details and the process right. Although this slow and deliberate culture is frustrating to many employees and clients alike, it does provide order and thoughtfulness.

Maintaining and Changing Organizational Culture   Values are the essential ingredients of both individual and organizational behavior. People and institutions develop and absorb their values over a long period of time. Once accepted, values are not readily relinquished.

But change can occur, even if slowly. The model in Figure 18.3 shows how cultural change can be stimulated or blocked in organizations. As the upper left block of the figure indicates, two basic approaches to cultural change are available to managers. First, they can hire new workers who accept the new culture and have not been contaminated by the old. Or, managers can "socialize" present organizational members by teaching them the new culture. Management has to identify employees who are flexible and are leaning toward the new system of values and beliefs. Those members who accept the change can be rewarded appropriately.

The second approach, indicated in the upper right block, is to remove members who do not accept or may oppose the new culture. After all reasonable means of encouraging the new culture's acceptance have been exhausted, the organization may have to encourage the resignations of resisters or terminate them. Persistent deviations from the new cultural norms will cause conflict, inefficiency, and ineffectiveness. Therefore the deviants must go if the new culture is to thrive.

An organization's culture affects its ability to differentiate and integrate its work. The Salvation Army and the Hell's Angels motorcycle gang have different structures,

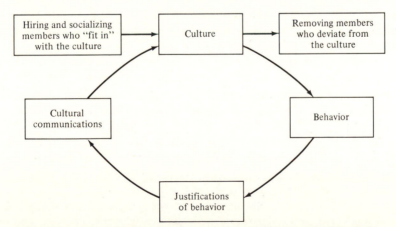

Figure 18.3   How culture tends to perpetuate itself. (*Source:* After Vijay Sathe, "How to Decipher and Change Corporate Culture," in *Gaining Control of the Corporate Culture* ed. Ralph H. Kilmann, Mary J. Saxton, and Roy Sherpa [San Francisco: Jossey-Bass Publications, 1985], p. 245. Used by permission.)

and those differences are not unrelated to the cultural differences between the two organizations. Organization theorists must become increasingly aware of the relationship between culture and structure.

Now, here are some trends with which today's excellent organizations and the organizations of tomorrow must come to terms.

The Work Force

The Promotional Clog   The nature of the work force is always an influence on organizational design. One work-force characteristic having its origin decades ago will continue to have an impact.

The postwar baby boom of 1945–1955 created a surge of people seeking employment in the 1965–1975 period. This bulge of employees in entry-level positions soon became eligible for their first and second promotions. The 1980s saw a promotional clog develop. The shape of the average organization is pyramidal. In typical Company ABC, for example, every five employees at one level have a supervisor at the next higher level. Thanks to the baby boom, more and more ABC employees in the 1980s have been competing for fewer and fewer promotions.

Even worse, the supervisor blocking an employee's promotion is likely to be about the same age as the employee. The end result has often been fewer promotional opportunities for employees—with all the motivational, career, and salary implications of that shortage.

As this situation continues, organizations must find new ways to challenge, excite, and reward hard-working employees who will be in the same jobs for the next 20 or so years. To keep these employees motivated and productive, jobs—and perhaps entire organizations—will have to be redesigned.

Worker Expectations   The educational level of the work force is rising. Historically, our society has encouraged the belief that more education leads to more challenging, more satisfying, higher-paid jobs. Consequently, people have increasingly sought out educational opportunities and now come to the work force with expectations quite different from those of their parents.

Organizations hiring these better-educated employees will feel pressure to redesign jobs to make them more significant and challenging. Employee demands for participation in decision making will lead to more delegation, decentralization, and committees, and to the wider control spans that will permit and encourage greater job autonomy.

Employee expectations concerning the boss will also differ. Typical employee Mary Smith is highly trained, professionally aware, and democratically raised. Her expectations about how her boss should exercise authority are quite different from those of her parents when they took their jobs.

In the 1960s and 1970s, government and business hired many college-trained, professional staff experts to perform a wide variety of advisory jobs: government planner, corporate planner, budget adviser, personnel consultant. The economic realities of the recessionary early 1980s and increased foreign competition for many industries have made these educated experts too expensive a luxury for many organizations to carry. Where all of these highly trained, professionally oriented people will go remains to be seen, but the organizations wanting to absorb them may well have to meet their needs with changes in organizational design.

The modern work force expects individual treatment; leaders of that work force must truly have a contingency attitude about managing it.

Other Demographic Trends   Several other, similar trends are also influencing organizational design. People are living longer, and these longer life spans create a demand for longer terms of employment, either with the same organization or with newly created ones specially designed to accommodate the limitations that age places on employees.

The increase in working mothers and single-parent households also pressures organizational designers to find structures that can adapt to these demographic developments. In order to accommodate these nontraditional employees, organizations are providing remote job locations, job sharing, day-care facilities, counseling staff, and other services that exert an influence on organizational design.

The rise of dual-career marriages, the easing of worker job commitment, the increased emphasis on career professionals and the associated decrease in the hierarchical aspirations of employees—all these factors further complicate the design of new organizations and the redesign of old ones.

Technological Change

Perhaps no trend will have a greater impact on organizational design issues than the development of extremely powerful, cheap computers. The time is not far away when every organizational member will have immediate, direct access to virtually all of the organization's data. This development will have enormous impact on delegation, decentralization, span of control, coordinative committees, and line-staff ratios—just to mention a few of the more obvious consequences.

Recentralization   The paperless office and electronic mail open up some interesting possibilities for organizations. Many firms decentralize in order to cope with complexity, geographical dispersion, or large size. Immediate access to computerized information, coupled with powerful decision-making program routines, may all but eliminate the need to decentralize. Some organizations will use their computer capabilities to recentralize control. Other organizations, aware of decentralization's motivational benefits for modern, highly educated employees, will continue to delegate and decentralize. Once the dominant coalitions within organizations have this choice, it will be interesting to see what they do with it.

Fragmenting the Facts   In the 1960s, the advent of mainframe computers forced a reconsideration of structures and designs as organizations tried to find the best location for this new function. Mini- and microcomputers create similar challenges for the organizations of the 1980s and beyond.

Desk-top microcomputers now enable many organizational members to accumulate, analyze, interpret, and report on data. This trend could have nightmarish outcomes. Imagine a meeting of managers trying to solve a major organizational problem. The managers all have their own data bases, data-processing programs, outputs—and their own different results and conclusions. We have entered a "my-computer-is-smarter-than-your-computer" environment. At some point, organizations must develop responses to cope with these forests of free-standing computer systems.

We may soon see the development of a new organizational function called something like "data-base controller," with responsibility for handling data, setting program standards, coping with system differences, and with authority to govern data-base use. The very strength of free-standing, personalized computers—their autonomy—is also their weakness: they encourage decision making in isolation. In essence, the fragmenting of facts permitted by the microcomputer is itself a micro example of why organization theory developed in the first place: to balance the need for dividing work into autonomous, differentiated units with the need to integrate these units all back together again.

The Routinizing of Middle Management   In many respects, middle managers are responsible for uniting the organization's operating level (those actually making the product or delivering the service) with the upper managerial level (those setting organizational goals and strategies). Some middle managers translate goals and strategies into operational terms for the people actually doing the work. For example, a production scheduler translates sales expectations and raw material supplies into daily production assignments for machine operators. Other middle managers have monitoring responsibilities. For instance, an auditor observes ongoing financial activities to keep money from dribbling away or being wasted.

As the routine decisions associated with goal operationalizing, monitoring, and other support activities become increasingly computerized, the number of middle managers will diminish. Computers are increasingly setting the pace and monitoring the performance of employees in routine production and service jobs. A familiar example is the night watchman who punches in at computer-monitored stations. If the watchman fails to punch in, the computer sounds an alarm. The watchman is supervised not by a person but by the knowledge that a machine awaiting him on his rounds will sound off if he doesn't keep moving. A more modern illustration is the operator of a CRT machine who must key in the desired information within a set length of time. The computer continuously records and makes available each operator's average speed, error rate, and other pertinent productivity data. Such equipment considerably simplifies the monitoring function of the operator's supervisor.

Computer applications in the standardization of routine work, and the consequent reduction in middle management numbers, are changing the shapes of organization charts. According to John Naisbitt, "The computer will smash the pyramid: We created the hierarchical, pyramidal, managerial system because we needed it to keep track of people and things people did; with the computer to keep track, we can restructure our institutions horizontally."[7]

One new arrangement would be the grouping at upper levels—alongside the organization's strategic-level administrators and policymakers—of numerous staff-type people in charge of nonroutine events. In fact, such specialized staff functions have increased so much in certain organizations that the chain of command in the staff-support areas now rivals the former numbers of people in line management. The rise in staff levels can more than offset the savings resulting from the decreases in production costs to which computerization has led. Some line managers complain that every time they use advanced technology to get rid of a production job, someone finds a way to add a high-priced staff person, so the organization's total labor cost rises anyway.

The shapes of organizations resulting from the foregoing developments might resemble those in Figure 18.4.

Other Technological Changes   The computer and information-processing technology have become dominating influences on organizational design. Other technological changes will also exert their pressures. The speed-up in communications linkages will permit new organizational responses in the traditional production, scheduling, warehousing, and inventory functions, among others. For example, "just-in-time" scheduling in the auto industry is based on the ability to schedule the delivery of parts at the exact time when they are needed in the production cycle. This development changes the activities of support personnel responsible for keeping parts available to ensure smooth production.

Other technological factors—not as apparent as computer-assisted decision systems and communications technology—will also affect the design of future organizations. As one small example, space laboratories may soon use weightlessness to produce perfect ball bearings, reducing or eliminating the need for quality control in ball-bearing production. The continuing development of robots and robotics is another technological offshoot of the computer revolution that will also change the design of tasks in many industrial organizations. Before long, such activities will cease being EPCOT Center demonstrations and will become practical parts of the working organization.

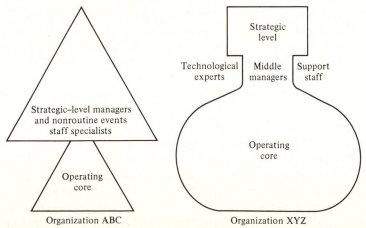

Figure 18.4 Possible future organization patterns. (*Source:* Organization XYZ after Henry Mintzberg, *The Structuring of Organizations: A Synthesis of Research,* © 1979, p. 443. Adapted by permission of Prentice-Hall, Inc., Englewood Cliffs, NJ)

Bureaucracy to Adhocracy

The Death of Bureaucracy   In a now-classic article, Warren G. Bennis maintained that bureaucracies—impersonal and characterized by rules, regulations, routine, inflexibility, and a well-defined chain of command—are doomed.[8]

The bureaucratic structure craves environmental stability. It thrives on the status quo. By its very nature, a bureaucracy cannot adapt effectively and quickly to environmental changes. And yet, rapid and unexpected change is the modern norm. Furthermore, organizations have increased in size and complexity; many have become international in scope. With its rules, regulations, and other red tape, the bureaucratic form's decision-making processes are inadequate for such large, widely spread organizations.

In addition, more people are now employed in the economy's service sector than in the manufacturing sector. Jobs are becoming more specialized, personalized, and nonroutine. These characteristics are not compatible with the routineness of bureaucracy. Finally, fundamental changes in management philosophy have occurred over the past few decades. Today, managers are more concerned for employees as human beings; they use collaboration and reasoning rather than force and threats. This new philosophy does not fit well with bureaucratic depersonalization, routine, and a well-defined chain of command.

Organizations and the Future Environment   Bennis subsequently described his vision of organizational life in the future.[9] He projected the following conditions.

The future organization will operate in an even more complex, turbulent, uncertain environment. Large-scale, complex, multinational firms, stressing interdependence rather than competition, will be the norm. Ties between business and government—like those seen in the "Chrysler bailout" of the early 1980s—will become even closer.

Work-force characteristics will change. Having more education and greater job mobility due to improved transportation, Americans will not be so prone to consider lifelong employment with one organization. Organizations will have to develop and train new managers continually, and devise means to keep competent managers and other skilled personnel from leaving.

Organizational tasks will become more technical and complicated, and less highly programmed. To complete these difficult tasks, organizations will place greater reliance on project groups and teams with multiple specialists.

The demands of the new era will require an organic structure that can respond to change quickly.

The Adhocracy   Such a structure is the adhocracy, a term popularized by Alvin Toffler in *Future Shock* (1970) and based on "ad hoc," meaning "for a specific purpose or situation." Warren G. Bennis defines the adhocracy as "a rapidly changing, adaptive, temporary system organized around problems to be solved by groups of relative strangers with diverse professional skills."[10] The adhocracy employs professionals and experts who "freelance" in small groups for the organization on particular projects. The units of the adhocracy are usually temporary, lasting only until they complete their projects. The unit members then return to the pool of professionals or experts from which they came.

Rules, regulations, and policies are few; professional specialists have their own codes of behavior, so other controls are not usually needed. Since the ad-hoc units are formed to solve a problem or complete a project quickly, they are usually given considerable decision-making authority.

The adhocracy is obviously unsuited for certain kinds of organizational effort. For example, NASA's Manned Space Flight Center was a famous adhocracy of the 1960s. A snuff company or a salt mine would probably not use the adhocracy form.

Henry Mintzberg distinguishes between the *operating* adhocracy and the *administrative* adhocracy.[11] The operating adhocracy consists of managers, planners, designers, support staff, and operating specialists who work side by side, in small groups, to solve problems or accomplish projects *for clients.* The client approaches the organization with a problem, and the organization puts together a team to solve it. The administrative and operating levels blend together and act as one.

The administrative adhocracy works not for clients but for itself. The administrative component is an adhocracy as described above, but the operating core may be a traditional bureaucracy. The two types of adhocracy are presented in Figure 18.5.

Responding to the Environment

Future organizations must contend with many changes other than technological ones. The ever-changing environment will also demand new responses in the future.

As organizations become more conscious of how important their interactions with the environment are, they will add more boundary spanners and sensing units—to monitor the environment and develop responses to perceived environmental changes. Highly visible organizations and organizations operating in highly political environments have already learned to monitor the political, economic, and competitive uncertainties in the social system of which they are a part. An organization may assess the environment and respond by creating a new product unit (caffeine-free soft drinks), or a new international unit (a Brazilian instant-coffee division, to reduce transportation

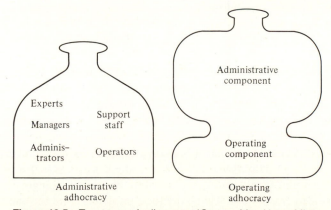

Figure 18.5 Two types of adhocracy. (*Source:* After Henry Mintzberg, *The Structuring of Organizations: A Synthesis of Research,* © 1979, p. 443. Adapted by permission of Prentice-Hall, Inc., Englewood Cliffs, NJ)

costs and save on taxes), or a new joint venture (joint ownership of drilling operations in China). Such strategic responses would fit in with the organization's existing differentiation and integration strategies, but they would be driven by events sensed in the environment.

As the environment changes, future organizations must be flexible enough to adapt and change with it. One response might be to achieve enough portability to go where the environment demands. The organization responding this way to environmental change might resemble a circus; it moves into a prime location, sets up its tent, puts on its show, folds up, moves on, and repeats the process in the next market—all the time keeping the same basic structure, personnel, and product. A variation would resemble the fixed-location fair that changes its format periodically to maintain or revive the interest of its fixed-location market. In this case, the location stays the same, but the structure, personnel, and product may change.

Life-Cycle Changes

Time changes all living things, so of course the organizations formed by the cooperative efforts of living things also change. New organizations are born; old organizations die, or are perhaps revitalized. In the past, organizations have not often planned their responses to the different stages of their life cycles. Nor have organization theorists offered much guidance about desirable structural changes as organizations move from one life-cycle stage to another.

Some responses to movements through the life-cycle stages also offer exciting ideas and challenges to organizational designers. For instance, many organizations are using new venture-capital or joint-venture situations to avoid the stagnation of maturity or decline and to get on the growth track again. In such a venture, two or more different sets of organizational structures and strategies are merged to form the new organization.

Such new forms offer interesting challenges for organization theorists. What should be the design of the steel mill mentioned earlier in the chapter that has a traditional blast furnace, a specialty steel mini-mill, and a high-technology laboratory? Even if we can make fairly confident recommendations about how the blast furnace, the mini-mill, and the lab should look, how should the overall coordinating unit be organized?

The practicalities of the different life-cycle stages may make even the best recommendations difficult to implement. Consider an older university having a large Latin department filled with tenured professors of high rank and also having a relatively small business administration department. As the priorities of society and the student body shift, the Latin teachers have few students and the business administration classes are bulging. The university realizes that it is poorly organized—overstaffed in Latin and understaffed in business administration. Yet it is stuck with resources in place and is reluctant to fire tenured faculty outright. Therefore instead of changing to meet different conditions, the university elects to ignore the complaints from the business administration faculty, leave people and resources where they are, and gradually reallocate personnel to the business administration department as, with the passage of time, professors of Latin move into academic administration, retire, take positions in industry, or leave the university for other reasons.

The point is that the relative inflexibility of organizational resource allocation compounded by the difficulty of recognizing when the organization is passing from one life-cycle stage to another presents organizational designers with constant challenges as they try to modify the old to meet the new.

As the rate of change in market technology and customer preferences continues to accelerate, structures and design strategies will also have to change more rapidly. Company annual reports often point out that today's most popular, best-selling company products were nonexistent a decade ago. Similarly, the best-sellers of ten years from now have probably not been invented yet.

The need to match structure to strategy is receiving increasing attention in the organizational design literature. Indeed, the literature of organizational change now seems to be moving away from an almost exclusive emphasis on strategies for bringing about behavioral change to include the structural and design issues as well.

Toward a Dynamic Model

The organizational model used in this book as a classification scheme is relatively static. It includes the elements that students and practitioners of organizational design should consider. However, it does not show how these differentiating and integrating issues work together dynamically within a particular organization. Our urn analogy is a start at categorizing organizations so we can begin the process of understanding what each class of organizations looks like in a total sense.

Whatever the dominant organization theory model of the future is, ideally it will describe and explain the dynamic interrelationships among structural and design variables, the organizational leadership's preferences, the make-up of the members, and the organization's culture, myths, legends, and history. The emerging "literature of organizational culture" has begun this study. It may become the vehicle that can finally unite the now separate study areas of organizational behavior and organization theory.

A PROMISING FUTURE

The future for organization theory studies is very promising. Today researchers all over the world and in a variety of fields are energetically working to solve organizational problems. New designs are being formulated and tested. The literature is alive with ideas about how organizations should be set up and maintained.

Necessity is the mother of organizational design. Future necessities will call for new responses to design questions. For the student of organization theory, excitement and challenge lie ahead.

DISCUSSION QUESTIONS

1. We have used the OT-Model as a basis for describing how organizations put themselves together. What are the model's strengths and weaknesses?
2. Is there in any sense a "one best way" to organize?
3. Modern organizations operate in a heterogeneous, complex, and diverse world. How does that fact affect modern organization theory?

4. Present the advantages and disadvantages of "the urn analogy."

5. Are the five differentiating factors or the five integrating factors more important to an "urn 1" organization? An "urn 16" organization?

6. What are some shortcomings of modern organization theory?

7. Since all organizations are different and conditions constantly change, can we really learn much by studying excellent modern organizations?

8. Discuss how you fit into the demographic trends outlined in the chapter.

9. If you were going to design a new organization, to what extent would you use (1) an organization theory text and (2) the seat of your pants?

10. What will be the effect of increasing computerization on middle-management positions? How will this effect influence your career choices and directions?

11. Are future organizations more apt to be bureaucracies or adhocracies? Why?

12. The OT-Model is fairly static. What factors would you include and emphasize in order to make it more dynamic?

13. Do you agree that the future of organization theory studies is very promising?

NOTES

1. Amitai Etzioni, *A Comparative Analysis of Complex Organizations* (New York: The Free Press, 1961).

2. Peter M. Blau and W. Richard Scott, *Formal Organizations* (San Francisco: Chandler Publishing Co., 1972), pp. 40–58.

3. Thomas J. Peters and Robert H. Waterman, Jr., *In Search of Excellence: Lessons from America's Best-Run Companies* (New York: Harper & Row, 1982). For excellent critiques and updates of *In Search of Excellence,* see D. T. Carroll, "A Disappointing Search For Excellence," *Harvard Business Review* 61 (November/December 1983): 76–88; "Who's Excellent Now?" *Business Week,* 5 November 1984, pp. 76–78; and Kenneth E. Aupperle, William Acar, and David E. Booth, "An Empirical Critique of *In Search of Excellence:* How Excellent Are the Excellent Companies?" *Journal of Management* 12 (Winter 1986): 499–512.

4. Ibid., p. 14.

5. Ralph H. Kilmann, Mary J. Saxton, and Roy Sherpa, *Gaining Control of the Corporate Culture* (San Francisco: Jossey-Bass, 1985), p. 5.

6. Terrence E. Deal and Allan A. Kennedy, *Corporate Cultures: The Rites and Rituals of Corporate Life* (Reading, MA.: Addison-Wesley, 1982).

7. John Naisbitt, *Megatrends* (New York: Warner Books, 1982), p. 251.

8. Warren G. Bennis, "The Coming Death of Bureaucracy," *Think,* November/December 1966, pp. 30–35.

9. Warren G. Bennis, "Organizations of the Future," *Personnel Administrator* 30 (September/October 1967): 6–19.

10. Warren G. Bennis, "Post-Bureaucratic Leadership," *Transaction,* July/August 1969, p. 45.

11. Henry Mintzberg, *The Structuring of Organizations: A Synthesis of Research* (Englewood Cliffs, NJ: Prentice-Hall, 1979), pp. 431–443.

ADDITIONAL READINGS

Argyris, Chris. "Today's Problems with Tomorrow's Organizations." *Journal of Management Studies* 4 (February 1967): 31–55.

Bass, B. "Organizational Life in the 70s and Beyond." *Personnel Psychology* 25 (Spring 1972): 19–30.

Golembiewski, Robert T. *Renewing Organizations: The Laboratory Approach to Planned Change.* Itasca, IL: F.E. Peacock, 1972.

Gregory, K.L. "Native-View Paradigms: Multiple Cultures and Culture Conflicts in Organizations." *Administrative Science Quarterly* 28 (September 1983): 359–376.

Kemball-Cook, R.B. *The Organization Gap.* Beverly Hills, CA: Davlin Publications, 1972.

Kimberly, John R., and Robert E. Quinn. *Managing Organizational Transitions.* Homewood, IL: Richard D. Irwin, 1984.

Leavitt, Harold, Lawrence Pinfield, and Eugene Webb, eds. *Organizations of the Future: Interaction with the External Environment.* New York: Praeger, 1974.

Lippitt, Gordon. *Organizational Renewal.* 2d ed. Englewood Cliffs, NJ: Prentice-Hall, 1982.

Ouchi, William. *Theory Z: How American Business Can Meet the Japanese Challenge.* Reading, MA: Addison-Wesley, 1981.

Pascale, R. "Fitting the New Employees into the Company Culture," *Fortune,* 28 May 1984, pp. 28–42.

Perkins, Dennis N., Veronica F. Nieva, and Edward E. Lawler III. *Managing Creation: The Challenge of Building a New Organization.* New York: Wiley, 1983.

Sarason, Seymour B. *The Creation of Settings and the Future Societies.* San Francisco: Jossey-Bass, 1972.

Scott, William G. "Organization Theory: A Reassessment." *Academy of Management Journal* 17 (June 1974): 242–253.

Tichy, Noel M. *Managing Strategic Change.* New York: Wiley, 1983.

COMPREHENSIVE CASES

WESTERN TELEPHONE CORPORATION

Western Telephone Corporation (WesTel) is "the telephone company" to most people in nine Western states. Its 100,000 employees are spread among several operating units; the four most important are the holding company Western Telephone Corporation itself, Western Services, West Central Telephone, and South Central Telephone. Because of a drastic change in its environment, WesTel must make several major decisions. One of them is what to do with its staff engineers.

The delivery of telecommunications service is a combination of four general functions: marketing, installation/maintenance, billing/accounting, and engineering. Within the engineering organization are two functional divisions: staff engineering (with about 2000 people) and line engineering (with about 8000 people).

The staff engineers design the microwave radio systems, configure equipment within the telephone buildings, design long-distance circuits, handle inventory records, and so on. The WesTel staff engineers are located in one city within each state. They normally do all of their work in an office and rarely go into the field.

The line engineers are the people in the field. They are located in numerous towns throughout the entire Western region. In a pure sense, the line "engineers" are not usually college-trained engineers but are rather company-trained technicians. They trench cable into the ground, provide cable to residential subdivisions, maintain existing service, and decide which side of the street to run the cable down. The line engineers are often the ones who implement the plans that the staff engineers create back in each state's main office.

Like so many things in a company with a long history, the role of the staff engineer in WesTel has evolved over time. In the old Bell System, state utility regulators were paramount forces that had to be accommodated in order to be successful in rate cases. State regulators took a provincial view of telephone operations and wanted "local" people to be accountable for each state's telephone network. State regulators did not (and still do not) want out-of-state people controlling in-state operations.

As a response to this environment, a semiautonomous telephone organization was placed in each state to interface with the state's regulators. Included in each separate state telephone organization was a group of staff engineers to support the engineering requirements of the state telephone network. At a distance, the giant holding company AT&T established corporate policy and contended with the federal government on behalf of the local telephone operations.

Having staff engineers in each state was desirable for technical as well as political reasons. Forty years ago, electronic data did not exist. At that time, the engineering plans, diagrams, and records for, say, California were literally in California. Technology was not yet at the point of permitting centralization of the engineering files in some remote location. Accessibility was important. Travel was more difficult, and out-of-state trips were commonly made by train. These logistical reasons for having state staff engineers remained significant until the 1960s.

The environment of the late 1980s for the telecommunications industry is markedly different from that of the 1960s because of both the Bell System break-up and electronic data. Almost overnight, WesTel inherited a business that required complete review. The continued role of the state staff engineer must now be examined in light of contemporary realities. What are these realities for the staff engineers?

The staff-engineer role was strongly affected in 1984 by the break-up of the Bell System because it separated the staff engineer from the support of Bell Telephone Labs and Western Electric. In the old Bell System, development and manufacture of telecommunications equipment depended heavily on these two organizations, which were concentrated in the Northeast. Although local telephone operations throughout the United States were responsible for putting the telephone equipment together, they did not take the lead in highly sophisticated R&D activities; they left that to Bell Labs and Western Electric.

This was certainly the case for WesTel's part of the old Bell System. With the 1984 divestiture, WesTel suddenly had to start making its own R&D-related telephone decisions. The company had an immediate need for new, highly technical groups to do essentially what Bell Labs and Western Electric had done for the old Bell System.

Since divestiture, competition has become strong in several areas of the telecommunications industry in which WesTel finds itself. Many companies now manufacture and sell equipment to end-users, provide long-distance service, and publish yellow pages. WesTel is in a race against external competitors for customers and market share. If the company falls behind in the race, WesTel knows that it will be eclipsed by other companies, perhaps to suffer the fate of the railroads in the transportation business. Staff engineers play a critical role in keeping WesTel ahead of its competitors in a technical sense, and they must function successfully without the assistance of Bell Labs or Western Electric.

Coupled with the ideas above is a strong WesTel emphasis on increasing net income through efficiency and cost savings. Since the telecommunications industry is much less heavily regulated today than in the past, a profit is no longer guaranteed. State regulators are interested in keeping the cost of telephone service to residential customers low; they do not want rates to go up. With rates flat, WesTel revenues tend to be flat. Cutting costs while charging customers the same rate is really the only way WesTel can increase profits.

This reality has a direct bearing on staff engineers, because one means of cost-cutting is to eliminate duplicated or overlapping groups. In-state staff engineers are almost redundant because their functions can now be performed literally hundreds of miles from the physical work site. Electronic data make distance irrelevant.

Under these changed environmental conditions, how should WesTel staff engineers be organized?

OFFSHORE POWER SYSTEMS

Offshore Power Systems (OPS), presently a subsidiary of Westinghouse Electric Corporation, evolved in 1972 as a joint venture between Tenneco, Inc. and Westinghouse. OPS was intended to become a large manufacturer of floating nuclear power

(continued)

plants (FNP's) with employment expected to reach 10,000 to 12,000 people at full capacity.

The concept of the FNP is to mass-produce a nuclear power plant in one location, tow it from the production facility to an offshore anchorage site designated by the purchaser, build a breakwater around it for protection, and lay electric conduit to landfall. At that time the idea seemed an excellent alternative to land-sited nuclear plants because of public concerns with most site locations in the densely populated Northeast. If its growth had gone according to plan, OPS would rapidly have reached the ranks of the Fortune 500, producing an estimated four FNP's per year valued at approximately $500 million each.

Background

In early 1970, Public Service Electric and Gas (PSE&G) of New Jersey approached Westinghouse to explore the possibility of Westinghouse's building floating nuclear power plants for PSE&G. Since PSE&G was a valued customer, Westinghouse immediately undertook a preliminary feasibility study and concluded after a month that the idea was worth pursuing. A full-scale feasibility study was then initiated under Mr. Z, the man who would later become president and chief executive officer of the joint venture.

As the study group expanded to allow an in-depth investigation of the FNP concept, Mr. Z decided that the project's credibility in the marketplace could rest only partly on Westinghouse's reputation in the nuclear field. Having had a prior work relationship with Newport News Shipbuilding and Drydock Corporation, Mr. Z approached that company and asked if they would be interested in joining this study. Newport News Shipbuilding, by then a subsidiary of Tenneco, Inc., agreed to join. The full-scale feasibility study was completed in November 1971 by a group now numbering more than 100 people.

To confirm the study's technical and financial projections, a joint Westinghouse-Tenneco audit team was organized to review the proposal. The review was completed by mid-March 1972, and the results of the study and the audit were presented to the chairmen of the boards of Westinghouse and Tenneco. By the end of July 1972, both boards had given final approval for an equal-ownership joint venture, and Offshore Power Systems came into legal existence on August 1.

The Initial Organization

The joint agreement was an important document for this new organization since it laid out the organizational nucleus as well as formalizing certain issues which would later become important in the ongoing relationship between Westinghouse and Tenneco. The joint agreement designated three senior staff officers for OPS, defined their responsibilities, and structured the OPS board of directors. The agreement stated that Westinghouse would name the president/CEO and that Tenneco would name the chief operating officer (vice president/operations) and the chief financial officer (vice president/finance). Although both corporations recognized that the president's impact on the organization would be hard to equalize, this trade-off seemed both reasonable and appropriate in fitting the managerial orientation of both parent companies. The OPS board of directors would consist of six members, three selected by each partner, with the OPS president serving as nonvoting chairman of the board.

Westinghouse immediately named Mr. Z as president of the new organization. Tenneco subsequently selected as vice president/finance a corporate headquarters staff financial man who had directed the Tenneco audit team's review of the OPS proposal. The vice president/operations came from the Newport News location as did all other Tenneco-related personnel. Like the vice president/finance, the vice president/operations was familiar with OPS as he had previously worked on the in-depth feasibility study of the FNP concept. The joint-venture agreement allowed the president to appoint any additional senior staff officers he felt were needed. In effect, the document gave the president of the new venture nearly complete autonomy to design and organize the company in any way he chose, subject only to the constraints of the joint-venture agreement and the political requirements of dealing with an evenly split board of directors.

Mr. Z's initial tasks were to finish selecting the executive group and to structure an organization that would enable the feasibility-study group of approximately 150 people to grow into a full-scale manufacturing organization of 10,000 to 12,000 people within three years. At the same time, he needed to ensure the continuing support of an evenly divided board of directors, command the loyalty of two key executives from Tenneco, and resolve the inevitable conflicts between new OPS employees who were former members of two organizations different in character, orientation, and design.

The way in which Mr. Z approached his tasks reflected what he felt was a logical solution to relatively routine problems. Rather than spending enormous amounts of time to evaluate alternative design strategies that took projected OPS needs into account, he relied largely on his previous experiences and acquaintances both to design and staff his organization. Mr. Z's approach was to take an overall design with which he was already familiar, then fit people he already knew and respected into that design.

The functional structure that Mr. Z chose was common at Westinghouse and in fact was used at the Astronuclear Division which Mr. Z had previously managed. Indeed, by his own account, the only real differences between the two organizations were in total size and in the financial area, where the nature of the joint-venture corporate structure necessitated a separate treasury function and banking responsibility unnecessary in a typical Westinghouse division.

Once he had decided what the "ideal" organization should look like, he fitted one person at a time into the chosen organizational structure. After each personnel decision was made, that person's abilities and traits would be considered as the next position was filled. Since one person's weaknesses would necessitate another person's strengths, this process obviously would start at some particular job responsibility/person match and continue throughout the staffing of the entire organization. Mr. Z's preconceived organization design would, consequently, become modified to accommodate unique personal characteristics of the people selected for the various positions.

The initial organization design had the eight functional vice-presidential positions reflected in Figure C4.1. As specified in the joint agreement, Tenneco named the vice presidents of finance and operations. Five of the other six vice-presidential

(continued)

positions designated in this first structure were filled by Westinghouse personnel who were directly or by reputation known to Mr. Z. The vice president/facilities construction was a career-long personal friend. The vice president/administration had also been associated with Mr. Z at Westinghouse. Mr. Z had known the new vice president/legal counsel from his Astronuclear Division days and recognized him as one of the premier legal experts on nuclear matters. The vice president/engineering had been the manager of the study team and had stayed with the project ever since. The vice president/marketing was recommended to Mr. Z by the vice presidents of administration and engineering. The remaining senior staff position, vice president/planning and program control, was created for the lead engineer of the feasibility study team from Newport News Shipbuilding, who had become a loyal supporter of Mr. Z and the FNP concept.

In addition, many subordinate positions were filled by members of the project study team, most of whom came from the Power Systems Division at Westinghouse. While Mr. Z did not personally know all these people, he knew and trusted the judgment of those who recommended them. The end result of all these appointments was a markedly cohesive group consisting mainly of longtime colleagues and friends.

The first structure was designed to permit the organization's effective initial growth. As Mr. Z, the architect of the organizational design, saw it, this initial organization would permit a fast-track effort to design a product, secure a license from the Atomic Energy Commission, build a plant, and expand a work force all at the same time. He anticipated making several major organizational changes when actual production of the two FNP's for PSE&G began. At that time the FNP construction facility would have been completed, eliminating the need for a staff-level vice president/facilities construction. The planning function would be brought under a vice president/production, eliminating the vice-presidential position in that area. Purchasing also would be placed under the vice president/production, removing it from the vice president/administration's responsibility. Finally, a newly created vice president/employee relations position would also take the personnel function away from the vice president/administration.

These organizational modifications never evolved. In 1973 the country entered a recession, at least partly as a result of the Arab oil embargo and the subsequent oil price increase enacted by the OPEC nations. The immediate impact of the recession and the large increase in energy prices was to bring to a stop the anticipated rise in the demand for electricity. This reduced demand, in conjunction with the lag in utility rate adjustments, put OPS's only customer, PSE&G, into financial difficulty. Therefore, in September of 1974, PSE&G asked for a five-year delay on delivery of the two floating nuclear power plants it had ordered. This delay would mean the effective postponement of the entire FNP project, because the PSE&G order was the only one OPS had.

Since most of OPS's developmental costs were paid by PSE&G in the form of progress payments, the prospect of delay caused an extensive reevaluation of OPS by the two venture partners. If the project was to continue on to complete the first FNP by the original target date, Westinghouse and Tenneco would have to put up the money to build the FNP—in effect, as a speculation. A second possible course of action was to delay construction of the FNP but continue on with the slow process of licensing the concept and designing the plant. Tenneco proposed a third strat-

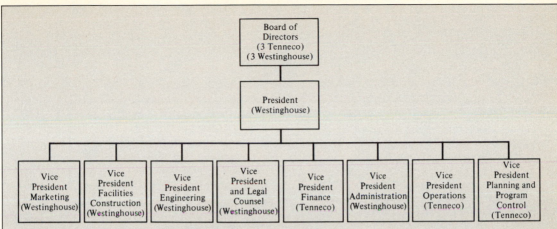

Figure C4.1   OPS organization chart: August 1972–December 1974.

egy: to force PSE&G to abide by the original payment schedule specified in the contract. If Westinghouse would not agree to support this proposal, then Tenneco wanted out. Westinghouse considered PSE&G to be a longtime good customer of their electrical products and chose not to put this valued customer into such a position. The result was that Westinghouse agreed to buy out Tenneco and pursue alternative two. By February 1, 1975, Tenneco had withdrawn from the joint venture, leaving Westinghouse in sole control.

The Second Organization

The PSE&G contract delay caused a reduction in the OPS work force from 700 to 280 in December 1974, reduced the number of partners to one, and delayed the delivery date by five years from the original one. These developments represented a major organizational turning point in terms of personnel and policymaking. No longer would Mr. Z have to satisfy two parent organizations. With a simple reporting structure (even though the joint venture was continued as a legal entity, both partners were entirely owned by Westinghouse), Mr. Z could operate OPS like the Westinghouse division he had been accustomed to managing.

Major changes were also made in the top management staff at this time. The vice presidents of finance and planning returned to Tenneco and Newport News Shipbuilding, respectively. The third Tenneco person, the vice president/operations, stayed at the urging of Mr. Z, to give the now totally Westinghouse-dominated organization a valid claim to shipbuilding expertise. Other personnel changes included the departure of the vice presidents of construction and marketing. The former position was deleted from the organization; the latter position was retained but the rank was changed from vice president to director. A similar change occurred in the finance area where the vice president/finance position was changed to controller. The vacated vice president/planning position was deleted. The planning (program control) function and physical facilities were placed under the vice president/operations. These changes are reflected in Figure C4.2.

(continued)

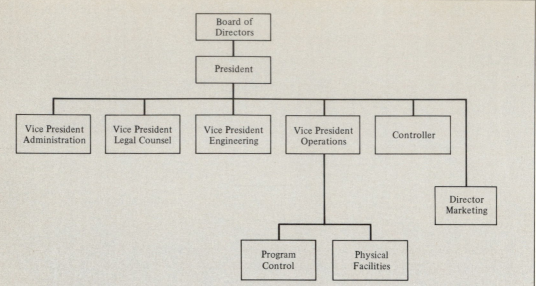

Figure C4.2   OPS organization chart: January 1975–October 1975.

The second organization, then, had a structure with six people at the senior-staff level. All but one of these were former Westinghouse personnel. A pattern of downgrading vacated vice presidencies to a lower rank with commensurately lower salaries was established at this time. Although this downgrading caused some resentment among the newly appointed people, the move was necessary to reflect the reality of OPS's new status within Westinghouse's structure and the reduced level of actual task responsibilities. Henceforth, OPS titles would accord with other positions in the parent's hierarchy. This new organization structure lasted approximately nine months before it gave way to a third organization.

The Third Organization

While the second organization evolved as a result of external forces, the next organization came about primarily as a design response to internal conflict. The placement of the planning function under the vice president/operations in the second organization did not work out satisfactorily. Conflict over who was structuring behavior for whom through control of the planning function arose almost immediately and continued throughout the nine months of the second organization's existence. An organizational development session conducted by an external consultant who used a confrontation strategy brought out the accumulated conflict caused by the existing structure. To resolve the problem, Mr. Z created a new series of reporting relationships. The planning function responsibility was removed from the vice president/operations, and a new staff-level position, director of management information systems, was created with responsibility for planning.

Mr. Z made one additional organizational change: He removed responsibility for quality control from the vice president/engineering. The Atomic Energy Commission had expressed its preference that quality assurance should report directly to the chief

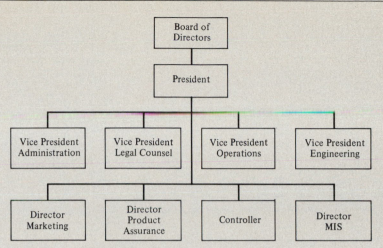

Figure C4.3 OPS organization chart: November 1975–March 1979.

executive officer in nuclear industries; this seemed like a good opportunity to accommodate their desire. A new senior staff-level position, director of product assurance, was created to handle this function.

The third organization is reflected in Figure C4.3. This organization shows a return to an eight-person top management staff. However, only four of these eight positions retained the rank of vice president.

The third organization remained intact until March 1979, though some of the personnel changed. During this period, the pattern of downgrading vacant positions was continued. For example, when the vice president/operations left in 1978, the position was downgraded to director of operations.

The Fourth and Final Organization

At the end of December 1978, OPS received notification that PSE&G was canceling its contract, the only contract OPS had for a floating nuclear power plant. The end of that contract put the organization into a new phase, which could be described as a holding pattern at best. Licensing and marketing efforts for the FNP's continued, but other functional activities were curtailed. On February 1, 1979, additional members of the OPS work force were laid off, leaving only 185 employees. Commensurate staff reorganization occurred on March 1, 1979. At that time, Mr. Z and two other top officers were promoted out of OPS, and the vice president/engineering was elevated to the presidency.

The resulting organization is depicted in Figure C4.4. All except two vice-presidential positions (those still occupied by the original position holders) had now been downgraded. The vice president/engineering position was split into two functional areas: engineering and licensing. Product assurance was downgraded from a director at the senior staff level to a manager subordinate to a staff-level supervisor.

(continued)

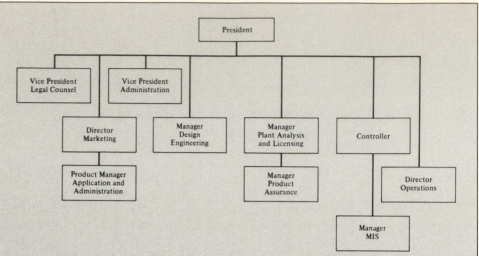

Figure C4.4   OPS organization chart: April 1979.

The director of MIS position was also downgraded to a manager level and, therefore, no longer reported to the president.

The final organizational structure reflects both the diminished level of operations at OPS as well as the continuing corporate belief that the FNP concept may yet become viable.

If Mr. Z had hired you to design each of the four successive Offshore Power Systems organizations, how would you have designed them and why? What effect on the outcome do you think your organizational designs would have had? What could/should Offshore Power Systems have done to protect itself against the changing conditions it encountered?

This case is adapted from Robert C. Ford, Sally A. Coltrin, and Steven K. Paulson, "Organizational Change in Theory and Practice: The Case of Offshore Power Systems, Inc.," *Journal of Management Case Studies,* in press. Used by permission.

Name Index

Subject Index